PHILIP'S

STREET

South

Hampshire

First published in 1994 by

Philip's, a division of
Octopus Publishing Group Ltd
2-4 Heron Quays, London E14 4JP

Second colour edition 2002
Third impression with revisions 2005

ISBN-10   0-540-08107-8 (pocket)
ISBN-13   978-0-540-08107-3 (pocket)

© Philip's 2005

 **Ordnance Survey**®

This product includes mapping data licensed from Ordnance Survey® with the permission of the Controller of Her Majesty's Stationery Office. © Crown copyright 2005. All rights reserved. Licence number 100011710

Printed and bound in Spain
by Cayfosa-Quebecor

Contents

III **Key to map symbols**

IV **Key to map pages**

VI **Route planning**

VIII **Administrative and Postcode boundaries**

1 **Street maps** at 2½ inches to 1 mile

215 **Street map of Portsmouth city centre** at 5 inches to 1 mile

216 **Town maps** of Winchester, Andover, Basingstoke, Farnborough and Newbury

219 **Index** of towns and villages

220 **Index** of streets, hospitals, industrial estates, railway stations, schools, shopping centres, universities and places of interest

Digital Data

The exceptionally high-quality mapping found in this atlas is available as digital data in TIFF format, which is easily convertible to other bitmapped (raster) image formats.

The index is also available in digital form as a standard database table. It contains all the details found in the printed index together with the National Grid reference for the map square in which each entry is named.

For further information and to discuss your requirements, please contact Philip's on 020 764 932 or james.mann@philips-maps.co.uk

Symbol	Description
(22a)	**Motorway** with junction number
	Primary route – dual/single carriageway
	A road – dual/single carriageway
	B road – dual/single carriageway
	Minor road – dual/single carriageway
	Other minor road – dual/single carriageway
	Road under construction
	Pedestrianised area
DY7	**Postcode boundaries**
	County and unitary authority boundaries
	Railway
	Railway under construction
	Tramway, miniature railway
	Rural track, private road or narrow road in urban area
	Gate or obstruction to traffic (restrictions may not apply at all times or to all vehicles)
	Path, bridleway, byway open to all traffic, road used as a public path

The representation in this atlas of a road, track or path is no evidence of the existence of a right of way

179 230 215	**Adjoining page indicators**

The map area within the pink band is shown at a larger scale on the page indicated by the red block and arrow

Abbr	Full	Abbr	Full
Acad	**Academy**	Mkt	**Market**
Allot Gdns	**Allotments**	Meml	**Memorial**
Cemy	**Cemetery**	Mon	**Monument**
C Ctr	**Civic Centre**	Mus	**Museum**
CH	**Club House**	Obsy	**Observatory**
Coll	**College**	Pal	**Royal Palace**
Crem	**Crematorium**	PH	**Public House**
Ent	**Enterprise**	Recn Gd	**Recreation Ground**
Ex H	**Exhibition Hall**	Resr	**Reservoir**
Ind Est	**Industrial Estate**	Ret Pk	**Retail Park**
IRB Sta	**Inshore Rescue Boat Station**	Sch	**School**
		Sh Ctr	**Shopping Centre**
Inst	**Institute**	TH	**Town Hall/House**
Ct	**Law Court**	Trad Est	**Trading Estate**
L Ctr	**Leisure Centre**	Univ	**University**
LC	**Level Crossing**	Wks	**Works**
Liby	**Library**	YH	**Youth Hostel**

Symbol	Description
Walsall	**Railway station**
(symbol)	**Private railway station**
(symbol)	**Bus, coach station**
◆	**Ambulance station**
◆	**Coastguard station**
◆	**Fire station**
◆	**Police station**
✚	**Accident and Emergency entrance to hospital**
H	**Hospital**
✛	**Place of worship**
i	**Information Centre** (open all year)
P	**Parking**
P&R	**Park and Ride**
PO	**Post Office**
Ⓧ	**Camping site**
⚌	**Caravan site**
▶	**Golf course**
✕	**Picnic site**
Prim Sch	**Important buildings, schools, colleges, universities and hospitals**
River Medway	**Water name**
	River, stream
	Lock, weir
	Water
	Tidal water
	Woods
	Houses
Church	**Non-Roman antiquity**
ROMAN FORT	**Roman antiquity**

■ The small numbers around the edges of the maps identify the 1 kilometre National Grid lines ■ The dark grey border on the inside edge of some pages indicates that the mapping does not continue onto the adjacent page

The scale of the maps on the pages numbered in blue is 3.92 cm to 1 km • 2½ inches to 1 mile • 1: 25344

0	¼	½	¾	1 mile
0	250m	500m	750m 1 kilometre	

The scale of the maps on pages numbered in red is 7.84 cm to 1 km • 5 inches to 1 mile • 1: 12672

0	220 yards	440 yards	660 yards	½ mile
0	125m	250m	375m ½ kilometre	

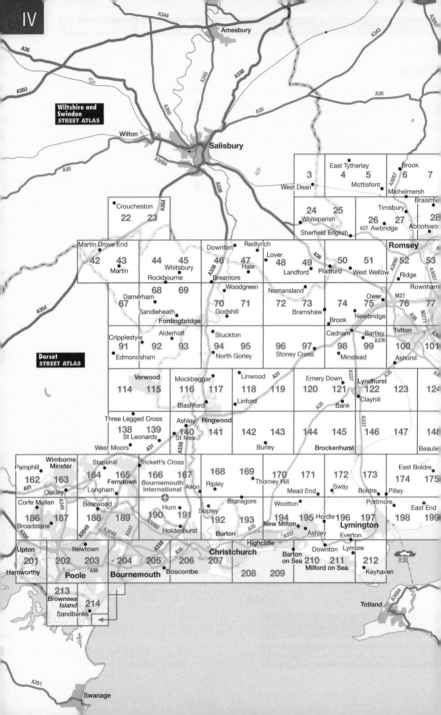

A344
Amesbury
A36
A303
A36
A343
A3057
A345
A338
A338
A30
A30
A30

Wiltshire and Swindon STREET ATLAS

Wilton
A360
A354
A3094
A338
Salisbury

| Croucheston | | | West Dean | 3 | East Tytherley 4 | 5 | Brook 6 | 7 |

Croucheston
22 23

3
East Tytherley
4   5
West Dean
Mottisfont
Brook
6   7
Michelmersh
Braishfie

24   25
Whiteparish
Sherfield English
26   27
A27 Awbridge
Timsbury
Abbotswo
28
Romsey

Martin Drove End
42   43
Martin
44   45
Whitsbury
Rockbourne
Downton Redlynch
46   47
Hale
Breamore
Lover
48   49
Landford Plaitford
A36
50   51
West Wellow
A3090
52   53
Ridge
Rownham
A3057

68   69
Damerham
67
Sandleheath
Fordingbridge
Woodgreen
70   71
Godshill
Nomansland
72   73
Bramshaw
74
Brook
Ower
75
Newbridge
M27
76   77
A36
MZ271

Cripplestyle
91   92   93
Edmondsham
Alderholt
Stuckton
94   95
North Gorley
96   97
Stoney Cross
Cadnam
98   99
Minstead
Bartley
A336
Totton
100 101
Ashurst

Verwood
114 115
Mockbeggar
116 117
Blashford
Linwood
118 119
Linford
A31
Emery Down
120 121
Bank
Lyndhurst
122 123
Clayhill
A337
124
A35

Three Legged Cross
138 139
St Leonards
West Moors
Ashley
140
St Ives
A338
Ringwood
141 142 143
Burley
144 145
A337
Brockenhurst
146 147
148
Beaulie

Pamphill
162 163
Oakley
A31
Wimborne Minster
Stapehill
164 165
Ferndown
Longham
A349
Trickett's Cross
166 167
Bournemouth International
Avon
168 169
Thorney Hill
Ripley
170 171
Mead End
172 173
Sway
Boldre
Pilley
East Boldre
174 175

Corfe Mullen
186 187
Broadstone
Bearwood
188 189
A349
A3049
A347
190 191
Hurn
Sopley
Holdenhurst
192 193
Burton
A35
Bransgore
Wootton
194 195
New Milton
Ashley
Hordle
Everton
196 197
Portmore
Lymington
East End
198 199

Upton
201
Hamworthy
Newtown
202 203
A35
Poole
204 205
206 207
Christchurch
Highcliffe
Barton on Sea
208 209
210 211
Milford on Sea
212
Keyhaven
Downton Lymore
A337
Bournemouth Boscombe

213
Brownsea Island
Sandbanks
214
0:30

A3054
Totland

A351
Swanage

Dorset STREET ATLAS

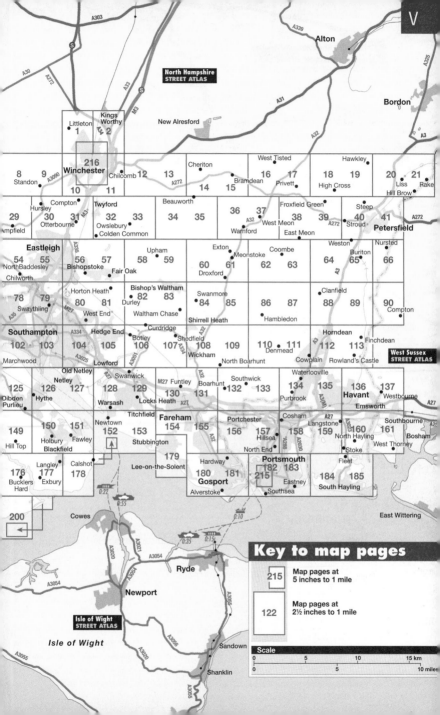

V

A303

A339

Alton

A325

A30 A272

North Hampshire
STREET ATLAS

M3

New Alresford

A31

A32

A3

Bordon

Littleton
1

Kings
Worthy
2

8
Standon

9

Winchester
216

Chilcomb **12**

13

Cheriton

West Tisted

Hawkley

16 **17**
Privett

Bramdean

18 **19**
High Cross

20
Liss

21
Rake

Hill Brow

A3

10 **11**

A272

14 **15**

29
ampfield

30

Hursley

Compton

31

Twyford

32 **33**
Owslebury
Colden Common

34 **35**

Beauworth

Warnford

36

37
West Meon

A32

Froxfield Green

38 **39**
East Meon

A272

Steep

40
Stroud

41
Petersfield

A272

Eastleigh

54
NorthBaddesley

55

56
Bishopstoke

57
Fair Oak

Upham

58 **59**

Exton
Meonstoke

60 **61**
Droxford

Coombe

62 **63**

Weston

64

Buriton

65

Nursted

66

Chilworth

78
Swaythling

79

Horton Heath

80 **81**
West End

Durley

Bishop's Waltham

82 **83**

Waltham Chase

Swanmore

84 **85**

Shirrell Heath

86 **87**

Hambledon

Clanfield

88 **89**

90
Compton

Southampton

102 103

104 **105**
Lowford

Hedge End

Botley

106

Curdridge
Shedfield

107
Wickham

108 **109**

North Boarhunt

Denmead

110 **111**

Cowplain

Horndean

112 **113**
Rowland's Castle

Finchdean

West Sussex
STREET ATLAS

Marchwood

125
Dibden
Purlieu

126
Hythe

Old Netley
Netley

127

Swanwick

128 **129**
Warsash

M27 Funtley

130 **131**
Locks Heath

Boarhunt

Southwick

132 **133**

Waterlooville

134 **135**
Purbrook

136
Havant

Emsworth

137
Westbourne

A27

149
Hill Top

150
Holbury
Blackfield

151
Fawley

Newtown

152 **153**
Stubbington

Titchfield

Fareham

154 **155**

Portchester

156

Cosham

157
North End

158

A27

Langstone

159
Stoke

A3055

160
North Hayling

West Thorney

Southbourne

161
Bosham

A27

176
Bucklers
Hard

Langley

177
Exbury

Calshot

178

A3054

179
Lee-on-the-Solent

Hardway

180 **181**
Gosport
Alverstoke

Portsmouth

182 **183**
215
Eastney
Southsea

Fleet

184 **185**
South Hayling

East Wittering

200

Cowes

A3020

A3021

A3054

Ryde

A3055

Newport

Isle of Wight
STREET ATLAS

A3054

A3055

A3020

A3066

Sandown

Shanklin

A3055

Isle of Wight

Key to map pages

215 — Map pages at
5 inches to 1 mile

122 — Map pages at
2½ inches to 1 mile

Scale

| 0 | 5 | 10 | 15 km |

| 0 | 5 | 10 miles |

Major administrative and Postcode boundaries

County and unitary authority boundaries
District boundaries
Postcode boundaries
Area covered by this atlas

Scale

0   5   10   15 km
0   5   10 miles

Counties / Areas

Bracknell Forest
Surrey
West Sussex
Wokingham
West Berkshire
Hart
East Hampshire
Basingstoke and Deane
Winchester
Hampshire
Test Valley
New Forest
City of Southampton
Fareham
Havant
City of Portsmouth
Isle of Wight
Wiltshire
Dorset
Poole
Bournemouth

Postcode districts

GU15, GU16, GU17, GU46, RG40, GU51, GU14, GU11, GU12, GU52, GU9, GU10, GU27, GU26, GU20, GU33, GU31, GU30, GU35, GU34, GU32, GU29, RG27, RG7, RG26, RG24, RG21, RG23, RG22, RG25, RG19, RG20, RG28, RG14, SN8, SP11, SP10, SP9, SP4, SP5, SP6, SP8, SP2, SO20, SO21, SO22, SO23, SO24, SO51, SO52, SO50, SO43, SO40, SO41, SO42, SO45, SO31, SO30, SO32, SO17, SO18, SO19, SO14, SO15, SO16, PO18, PO8, PO7, PO6, PO9, PO10, PO11, PO1, PO2, PO3, PO4, PO5, PO12, PO13, PO14, PO15, PO16, PO17, BH6, BH5, BH1, BH4, BH7, BH8, BH9, BH10, BH11, BH23, BH24, BH25, BH21, BH22, BH31, BH18, BH16, BH15, BH12, BH13, BH14, BH17, BH3, BH2

Towns / Places

Camberley, Frimley, Farnborough, Aldershot, Farnham, Haslemere, Grayshott, Liphook, Wokingham, Yateley, Fleet, Odiham, Bentley, Bordon, Liss, Petersfield, Alton, Medstead, East Tisted, West Meon, Hordean, Mortimer, Tadley, Bramley, Chineham, Basingstoke, Ellisfield, Bentworth, Alresford, New Alresford, Meonstoke, Hambledon, Wickham, Fareham, Gosport, Portsmouth, Havant, Hayling Island, Thorney Island, Newbury, Kingsclere, Burghclere, Oakley, North Waltham, Whitchurch, Micheldever, South Wonston, Winchester, Bishop's Waltham, Twyford, Itchen Abbas, Eastleigh, West End, Netley, Hythe, Fawley, Verham Dean, Tangley, Thruxton, Andover, Over Wallop, Wherwell, Broughton, Romsey, Mottisfont, West Wellow, Totton, Southampton, Beaulieu, Lymington, St Mary Bourne, West Dean, Wick, Fordingbridge, Ilsley, Ringwood, Burley, Lyndhurst, Brockenhurst, Cadnam, Sway, Barton on Sea, Christchurch, Bournemouth, Martin, Croucheston, Verwood, Ferndown, Wimborne Minster, Poole

Isle of Wight

ST, SU, SZ, SY

A33 Basingstoke (A30)

A34

B304

Kings
Worthy

Kings Worthy
Prim Sch

Meadow
Farm

Cemy
1 GILLINGHAM CL
2 CEDARWOOD

Springvale

Woodhams
Farm

Recn
Gd

Prince's Mead
Sch

Worthy
Park

Worthy Park
Home Farm

Headbourne
Worthy

HEADBOURNE
WORTHY HO

Abbots
Worthy

B3047

PH

Upper
Farm

Lower
Farm

Foresters
Pk

Pudding
House
Farm

SO23

SO21

Easton
Down

Three Castles Path
Itchen Way

Dairy
Farm

Lone
Barn

SO22

Abbots
Barton
House

Kings Way
Nuns Wlk

River Itchen

WINCHESTER BY PASS

Winnall
Cottage Farm

Abbots
Barton

Abbots Barton
Farm House

Shoulder of Mutton
Farm

WINCHESTER

North Walls
Recn
Gd

The
Wykeham
Ind Est

9

SPITFIRE LINK

Hyde

River Park
L Ctr

ERASMUS WAY

Dykes
Farm

Chaucer
Ind Est

Superstore

Winnall
Dennet
Trad Est

Winnall Down
Copse

M3

A33

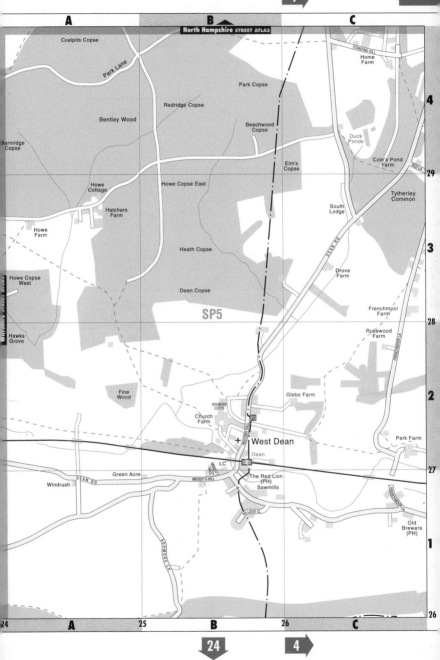

North Hampshire STREET ATLAS

Coalpits Copse

Park Lane

STANDING HILL

Home
Farm

Park Copse

Redridge Copse

Bentley Wood

Beechwood
Copse

Duck
Ponds

Barnridge
Copse

Cole's Pond
Farm

B3084

Elm's
Copse

29

Howe
Cottage

Howe Copse East

South
Lodge

Tytherley
Common

Hatchers
Farm

Howe
Farm

Heath Copse

DEAN RD

Drove
Farm

3

Howe Copse
West

Frenchmoor
Farm

Dean Copse

28

Rosewood
Farm

Hawks
Grove

SP5

FRENCHMOOR LA

Fine
Wood

Glebe Farm

2

ROOKERY
COTTS

Church
Farm

West Dean

Park Farm

Dean

LC

27

Green Acre

MOODY'S HILL

The Red Lion
(PH)
Sawmills

FRENCHMOOR LA

Windrush

DEAN RD

HILLSIDE CL

Old
Brewers
(PH)

ASHMORE LA

1

26

North Hampshire STREET ATLAS

A   **B**   **C**

West Tytherley
CE Prim Sch

Church
Farm

Stony
Batter

Stride's
Farm

Manor
Farm

East
Tytherley

Poplar
Farm

West
Tytherley

Lye
Farm

Sopp's
Farm

MANOR
RD

The Green

THE COACH RD

White House

BONNER
COTTS

Oaklands
Farm

29

Drove

3 SP5

Frenchmoor

Lockerley Hall
Park

Lain
Copse

Upper Frenchmoor Copse

Lower
Frenchmoor
Copse

Bulls Drove

HOME FARM
BSNS CTR.

Lockerley
Hall

28

Pug's Hole

Holbury Wood

The Star Inn
(PH)

2

Holbury
Farm

MARK WAY

SO51

PARK
VIEW

Lockerley Water
Farm

27

Holbury Mill

Mill Farm

Manor
Farm

LC

River Dun

EAST DEAN RD

East Dean

1

Dean Hill Barn
Farm

Deangate
Farm

Top Green

Lockerley

Dean Hill

Curlew's
Farm

Critchell's
Green

Butt's
Green

26

27   **A**   **28**   **B**   **29**   **C**

Hackpits
Copse

Redhills
Copse

Deborah
Copse

Pittleworth
Manor

Pittleworth
Farm

B3084

Little Bentley
Farm

Great Bentley
Farm

Holm Moor
Copse

SP5

Bentley
Firs

SO20

Blackpits Wood

The
Bungalow

Lain Copse

Great
Copse

Clapgate
Copse

Snook's
Copse

Spearywell Wood

SO51

Newlyns
Farm

BACK LA

Blackmoor Firs

Culver
Leaze

Bushy
Copse

Woodland
Walk

P

Cadbury
Farm

Dummer
Copse

Spearywell

Test Way

Mottisfont Abbey
(National Trust)

Gardens

Priory

OAKLEY RD

Abbey
Farm

KEEPERS LA

BENGER'S LA

Mottisfont

River Dun

Drove Copse

HATT LA

Hatt Farm
Hatt Hill

Glebe
Farm

Monarch's Way

CHURCH LA

River Test

P

Lockerley Endowed
CE Prim Sch

Butt's
Green

The
School Farm

LOCKERLEY RD

Dunbridge

LC

LC

Dunbridge

Test Way

River Dun

RUSSELL DR 1
MILL RISE 2

LOCKERLEY RD

DUNBRIDGE LA

PH

B3084

Lodge

Drovelands

Compton Park

Humbers Wood

Compton Manor

Compton

Compton Home Farm

Brook Dairy Farm

Horse Lynch

BROOK COTTS

Brook

SO20

News Wood

Oakley Copse

Eldon Firs

River Test

Lower Brook

Strouds Wood

Lower Eldon Farm

Oakley Farm

Michelmersh Wood

Monarch's Way

Test Way

ROMSEY RD

A3057

Park Farm Bungalow

Parnell Lane

SO51

Stonymarsh Cottage

MUSH RD

Michelmersh Court

Manor Farm

Oak Tree Farm

SCHOOL LA

The Monarch's Way

Michelmersh

Stonymarsh

STAFF RD

Linhay Meads Dairy

HONEYST LA

A3057

King's Somborne

Bourne
Farm

FURZEDOWN RD

FURZEDOWN
COTTS

Furzedown
Farm

FURZEDOWN
HO

Humbers
Wood

Hoplands

Hoplands
Cottages

Charlwood
Copse

Clarendon Way

Combe
Bottom

Luke Copse

SO20

Dirty Mount

Parnholt Wood

ELDON RD

Jews
Wood

The
Bungalow

Eldon
House

Bailey's
Down

Taunton
Vale

Fishponds
Farm

Bailey's Down
Farm

PARNHOLT RD

Stubb's Copse

SO51

Farley
House

Parnell La

Bull Grove
Copse

Blue Haze
Farm

Monarch's Way

Windmill
Cottages

Hall
Place

FARLEY LA

Pitt
Farm

Braishfield
Manor

KING'S SOMBORNE RD

PATNS WAY RD

Fern Hill La

Fernhill
Farm

4

29

3

28

2

27

1

26

A   37   B   38   C

A   B   C

SO20

Forest of Bere Farm

Forest Belt

West Wood

P

4

Ashley Down

Beacon Hill

Beaconhill Plantation

P

Farley Mount Country Park

E

Clarendon Way

Mon • Farley Mount

Hanging Wood

29

Mount Down

Pitt Down

Parnholt Wood

3

Farley Down

Heath Close Corner

Talbeys

28

Landing Strip

SO21

Farley Farm Cottages

Farley Farm

SO51

Boosey Hanging

South Lynch

Berrydown Farm

2

+

Berry Down

Violet Hill

Sandhill Copse

Oakfield

27

Brooks Copse

Merdon Manor Farm

Miller's Copse

Blows Row

1

Gudge Copse

Ammery Lodge

Upper Slackstead

Upper Slackstead Farm

Pillinch Copse

26
39   A   40   B   41   C

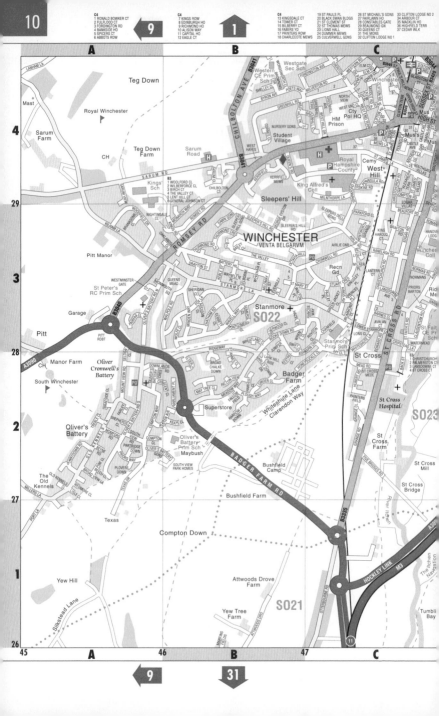

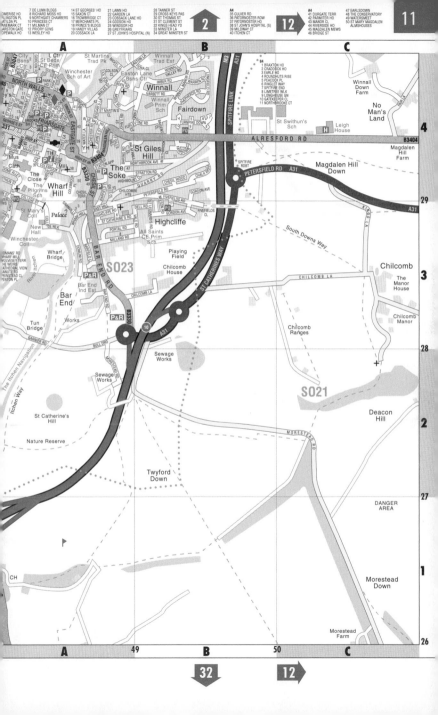

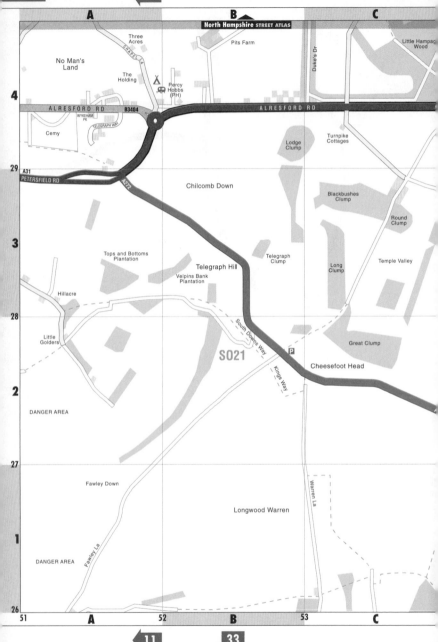

No Man's Land

Three Acres

Pits Farm

Little Hampage Wood

The Holding

Percy Hobbs (PH)

Duke's Dr

4

A L R E S F O R D   R D

B3404

A L R E S F O R D   R D

WYKEHAM PK

TELEGRAPH WK

Cemy

Lodge Clump

Turnpike Cottages

29

A31

PETERSFIELD RD

A272

Chilcomb Down

Blackbushes Clump

Round Clump

3

Tops and Bottoms Plantation

Telegraph Hill

Telegraph Clump

Long Clump

Temple Valley

Velpins Bank Plantation

Hillacre

28

South Downs Way

Little Golders

SO21

P

Great Clump

Cheesefoot Head

2

Kings Way

DANGER AREA

27

Fawley Down

Warren La

Longwood Warren

1

Fawley La

DANGER AREA

26

51

A

52

B

53

C

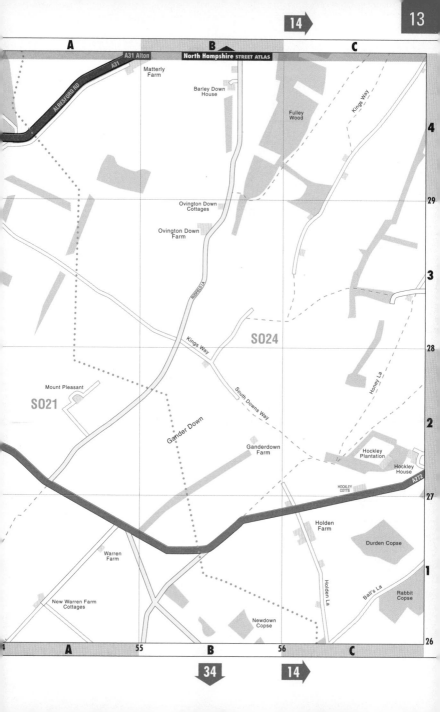

A   B   C

4

29

3

28

2

27

1

26

57   58   59

Sevington Farm

Cheriton Mill

B3046

Prite La

Wayfarer's Walk

Broad La

Hinton La

River Itchen

North End

Itchen Way

Middle Farm

NORTH END FARM COTTS

North End Farm

Cowdown Copse

Bramdean La

Broad La

Hill Houses

HILL HOUSES LA

Cheriton Prim Sch

Cheriton

Upper Lamborough La

Itchen Way

Cheriton La

THE GOOCHES

DARK LA

Lamborough La

Cheriton La

LOWER LAMBOROUGH LA

The Flowerpots (PH)

Malthouse Farm

TICHBORNE CL

WHITE LA

Marriners Farm

Primrose Cottages

SO24

Westfield Farm

B3046

Jolly Farmer (PH)

A272

28

Hinton Marsh

Hinton Ampner

Godwin Farm

New Cheriton

GREYS FARM CL

The Park

PETERSFIELD RD

Harnham Hill

Source of The River Itchen

KILMESTON RD

Hinton Ampner House

Manor Farm

HINTON HILL

A272

Durden Copse

BAITS LA

Durden Lodge

Powells Grove Copse

Shorley Copse

Shorley Wood House

Shorley Farm

Shorley

Wayfarer's Walk

Hacks Cottage

Beauworth

WESTFIELD DRO

Manor Farm

West Wood

Kilmeston

Manor Farm

WESTWOOD VIEW

St Andrew's House

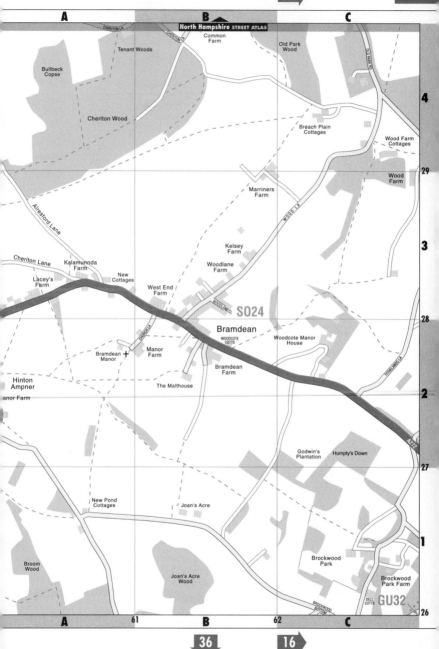

CHERITON LA

Tenant Woods

Common Farm

Old Park Wood

Bullbeck Copse

OLD PARK RD

Cheriton Wood

Breach Plain Cottages

Wood Farm Cottages

4

29

Wood Farm

Alresford Lane

Marriners Farm

WOOD LA

3

Cheriton Lane

Kalamunda Farm

Kelsey Farm

Lacey's Farm

New Cottages

Woodlane Farm

West End Farm

WOODLANE CL

SO24

28

Bramdean

CHURCH LA

WOODCOTE COTTS

Woodcote Manor House

ITHELANDS LA

Bramdean Manor +

Manor Farm

2

Hinton Ampner

Bramdean Farm

The Malthouse

anor Farm

A272

Godwin's Plantation

Humpty's Down

27

New Pond Cottages

Joan's Acre

1

Broom Wood

Brockwood Park

Joan's Acre Wood

Brockwood Park Farm

BROCKWOOD BOTTOM

DELL COTTS

GU32

26

North Hampshire STREET ATLAS

A   **B**   **C**

Wr Twr

Daylesford

4

Bramdean Common

Bonniesfield
Farm

West Tisted

The
Plantation

Clinkley Road

Manor
Farm

Saw
Mill

St
Christopher

Green Lane

Home Farm

29

Long
House

Manor Farm
Stud

Cour
Farm

Woodland
Gate

3

Wolfhanger
Farm

Frenchleys

PUNSHOLT LA

SO24

Parsonage
Farm

28

Tithelands Lane

Slys Farm

Punsholt
Farm

Punsholt
Cottages

Purser's

2

Hinton Woodlands
Farm

Woodlands
Farm

Purser's La

Old
Wheatshea

GU3

Three Horse Shoes
Farm

27

A272

The Grove

THREE HORSE SHOES LA

**West Meon
Woodlands**

The Dean

KITT'S LA

P

Woodlands
Farm

1

Inwood
Copse

Shutt's
Copse

GU32

The West Meon Hut
(PH)

A32

Garage

A27

Martin's Woo

26

Pest Houses

63   **A**   **64**   **B**   **65**   **C**

North Hampshire STREET ATLAS

A32 Alton

Wyatt's Wood

Bottom Farm

Woodside Farm

Ashtree Cottage

Lodge

BRICK KILN LA

LANE END

New Copse

Brick Kiln Farm

SO24

Old Lodge

4

29

The Grove

Cannon Dell

RAILWAY COTTS

Pig and Whistle (PH)

Basing Home Farm

Ashen Wood House

Basing Park

Monument

3

Ashen Wood

The Jumps

Basing Park

BASING DEAN

28

Broom Farm

FARM LA

Fawley Farm

HEMPLAND LA

GU34

Broadmore Copse

Mere Pond

Filmore Hill

Hall

Bailey Green

2

FILMOREHILL LA

PO

CHURCH RD

Farnfield Farm

MEREPOND LA

Filmore Hill Farm

Lime Copse

The Old Vicarage

Hurst Bottom

27

Stock Copse

STOCKS LA

Privett

Church Farm

Stocks Farm

Butt's Wood

Ham Wood

Tiddle's Copse

1

Dick's Copse

GU32

Common Copse

GU32

Roundabout Copse

A272

Petersfield Lodge

A
67
B
68
C
26

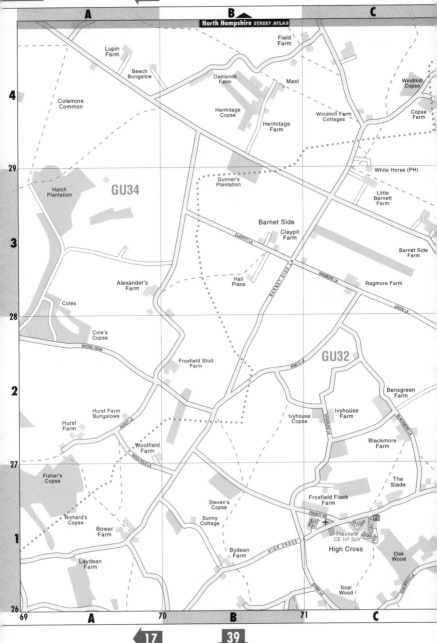

North Hampshire STREET ATLAS

A   B   C

4

Lupin Farm

Beech Bungalow

Colemore Common

Field Farm

Oaklands Farm

Mast

Hermitage Copse

Hermitage Farm

Windmill Farm Cottages

Windmill Copse

Copse Farm

29

GU34

Hatch Plantation

Gunner's Plantation

White Horse (PH)

Little Barnett Farm

3

Barnet Side

Claypit Farm

Barnet Side Farm

CLAYPIT LA

BARNET SIDE LA

RAGMORE LA

Alexander's Farm

Hall Place

Ragmore Farm

GREEN LA

Coles

28

Cole's Copse

BASING DEAN

Froxfield Stud Farm

KING'S LA

GU32

Bensgreen Farm

2

Hurst Farm Bungalows

HURST LA

Ivyhouse Copse

Ivyhouse Farm

BLACKMORE LA

Hurst Farm

Woolfield Farm

WOOLSILO LA

Blackmore Farm

27

Fisher's Copse

The Slade

Steven's Copse

Froxfield Flock Farm

Richard's Copse

Bower Farm

Sunny Cottage

PRIVETT RD

Froxfield CE Inf Sch

FANG LA

1

Laydean Farm

Bydean Farm

HIGH CROSS

High Cross

Oak Wood

Soal Wood

SPORT LA

SPARKFORD LA

26

69   A   70   B   71   C

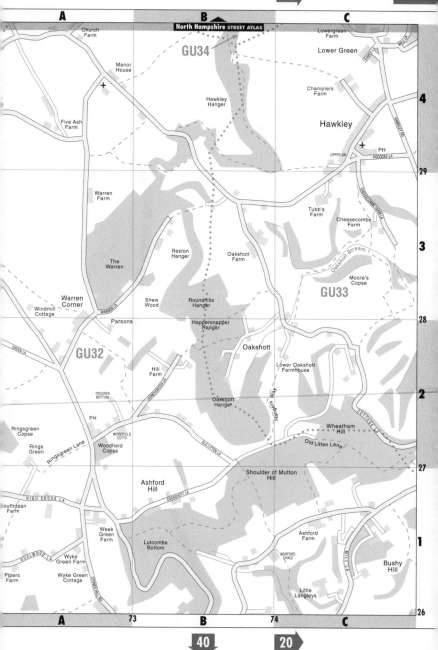

A | **B** | **C**

Church Farm

Manor House

GU34

Lowergreen Farm

Lower Green

Hawkley Hanger

Champlers Farm

4

Five Ash Farm

Hawkley

PH

UPPER GN

POCOCKS LA

29

Warren Farm

Tubb's Farm

Cheesecombe Farm

3

Reston Hanger

Oakshott Farm

Moore's Copse

The Warren

GU33

Warren Corner

Shaw Wood

Roundhills Hanger

Windmill Cottage

Parsons

Happersnapper Hanger

28

GREEN LA

GU32

Oakshott

Hill Farm

Lower Oakshott Farmhouse

TROOPER BOTTOM

Oakshott Hanger

2

PH

Ringsgreen Copse

WOODFIELD COTTS

Wheatham Hill

COTTAGE LA

Rings Green

Ringsgreen Lane

Woodfield Copse

Old Litten Lane

27

HIGH CROSS LA

Ashford Hill

Shoulder of Mutton Hill

Southdean Farm

COCKSHOTT LA

Week Green Farm

Ashford Farm

1

SUALWOOD LA

Wyke Green Farm

Lutcombe Bottom

ASHFORD CHACE

Bushy Hill

Pipers Farm

Wyke Green Cottage

Little Langleys

26

A | 73 | **B** | 74 | **C**

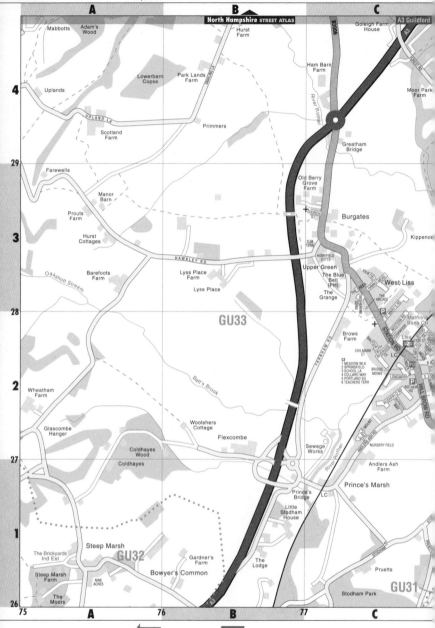

GU30

Longmoor
Inclosure

Little Dean
Bottom

4

Warren
Hill

The
Wylds

The Lake

Wylds
Farm

Langley

29

WARREN RD

Langley Bridge
Farm

The Temple
Inn
(PH)

Liss
Forest

The
Mint

Mangers

REEDS LA

Brewells
Farm

Little
Langley
Farm

THERBANK
FARM LA

Reeds

3

CHEST RISE

MINT RD

Home
Farm

Whangerei Nursery
Palmers Farm

LC

DUCKMEAD LA

Palmers

Newlands

West Sussex STREET ATLAS

Rake CE
Prim Sch

DUDLEY
TERR

WYLD GREEN LA

Wyld Green
Farm

Ciddy
Hall

ST PATRICK'S LA

Rake
Bsns Pk.

28

MILLBROOK
CL

SILVER BIRCH

East Liss

ROCKPIT
COTTS

GU33

St Patrick's
Copse

The
Flying Bull
(PH)

B2070

Liss

OAK TREE DR

YEW TREES

RAKE RD

PRIORS LA

FIR TREE
COTTS

Coldharbour
Park
Farm

COPSE CL

LITTLE BARN

HIGHFIELD DRS

High Firs
House

HATCH LA

Rake

2

MOSS CL

THE
BOUNDS

Highfield
Farm

East
Hill
Liss
Inf & Jun
Schs

CARDEN
DENNS RD

Highfield
Wood

Sussex Border Path

CASTLE LA

SANDY LA

27

HILL BROW RD

HUNTSBOTTOM LA

Hill
Side

Pot
Well

Black
Pond

Rake
Common

EDGEWOOD
CT

Rake
Hanger

GU31

1

Hill
Brow

B3006

PLANTATION LA

Farther
Commons

PH

Hambledon
Piece

LONDON RD

Clayton
Court

Combe
Hill

Harting
Combe

79

B

80

C

26

Bishopstone

The White Hart (PH)

PH

Flamstone Farm

FLAMSTONE ST

THE COURT

BETTYS CL

STANLEY CL

THE STYLES

Faulston House

MILL LA

FAULSTON COTTS

River Ebble

Faulston

Croucheston Farm

Corn Mill

Croucheston

Throope

Throope Bottom Cottages

Faulston Hole

Croucheston Hollow

Bishopstone Hollow

Faulston Drove

SP5

Faulston Down

Croucheston Drove

Ox Drove

Faulston Down Farm

Knighton High Wood

Croucheston Down Farm

Knighton Wood Farm

Toyd Clump

Garage

Croucheston Down

SP6

Trinity House

Swayne's Firs

A354

Granary

Wiltshire STREET ATLAS

Coombe
Bissett

Cemy

Shutts Lane

Pennings Drove

A354

Old Blandford Road

Downs

Gypsy Lane

Flowers
Bottom

BLANDFORD RD

The Beeches

Lower Coombe
Farm

25

Coombe Bissett
Down

Stratford Tony Down

Parsonage Barn

Homington Down

3

New Farm
Barn

Tottens Down
Barn

24

Southdown Farm

SP5

Pennings
Farm

Jervoise Farm

Greenacres Farm

College Farm

2

Ash Tree
Cottage

Grims Lodge
Farm

Grim's Ditch

Great Yews

23

Black Hill

Round
Clump

1

Long
Plantation

SP6

22

A **B** **C**

SP5

Deanhill Barn

Curlew's Farm

New Barn

COOKS LA 1
OVAL RD 2

Lockerley Manor

Critchell's Green

Gatmore Copse

Pits (disused)

Butler's Barn

4

Painshill Farm

MOUNT LA

Gatmore Cottage

25

Mount Pleasant Farm

Chapel Farm

Brokes Copse

3

Owls Lodge

Little Fosters

Rowden's Farm

Gambledown Farm

Badgers

24

Broxmore Park

SO51

Morrisholt Farm

Bryce's Farm

2

SP5

Cowesfield Gate

Ash Hill House

Deer Park Close

Sandy Close Farm

Berryfield Copse

Manor Farm

Pound Farm

Watson's Farm

CHURCH LA

23

Pound Hill

Warren Farm

Sole Hill Farm

Pound Hill

POUND LA

Broxmore Farm

Pinewood Farm

EASTWOOD

Glebe Farm

A27

1

Temple Park

Melchet Pond

Greenvale Farm

Sherfield English

Rectory

Blackwater Farm

Edward's Sch

THE RISE

Fouracres

Sack Hill Farm

Hatchet Inn (PH)

MILL LA

Midfield Farm

22

A **28** **B** **29** **C**

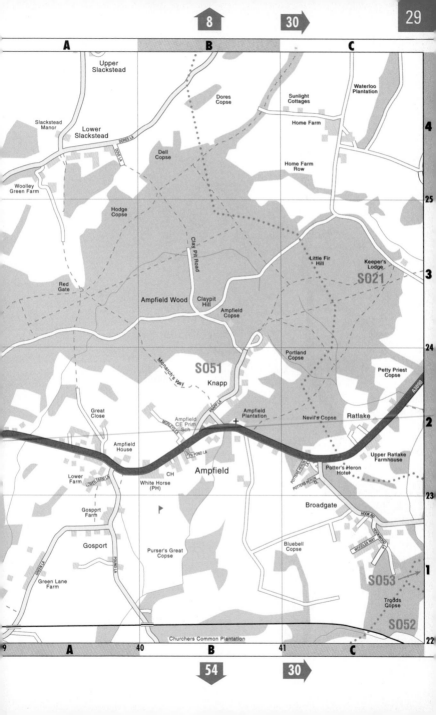

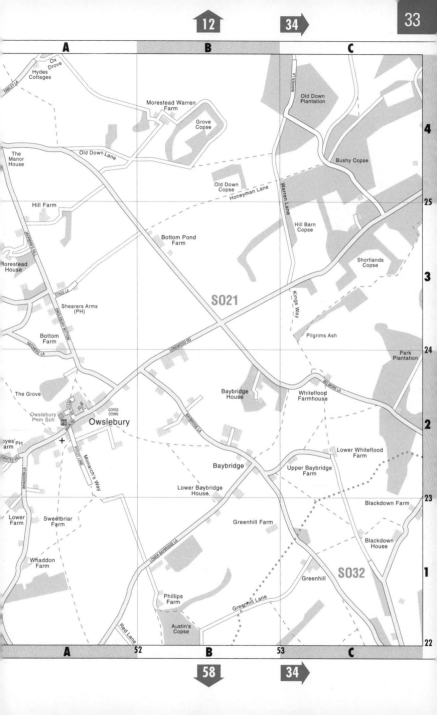

A
B
C

Ox Drove
Hydes Cottages

Morestead Warren Farm

Grove Copse

Old Down Plantation

4

The Manor House

Old Down Lane

Bushy Copse

Hill Farm

Old Down Copse

Honeyman Lane

Warren Lane

25

Morestead House

Bottom Pond Farm

Hill Barn Copse

Shortlands Copse

3

Shearers Arms (PH)

SO21

Kings Way

Pilgrims Ash

Park Plantation

Bottom Farm

LONGWOOD RD

24

The Grove

BELMORE LA

Baybridge House

Whiteflood Farmhouse

Owslebury Prim Sch

GORSE DOWN

Owslebury

2

oyes' PH arm

Monarch's Way

Baybridge

Upper Baybridge Farm

Lower Whiteflood Farm

Lower Farm

Sweetbriar Farm

Lower Baybridge House

Blackdown Farm

23

Greenhill Farm

Blackdown House

Whaddon Farm

LOWER BAYBRIDGE LA

SO32

1

Greenhill

Phillips Farm

Greenhill Lane

Red Lane

Austin's Copse

22

A
52
B
53
C

A B C

4

Piddles
Plantation

Ganderdown
wood

Honeyman
Farm

Stonywalls
Plantation

Stubb La

Lane End
Copse

Lane End
Down

Lane End

Lane End
Farm

Hamilton Fa
Cottages

Hamilton Farm

WESTFIELD DRO

South Downs Way

MONARCH LA

High
Stoke

25

SO21

Loverdene

Lancen Cottages

Greendowns

SO24

Windmi
Farm

The Milbury's
(Inn)

3

Forest
Copse

Douglas
Cottage

Glasspools Farm
House

May
Cottages

Millbarrow
Plantation

LONGWOOD PARK LA

24

Longwood Dean
Farm

2

Long
Wood

Dur Wood

Saltlane
Plantation

Rooker

West
Lodge

BEECH LA

WILMOTT LA

23

Durwood
Cottages

Valley Walk

The Holt

High
Wood

SO32

Lime Wood

Monarch's Way

1

Stony Hard
Farm

Hazards
Copse

The Holt
Lodge

Middle Preshaw

Lower Preshaw Lane

Well
Copse

Linches
Rows

Priest Wood

BEECH LA

Lower Preshaw
Farm

22

54 A 55 B 56 C

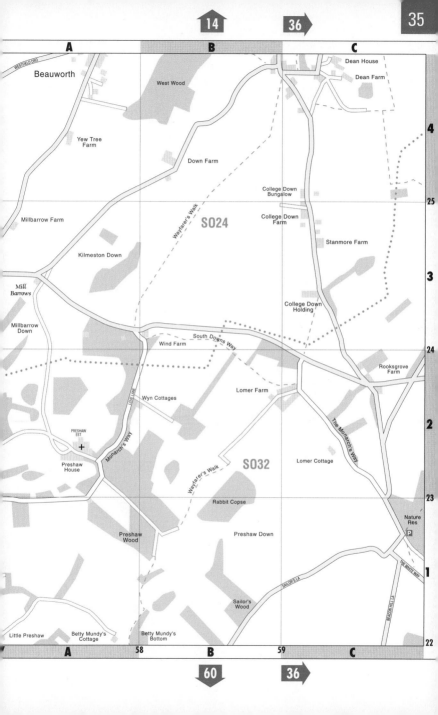

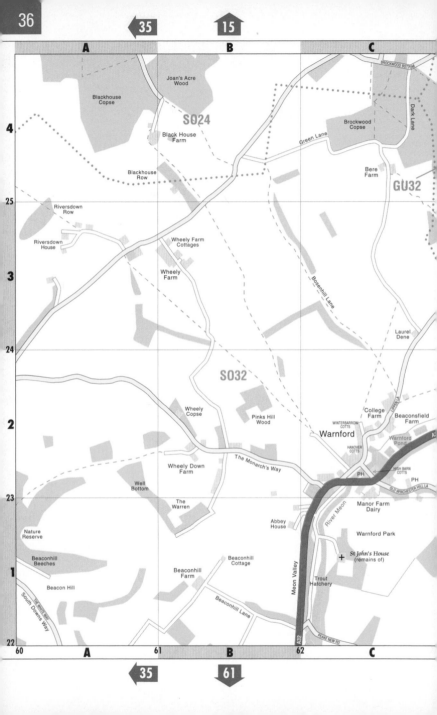

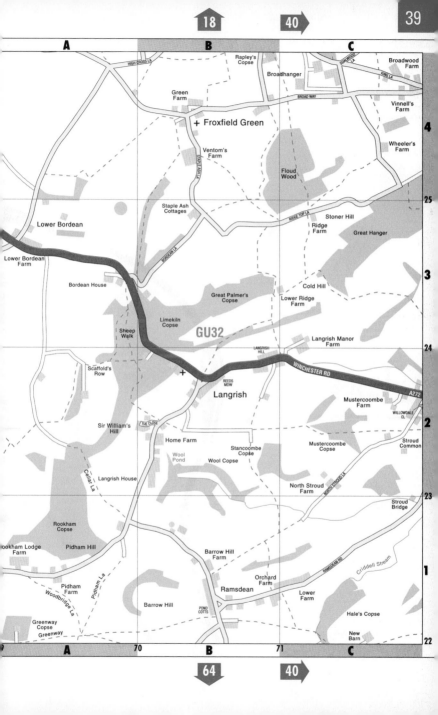

A
B
C

HIGH CROSS LA

Rapley's Copse

KOALWOOD LA

Broadwood Farm

KING LA

Broadhanger

Green Farm

BROAD WAY

Vinnell's Farm

+ Froxfield Green

4

Ventom's Farm

Wheeler's Farm

Floud Wood

25

STAPLE ASH LA

Staple Ash Cottages

RIDGE TOP LA

Stoner Hill

Lower Bordean

Ridge Farm

Great Hanger

BORDEAN LA

Lower Bordean Farm

3

Bordean House

Great Palmer's Copse

Cold Hill

Lower Ridge Farm

Limekiln Copse

GU32

Langrish Manor Farm

Sheep Walk

LANGRISH HILL

24

WINCHESTER RD

Scaffold's Row

REEDS MDW

A272

Langrish

Mustercoombe Farm

WILLOWDALE CL

Sir William's Hill

THE CLOSE

Home Farm

Stancoombe Copse

Mustercoombe Copse

Stroud Common

2

Wool Pond

Wool Copse

NORTH STROUD LA

Cellar La

Langrish House

North Stroud Farm

23

Stroud Bridge

Rookham Copse

ookham Lodge Farm

Pidham Hill

Barrow Hill Farm

RAMSDEAN RD

Criddell Stream

1

Pidham Farm

PIDHAM LA

Orchard Farm

Lower Farm

Hale's Copse

Woodbridge La

Barrow Hill

Ramsdean

POND COTTS

New Barn

Greenway Copse

Greenway

22

Chicken Grove

Chickengrove Bottom

Vernditch Lodge

Vernditch Chase

Sundown Farm

Haskells Farm

Martin Drove End

The Coote Arms (PH)

SP6

Middle Lane

Bokerley Junction

SP5

A354 Blandford Forum

A354

Martin Down
National Nature Reserve

TOWNSEND LA

BELEN LA

Bokerley Farm

Bowling Green Lane

Earthpits Lane

Bokerley Down

Jubilee Trail

BH21

Peaked Post

MORGAN'S LA

Pentridge

Whitey Top

Blagdon Plantation

03   A   04   B   05   C

A | B | C

4

Furze Down

SP5

Paradise

21

Toyd Farm

3

St Bride's
Farm

20

SP6

Knap
Barrow

East Martin

Grans
Barrow

TOWNSEND LANE

Martin

Bustard Manor
Farm

Toyd Down

2

SILLEN LA

King's
Farm

ST GEORGES
CDTTS

Kingstown
Copse

19

Windmill Hill

Tidpit

Knoll Down

1

Allen River

BH21

Chase
Barn

Tidpit Down

18

A | B | C

A **B** **C**

Titchborne
Farm

MOOR LA

Great Sherwood
Copse

Gill's Hole

Mollcroft
Copse

4

Lower Pensworth
Farm

Horse Pond
Copse

Wall Copse

East Copse

Thorn's
Copse

Newhouse

Bagfield Copse

21

GROVE LA

GOGG'S LA

Out Wood

TIMBURY LA

Timbury Farm
House

Shearwood Copse

Appsy Copse

Homan's Copse

Langley Wood

Round
Copse

3

Badger's
Copse

HORSE RD

Brickkiln
Cottage

Witterns Hill
Farm

LOVER RD

Langley Wood

Lover

CHURCH HILL

Cole's
Copse

Bishops Wood

CHURCH HILL

SCHOOL RD

Redlynch CE
Prim Sch

The Mount

SP5

Ford

Hamptworth
Farm

20

BLACK LA

Moor Copse

HAMPTWORTH RD

Loosehanger Farm

2

Hamptworth
Lodge

Loosehanger Copse

Home
Farm

Pimlico
Firs

The Bog

19

SP6

Loosehanger
Common

Pimlico
Bottom

1

Radnor
Firs

B3080

Quar Hill
Plantation

Horse Common

LYBURN RD

Lyburn
Farm

Windyeats Farm

Cloven Hill Plantation

18

21 **A** **22** **B** **23** **C**

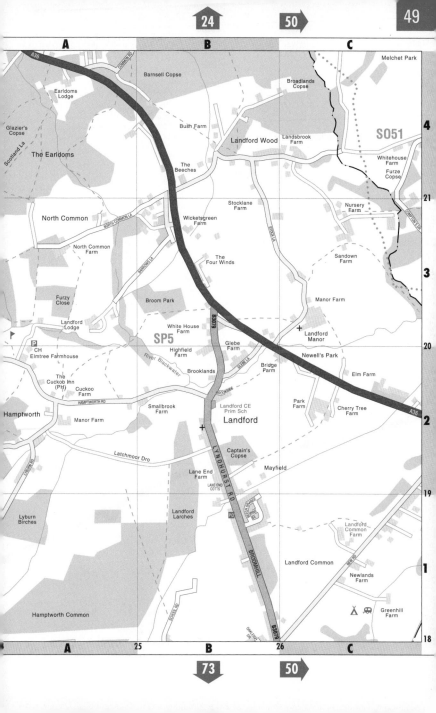

A   B   C

4

Melchetcourt Farm
Boulder Wood
Plaitford Wood
Plaitford Wood Farm
Yew Tree Farm
Fielder's Farm

Sherfield Mill
Dandy's Ford
Wellow Wood
Pilgrim's Farm
Hazel Wood
Plaitford Green
Paddock Farm
Short's Farm
Sinderkerkins Farm

21

Plaitford Copse
Bowles Farm
New Lodge

Gardiner's Farm

Cross Oak Farm
Pinns Farm

3

Manor Farm
Ford
Gauntletts Farm
Pound La
Bower's Farm
Lower Bridge Farm
SO51

King's Farm
Ford

River Blackwater

20

Plaitford
Ford
Powell's Farm
Redhouse Farm

Bottom Lane Farm
Chapman's Farm
Groves Down
Hatches Farm

Bridge Cotts
Long Bridg

2

Partridge Hill
Partridge Hill Farm
The Shoe (PH)

SALISBURY RD

Pembroke Farm

Peartree Cl
Bourne Cl

Romsey Rd
Bridge Farm
Pottery Farm

West Wellow
Oaklands

19

SP5

Osborne Ho

CRAWLEY HILL

1

Plaitford Common

West Wellow Common

Canada

Chatmohr

18

Sturtmoor Pond
SO43

Abbotts Farm

BLACK HILL RD

27   A   28   B   29   C

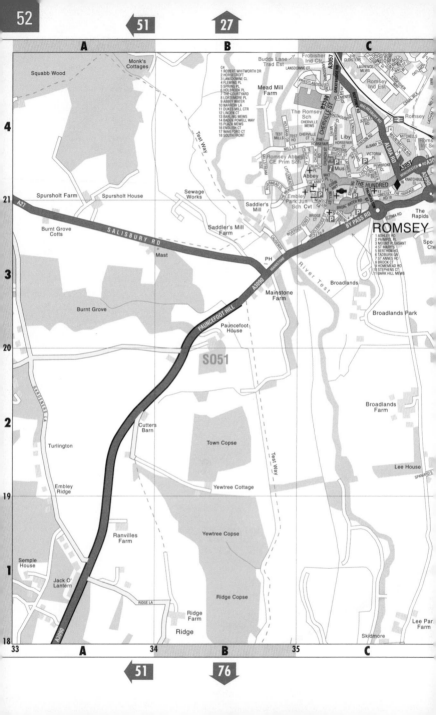

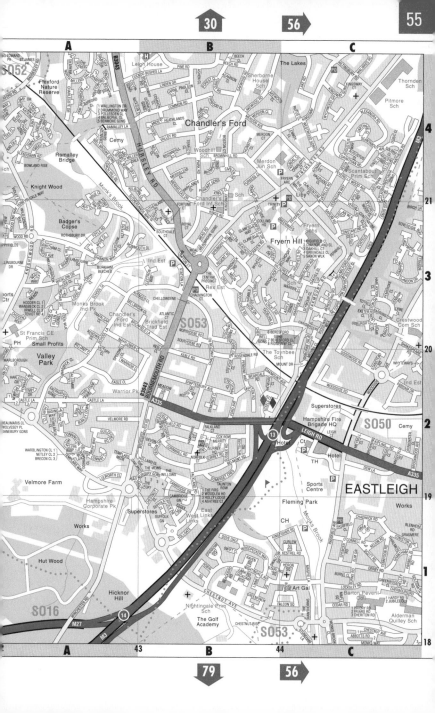

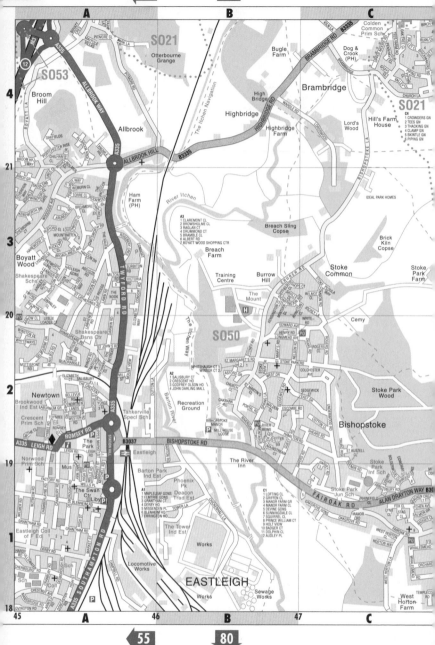

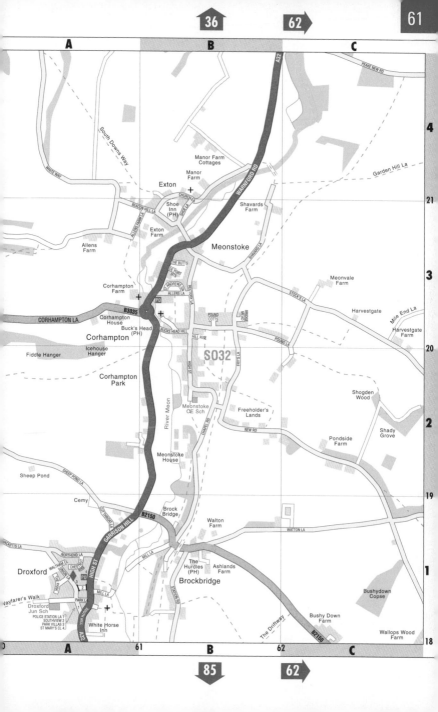

A **B** **C**

Henwood
Down

Garston
Farm

Duncoombe
Farm

Duncoombe
Cottage

GARSTON CL.
COOMBE RD.

HILL
VIEW
TEMPLE

Belmont
Farm

1 COOMBE ROAD TERR
2 PRINCES COTTS

Pastures

Lower House
Farm

4

Hockham

Coombe
Cross

Coombe
Cottages

Coombe

Coombe Farm
House

Small Down

Lower
Farm

Mill
Cottage

South
Farm

21

3

South Downs Way

Spring

Source of
River Meon

River Meon

20

Salt
Hill

GU32

Long
Down

Mast

Wether
Down

Upper
Barns

2

Chidden
Down

Monarch's Way

Mast

Mercury
Park

Hyden
Hill

PO7

Leydene
Bottom

HYDEN
CROSS

Hyden
Wood

19

Limekiln
Copse

PO8

HYDEN
WOOD

Dead Woman's
Gate

Hyden
Wood

1

Coombe Wood

A 67 **B** 68 **C**

18

A B C

Allen River

Tidpit Common Down

Knight's Copse

Soldier's Ring

South Allenford Farm

4

Blackheath Down

Kites Nest Farm

New Road Plantation

Boulsbury Down

17

Blagdon Hill Wood

High Boulsbury Wood

3

Martin Wood

Boulsbury Cottages

Boulsbury Farm

Holm Hill Copse

SP6

16

Stone Hill Wood

Kingland Copse

Peaked Plantation

Highwood Copse

BH21

Ball Hill Copse

2

Bottom Copse

Stapleton Farm

High Wood

Boulsbury Wood

Buttons Copse

Boveridge Farm

15

Boveridge House

Noddle Hill

Biddlesgate Copse

Bovis Row

Boveridge

Hyde Cross

Park Row

Hyde Farm

1

Burwood

Perry Copse

Biddlesgate Farm

Bratch Copse

Wadleys Dro

Pinetree Farm

14

A 07 B 08 C

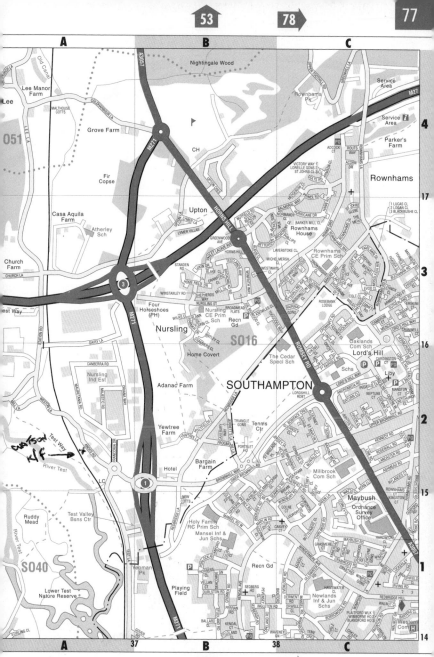

SO52

M27

Chilworth Common

Chilworth Tower

Dymer's Wood

Chilworth Common

Chilworth Ring

Lord's Wood

Castle Hill

SO16

Lordswood

Matheson Rd
Sinclair Jun Sch
Sinclair Inf Sch

Oakwood Schs

CH

RIDGEMOUNT LA 1
CHILWOOD GATE 2
BSAMPTON TWR 3
BRAMPTON MANOR 4

Vermont Sch

Red Lodge Sch

Sports Ctr

Greywell Ct 1
Pinelands Ct 2
Lyscom Ct 3

Aldermoor

Tanner's Brook

Princess Anne H

Northbrook Ind Est

Cemy

Holly Brook

Southampton Gen H

Shirley Warren

Malvern Bans Ctr

Charlbeate H

SOUTHAMPTON

Super store

Southampton Common

The Dukes

Bellemoor Sec Sch (Boys)

SO15

SO17

Coxford

Old Shirley

Wordsworth Inf Sch

Upper Shirley

Taunton Coll

SO15

The Cowherds (PH)

Cemetery Lake

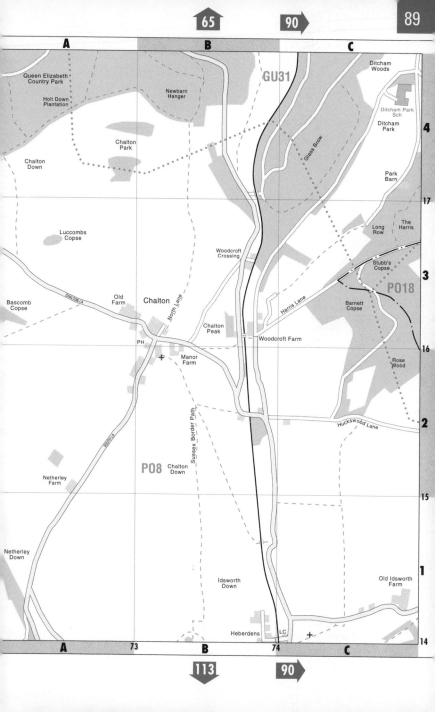

GU31

Booker
Down

Booker Down
Rough

Hudsons
Copse

Upper West
Wood

Uppark
(National Tr

Harehurst
Wood

Nightingale
Bottom

Grass
Piece

Lower West
Wood

Sussex Border Path

The
Harrows

Star
Copse

Park
Copse

Killing
Wood

The
Harris

Hale
Wood

Ladyholt

Eckensfield

Hucksholt
Farm

Wills
Wood

Ladyholt Park

Littlegreen
Wood

Little Down
Copse

PO18

Compton Park

Littlegreen
Sch

Cowdown La

Cowdown
Farm

Hundred Acre
Farm

Huckswood

Compton
Farm

Huckswood
Copse

Jubilee
Clump

Compton

PO8

THE SQUARE

PH

SCHOOL LA

Compton & Up Marc
CE Prim Sch

Robin
Wood

Compton
Down

Hill
Barn

Drift Road
Plantation

West
Hanger

Bottom
Copse

B2146

4

13

3

12

2

11

1

BOWERWOOD RD

Hill Farm

Home Farm

BOWERWOOD COTTS

Bowerwood House

PADSTOW PL

1 YEW TREE CT
2 MULBERRY MEWS
3 DIAMOND CL
4 QUADRANT
5 QUADRANT
6 WEST ST
7 BROOK TERR
8 TIMBERMILL CT

CANDLEHEATH RD

FORDINGBRIDGE RD

New Farm

Salisbury Arms Farm

PRESSEYS CNR

Cross Farm

Bonfire Hill

Highfield Farm

Wolvercrate Copse

Midgham Wood

Padstow Farm

Sewage Works

Weir

Camel Green

St James CE Fst Sch

Hillbury Copse

Hillbury Copse

SP6

Midgham Farm

Bickton

Bickton Farm

Midgham Long Copse

River Avon

Oak Tree Farm

Drove End Farm

East Moor Copse

Avon Valley Path

Sleepbrook Farm

Alderholt Common

RINGWOOD RD

Warren Park Farm

NORTH END LA

Whitefield Bottom

Plumley Wood

Bleakhill Farm

Bleak Hill

North End Farm

LINBER LA

FORDINGBRIDGE RD

North Plumley Farmhouse

Cobley Wood Farm

BH24

Cobley Hill

Harbridge Green

HARBRIDGE LA

Hamer Copse

Hamer

Kent Hill

KENT LA

Kent

Harbridge

Harbridge House

SO43

Long Bottom

Alderhill Bottom

Gaze
Hill

Amberwood
Inclosure

Hampton Ridge

Pitchers
Knowle

Alder
Hill

4

Thompson's Castle

Alderhill
Inclosure

13

Windmillhill
Pond

SP6

Sloden Inclosure

Latchmore Brook

Deadbuck
Hill

Windmill Hill

Latchmore Bottom

Latchmore
Shade

Watergreen Bottom

3

Ford

Great
Witch

Little
Witch

Hallickshole
Hill

Hasley Hole

Purlieu
Farm

Hasley Inclosure

12

Splash Bridge

BH24

Woodford Bottom

Broomy Inclosure

2

Broomy
Lodge

Ogden's Purlieu

Nices Hill

11

Broomy
Plain

Amberslade Bottom

High Corner
Wood

North Hollow

Black
Barrow

Summerhill

High Corner
Inn
(PH)

Broomy Walk

1

Linwood
Bog

Linwood

Milkham Inclosure

10

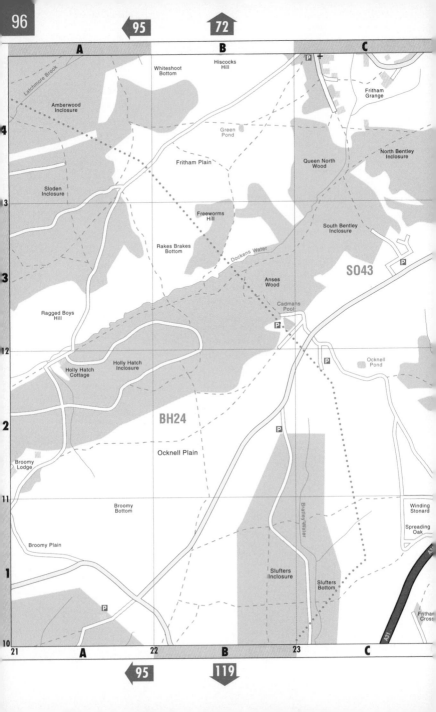

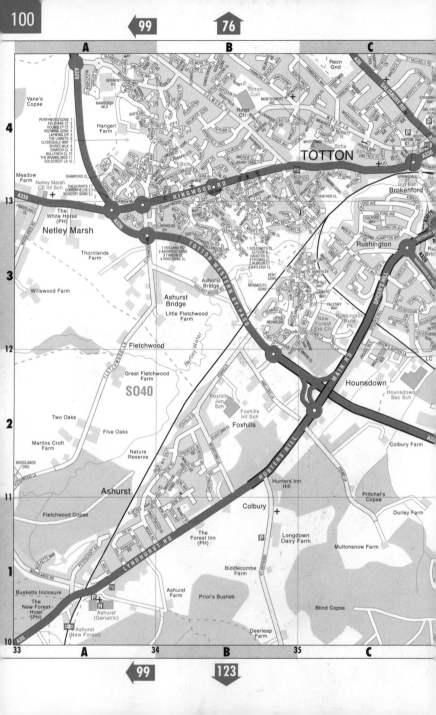

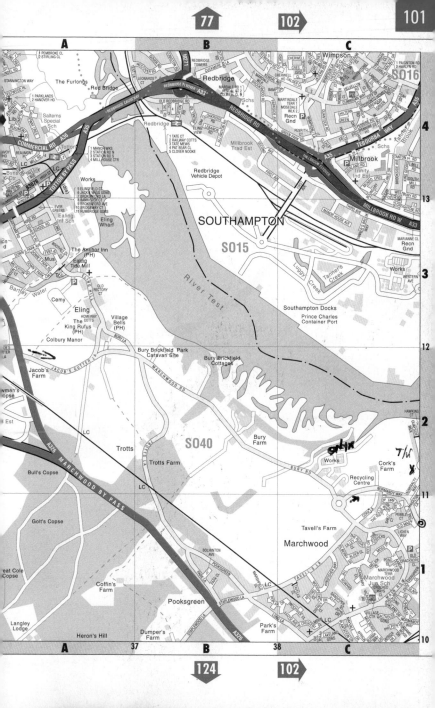

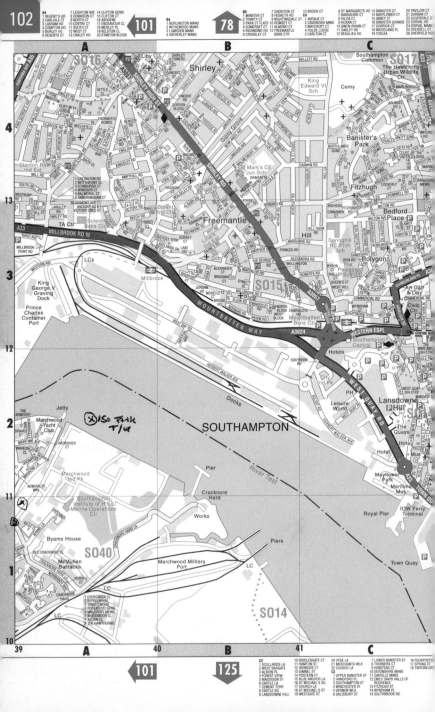

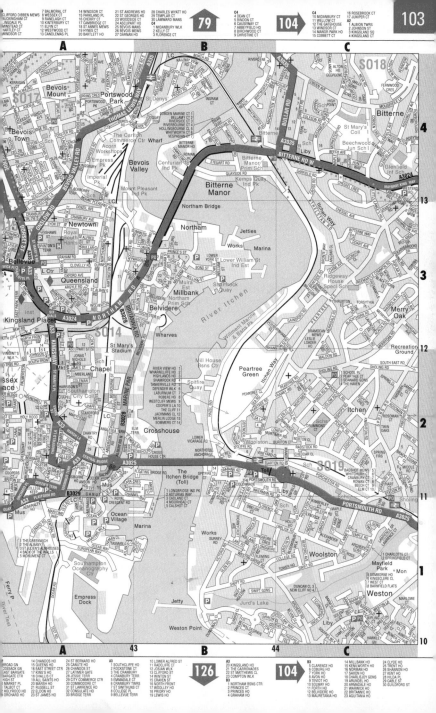

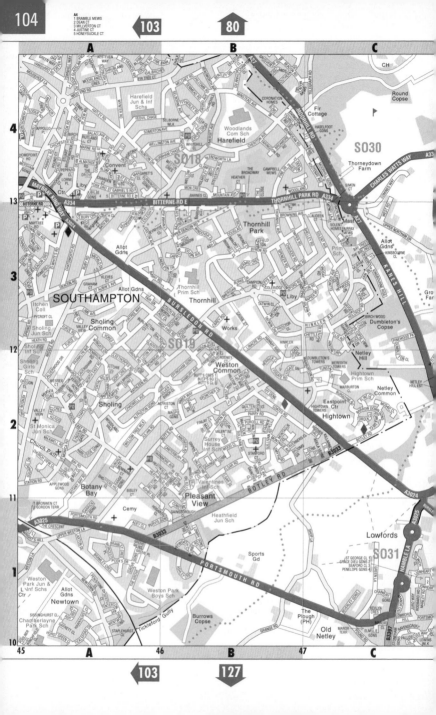

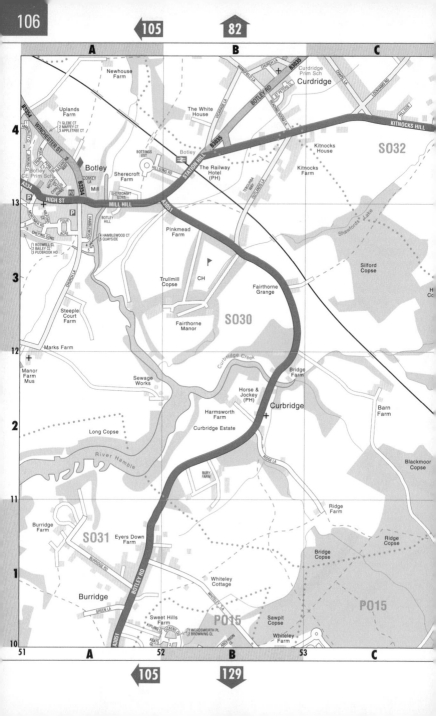

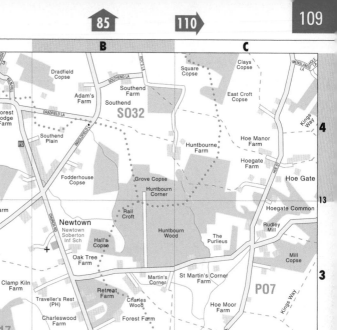

A B C

4

13

3

12

2

11

1

10

Map labels:

MENSLANDS LA
FORESTERS LA
KILN HILL
LIBERTY RD
Dradfield Copse
Clays Copse
Square Copse
Southend Farm
Adam's Farm
Southend
East Croft Copse
SOUTHEND LA
BOYS LA
DRADFIELD LA
SO32
Kings Way
Haraldslea Farm
Forest Lodge Farm
Southend Plain
Hoe Manor Farm
Huntbourne Farm
Hoegate Farm
West Walk
BROADFIELD LA
Hoe Gate
HOE LA
Kiln Copse
Fodderhouse Copse
Grove Copse
Huntbourn Corner
Hoegate Common
Clamp Farm
Newtown
Newtown Soberton Inf Sch
Rail Croft
Huntbourn Wood
The Purlieus
Rudley Mill
CHAPEL RD
HUNDRED ACRES RD
LODGE HILL
Hall's Copse
Mill Copse
Lodge Hill
Oak Tree Farm
Martin's Corner
St Martin's Corner Farm
PO7
Clamp Kiln Farm
Traveller's Rest (PH)
Retreat Farm
Charles Wood
Hoe Moor Farm
Kings Way
P
Charleswood Farm
Forest Farm
PO17
GOATHOUSE LA
Meadows Farm
BUNNS LA
Kiln Farm
Goathouse Farm
Hoemoor Farm
Hipley
Bunns Lane Farm
Chairmakers' Arms (PH)
TRUMPET LA
Sand Pit
Ivy Cottage
KILN LA
Kings Way
BIRCH HILL
SHOOT HILL
Hipley Farm
tle est
Horse & Jockey (PH)
Goathouse Copse
Shoothill Lodge
Kiln Wood
Russell's Copse
Hipley Copse
Beckford Bridge
Hale Row
Pounds Farm
Houndels Row
BECKFORD LA
WINE CROSS
Gravelpit Row
Kings Way
ORCHARD BGLWS
North Boarhunt
Quagg Farm
Ashlands
Goldsmith's Copse
Mitchelland Copse
WINE CROSS
Dirty Ground Copse
Furzy Ground
Bonham Row
Hipley Barn Farm
BLACKHOUSE LA
Walton Heath Plantation
Ashlands Plantation
Tylers Copse
B2177

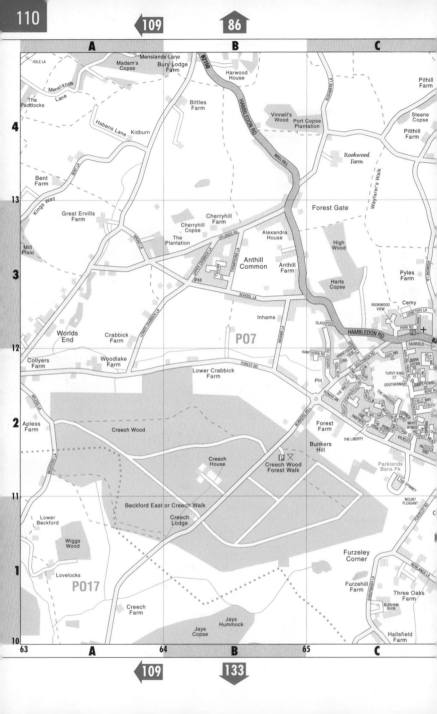

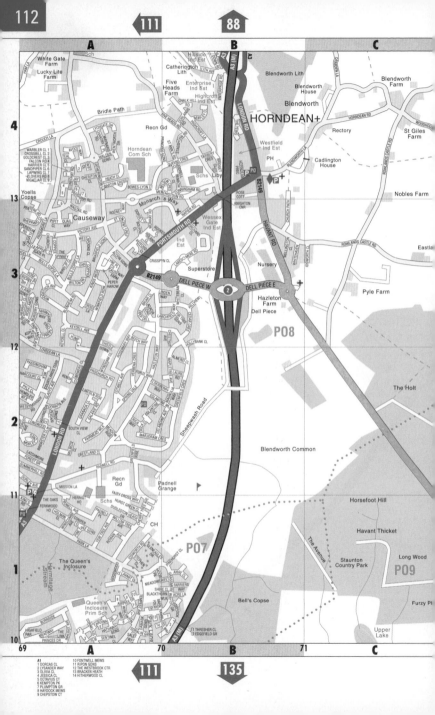

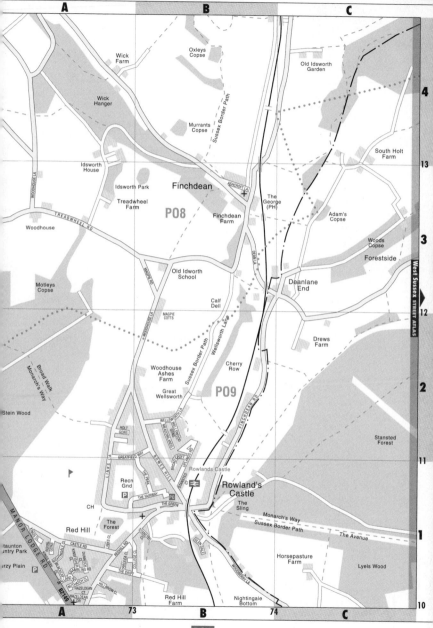

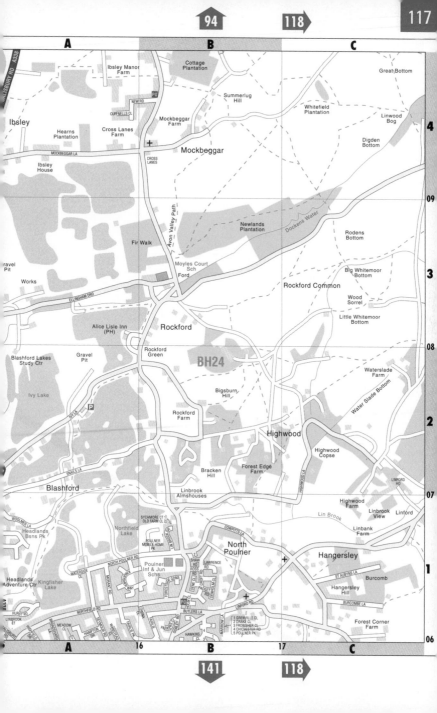

A **B** **C**

Milkham
Inclosure

Linwood

Amie's
Wood

P

Toms
Farm

Webb's
Copse

P

4

Appleslade
Farm

The
Red Shoot Inn
(PH)

Linwood
Farm

Appleslade
Bottom

P

Amie's
Corner

King
Gard

Mount
Hill

Lin Wood

09

Castle
Piece

Roe
Inclosure

Appleslade
Inclosure

3

Red Shoot
Plain

Red Shoot
Wood

Linford Brook

Green
Ford

Buckherd
Bottom

Greenford
Bottom

08

Great Linford
Inclosure

White
Hill

BH24

Collier's
Thorns

Pinnick
Wood

2

Linford Bottom

Akercombe
Bottom

Handy
Cross

Little Linford
Inclosure

Handy Cross Plain

07

P

Marrowbones
Hill

Ridley Plain

Linford

Picket
Bottom

Old Gate

Little
Wood

Harve
Slad

1

Brook
Farm

Picket
Hill

Shobley

Ridley
Bottom

Ridley
Wood

Shobley
Bottom

A31

Picket
Post

06

18 **A** 19 **B** 20 **C**

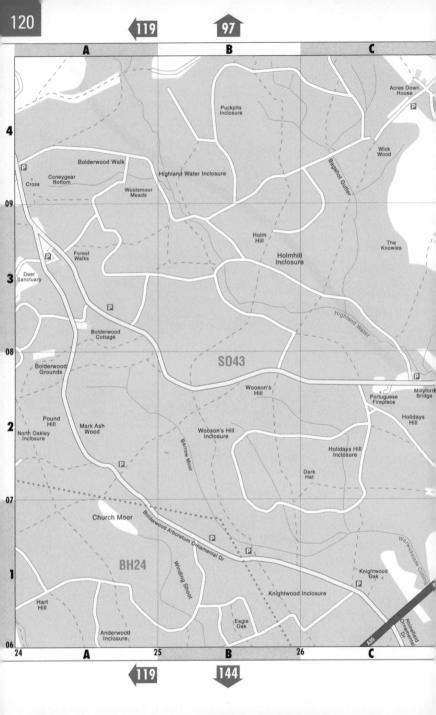

A B C

SO14

Docks

Mast

Weston Shelf

Weston Hard

SO19

ROTHSCHILD CL

HURSTBOURNE

CANBERRA TWRS

Weston Shore Inf Sch

Weston Park

SO3

4

Ferry

Solent Way

C4
1 SQUIRES WLK
2 HAMPTON TWRS
3 HAVRE TWRS
4 OSLO TWRS
5 COPENHAGEN TWRS
6 ROTTERDAM TWRS
7 WESTON HOMES
8 GRATELEY CL
9 DRAYTON CL

09

Hythe Marina

Southampton Water

3

Hythe Pier Rly Hythe Pier

A3
1 WHITE HEATHER CT
2 VELSHEDA CT
3 ASTRA CT
4 WATERSIDE
5 MOUNT HOUSE CL
6 HAZELDALE VILLAS
7 HOMEBOROUGH HO
8 DRUMMOND CT
9 ADMIRALS WAY

Hythe Hard

Hythe

DIBDEN LODGE CL

08

Hythe Prim Sch

Liby

Pier

A2
1 MARSH PAR
2 NEW MARSH HO
3 DRUMMOND RD
4 COURT HOUSE CL
5 SIR CHRISTOPHER CT
6 LAWRENCE HO
7 MARINERS MEWS
8 HANOVER CT
9 THE SYCAMORES
10 FAIRFIELD CL
11 GREEN CL
12 HOLLYBANK CL

2

SO45

HOWARD OLIVER HO

Langdown Jun Sch

Solent Way

LANGDOWN FIRS

FAIRVIEW WAY

07

Langdown

LC

Hythe

Furzey Piece

Langdown Inf Sch

CURLEW WLK

SPINNEY DALE

1

HART HILL

Furzedown Farm

Frostlane

Hotel

Kitcher's Copse

Crampool Copse

Forest Lodge

Works

06

42 A 43 B 44 C

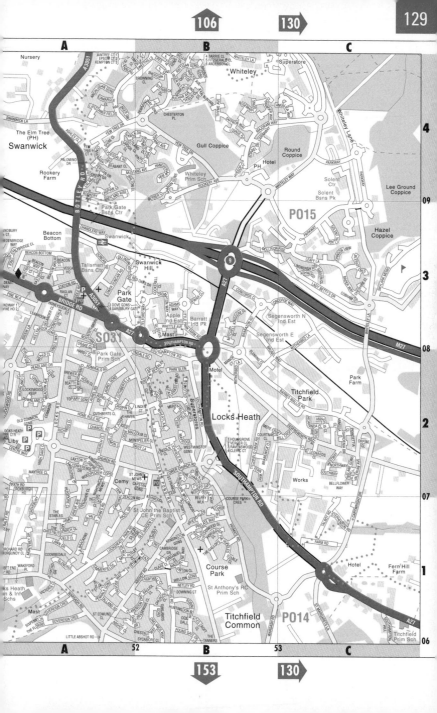

A   B   C

4

09

Heytesbury Farm

Crockerhill

The Old Vine (PH)

CHALK PIT COTTS

Carpenters Copse

Homerhill Copse

Pigeonhouse Coppice

Bere Farm

BERE FARM LA

Albany Farm

Charity Farm

Moor Coppice

PO17

3

Wallington River

Whitedell Farm

Dean Farm

Boundary Oak Prep Sch

Hellyers Farm

08

POOK LA

North Fareham

North Fareham Farm

Spurlings Farm

NINE ELMS LA

WICKHAM RD

10

FURZE HALL

Down Barn Farm

BOARHUNT RD

2

SPURLINGS YD

GREENWOOD CL

1 HANOVER GDNS
2 THE POTTERIES
3 BEEHIVE COTTS

Cemy

Pennant Pk

PO16

Bridge Industries

RIVERDALE COTTS

North Wallington

Fareham Hts

STANDARD WAY

11

07

FAREHAM

Fareham Ind Pk

St Christophers

Superstore

Old Turnpike Bsns Pk

Fort Wallington Ind Est

Wallington

M27

MILLER DR

L Ctr

Harrison Prim Sch

P

P

WALLINGTON WAY A32

Kings Way

PARADISE LA

THE CAUSEWAY

Ellerslie House

1

NEW RD

GORDON RD

TRINITY GDNS

RUSSELL ST

P H

C Ctr

Liby

High Est

Mus

C

Ind Est

CREST CL

THE RIDGEWAY

THE THICKET

Downend

THE SPINNEY

23 24 25
26

WESTERN WAY

A27

BELVOIR CL

A27 EASTERN WAY

DEANE PARK RD

CAMS HILL

A27

PORTCHESTER RD

PARADISE LA

SHEARWATER AVE

Cams Hill Sch

MAGPIE CT

06

A   B   C

58   59

A   B   C

Carmans Copse

STAPLE CROSS

B2177

Staplecross Copse

Walton Heath

Mitchell

4

Prior's Hold Farm

Carmans Farm

Lodge Farm

Vernons Farm

Friar's Coppice

Wallington River

Boarhunt Mill Grub Coppice

Mill Coppice

Ham Coppice

Castle Farm

NORTON

Kings Way

Dirtystile Copse

Newman's Bridge

BACK LA.

BRIDGE RD

FAREHAM RD

NORTON CL.

09

Manor Farm

Ashleydown Coppice

Ham Farm

WEST ST.

HIGH ST.

ROYAL NAVAL COTTS

P.O

CASTLE RD

3

Boarhunt

Ashley Down Farm

Stroud Coppice

Southwick

Th' Wilde

Sout Pa La

B2

Ashley Down

Perrige's Coppice

Marls Rows

PORTCHESTER RD

PO17

08

Offwell Farm

NORTH RD

Damson Row

CROOKED WALK LA.

2

Monument Farm

SHIRRELL LA.

Mountemoor's Coppice

PO6

Fort Nelson

Mus

P

Nelson's Monument

Mast

Fort Southwic

Mast

JAMES CALLAGHAN DR.

WINTER

07

PORTSDOWN HILL RD

DOWNEND RD

M27

P

The Mount

NELSON LA.

Ports Down

SKEW RD

High Tor

BENEDICT WAY

PO6

1 2 3 4 5 6 7 8 9

SUNRIDGE ALMON

VALLEY RD

ALMO

1

PO16

Porchester

Upper Cornaway LA.

LECKFORD CL.

WALTHAM CL.

CAER PERIS VIEW

NYEWOOD AVE

ANSON GR

CARLTON RD

KEATS AVE

CONRAD CL

BROWNING AVE

COLERIDGE RD

CHAUCER AVE

SHELLEY AVE

DRYDEN AVE

MOUSEHOLE RD

LANCASTER CL.

KILMISTON DR

CHOL CL

BOSCATE GDNS

PICKFIELD GDNS

BURTON RD

MORNINGSIDE AVE

SEAVIEW AVE

HILLSIDE

Winnham Farm

SOLENT VIEW

GRINDLE

ROBINSON CT

BANNON'S BARN CL

LAVEROCK LEA

SAUNDERS RD

RAYMOND RD

Cams Bridge

HAWTHORN CL

LINDEN LEA

HILL VIEW RD

A VIEW GDNS

Crem

BOXWOOD CL

06

60   A   61   B   62   C

C1
1 TRINIDAD HO
2 ST LUCIA HO
3 BERMUDA HO
4 ST KITTS HO
5 ANTIGUA HO
6 FOXCOTE HO
7 KINGSCOTE HO
8 ALMONDSBURY HO
9 OAKLANDS HO
10 THORNBURY HO
11 PARKFIELD HO

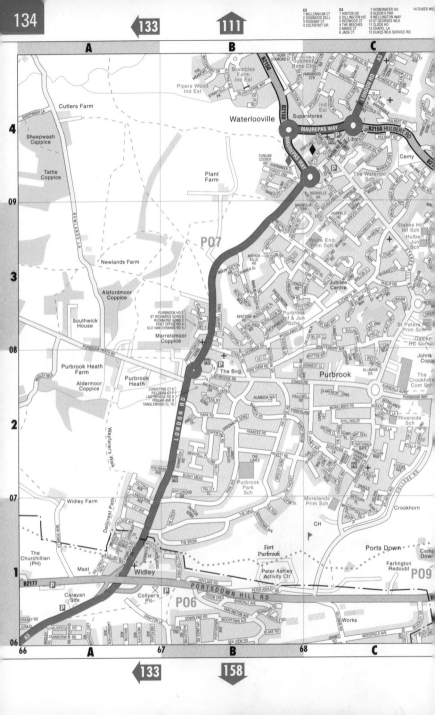

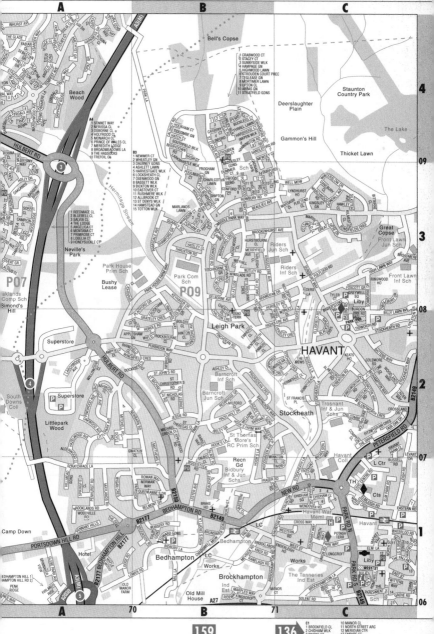

A&4
1 SONNET WAY
2 NERISSA CL
3 OSBORNE CL
4 HOLYROOD CL
5 MONARCH CT
6 PRINCE OF WALES CL
7 MEREDITH LODGE
8 BROADMEADOWS LA
9 THE HASSOCKS
10 TREFOIL C*

B3
1 NEWMER CT
2 WHEATLEY GN
3 DALRNEY GDNS
4 ASHLETT LAWN
5 HARVESTGATE WLK
6 LOCKSHEATH CL
7 OXENWOOD GN
8 BASSETT WLK
9 BICKTON WLK
10 EASTOVER CT
11 RUSHMERE WLK
12 ALLBROOK CT
13 ST DENYS WLK
14 HAWSTEAD GN
15 TOTTON WLK

1 REEDMACE CL
2 BLUEBELL CL
3 SALVIA CL
4 THE LODGE
5 ANGELICA CT
6 MONTANA CT
7 PRIMROSE CT
8 LOBELIA CT
9 HONEYSUCKLE CT*

B4
1 CRABWOOD CT
2 STACEY CT
3 SUNNYSIDE WLK
4 HAMPAGE GN
5 HIGHWOOD LAWN
6 STROUDEN COURT PREC
7 TELEASE GN
8 MORTIMER LAWN
9 UPTON CL
10 ABIAS GN
11 STRATFIELD GDNS

PO7

P09

Leigh Park

HAVANT

Stockheath

Bedhampton

Brockhampton

C1
1 BROOKFIELD CL
2 CHIDHAM WLK
3 WHYKE CT
4 COMPTON CT
5 WESTBOURNE CT
6 THE FORUM
7 RIVERSDALE GDNS
8 WELLINGTON CT
9 EAST VIEW TERR
10 MANOR CL
11 NORTH STREET ARC
12 MERIDIAN CTR
13 EMPIRE CT
14 GROVE CT
15 SLINDON GDNS
16 CLARENDON RD

4

09

3

08

2

07

1

06

A   B   C

72   73   74

Rowlands Castle
St John's CE
Prim Sch
Durrant PRU
PH

MANOR LODGE RD
B2149
B2149
WHICHERS GATE RD

Gipsies
Plain
PARK VIEW 1
CHESTNUT CT 2
WHICHERS GATE RD 3

Durrants

Mays Coppice
Farm

Sandpit
Roundell

STUBBERME

Staunton
Ctry Pk

Hammond's Land
Coppice

Shuffles
Plantation

PETERSFIELD RD

Staunton Park
Com Sch

Sewage
Works

Blackbush
Copse

Sussex Border Path

MIDDLE PARK WAY

Vistors
Ctr

Leigh Park
Gardens

KEN
BERRY
CT

Southleigh Forest

MENGHAM COMMON RD

Barton's
Copse

P

PO9

COMLEY HILL

Hollybank
House

B2149

Football
Gd

West
Leigh
HAVANT

Bupa H

LONG COPSE CT 1
BIRCH TREE CL 2
CHURCHILL DR 3
WALLBROOK WLK 4
THE GREENWAY 5
WOODRIFFE WLK 6
LAURENCE GN 7

Nest
Bsns Pk

Ind Est

Hemsley
House

Southleigh
Park

LONG COPSE LA

East Leigh
House

Home
Farm
Barn

HORNDEAN RD

SOUTHLEIGH RD

The
Oakwood Ctr

Downley
Point

Locks
Farm

WOODLEIGH

St Alban's
CE Prim Sch

Hayward
Bsns Ctr

1 WEAVERS GN
2 SPINDLE WARREN
3 BLADON CL
4 MARLBOROUGH PK

BARWELL GR 8
PANTON CL 9
GODWIN CL 10
ALLENDALE AVE 11
HEDGEROW CT 12

1 SOLENT HO
2 LANGSTONE HO
3 CHICHESTER HO
4 FLEXFORD GDNS
5 LANGLEY CT
6 HODGES CL

Southleigh
Farm

Ind Est

SWALLOW

PO10

St James
CE Prim Sch

Nursery

HEATHERTON MEWS 1
SILVERTREES 2
AVALON CT 3
WESTBOURNE AVE 4
MALVERN MEWS 5

A1
1 KINGFISHER CT
2 CARISBROOK CL
3 BEECHWORTH RD
4 NORFOLK HO
5 CONNAUGHT PL
6 GROVE RD
7 LOWER GROVE RD
8 NIGHTINGALE PK
9 GREEN POND CNR
10 TAVISTOCK GDNS
11 LUARD CT

Denvilles

Manor
Farm

Motel

Emsworth

LC

Somerstown
Flats

Warblington
Sch

Warblington Halt

Emsworth
Prim Sch

Schs

Mus

Warblington

Glenwood
Sch

Emsworth

ROMAN RD A259
HAVANT RD

P

B2147 NEW BRIGHT

NORTH ST

B2148

PO9

The Groves

Stubbermere

Racton
Common

Pond
Cottage

Brickkiln
Ponds

Pond Copse

Westbourne
Common

Valley
Farm

Cricket
Gd

Monk's
Farm

llybank
arm

Commonside

Westbourne
Cty Prim Sch

Westbourne

Hampshire
Farm

The Wren
Ctr

New
Brighton

Lumley
Farm

Chantry
Farm

Cemy

Brook
Cotts

Lumley
Croft

Lumley Mill
Farm

Lumley

New Barn
Cottage

Walderton

PO18

Racton
Mon

Aldsworth

Ell Bridge

Ellbridge
Buildings

Aldsworth
Manor

Aldsworth Common

Didmans
Copse

Ractonpark
Wood

River Ems

Foxbury La

Deepsprings

PO10

Woodmancote

Woodmancote
Farm

Bishop Barn
Farm

Manor
House

The
Woodmancote
Arms (PH)

South Lane
Farm

Cemetery La

Walnut Tree
Dr

Southla

Old Farm La

West View
Cotts

Hither Gn

Fraser Gdns

Breach Ave

Works

Bourne
Com Coll

Breach

PO18

Loveders
Farm

Inlands Farm

Inlands

Priors Leaze La

Cooks La

Hurstwood
Ave

Guildford Rd

114

A **B** **C**

Three Legged
Cross

Homestead
Farm

Skies
Farm

Clump Hill
Farm

Upper Mannington
Farm

BH21

Earles Rd

West Ave

PH
1 BRACKENDALE CT
2 GREYDOT CL
3 HERMITAGE CL
4 SAINTS CL

Mannington

4

Jubilee
Farm

Lower
Mannington

Mannington
Copse

Haddons
Farm

Gundry's
Farm

Mannington
Farm

Barewood
Copse

05

Nursery

Kingfisher Pk

Cross Keys
(PH)

Summerlug
Hill

Sturt's
Farm

Minster Pk

Holt
Heath

3

Newman's
Farm

Depot

Holt Heath

Newman's Farm
South

04

Gullivers
Farm

BH22

2

West
Moors

West Moors St Mary's
CE Fst Sch

West M
Planta

03

Clayford
Farm

GARDEN COURT
COTTS

CASTLEMAN CT

Charnwood

Lib
y

Sch

Knightstone
Gr

Hamwoods
Copse

Dolman's
Crossing

Dolman's
Farm

Pennington's
Copse

West M
Mid

1

Ameysford

Uddens Water

Uddens
Plantation

Broadmoor
Coppice

West

02

06 **07** **08**

A **B** **C**

A31 A31

165

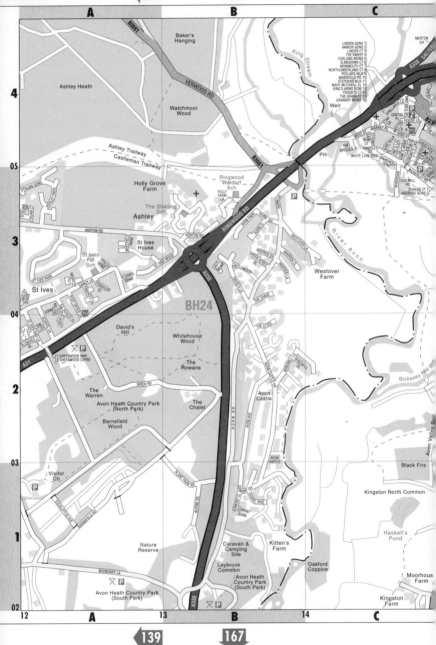

139
116
139
167

B3081

Baker's
Hanging

MERTON
GR

A338 SALISBURY

LINDEN GDNS 1
MANOR RD 2
LINDEN CT 3
THE SWEEP 4
FURLONG MEWS 5
ELMSDOWN CT 6
MONMOUTH CT 8
NORTHUMBERLAND CT 9
PEDLARS WLK 9
MANSFIELD RD 10
STEPHENS WLK 11
MARY MITCHELL CL 12
KING'S ARMS ROW 13
FRIDAY'S CT 14
THE GRANARY 15
GRANARY MEWS 16

VERWOOD RD

King

Stream

Ashley Heath

Watchmoor
Wood

Weir

CENTRE

Ashley Trailway
Castleman Trailway

B3081

PH

THE
BRIDGES

WEST ST
MARKET PL
CT
HANDLEY
WHITE LION GDNS

05

Holly Grove
Farm

Ringwood
Waldorf
Sch

FOLLY
FARM
LA

P

River

Avon

Old Mill
HO
QUAKER CT 1
ANDRISE GDNS 2

The Sheiling
Sch

Ashley

HORTON RD

HORTON RD

RINGWOOD RD

St Ives
House

Westover
Farm

3

St Ives Fst
Sch

BH24

A338

Westover
Farm

04

David's
Hill

Whitehouse
Wood

St Ives

The Rowans

BIRCH RD

2

The
Warren

Avon Heath Country Park
(North Park)

The Chalet

Avon
Castle

Barnsfield
Wood

1 GREENWOOD WAY
2 GREENWOOD COPSE

A31

Bickerley

Avon Valley Rd

03

Visitor
Ctr.

P

Black Firs

PLANT FARM RD

Kingston North Common

ALPINE RD

Haskell's
Pond

1

Nature
Reserve

Caravan &
Camping
Site

Kitten's
Farm

BOUNDARY LA

Leybrook
Common

Oakford
Coppice

Moorhous
Farm

Avon Heath Country Park
(South Park)

Avon Heath
Country Park
(South Park)

Kingston
Farm

02

A338

12
A
13
B
14
C

Sir Dudley's Ride

Berry Wood

Turf Croft

White Moor Bottom

ack ill

Burley Moor

Brookside Farm

FOREST RD

LYNDHURST RD

WOOD'S CNR

North Farm

Lucy Hill

South Oakley Inclosure

Burley Walk

Great Early

Depot

Burley New Inclosure

Little Early

Cockroad Hill

Burley Outer Rails Inclosure

Burley Lodge

Springwood Cottages

Southmead Cottage

05

4

3

04

Burley Grange

MILL LA

Mill Lawn House

Mill Lawn

Mill Lawn Brook

Redrise Hill

Burley Manor Hotel

CHAPEL LA

BURLEY LAWN

Burley Lawn

Fords

Burley

The Queens Head Hotel

YS P

P

appen Farm

Hotel

Shappen Hill

MOORHILL RD

BEECHWOOD LA

CHURCH LA

Burley Prim Sch

CH

COTT LA

Turf Hill

Shappen Bottom

LESTER SQ

Burley Rocks

Shoot Wood

Southfield LA

BISTERNE CL

The White Buck Inn

YH

Bisterne Close

Creek Bottom

Rock Hills

The Burrpws

P

Clay Hill

Pigsty Hill

Cot Bottom

Broadoak Bottom

STREAM RD

Holman's Bottom

2

03

1

02

A
B
C

4

Denny
Wood

Denny
Lodge

Stephill
Bottom

B3056

Woodfidley
Passage

05

Furzy
Brow

Bishop of
Winchester's
Purlieu

Denny Lodge
Inclosure

Penny
Moor

3

Woodfidley

SO42

Rowbarrow

04

LC

Frame Heath
Inclosure

2

Frame
Wood

03

Ladycross
Inclosure

Moon
Hill

Ladycross
Lodge

1

Worts Gutter

B3055

Hawkhill
Inclosure

Lodge
Heath

Stockley
Inclosure

Little
Wood

02

A
34
B
35
C

A   B   C

Dibden
Inclosure

A326
BEAULIEU
RD
PRU
CRETE
COTTS
MONTAGU
CT
BEAULIEU RD
BERTHOL RD
CORBOULD RD
BARCLAY
CO MEWS
P
B3054
HYTHE BY PASS
ROMAN RD
COBOURG RD
BOLEY CT RD
BETTS SKL LA
WLK
COOK WLK
FOREST
MEW
The
Noads

Solent Way
Nature
Reserve

A326

4

Fawley
Inclosure

Crabhat
Inclosure

Flash Pond

05

Harford
House

SO45

3

Beaulieu Heath

Hartford Heath

Holbury
Purlieu

Stonyford
Pond

04

Great Goswell
Copse

SO42

Solent Way

BEAULIEU RD

2

Hilltop
Farm

Hill Top

Hilltop
Wood

Hilltop
House

Royal Oak
(PH)

03

Boarman
Pond

Moonhills
Gate

Moonhills
Copse

P

1

MOONHILLS LA

Home
Farm

PALACE LA

Otterwood
Gate

Stock Water

Cowleys La

Carpenters
Cottage

Otterwood
Farm House

Cowleys
Copse

DOCK LA

BUNKER LA

Otterwood

A   B   C

02

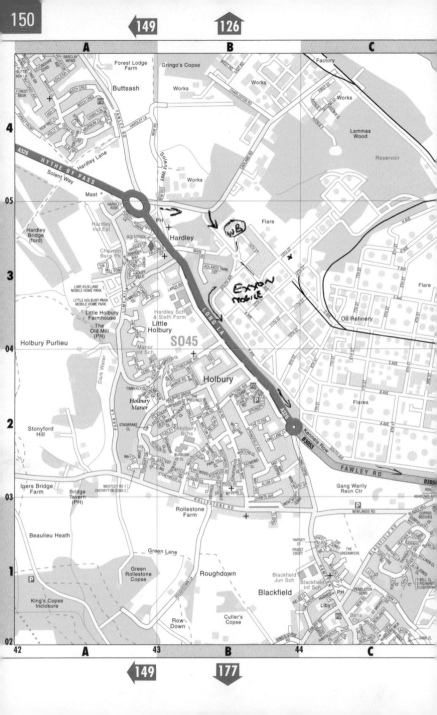

151
128

S031
Hamble Point Marina
River Hamble

A
B
C

1 BEECHWOOD CL
2 LARCHDALE CL
3 BIRCHDALE CL
4 SANDYCROFT

NEW RD

FLEET END RD

Sch

OSBORNE RD

Newtown

GILCHRIST GDNS

Warsash Maritime Ctr (Southampton Inst)

Hook Lake

S031

Solent Court Farm

Solent Court

05

Hamble Spit

Nature Reserve

Solent Way

Hook Park

Workman's Lane

CHILLING

3

04

Southampton Water

Solent Breezes Cvn Site

2

02

S045

Calshot

Stanswood Bay

P

01

Hillhead

B3053

P

48

49

03

Lifeboat Sta

Pier

Calshot Castle

1

S045

Nature Reserve

S045

Calshot Activities Ctr

02

48

A

49

B

50

C

151

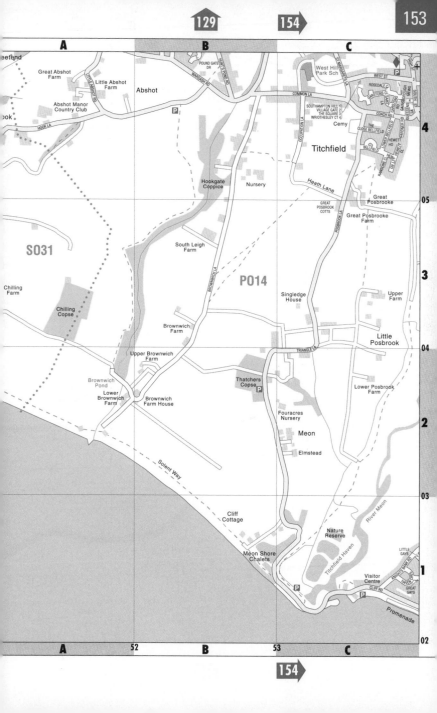

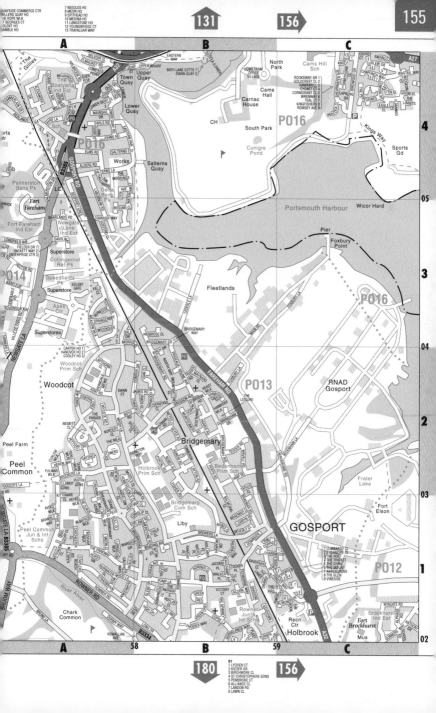

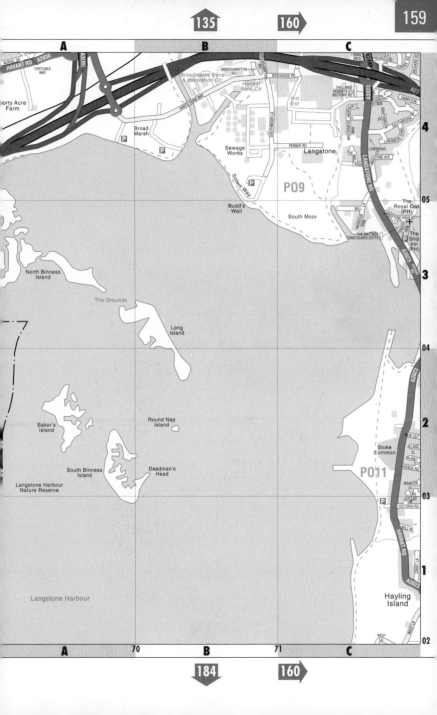

A　　　　　　　　B　　　　　　　　C

HAVANT RD　A2030　　FORTUNES WAY　A3(M)

orty Acre Farm

Broadmarsh Bsns & Innovation Ctr

BROCKHAMPTON RD

BROOKSIDE RD

HARTS FARM WAY

Havant Bsns Ctr

THE LIMES
REGENTS ST 2
RECTORY RD 1

HAMILTON

4

Broad Marsh

P

P

Sewage Works

SOUTHMOOR LA

PENNER RD

Ind Est

Langstone

A3023

SOUTHBROOK

LONGMEAD

LONGMEAD

STONE AVE

05

Solent Way

P

Budd's Wall

South Moor

P09

THE MALLARDS

MILL

LANGSTONE HIGH ST

The Royal Oak (PH)

The Ship Inn (PH)

THE SALTINGS 1
COASTGUARD COTTS 2

P

North Binness Island

3

The Grounds

Long Island

04

Baker's Island

Round Nap Island

Stoke Common

A3023

NEW CUT

ISLAND CL

ISLAND AVENUE RD

P011

2

South Binness Island

Deadman's Head

MEADOW CL

VICTORIA RD

03

Langstone Harbour Nature Reserve

P

MILL CL

HAVANT RD

1

Langstone Harbour

A3023

Hayling Island

WEST LA

WEST LA

02

A　　　　70　　　　B　　　71　　　C

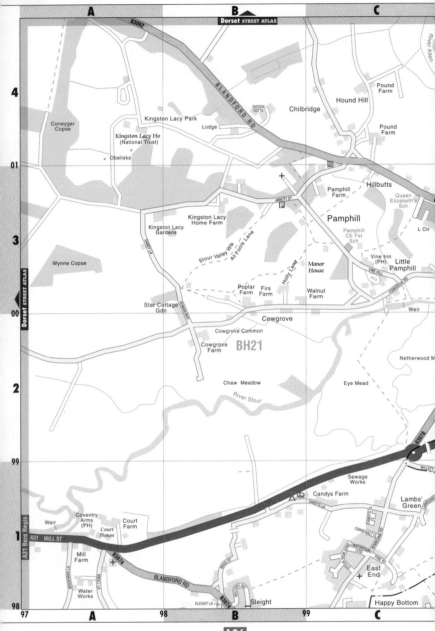

B3082

4

BLANDFORD RD

TADDEN COTTS

Pound Farm

Hound Hill

Chilbridge

Coneygar Copse

Kingston Lacy Park

Lodge

Pound Farm

01

Kingston Lacy Ho (National Trust)

Obelisks

PO

Hillbutts

Pamphill Farm

Queen Elizabeth's Sch

ABBOTT ST

P

Pamphill

Kingston Lacy Home Farm

L Ctr

3

Kingston Lacy Gardens

Pamphill CE Fst Sch

Stour Valley Wlk

All Fools Lane

Wynne Copse

Holly Lane

Manor House

Vine Inn (PH)

Little Pamphill

VINE HILL

COWGROVE RD

Poplar Farm

Firs Farm

Walnut Farm

Weir

00

Star Cottage Gdn

Cowgrove

Cowgrove Common

BH21

Netherwood M

Cowgrove Farm

Chaw Meadow

Eye Mead

2

River Stour

99

Sewage Works

B3078

WILLETT

Candys Farm

Lambs' Green

CANDYS LA

Coventry Arms (PH)

Court Farm

CORFE HALT CL

1

Weir

A31

MILL ST

Court House

B3074

CORFE HALL RD

WAYGROUND RD

PORK RD

East End

Mill Farm

BLANDFORD RD

Water Works

B3074

SLEIGHT LA

Sleight

Happy Bottom

98

A31 Bere Regis

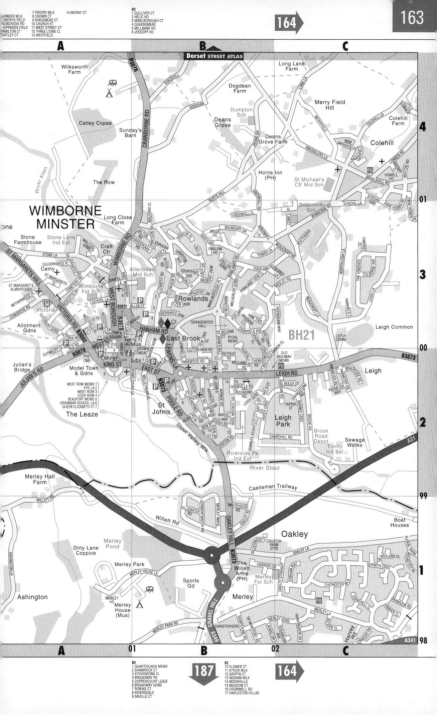

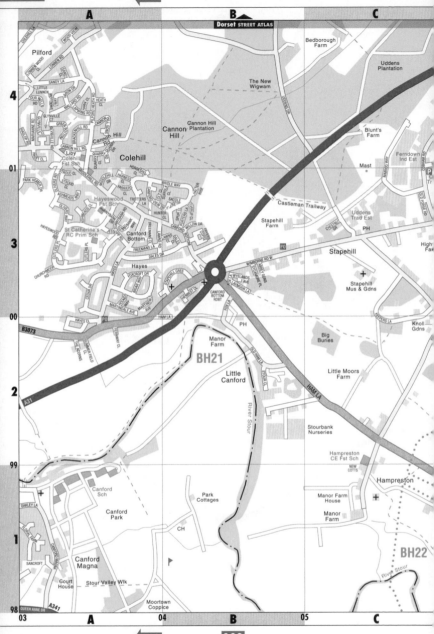

A   B   C

4

Pilford

Cannon Hill
Plantation

The New
Wigwam

Bedborough
Farm

Uddens
Plantation

Cannon Hill
Plantation

Cannon
Hill

Blunt's
Farm

Ferndown
Ind Est

01

Colehill
Fst Sch

Colehill

Hayeswood
Fst Sch

Castleman Trailway

Stapehill
Farm

Uddens
Trad Est

Mast

PH

High
Far

St Catherine's
RC Prim Sch

Canford
Bottom

Stapehill

Stapehill
Mus & Gdns

3

Hayes

Knoll
Gdns

00

Hayes Cl

Canford
Bottom
Rdbt

PH

Manor
Farm

Big
Buries

Little Moors
Farm

B3073

A31

BH21

Little
Canford

River Stour

2

Stourbank
Nurseries

99

Hampreston
CE Fst Sch

NEW
COTTS

Hampreston

Canford
Sch

Park
Cottages

Manor Farm
House

Canford
Park

CH

Manor
Farm

BH22

1

Canford
Magna

Court
House

Stour Valley Wlk

River Stour

Moortown
Coppice

98

QUEEN ANNE DR   A341

03   A   04   B   05   C

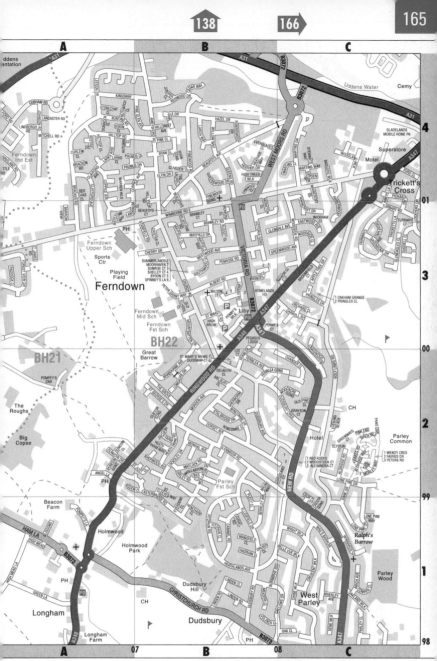

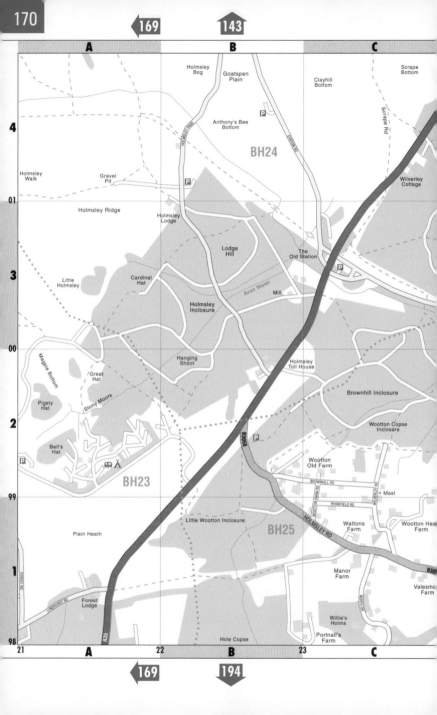

A B C

Row Down
KING'S COPSE RD

East Stock
Copse

SO42

JANES CL

Cemy

Ford

Blackfield

WHEELERS WLK

DEDRIC CL 1
DANE CL 2

NORTHAMPTON
LA

WHITEHAVEN
HOME PK

Recn
Gd

THORNBURY AV

Meadow Close
Copse

Kings Copse
Inclosure

4

Blackwell
Common

Gatewood
Bridge

Gatewood Farm
House

Gatewood Hill

Langley

MOPLEY CL

MOPLEY

CLARE GDNS

PH

1 ST FRANCIS CL
2 THE MEWS
3 FOXY PADDOCK
4 FOXLAWDS
5 FOX'S WLK
6 FOXGLADE

01

Nursery

WEST COMMON

HOME FARM LA

Whitefield
Farm

West Common

HOMER
MOBILE HOME PARK

ard Wood

Main Drive

Nursery

Dark Water

3

Exbury
Bridge

Chale
Wood

East
Wood

Whitefield
Rough

tchers
opse

THE
CRESCENT
COTTS

NEW
COTTS

Exbury
Gardens

Exbury
House

Recn Gd

SO45

00

Exbury

Upper
Exbury

East Hill
Farm

St Mary's
Spring

The
Green

2

Salterns
Copse

Haxland
Pits

Lepe
Farm

Grassy
Copse

Aldermoor

Pophams
Wood

The
Moor

Three
Stones

Little Haxland
Copse

99

ower Exbury
House

Inchmery
House

Lepe
House

Lower Exbury

Quay

Groyhes

1

98

A 43 B 44 C

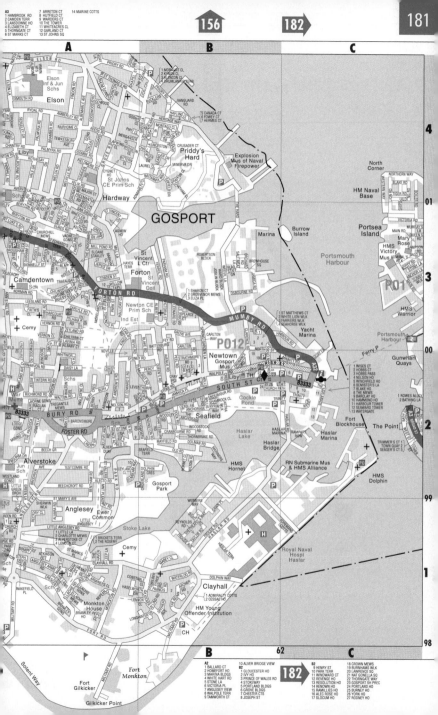

A   B   C

4

01

3   DAW LA

WEST LA

WOODLANDS

BRIGHT'S LA

HIGHWORTH LA

HAMBOR RD

Higworth
Cvn Site

00   Newtown

THE KENCH

The Kench   Pier

Sinah
Farm   Holiday
Village

PO11

Rook
Farm

NORTH SHORE RD

FERRY RD

HARBOUR RD

PARK RD

LIME GR

CATHERINE'S RD

ST THOMAS AVE

STAUNTON AVE

RICHMOND DR

STATION RD

MENGHAM LA

West
Town

SOUTHLEIGH

BENWELL CT

BEACH RD

2   Sinah Common

ST CATHERINES
CT

ST HELEN'S RD

THE
GORSEWAY

BATHURST PL

VICTORIA AVE

HOLLOW LA

GORSEWAY

CH

BACON LA

WESTFIELDS

ORCHARD

99   P   P   Hotel   P   Westfield

Gunner
Point

BAY VIEW
CT

NORFOLK GDNS

PH   The Beach

CHICHESTER
AVE

P

South Hayling

BAY VIEW MEWS 1
WARD CT 2
NORFOLK MEWS 3
THE ROYAL 4
LAUREN MEWS 5
ANNES CT 6
STAMFORD LODGE 7
ROPLEY CT 8
FAIRMEAD 9
OCEAN CT 10
NICHOLAS CL 11
PADWICK CT 12
VICTORIA CT 13
MARK ANTHONY CT 14
WESTFIELD OAKS 15
ST JOHNS CL 16
HOLM CT 17

1   Hayling Bay

98

A   70   B   71   C
69

HAYLING ISLAND

Fleet

Verner Common

WOODGATSON LA

COPSE LA

A3023

HAVANT RD

e Maypole (PH)

MILL RYTHE LA

Manor Farm

Mill Rythe Jun & Inf Sch

Mill Rythe Holiday Village

Manor House

Pound Marsh

Middle Marsh

MOR RD

HARRY BROWN

REST-A-WILE AVE

POUND LEA

KINGS RD

CHURCH RD

LULWORTH CL

The Hayling Sussex

PO11

KATRINA GDNS

DUNWOALD

HERONS CT

EASTWOOD

Gable Head

ham Sch

GABLE MEWS

TOURNERBURY LA

BEECH CL

TRUNDLE WAY

CH

Tourner Bury Marsh

Tournerbury Farm

Tourner Bury

LEGION RD

HAWTHORNE GR

by

PALMERSTON RD

Mengham Jun Sch

Tourner Bury Plantations

Tourner Bury Wood

HAYWOOD GDNS

SPENCER CL

ST MARGARET'S

WILLOW WOOD RD

MENGHAM CT

Mengham House

Mengham

My Lord's Pond

Meringham Salterns

SIMMONDS

FERNS CL

SALTERNS LA

Selsmore

MARINE WLK

Yacht Harbour

Black Point

LOW LA

RAMSEY

MENGHAM RD

SELSMORE RD

MENGHAM LA

WHITEHORN

BLACKTHORN DR

KINGFISHER

SEA VIEW RD

FISHERY

RNLI Sta

NORTH CRES

NORMAN RD

SEA FRONT

CHANDLERS CL

Holiday Village

FISHERMANS WLK

EARNLEY

SIDDLESHAM

WITTERING

Sea View

GRAND PAR

ORCHARD

SEA FRONT

THE SANDERLINGS

WEBB CT

WYBORN CL

ROUNDHOUSE CT

SUNTRAP GDNS

SCARFS

OLD SCHOOL RD

ST HERMANS

HAROLD

FORELAND CL

THORBY

Boating Lake

Eastoke

EASTOKE AVE

Caravan Park

HASLEMERE GDNS

ROSAMIE RD

POINT RD

SEAFARERS WLK

BRACKLESHAM RD

Prom

PEMBRIDGE RD

WIGHT VIEW

MEADS RD

THE GLADE

SILHOUETTE CT

SHEARWATER CT

MILEE

WINSON CL

BOTTERWOOD RD

PEEBLE CT

WEST HAYE RD

CREEK RD

SANDY PT RD

WHEATLANDS AVE

WHEATLANDS CRES

HAVEN RD

TRELOAR RD

SANDY BEACH

MALONEY MEWS 1
ALEXANDER RD 2

Sea View

West Sussex STREET ATLAS

Emsworth Channel

73   74

01   4   3   00   2   99   1   98

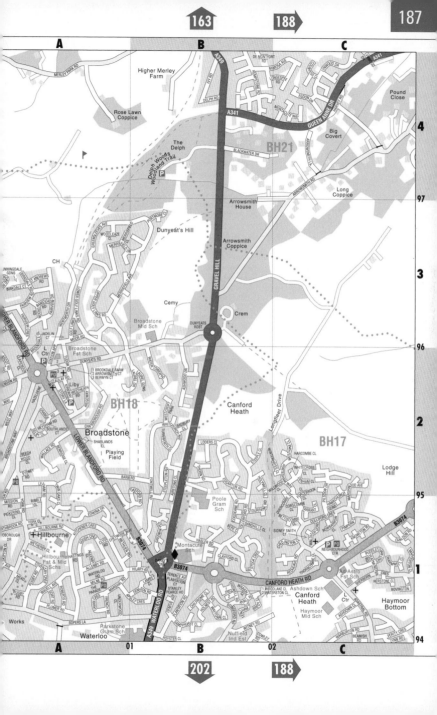

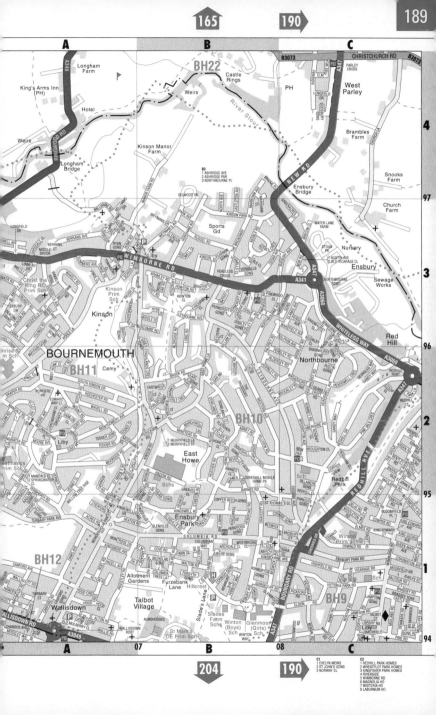

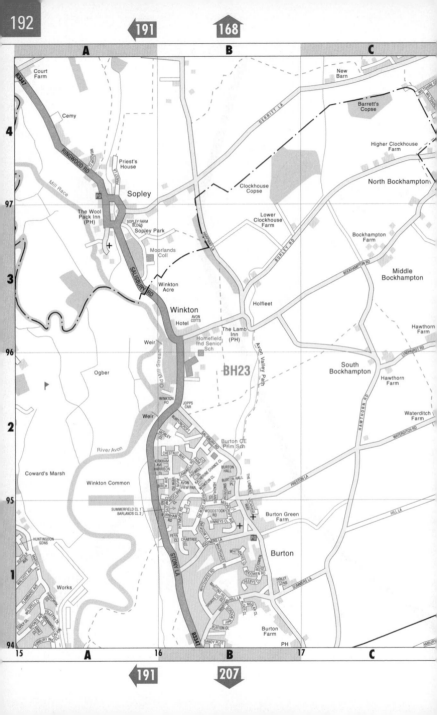

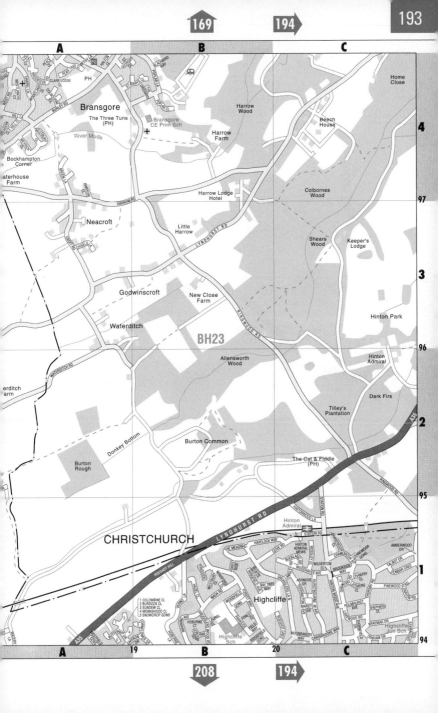

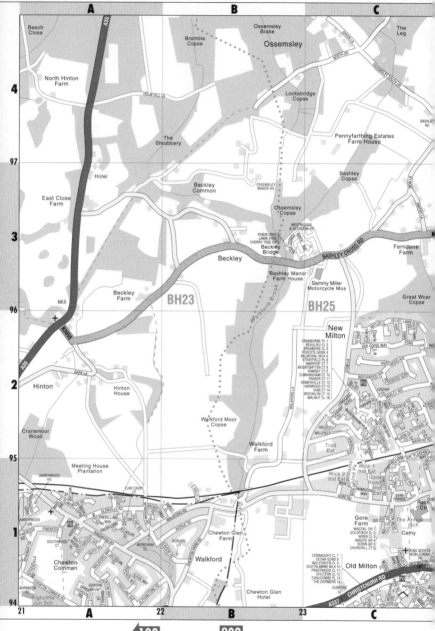

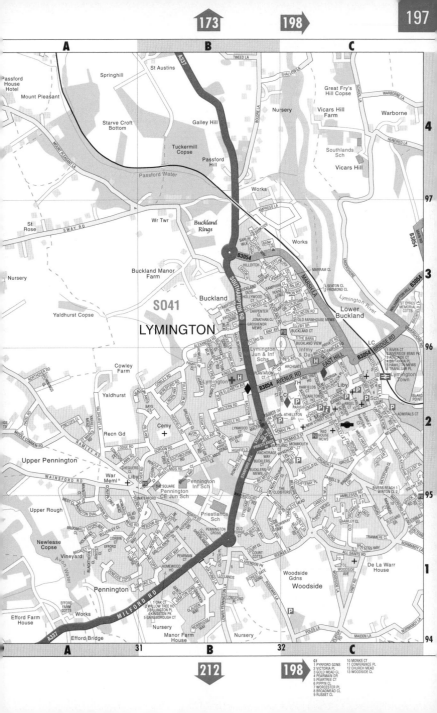

197
174

A   B   C

4

Norley Inclosure

NORLEYWOOD RD

Norleywood

SWEBDEN HO⁶

Bull
Hill
Farm

P

B3054

WARBORNE LA

SCHOOL LA

CHURCH LA

JOYS LA

THATCHERS LA

Portmore

MAIN RD

Newtown Park
Farm

Brick Kiln
Clump

Ford

Carters
Farm

HUNDRED LA

Pleasure
Copse

97

B3054 WALHAMPTON HILL

Portmore
Pond

Newtown
Park

Winter's
Wood

South
Baddesley

Plummers Water

BRICK HILL

B3054

MAIN RD

Hordle
Walhampton
Sch

WALHAMPTON
HILL

Pike
Lake

BROOKS LA

3

SO41

South Baddesley
CE Prim Sch

Dod's
Pond

Solent Way

Snooks
Farm

Shotts
Copse

Pylewell
Park

Pylewell Ho
Farm

96

Mon

MONUMENT LA

Walhampton

SOUTH BADDESLEY RD

Pylewell
House

SHOTTS LA

FERRY WAY

UNDERSHORE RD

Bampton's
Farm

Lisle Court
Farm

LISLE COURT RD

Lisle
Court

2

Marina

P

Lymington
Pier

Ferry
Terminal

Country
Club

1 2

1 SOLENT VIEW
2 HOLBEIN LODGE

95

P

IRB Sta

Yacht
Haven

Lymington River

COASTGUARD
COTTS

1

Waterford

Normandy
Farm

Solent

94

A   34   B   35   C

33

197

A1
1 WEST BUTTS ST
2 MARSTON RD
3 ST AUBYNS CT
4 GUILDHALL CT
5 LEVETS LA
6 POPLAR CL
7 ST JAMES CL
8 BARBERS PILES
9 NEW ST
10 CINNAMON LA
11 ST GEORGE'S ALMSHOS
12 THAMES MEWS
13 THAMES ALLEY
14 SARUM ST
15 BARBERS GATE
16 BARBERS WHARF
17 PARADISE ST
18 BELL LA
19 DENNETTS LA
20 GRAND PAR
21 KEY LA
22 BENNETT'S ALLEY
23 HOSIER'S LA

B1
1 TOWNGATE SH CTR
2 FALKLAND SQ
3 WINCHESTER PL
4 NIGHTINGALE LA
5 OLD TOWN MEWS
6 POST OFFICE LA
7 THE BROMBYS
8 WESTONS LA
9 CARTER'S LA
10 NELSON CT
11 GRENVILLE CT
12 LAGLAND CT
13 DANIEL GDNS
14 PROSPEROUS ST
15 THE SEED WAREHOUSE
16 BULL LA
17 BALL LA
18 BUTTON'S LA
19 QUAY POINT
20 THE KIOSKS
21 TAYLOR'S BLDGS
22 DRAKE CT
23 GRAY'S YD

C2
1 BANOCROFT CT
2 CROWE HILL CT
3 MERTON CT
4 THOROGOOD CT
5 BIRDS HILL GDNS
6 LANSDELL CT
7 GARDENS CT
8 SUNNINGDALE
9 PARK VIEW

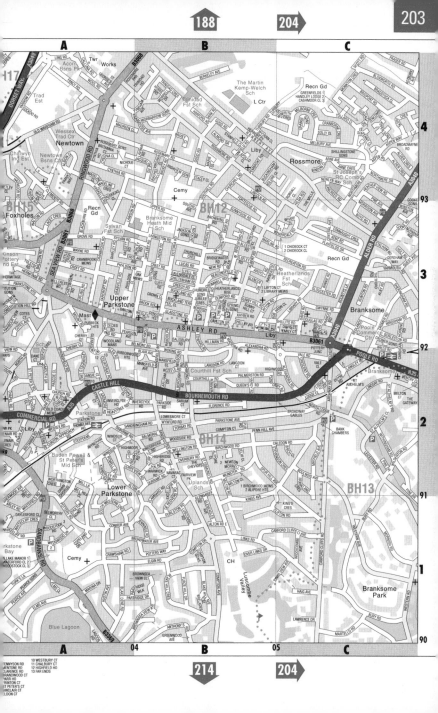

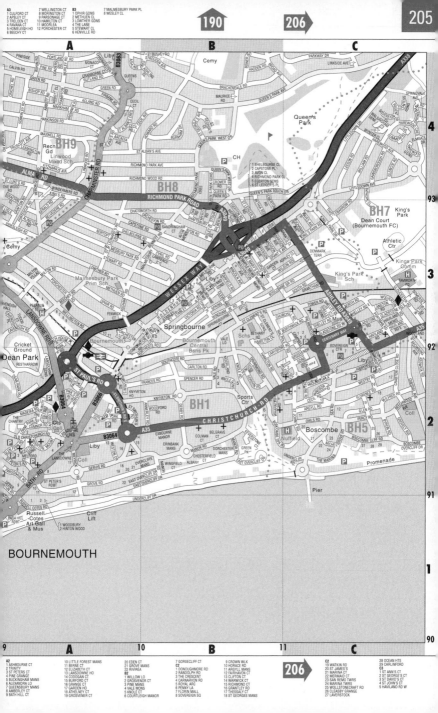

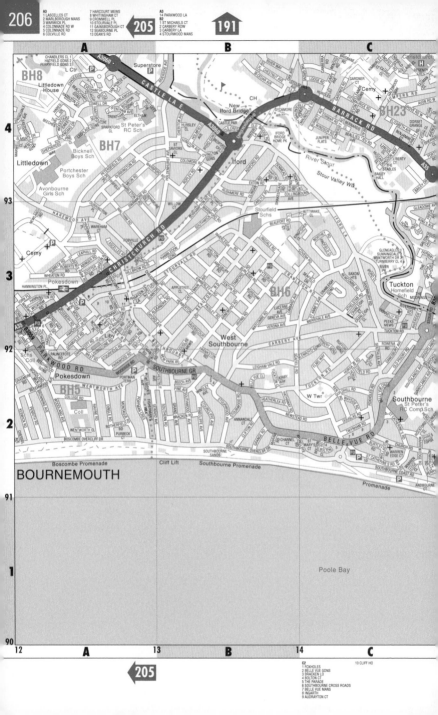

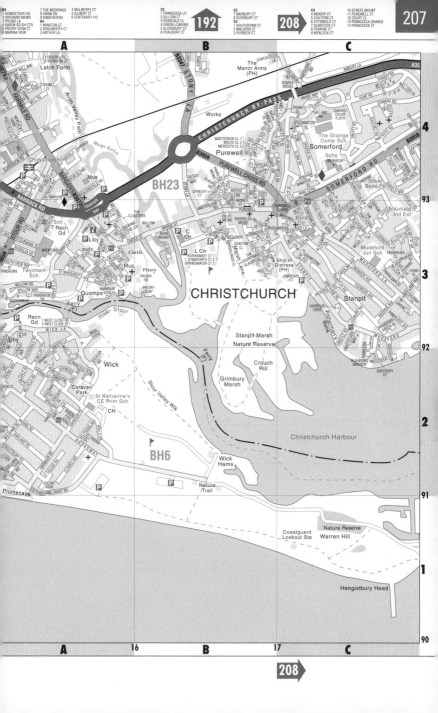

207
193

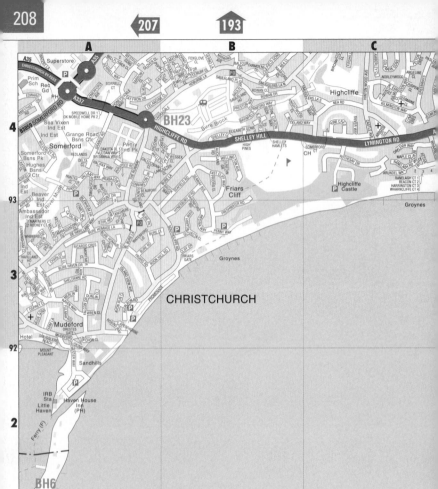

CHRISTCHURCH

BH23

BH6

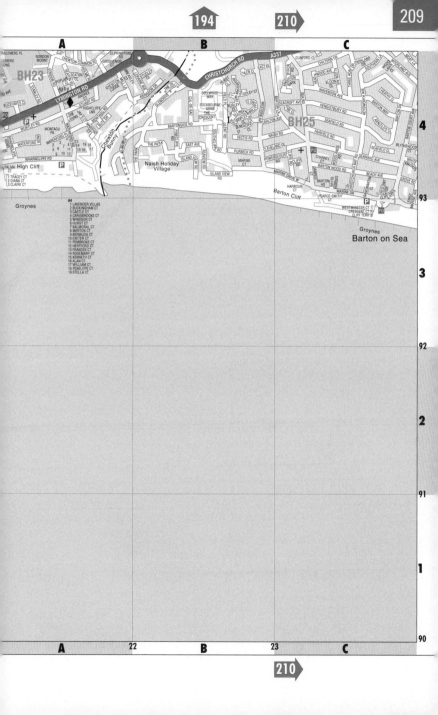

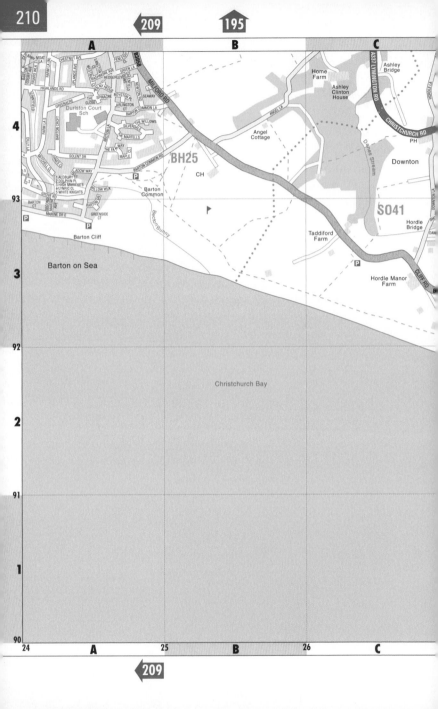

A **B** **C**

4

93

3

92

2

91

1

90

BH25

S041

Home
Farm

Ashley
Bridge

Ashley
Clinton
House

Downton

Hordle
Bridge

Angel
Cottage

CH

Barton
Common

Barton Cliff

Barton on Sea

Taddiford
Farm

Hordle Manor
Farm

Christchurch Bay

Duriston Court
Sch

The Willows

The Martells

The Fw

Maple

Solent Dr

Meadow Way

Willow Wlk

Greenacre

Highlands Rd

Chestnut Ave

Uplands Ave

The Close

Arlington
Ct

Silverdal

Green La

Seaway

Barton Common La

Barton Common Rd

Marine Dr E

Greenside
Ct

Barton
Ct

1 ALDBURY CT
2 DOLPHIN PL
3 HIGH MARRYATS
4 LYRIC CL
5 WHITE KNIGHTS

Beacon Bunny

Milford Rd

Angel La

Christchurch Rd

A337 Lymington Rd

Danes Stream

Cliff Rd

PH

A
B
C

MILFORD RD A337

Leagreen

Leagreen
Farm

CHRISTCHURCH RD

RODBOURNE CL 1
ASH GR 2
OAK GDNS 3
CHERRY TREE CL 4
CYPRESS GR 5
LABURNUM GR 6
MULBERRY GR 7
PLANTATION 8

Everton
Grange

Downton Manor
Farm

Newlands
Manor

Buona Vista
Farm

BRAXTON
CTYD

4

NEWLANDS
MANOR

Cox's
Bridge

Lymore

93

Shorefield
Copse

Blackbush
Copse

Barnes
Farm

SO41
Nursery

Hotel

Milford on Sea
Prim Sch

Lymore
Farm

Danes Stream

AMBERWOOD

B3
1 ADDINGTON CT
2 BLANDFORD CT
3 DACRES WLK
4 DRYDEN PL
5 WINDMILL CL
6 GLEBEFIELDS

GREENWAYS

Knold

The
Vicarage

3

Studland
Common

SHOREFIELD
CRES

Recn
Gd

BROADFIELDS
CL

CANONS
WLK

1 MOLEFIELDS
2 MILFORD HO

THE
BUCKLERS

1 THE LYDGATE
2 SEAWINDS

SHARVELLS RD

SHELLEY WAY

92

ordie Cliff

CLIFF RD

WESTMINSTER
RD

WHITBY RD

VICTORIA RD

PARK LA

HIGH ST

MILFORD CRES

War
Meml

Milford
Trad Est

Solent Way

A2
1 CAMDEN HURST
2 SOLENT PINES
3 MARYLAND CT
4 WHITBY CT
5 BEATRICE CT
6 ALLISON CT

Rook Cliff

E2
1 KIVERNELL PL
2 HOLLY GDNS
3 ROOKWOOD
4 HAVEN CT
5 HURST CT
6 SOLENT CT
7 OSBORNE CT
8 TOTLAND CT
9 SEA PINES
10 PINEHURST
11 NEEDLES CT
12 RICHMOND CT
13 ROOKCLIFF
14 PARK CT
15 HOMEGRANGE HO
16 THE BOLTONS
17 HURDLES MEAD

THE
WHITE HO

Milford on Sea

Sturt
Pond

2

91

Solent Way

1

A
28
B
29
C

90

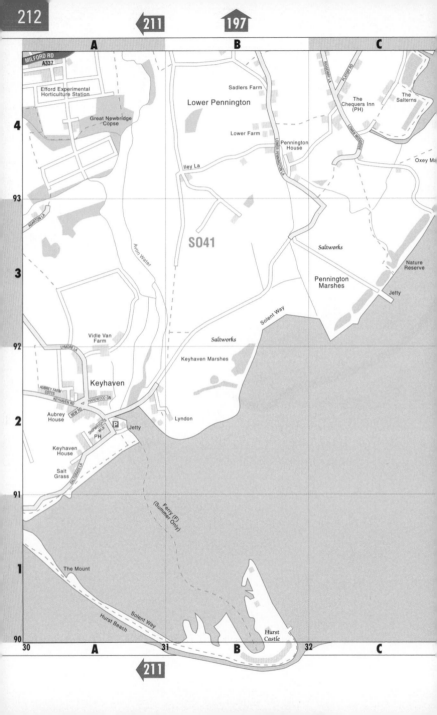

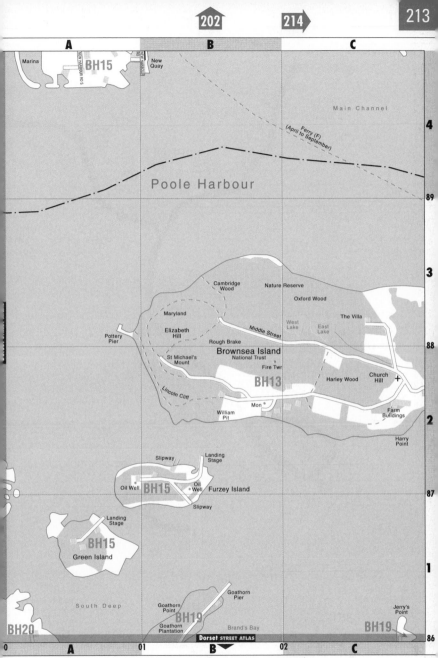

A   B   C

THE CAPSTANS 1
LAGOON CT 3
SALTERNS CT 3
BROWNSEA CT 4

Blue
Lagoon

SALTERNS
WAY
SALTERNS
POINT

Pier   Marina

Lifeboat
Sta

Landing
Stage

COOLHURST

4

CHESTERFIELD
CL

SPENCER RD

MOORFIELDS

NEWTON RD

CHARTCOMBE

MOORINGS
RD

ORATORY RD

CHAUCER

WESTLANDS

LITTLE
18

WESTERN RD   B30

KINGSLAND
HERITAGE
4 5 6

BH14

Lilliput

HILL HILL

FAIRWAY
AVE

HARBOUR
PROSPECT

Sch

LILLIPUT RD

Luscombe Valley

Canford
Cliffs

Compton Acres
Gdns

CARISBROOKE

POOLE

THE CIRCLE

MARTELLO
RD

Canford
Chine

WENTWORTH
MINTERNE RD
MINTERNE
GRANGE

WITLEY

HARBOUR
WATCH

Little
CT

MOUNT GRACE

ALINGTON
CT ALINGTON CL

DORRIE RD

HAVEN RD

THE CIRCLE

RAVINE
RD

Canford Cli
Chine

89

Pier

SHORE RD   B3369

BH13
HAVEN RD

St Ann's

H

FLAGHEAD

C4
1 MERROW CHASE
2 CANFORD PL
3 RIVIERA CT
4 IMPERIAL CT
5 RAVINE GDNS
6 KILLOCK
7 FINESHADE
8 SEA POINT
9 TREETOPS
10 MARTELLO HO
11 KENILWORTH CT
12 BRACKENS WAY
13 STONELEIGH
14 BRANKSOME CT
15 PINE LO
16 LEYTON CONYERS
17 STANTON LACY
18 BURNAGE CT

Poole Harbour

Main Channel

HIVE
GDNS
VISTA
RD

LITTLE
FOSTERS

Promenade

1 WYKEHAM LO
2 HARBOUR CT
3 HAVENHURST
4 CHADDESLEY PINES
5 CANFORD CT

Poole
Head

3

88

Brownsea
Island

BH13

Brownsea
Road

North
Haven
Point

2

Branksea
Castle

Ferry (F)
(April to September)

Piers

OLD
COASTGUARD RD

PANORAMA RD

BERNIE HAVEN
CT

SEACOMBE RD

GRASMERE RD

SALTER RD

BANKS RD

BEACH
VIEW

DUNE
CREST

CARINA
CT

SHOREACRES

Promenade

Sandbanks

1 FAIRWINDS
2 GOLDEN SANDS
3 WOODRISING
4 MANSARD CT
5 GOLDEN GATES

Sandbanks
Bans Ctr

Hotel

204

Seaward
Path

BEACH HIGH
CL TREES

PINE BEACH
LO

THE AVENUE

B3065

TEAK
CL

DENECOTE

PINECLIFF RD

Promenade

Branksome
Chine

B3065 PINECLIFF RD

Liby

SOUTH
LO

4

89

06   D   07

South Haven
Point

Ferry (V)

87

Shell Bay
Sailing Ctr

Gravel
Point

Dorset Coastal Path
South West Coast Path

Shell
Bay

1

BH19

Bramble Bush
Bay

86

03   A   04   B   05   C

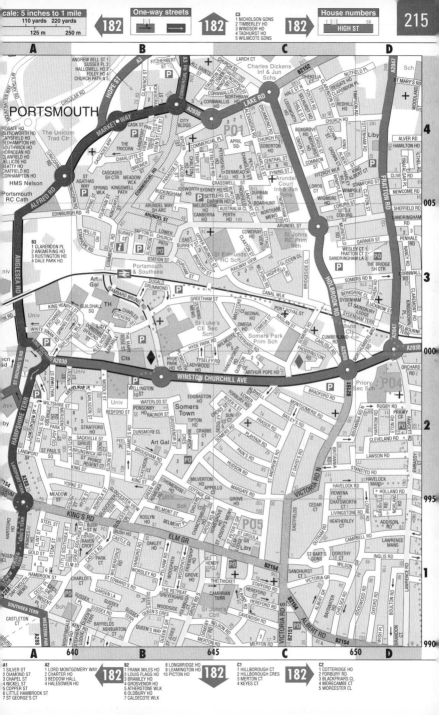

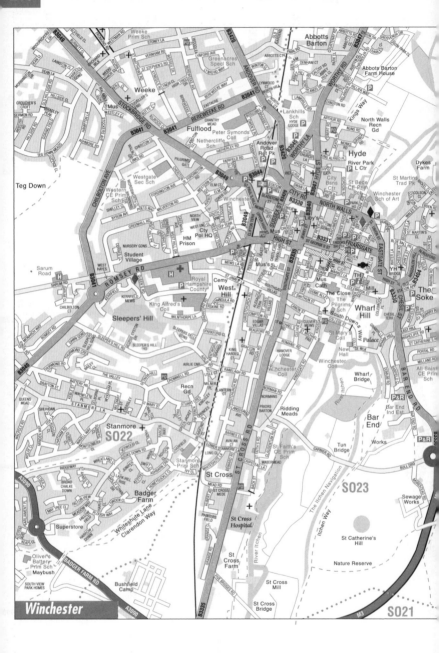

Winchester

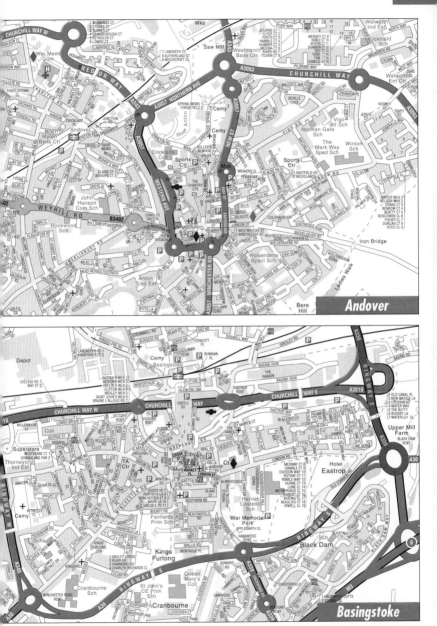

Andover

Basingstoke

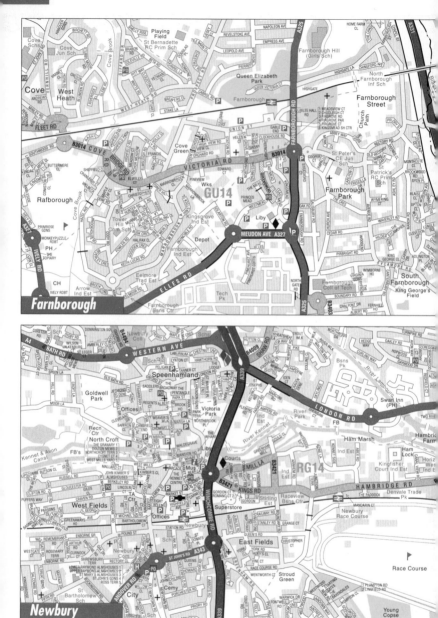

Farnborough

Newbury

Church Rd 6 Beckenham BR2..........**53** C6

Place name	Location number	Locality, town or village	Postcode district	Page and grid square
May be abbreviated on the map	Present when a number indicates the place's position in a crowded area of mapping	Shown when more than one place has the same name	District for the indexed place	Page number and grid reference for the standard mapping

Public and commercial buildings are highlighted in magenta. Places of interest are highlighted in blue with a star★

Abbreviations used in the index

Acad	**Academy**	Comm	**Common**	Gd	**Ground**	L	**Leisure**	Prom	**Prom**
App	**Approach**	Cott	**Cottage**	Gdn	**Garden**	La	**Lane**	Rd	**Road**
Arc	**Arcade**	Cres	**Crescent**	Gn	**Green**	Liby	**Library**	Recn	**Recreation**
Ave	**Avenue**	Cswy	**Causeway**	Gr	**Grove**	Mdw	**Meadow**	Ret	**Retail**
Bglw	**Bungalow**	Ct	**Court**	H	**Hall**	Meml	**Memorial**	Sh	**Shopping**
Bldg	**Building**	Ctr	**Centre**	Ho	**House**	Mkt	**Market**	Sq	**Square**
Bsns, Bus	**Business**	Ctry	**Country**	Hospl	**Hospital**	Mus	**Museum**	St	**Street**
Bvd	**Boulevard**	Cty	**County**	HQ	**Headquarters**	Orch	**Orchard**	Sta	**Station**
Cath	**Cathedral**	Dr	**Drive**	Hts	**Heights**	Pal	**Palace**	Terr	**Terrace**
Cir	**Circus**	Dro	**Drove**	Ind	**Industrial**	Par	**Parade**	TH	**Town Hall**
Cl	**Close**	Ed	**Education**	Inst	**Institute**	Pas	**Passage**	Univ	**University**
Cnr	**Corner**	Emb	**Embankment**	Int	**International**	Pk	**Park**	Wk, Wlk	**Walk**
Coll	**College**	Est	**Estate**	Intc	**Interchange**	Pl	**Place**	Wr	**Water**
Com	**Community**	Ex	**Exhibition**	Junc	**Junction**	Prec	**Precinct**	Yd	**Yard**

Index of localities, towns and villages

Abbotswood 28 A2	Compton (Sussex) 90 C1	Hayling Island 185 A4	New Milton 194 C2	Standon 9 A1
Alderholt 92 C3	Coombe Bissett 23 C4	Hedge End 105 B3	Nomansland 73 B4	Steep 40 B4
Ampfield 29 B2	Corfe Mullen 186 B3	Hermitage 161 A4	North Baddesley 53 C3	Steep Marsh 20 A1
Ashington 163 A1	Cosham 158 A3	Highcliffe 208 C4	North Boarhunt 109 A1	Stubbington 154 B2
Ashurst 100 A2	Cowplain 111 C2	High Cross 18 C1	North Hayling 160 B2	Swanmore 84 B3
Awbridge 26 C2	Cranborne 91 A4	Hill Brow 21 A1	Nursling 77 B3	Swanwick 129 A4
Barton on Sea 209 C3	Crouchestern 22 A4	Holbury 150 B2	Oakley 163 C1	Sway 172 A1
Beaulieu 148 C1	Curdridge 106 B4	Hordle 195 C2	Otterbourne 31 B2	Thorney Island 161 A2
Beauworth 35 A4	Damerham 68 B3	Horndean 112 B4	Ower 75 C3	Three Legged Cross ..138 C4
Bishopstoke 56 C2	Dean 59 C2	Horton Heath 81 B4	Owslebury 33 A2	Timsbury 27 B3
Bishop's Waltham 83 B4	Denmead 111 A3	Hurn 191 A4	Pamphill 162 C3	Titchfield 153 C4
Blackfield 177 C4	Dibden Purlieu 125 C1	Hursley 30 A4	Pentridge 42 A1	Totton 100 C4
Blashford 117 A2	Downton 47 A4	Hythe 126 A3	Petersfield 40 B2	Twyford 32 A3
Boldre 173 B1	Droxford 61 A1	Ibsley 117 A4	Plaitford 50 A2	Upham 58 C3
Botley 106 A4	Durley 82 A3	Keyhaven 212 A2	Poole 202 A2	Upton 201 B4
Bournemouth 206 A2	East Boldre 175 B3	Kilmeston 14 B1	Portchester 156 B4	Verwood 114 C2
Braishfield 28 B4	East Dean 4 A1	Kingston 167 C4	Portmore 198 A4	Walderton 137 C4
Bramdean 15 B2	East End 199 A4	Kings Worthy 2 B3	Portsea Island 182 C3	Waltham Chase 83 C2
Bramshaw 73 C2	Eastleigh 55 C2	Landford 49 B2	Portsmouth 157 B2	Warnford 36 C2
Bransgore 193 A4	East Meon 38 B1	Langrish 39 B2	Privet 17 B1	Warsash 128 B1
Breamore 70 A4	East Tytherley 4 C4	Langstone 159 C4	Purbrook 134 C2	Waterlooville 134 B4
Broadstone 187 A2	East Wellow 51 A3	Lee-on-the-Solent ...179 B1	Rake 21 C2	Westbourne 137 A2
Brockbridge 61 B1	Edmondsham 91 A2	Lepe 178 A1	Ramsdean 39 B1	West Dean 3 B2
Brockenhurst 145 C1	Emery Down 121 B3	Linwood 118 A4	Redlynch 47 C3	West End 80 C1
Brook 74 A1	Emsworth 136 C1	Liss 21 A2	Ringwood 141 B4	West Meon 37 A2
Bucklers Hard 176 B2	Exbury 177 A3	Littleton 1 A3	Ripley 168 B1	West Moors 138 C2
Buriton 65 B3	Fair Oak 57 B1	Lockerley 4 C1	Rockbourne 44 C1	West Parley 189 C4
Burley 143 A2	Fareham 131 A2	Locks Heath 129 B2	Romsey 52 C3	West Tisted 16 B4
Bursledon 128 A4	Fawley 151 A2	Lover 48 A3	Rowland's Castle 113 B1	West Tytherley 4 A4
Burton 192 B1	Ferndown 165 A3	Lymington 197 B3	Rownhams 77 C4	West Wellow 50 C2
Cadnam 98 C4	Finchdean 113 B3	Lyndhurst 121 C3	St Leonards 139 B2	Whiteparish 24 A2
Calshot 178 C4	Fordingbridge 69 C1	Marchwood 101 C1	Sandleheath 69 A2	Whitsbury 45 A2
Chalton 89 B3	Fratton 182 C2	Martin 43 A2	Shedfield 107 B4	Wick 46 B4
Chandler's Ford 55 B4	Fritham 72 C1	Meonstoke 61 B3	Sherfield English 25 B1	Wickham 108 A2
Cheriton 14 B3	Froxfield Green 39 B4	Michelmersh 6 B1	Soberton 85 B3	Wimborne Minster ...163 A3
Chilcomb 11 C3	Godshill 70 C1	Milford on Sea 211 B2	Sopley 192 A4	Winchester 10 B3
Chilworth 54 B1	Gosport 181 B3	Minstead 98 A2	Southampton 102 B2	Woodgreen 70 C4
Christchurch 207 B3	Hambledon 86 B1	Mottisfont 5 C1	Southbourne 161 C4	Woodlands 114 A3
Clanfield 88 A3	Hamble-le-Rice 128 A1	Netley 127 A3	South Harting 66 C2	Wootton 171 A1
Colden Common 32 A1	Hamworthy 201 B2	Netley Marsh 100 A3	South Hayling 184 C1	
Colehill 164 A4	Havant 135 C2	Newbridge 74 C2	Southsea 182 B1	
Compton (Hants) 31 B4	Hawkley 19 C4		Southwick 132 C3	

1

1st St SO45 .... 151 A2

2

2nd St SO45 .... 151 A2

3

3rd St SO45 .... 150 C2

4

4th St SO45 .... 150 C2

5

5th St SO45 .... 150 C2

6

6th St Fawley SO45 .... 150 C2
Fawley SO45 .... 150 C3

7

7th St SO45 .... 150 C2

8

8th St SO45 .... 150 C2

9

9th St SO45 .... 150 B2

1

10th St SO45 .... 150 B3
11th St SO45 .... 150 B3
12th St SO45 .... 150 B3
13th St SO45 .... 150 B3
14th St SO45 .... 150 B3
17th Centure Experience
Mus* PO13 .... 180 B3

A

A Ave SO45 .... 150 B2
A'beckett Ct 3 PO1 ...... 182 A2
Aaron Cl BH17 .... 202 C4
Aaron Ct SO40 .... 101 C1
Abbas Gr PO9 .... 135 B4
Abbey Cl SO45 .... 126 A2
Abbey Ct 15 SO15 .... 102 C4
Abbey Ent Ctr SO51 ...... 53 B3
Abbey Gdns BH21 .... 164 B3
Abbey Hill SO31 .... 127 A4
Abbey Hill Cl SO23 .... 2 A1
Abbey Hill Rd SO23 .... 1 C1
Abbey Mill Bsns Site
SO32 .... 83 A4
Abbey Pas SO23 .... 11 A4
Abbey Rd Fareham PO15 .. 130 B1
West Moors BH22 .... 166 A4
Abbey The SO51 .... 52 C2
Abbey Water 3 SO51 ...... 52 C4
Abbeyfield Dr PO15 ...... 130 B1
Abbeyfield Ho 7 SO18 .... 103 C4
Abbeyfields Cl SO31 ...... 127 B3
Abbots Cl
Christchurch BH23 .... 208 C4
Waterlooville PO7 .... 134 B2
Abbots Row 6 SO22 .... 10 C4
Abbots Way
Fareham PO15 .... 130 B1
Nailsea SO31 .... 127 B3
Abbots Well Rd SP6 ...... 94 A4
Abbotsbury Rd
Bishopstoke SO50 .... 56 C1
Broadstone BH18 .... 186 C3
Abbotsfield SO40 .... 100 C4
Abbotsfield Cl SO16 ...... 78 B3
Abbotsford SO40 .... 101 C1
Abbotstone Ave PO9 ..... 136 A2
Abbotswood Cl SO51 ...... 28 B1
Abbotswood Jun Sch
SO40 .... 100 C4
Abbott Cl BH9 .... 205 A4
Abbott Rd BH9 .... 205 A4
Abbott St BH21 .... 162 B3
Abbotts Ann Rd SO22 .... 9 B3
Abbotts Cl SO23 .... 2 A1
Abbotts Cl
15 Southampton SO17 .... 79 A1
Winchester SO22 .... 1 C1
Abbotts Dro SO51 .... 50 C1
Abbotts Rd Eastleigh SO50 55 C1
Winchester SO23 .... 2 A1
Abbotts Way
Southampton SO17 .... 79 A1
West Moors BH22 .... 166 A4

Abercrombie Gdns SO16 ... 78 A2
Aberdare Ave PO6 .... 158 A4
Aberdare Rd BH10 .... 189 C2
Aberdeen Cl PO15 .... 130 C2
Aberdeen Rd SO17 .... 79 B1
Aberdour Cl SO18 .... 104 A4
Abingdon Cl PO12 .... 181 A2
Abingdon Dr BH23 ...... 209 A4
Abingdon Gdns SO16 .... 78 C2
Abingdon Rd BH17 ...... 202 B4
Abinger Rd BH7 .... 206 A3
Abney Rd BH10 .... 189 B2
Above Bar St SO14 ...... 102 C3
Abraham Cl SO30 ...... 105 B3
Abshot Cl PO14 .... 129 A1
Abshot Rd PO14 .... 129 A1
Acacia Ave BH31 .... 115 B2
Acacia Gdns PO8 .... 112 A3
Acacia Rd Hordle SO41 .. 195 C2
Southampton SO19 ...... 103 C3
Acer Way PO9 .... 136 A2
Ackworth Rd PO3 ...... 158 A3
Acland Rd BH9 .... 205 A4
Acorn Bsns Ctr PO6 ..... 157 B4
Acorn Bsns Pk BH12 .... 203 A4
Acorn Cl
Christchurch BH23 .... 206 C4
Cosham PO6 .... 158 C4
Gosport PO13 .... 155 B1
Marchwood SO40 .... 102 A1
New Milton BH25 .... 195 B2
St Leonards BH24 .... 139 C2
Acorn Cotts BH21 ...... 114 C4
Acorn Cl SO31 .... 127 C2
Acorn Dr SO16 .... 77 C4
Acorn Gdns PO8 .... 112 A3
Acorn Gr SO53 .... 54 C2
Acorn Way BH31 .... 115 A3
Acorn Workshops SO14 .. 103 A4
Acorns The
Burstledon SO31 .... 127 C4
Wimborne Minst BH21 ... 164 A2
Acre La PO7 .... 112 B1
Acres Rd BH11 .... 189 A1
Acton Rd BH10 .... 189 A1
Ad Astro Fst Sch BH17 .. 187 C1
Adair Rd PO4 .... 183 A1
Adames Rd PO1 .... 182 C3
Adams Cl SO30 .... 81 A2
Adams Rd SO45 .... 126 A1
Adams Terr PO6 .... 158 B3
Adams Way PO15 .... 129 B3
Adams Wood Dr SO40 ... 101 C1
Adamsfield Gdns BH10 .. 189 B1
Adamson Cl SO53 .... 55 B4
Adastral Rd BH17 ...... 202 C4
Adastral Sq BH17 ...... 202 C4
Adcock Ct SO16 .... 77 C4
Adderbury Ave PO10 .... 136 C2
Addington Ct 1 SO41 ... 211 B3
Addington Pl BH23 ...... 207 B3
Addiscombe Rd BH23 ... 207 A4
Addison Cl Romsey SO51 .. 28 A1
Winchester SO22 .... 10 B3
Addison Rd
Brockenhurst SO42 ..... 172 C4
Eastleigh SO50 .... 56 A3
Locks Heath SO31 ...... 128 C3
Portsmouth PO5 .... 215 D1
Addison Sq BH24 ...... 141 A4
Adelaide Cl BH23 ...... 206 C4
Adelaide Cl SO41 ...... 197 C2
Adelaide La 10 BH1 .... 204 C2
Adelaide Pl 9 PO16 .... 131 B1
Adelaide Rd SO17 ...... 103 B4
Adeline Rd BH5 .... 205 C2
Adey Cl SO19 .... 104 A1
Adhurst Rd PO9 .... 136 A2
Adlam's La SO41 ...... 172 A1
Admiral Lord Nelson Sch
PO3 .... 158 A1
Admiral Park The PO3 .. 158 B4
Admiral's Cnr 4 PO5 ... 182 B1
Admiral's Wlk PO1 .... 181 C3
Admirals Cl SO45 ..... 151 A2
Admirals Ct
Hamble-le-Rice SO31 ... 128 A1
19 Lymington SO41 .... 197 C2
19 Portsmouth PO5 .... 182 B1
Admirals Rd SO31 ..... 129 A2
Admirals Way 5 SO45 .. 126 A3
Admirals Wlk
Bournemouth BH2 ...... 204 B1
Gosport PO12 .... 180 C2
Aderbury Ct 8 BH23 .... 207 A4
Aldbourne Cl BH8 ...... 206 B3
Alderfield GU32 .... 40 C2
Aldermoor Ave SO16 ... 78 A2
Aldermoor Cl SO16 .... 78 B2
Aldermoor Rd
Gosport PO13 .... 180 B4
Southampton SO16 ..... 78 A2
Waterlooville PO7 ...... 134 B2
Aldermoor Rd E PO7 ... 134 B3
Alderney Ave BH12 .... 188 B1
Alderney Cl SO16 ...... 77 C2
Alderney Rd BH12 ..... 188 B1
Alderney Mid Sch BH12 . 188 B1
Alderney Rdbt BH12 ... 188 B1
Alders Rd PO16 .... 155 A4
Aldershot Ho 50 PO9 .. 136 A3

Ainsley Gdns SO50 ..... 56 A3
Aintree Cl SO50 .... 81 B4
Aintree Cl SO31 .... 129 A4
Aintree Dr PO7 .... 112 A1
Aintree Rd SO40 ...... 101 B4
Airetons Cl BH18 ...... 187 B2
Airfield Ind Est BH23 .. 207 C3
Airfield Rd BH23 ...... 207 C3
Airfield Way BH23 ..... 207 C4
Airlie Cnr SO22 .... 10 C3
Airlie Rd SO22 .... 10 C3
Airport Service Rd PO3 . 158 A2
Airspeed Rd
Christchurch BH23 ...... 208 A4
Portsmouth PO3 .... 158 A1
Ajax Cl PO14 .... 179 B3
Akeshill Cl BH25 ...... 195 A3
Alameda Rd PO7 ...... 134 B2
Alameda Way PO7 .... 134 B2
Alan Chun Ho SO31 ... 128 A1
Alan Ct 10 BH23 ...... 209 A4
Alan Drayton Way SO50 . 56 C1
Alan Gr PO15 .... 130 C1
Alandale Rd SO19 ..... 104 B2
Albacore Ave SO31 ... 128 C1
Albany BH1 .... 205 B2
Albany Cl BH25 ...... 194 C1
Albany Ct
Bishop's Waltham SO32 .. 83 A4
Gosport PO12 .... 181 A3
Albany Dr
Bishop's Waltham SO32 .. 83 A4
Three Legged Cross BH21 114 C1
Albany Gdns BH15 .... 201 C1
Albany Park Cl SO17 .. 102 C4
Albany Pk BH17 ...... 202 A4
Albany Rd
Bishop's Waltham SO32 .. 83 A4
Holbury SO45 .... 150 B2
Portsmouth PO5 ...... 215 C1
Romsey SO51 .... 52 C4
Southampton SO15 .... 102 B3
Albany The SO14 ...... 103 A2
Albatross Wlk PO13 ... 155 A1
Albemarle Ave PO12 .. 181 A4
Albemarle Rd BH4 .... 204 C4
Albemarle Ct SO17 ... 79 B2
Albert Cl SO31 .... 127 B3
Albert Ct SO17 .... 79 B1
Albert Gr PO5 .... 215 C1
Albert Rd
Bishop's Waltham SO32 .. 83 A4
Bournemouth BH1 ...... 204 C2
Corfe Mullen BH21 .... 186 B3
Cosham PO6 .... 157 C4
Fernhaven SO50 ...... 56 A3
Ferndown BH22 .... 165 B3
Hedge End SO30 ...... 105 A3
New Milton BH25 ...... 194 C1
Poole BH12 .... 203 B3
Portsmouth PO4 ...... 183 A1
Stubbington PO14 ..... 179 C3
Albert Rd N SO14 ..... 103 A2
Albert Rd S SO14 ..... 103 A2
Albert St PO12 .... 181 B3
Albion Cl Poole BH12 ... 203 A4
Portchester PO16 ..... 156 A3
Albion Pl 6 SO14 ..... 102 C2
Albion Rd
Christchurch BH23 ..... 191 C1
Fordingbridge SP6 ..... 69 C1
Lee-on-the-Solent PO13 177 C2
Albion Terr 11 SO14 ... 103 A2
Albion Way BH11 ..... 114 B4
Albretia Ave PO8 ..... 111 C2
Albury Pl SO53 .... 30 A1
Alby Rd BH12 .... 203 C3
Alcantara Cres SO14 ... 103 A2
Alcester Rd BH12 ..... 203 B3
Alchorne Pl PO3 ...... 158 A2
Aldbury Ct BH25 ...... 210 A4
Alder Cl Burton BH23 .. 192 B1
Colden Common SO21 .. 57 A4
Hythe SO45 .... 125 B2
Marchwood SO40 ...... 101 C1
Romsey SO51 .... 53 B3
Alder Cres BH10 ...... 203 C4
Alder Dr SP6 .... 69 C2
Alder Hill Dr SO40 .... 100 A4
Alder Hills BH12 ...... 204 A4
Alder Hills Ind Est BH12 204 A4
Alder La PO12/PO13 ... 180 B3
Alder Rd Poole BH12 .. 203 C3
Southampton SO16 .... 78 A2
Alderbury Ct 8 BH23 ... 207 A4
Aldbury Ct 8 BH23 .... 207 A4

Alderwood Ave SO53 ... 55 A3
Alderwood Cl PO9 .... 135 A2
Aldis Gdns BH11 ..... 201 C1
Aldrich Rd PO1 ...... 182 A3
Aldridge Cl PO8 ...... 88 B3
Aldridge Rd
Bournemouth BH10 .... 189 B3
Ferndown BH22 ...... 165 C2
Aldridge Way BH22 ... 165 C2
Aldroke St 10 PO6 .... 157 C4
Aldsworth Cl PO6 .... 158 B4
Aldsworth Gdns PO6 .. 158 B4
Aldwell St PO5 ...... 215 C2
Alec Rose Ho 16 PO12 . 181 B2
Alec Rose La PO1 ..... 215 B3
Alec Wintle Ho PO2 ... 182 B4
Alecto Rd PO12 ...... 181 A2
Alencon Cl PO12 ..... 181 B4
Alexander Cl
Christchurch BH23 .... 207 C3
Totton SO40 .... 100 B4
Waterlooville PO7 .... 134 B3
Alexander Ct
Southampton SO15 .... 102 B3
Southampton, Woolston
SO19 .... 103 C1
Alexander Gr PO16 ... 155 A4
Alexander Ho PO11 ... 185 C1
Alexandra Ave PO11 .. 184 C1
Alexandra Cl SO45 ... 126 A2
Alexandra La 6 BH1 ... 205 A2
Alexandra Rd
Bournemouth BH6 .... 206 B3
Chandler's Ford SO53 .. 55 C4
Fordingbridge SP6 .... 69 C1
Hedge End SO30 ..... 105 A3
Lymington SO41 ...... 197 B3
Poole BH14 .... 203 C2
Portsmouth PO1 ..... 215 C4
Southampton SO15 ... 102 B3
Alexandra St PO12 ... 181 A3
Alexandra Terr SO23 .. 10 C4
Alexandra Way SO30 .. 106 A4
Alexandria Ct BH22 .. 165 C2
Alford Rd BH3 .... 204 B4
Alfred Cl SO40 .... 100 B4
Alfred Rd
Portsmouth PO1 ..... 215 A4
Stubbington PO14 .... 154 B2
Alfred Rose Ct SO18 .. 79 C2
Alfred St SO14 .... 103 A3
Alfrey Cl PO10 ...... 161 B4
Alfriston Ct SO19 .... 104 B2
Alfriston Gdns SO19 .. 104 A2
Algiers Rd PO3 ...... 183 A4
Alhambra Rd PO4 .... 183 A1
Alice in Wonderland Family
Pk* BH23 .... 190 C4
Alington 18 BH4 ..... 204 B2
Alington Cl BH14 .... 214 B4
Alington Ho BH14 .... 214 B4
Alington Rd BH3 ..... 205 A3
Alipore Cl BH14 ..... 203 B2
Alipore Hts BH14 .... 203 B2
Alison Way 11 SO22 .... 10 C4
All Saints CE Prim Sch
SO23 .... 11 A4
All Saints Ho 19 SO14 .. 103 A2
All Saints Rd SO41 ... 197 C1
All Saints' St PO1 ... 215 B4
All Saints' St PO1 ... 215 B4
Allan Gr SO51 .... 52 A4
Allaway Ave PO6 ..... 157 A4
Allbrook Ct 12 PO9 ... 135 B3
Allbrook Hill SO50 ... 56 A4
Allbrook Knoll SO50 .. 56 A4
Allbrook Way SO50 .. 56 A4
Allcot Rd PO3 .... 158 A1
Allen Ct BH21 .... 164 A2
Allen Rd Hedge End SO30 105 B4
Wimborne Minst BH21 . 163 B2
Allen Water Dr SP6 ... 69 C1
Allen's Rd PO4 .... 182 C1
Allenbourn Mid Sch
BH21 .... 163 B3
Allenby Cl BH17 ..... 187 A1
Allenby Gr PO16 ..... 156 B4
Allenby Rd Gosport PO12 180 C3
Poole BH17 .... 187 A1
Allendale Ave PO10 ... 136 C2
Allens Farm La SO32 .. 61 A3
Allens La Meonstoke SO32 61 B3
Upton BH16 .... 201 B3
Allens Rd BH16 ...... 201 B3
Allenview Rd BH21 ... 163 B3
Allerton Cl SO40 ..... 76 B1
Alley The SP6 .... 70 C4
Alliance Cl PO13 ..... 180 B4
Allington La SO30 .... 80 A4
Allington Manor Farm Bsns
Ctr SO50 .... 80 C4
Allington Rd Poole BH14 214 B4
Southampton SO15 ... 101 B4
Allison Cl 6 SO41 .... 211 A2
Allison Ho SO30 ..... 105 B4
Allmara Dr PO7 ...... 134 C2
Allotment Rd
Hedge End SO30 ..... 105 A3
Locks Heath SO31 .... 128 C3
Alma Ho SO14 .... 103 A4
Alma La SO32 .... 58 A1
Alma Rd
Bournemouth BH9 .... 205 A4
Romsey SO51 .... 52 C4
Southampton SO14 ... 103 A4
Alma St PO12 .... 181 A3
Alma Terr PO4 .... 183 A2

Almatade Rd SO18 .... 104 A4
Almer Rd BH15 ...... 201 C2
Almond Cl Cosham PO9 . 158 C4
Waterlooville PO8 ..... 112 B2
Almond Ct 18 SO15 ... 102 B3
Almond Gr BH12 ..... 203 B4
Almond Rd SO15 ..... 102 B3
Almondsbury Ho 8
PO6 .... 132 C3
Almondsbury Rd PO6 . 132 C1
Almondside PO13 .... 155 C1
Almshouses BH10 .... 189 B1
Alpha Ctr The BH17 .. 202 A4
Alphage Rd PO12 .... 155 C1
Alpine Cl SO18 ...... 104 A4
Alpine Rd Ashurst SO40 . 99 C2
St Leonards BH24 .... 140 B1
Alresford Rd
Chilcomb SO21, SO23 .. 12 B4
Havant PO9 .... 135 C2
Winchester SO21, SO23 . 11 B4
Alsford Rd PO7 ...... 134 B3
Alswitha Terr 27 SO23 .. 2 A1
Alten Rd PO7 .... 111 B1
Althorpe Dr PO3 ..... 158 B2
Alton Cl SO50 .... 57 A1
Alton Ct 12 SO23 ...... 2 A1
Alton Gr PO16 .... 156 B3
Alton Ho SO18 .... 103 C4
Alton Rd
Bournemouth BH10 ... 189 A1
Poole BH14 .... 203 B2
Alton Rd E BH14 ..... 203 B1
Alum Chine Rd BH4 .. 204 A2
Alum Cl SO45 .... 150 B2
Alum Way
Portchester PO16 .... 131 C1
Southampton SO18 ... 104 A4
Alumdale Rd BH4 .... 204 A1
Alumhurst Rd BH4 .. 204 A1
Alvandi Gdns 12 BH25 . 195 A2
Alvara Rd PO12 ...... 181 A1
Alver Bridge View 10
PO12 .... 181 A2
Alver Quay PO12 .... 181 A2
Alver Rd Gosport PO12 . 181 A2
Portsmouth PO1 ..... 182 C3
Alvercliffe Dr PO12 ... 180 C1
Alverstoke CE Jun Sch
PO12 .... 181 A2
Alverstoke Ct PO12 ... 181 A1
Alverstoke Inf Sch
PO12 .... 181 A1
Alverstone Ave BH23 . 183 A3
Alverton Ave BH15 ... 202 C2
Alverton Hall BH4 .... 204 B1
Alveston Ave PO14 ... 154 B4
Alyne Ho SO15 ...... 102 C4
Alyth Rd BH3 .... 204 B3
Amaryllis Cl PO15 ... 129 C2
Ambassador Cl BH23 . 208 A3
Ambassador Ind Est
BH23 .... 208 A3
Amber Rd BH21 ..... 186 B2
Amberley Cl Botley SO30 106 A4
Christchurch BH23 .... 208 C4
North Baddesley SO52 . 53 C3
Amberley Ct
8 Bournemouth BH1 ... 205 A2
Totton SO40 .... 100 B3
Amberley Rd Clanfield PO8 88 B3
Gosport PO12 .... 180 C1
Portsmouth PO2 ..... 157 C2
Amberslade Wlk SO45 . 125 C1
Amberwood
Ferndown BH22 ...... 165 C3
Milford on Sea SO41 ... 211 A3
Amberwood Cl SO40 .. 76 B1
Amberwood Dr BH23 . 193 C1
Amberwood Gdns BH23 194 A1
Amberwood Ho BH23 . 194 A1
Amblecote SO31 ..... 128 C2
Ambleside
Bishop's Waltham SO32 . 83 A4
Christchurch BH23 .... 191 C2
Hedge End SO30 ..... 105 B3
Ambleside Gdns SO19 . 104 A2
Ambleside Rd SO41 .. 197 B4
Ambury La BH23 ..... 207 C4
Amersham Ct PO12 ... 180 C2
Amesbury Rd BH6 ... 206 B3
Amethyst Gr PO7 .... 135 A4
Amethyst Rd BH23 ... 207 C4
Amey Ind Est GU32 ... 40 C2
Ameys La BH22 ...... 165 C4
Ameysford Rd BH22 . 165 B4
Amira Ct 9 BH2 ...... 204 C2
Amoy St SO15 .... 102 C3
Ampfield CE Prim Sch
SO51 .... 29 B2
Ampfield Cl PO9 ..... 135 A2
Ampfield Rd BH8 .... 190 B2
Amport Cl SO22 .... 9 B3
Amport Ct PO9 ...... 135 B3
Ampress La SO41 .... 197 B3
Ampthill Rd SO15 .... 102 A4
Amsterdam Sq BH23 . 207 B3
Amyas Ct PO4 .... 183 B2
Ancasta Rd SO14 .... 103 A4
Anchor Cl
Bournemouth BH11 ... 188 C3
Christchurch BH23 .... 208 A3
Anchor La PO1 ...... 182 B2
Anchor Mews SO41 .. 197 C2
Anchor Rd BH11 ..... 188 C3
Anchorage Rd PO3 ... 158 A2
Anchorage The PO12 . 181 B2
Anchorage Way SO41 . 197 B2

Ancrum Lo BH4 ....204 A2
Andalusian Gdns SO31 ..129 A4
Andbourne Ct BH6 ......206 C2
Anderby Rd SO16 ....77 B1
Anderson Cl Havant PO9 .136 A2
  Romsey SO51 ....28 B1
  Swanwick PO15 ....129 B4
Anderson's Rd SO14 .....103 A2
Anderwood Dr SO41 .....172 A1
Andes Cl SO14 ....103 B2
Andes Rd SO16 ....77 A2
Andlers Ash Rd GU33 .....20 C2
Andover Cl BH23 ....208 A4
Andover Ho PO9 ....136 A3
Andover Rd
  Portsmouth PO4 ....182 C1
  Southampton SO15 .....102 B3
  Winchester SO21, SO22,
  SO23 ....1 C1
Andover Rd N SO22 ....1 C1
Andover Road Ret Pk
  ....1 C1
Andree Ct BH23 ....209 A4
Andrew Bell St PO1 .....215 B4
Andrew Cl
  Hythe SO45 ....126 A1
  Portsmouth PO1 ....182 C1
  Totton SO40 ....100 B4
Andrew Cres PO7 ....111 B1
Andrew La BH25 ....195 B1
Andrew Pl PO14 ....179 A3
Andrews Cl SO32 ....83 B4
Andrews Cl BH11 ....189 A2
Andromeda Rd SO16 ......77 C2
Androse Gdns BA24 ......140 C3
Anfield Cl SO50 ....57 B1
Anfield Cl SO50 ....57 A1
Angel Cres SO18,SO19 ..104 A3
Angel Ct SO41 ....197 C2
Angel La
  Barton on Sea BH25 ...210 B4
  Ferndown BH22 ....165 A2
Angelica Ct PO7 ....35 A3
Angelica Way PO15 .....129 C4
Angelica Way PO15 .....129 C4
Angeline Cl BH23 ....208 C4
Angelo Cl PO7 ....135 A4
Angelus Cl PO14 ....179 A3
Angerstein Rd PO2 ......157 B1
Anglers Way SO31 ......128 B4
Anglesea Ct SO15 ....78 A1
Anglesea Rd
  Lee-on-the-Solent PO13 .180 A2
  Portsmouth PO1 ....215 A3
  Southampton SO15 ......78 A1
Anglesea Terr SO14 .....103 A2
Anglesey Arms Rd
  PO12 ....181 A1
Anglesey Rd PO12 ....181 A1
Anglesey View PO12 ....181 A1
Anglewood Mans [9]
  BH4 ....204 B2
Anglo-European Coll of
  Chiropractic BH5 .....206 A2
Angmering Ho [2] PO1 ..215 B3
Angus Cl PO15 ....130 C2
Anjou Cl BH11 ....188 B3
Angus Cres PO15 ....130 B1
Anker La PO14 ....154 B2
Ankerwyke PO13 ....155 A1
Anmore Cl PO9 ....135 B2
Anmore Cnr PO7 ....111 A2
Anmore Dr PO7 ....111 B1
Anmore La PO7 ....111 A2
Anmore Rd PO7 ....111 A2
Ann's Hill Rd PO12 .....181 A3
Anna La BH23 ....168 A2
Annadale Cl BH6 ....206 B2
Anne Cl BH23 ....192 A1
Anne Cres PO7 ....134 C3
Annerley Rd BH1 ....205 B2
Annes Ct PO11 ....184 C1
Annet Cl BH15 ....201 C1
Anson Cl
  Christchurch BH23 ....207 C3
  Gosport PO13 ....180 B3
  Ringwood BH24 ....141 B4
Anson Dr SO19 ....104 B3
Anson Ho PO14 ....132 C1
Anson Ho SO14 ....103 A2
Anson Rd
  Horton Heath SO50 .....81 B4
  [1] Portsmouth PO1 ...183 A3
Anstey Cl BH11 ....189 A3
Anstey Rd
  Bournemouth BH11 ....189 A3
  Romsey SO51 ....28 A1
Antell's Way SP6 ....93 A3
Anthill Cl PO7 ....110 B3
Anthony Gr PO12 ....156 A1
Anthony Way PO10 .....136 C2
Anthony's Ave PO13 ....203 B1
Antigua Ho [5] PO6 ....132 C1
Antler Dr BH25 ....194 C2
Anton Cl SO51 ....53 A4
Anvil Cl East Meon GU32 ..63 C4
  Waterlooville PO7 .....112 B1
  West End SO30 ....80 B1
Anvil Cres BH18 ....186 C3
Anvil Ct [2] PO4 ....183 B2
Anzac Cl PO14 ....154 B2
Apex Cnr PO14 ....155 A3
Apless La PO7 ....110 A2
Apollo Cl BH12 ....203 B4
Apollo Dr PO7 ....134 B1
Apollo Rd SO53 ....55 C4
Apple Cl BH12 ....204 A2

Apple Gr
  Christchurch BH23 ....191 C1
  Emsworth PO10 ....161 A4
Apple Ind Est PO15 ....129 B3
Apple Tree Cl SP5 ....47 B4
Apple Tree Gr BH23 ...165 C3
Apple Tree Rd SP6 ......92 C3
Applegate Pl PO8 ......112 A3
Applemore Coll SO45 ..125 B2
Applemore Recn Ctr
  ....125 B2
Appleshaw Cl SO22 ......1 B2
Appleshaw Gr PO9 .....135 B2
Appleslade Way BH25 ..195 A3
Appleton Rd
  Fareham PO15 ....130 B1
  Southampton SO18 .....79 C1
Appletree Cl
  Bournemouth BH6 .....206 B3
  New Milton BH25 .....195 A1
Totton SO40 ....76 B1
Appletree Cl SO30 ......106 A4
Appletree Rd SP5 ....47 B4
Applewood Gdns SO19 .104 A3
Applewood Gr PO7 .....134 B2
Applewood Pl SO40 ...100 B3
Applo Cl PO5 ....215 B2
Approach Rd BH14 .....203 A2
Approach The PO3 .....158 A1
April Cl
  Bournemouth BH11 ...189 A2
  Southampton SO18 ...104 A4
April Sq SO31 ....128 C2
April Sq PO1 ....215 C4
Apsley Cres BH17 .....187 B1
Apsley Ct [4] BH8 .....205 A3
Apsley Pl SO53 ....30 A1
Apsley Rd PO4 ....183 A2
Aquila Way SO31 ......127 C1
Aquitania Ho [26] SO14 .103 B3
Arabian Gdns PO15 ....29 B4
Aragon Way BH9 ......190 A2
Arbour Ct [34] SO22 ....10 C4
Arcade BH4 ....204 A2
Arcade The
  [5] Bournemouth BH1 .204 C2
  Liss GU33 ....20 C3
Arcadia Ave BH8 ......205 A4
Arcadia Cl SO16 ....78 B2
Arcadia Rd BH23 ......191 C1
Arch Farm Ind Est SP6 ..57 A3
Archdale Cl BH10 .....189 B1
Archer Ho PO12 ....181 B1
Archers SO15 ....102 C3
Archers Cl SO40 ....98 B1
Archers Rd Eastleigh SO50 .56 A2
  Southampton SO15 ...102 C4
Archery Gdns SO19 ....103 C1
Archery Gr SO19 ....103 C1
Archery La
  Fareham PO16 ....131 B1
  Winchester SO22 ....10 C4
Archery Rd SO19 ......103 C1
Archgate SO41 ....197 C2
Archway Rd BH14 .....203 C2
Arden Cl Gosport PO12 ..180 C2
  Southampton SO18 .....80 A1
Arden Rd BH9 ....189 C2
Arden Wlk BH25 ......195 A1
Ardingly Cres SO30 .....81 B1
Ardington Rise PO7 ...134 C2
Ardmore Rd BH14 .....203 A2
Ardnave Cres SO16 .....78 C3
Argosy Cl SO31 ....128 C1
Argus Rd PO13 ....179 C2
Argyle Cres PO15 ......130 C1
Argyle Rd
  Christchurch BH23 ....207 C3
  Southampton SO14 ...103 A3
Argyll Mans [11] BH5 ..205 C2
Argyll Rd
  Bournemouth BH5 .....205 C2
  Poole BH12 ....203 B3
Ariel Cl BH6 ....207 A2
Ariel Dr BH6 ....207 A2
Ariel Rd PO1 ....182 C3
Arismore Ct PO13 .....179 C2
Ark Dr BH22 ....165 C2
Ark Royal Cres PO13 ..179 C2
Arle Cl PO8 ....88 B2
Arley Rd BH14 ....203 A1
Arlington Cl BH25 .....210 A4
Arlington Pl [2] SO23 ..11 A4
Arliss Rd SO16 ....78 A1
Arlott Ct SO15 ....102 C4
Armada Cl SO16 ....77 C4
Armada Dr SO45 ......126 A1
Armadale Ho [8] SO14 .103 B3
Arminers Cl PO12 .....181 A1
Armitage Ave SO45 ...125 C1
Armory La PO1 ....182 A2
Armoury The SO40 ....102 A2
Armstrong Cl
  Brockenhurst SO42 ...145 C1
  Waterlooville PO7 ....111 B1
Armstrong Cl SO16 .....77 C3
Armstrong La SO42 ...145 C1
Armstrong Rd SO42 ...145 C1
Arnewsworth La PO7,SO32 .85 C1
Arnaud Cl PO2 ....182 B4
Arne Ave PO3 ....203 C4
Arne Cres BH12 ....203 C4
Arnewood Bridge Rd
  SO41 ....196 A4
Arnewood Ct
  Bournemouth BH2 ....204 B1

Arnewood Ct continued
  Sway SO41 ....196 B3
Arnewood Ho SO41 ....196 B2
Arnewood Rd BH6 .....206 B3
Arnewood Sch The
  BH25 ....194 C1
Arnheim Cl SO16 ....78 B2
Arnheim Rd SO16 ....78 B2
Arnold Cl BH22 ....138 C2
Arnold Rd Southampton SO17 .79 B1
  West Moors BH22 .....138 C2
Arnolds Cl BH25 ......209 C4
Arnside Rd PO7 ....134 C4
Arnwood Ave SO45 ....149 C4
Arragon Ct PO7 ....135 A4
Arran Cl PO6 ....133 C1
Arran Way BH23 ......194 A1
Arras Rd PO15 ....130 B2
Arreton SO31 ....127 B3
Arreton Ct [7] PO12 ...181 A3
Arrow Cl Eastleigh SO50 ..56 A2
  Southampton SO19 ...103 B1
Arrowsmith Cl BH18 ..187 A3
Arrowsmith La BH21 ..187 C4
Arrowsmith Rd BH21 ..187 C4
Arthur Cl BH2 ....204 C3
Arthur Dr PO4 ....183 A2
Arthur Kille Ho PO7 ..134 B3
Arthur La [3] BH23 ...207 A4
Arthur Pope Ho PO5 ..215 C2
Arthur Rd
  Christchurch BH23 ...207 A4
  Eastleigh SO50 ....56 A2
  Southampton SO15 ...102 B3
  Winchester SO23 ....2 A1
Artillery Cl [1] PO6 ...157 B4
Artillery Terr [4] PO4 ..183 A2
Arts Inst of Bournemouth The
  BH12 ....204 B4
Arun Cl GU31 ....40 C2
Arun Rd SO18 ....80 A1
Arun Way SO51 ....50 B2
Arundel Cl BH25 ......194 C2
Arundel Ct Inf Sch PO1 .215 C4
Arundel Ct Jun Sch
  PO1 ....215 C4
Arundel Dr PO16 .....131 A1
Arundel Ho
  Southampton, Banister's Pk
  SO15 ....102 C4
  [18] Southampton, Northam
  SO14 ....103 B3
Arundel Rd Eastleigh SO50 .56 A3
  Gosport PO13 ....180 C3
  Totton SO40 ....100 A4
Arundel St PO1 ....215 C3
Arundel Way BH23 ....208 C4
Arundel Way Sh Arc
  PO1 ....215 B3
Ascham Rd BH8 ....205 A3
Ascot Cl PO14 ....129 B1
Ascot Rd
  Broadstone BH18 .....187 A2
  Fair Oak SO50 ....81 B4
  Portsmouth PO3 ......183 A4
Ascupart Ho [2] SO17 ..103 A4
Ascupart St SO14 .....103 A2
Asford Gr SO50 ....56 B2
Ash Cl Alderholt SP6 ...93 A3
  Burslendon SO31 .....127 C4
  Colden Common SO21 ..32 A1
  Fareham PO14 ....154 C4
  Gosport PO13 ....179 B1
  Hythe SO45 ....150 A4
  North Baddesley SO52 ..53 C3
  Romsey SO51 ....29 B1
  Southampton SO19 ...104 B3
  Upton BH16 ....201 A4
Ash Gr Ashurst SO40 ..100 B2
  Hordle SO41 ....196 A4
  Ringwood BH24 ....141 B4
Ashbarn Cres SO22 .....10 C3
Ashbourne Cl [1] BH1 ..205 A1
Ashbourne Rd BH5 ....206 A3
Ashbridge Rise SO53 ...53 A2
Ashburnham Cl SO19 ..103 B3
Ashburton Cl SO45 ...125 B2
Ashburton Ct SO45 ...215 B1
Ashburton Gdns BH10 .189 B1
Ashburton Ho [12] SO31 .127 A3
Ashburton Rd
  Gosport PO12 ....180 C1
  Portsmouth PO5 ......182 B1
Ashby Cres SO40 ......100 B4
Ashby Pl PO5 ....182 B1
Ashby Rd
  Southampton SO19 ...104 A2
  Totton SO40 ....100 B4
Ashcroft Cl [9] GU32 ...40 C2
Ashcroft La PO8 ....113 B3
Ashdene [16] SO15 ....102 A4
Ashdene Cl BH21 .....163 B3
Ashdene Rd SO40 .....100 B2
Ashdown
  Bournemouth BH2 ....204 B1
  Fawley SO45 ....150 C2
  Gosport PO13 ....155 B1
Ashdown Cl
  Chandler's Ford SO53 ..30 B1
  Poole BH17 ....187 C1
Ashdown Dr SO53 ......30 B1

Ashdown Rd
  Blackfield SO45 ......150 C1
  Chandler's Ford SO53 ..30 B1
Ashdown Sch BH17 ...187 C1
Ashdown Way SO51 ....53 A4
Ashdown Wlk BH25 ...195 B1
Ashe Rd PO9 ....136 A3
Ashen Cl SO53 ....55 B4
Ashford Chace GU32 ...19 C1
Ashford Cl Cosham PO6 .133 C1
  Fordingbridge SP6 .....69 B1
Ashford Cres SO45 ...126 A2
Ashford Rd
  Bournemouth BH6 ....206 B4
  Fordingbridge SP6 .....93 B4
Ashford Works Ind Est
  SP6 ....69 B1
Ashington Cl PO8 .....112 A2
Ashington Gdns BH21 .186 C4
Ashington La BH21 ....163 A1
Ashington Pk BH25 ...195 A1
Ashlea Cl PO9 ....135 B3
Ashleigh Cl SO45 .....150 A4
Ashleigh Rise BH10 ...189 B1
Ashlett Cl SO45 ......151 B2
Ashlett Gdns BH25 ...195 B2
Ashlett Lawn [4] PO9 .135 B3
Ashlett Mews SO45 ...151 A2
Ashlett Rd SO45 ......151 B2
Ashley Arnewood Ct [9]
  BH25 ....195 A1
Ashley Cl
  Bournemouth BH1 ....205 C3
  Havant PO9 ....135 B2
  Horndean PO8 ....111 C3
  Ringwood BH24 ....141 B3
  Swanwick SO31 ....129 A4
  Winchester SO23 ....1 B2
Ashley Common Rd
  BH25 ....195 B2
Ashley Cres SO19 .....104 B1
Ashley Ct
  Bursledon SO31 ......105 A1
  Gosport PO13 ....181 A3
  West Moors BH22 .....166 A4
Ashley Dr BH24 ....116 B2
Ashley Dr N SO19 .....139 C3
Ashley Drive S BH24 ..139 C3
Ashley Drive W BH24 .139 C3
Ashley Gdns
  Chandler's Ford SO53 ..55 C3
  Waltham Chase SO32 ..83 C2
Ashley Heath Ind Est
  BH21 ....139 A4
Ashley Ho SO51 ....52 C3
Ashley Inf Sch BH25 ..195 B2
Ashley Jun Sch BH25 .195 B2
Ashley La Hordle SO41 .195 C2
  Lymington SO41 ......197 C2
  New Milton BH25 .....195 C2
Ashley Mdws SO51 ....53 A4
Ashley Park BH24 .....140 A3
Ashley Rd
  Bournemouth BH1, BH7 .205 C3
  New Milton BH25 .....195 B2
  Poole BH14 ....203 B3
Ashleycross Cl SO45 ..150 B2
Ashling Cl
  Bournemouth BH8 ....205 A4
  Denmead PO7 ....110 C2
Ashling Cres SO19 ....104 A4
Ashling Gdns PO7 ....110 C2
Ashling La PO2 ....157 B1
Ashling Park Rd PO7 .110 C2
Ashlyn Cl BH21 ....130 B1
Ashmead Rd SO16 .....77 C2
Ashmeads Cl BH21 ...164 A3
Ashmeads Way BH21 .164 A3
Ashmede BH4 ....204 B1
Ashmore Cl [1] PO9 ..163 B2
Ashmore Ave
  Barton on Sea BH25 ..210 A4
  Hamworthy BH15 .....201 C1
Ashmore Cres BH15 ..201 C1
Ashmore Gr BH23 .....193 C1
Ashmore La
  Sheet SP5 ....24 A3
  West Dean SP5 ....24 A3
  Whiteparish SP5 ......24 A3
Ashmore Rd SO22 ......1 B1
Ashridge Ave [1] BH10 .189 B3
Ashridge Cl SO15 .....102 C4
Ashridge Gdns BH10 .189 B3
Ashridge Par [5] BH10 .189 B3
Ashstead CI PO16 .....156 A4
Ashton CI SO32 ....59 A1
Ashton Cross
  New Milton BH25 .....195 A2
  Poole BH13 ....204 A1
Ashton Ho SO19 ....103 C1
Ashton La SO32 ....59 A1
Ashton Rd BH9 ....190 A2
Ashton Way PO14 .....179 B2
Ashtree Cl BH25 ....195 A2
Ashtree Cl SO45 ....55 C2
Ashurst (New Forest) Sta
  SO40 ....100 B2
Ashurst Bridge Rd SO40 .100 A3
Ashurst Cl Ashurst SO40 ..100 A3
  Southampton SO19 ...104 A1
  Winchester SO22 ....2 A1
Ashurst Ct PO12 ......180 B2
Ashurst Hospl (Geriatric)
  SO40 ....100 A1

Anc – Ave **221**

Ashurst Rd
  Bournemouth BH8 ....190 B2
  Cosham PO6 ....157 C4
  West Moors BH22 ....138 C2
Ashwell Ct BH23 ......191 C1
Ashwood
  Swanwick, Whiteley PO15 .129 C3
  Titchfield SO31 ......129 B1
Ashwood Cl Havant PO9 .135 A2
  South Hayling PO11 ..185 A2
Ashwood Dr BH18 ....187 B2
Ashwood Gdns
  [15] Southampton SO16 .78 C2
  Totton SO40 ....100 B4
Ashwood Lodge [1]
  PO16 ....131 B1
Aspen Ave SO31 ......152 B4
Aspen Cl
  Colden Common SO21 ..57 A4
  Hedge End SO30 ......105 B4
Aspen Dr BH31 ....115 A3
Aspen Gdns BH12 ....203 C4
Aspen Holt SO16 ....79 A3
Aspen Rd BH12 ....203 C4
Aspen Rd BH12 ....203 C4
Aspen Way Poole BH12 .203 C4
  Waterlooville PO8 ....112 A3
Aspen Wlk SO40 ......100 A4
Aspengrove PO13 .....155 C1
Asquith Cl BH23 ......207 B3
Assheton Ct PO16 ....156 B4
Astbury Ave BH12 ....189 A1
Aster Rd SO16 ....79 B2
Astley Rd PO5 ....215 A2
Aston Mead BH23 ....191 C2
Aston Rd
  Portsmouth PO4 .....182 C1
  Waterlooville PO7 ....134 B4
Astra Cl [3] SO45 ....126 A3
Astra Wlk PO12 ....181 B2
Astral Gdns SO31 ....127 C2
Astrid Cl PO11 ....185 B2
Asturias Way SO14 ...103 B3
Asylum Rd SO15 .....103 A3
Atalanta Cl PO4 .....183 B3
Atheling Rd SO45 ....126 A2
Athelney Ct [18] BH1 .205 A2
Athelstan Rd
  Bournemouth BH6 ....206 C3
  Southampton SO19 ...103 C3
Athelston Cl SO41 ....197 B2
Athena Ave PO7 .....134 C2
Athena Cl SO50 ....57 A2
Atherfield Rd SO16 ....77 C2
Atherley Ct SO15 .....102 C4
Atherley Rd
  South Hayling PO11 ..184 C3
  Southampton SO15 ...102 B3
Atkins Pl SO15 ....77 A3
Atkinson Cl PO12 .....181 A1
Atlantic Cl SO14 ......103 A1
Atlantic Ct SO53 ......55 A3
Atlantic Park View SO18 .80 A4
Atlantis Ave PO7 .....134 C1
Attwood Cl PO4 ....92 C3
Attwoods Dro SO21 ....10 B1
Aubrey Cl
  Milford on Sea SO41 .211 C2
  South Hayling PO11 ..184 C2
Aubrey Farm Cotts
  SO41 ....212 A1
Auckland Ave SO42 ..146 A1
Auckland Pl SO42 ....146 A1
Auckland Rd
  Christchurch BH23 ...208 B4
  Southampton SO15 ...101 C4
Auckland Rd E PO5 ..182 B1
Auckland Rd W PO5 ..182 B1
Audley Pl [8] SO50 ....56 C1
Audrayton Ct [3] BH6 .206 C2
Audret Ct PO16 ....156 A3
Augustine Rd
  Cosham PO6 ....158 A4
  Southampton SO14 ...103 A3
Augustus Cl SO53 ....55 C4
Augustus Way SO53 ..55 C4
Auriol Dr PO9 ....159 A4
Aust Rd PO14 ....154 B4
Austen Ave
  Bournemouth BH10 ...189 C3
  Winchester SO22 ......10 B2
Austen Cl Totton SO40 .100 B3
  Winchester SO22 ......10 B2
Austen Gdns PO15 ...129 B4
Auster Cl BH23 ....208 A4
Austerberry Way BH10 .180 C4
Austen Rd BH14 ......203 A1
Austin Cl BH11 ....203 A1
Austin Ct [6] PO6 ....133 A1
Australia Cl PO1 ......215 C3
Autumn Cl BH22 .....165 A4
Autumn Copse BH25 .195 B1
Autumn Pl [18] SO17 ..79 A1
Autumn Rd
  Bournemouth BH10 ..188 B2
  Marchwood SO40 ....102 A1
Avalan Ct SO23 ....10 C3
Avalon BH14 ....214 B4
Avalon Ct PO10 ......136 C3
Avebury Ave BH10 ...189 C1
Avebury Gdns SO53 ..55 A3
Avenger Cl SO53 .....55 A3

Avens Cl SO50 ....81 B3
Avenue C SO45 ....150 C4
Avenue Campus (Univ of Southampton) SO17 ....79 A1
Avenue Ct Gosport PO12 ....181 A1
Poole BH13 ....204 A2
1 Southampton SO17 ....102 C4
Avenue D SO45 ....150 C4
Avenue De Caen PO5 ....182 B1
Avenue E SO45 ....150 C4
Avenue La 20 BH2 ....204 C2
Avenue Rd
Bournemouth BH2 ....204 C2
Brockenhurst SO42 ....172 C4
Christchurch BH23 ....206 C4
Christchurch, Walkford BH23 ....194 B1
Fareham PO14 ....130 C1
Gosport PO12 ....181 B2
Lymington SO41 ....197 C2
New Milton BH25 ....195 A2
North Hayling PO11 ....160 A2
Southampton SO14 ....103 A4
Wimborne Minst BH21 ....163 B2
Winchester SO22 ....10 C4
Avenue Sh Ctr The 21 BH2 ....204 C2
Avenue The
Bishop's Waltham SO32 ....83 A4
Bournemouth BH9 ....189 C2
Fareham PO14 ....130 B1
Gosport PO12 ....181 A2
Petersfield GU31 ....40 C2
Poole BH13 ....204 A1
Southampton SO17 ....102 C4
Twyford SO21 ....32 A3
West Moors BH22 ....138 C2
Avery La PO12 ....181 A4
Avington Cl SO50 ....56 B3
Avington Ct SO16 ....78 C2
Avington Gn PO9 ....136 A3
Avocet Cl PO4 ....183 A3
Avocet Ho 6 PO4 ....183 A3
Avocet Quay PO10 ....161 A4
Avocet Way PO8 ....112 A4
Avocet Wlk PO13 ....155 A1
Avon Ave BH24 ....140 B2
Avon Bldgs BH23 ....207 A4
Avon Castle BH24 ....140 B2
Avon Castle Dr BH24 ....140 B2
Avon Cl
Bournemouth BH8 ....205 B3
Lee-on-the-Solent PO13 ....179 C1
Lymington SO41 ....197 B2
Petersfield GU31 ....40 C1
Avon Cotts BH23 ....192 B3
Avon Cres SO51 ....53 B4
Avon Cswy BH23 ....191 B4
Avon Ct
Christchurch BH23 ....207 B3
Fordingbridge SP6 ....69 C1
Netley SO31 ....127 B3
2 Waterlooville PO8 ....111 C2
Avon Dyke SP5 ....46 C3
Avon Farm Cotts BH23 ....167 C2
Avon Gdns BH23 ....169 A1
Avon Gn SO53 ....55 B3
Avon Heath Ctry Park Visitor Ctr* BH24 ....140 A1
Avon Heath Ctry Pk (North Pk) BH24 ....140 A2
Avon Heath Ctry Pk (South Pk) BH24 ....167 A4
Avon Ho
Bournemouth BH2 ....204 C1
8 Southampton SO14 ....103 B3
Avon Mdw SP5 ....46 C4
Avon Meade SP6 ....69 C1
Avon Mews BH8 ....205 B3
Avon Park BH24 ....140 B3
Avon Rd
Bournemouth BH8 ....205 B3
Southampton SO18 ....79 C1
West Moors BH22 ....138 C1
Avon Rd E BH23 ....207 A4
Avon Rd W BH23 ....206 C4
Avon Run Cl BH23 ....208 A3
Avon Run Rd BH23 ....208 A3
Avon View SP6 ....70 B1
Avon View Par BH23 ....192 B2
Avon View Rd BH23 ....192 B2
Avon Way SO30 ....80 C1
Avon Wharf BH23 ....207 B3
Avon Wlk PO16 ....156 A4
Avonborne Way SO53 ....55 A4
Avonbourne Girls Sch BH7 ....206 A4
Avoncliffe Rd BH6 ....206 C2
Avondale Ct SO17 ....79 A1
Avondale Cvn Pk SO21 ....32 A1
Avondale Rd
Portsmouth PO1 ....182 C4
Waterlooville PO7 ....134 C4
Avonlea Sch BH24 ....141 A4
Award Rd BH21 ....164 C3
Awbridge Prim Sch SO51 ....26 B3
Awbridge Rd PO9 ....135 B2
Axford Cl BH8 ....190 B2
Aylen Rd PO3 ....158 A1
Aylesbury Rd
Bournemouth BH1 ....205 C2
Portsmouth PO2 ....182 C4
Ayling Cl PO13 ....180 B4
Aylward St PO1 ....182 A3
Aynsley Ct SO15 ....102 B4
Aysgarth Rd PO7 ....134 C4
Aysha Cl BH25 ....195 A1
Azalea Cl Havant PO9 ....136 B2
St Leonards BH24 ....140 A3
Azura Cl BH21 ....139 A3

B

B Ave Fawley SO45 ....150 B3
Fawley SO45 ....150 C2
Back La Mottisfont SO51 ....5 C3
Southwick PO17 ....132 C3
Sway SO41 ....172 B1
Back of the Walls
Southampton SO14 ....103 A1
Southampton SO14 ....103 A2
Back St SO23 ....10 C2
Bacon Cl SO19 ....103 C1
Bacon La PO11 ....184 C2
Badbury Cl BH18 ....187 B2
Badbury Ct 7 BH23 ....207 C3
Badbury View BH21 ....163 B3
Badbury View Rd BH21 ....186 B4
Baddesley Cl SO52 ....53 C3
Baddesley Gdns PO9 ....135 B3
Baddesley Rd SO53 ....30 A1
Baden Cl BH25 ....195 A1
Baden Powell & St Peter's Mid Sch BH14 ....203 A2
Baden Powell Way 14 SO51 ....52 C4
Bader Cl SO30 ....105 B4
Bader Rd BH17 ....202 C4
Bader Way PO15 ....129 C3
Badger Brow PO7 ....135 A3
Badger Cl
Bishopstoke SO50 ....56 C1
Fareham PO15 ....130 B1
Badger Ct 10 SO50 ....56 C1
Badger Farm Rd SO22, SO23 ....10 B2
Badger Rd PO14 ....154 C3
Badger Way BH31 ....114 C3
Badger Wood Pl SO18 ....79 C1
Badgers Cl
St Leonards BH24 ....139 C3
Sway SO41 ....172 B1
Badgers Copse BH25 ....195 B3
Badgers Run SO31 ....128 C3
Badgers The SO31 ....127 B3
Badgers Wlk
Ferndown BH22 ....165 C4
Hythe SO45 ....125 C1
Badminston Dro SO45 ....178 B4
Badminston La SO45 ....151 B1
Badshear La SO24 ....14 C4
Baffins Rd PO3 ....183 A4
Bagber Rd SO40 ....100 C4
Bagot Ho PO12 ....180 C3
Bagshot Mews SO19 ....103 C2
Baigent Cl SO23 ....11 B4
Bailey Cl Botley SO30 ....106 A3
New Milton BH25 ....195 B2
Winchester SO22 ....10 B3
Bailey Cres BH15 ....202 B4
Bailey Dr BH23 ....206 C4
Bailey Gn SO18 ....80 A1
Bailey Hall BH23 ....206 C4
Bailey's Rd PO5 ....215 C2
Baiter Gdns BH15 ....202 B1
Baker Rd BH11 ....189 A3
Baker St PO1 ....182 B4
Bakers Dro SO16 ....77 C3
Bakers Farm Rd BH31 ....114 C4
Balaclava Rd SO18 ....104 A4
Balcombe Rd BH13 ....204 A2
Balderton Cl 15 PO2 ....157 C2
Baldwin Cl BH23 ....207 B3
Balena Cl BH17 ....202 A4
Balfour Cl
Christchurch BH23 ....208 B4
Gosport PO13 ....180 B3
Balfour Dr GU33 ....20 C2
Balfour Rd
Bournemouth BH9 ....189 C1
Portsmouth PO2 ....157 C1
Southampton SO19 ....104 B2
Balfour Red Cross Mus* SO22 ....1 B1
Ball La 17 BH15 ....202 B1
Ballam Cl BH16 ....201 B4
Ballard Cl
New Milton BH25 ....195 A2
Poole BH15 ....202 B1
Southampton SO16 ....77 B1
Ballard Coll BH25 ....195 A2
Ballard Ct 1 PO12 ....181 A2
Ballard Rd BH15 ....202 B1
Ballard Sch BH25 ....195 A2
Balliol Cl PO14 ....129 B1
Balliol Rd PO2 ....182 C4
Balmer Lawn Rd SO42 ....146 A2
Balmoral Ave BH8 ....190 C1
Balmoral Cl
Chandler's Ford SO53 ....55 A4
Gosport PO13 ....155 B1
Southampton SO16 ....78 B3
Balmoral Ct
7 Christchurch BH23 ....209 A4
7 Southampton SO17 ....103 A4
Southampton, Millbrook SO15 ....102 A3
Balmoral Dr PO7 ....134 B2
Balmoral Ho BH2 ....204 B2
Balmoral Rd
Fareham PO15 ....130 C2
Poole BH14 ....203 B2
Balmoral Way
Petersfield GU32 ....40 C2
Rownhams SO16 ....77 C3
Balmoral Wlk BH25 ....194 C2
Balston Rd BH14 ....203 A3
Balston Terr BH15 ....202 A1
Baltic Rd SO30 ....80 C1
Bambridge Pk Gdn Ctr Miniature Rly* SO50 ....31 C1
Bamford Ho PO4 ....183 A1
Bampton Cl SO16 ....101 C4
Bampton Ct SO53 ....55 B3
Banbury Ave SO19 ....104 B2
Banbury Rd BH17 ....202 B4
Banfurly Gdns SO45 ....125 C1
Bangor Rd SO15 ....102 A3
Banister Ct 13 SO15 ....102 C4
Banister Gdns SO15 ....102 C4
Banister Grange 16 SO15 ....102 C4
Banister Inf Sch SO15 ....102 C4
Banister Mews SO15 ....102 C4
Banister Rd SO15 ....102 C4
Bank Chambers BH14 ....203 C2
Bank Cl BH23 ....207 A3
Bank Side SO18 ....79 B2
Bank St SO32 ....83 B4
Bankhill Dr SO41 ....197 B3
Banks Rd BH13 ....214 B2
Banks The SO51 ....26 A3
Bankside SO41 ....197 B3
Bankside Ho 4 SO22 ....10 C4
Bankside Rd BH9 ....190 A2
Bankview SO41 ....197 B3
Bannerman Rd GU32 ....40 C2
Banning St SO51 ....52 C3
Bannister Ct SO40 ....101 A4
Banocroft Ct 1 BH15 ....202 C2
Banstead Rd BH18 ....187 A3
Bapaume Rd PO3 ....157 C3
Bar End Ind Est SO23 ....11 A3
Bar End Rd SO23 ....11 A3
Bar Gate & Guildhall (Mus)* SO14 ....102 C2
Barbe Baker Ave SO30 ....80 B1
Barberry Dr SO40 ....76 A1
Barberry Way BH31 ....115 B3
Barbers Gate 15 BH15 ....202 A1
Barbers Piles 5 BH15 ....202 A1
Barbers Wharf 16 BH15 ....202 A1
Barclay Ho PO12 ....181 C2
Barclay Mans BH2 ....204 C3
Barclay Mews
Hythe SO45 ....149 C4
Hythe SO45 ....150 A4
Bardon Way PO14 ....154 B4
Barfield Cl SO23 ....11 A3
Barfields SO41 ....197 C2
Barfields Ct SO41 ....197 C2
Barfleur Cl PO15 ....130 B1
Barfleur Rd PO14 ....155 A3
Barford Cl SO53 ....55 A4
Barford La SP5 ....47 A4
Bargate Ctr 8 SO14 ....103 A2
Bargate St SO14 ....102 C2
Bargates BH23 ....207 A4
Barham Cl PO12 ....181 A3
Barham Rd GU32 ....40 C2
Barham Way PO2 ....157 B2
Baring Rd
Bournemouth BH6 ....207 A2
Winchester SO23 ....11 A4
Bark Hill Mews SO51 ....52 C3
Barker Mill Cl SO16 ....77 C3
Barkis Ho 11 PO1 ....182 B4
Barkshire Ct 7 SO15 ....102 C4
Barlands Cl BH23 ....192 B1
Barle Cl SO18 ....80 A1
Barley Down Dr SO22 ....10 B2
Barleycorn Wlk SO40 ....98 C4
Barling Mews 13 SO51 ....52 C4
Barlow Cl PO14 ....179 A3
Barn Cl Emsworth PO10 ....160 B4
Upton BH16 ....201 A4
Barn Fold PO7 ....112 B1
Barn Piece SO53 ....54 C3
Barn Rd BH18 ....187 A2
Barnaby Cl SP5 ....46 B4
Barnbrook Rd SO31 ....128 C2
Barncroft Inf Sch PO9 ....135 B2
Barncroft Jun Sch PO9 ....135 B2
Barncroft Way PO9 ....135 B2
Barnes Cl
Bournemouth BH10 ....189 B2
Locks Heath SO31 ....128 B2
Southampton SO18 ....104 B3
West Wellow SO51 ....50 C2
Winchester SO23 ....10 C3
Barnes Cres
Bournemouth BH10 ....189 B2
Wimborne Minst BH21 ....163 C2
Barnes La
Locks Heath SO31 ....128 C2
Milford on Sea SO41 ....211 B3
Barnes Rd
Bournemouth BH10 ....189 B2
Portsmouth PO1 ....182 C3
Southampton SO19 ....104 B3
Barnes Wallis Rd PO15 ....129 C2
Barnes Way PO9 ....135 B2
Barnet Side La GU32 ....18 B3
Barney Evans Cres PO8 ....111 B2
Barney Hayes La SO40 ....99 A4
Barnfield BH23 ....208 B4
Barnfield Cl
Southampton SO19 ....103 C1
Southbourne PO10 ....137 C1
Barnfield Ct
Fareham PO14 ....154 C4
Southampton SO19 ....103 C1
Barnfield Flats SO19 ....103 C1
Barnfield Rd
Petersfield GU31 ....41 B2
Southampton SO19 ....103 C1
Barnfield Way SO19 ....103 C1
Barnfields Flats SO19 ....103 C1
Barns Rd BH22 ....166 A3
Barnsfield Cres SO40 ....100 B4
Barnsfield Rd BH24 ....140 A2
Barnside Way GU33 ....20 C2
Barnsland SO30 ....80 B2
Barnwood Rd PO15 ....130 B1
Baron Rd SO31 ....127 C2
Barons Ct 8 BH12 ....204 A2
Barons Mead SO16 ....77 C2
Barons Rd BH11 ....188 B3
Baronsmere PO12 ....181 A2
Barrack La BH24 ....141 B2
Barrack Rd
Christchurch BH23 ....206 C4
Ferndown BH22 ....166 A1
Barratt Ind Pk PO15 ....129 B3
Barrie Cl PO15 ....129 B4
Barrie Rd BH9 ....189 C2
Barrington Cl SO50 ....55 C3
Barrington Ct 31 SO17 ....79 A1
Barrington Ho 23 PO1 ....182 B4
Barrow Down Gdns SO19 ....104 C2
Barrow Dr BH8 ....190 C1
Barrow Hill Rd SO40 ....75 B2
Barrow Rd BH8 ....190 C1
Barrow View BH22 ....165 A3
Barrow Way BH8 ....190 C1
Barrowgate Rd BH8 ....190 B2
Barrowgate Way BH8 ....190 B2
Barrows La Landford SP5 ....49 B3
Sway SO41 ....196 A3
Barrs Ave BH25 ....195 A2
Barrs Wood Dr BH25 ....195 A2
Barrs Wood Rd BH25 ....195 A2
Barry Gdns BH18 ....186 C3
Barry Rd SO19 ....104 A3
Barters Cl SO16 ....77 C1
Barters La BH18 ....186 C2
Bartholomew Cl 25 SO23 ....2 A1
Bartlett Cl PO15 ....130 C2
Bartlett Dr BH7 ....206 A4
Bartlett Ho 20 SO17 ....103 A4
Bartletts Comm SP6 ....94 C4
Bartletts The SO31 ....128 A1
Bartley Ave SO40 ....100 C3
Bartley CE Jun Sch SO40 ....99 A4
Bartley Ct 6 BH21 ....163 A3
Bartley Rd SO40 ....99 B2
Barton Cl SO51 ....53 A4
Barton Common La BH25 ....210 A4
Barton Common Rd BH25 ....210 A4
Barton Court Ave BH25 ....210 A4
Barton Court Rd BH25 ....195 A1
Barton Cres SO18 ....79 C1
Barton Croft BH25 ....210 A4
Barton Cross PO8 ....112 A4
Barton Ct BH25 ....210 A3
Barton Dr
Barton on Sea BH25 ....209 C4
Hamble-le-Rice SO31 ....127 C2
Hedge End SO30 ....105 B4
Barton Gn BH25 ....210 A3
Barton Gr PO3 ....158 A2
Barton Ho BH25 ....209 C4
Barton La BH25 ....209 C4
Barton Lo BH12 ....203 A3
Barton Park Ind Est SO50 ....56 B1
Barton Peveril Coll SO50 ....55 C1
Barton Rd SO50 ....56 B2
Barton Way BH25 ....209 C4
Barton Wood Rd BH25 ....209 C4
Bartons Rd
Fordingbridge SP6 ....69 C1
Havant PO9 ....136 A2
Bartons The
Fordingbridge SP6 ....69 C1
Hedge End SO30 ....105 A3
Bartonside Rd BH25 ....209 B4
Bartram Rd SO40 ....101 A3
Barwell Gr PO10 ....136 C2
Barwell Terr 10 SO30 ....105 B3
Bascott Cl BH11 ....189 A1
Bascott Rd BH11 ....189 A1
Bashley Common Rd BH25 ....195 A4
Bashley Cross Rd BH25 ....194 C3
Bashley Dr BH25 ....195 A3
Bashley Rd BH25 ....195 A3
Basin St PO2 ....182 B4
Basing Dean GU34 ....17 C2
Basing Ho SO15 ....102 B4
Basing Mews 8 SO32 ....83 B4
Basing Rd PO9 ....135 C2
Basing Way SO53 ....55 A2
Basingstoke Rd SO23 ....2 B4
Basingwell St SO32 ....83 B4
Bassett Ave SO16 ....78 C3
Bassett Cl SO16 ....78 C2
Bassett Cres E SO16 ....78 C2
Bassett Cres W SO16 ....78 C2
Bassett Ct SO16 ....78 C2
Bassett Dale SO16 ....78 C3
Bassett Gdns SO16 ....78 C2
Bassett Gn SO16 ....79 A3
Bassett Green Cl SO16 ....79 A3
Bassett Green Ct SO16 ....79 A3
Bassett Green Dr SO16 ....79 A3
Bassett Green Prim Sch SO16 ....79 A2
Bassett Green Rd SO16 ....79 A3
Bassett Heath Ave SO16 ....78 C3
Bassett Mdw SO16 ....78 C2
Bassett Mews SO16 ....78 C3
Bassett Rd BH12 ....203 A3
Bassett Row SO16 ....78 C3
Bassett Wlk 8 PO9 ....135 B3
Bassett Wood Dr SO16 ....79 A3
Bassett Wood Mews 7 SO16 ....78 C2
Bassett Wood N SO16 ....79 A3
Bassett Wood Rd SO16 ....79 A3
Bastone Way BH22 ....165 A3
Batchelor Cres BH11 ....188 C2
Batchelor Gn SO31 ....127 C4
Batchelor Rd BH11 ....188 C2
Batcombe Cl BH11 ....188 C2
Bath & Wells Ct PO13 ....180 B3
Bath Cl SO19 ....104 A3
Bath Hill Ct 9 BH1 ....205 A2
Bath Hill Rdbt BH1 ....205 A1
Bath La 11 PO16 ....131 B1
Bath La (lower) 13 PO16 ....131 B1
Bath Lane Cotts PO16 ....155 B4
Bath Rd
Bournemouth BH1 ....205 A2
Emsworth PO10 ....160 C4
Lymington SO41 ....197 C2
Portsmouth PO4 ....182 C2
Southampton SO19 ....104 A3
Bath Sq PO1 ....181 C2
Bath St SO14 ....103 A4
Bathing La PO1 ....181 C2
Bathurst Cl PO11 ....184 C2
Bathurst Way PO2 ....157 A1
Batten Cl BH23 ....207 B4
Batten Rd SP5 ....46 C4
Battenburg Ave PO2 ....157 C1
Battenburg Rd PO12 ....181 B3
Battens Way PO9 ....135 C2
Batterley Dro BH21 ....91 C2
Battery Cl PO12 ....180 C4
Battery Hill
Bishop's Waltham SO32 ....83 A4
Winchester SO22 ....10 B3
Battery Row PO1 ....182 A2
Battle Cl SO31 ....129 A2
Battramsley Cross SO41 ....173 B1
Baverstock Rd BH12 ....204 A4
Baxter Rd SO19 ....104 C3
Bay Cl Southampton SO19 ....104 A2
Three Legged Cross BH21 ....138 C4
Upton BH16 ....201 A3
Bay Hog La BH15 ....202 A1
Bay House Sec Sch PO12 ....180 C2
Bay Rd Gosport PO12 ....180 C2
Southampton SO19 ....104 A2
Bay Tree Lodge PO14 ....179 B3
Bay Tree Way BH23 ....193 B1
Bay Trees SO19 ....104 C3
Bay View Ct PO11 ....184 B1
Bay View Mews PO11 ....184 B1
Baybridge La SO21 ....33 B2
Baybridge Rd PO9 ....136 A3
Baycroft Sch PO14 ....179 C3
Bayfields PO5 ....215 B1
Bayly Ave PO16 ....156 B3
Bays Ct SO41 ....197 B2
Bays Rd SO41 ....197 B2
Bayswater Ho PO5 ....215 C1
Baythorn Cl PO2 ....182 B4
Beach Ave BH25 ....209 C4
Beach Cl BH13 ....214 D4
Beach La SO31 ....127 A3
Beach Rd
Emsworth PO10 ....160 C4
Lee-on-the-Solent PO13 ....179 C1
Poole BH13 ....214 D4
Portsmouth PO5 ....182 B1
South Hayling PO11 ....184 C2
Upton BH16 ....201 A3
Beach View BH13 ....214 B2
Beachcroft BH13 ....204 A2
Beachway PO16 ....156 B3
Beacon Bottom SO31 ....129 A3
Beacon Cl Hordle SO41 ....196 B1
Locks Heath SO31 ....129 A3
Rownhams SO16 ....77 B3
Beacon Ct
Christchurch BH23 ....208 C4
Fordingbridge SP6 ....69 C2
Beacon Dr BH23 ....208 C4
Beacon Gdns BH18 ....186 C2
Beacon Hill La
Corfe Mullen BH21 ....186 A2
Droxford SO32 ....60 C3
Meonstoke SO32 ....61 B3
Beacon Mews SO30 ....104 B4
Beacon Mount SO31 ....129 A3
Beacon Park Cres BH16 ....201 A4
Beacon Park Rd BH16 ....201 A4
Beacon Rd
Bournemouth BH2 ....204 C1
Broadstone BH18 ....186 C2
Upton BH16 ....201 A4
West End SO30 ....104 B4
Beacon Sq PO10 ....160 C4
Beacon Way
Broadstone BH18 ....186 C2
Locks Heath SO31 ....129 A3
Beaconsfield Ave PO6 ....158 A4
Beaconsfield Rd
Christchurch BH23 ....207 A4

Beaconsfield Rd *continued*
Fareham PO16 155 A4
Poole BH12 203 B3
Waterlooville PO7 134 C4
Bealing Cl SO16 79 A2
Beamish Rd BH17 202 C4
Bear Cross Ave BH11 188 C3
Bear Cross Rdbt BH11 188 C3
Bearslane Cl SO40 76 B1
Bearwood Prim Sch BH11 188 B3
Beatrice Ct 5 SO41 211 A2
Beatrice Mews 15 PO6 157 C4
Beatrice Rd
Portsmouth PO4 182 C1
Southampton SO15 102 B4
Beatrice Royal Art Gal* SO50 55 C1
Beattie Rise SO30 81 B1
Beatty Cl
Locks Heath SO31 129 A2
Ringwood BH24 141 B4
Beatty Dr PO12 180 C2
Beatty Ho 9 PO1 215 C4
Beatty Rd BH9 190 A1
Beaty Ct SO19 104 B3
Beau Ct
31 Bournemouth BH4 204 B2
9 New Milton BH25 195 A2
Beauchamp Ave PO13 155 B1
Beauchamps Gdns BH7 206 A4
Beaucroft La BH21 163 C3
Beaucroft Rd
Waltham Chase SO32 83 C2
Wimborne Minst BH21 163 C3
Beaucroft Sch BH21 163 C3
Beaufort Ave PO16 130 C1
Beaufort Cl BH23 208 A4
Beaufort Dr
Bishop's Waltham SO32 83 B4
Wimborne Minst BH21 163 B3
Beaufort Mews BH21 163 A2
Beaufort Rd
Bournemouth BH6 206 B3
Havant PO9 135 B1
10 Portsmouth PO5 182 B1
Winchester SO23 10 C3
Beaufoys Ave BH22 165 B4
Beaufoys Cl BH22 165 B4
Beaufoys Ct BH22 165 B3
Beaulieu Abbey* SO42 148 C1
Beaulieu Ave
Christchurch BH23 206 C4
Havant PO9 135 B3
Portchester PO16 156 A4
Beaulieu Cl
New Milton BH25 194 C2
Southampton SO16 78 A3
Winchester SO22 1 B2
Beaulieu Ct 5 PO8 111 C2
Beaulieu Ho 12 SO15 102 C4
Beaulieu Pl PO13 155 A1
Beaulieu Rd
Beaulieu SO42,SO45 149 B3
Bournemouth BH4 204 A1
Christchurch BH23 206 C4
Eastleigh SO50 56 A2
Hamble-le-Rice SO31 127 C2
Hythe SO45 125 C1
Lyndhurst SO42 122 B2
Marchwood SO40 124 C3
Portsmouth PO2 157 C1
Beaulieu Road Sta SO42 123 B1
Beaulieu Village Prim Sch SO42 148 C1
Beaumaris Cl SO53 55 A2
Beaumaris Gdns SO40 125 C3
Beaumond Gn 29 SO22 10 C4
Beaumont Cl
Fareham PO15 130 B2
Southampton SO16 78 C2
Beaumont Ct PO12 181 A4
Beaumont Pl SO40 101 A4
Beaumont Rd
Poole BH13 214 C4
Totton SO40 101 A4
Beaumont Rise PO15 130 B2
Beauworth Ave SO18 104 B4
Beaver Dr SO50 57 A1
Beaver Ind Est BH23 208 A3
Beccles Cl BH15 201 C1
Becher Rd BH14 203 C2
Beck Cl SO31 128 C2
Beck St PO1 182 A3
Beckenham Terr PO10 137 A2
Beckford La PO17 109 C1
Beckham La GU32 40 B2
Beckhampton Rd BH15 201 C2
Beckley Copse BH23 194 A1
Becton La BH25 210 A4
Becton Mead BH25 195 A1
Bedale Way BH15 202 C3
Bedales Sch GU32 40 C4
Beddow Hall 3 PO5 215 A2
Bedenham La PO13 155 C2
Bedenham Prim Sch PO13 155 B2
Bedfield Ho SO23 2 A3
Bedfield La SO23 2 A3
Bedford Ave SO19 103 C1
Bedford Cl
Fordingbridge SP6 69 C2
Havant PO9 160 A4
Hedge End SO30 105 B3
Bedford Cres BH7 206 B4
Bedford Pl SO15 102 C3
Bedford Rd GU32 40 B2
Bedford Rd N BH12 188 B1
Bedford Rd S BH12 188 B1
Bedford St Gosport PO12 181 A3
Portsmouth PO5 215 B2
Bedhampton Hill PO9 135 A1
Bedhampton Hill Rd PO9 135 A1
Bedhampton Ho 4 PO1 215 C4
Bedhampton Rd
Havant PO9 135 B1
Portsmouth PO2 182 C4
Bedhampton Sta PO9 135 B1
Bedhampton Way PO9 135 C2
Bedwell Cl SO16 77 C3
Beech Ave
Bournemouth BH6 206 B2
Christchurch BH23 206 B4
Southampton SO18 103 C4
Beech Cl Alderholt SP6 93 A3
Broadstone BH18 186 C2
Chandler's Ford SO53 30 B1
Hamble-le-Rice SO31 127 C1
Hordle SO41 211 B4
Romsey SO51 53 B3
Verwood BH31 114 C3
Waterlooville PO8 111 C1
Winchester SO22 10 A2
Beech Cnr SO32 81 C3
Beech Copse SO22 1 A1
Beech Cres SO45 150 A4
Beech Ct
Southampton SO19 103 C2
Wimborne Minst BH21 163 C2
Beech Dr PO6 156 C4
Beech Gdns SO31 127 C1
Beech Gr Gosport PO12 181 A2
Owslebury SO21 33 A2
South Hayling PO11 185 A2
Beech Grange SP5 49 B1
Beech Ho SO16 78 C4
Beech La BH24 139 C1
Beech Rd Ashurst SO40 100 A1
Chandler's Ford SO53 55 B4
Clanfield PO8 88 B3
Fareham PO15 130 C1
Hedge End SO30 105 B4
Southampton SO15 102 A3
Beech Way PO8 112 A3
Beech Wood Cl BH18 187 A2
Beecham Rd PO1 182 C4
Beechbank Ave BH17 186 C1
Beechcroft BH1 205 A3
Beechcroft Cl
Chandler's Ford SO53 55 B3
Fareham PO15 130 B1
Beechcroft La BH24 141 A4
Beechcroft Mews 2 BH24 141 A4
Beechcroft Rd PO12 181 A2
Beechcroft Way SO53 55 B4
Beechdale Cl SO40 76 B1
Beechdale Wlk SO40 76 B1
Beechen La SO43 122 A2
Beeches Hill SO32 59 B1
Beeches The
Awbridge SO51 26 C3
Bournemouth BH7 206 A4
Fair Oak SO50 57 B1
4 Waterlooville PO7 134 C4
West Wellow SO51 50 B2
Beechey Ct 6 BH8 205 A3
Beechey Rd BH8 205 A3
Beechfield 30 BH4 204 B2
Beechfield Ct SO15 102 A4
Beechmount SO16 78 C3
Beechmount Rd SO16 78 C3
Beechwood SP6 69 B1
Beechwood Ave
Bournemouth BH5 205 C2
New Milton BH25 194 C2
Waterlooville PO7 134 C3
Beechwood Cl
Chandler's Ford SO53 30 A1
Locks Heath SO31 152 B4
Beechwood Cres SO53 30 A1
Beechwood Ct
Bournemouth BH2 204 C1
Liss GU33 21 A3
Beechwood Gdns
Bournemouth BH5 206 A2
Southampton SO18 103 C4
Beechwood Ho SO17 103 B4
Beechwood Jun Sch SO18 103 C4
Beechwood La BH24 143 A2
Beechwood Lodge 3 PO16 131 A1
Beechwood Rd
Cadnam SO40 99 A3
Holbury SO45 150 B2
Portsmouth PO2 157 C2
West Moors BH22 138 C1
Beechwood Rise SO18 80 B1
Beechwood Way SO45 125 B1
Beechworth Rd 3 PO9 136 A1
Beehive Cotts PO16 131 A2
Beehive Wlk PO1 182 A2
Beeston Ct PO1 182 C4
Beggar's La SO23 11 A4
Begonia Rd SO16 79 A2
Behrendt Cl PO12 181 A3
Belben Cl BH12 188 B1
Belben Rd BH12 188 B1
Belbins SO51 27 C2
Belbins Bsns Pk SO51 28 A2
Belfield Rd BH6 207 A2
Belfry Wlk PO14 129 B1
Belgrave Ct BH1 205 B2
Belgrave Ind Est SO17 79 B1
Belgrave Rd Poole BH13 204 A1
Southampton SO17 79 B1
Belgravia Rd PO2 157 C1
Bell Cl SO45 150 C1
Bell Cres PO7 134 C3
Bell Davies Rd PO14 179 A3
Bell Heather Cl BH16 201 A4
Bell Hill GU32 40 C3
Bell Hill Ridge GU32 40 C3
Bell Ho PO18 161 C4
Bell La 18 BH15 202 A1
Bell Rd PO6 157 B4
Bell St Romsey SO51 52 C4
Southampton SO14 103 A2
Bellair Ho PO9 136 A1
Bellair Rd PO9 136 A1
Bellamy Ct SO17 103 B4
Belle Vue Cl BH6 206 B2
Belle Vue Cres BH6 206 C2
Belle Vue Gdns 2 BH6 206 C2
Belle Vue Gr BH22 138 C1
Belle Vue Mans 7 BH6 206 C2
Belle Vue Rd
Bournemouth BH6 206 C2
Poole BH14 203 B2
Belle Vue Wlk BH22 165 C1
Bellemoor Rd SO15 78 B1
Bellemoor Sec Sch (Boys) SO15 78 B1
Belleview Terr PO5 215 A1
Bellevue La PO10 136 C1
Bellevue Rd
Eastleigh SO50 56 A2
Southampton SO15 103 A3
Bellevue Terr 9 SO14 103 A3
Bellfield PO14 153 C4
Bellflower Cl BH23 208 A4
Bellflower Way SO53 54 C4
Bells Ho BH21 163 B3
Bells La PO14 179 B3
Belmont Ave BH8 190 B1
Belmont Cl Horndean PO8 88 B2
Hythe SO45 126 A1
Stubbington PO14 154 B2
Verwood BH31 115 A3
Belmont Gr PO9 135 B1
Belmont Pl PO5 215 B1
Belmont Rd
Chandler's Ford SO53 55 B2
New Milton BH25 195 B2
Poole BH14 203 B3
Southampton SO17 103 A4
Belmont St PO5 215 B1
Belmore Cl PO1 182 C4
Belmore La
Lymington SO41 197 C2
Owslebury SO21 33 C2
Upham SO32 34 A2
Belmore Rd SO41 197 B2
Belmour Lo 26 BH4 204 B2
Belney Ho PO6 157 A4
Belstone Rd SO40 100 C4
Belton Rd SO19 104 A2
Belvedere Cl GU32 40 C2
Belvedere Rd
Bournemouth BH3 205 A3
Christchurch BH23 207 A4
Hythe SO45 126 A1
Belvidere Ho 12 SO14 103 B3
Belvidere Rd SO14 103 B3
Belvidere Terr SO14 103 B3
Belvoir Cl PO16 155 A4
Bembridge SO31 127 B3
Bembridge Cl SO16 79 B3
Bembridge Cres PO4 182 C1
Bembridge Ct PO11 185 B1
Bembridge Dr PO11 185 B1
Bembridge Ho PO11 185 B1
Bembridge Lodge Flats 8 PO13 179 C1
Bemister Rd BH9 205 A4
Bemister's La PO12 181 C2
Benbow Cl PO8 112 B4
Benbow Cres BH12 188 C1
Benbow Gdns SO40 76 B1
Benbow Ho 6 PO1 182 A3
Benbow Pl 5 PO1 182 A3
Benbridge Ave BH11 188 C3
Bencraft Ct SO16 79 A3
Bendigo Rd BH23 206 C4
Benedict Cl SO51 53 B4
Benedict Way PO16 132 C1
Beneficial St 14 PO1 182 A3
Benellen Ave BH4 204 B2
Benellen Gdns BH4 204 B2
Benellen Rd BH4 204 B3
Benellen Twrs BH4 204 B2
Bengal Rd BH9 204 C4
Benger's La SO51 5 B1
Benham Dr 18 PO3 157 C2
Benham Gr PO16 156 B3
Benhams Farm Cl 8 SO18 80 A1
Benhams Rd SO18 80 A1
Benjamin Ct BH23 206 C4
Benjamin Rd BH15 201 C1
Benmoor Rd BH17 202 A4
Benmore Cl BH25 195 B1
Benmore Gdns SO53 55 A4
Benmore Rd BH9 190 A1
Bennett Ho 11 BH4 204 B2
Bennett Rd BH8 205 B3
Bennett's Alley 22 BH15 202 A1
Bennetts La BH24 143 B1
Bennion Rd BH10 189 B2
Benridge Cl BH18 187 A2
Benson Cl BH23 169 A1
Benson Rd Poole BH17 202 B4
Southampton SO15 102 A4
Bent La PO7 110 A4
Bentham Rd PO12 181 A2
Bentham Way SO31 128 B4
Benthem Ct SO16 79 A2
Bentley Cl Horndean PO8 112 B4
Kings Worthy SO23 2 A3
Bentley Cres PO16 130 C1
Bentley Ct Havant PO9 136 A3
16 Southampton SO17 79 A1
Bentley Gr SO18 104 B4
Bentley Rd BH9 189 C2
Bentworth Cl PO9 135 B2
Benwell Ct PO11 184 C2
Bepton Down GU31 41 A2
Berber Cl PO15 129 B4
Bercote Cl SO22 1 A3
Bere Cl
North Baddesley SO53 55 A4
Poole BH17 187 B1
Winchester SO22 1 B1
Bere Farm La PO17 131 C4
Bere Rd PO7 110 C2
Beresford Cl
Chandler's Ford SO53 55 C3
Poole BH12 203 B3
Waterlooville PO7 134 C3
Beresford Gdns
Chandler's Ford SO53 55 C3
Christchurch BH23 207 C3
Beresford Rd
Bournemouth BH6 206 A2
Chandler's Ford SO53 55 C3
Lymington SO41 197 B2
Poole BH12 203 B3
Portsmouth PO2 157 C1
Stubbington PO14 154 B2
Bereweeke Ave SO22 1 C1
Bereweeke Cl SO22 1 C1
Bereweeke Rd SO22 1 C1
Bereweeke Way SO22 1 C1
Bergen Cres SO30 105 B3
Berkeley Ave BH12 203 B4
Berkeley Cl
Southampton SO15 102 C4
Stubbington PO14 179 A3
Verwood BH31 114 C4
Berkeley Ct PO13 179 C1
Berkeley Gdns SO30 105 B3
Berkeley Rd
Bournemouth BH3 204 C4
Southampton SO15 102 C3
Berkeley Sq PO9 136 A1
Berkeley The PO5 182 C1
Berkley Ave BH22 165 B1
Berkshire Cl PO1 215 D3
Bermuda Ct
9 Christchurch BH23 209 A4
22 Southampton SO17 79 A1
Bermuda Ho 3 PO6 132 C1
Bernard Ave PO6 158 A4
Bernard Powell Ho PO9 136 A1
Bernard St SO14 103 A2
Bernards Cl BH23 206 C4
Berne Ct 11 BH1 205 A2
Berney Rd PO4 183 B2
Bernina Ave PO7 111 B1
Bernina Cl PO7 111 B1
Bernwood Gr SO45 177 C4
Beron Ct BH15 202 C2
Berrans Ave BH11 189 A3
Berrans Ct BH11 189 A3
Berry Cl SO30 105 B3
Berry La
Stubbington PO14 179 A3
Twyford SO21 32 A4
Berrydown Rd PO9 135 B4
Berryfield Rd SO41 196 A1
Berrylands GU33 21 A4
Berrywood Bsns Village SO30 81 A2
Berrywood Gdns SO30 105 A4
Berrywood Prim Sch SO30 81 B1
Berthon Ho SO51 52 C3
Bertie Rd PO4 183 A2
Bertram Rd BH25 195 B2
Berwick Rd BH3 204 C3
Berwyn Ct BH18 187 A2
Berwyn Wlk PO14 154 C4
Beryl Ave PO12 180 C4
Beryton Cl PO12 181 A3
Beryton Rd PO12 181 A3
Besomer Dro SP5 47 C3
Bessborough Rd BH13 214 C4
Bessemer Cl BH31 115 B2
Beswick Ave BH10 189 B1
Bethany Ct BH12 204 A4
Bethany Ho BH1 205 B3
Bethany Jun CE Sch BH1 205 B3
Bethia Cl BH8 205 B3
Bethia Rd BH8 205 B3
Betsy Cl BH23 169 A1
Betsy La BH23 169 A1
Betteridge Dr SO16 77 B3
Bettesworth Rd PO1 182 C4
Bettiscombe Cl BH17 187 C1
Betula Cl PO7 135 A3
Beulah Rd SO16 78 A1
Bevan Cl SO19 103 C1
Bevan Rd PO8 112 A3
Beverley Cl PO14 129 B2
Beverley Gdns
Bournemouth BH10 189 B2
Bursledon SO31 104 C1
Romsey SO51 28 B1
Beverley Gdns *continued*
Swanmore SO32 84 A3
Beverley Gr PO6 134 C1
Beverley Grange 29 BH4 204 B2
Beverley Hts SO18 79 C2
Beverley Rd Hythe SO45 149 C4
Stubbington PO14 179 B3
Beverly Cl PO13 155 B1
Beverston Ho 4 PO6 133 A1
Beverston Rd PO6 133 A1
Bevis Cl Blackfield SO45 150 C1
Locks Heath SO31 152 B4
Bevis Rd Gosport PO12 181 A3
Portsmouth PO2 157 B1
Bevis Rd N PO2 157 B1
Bevois Gdns SO14 103 A4
Bevois Hill SO14 103 A4
Bevois Mans 25 SO14 103 A4
Bevois Mews 26 SO14 103 A4
Bevois Town Prim Sch SO14 103 A4
Bevois Valley Rd SO14 103 A4
Bexington Cl BH11 188 C2
Beyne Rd SO22 10 A2
Bickerley Gdns BH24 140 C3
Bickerley Rd BH24 140 C3
Bickerley Terr BH24 140 C4
Bicknell Boys Sch BH7 206 A4
Bicknell Ct 10 BH4 204 B2
Bickton Wlk 9 PO9 135 B3
Bicton Rd BH10 189 A2
Bidbury Inf Sch PO9 135 B1
Bidbury Jun Sch PO9 135 B1
Bidbury La PO9 135 B1
Biddenfield La SO32, PO17 107 B3
Biddlecombe Cl PO13 180 B4
Biddlesgate Ct 10 SO14 102 C2
Bideford Cl SO16 77 C1
Big Tree Cotts SO32 85 B3
Biggin Wlk PO14 154 C4
Bilberry Cl SO31 128 C1
Bilberry Ct 15 SO22 10 C4
Bilberry Dr SO40 101 C1
Bill Stillwell Ct 6 PO2 157 B1
Billett Ave PO7 134 C4
Billing Cl PO4 183 A2
Billington Gdns SO30 81 B1
Billington Pl SO41 197 B1
Billy Lawn Ave PO9 135 C3
Bilton Bsns Pk PO3 158 B1
Bilton Way PO3 158 B1
Bindon Cl Poole BH12 203 C4
Southampton SO16 78 A1
Bindon Ct 5 SO18 103 C4
Bindon Rd SO16 78 A1
Bingham Ave BH14 214 B4
Bingham Cl
Christchurch BH23 207 C4
Verwood BH31 115 A2
Bingham Dr
Lymington SO41 197 C2
Verwood BH31 115 A2
Bingham Rd
Bournemouth BH9 205 A4
Christchurch BH23 207 C4
Verwood BH31 115 A2
Binnacle Way PO6 157 A4
Binness Way PO6 158 C4
Binnie Rd BH12 203 C3
Binstead Cl SO16 79 B3
Binsteed Rd PO2 182 C4
Birch Ave Burton BH23 192 B2
Ferndown BH22 165 C1
New Milton BH25 194 B3
Birch Cl
Colden Common SO21 56 C4
Corfe Mullen BH21 186 B3
Liss GU33 21 A2
Poole BH14 203 C2
Romsey SO51 53 B3
Southampton SO16 78 A1
St Leonards BH24 139 B2
Waterlooville PO8 111 C2
Birch Ct
Southampton SO18 104 A4
3 Winchester SO22 10 B3
Birch Dale SO45 126 A1
Birch Dr
Bournemouth BH8 191 A1
Gosport PO13 155 B2
Birch Gr Eastleigh SO50 56 A3
New Milton BH25 195 A1
West Moors BH22 138 B1
Birch Hill PO17 109 C2
Birch Ho SO16 78 C4
Birch Rd Chilworth SO16 79 A4
Hedge End SO30 105 B4
Southampton SO16 78 A2
St Leonards BH24 140 A2
Birch Tree Cl PO10 136 C2
Birch Tree Dr PO10 136 C2
Birch Wlk BH22 165 C2
Birch Wood SO19 104 C3
Birchdale Cl SO31 152 B4
Birchdale Rd BH21 163 B3
Birchen Cl SO31 129 B2
Birchen Rd SO31 129 B2
Birches Cl The SO52 53 C3
Birches The SO18 104 A4
Birchglade SO40 76 B1
Birchlands SO40 100 B3
Birchmore Cl 3 PO13 155 B1
Birchwood Cl BH23 208 C4

Birchwood Ct 6 S018 ....103 C4
Birchwood Dr SP6 ......93 A3
Birchwood Gdns S030 ..105 B4
Birchwood Lodge 7
PO16 ....131 A1
Birchwood Mews BH14 .203 B2
Birchwood Rd
Poole BH14 ....203 B2
Upton BH16 ....201 A3
Birchy Hill S041 ....172 B1
Bird Field S053 ....54 C4
Bird's Hill Rd BH15 ...202 C2
Birdham Rd PO11 ......185 C1
Birdlip Cl PO8 ....112 A2
Birds Hill Gdns 5 BH15 .202 C2
Birdwood Gr PO16 .....155 C4
Birinus Rd S023 ....2 A1
Birkdale Ave PO6 ......134 B1
Birkdale Cl BH18 ......187 A3
Birkdale Rd BH18 ......187 A3
Birmingham Ct PO13 ...180 B3
Biscay Cl PO14 ....154 A2
Bishearne Gdns GU33 ..20 C3
Bishop Cl BH12 ....204 B4
Bishop Ct BH24 ....141 A4
Bishop Rd BH9 ....205 A4
Bishop St PO1 ....182 A3
Bishop's La S032 ......83 B4
Bishop's Waltham Inf Sch
S032 ....83 B4
Bishop's Waltham Pal*
S032 ....83 B4
Bishop's Wood Rd PO17 .84 B1
Bishops Cl
Bournemouth BH7 ......205 C4
Totton S040 ....100 C4
Bishops Cres S019 .....103 C2
Bishops Ct S050 ....56 B3
Bishops Gate PO14 ....129 B2
Bishops La S032 ....84 A1
Bishops Rd S019 ......103 C2
Bishopsfield Rd PO14 ..154 C4
Bishopstoke La S050 ...56 C4
Bishopstoke Manor S050 .56 B2
Bishopstoke Rd
Eastleigh S050 ....56 B2
Havant PO9 ....135 C3
Bisley Cl S019 ....104 A2
Bisterne Cl BH24 ......143 C1
Bittern Cl PO12 ....181 B4
Bittern CE Inf & Jun Sch
S019 ....103 C3
Bitterne Cl PO9 ....135 C3
Bitterne Cres S019 ....104 A3
Bitterne Manor Ho
S018 ....103 B4
Bitterne Manor Prim Sch
S018 ....103 B4
Bitterne Park Inf Sch
S017 ....79 B1
Bitterne Park Jun Sch
S017 ....79 B1
Bitterne Park Sec Sch
S018 ....79 C1
Bitterne Park Triangle
S018 ....79 B1
Bitterne Rd E S018 ....104 A4
Bitterne Rd W S018 ....103 C4
Bitterne Sta S018 .....103 B4
Bitterne Way
Lymington S041 ....197 B1
Southampton S019 .....103 C3
Verwood BH31 ....115 A3
Black Dale S045 ....151 A2
Black Hill PO11 ....115 A3
Black La Bransgore BH23 .169 C2
Redlynch SP5 ....48 A2
Black Moor Rd BH31 ...115 B2
Black Swan Bldgs 20
S022 ....10 C4
Blackberry Cl PO8 .....88 B2
Blackberry Dr S050 ....57 A1
Blackberry La BH23 ....207 C3
Blackberry Terr S014 ..103 A4
Blackbird Cl
Broadstone BH17 ......201 C4
Waterlooville PO8 .....111 C2
Blackbird Rd S050 .....55 B1
Blackbird Way
Bransgore BH23 ....193 B4
Lee-on-the-Solent PO13 .179 C2
Blackbrook House Dr
PO15 ....130 C1
Blackbrook Park Ave
PO15 ....130 C1
Blackbrook Rd PO15 ...130 B1
Blackburn Ct PO13 ....180 B3
Blackburn Rd BH12 ....203 A3
Blackbush Cl S016 .....77 C3
Blackcap Cl PO9 ....113 A1
Blackdown Cl S045 ....125 B1
Blackdown Cres PO9 ...135 C2
Blackdown Inf Sch S045 .150 C1
Blackfield Jun Sch
S045 ....150 B1
Blackfield La BH22 ....138 C2
Blackfield Rd
Blackfield S045 ....150 C1
Bournemouth BH9 .....190 B2
Blackfriars Cl 3 PO1 ..215 C2

Blackfriars Rd PO1 .....215 C3
Blackhill Rd S051 .....74 C4
Blackhorse La S032 ....83 C1
Blackhouse La PO17 ...109 A1
Blackmoor Wlk 12 PO9 .136 A3
Blackmore La GU32 ....18 C2
Blacksmith Cl BH21 ...186 B3
Blackthorn Cl
Lymington S041 ....197 A1
Southampton S019 ....103 C3
Blackthorn Dr
Gosport PO12 ....156 A1
South Hayling PO11 ...185 B2
Blackthorn Gn S021 ...57 A4
Blackthorn Rd
South Hayling PO11 ...185 B1
Southampton S019 ....103 C3
Blackthorn Terr PO1 ..182 A3
Blackthorn Way
New Milton BH25 ......195 B2
Verwood BH31 ....115 A3
Blackthorn Wlk PO7 ...112 B1
Blackwater Cl 10 PO6 .157 B4
Blackwater Dr
Oakley BH21 ....187 B4
Totton S040 ....76 B1
Blackwater Gr SP6 ....92 C3
Blackwater Mews S040 .76 B1
Blackwood Ho 18 PO1 .182 B4
Bladon Cl PO9 ....136 B2
Bladon Rd S016 ....78 B1
Blair Ave BH14 ....203 B2
Blair Cl BH25 ....194 C2
Blake Cl S016 ....77 B3
Blake Dene Rd BH14 ..203 A1
Blake Hill Ave BH14 ..203 B1
Blake Hill Cres BH14 .203 B1
Blake Ho PO12 ....181 C2
Blake Rd Cosham PO6 .134 B1
Gosport PO12 ....181 B3
Portsmouth PO1 ......181 C4
Blakemere Cres PO9 ..133 B1
Blakeney Rd S016 ....77 B1
Blakesley La PO3 .....158 B2
Blanchard Rd S022 ...83 A4
Blandford Cl BH15 ...201 C1
Blandford Ct 2 S041 .211 B3
Blandford Ho S016 ...77 C1
Blandford Rd
Coombe Bissett SP5 ..23 B4
Corfe Mullen BH21 ...186 B4
Hamworthy BH15,BH16 .201 B2
Pamphill BH21 ....162 B4
Blandford Rd N BH16 .201 A4
Blaney Way BH21 .....186 B3
Blankney Cl PO14 ....179 A3
Blann Cl S016 ....77 B3
Blashford Lakes Study Ctr
BH24 ....117 A2
Blaven Wlk 4 PO14 ..154 C4
Bleaklow Cl S016 ....101 C4
Blechynden Terr S015 .102 C3
Blencowe Dr S053 ...54 C3
Blendworth Cres PO9 .135 C2
Blendworth Ho 2 PO1 .215 C4
Blendworth La
Horndean PO8 ....112 C4
Southampton S018 ...104 B4
Blendworth N 5 PO4 .183 A3
Blenheim Ave S017 ...79 A1
Blenheim Cl
Chandler's Ford S053 .54 C2
Totton S040 ....100 C3
Blenheim Cres S041 ..195 C2
Blenheim Ct
26 Bournemouth BH4 .204 B2
Christchurch BH23 ....207 A4
Portsmouth PO4 ......183 A2
Southampton S017 ...79 A1
Blenheim Dr BH23 ....208 A3
Blenheim Gdns
Gosport PO12 ....181 A4
Havant PO9 ....136 B1
Hythe S045 ....125 B1
Southampton S017 ...79 A1
Blenheim Ho
6 Eastleigh S050 ....56 A1
Romsey S051 ....53 A4
Blenheim Rd
Eastleigh S050 ....56 A1
Waterlooville PO8 ....112 A3
Blenheim Barn PO7 ..110 C1
Bleriot Cres PO15 ....129 C3
Blighmont Ave S015 ..102 A3
Blighmont Cres S015 .102 A3
Blind La Curdridge S032 .82 C1
Fair Oak S030 ....81 B3
Ibsley SP6 ....94 B1
Wickham PO17 ....107 C3
Wimborne Minst BH21 .163 A3
Bliss Cl PO7 ....134 C3
Blissford Cl PO9 ......136 A3
Blissford Cross SP6 ...94 C4
Blissford Hill SP6 ....94 C4
Blissford Rd SP6 .....94 C4
Bloomfield Ave BH9 ..189 C1
Bloomfield Pl BH9 ....189 C1
Bloomsbury Wlk S019 .103 C1
Blossom Cl S030 .....105 C3
Blount Rd PO1 ....182 A2
Blue Anchor La PO1 ..203 C4
Blue Anchor La 16
S014 ....102 C2
Blue Ball Hill S023 ...11 A4
Bluebell Cl
Christchurch BH23 ...208 A4
Waterlooville PO7 ....135 A3
Bluebell Copse S031 .128 C1

Bluebell La BH17 .....186 C1
Bluebell Rd S016 .....79 B2
Blueberry La S041 ....197 A1
Blueprint Portfield Rd
PO3 ....158 A1
Bluestar Gdns S030 ..81 B1
Blundell La S031 .....105 B1
Blyth Cl
Christchurch BH23 ...191 B2
Southampton S016 ...77 B1
Blythe Rd BH21 ......186 B3
Blythswood Ct BH25 .209 C4
Boakes Pl S040 ....100 B3
Boardwalk The PO6 ..157 A4
Boardwalk Way S040 .102 A2
Boarhunt Cl PO1 .....215 C3
Boarhunt Rd PO17 ...131 C2
Boatyard Ind Est The
PO18 ....155 A4
Bob Hann Cl BH12 ...203 B3
Bockhampton Rd BH23 .192 C3
Bodley Rd BH13 ......214 C4
Bodmin Rd
Bishopstoke S050 ....56 C1
Portchester PO6 .....157 A4
Bodorgan Rd BH2 ....204 C2
Bodowen Cl BH23 ...192 B1
Bodowen Rd BH23 ...192 B1
Bodycoats Rd S053 ..55 B3
Bognor Rd BH18 .....186 C2
Bohemia La SP5 ......47 C2
Boiler Rd Fawley S045 .151 C1
Poole BH15 ....204 A2
Bolde Cl PO13 ....158 B2
Bolderwood Rd S016 .78 C2
Boldens Rd PO12 ....181 A1
Boldre Cl BH9 ....190 A2
Boldrewood Arboretum
Ornamental Dr* S043 .120 B1
Bolderwood Cl S050 ..56 C1
Boldre Cl
Barton on Sea BH25 ..209 B4
Havant PO9 ....135 B2
Poole BH12 ....203 B4
Boldre La S041 ......197 B4
Bolhinton Ave S040 ..101 B1
Bolton Cl BH6 ....206 C2
Bolton Cres BH22 ....166 A3
Bolton Dr 14 BH6 ....206 C2
Bolton Dr PO12 ......181 B4
Bolton Rd BH6 ......206 C2
Boltons The
16 Milford on Sea S041 .211 B2
Waterlooville PO7 ....134 C2
Bonchurch Cl S016 ...79 B3
Bonchurch Rd PO4 ...183 A3
Bond Ave BH22 ......138 B2
Bond Cl S041 ....172 A2
Bond Rd Poole BH15 .202 C3
Bond St S014 ....103 B3
Bondfields Cres PO9 .135 C3
Bones La BH24 ......65 B3
Bonfire Cnr PO1 .....182 A3
Bonham Rd BH13 ....204 C4
Boniface Cl S040 ....100 B4
Boniface Cres PO7 ...77 C2
Bonington Cl BH23 ..207 C4
Bonner Cotts SP5 ....4 C4
Boothby Cl S040 .....101 A3
Border Dr BH16 .....201 B3
Border Lo BH23 ......194 B1
Border Rd BH16 .....201 B3
Bordon Rd PO9 ......135 C3
Boreham Rd BH6 ....206 B3
Borley Rd BH17 .....202 A4
Borough Gr GU32 ...40 C1
Borough Hill GU32 ..40 C2
Borough Rd
Petersfield GU32 ....40 B1
Petersfield GU32 ....40 C2
Borough The SP5 ....46 C4
Borrowdale Rd S016 .77 C1
Borthwick Rd BH1 ...205 C3
Boscobel Rd S022 ...1 C1
Boscombe Cliff Rd BH5 .205 C2
Boscombe Gr Rd BH1 .205 B3
Boscombe Overcliff Dr
BH5 ....205 A2
Boscombe Spa Rd BH5 .205 B2
Bosham Rd PO2 .....182 C4
Bosham Wlk PO13 ...155 A1
Bosley Cl BH23 ......191 C1
Bosley Way BH23 ....191 C1
Bosmere Gdns PO10 .136 C1
Bosmere Jun Sch PO9 .159 C4
Bosmere Rd PO11 ...185 C1
Bossington Cl S016 ..77 C3
Boston Cl S053 ......55 B4
Boston Lo 8 BH4 ....204 B2
Boston Rd PO6 ......133 C1
Bosuns Cl PO10 .....155 A3
Boswell Cl Botley S030 ..106 B4
Southampton S019 ...103 C3
Bosworth Mews BH9 ..190 A2
Botany Bay Rd S019 ..104 A2
Botley CE Prim Sch
S030 ....106 A4
Botley Dr PO9 ....135 B3
Botley Gdns S019 ....104 C2
Botley Hill S030 .....106 A3
Botley Rd Curdridge S032 .82 C1
Fair Oak S050 ....57 B1
Fair Oak, Wildern S050 .81 B4
North Baddesley S052 .53 B3

Botley Rd continued
Romsey S051 ....53 B3
Southampton S019 ...104 B2
Swanwick S031 ......129 A4
West End S030 ....81 A1
Botley Sta S030 .....106 B4
Bottings Est S030 ...106 A4
Bottom La S051 .....50 C2
Boulnois Ave BH14 ..203 C2
Boulton Rd PO5 .....215 D1
Bound La PO11 ......185 A1
Boundary Acre S031 .105 A2
Boundary Cl S015 ...101 C4
Boundary Dr BH21 ..163 B3
Boundary La BH24 ..139 C1
Boundary Oak Prep Sch
PO17 ....131 B3
Boundary Rd
Bournemouth BH10,BH9 .189 C1
Bursledon S031 ......127 C4
Boundary Rdbt BH3,
BH10 ....204 B4
Boundary Way
Havant PO9 ....135 C1
Waterlooville PO6 ...134 A1
Boundstone S045 ....125 C2
Boundway S041 .....171 C1
Bountys La BH21 ....203 C3
Bourne Ave
Bournemouth BH2 ...204 C2
Southampton S015 ...78 B1
Bourne Cl
Bournemouth BH4 ...204 B2
Southampton S015 ...78 B1
Bourne Cres
Bournemouth BH10 ..189 A4
Otterbourne S021 ...31 A2
Bourne Rd
Bournemouth BH4 ...204 B2
Waterlooville PO8 ...112 A3
West Wellow S051 ...50 B2
Bourne Com Coll PO10 .137 B1
Bourne Cotts SP5 ...44 C1
Bourne Ct
24 Bournemouth BH2 .204 C2
Wimborne Minst BH21 .163 B3
Bourne La
Netley Marsh S040 ..99 B3
Twyford S021 ....32 A3
Bourne Pines 8 BH1 .204 C2
Bourne Rd Cosham PO6 .157 A4
Bournemouth BH9 ...190 B3
Southampton S015 ..102 B3
Bourne Valley Rd BH12 .204 A3
Bourne View PO10 ..137 B1
Bournefields S031 ...32 A4
Bournemouth & Poole Coll of
F Ed BH14 ....205 A2
Bournemouth & Poole Coll of
F Ed (Annex) BH14 ..202 C3
Bournemouth & Poole Coll of
The BH1 ....205 A2
Bournemouth Aquarium*
BH2 ....204 C1
Bournemouth Ave PO12 .181 A4
Bournemouth Aviation Mus*
BH23 ....191 A4
Bournemouth Central Bsns
Pk BH1 ....205 B3
Bournemouth Crown & Cty
Cts BH7 ....191 B1
Bournemouth Gram Sch
(Boys) BH8 ....190 B1
Bournemouth Gram Sch
(Girls) BH9 ....190 B1
Bournemouth Ho 99
PO9 ....136 A3
Bournemouth Int Airport
BH23 ....190 C4
Bournemouth Int Ctr*
BH2 ....204 C1
Bournemouth Meml Homes
BH8 ....190 C1
Bournemouth Nuffield Hospl
BH8 ....205 A3
Bournemouth Rd
Chandler's Ford S053 .55 B2
Lyndhurst S043 ......121 C3
Poole BH14 ....203 B2
Bournemouth Sta BH1 .205 A2
Bournemouth Univ
BH12 ....204 B4
Bournemouth West Rdbt
BH2 ....204 B2
Bournewood Dr BH4 .204 B2
Bourton Gdns BH7 ..206 A4
Bouverie Cl 8 BH25 ..195 A1
Boveridge Gdns BH9 .190 A2
Bovington Cl BH17 ..187 C1
Bowater Cl S040 ....76 B1
Bowater Way S040 ..76 B1
Bowcombe S031 ....127 B4
Bowden La BH17 ....79 C1
Bowden Rd BH12 ...188 B1
Bower Cl Holbury S045 .150 B2
Southampton S019 ..103 C2
Bowerdean Ct BH8 ..205 B4
Bowers Cl PO8 ......112 A2
Bowers Hill SP5 .....47 C4
Bowerwood Cotts SP6 .93 B4
Bowerwood Rd SP6 ..93 B4
Bowes Ct PO1 ....113 B2
Bowes-Lyon Ct PO8 .112 A4
Bowland Rise
New Milton BH25 ....195 B1
North Baddesley S052 .55 A4
Bowland Way S045 ..177 C4
Bowler Ave PO3 .....182 C3
Bowler Ct PO1 ......182 C3

Bowman Ct S019 .....104 A2
Box Cl BH17 ....202 A4
Boxgrove Ho PO1 ....215 C4
Boxwood Cl
Portchester PO16 ....132 A1
Waterlooville PO7 ....134 C3
Boyatt Cres S050 ....56 A4
Boyatt La Eastleigh S050 .56 A4
Otterbourne S021,S050 .31 A1
Boyatt Wood Sh Ctr 7
S050 ....56 A3
Boyd Cl PO14 ....179 A3
Boyd Rd Gosport PO13 .155 A2
Poole BH12 ....203 C3
Boyes Cres S050 ....32 A1
Boyle Cres PO7 .....134 B3
Boynes Mead Rd S023 .2 B4
Boyne Rise S023 ....2 A4
Boyton Cl S053 .....55 A4
Brabant Cl PO15 ....129 A4
Brabazon Dr BH23 ..208 A4
Brabazon Rd
Locks Heath PO15 ...129 B3
Oakley BH21 ....163 C1
Brabourne Ave BH22 .165 B2
Bracken Cl
North Baddesley S052 .54 A2
St Leonards BH24 ...139 B2
Bracken Cres S050 ..56 C1
Bracken Glen BH15 ..202 C3
Bracken Hall S016 ..79 A4
Bracken Heath 16 PO7 .112 A1
Bracken La S016 ....78 A1
Bracken Lodge 8 BH6 .206 C2
Bracken Pl S016 ....79 A4
Bracken Rd
Bournemouth BH6 ...206 B2
Ferndown BH22 .....165 A4
North Baddesley S052 .54 A2
Petersfield GU31 ....41 B1
Bracken Way BH23 ..194 A1
Brackendale Ct BH21 .138 C4
Brackendale Rd BH18 .205 B4
Brackenhill BH13 ...204 A1
Brackenhill Rd BH21 .164 A4
Brackens The
Hythe S045 ....125 B2
Locks Heath S031 ...129 A1
Brackens Way
17 Poole BH13 ......214 C4
Brackenway Rd S053 .55 B4
Bracklesham Cl S019 .103 C2
Bracklesham Rd
Gosport PO13 ....180 B4
South Hayling PO11 .185 C1
Brackley Ave S050 ..57 A2
Brackley Cl BH23 ...191 A4
Brackley Way S040 ..100 B4
Bradbourne Rd BH2 .204 C2
Bradford Cl BH23 ...180 B3
Bradford Rd
Bournemouth BH9 ...190 B2
Portsmouth PO5 ....215 C2
Brading Ave
Gosport PO13 ....155 B1
Portsmouth PO4 ....183 A1
Bradley Cl 12 PO9 ..136 A3
Bradley Gn S016 ....78 A2
Bradley Peak S022 ..1 B1
Bradley Rd S022 ....1 B2
Bradly Rd PO15 ....130 B1
Bradpole Rd BH8 ...190 C2
Bradshaw Cl S050 ..57 C1
Bradstock Cl BH12 .203 C4
Braehead S045 .....125 C1
Braemar Ave
Bournemouth BH6 ...207 A2
Cosham PO6 ....158 A4
Braemar Cl
Bournemouth BH6 ...207 A2
Fareham PO15 ......130 C2
Gosport PO13 ......155 B1
Braemar Dr BH23 ...193 C1
Braemar Rd PO13 ...155 B1
Braeside Cl
Southampton S016 ..103 C3
Winchester S022 ...10 A2
Braeside Cres S019 .103 C3
Braeside Rd
Southampton S016 ..103 C3
St Leonards BH24 ...139 C2
West Moors BH22 ...138 C2
Braidley Rd BH2 ....204 C2
Braidwood Rd BH15 .202 C2
Braintree Rd PO6 ...133 B1
Braishfield Cl S016 .77 C1
Braishfield Gdns BH8 .190 B1
Braishfield Prim Sch
.... 28 B3
Braishfield Rd
Havant PO9 ....136 A2
Romsey S051 ....52 B2
Brake Ho PO9 ......135 B1
Bramar Ct BH4 .....204 B1
Bramber Rd PO12 ..181 A4
Bramble Cl Alderholt SP6 .93 A3
5 Eastleigh S050 ...56 A3
Bramble Ho PO4 ...136 B2
Bramble La S041 ...150 B2
Stubbington PO14 ..179 A3
Bramble Ct
2 Petersfield GU31 ..41 B2
West Moors BH22 ...138 B1
Bramble Dr S041 ...138 C1
Bramble Hill S053 ..55 A3

Bramble La
Christchurch BH23 194 A1
Clanfield PO8 88 A4
Locks Heath SO31 128 C3
Bramble Mews 1 SO18 104 A4
Bramble Rd
Petersfield GU31 41 B2
Portsmouth PO4 182 C2
Bramble Way
Bransgore BH23 169 A1
Gosport PO13 155 A1
Bramble Wlk SO41 197 B3
Bramblegate SO50 57 B1
Brambles Bsns Ctr The
PO7 111 B1
Brambles Cl SO21 57 A4
Brambles Ent Ctr The
PO7 111 B1
Brambles Farm Ind Est
PO7 134 B4
Brambles Rd PO13 179 B2
Brambling Cl SO16 78 A3
Brambling Rd PO9 113 A1
Bramblings The SO40 100 B4
Brambridge SO50 56 C4
Brambridge Ho SO21 31 B1
Brambridge Rd SO21,
SO50 56 C4
Bramdean Dr PO9 135 B3
Bramdean Mews SO19 103 C3
Bramdean Rd SO18 104 B4
Bramham Moor PO14 179 A3
Bramley Cl
Lymington SO41 197 C1
Waterlooville PO7 134 C4
Bramley Cres SO19 104 A1
Bramley Ct BH22 165 B3
Bramley Gdns
Fair Oak SO50 81 B3
Gosport PO12 181 A1
Hermitage PO10 161 A4
Bramley Ho
Gosport PO12 181 A1
Hedge End SO30 105 A3
3 Portsmouth PO5 215 B2
Bramley Rd
Bournemouth BH10 189 B3
Ferndown BH22 165 B3
Bramleys The SP5 24 A2
Brampton La PO3 158 B2
Brampton Manor SO16 78 C3
Brampton Rd BH15 202 B3
Brampton Twr SO16 78 C3
Bramshaw Cl SO22 1 B2
Bramshaw Ct 37 PO9 136 A3
Bramshaw Gdns BH8 190 B2
Bramshaw Way BH25 209 B4
Bramshott Rd
Portsmouth PO4 182 C2
Southampton SO19 126 C4
Bramston Rd SO15 102 B4
Bramwell Ct SO18 104 A3
Branches La SO51 25 C2
Branders Cl BH6 207 A2
Branders La BH6 207 A3
Brandon Ct PO5 215 D1
Brandon Rd PO5 182 B1
Brandwood Ct 4 BH14 203 A2
Branewick Cl PO15 129 B2
Branksea Ave BH15 201 C1
Branksea Cl BH15 201 C1
Branksome Ave SO15 78 B1
Branksome Cl
New Milton BH25 195 A1
Winchester SO22 10 A3
Branksome Ct 14 BH13 214 C4
Branksome Dene Rd
BH4 204 A1
Branksome Heath Mid Sch
BH12 203 B3
Branksome Hill Rd
Bournemouth BH4 204 A3
Poole BH12 204 A3
Branksome Sta BH12 203 C2
Branksome Twrs BH13 214 D4
Branksome Wood Gdns
BH2 204 B2
Branksome Wood Rd
Bournemouth BH2,BH4 204 B2
Poole BH12 204 B2
Bransbury Cl SO16 78 B2
Bransbury Rd PO4 183 A2
Bransgore Ave PO9 135 B2
Bransgore CE Prim Sch
BH23 193 B4
Bransgore Gdns BH23 169 B1
Bransley Cl SO51 28 A1
Branwell Cl BH23 192 A1
Branwood Cl SO41 196 C1
Brasenose Cl PO14 129 B1
Brasher Cl SO50 57 A1
Brassey Cl BH9 190 A1
Brassey Rd
Bournemouth BH9 190 A1
Winchester SO22 1 C1
Brassey Terr BH9 189 C1
Brasted Ct PO4 183 B3
Braunston Cl 10 PO6 133 A1
Braxall Lawn PO9 135 B3
Braxton Ctyd SO41 211 C4
Braxton Ho 1 SO23 11 B4
Breach Ave PO10 137 C1
Breach La BH24 141 C4
Breamore CE Prim Sch
SP6 70 A4
Breamore Cl
Eastleigh SO50 56 A3
New Milton BH25 194 C2

Breamore Countryside Mus*
SP6 46 A1
Breamore Ho* SP6 46 A2
Breamore Rd SO18 104 B4
Brean Cl SO16 77 C1
Brearley Ct BH23 209 A4
Brecon Ave PO6 158 A4
Brecon Cl
Bournemouth BH10 189 C3
Chandler's Ford SO53 55 A2
Fareham PO14 154 C4
Hythe SO45 125 C2
New Milton BH25 195 B1
Brecon Rd SO19 104 B3
Bredenbury Cres PO6 133 B1
Bredon Wlk PO14 154 C4
Bredy Cl BH17 187 B1
Breech Cl 12 PO3 157 C2
Bremble Cl BH12 188 B1
Brenchley Cl PO16 156 A4
Brendon Cl
Bournemouth BH8 190 C1
Hythe SO45 125 B1
Brendon Gr SO16 101 C4
Brendon Rd PO14 154 B4
Brent Ct PO10 160 C4
Brentwood Cres SO18 80 A1
Breton Cl PO15 129 A4
Brewells La GU33 21 C2
Brewer Cl SO31 129 A2
Brewer St PO1 215 B4
Brewers La
Gosport PO13 155 B1
Twyford SO21 31 C3
West Tisted SO24 17 B4
Brewhouse Sq PO12 181 B3
Brewster Cl PO8 112 A2
Briar Cl
Christchurch BH23 207 C3
Gosport PO12 180 C2
Poole BH15 202 C3
Waterlooville PO8 112 A3
Briar Way Romsey SO51 28 B1
Wimborne Minst BH21 164 A3
Briar Wood GU33 21 A4
Briar's The PO7 111 B1
Briardene Ct SO40 100 C4
Briarfield 28 BH4 204 B2
Briarfield Gdns PO8 112 A3
Briars The SO42 145 C1
Briarswood SO16 78 A1
Briarswood Rd BH16 201 B4
Briarswood Rise SO45 125 B1
Briarwood Cl PO16 155 A4
Briarwood Gdns PO11 184 C2
Briarwood Rd SO40 100 B3
Brick Kiln La SO24 17 A4
Brick La BH23 169 C2
Brickets Terr PO12 181 A1
Brickfield La
Chandler's Ford SO53 55 B3
Lymington SO41 197 C3
Brickfield Rd SO17 79 B1
Brickfield Trad Est SO53 55 B3
Brickmakers Rd SO21 56 C4
Brickwoods Cl SO51 53 A4
Brickworth Rd SP5 24 A2
Brickyard La
Broadstone BH21 162 A1
Ferndown BH21 165 A3
Brickyard Rd SO32 84 A2
Brickyard The SO40 99 A4
Brickyards Ind Est The
GU32 20 A1
Bridefield Cl PO8 111 B2
Bridefield Cres PO8 111 B2
Bridge App BH15 202 A1
Bridge Cl SO31 105 A1
Bridge Cotts SO51 50 C2
Bridge Ct SO51 52 C3
Bridge Ho Gosport PO13 155 B2
Southampton SO15 102 B3
Bridge Industries PO16 131 B2
Bridge La SO21 31 C4
Bridge Mdws GU33 20 C2
Bridge Mead SO32 61 B3
Bridge Pl BH10 189 B4
Bridge Rd
Emsworth PO10 136 C1
Locks Heath SO31 128 B3
Lymington SO41 197 C3
Romsey SO51 53 A4
Southampton SO19 103 B2
Bridge Sh Ctr The PO1 215 D3
Bridge St
Christchurch BH23 207 B3
Fordingbridge SP6 69 C1
Southwick PO17 132 C3
Titchfield PO14 154 A4
Wickham PO17 108 A2
46 Winchester SO23 11 A4
Bridge Terr
Compton (Hants) SO21 31 C3
33 Southampton SO14 103 A2
Bridgefoot Dr PO16 131 B1
Bridgefoot Path PO10 160 C4
Bridgemary Ave PO13 155 B2
Bridgemary Com Sch
PO13 155 B1
Bridgemary Gr PO13 155 B3
Bridgemary Rd PO13 155 B2
Bridgemary Way PO13 155 B3
Bridgers Cl SO16 77 C3
Bridges Ave PO6 132 C1
Bridges Cl Eastleigh SO50 55 C2
West Moors BH22 138 C2
Bridges The BH24 140 C4
Bridgeside Cl PO1 215 C3

Bridget Cl PO8 112 B4
Bridgewater Rd BH12 203 B3
Bridgeway Ct SO40 101 A4
Bridgwater Ct SO15 102 B3
Bridle Cl BH16 201 B4
Bridle Cres BH7 206 B4
Bridle Way BH21 164 B3
Bridleways BH31 114 C3
Bridlington Ave SO15 102 B4
Bridport Ct SO15 102 B3
Bridport Rd Poole BH12 203 C4
Verwood BH31 114 C3
Bridport St PO1 215 B3
Brierley Ave BH22 165 C1
Brierley Cl BH10 189 C3
Brierley Rd BH10 189 C2
Brigantine Rd SO31 128 C1
Brigham Cl 20 PO2 157 C2
Brighstone Cl SO16 79 B3
Bright Rd BH15 202 B3
Brightlands Ave BH6 206 C3
Brighton Ave PO12 180 C4
Brighton Rd
Southampton SO15 102 C4
Sway SO41 172 A2
Brights La PO11 184 C3
Brightside PO7 134 B3
Brightside Rd SO16 77 C1
Brightstone Rd PO6 157 C4
Brindle Cl SO16 79 A3
Brinsons Cl BH23 192 B2
Brinton La SO45 126 A3
Brinton's Rd SO14 103 A3
Brinton's Terr SO14 103 A3
Brisbane Ho 20 PO1 182 B4
Brisbane Rd BH23 191 C1
Bristol Ct PO13 180 B3
Bristol Rd PO4 182 C1
Britain St PO1 182 A3
Britannia Ct BH12 203 A4
Britannia Gdns SO30 81 A2
Britannia Pl SO41 197 C2
Britannia Rd Poole BH14 203 A2
Portsmouth PO5 215 C2
Southampton SO14 103 A3
Britannia Rd N PO5 215 C2
Britannia Way
Christchurch BH23 208 A4
Gosport PO12 181 B4
Britannic Ho 22 SO14 103 B3
Britnell Ho 6 GU31 40 C2
Briton St SO14 103 A2
Britten Rd PO13 179 C1
Britten Way PO7 134 C2
Brittons Cotts SO42 145 B1
Brixey Cl BH12 203 B4
Brixey Rd BH12 203 B4
Brixworth Cl 11 PO6 133 A1
Broad Ave BH8 205 B4
Broad Chalke Down
SO22 10 B2
Broad Croft PO9 113 B2
Broad Gdns PO6 158 C4
Broad Gn 5 SO14 103 A2
Broad La Denmead PO7 110 A3
Lymington SO41 197 C1
North Baddesley SO52 53 C3
Southampton SO14 102 C2
Swanmore SO32 84 A3
Broad Mead Rd GU23 114 C1
Broad Oak SO30 105 C4
Broad St PO1 181 C2
Broad View La SO22 10 A2
Broad Way
Froxfield Green GU32 39 C4
Hamble-le-Rice SO31 127 C3
Broad Woods La SO51 51 A3
Broadbent Cl SO16 77 C3
Broadcut PO16 131 B1
Broadfields Cl SO41 211 B3
Broadhill La SP6 94 B4
Broadhurst Ave BH10 189 C2
Broadland Cotts GU32 41 A3
Broadlands* SO51 52 C3
Broadlands Ave
Bournemouth BH6 206 C2
Eastleigh SO50 56 A3
Waterlooville PO7 134 C4
Broadlands Cl
Bournemouth BH8 190 B2
Christchurch BH23 194 A1
Broadlands Rd
Brockenhurst SO42 145 C1
Southampton SO17 79 A2
Broadlaw Walk Prec 14
PO14 154 C4
Broadley Cl SO45 150 B2
Broadly Cl SO41 197 A1
Broadmarsh Bsns &
Innovation Ctr PO9 159 B4
Broadmayne Rd BH12 204 A4
Broadmead Cl 8 SO41 197 C1
Broadmead Flats SO16 77 B3
Broadmead Rd SO16 77 B3
Broadmeadow Cl SO40 100 C4
Broadmeadows La 8
PO7 135 A4
Broadmere Ave PO9 135 C3
Broadmoor Rd BH21 186 B4
Broadoak Cl SO45 150 B2
Broads The BH21 162 C3
Broadsands Dr PO12 180 B2
Broadsands Wlk PO12 180 C2
Broadshard La BH24 141 A4
Broadstone Fst Sch
BH18 187 A2
Broadstone Mid Sch
BH18 187 B3

Broadstone Way
Broadstone BH18,NH17 186 C1
Broadstone, Fleet's Cnr
BH15,BH17 202 A4
Broadwater Ave BH14 203 B1
Broadwater Rd
Romsey SO51 52 C3
Southampton SO18 79 C2
Broadway BH6 207 A2
Broadway Ct BH12 204 A3
Broadway Gables BH14 203 C2
Broadway Gdns 6
BH21 163 B2
Broadway La
Bournemouth BH8 190 B2
Horndean PO8 111 B4
Broadway Mews BH14 202 C2
Broadway Pk 4 BH21 163 B2
Broadway The
Bournemouth BH10 189 B3
5 Southampton, Bitterne Pk
SO18 79 C1
Southampton, Portswood
SO17 79 A1
Southampton, Thornhill Pk
SO18 104 B4
Winchester SO23 11 A4
Brock Hill Forest Wlks*
SO43 144 C4
Brockenhurst Ave PO9 135 B3
Brockenhurst CE Prim Sch
SO42 172 C4
Brockenhurst Coll SO42 146 A1
Brockenhurst Rd BH9 190 A1
Brockenhurst Sta SO42 173 A4
Brockhampton La PO9 135 C1
Brockhampton Rd PO9 135 B1
Brockhills La BH25 195 B3
Brockhurst Ind Est
PO12 155 C1
Brockhurst Inf Sch
PO12 180 C4
Brockhurst Jun Sch
PO12 181 A4
Brockhurst Rd PO12 180 C4
Brockishill Rd SO40 99 A3
Brocklands PO9 135 B1
Brockley Rd BH10 189 C2
Brocks Cl SO45 125 B1
Brocks Pine BH24 139 C2
Brockwood Bottom SO32 36 C4
Brodrick Ave PO12 181 A2
Brog St BH21 162 B1
Brokenford Ave SO40 101 A4
Brokenford Bsns Ctr
SO40 100 C4
Brokenford La SO40 100 C4
Brombys The 7 BH15 202 B1
Bromley Ho BH12 204 A3
Bromley Rd SO18 79 C1
Brompton Rd PO4 182 C2
Bromyard Cres PO6 133 B1
Bronte Ave BH23 192 A1
Bronte Cl SO40 100 B3
Bronte Gdns PO15 129 B4
Bronte Way SO19 103 C3
Bronwen Ct SO19 104 A1
Brook Ave
Locks Heath SO31 128 B2
New Milton BH25 195 A2
Brook Ave N BH25 195 A2
Brook Cl
Bournemouth BH10 189 B2
Locks Heath SO31 128 C2
North Baddesley SO52 54 A2
Brook Cnr SO43 74 A1
Brook Cotts
King's Somborne SO51 6 B3
Westbourne PO10 137 A2
Brook Ct Romsey SO51 52 C3
13 Southampton SO15 102 B3
Brook Dr BH31 115 A2
Brook Farm Ave PO15 130 C1
Brook Gdns PO10 160 B4
Brook Hill SO41 198 C4
Brook La Botley SO30 105 C3
Bransgore BH23 193 A4
Corfe Mullen BH21 186 B3
Hambledon PO7 86 B3
Locks Heath SO31 128 C2
Woodgreen SP6 70 C4
Brook Mdw PO15 130 C1
Brook Rd
Bournemouth BH10 189 B2
Fair Oak SO50 57 B1
Lymington SO41 197 C1
Poole BH12 203 B3
Southampton SO18 104 A4
Wimborne Minst BH21 163 C2
Brook Road Depot
BH21 163 C2
Brook St SO32 83 B4
Brook Terr SP6 93 C4
Brook Valley SO16 78 A1
Brook Way
Christchurch BH23 208 B4
Romsey SO51 28 A1
Brook Wlk SO40 76 B1
Brookdale Cl
Broadstone BH18 187 A2
Waterlooville PO7 134 C4
Brookdale Farm BH18 187 A2
Brooke Cl SO23 2 A4
Brookers La PO13 155 A2
Brookfield Cl 1 PO9 135 C1
Brookfield Com Sch
SO31 128 C2
Brookfield Gdns SO31 128 C2

Brookfield Pl SO17 79 A1
Brookfield Rd
Fair Oak SO50 57 B1
Portsmouth PO1 182 C3
Brookfields SO51 50 B2
Brookland Cl SO41 197 B2
Brooklands
Bournemouth BH4 204 A2
Lyndhurst SO43 122 A2
Brooklands Rd
Bishop's Waltham SO32 83 B4
Havant PO9 135 A1
Brookley Rd SO42 146 A1
Brooklyn Cl SO21 31 B2
Brooklyn Ct BH25 194 C2
Brooklyn Dr PO7 134 C4
Brooklynn Cl SO32 83 C1
Brookman Ct SO18 104 A4
Brookmead Way PO9 159 C4
Brooks Cl BH24 141 A3
Brooks Sh Ctr The SO23 11 A4
Brookside
Fordingbridge SP6 69 A1
Gosport PO13 155 A3
Ibsley SP6 94 B1
Landford SP5 49 B2
Totton SO40 100 C3
Brookside Ave SO15 101 C4
Brookside Cl
Bransgore BH23 169 A1
Denmead PO7 110 C2
Brookside Ho SO18 79 C2
Brookside Park Homes
BH21 186 A2
Brookside Rd
Bransgore BH23 193 A4
Brockenhurst SO42 145 C1
Havant, Bedhampton PO9 135 B1
Havant, Langstone PO9 159 C4
Wimborne Minst BH21 163 C2
Brookside Way
Christchurch BH23 193 C1
Southampton SO18 79 C2
West End SO30 80 C2
Brookvale Ct 14 SO17 79 A1
Brookvale Rd SO17 79 A1
Brookwood Ave SO50 55 C2
Brookwood Ind Est SO50 56 A2
Brookwood Rd SO16 101 B4
Broom Cl
Portsmouth PO4 183 B2
Waterlooville PO7 135 A3
Broom Hill SO41 199 A4
Broom Hill Way SO50 56 A4
Broom Rd
Petersfield GU31 41 B1
Poole BH12 188 B1
Broom Sq PO4 183 B3
Broom Way PO13 179 C2
Broomfield Cres PO13 180 A4
Broomfield Ct BH22 165 C3
Broomfield Dr SP6 93 A3
Broomfield La SO41 197 C2
Broomhill SP5 49 B1
Broomhill Cl SO41 197 A1
Brooms Gr SO19 104 B2
Broomy Cl SO45 125 B2
Brougham La PO12 181 A3
Brougham Rd PO5 215 B2
Brougham St PO12 181 A3
Broughton Ave BH10 189 C2
Broughton Cl
Bournemouth BH10 189 C2
5 Southampton SO16 78 A1
Broughton Ct PO3 158 B2
Broughton Rd SO43 121 C3
Brow The PO7 134 B1
Browndown Rd PO13 180 B2
Brownen Rd BH9 205 A4
Brownfield Ho 22 GU31 40 C2
Brownhill Cl SO53 55 B4
Brownhill Ct SO16 77 C2
Brownhill Gdns SO53 55 B4
Brownhill Rd
Brockenhurst BH25 170 C2
Chandler's Ford SO53 55 B4
North Baddesley SO52 54 A2
Brownhill Way SO16 77 B2
Browning Ave
Bournemouth BH5 206 A2
Portchester PO6 132 C1
Southampton SO19 104 B3
Browning Cl
Eastleigh SO50 55 C2
Swanwick PO15 129 B4
Totton SO40 100 B4
Browning Dr SO22 10 B4
Browning Rd BH12 203 B3
Brownings Cl SO41 197 A2
Brownlow Ave SO19 104 A3
Brownlow Cl PO1 182 B4
Brownlow Ct 23 BH4 204 B2
Brownlow Gdns SO19 104 A3
Browns La Beaulieu SO41 199 B3
Damerham SP6 68 A3
Brownsea Ave BH21 186 B3
Brownsea Cl BH25 194 C2
Brownsea Ct BH14 214 A4
Brownsea Island (NT)*
BH15 213 B2
Brownsea Rd BH13 214 A2
Brownsea View Ave
BH14 203 B1
Brownsea View Cl BH14 203 B1
Brownwich La PO14 153 B3

Browsholme Cl ② SO50 ....56 A3
Broxburn Cl SO13 ....30 C1
Broxhead Rd 56 PO9 ....136 A3
Bruce Cl PO16 ....131 A2
Bruce Rd PO14 ....182 C1
Brudenell Ave BH13 ....214 B4
Brudenell Rd BH13 ....214 B3
Brue Cl SO53 ....55 A4
Brune La Gosport PO13 ....180 A4
Portsmouth PO13,SO15 ....155 A1
Brune Park Com Sch
PO12 ....180 C4
Brune Way BH22 ....165 B2
Brunei Ho SO14 ....79 A3
Brunel Cl Hedge End SO30 ....81 C1
Verwood BH31 ....115 B2
Brunel Rd
Portsmouth PO2 ....157 C2
Southampton SO15 ....101 B4
Totton SO40 ....76 C2
Brunel Way PO15 ....129 B2
Brunstead Pl BH12 ....204 A2
Brunstead Rd BH12 ....204 A2
Brunswick Cl SO40 ....57 A2
Brunswick Gdns PO9 ....135 B1
Brunswick Pl
Lymington SO41 ....197 C2
Southampton SO15 ....103 A3
Brunswick Rd SO50 ....57 A2
Brunswick Sq SO14 ....103 A2
Brunswick St PO5 ....215 B2
Brushers BH23 ....169 C2
Bruyn Ct SP6 ....70 A1
Bruyn Rd SP6 ....70 A1
Bryanston Rd SO19 ....103 C3
Bryanstone Rd BH3 ....204 C4
Bryant Rd BH12 ....204 A4
Bryher Br PO6 ....157 A4
Bryher Island PO6 ....157 A4
Brympton Cl SP6 ....69 B1
Bryony Cl
Broadstone BH18 ....186 C2
Locks Heath SO31 ....128 C1
Bryony Gdns SO50 ....81 B3
Bryony Way PO7 ....135 A4
Bryson Rd PO6 ....157 B4
Bub La SO23 ....207 C3
Bubb La SO32 ....81 B2
Buccaneers Cl BH23 ....207 C3
Buccleuch Rd BH13 ....204 A1
Buchages Cl BH23 ....209 A4
Buchan Ave PO15 ....129 B4
Buchan Ct SO45 ....125 B1
Buchanan Ave BH7 ....205 C3
Buchanan Rd SO16 ....77 C3
Buckby La PO13 ....158 B2
Bucketts Farm Cl SO32 ....84 A3
Buckingham Ct
② Christchurch BH23 ....209 A4
Fareham PO15 ....130 C2
Poole BH15 ....203 B4
② Southampton SO17 ....103 A4
Buckingham Gr PO1 ....182 B4
Buckingham Mans ⑤
BH1 ....205 A2
Buckingham Rd
Petersfield GU32 ....40 B2
Poole BH12 ....203 B4
Buckingham St PO1 ....182 C4
Buckingham Wlk BH25 ....194 C2
Buckland Cl
Eastleigh SO50 ....56 A3
Waterlooville PO7 ....111 B1
Buckland Ct SO41 ....197 C3
Buckland Dene SO41 ....197 B3
Buckland Gdns SO40 ....76 B1
Buckland Gr SO31 ....193 C1
Buckland Path PO2 ....182 B4
Buckland Terr PO12 ....182 C4
Buckland Rd BH12 ....203 B3
Buckland St PO2 ....182 C4
Buckland Terr SO41 ....197 C3
Bucklers Ct Havant PO9 ....135 B4
Lymington SO41 ....197 C2
Portsmouth PO2 ....157 B1
Bucklers Hard Maritime
Mus* SO42 ....176 B3
Bucklers Mews SO41 ....197 B2
Bucklers Rd PO12 ....181 B4
Bucklers Way BH8 ....190 B2
Bucklers St SO16 ....78 A1
Buckmore Ave GU32 ....40 B2
Bucks Head Hill SO32 ....61 B3
Bucksey Rd PO13 ....180 B4
Buckstone Cl SO41 ....196 C1
Buckthorn Cl
Broadstone BH17 ....186 C1
Totton SO40 ....100 A4
Budden's Cl PO17 ....108 C4
Buddens Rd PO17 ....108 A2
Buddle Hill SP6 ....94 B2
Budds La SO51 ....27 C1
Budds Lane Trad Est
SO51 ....27 C1
Bude Cl PO6 ....132 C1
Buffalo Mews BH15 ....202 A1
Bugdens La BH31 ....115 B4
Bugle St SO14 ....102 C2
Bulbarrow Wlk PO14 ....154 C4
Bulbeck Rd PO9 ....135 C1
Buldowne Wlk SO41 ....172 A2
Bull Dro SO23 ....11 A3
Bull Hill Boldre SO41 ....174 A1
Rake GU33 ....13 C2

Bull La Minstead SO43 ....98 B2
Poole BH15 ....202 B2
Waltham Chase SO32 ....83 B2
Bullar Rd SO18 ....103 C4
Bullar St SO14 ....103 A3
Bullfinch
Broadstone BH17 ....186 C1
Totton SO40 ....100 A4
Bullfinch Ct PO13 ....179 C2
Bullrush Cl SO45 ....125 A4
Bulls Copse La PO8 ....112 A3
Bulls Dro SP5 ....4 A3
Bunkers Hill PO7 ....110 B2
Bunns La PO7 ....109 C3
Bunny La
Michelmersh SO51 ....27 C3
Sherfield English SO51 ....25 A2
Bunstead La SO21 ....30 B4
Bunting Gdns PO8 ....111 C2
Bunting Rd BH22 ....165 A4
Bupa Hospl PO9 ....136 B3
Burbidge Gr PO4 ....183 A1
Burbidge Cl BH17 ....202 C4
Burbush Cl SO45 ....150 B2
Burcombe La BH24 ....117 C1
Burcombe Rd BH10 ....189 B3
Burcote Dr PO13 ....158 A2
Burdale Dr PO11 ....185 B2
Burdock Cl BH23 ....193 A1
Bure Cl BH23 ....208 A3
Bure Haven Dr BH23 ....208 A3
Bure Homage Gdns
BH23 ....208 A3
Bure Homage La BH23 ....208 A3
Bure La BH23 ....208 A3
Bure Pk BH23 ....208 A3
Bure Rd BH23 ....208 A3
Burford Cl BH23 ....191 C1
Burford Ct ⑬ BH1 ....205 A2
Burford La SO42 ....146 A1
Burgate Cl PO9 ....135 B2
Burgate Cross SP6 ....70 A2
Burgate Fields SP6 ....70 A2
Burgate Sch The SP6 ....70 A2
Burgesmede Ho ⑯ GU32 ....40 C2
Burgess Cl
Bournemouth BH11 ....188 C2
South Hayling PO11 ....185 B1
Burgess Ct SO16 ....79 A2
Burgess Fld BH21 ....114 A3
Burgess Gdns ⑭ SO16 ....78 C2
Burgess Rd SO16,SO17 ....79 A2
Burghclere Rd
Havant PO9 ....136 A3
Southampton SO19 ....126 C4
Burgoyne Rd
Portsmouth PO5 ....182 B1
Southampton SO19 ....104 C2
Burgundy Cl SO31 ....193 A3
Burgundy Terr ❶ PO2 ....157 C1
Buriton Cl PO11 ....132 B1
Buriton Ct SO19 ....104 C2
Buriton Ho SO22 ....1 B2
Buriton St PO1 ....215 B4
Burke Dr SO19 ....104 B3
Burleigh Rd
Bournemouth BH6 ....206 B3
Portsmouth PO1 ....182 C4
Burley Cl Ashurst SO40 ....100 A4
Barton on Sea BH25 ....209 B4
Chandler's Ford SO53 ....55 A2
⑰ Havant PO9 ....136 A3
Verwood BH31 ....114 C3
Burley Down SO53 ....55 A2
Burley Ho ❾ SO16 ....102 A4
Burley Lawn BH24 ....143 A2
Burley Prim Sch BH24 ....143 A2
Burley Rd
Bransgore BH23 ....193 A4
Brockenhurst SO42 ....172 B4
Burton BH23 ....192 B3
Poole BH12 ....203 B3
Winchester SO22 ....1 B1
Burling Terr ❶ BH12 ....204 A2
Burley Terr ❶ BH24 ....143 B1
Burlington Arc ❷ BH2 ....204 C2
Burlington Ct SO19 ....104 C1
Burlington Mans ❶
SO15 ....102 B4
Burlington Rd
Portsmouth PO2 ....157 C1
Southampton SO15 ....102 C3
Burma Ho SO18 ....79 C2
Burma Rd SO51 ....52 C3
Burmah Rd N SO45 ....151 B3
Burmah Rd S SO45 ....151 A3
Burmese Cl PO15 ....129 B4
Burn Cl BH31 ....115 A2
Burnaby Ct BH4 ....204 B1
Burnaby Rd
Bournemouth BH4 ....204 B1
Portsmouth PO1 ....182 A2
Burnage Ct ⑮ BH13 ....214 C4
Burnbake Rd BH31 ....115 A3
Burnbank Gdns SO40 ....100 C4
Burnbrae Rd BH22 ....165 B1
Burnett Ave BH23 ....206 C4
Burnett Cl Hythe SO45 ....126 A1
Southampton SO18 ....79 C1
Winchester SO22 ....1 B1
Burnett Rd
Christchurch BH23 ....206 C4
Gosport PO12 ....180 C3
Burnetts Fields SO50 ....81 B4
Burnetts Gdns SO50 ....81 B4
Burnetts La SO50,SO30 ....81 C4

Burney Rd 28 PO12 ....181 B2
Burngate Rd PO12 ....180 C2
Burngate Rd BH15 ....201 C1
Burnham Beeches SO53 ....55 A3
Burnham Chase SO18 ....104 B4
Burnham Dr BH8 ....205 B4
Burnham Rd
Burton BH23 ....192 B1
Cosham PO6 ....134 B1
Fordingbridge SP6 ....69 C2
Burnham Wood PO10 ....131 A2
Burnhams Wlk ⑰ PO12 ....181 B2
Burnleigh Gdns BH25 ....195 B2
Burns Cl SO50 ....56 C1
Burns Pl SO16 ....78 A1
Burns Rd
Bournemouth BH6 ....206 B4
Eastleigh SO50 ....55 C1
Southampton SO19 ....104 B3
Burnside
Christchurch BH23 ....208 B4
Gosport PO13 ....155 A3
Waterlooville PO7 ....112 A1
Burnt House La
Boldre SO41 ....174 A1
Bransgore BH23 ....169 A1
Stubbington PO14 ....154 B2
Burr Cl SO21 ....56 A4
Burrard Gr SO41 ....197 C1
Burrfields Rd PO3 ....158 A1
Burridge Rd SO31 ....106 A1
Burrill Ave PO6 ....158 A4
Burrows Cl PO9 ....136 A2
Burrows La BH31 ....114 C4
Bursledon Hts SO31 ....105 A1
Bursledon Jun & Inf Sch
SO31 ....128 A4
Bursledon Rd
Hedge End SO30 ....104 B3
Southampton SO19,SO31 ....104 B3
Waterlooville PO7 ....130 A4
Bursledon Sta SO31 ....128 A4
Bursledon Windmill*
SO31 ....106 A3
Burt's La Holt Heath BH21 ....138 A4
Verwood BH31 ....138 A4
Burtley Rd BH6 ....206 C2
Burton CE Prim Sch
BH23 ....192 B1
Burton Cl Burton BH23 ....192 B1
St Leonards BH24 ....139 C3
Burton Hall BH23 ....192 B2
Burton Hall Pl BH23 ....192 B2
Burton Rd
Christchurch BH23 ....207 C4
Poole BH13 ....204 A2
Southampton SO15 ....102 C3
Burtoncroft BH23 ....192 B2
Burts Hill BH21 ....163 B3
Burwood Gr PO11 ....185 A2
Bury Cl PO12 ....181 A2
Bury Cres PO12 ....181 A2
Bury Hall La PO12 ....181 A1
Bury Ho ⑩ PO12 ....181 A2
Bury La SO40 ....101 A3
Bury Rd Gosport PO12 ....181 A2
Marchwood SO40 ....101 C2
Bus Dro SO45 ....178 C4
Bush Ho PO5 ....215 B1
Bush St E PO5 ....215 B1
Bush St W PO5 ....215 B1
Bushell Rd BH15 ....202 B4
Bushey Cl BH11 ....189 A3
Bushey Rd BH8 ....190 B1
Bushmead Dr BH24 ....139 C3
Bushy Mead PO7 ....134 B2
Bussage Ct SO41 ....11 A4
Bussetts Way SO40 ....100 A1
Butcher St PO1 ....182 A3
Butcher's Cnr SO43 ....73 C2
Bute Dr BH23 ....209 A4
Butlers Cl SO51 ....4 C1
Butlers La BH24 ....117 B1
Butser Ancient Farm*
PO8 ....88 C3
Butser Ct PO8 ....88 B2
Butser Wlk
Fareham PO14 ....154 C4
Petersfield GU31 ....41 A2
Butt La SP5 ....22 A4
Butt's Cl SO19 ....104 B2
Butt's Cres SO19 ....104 B2
Butt's Rd SO19 ....104 B2
Butt's Sq SO19 ....104 B2
Buttercup Cl
Hedge End SO30 ....105 A3
Hythe SO45 ....126 A1
Buttercup Dr BH23 ....193 A1
Buttercup Way SO31 ....128 C2
Butterfield Rd SO16 ....78 C2
Butterfly Dr PO6 ....133 A1
Buttermere Cl SO16 ....77 C1
Buttermere Ho ⑰ PO6 ....133 A1
Buttery The BH23 ....207 B4
Button's La
❶ Poole BH15 ....202 B1
West Wellow SO51 ....50 C2
Butts Ash Gdns SO45 ....126 A1
Butts Ash La SO45 ....126 A1
Butts Bridge Hill SO45 ....126 A1
Butts Farm La SO32 ....83 B4
Butts Paddock SO42 ....145 C1
Butts Rd SO22 ....1 B1
Buttsash Ave SO45 ....150 A4

Buttsbridge Rd SO45 ....126 A1
By Pass Rd SO51 ....52 C3
By The Wood SO40 ....76 B1
Byams La SO40 ....102 A1
Bye Rd SO31 ....128 B4
Byerley Cl PO10 ....137 A3
Byerley Rd PO1 ....182 C3
Byeways SO45 ....125 C1
Byrd Cl PO7 ....134 C3
Byres The PO14 ....154 B2
Byron Ave SO22 ....10 B4
Byron Cl
Bishop's Waltham SO32 ....83 C4
Fareham PO16 ....131 A1
Byron Ct Ferndown BH22 ....165 B3
Southampton SO15 ....102 C3
Byron Ho ⑩ BH25 ....195 A1

C

C Ave SO45 ....150 C2
Cable St ② SO14 ....103 B3
Cabot Bsns Village
BH17 ....202 A4
Cabot Dr SO45 ....125 B2
Cabot La BH17 ....202 A4
Cabot Way BH25 ....194 C2
Cadgwith Pl PO6 ....157 A4
Cadhay Cl BH25 ....194 C2
Cadland Ct SO14 ....103 B2
Cadland Rd Fawley SO45 ....151 A3
Hythe SO45 ....150 B4
Cadlands Park Est SO45 ....150 B3
Cadnam Ct PO12 ....180 B2
Cadnam La SO40 ....74 C1
Cadnam Lawn PO9 ....135 B3
Cadnam Rd PO4 ....183 A2
Cadogan Rd BH24 ....141 A4
Cador Dr PO16 ....156 A3
Caen Rd PO14 ....154 C4
Caer Peris View PO16 ....132 B1
Caerleon Ave SO19 ....104 B3
Caerleon Dr SO19 ....104 B3
Caesar's Way BH18 ....186 C2
Cains Cl PO14 ....154 B2
Caird Ave PO15 ....195 B1
Cairns Cl BH23 ....206 C4
Cairo Terr PO2 ....182 B4
Caister Cl BH22 ....165 B3
Caistor Cl SO16 ....78 A2
Calabrese SO31 ....129 A4
Calbourne SO31 ....127 B4
Caldecote Wlk ⑦ PO5 ....215 B2
Calder Cl SO16 ....76 C1
Calder Rd BH17 ....202 C4
Calderwood Dr SO19 ....104 A2
Caledon Rd BH14 ....203 C2
Caledonia Dr SO45 ....125 B2
Caledonian Cl BH23 ....208 A4
California Cl SO40 ....76 C4
Calkin Cl BH23 ....192 A1
Calluna Rd BH12 ....203 A4
Calmore Cl BH8 ....190 B2
Calmore Cres SO40 ....76 A1
Calmore Dr SO40 ....76 A1
Calmore Gdns SO40 ....100 B4
Calmore Inf Sch SO40 ....76 C1
Calmore Jun Sch SO40 ....100 B4
Calmore Rd SO40 ....100 B4
Calpe Ave SO43 ....121 C3
Calshot Activities Ctr
SO45 ....152 A1
Calshot Castle* SO45 ....152 A1
Calshot Cl SO45 ....152 A1
Calshot Ct SO14 ....103 B1
Calshot Dr SO53 ....55 B2
Calshot Rd Fawley SO45 ....151 A2
Havant PO9 ....135 A4
Calshot Way ⑬ SO16 ....155 A1
Calvin Rd BH9 ....204 C4
Camargue Cl SO31 ....129 A4
Camber Pl ⑰ PO1 ....182 A2
Cambria Dr SO45 ....125 B2
Cambrian Cl SO31 ....129 A4
Cambrian Terr PO5 ....215 C1
Cambrian Wlk PO14 ....154 C4
Cambridge Cl ⑰ SO14 ....103 A4
Cambridge Dr SO53 ....55 B1
Cambridge Gdns BH23 ....191 C1
Cambridge Gn
Chandler's Ford SO53 ....55 B1
Titchfield PO14 ....129 C4
Cambridge Junc PO1 ....182 A2
Cambridge Rd
Bournemouth BH2 ....204 B2
Gosport PO12 ....180 C3
Lee-on-the-Solent PO13 ....179 C1
Portsmouth PO1 ....182 A2
Stubbington PO14 ....154 B2
Camdeon La SO43 ....98 A4
Camden St SO15 ....102 C3
Camden Terr ❷ PO5 ....215 B2
Cameron Rd BH23 ....169 A1

Camelia Cl continued
North Baddesley SO52 ....54 A3
Camelia Gdns SO18 ....80 A1
Camelia Gr SO50 ....57 C1
Camellia Cl BH21 ....114 C1
Camellia Ct ② SO18 ....79 C1
Camellia Gdns BH25 ....195 A1
Camelot Cres PO16 ....132 A1
Cameron Cl PO13 ....155 B2
Cameron Ct SO16 ....77 C3
Cameron Rd BH23 ....207 B4
Camley Cl SO19 ....103 C1
Cammel Rd BH22 ....165 B1
Camp Rd PO13 ....155 B2
Campbell Cres PO7 ....134 B3
Campbell Mews SO18 ....104 B4
Campbell Rd
Bournemouth BH1 ....205 C3
Burton BH23 ....192 B2
Eastleigh SO50 ....56 A1
Portsmouth PO5 ....215 D1
Southampton SO19 ....104 B3
Campbell Way SO50 ....57 B1
Campion Cl Fair Oak SO50 ....81 B3
Locks Heath SO31 ....128 C1
Waterlooville PO7 ....135 A3
Campion Dr SO51 ....28 B1
Campion Gr BH23 ....207 C3
Campion Rd SO19 ....104 B3
Campion Way
Kings Worthy SO23 ....2 B4
Lymington SO41 ....197 C3
Cams Bay Cl PO16 ....131 C1
Cams Hill Hambledon PO7 ....86 A1
Portchester PO16 ....131 C1
Cams Hill Sch PO16 ....155 C4
Canada Cnr GU31 ....66 C3
Canada Cl PO12 ....181 B4
Canada Pl ⑥ SO16 ....78 C2
Canada Rd
Southampton SO19 ....103 C1
West Wellow SO51 ....50 B1
Canal Cl SO51 ....28 A1
Canal Wlk
Portsmouth PO1 ....215 C3
Romsey SO51 ....52 C4
Southampton SO14 ....103 A2
Canberra Cl PO12 ....180 C2
Canberra Ct PO12 ....180 C2
Canberra Ho PO1 ....215 B3
Canberra Rd
Christchurch BH23 ....191 C1
Southampton SO16 ....77 A2
Thorney Island PO10 ....161 A2
Canberra Twrs SO19 ....126 C4
Candlemas Pl ⑱ SO17 ....103 A4
Candover Ct SO19 ....127 A4
Candy La SO19 ....104 B2
Candys Cl BH21 ....162 C1
Candys La BH21 ....162 C1
Canford Ave BH11 ....189 A1
Canford Bottom BH21 ....164 B3
Canford Bottom Rdbt
BH21 ....164 B3
Canford Cl
Sheffield SO32 ....107 C4
Southampton SO16 ....77 B1
Canford Cliffs Ave
BH14 ....203 C1
Canford Cliffs Rd BH13 ....203 C1
Canford Cres BH13 ....214 C4
Canford Ct BH13 ....214 C3
Canford Gdns BH11 ....189 A1
Canford Heath Fst & Mid
Schs BH17 ....202 B4
Canford Heath Nature
Reserve* BH11 ....188 A2
Canford Heath Rd BH17 ....187 C1
Canford Magna BH21 ....164 A1
Canford Pl ② BH13 ....214 C4
Canford Rd
Bournemouth BH11 ....189 A1
Poole BH15 ....202 B2
Canford Sch BH21 ....164 A3
Canford View Dr BH21 ....164 A3
Canford Way BH12 ....188 B1
Canhouse La GU33 ....21 C2
Cannock Wlk ⑩ PO14 ....154 C4
Cannon Cl BH18 ....187 A1
Cannon Hill Gdns BH21 ....164 A4
Cannon Hill Rd BH21 ....164 A4
Cannon Ho SO41 ....197 C2
Cannon St
Lymington SO41 ....197 C2
Southampton SO15 ....102 B4
Cannon's Barn Cl PO16 ....132 B1
Canoe Cl SO31 ....128 C1
Canon Cl ⑤ SO50 ....57 B1
Canon St SO23 ....10 C4
Canons View SO41 ....211 B3
Canons La Sec Sch 79 A2
Canterbury Ave SO19 ....104 B2
Canterbury Cl
Lee-on-the-Solent PO13 ....180 A2
Petersfield GU32 ....138 C1
Canterbury Dr SO45 ....125 B2
Canterbury Rd
Portsmouth PO4 ....182 C2
Stubbington PO14 ....154 B2
Canterton La SO43 ....98 A4
Canton St SO15 ....102 C3
Cantle Cl SO23 ....169 A1
Canute Dr BH23 ....103 A2
Canute Ho 28 SO14 ....103 A2
Canute Rd
Southampton SO14 ....103 A2
⑰ Winchester SO23 ....11 A3
Canvey Ct SO16 ....77 C1

Capel Ley PO7 134 C2
Capella Ct BH2 204 C1
Capella Gdns SO45 125 B2
Capers End La SO32 82 C1
Capesthorne BH23 208 A3
Capital Ho 11 SO22 10 C4
Capon Cl SO18 79 C2
Capstan Gdns SO31 129 B2
Capstans The BH14 214 A4
Capstone Pl BH8 205 B3
Capstone Rd BH8 205 A3
Captain's Pl SO14 103 A2
Captain's Row SO41 197 C2
Captains Cl PO12 180 C4
Captains Row 15 PO1 182 A2
Caradon Pl BH31 114 B4
Carberry Dr PO16 156 B4
Carbery Ave BH6 206 B3
Carbery Ct PO9 135 B4
Carbery Gdns BH6 206 C3
Carbery La 3 BH6 206 B2
Carbery Row 2 BH6 206 B2
Carbis Cl PO6 157 A4
Cardew Rd GU33 21 A2
Cardiff Rd PO2 157 B1
Cardigan Rd
Bournemouth BH9 204 C4
Poole BH12 203 C2
Cardinal Dr PO7 112 A1
Cardinal Way SO31 129 A1
Cardington Ct SO16 77 C2
Carey Rd
Bournemouth BH9 189 C2
Southampton SO19 104 B3
Careys Cotts SO42 145 C1
Careys Rd BH8 190 B2
Carina Ct BH13 214 B2
Carisbrook Cres BH15 201 B2
Carisbrooke Netley SO31 127 B4
Poole BH13 214 C4
Carisbrooke Ave PO14 179 A3
Carisbrooke Cl 2 PO9 136 A1
Carisbrooke Cres SO53 55 C3
Carisbrooke Ct
4 Christchurch BH23 209 A4
New Milton BH25 194 C2
Romsey SO51 28 A1
Carisbrooke Dr SO19 103 C3
Carisbrooke Rd
Gosport PO13 155 B1
Portsmouth PO4 183 A2
Carisbrooke Way BH23 193 C1
Carless Cl PO13 180 B4
Carlinford 29 BH5 205 C2
Carlisle Ct 2 SO16 102 A4
Carlisle Rd
Portsmouth PO1 215 C3
Southampton SO16 102 A4
Carlton Ave BH25 209 C4
Carlton Commerce Ctr The SO14 103 A4
Carlton Cres SO15 102 C3
Carlton Ct 5 SO15 102 C4
Carlton Gr BH12 203 B3
Carlton Ho SO41 197 C2
Carlton Pl SO15 102 C3
Carlton Rd
Bournemouth BH1 205 B2
Gosport PO12 181 B3
Portchester PO16 132 C1
Southampton SO15 102 C4
Carlton Way PO12 181 B3
Carlyle Rd
Bournemouth BH6 206 B3
Gosport PO12 181 A3
Carlyn Dr SO53 55 B4
Carmans La SO21 31 B4
Carmarthen Ave PO6 158 A4
Carmel Cl BH15 201 B1
Carmine Ct PO13 180 B3
Carnarvon Rd
4 Bournemouth BH1 205 C2
Gosport PO12 181 A2
Portsmouth PO2 182 C4
Carnation Rd SO16 79 B2
Carne Cl SO53 55 B4
Carne Pl PO6 157 A4
Carnegie Cl BH14 203 B3
Caroline Ave BH23 207 C3
Caroline Gdns PO15 130 B1
Caroline Rd BH11 189 A2
Carolyn Cl SO19 103 C1
Carpathia Cl SO18 80 A1
Carpenter Cl Hythe SO45 126 A2
Lymington SO41 197 B3
10 Portsmouth PO4 183 A2
Carradale BH23 208 A4
Carran Wlk PO14 154 C4
Carraway PO15 129 B4
Carrbridge Cl BH3 204 B4
Carrbridge Gdns BH3 204 B4
Carrbridge Rd BH3 204 B4
Carrick Way BH25 195 B1
Carrington Cl SO41 211 C3
Carrington Ho 33 SO17 79 A1
Carrington La SO41 211 C2
Carrol Cl SO50 57 B1
Carroll Ave BH22 165 C3
Carroll Cl BH12 204 A3
Carronade Wlk PO3 157 C3
Carronades The 21 SO14 103 A3
Carshalton Ave PO6 158 A4
Carsworth Way BH17 188 A1
Carter Com Sch BH15 201 C1
Carter Ho Gosport PO13 155 A3
7 Portsmouth PO1 182 A3
Carter's Cl SP6 47 B2
Carter's Clay Rd SO51 26 A3
Carter's Copse Nature Trail* PO13 180 B3
Carter's La 9 BH15 202 B1
Carters Ave BH15 201 B2
Carthage Cl SO53 55 C4
Cartref Cl BH31 114 C3
Cartwright Cl BH10 189 B2
Cartwright Dr PO14, PO15 129 C1
Carvers Ind Est BH24 141 A4
Carvers La BH24 141 A4
Carysfort Rd BH1 205 B2
Cascades App PO1 215 B4
Cascades Sh Ctr PO1 215 B4
Cases Bakery Cl PO17 108 A2
Cashmoor Cl BH12 203 C4
Cask St PO1 215 B4
Caslake Cl BH25 194 C1
Caspar John Cl PO14 179 A3
Caspian Cl SO31 129 A4
Cassel Ave BH13 204 A1
Casselles Ct 33 BH25 195 A1
Casterbridge Rd BH22 165 B2
Castle Ave
Christchurch BH23 208 C4
Havant PO9 136 A1
Winchester SO23 10 C4
Castle Cl
Milford on Sea SO41 211 C2
Portsmouth PO5 215 B1
Castle Court Sch BH21 186 A4
Castle Ct
3 Christchurch BH23 209 A4
4 Southampton, Bitterne Pk SO18 79 C1
Southampton, Millbrook SO15 102 A3
Castle Farm La PO17 108 A1
Castle Gate Cl BH8 190 B1
Castle Gdns GU32 40 C2
Castle Gr PO16 156 B4
Castle Hill Poole BH14 203 A2
Winchester SO22 10 C4
Castle Hill La BH24 142 C2
Castle Hts 3 SO18 79 C1
Castle La
Chandler's Ford SO53 55 A2
Fawley SO45 178 C4
North Baddesley SO53,SO52 54 B2
6 Southampton SO14 102 C2
Castle La E BH7 206 B4
Castle La W BH8, BH9 190 B1
Castle Marina PO13 179 C1
Castle Mdw SP5 46 C4
Castle Mews
Southampton SO14 102 C2
St Leonards BH24 140 B3
Castle Par BH7 206 B4
Castle Prim Sch PO16 156 B4
Castle Rd
Bournemouth BH9 190 A1
Netley SO31 127 A3
Portsmouth PO5 215 B1
Rowland's Castle PO9 113 A1
Southampton SO18 79 C1
Southwick PO17 132 C3
Castle Sq 8 SO14 102 C2
Castle St
Christchurch BH23 207 B3
Poole BH15 202 B1
Portchester PO16 156 B4
Southampton SO14 103 A4
Titchfield PO14 154 A4
Castle Trad Est PO16 156 C4
Castle View PO12 181 A4
Castle View Rd PO16 156 C3
Castle Way SO14 102 C2
Castle Woods SP5 47 B3
Castledene Cres BH14 203 A1
Castlemain Ave BH6 206 B3
Castleman Ct BH22 138 B2
Castleman Way BH24 141 A3
Castlemans La PO11 160 A1
Castleshaw Cl SO16 101 C4
Castleton Ave BH10 189 B3
Castleton Ct PO5 215 A1
Castleway PO9 136 A1
Castlewood BH24 140 B3
Catalina Cl BH23 208 A3
Catalina Dr BH15 202 C1
Catamaran Cl SO31 128 C1
Cateran Cl SO16 101 C4
Cathay Gdns SO45 125 B2
Cathedral View 5 SO23 11 A3
Catherine Cl SO30 80 C1
Catherine Cres SP5 46 B4
Catherine Gdns SO30 80 C1
Catherine Wheel Gdns BH23 191 C2
Catherington CE Inf Sch PO8 88 A1
Catherington Hill PO8 88 A2
Catherington La
Horndean PO8 112 A4
Waterlooville PO8 112 A4
Catherington Way PO9 135 C2
Catisfield Ho 3 PO1 215 C4
Catisfield La PO15 130 A1
Catisfield Rd
Fareham PO15 130 B1
Portsmouth PO4 183 A2
Catmint Cl SO53 54 C4
Caton Cl BH12 204 A4
Cattistock Rd BH8 190 C1
Catways SO21 30 A4
Causeway SO51 52 B3
Causeway Cres SO40 101 A4
Causeway Ct 6 SO18 103 C4
Causeway Farm PO8 112 A3
Causeway The
Petersfield GU31 40 C1
Portchester PO16 131 C1
Cavalier Cl SO45 125 B2
Cavalier Ct PO6 158 B4
Cavan Cres BH17 187 A1
Cavanna Cl PO13 155 A2
Cavell Dr PO6 133 C1
Cavendish Cl
Romsey SO51 28 A1
Waterlooville PO7 134 C4
Cavendish Corner Cvn Pk 4 BH24 141 A4
Cavendish Dr PO7 134 C4
Cavendish Gr
Southampton SO17 102 C4
Winchester SO23 2 A2
Cavendish Hall BH1 205 A3
Cavendish Mews 2 SO15 102 C4
Cavendish Pl BH1 205 A3
Cavendish Rd
Bournemouth BH1 205 A3
Portsmouth PO5 215 C1
Caversham Cl
Hamworthy BH15 201 C2
Southampton SO19 104 A2
West End SO30 80 B1
Cawdor Rd BH3 204 B4
Cawte Rd SO15 102 B3
Cawte's Pl PO16 131 B1
Caxton Ave SO19 104 A3
Caxton Cl BH23 208 A4
Cecil Ave Ashurst SO40 100 B1
Bournemouth BH8 205 B4
Southampton SO16 78 A1
Cecil Cl BH21 186 C3
Cecil Ct BH8 205 A4
Cecil Gr PO5 215 A1
Cecil Hill BH8 205 A4
Cecil Pl PO5 215 A1
Cecil Rd
Bournemouth BH5 205 C2
Poole BH12 203 B3
Southampton SO19 103 C2
Cecil Villas SO17 79 B1
Cedar Ave
Bournemouth BH10 189 B3
Christchurch BH23 206 B4
Southampton SO15 102 B4
St Leonards BH24 139 C2
Cedar Cl Bursledon SO31 127 C4
Gosport PO12 156 A1
Hedge End SO30 105 B4
Kings Worthy SO23 2 A4
Upton BH16 201 A4
Waterlooville PO7 134 C3
Cedar Cres
North Baddesley SO52 53 C3
Waterlooville PO8 112 B3
Cedar Ct
Bournemouth BH4 204 A1
12 Fareham PO16 131 B1
Portsmouth PO5 215 C1
Cedar Dr Hordle SO41 211 B4
Wimborne Minst BH21 164 A3
Cedar Gdns
Barton on Sea BH25 194 C1
Havant PO9 136 A1
Southampton SO14 103 A4
Cedar Gr PO3 183 A4
Cedar Lawn SO51 28 B1
Cedar Manor BH4 204 B2
Cedar Pl BH23 169 A1
Cedar Rd Eastleigh SO50 55 C1
Hythe SO45 150 A4
Southampton SO14 103 A4
Cedar Specl Sch The SO16 77 C2
Cedar St SO32 83 B4
Cedar Trad Pk BH21 164 C3
Cedar Way
Fareham PO14 154 C4
Ferndown BH22 165 B4
Cedar Wlk 37 SO22 10 C4
Cedar Wood Cl
Fair Oak SO50 57 C1
Totton SO40 100 B4
Cedarmount SO43 121 C2
Cedars The
Bournemouth BH4 204 B2
Fareham PO16 130 C2
Cedarwood SO23 2 B4
Cedarwood Lodge 6 PO16 131 A1
Ceder Ho SO14 103 A2
Cedric Cl SO45 177 C4
Celandine Ave
Locks Heath SO31 128 C1
Waterlooville PO8 112 A2
Celandine Cl
Chandler's Ford SO53 54 C3
Christchurch BH23 208 A4
Celia Cl PO7 135 A4
Cellars Farm Rd BH6 207 A2
Cement Terr 7 SO14 102 C2
Cemetery Ave BH15 202 C3
Cemetery Junc BH2 204 C3
Cemetery La
Denmead PO7 110 C3
Westbourne PO10 137 B2
Cemetery Rd
Southampton SO15 102 C4
Wimborne Minst BH21 163 A3
Centaur St PO2 182 B4
Centaury Gdns SO50 81 B4
Centenary Cl SO41 172 B1
Centenary Ho 6 BH23 207 A4
Centenary Way BH1, 205 C3
Central Ave
Corfe Mullen BH21 186 B4
Poole BH12 203 C3
Central Bridge SO14 103 A2
Central Dr BH2 204 C3
Central Prec The SO53 55 B3
Central Rd Cosham PO6 158 B4
Portchester PO16 156 A4
Southampton SO14 103 A1
Central St PO1 215 C4
Central Station Bridge SO15 102 C3
Central Way N SO45 151 C1
Centre La SO41 196 C1
Centre Pl BH24 140 C4
Centre Way SO31 129 A2
Centurian Ind Pk SO18 103 B4
Centurion Gate PO4 183 B2
Cerdic Mews SO31 128 A2
Cerne Abbas BH13 204 A1
Cerne Cl
Bournemouth BH9 190 A2
North Baddesley SO52 53 C2
West End SO18 80 A1
Cessac Ho PO12 181 B1
CH La SO32 83 C2
Chadderton Gdns PO1 182 A2
Chaddesley Glen BH13 214 C3
Chaddesley Pines BH13 214 C3
Chaddesley Wood Rd BH13 214 C3
Chadswell Mdw PO9 135 B1
Chadwell Ave SO19 104 A2
Chadwick Rd SO50 55 C1
Chafen Rd SO18 103 B4
Chaffey Cl BH24 141 B4
Chaffinch Cl
Broadstone BH17 186 C1
New Milton BH25 194 C1
Totton SO40 100 B4
Chaffinch Gn PO8 111 C2
Chaffinch Way
Lee-on-the-Solent PO13 179 C2
Portchester PO16 155 C4
Chalbury Cl BH17 188 A1
Chalbury Ct
6 Christchurch BH23 207 C3
11 Poole BH14 203 A2
Chaldecott Gdns BH10 189 B2
Chaldon Rd BH17 187 C1
Chale Cl PO13 155 B1
Chalewood Rd SO45 177 C4
Chalfont Ave BH23 191 B2
Chalfont Ct 7 SO16 78 A1
Chalice Cl BH14 203 A2
Chalice Ct SO30 105 A3
Chalk Cl SP5 47 B4
Chalk Hill Soberton SO32 85 B3
West End SO18 80 B1
Chalk Hill Rd PO8 112 B4
Chalk La PO17 131 A4
Chalk Pit Cotts PO17 131 A4
Chalk Ridge Horndean PO8 88 B2
Winchester SO23 11 B4
Chalkpit Rd PO6 133 A1
Chalkridge Rd PO6 134 A1
Challenge Ent Ctr The PO3 158 A2
Challenger Dr PO12 181 B4
Challenger Way SO45 125 B1
Challis Ct 18 SO14 103 A2
Chalmers Way SO31 127 C2
Chaloner Cres SO45 126 A1
Chalton Cres PO9 135 B2
Chalton Ho PO1 215 B4
Chalton La PO8 88 B3
Chalvington Ct SO53 55 B3
Chalvington Rd SO53 55 B2
Chalwyn Ind Est BH12 203 A4
Chalybeate Cl SO16 78 A1
Chalybeate Hospl SO16 78 A1
Chamberlain Gr PO14 155 A4
Chamberlain Hall SO16 79 A2
Chamberlain Rd SO17 79 A2
Chamberlayne Ct SO52 54 A2
Chamberlayne Ho 10 SO31 127 A3
Chamberlayne Park Sch
Southampton SO19 104 A1
Southampton SO19 127 A4
Chamberlayne Rd
Bursledon SO31 127 C4
Eastleigh SO50 56 A1
Netley SO31 127 A3
Chambers Ave SO51 53 A4
Chambers Cl SO16 77 B3
Champion Cl SO41 211 C2
Chancel Rd SO31 129 A2
Chancellors La SO32 81 C2
Chanctonbury Ho PO5 215 B1
Chander Cl BH22 165 C2
Chandler's Ford Ind Est SO53 55 A3
Chandler's Ford Inf Sch SO53 55 B3
Chandler's Ford Inf Sch (Annexe) SO53 55 B4
Chandlers Cl
Bournemouth BH7 206 A4
South Hayling PO11 185 B1
Chandlers Way SO31 129 A3
Chandos Ave BH12 204 A4
Chandos Ho 14 SO14 103 A2
Chandos St 26 SO14 103 A2
Channel Ct
Barton on Sea BH25 209 C4
Bournemouth BH6 206 B2
Channel Mouth Rd SO45 151 C1
Channel Way SO14 103 B2
Channels Farm Rd SO16 79 B3
Chant Cl BH23 207 B4
Chantrell Wlk PO15 130 B2
Chantry Cl BH23 193 C1
Chantry Mead SO22 1 C1
Chantry Rd
Gosport PO12 181 A4
Horndean PO8 112 A4
Southampton SO14 103 A2
Chantry The
Bournemouth BH1 205 A2
Locks Heath PO14 129 B2
Chapel Cl Braishfield SO51 28 B3
Corfe Mullen BH21 186 B3
West End SO30 80 B1
Chapel Cres SO19 104 A2
Chapel Ct 7 PO1 182 B4
Chapel Dro Fair Oak SO50 81 B4
Hedge End SO30 105 A3
Chapel Gate BH23 190 B4
Chapel La
Blackfield SO45 177 C4
Bransgore BH23 193 A4
Burley BH24 143 A2
Chilcomb SO21, SO23 12 A4
Corfe Mullen BH21 186 B3
Curdridge SO32 106 C4
East Boldre SO42 175 B3
Fawley SO45 151 A1
Hurn BH23 190 B4
Lockerley SO51 26 A3
Lyndhurst SO43 121 C2
Michelmersh SO51 27 B4
Nomansland SP5 73 B4
Otterbourne SO21 31 A1
Poole BH15 202 B1
Redlynch SP5 47 C3
Sway SO41 172 B1
Totton SO40 100 C3
13 Waterlooville PO7 134 C4
Wimborne Minst BH21 163 A3
Chapel Rd Droxford SO32 61 B2
Locks Heath SO31 128 C3
Poole BH14 203 A2
Soberton SO32 85 A1
Southampton SO14 103 A2
Swanmore SO32 84 A3
West End SO30 80 C1
Chapel Rise BH24 140 B1
Chapel Sq PO12 180 C4
Chapel St East Meon GU32 38 B1
Gosport PO12 181 A4
Petersfield GU32 40 C2
3 Portsmouth PO2 215 A1
Southampton SO14 103 A2
Chapelside PO14 154 A4
Chaplains Ave PO8 111 B2
Chaplains Cl PO8 111 B2
Charborough Rd BH18 187 A2
Charden Ct SO18 104 A4
Charden Rd
Bishopstoke SO50 57 A1
Gosport PO13 180 B4
Charfield Cl
Fareham PO14 154 B4
Winchester SO22 10 C3
Charielote Ho SO15 102 B3
Charing Cl BH24 141 A3
Chark La PO13 179 C2
Charlcot Lawn PO9 135 B3
Charlecote Dr SO53 55 A4
Charlecote Mews 18 SO22 10 C4
Charlemont Dr 15 PO16 131 B1
Charles Cl
Waterlooville PO7 134 B3
Winchester SO23 2 A1
Charles Cres BH25 195 A3
Charles Dickens Birthplace Mus* PO1 182 B4
Charles Dickens Inf Sch PO1 182 B4
Charles Dickens Jun Sch PO1 182 B4
Charles Dickens St PO1 215 B3
Charles Gdns BH10 189 B1
Charles Keightley Ct BH21 163 B2
Charles Knott Gdns SO15 102 C4
Charles Ley Ct SO45 151 A2
Charles Rd
Christchurch BH23 207 C4
Poole BH15 202 B2
Charles St
Petersfield GU32 40 C2
Portsmouth PO1 215 C4
Southampton SO14 103 A2
Charles Watts Way SO30 105 A4
Charles Wyatt Ho 28 SO14 103 A4
Charles's La BH24 141 C2
Charlesbury Ave PO12 180 C2
Charleston Cl PO11 184 C2
Charleston Rd SO45 150 B4
Charlesworth Dr PO7 111 B1
Charlesworth Gdns PO7 111 B1

Charliejoy Gdns 18
SO14 ....103 B3
Charlott Ct P05 ....215 B1
Charlotte Cl
Christchurch BH23 ....208 A3
8 New Milton BH25 ......195 A1
Poole BH12 ....204 B4
Charlotte Ct
Chandler's Ford SO53 ....55 C4
Southampton SO19 ....103 A1
Charlotte Mews P012 ...181 A1
Charlotte Pl SO14 ....103 A3
Charlotte St P01 ....215 B4
Charlton Cl
Bournemouth BH9 ....190 B2
Hordle SO41 ....195 C2
Charlton Rd SO15 ....102 B4
Charltons The BH2 ....204 C3
Charminster 8 P05 ....182 B1
Charminster Ave BH9 ....190 A1
Charminster Cl
8 Bournemouth BH8 ....190 A1
Waterlooville P07 ....134 C4
Charminster Pl BH8 ....190 B1
Charminster Rd BH8 ......205 A4
Charmouth Gr BH14 ....203 A2
Charmouth Terr 8 SO16 ..78 A1
Charnus Rd SO40 ....76 A1
Charnwen Cres SO30 ....80 B1
Charnock Cl SO41 ....195 C2
Charnwood P013 ....155 B1
Charnwood Ave 8 BH9 ...190 A2
Charnwood Cl
Chandler's Ford SO53 ....30 B1
Totton SO40 ....76 B1
West Moors BH22 ....138 C1
Charnwood Cres SO53 ......30 B1
Charnwood Dr SP6 ....69 C2
Charnwood Gdns SO30 ......30 B1
Charnwood Way SO45 ....177 C4
Chartcombe BH13 ....214 C4
Charter Ho 8 P015 ....215 A2
Charter Rd BH11 ....188 B3
Chartergrove Ho 18
GU31 ....40 C2
Charterhouse Way SO30 ...81 B1
Chartwell Cl
Eastleigh SO50 ....56 A3
Titchfield P014 ....129 B1
Chartwell Dr P09 ....136 B2
Chase Cl GU33 ....21 A2
Chase Farm Cl SO32 ....83 C2
Chase Gr SO32 ....83 C2
Chase Rd GU33 ....21 A2
Chase The Gosport P012 ..180 C2
Locks Heath P014 ....129 B1
St Leonards BH24 ....140 B3
Verwood BH31 ....115 B3
Chaseside BH7 ....206 A4
Chasewater Ave P03 ....183 A4
Chatburn Ave P08 ....111 C2
Chatfield Ho 10 P01 ......215 C4
Chatfield Rd P013 ....155 B2
Chatham Cl P012 ....181 B4
Chatham Dr P01 ....182 A2
Chatham Rd SO22 ....10 B3
Chatsworth Ave P06 ....158 A3
Chatsworth Cl P015 ....130 B1
Chatsworth Ct P05 ....215 C1
Chatsworth Rd
Bournemouth BH8 ....205 B3
Eastleigh SO50 ....56 A3
Poole BH14 ....203 A3
Southampton SO19 ....104 A3
Chatsworth Way BH25 ....194 C2
Chaucer Ave P06 ....132 C1
Chaucer Cl
Fareham P016 ....130 C1
Waterlooville P07 ....111 C1
Wimborne Minst BH21 .....163 B3
Chaucer Dr SO41 ....211 B3
Chaucer Ind Est SO23 ....2 B1
Chaucer Rd Poole BH13 ..214 C4
Southampton SO19 ....104 B3
Chaucombe Pl BH25 ....194 C1
Chaundler Rd SO23 ....2 A1
Chaveney Cl 8 SO46 ....125 C1
Chawton Cl
Southampton SO18 ....104 B4
Winchester SO22 ....1 B2
Cheam Rd BH18 ....186 C2
Cheam Way SO40 ....76 B1
Cheater's La SP6 ....92 B4
Cheddar Cl SO19 ....103 C2
Cheddington Rd BH9 ......190 A2
Chedington Cl BH17 ....187 C1
Chedworth Cres P06 ....133 A1
Cheeryble Ho 15 P01 .....182 B4
Cheesecombe Farm La
GU33 ....19 C3
Chellowdene SO53 ....55 B3
Chelmsford Rd
Portsmouth P02 ....157 C1
Upton BH16 ....201 A4
Chelsea Rd P05 ....240 C3
Cheltenham Cres P013 ....179 C2
Cheltenham Ct 20 SO17 ....79 A1
Cheltenham Gdns SO30 ....81 B2
Cheltenham Rd
Cosham P06 ....157 B4
Poole BH12 ....203 B3
Chelveston Cres SO16 ......78 A2
Chelwood Gate SO16 ....78 C3
Chene Rd BH21 ....163 B2
Cheney's Farm SO51 ....75 C3

Cheping Gdns SO30 ....106 A3
Chepstow Cl
North Baddesley SO52 ....55 A3
Totton SO40 ....100 B4
Chepstow Ct 8 P07 ....112 A1
Chequers Cl SO41 ....197 B2
Chequers Ho 20 P016 .....131 A1
Chequers Quay 8 P010 ..161 A4
Cherbourg Prim Sch
SO50 ....56 A1
Cherbourg Rd SO50 ....56 A1
Cherford Rd BH11 ....189 A1
Cherita Ct BH15 ....202 C3
Cheriton Ave
Bournemouth BH7 ....206 B4
Southampton SO18 ....104 B4
Cheriton Cl Havant P09 ...135 B2
Horndean P08 ....112 A4
Winchester SO22 ....1 B1
Cheriton Rd
Eastleigh SO50 ....55 C1
Gosport P012 ....180 C2
Winchester SO22 ....10 C4
Cheriton Way BH21 ....163 B3
Cherque La P013 ....180 A4
Cherrett Cl BH11 ....188 C2
Cherry Dr BH24 ....189 C1
Cherry Blossom Ct 8
P01 ....182 B4
Cherry Cl
Lee-on-the-Solent P013 ....180 A3
Poole BH14 ....203 A3
Cherry Ct Poole BH14 .....203 A3
8 Southampton SO17 ....103 A4
Cherry Dr SO50 ....81 B3
Cherry Gr BH22 ....188 A3
Cherry Gdns SO32 ....83 B4
Cherry Gr BH22 ....165 B3
Cherry Hill Gdns BH16 ...201 A3
Cherry Hill Gr BH16 ....201 A3
Cherry Tree Ave
Fareham P014 ....154 B4
Waterlooville P08 ....112 A1
Cherry Tree Cl
Hordle SO41 ....211 B4
St Leonards BH24 ....139 B2
Cherry Tree Ct 31 BH25 ..195 A1
Cherry Tree Dr BH25 ......194 C3
Cherry Wlk SO15 ....102 B3
Cherrygarth Rd P015 ......130 B1
Cherryton Gdns SO45 .....150 A2
Cherrywood SO30 ....105 A3
Cherrywood Gdns
South Hayling P011 ....185 A2
Totton SO40 ....100 B4
Cheril Cl
Chandler's Ford SO53 ....54 C3
Horndean P08 ....88 B1
Cherville Ct SO51 ....52 C4
Cherville Mews SO51 ....52 C4
Cherville St SO51 ....52 C4
Cherwell Cres SO16 ....101 C4
Cherwell Gdns SO53 ....55 B3
Cherwell Ho SO16 ....101 C4
Cheshire Cl P015 ....129 C3
Cheshire Dr BH8 ....191 A1
Cheshire Way P010 ....137 B1
Chesil St SO23 ....11 A4
Chesil Terr SO23 ....11 A4
Chesil Wood SO23 ....11 A4
Chesildene Ave BH8 ....190 B2
Chesildene Dr BH8 ....190 B2
Cheslyn Rd P03 ....183 A3
Chessel Ave
Bournemouth BH5 ....205 C2
Southampton SO19 ....103 C3
Chessel Cres SO19 ....103 C4
Chester Cres P013 ....180 A2
Chester Cl SO16 ....78 B1
Chester Ct SO16 ....78 B1
Chester Pl 8 P05 ....182 B1
Chester Rd Poole BH13 ....204 A1
Southampton SO18 ....80 A1
Winchester SO23 ....11 A4
Chesterfield Cl BH13 ....204 C2
Chesterfield Ct BH1 ....205 B2
Chesterfield Rd P03 ....183 A4
Chesterton Gdns P08 ......111 C2
Chesterton Pl SO31 ....129 B4
Chestnut Ave
Ashurst SO40 ....100 B2
Barton on Sea BH25 ....210 A4
Bournemouth BH6 ....206 B2
Christchurch BH23 ....206 B4
2 Colden Common SO21 ....31 C1
Eastleigh SO50,SO53 ....55 B1
Havant P09 ....135 A2
Ibsley BH24 ....116 A3
Littleton SO22 ....1 A2
Portsmouth P04 ....182 C2
Waterlooville P08 ....112 B3
Chestnut Cl
Chandler's Ford SO53 ....55 B2
Denmead P07 ....110 C2
Romsey SO51 ....53 B3
West End SO30 ....80 B2
Chestnut Ct
Rowland's Castle P09 ....136 A4
8 Southampton SO17 ....79 A1
Chestnut Gr BH21 ....164 C3
Chestnut Lodge 12 SO16 ..78 C2
Chestnut Rd
Brockenhurst SO42 ....146 A1
Southampton SO16 ....78 A1
Chestnut Rise
Droxford SO32 ....61 A1

Chestnut Rise continued
Eastleigh SO53 ....55 B1
Chestnut Way
Burton BH23 ....192 B2
Titchfield P014 ....129 B1
Chestnut Wlk
Botley SO30 ....105 C4
Gosport P012 ....156 A1
Chestnuts The SO31 ....129 A1
Chetnole Cl BH17 ....188 A1
Chettle Rd SO19 ....104 C3
Chetwode Way BH17 ......187 A1
Chetwynd Dr SO16 ....78 C2
Chetwynd Rd
Portsmouth P04 ....182 C2
Southampton SO16 ....78 C3
Chevening Ct 8 P04 ....183 A3
Cheviot Court Flats
BH23 ....207 C4
Cheviot Cres SO16 ....101 C4
Cheviot Dr SO45 ....125 B2
Cheviot Gn SO31 ....152 B4
Cheviot Rd SO16 ....101 C4
Cheviot Way BH31 ....114 C3
Cheviots The BH14 ....203 B2
Chevron Bsns Pk SO45 ...150 A3
Chewter Cl P04 ....182 C3
Chewton Common Rd
BH23 ....209 A4
Chewton Farm Rd BH23 ..194 B1
Chewton Lodge BH23 ......209 A4
Chewton Way BH23 ....194 A1
Cheyne Ave BH23 ....194 B4
Cheyne Gdns BH4 ....204 B1
Cheyne Way P013 ....179 C1
Chichester Ave P011 ....185 A2
Chichester Cl
Gosport P013 ....155 A1
Hedge End SO30 ....81 B1
Locks Heath SO31 ....128 C2
West Wellow SO51 ....51 A1
Chichester Ho P09 ....136 A2
Chichester Rd
North Hayling P011 ....160 B1
Portsmouth P02 ....182 C4
Ringwood BH24 ....117 B1
Southampton SO18 ....104 A4
Chichester Way BH23 ......208 A3
Chichester Wlk P011 ....163 C1
Chickenhall La SO50 ....56 B1
Chickerell Cl BH9 ....190 A2
Chidden Cl GU32 ....38 B1
Chidden Holt SO53 ....55 A3
Chideock Cl BH12 ....203 C3
Chideock Ct BH14 ....203 C3
Chidham Cl P09 ....135 C1
Chidham Dr P09 ....135 C1
Chidham Rd P09 ....135 C1
Chidham Sq P09 ....135 C1
Chidham Wlk 2 P09 ....135 C1
Chigwell Rd BH8 ....190 A1
Chilbolton Ave SO22 ....10 B4
Chilbolton Ct
18 Havant P09 ....136 A3
Winchester SO22 ....10 A4
Chilcomb Cl P013 ....179 C1
Chilcomb La
Chilcomb SO21 ....11 C3
Winchester SO23 ....11 B3
Chilcomb Rd SO18 ....104 B4
Chilcombe Cl P09 ....135 C2
Chilcombe La SO32 ....11 A4
Chilcombe Rd BH6 ....206 A3
Chilcote Rd P03 ....183 A4
Childe Sq P02 ....157 B1
Chilfrome Cl BH17 ....187 B1
Chilgrove Rd P06 ....158 B4
Chilham Cl SO50 ....56 A4
Chillenden Ct SO40 ....100 B3
Chillerton SO40 ....127 B4
Chilling La SO31 ....152 C3
Chillington Gdns SO53 .....30 A1
Chilly Hill SP6 ....94 C4
Chilmark Ct GU33 ....20 C2
Chilsdown Way P07 ....134 C2
Chiltern Cl
Barton on Sea BH25 ....194 C1
Poole BH12 ....204 A3
Totton SO40 ....100 B3
Chiltern Ct
8 Christchurch BH23 ....207 C4
Gosport P012 ....181 A3
7 Portsmouth P05 ....182 B1
Chiltern Dr
Barton on Sea BH25 ....209 C4
Verwood BH31 ....114 C3
Chiltern Wlk SO16 ....154 C4
Chilworth Cl SO16 ....54 B1
Chilworth Dr P08 ....88 B2
Chilworth Gr P012 ....181 A3
Chilworth Rd SO16 ....54 C1
Chilworth Way SO16 ....54 A1
Chimes The BH4 ....204 A2
Chine Ave SO19 ....103 C3
Chine Cl SO31 ....129 B4
Chine Cres BH2 ....204 B1
Chine Cres Rd BH2 ....204 B1
Chine The P013 ....155 C1
Chine Wlk BH22 ....165 C1
Chinham Rd SO40 ....99 B3
Chipstead Ho 10 P06 ....157 C4
Chipstead Rd 11 P06 ....157 C4
Chisholm Cl SO16 ....77 C3
Chiswell Rd BH17 ....187 C4
Chitty Rd P04 ....183 A1
Chivers Cl P05 ....215 B1
Chorley Cl BH15 ....202 B3

Chris Cres BH16 ....201 B4
Christ the King RC Prim Sch
BH11 ....189 A3
Christchurch Bay Rd
BH25 ....209 C4
Christchurch By-Pass
BH23 ....207 B4
Christchurch Castle*
BH23 ....207 B3
Christchurch Cty Jun Sch
BH23 ....207 A4
Christchurch Cty Prim Sch
BH23 ....207 A4
Christchurch Gdns
Waterlooville P07 ....134 A1
1 Winchester SO23 ....10 C3
Christchurch Hospl
BH23 ....206 C4
Christchurch Priory*
BH23 ....207 C4
Christchurch Rd
Barton on Sea BH25 ....209 B4
Bournemouth BH1, BH7 ...205 B2
Ferndown BH22 ....165 B1
Hordle SO41 ....211 B4
Hurn BH23 ....191 B3
Ringwood BH24 ....141 A2
Winchester SO23 ....10 C3
Christchurch Ski Ctr
BH23 ....167 A2
Christchurch Sta BH23 .....207 A4
Christie Ave P015 ....129 B4
Christine Ct 9 SO18 ....103 C4
Christopher Cres BH15 ...202 B3
Christopher Way P010 ....136 C1
Christophers BH21 ....163 B1
Christyne Ct P07 ....134 B2
Church Cl
Bishopstoke SO50 ....56 B2
Clanfield P08 ....88 A3
Locks Heath SO31 ....129 A2
Minstead SO43 ....98 B1
North Baddesley SO52 ....54 A2
Church End SO15 ....102 B4
Church Farm SP6 ....93 C4
Church Farm Cl SO45 ......125 A3
Church Hatch SP5 ....47 A4
Church Hill
Milford on Sea SO41 ....211 C2
Redlynch SP5 ....47 C3
Verwood BH31 ....114 C3
West End SO18,SO30 ....80 B1
Church La Awbridge SO51 ..26 C2
Boldre SO41 ....173 C1
Botley SO30 ....106 A3
Bramdean SO24 ....15 B2
Brockenhurst SO42 ....173 A4
Burley BH24 ....143 A2
Burseldon SO31 ....128 A4
Christchurch BH23 ....207 A3
Colden Common SO21 ....31 C1
Curdridge SO32 ....106 B4
Damerham SP6 ....68 B2
Durley SO32 ....81 C3
East Boldre SO42 ....175 B3
Fawley SO45 ....151 A2
Ferndown BH22 ....189 C4
Hambledon P07 ....86 B2
Havant P09 ....160 A4
Hedge End SO30 ....105 A3
Kings Worthy SO23 ....2 B3
Littleton SO22 ....1 A3
Lymington SO41 ....197 C2
Lyndhurst SO43 ....121 C3
Meonstoke SO32 ....61 B4
Mottisfont SO51 ....5 C1
New Milton BH25 ....194 C1
North Hayling P011 ....160 B2
Nursling SO16 ....54 B4
East Boldre SO42 ....175 B3
Portsmouth P01 ....215 C4
Romsey SO51 ....52 C4
Sheffield SO32 ....107 C4
Soberton P017 ....109 B3
South Hayling SO51 ....185 A3
Southampton SO19 ....103 B1

Church Rd continued
Southbourne P010 ....161 C4
Steep GU32 ....40 C4
Swanmore SO32 ....84 A4
Thorney Island P010 ....161 B4
Three Legged Cross BH21 .114 C3
Westbourne P010 ....137 A4
Church St
Christchurch BH23 ....207 A4
East Meon GU32 ....38 C4
Fordingbridge SP6 ....93 C2
Liss GU33 ....20 C4
Poole BH15 ....202 A4
Portsmouth P01 ....215 C4
Romsey SO51 ....52 C4
Southampton SO15 ....78 B4
Titchfield P014 ....154 A4
Upham SO32 ....58 C1
10 Wimborne Minst BH21 .163 A4
Church View
Portsmouth P04 ....183 A4
Shedfield SO32 ....107 C4
Wimborne Minst P010 ......137 A2
Church View Cl SO19 ......104 A1
Church Wlk SP5 ....48 A4
Churcher Cl P012 ....180 B4
Churcher Rd SO19 ....137 A4
Churcher Wlk P012 ....180 B4
Churcher's Coll GU31 ....41 A4
Churchers Coll Jun Sch
GU32 ....40 C4
Churchfield BH11 ....114 C4
Churchfield Cres BH15 ....202 C4
Churchfield La BH24 ....93 C3
Churchfield Rd
Petersfield GU31 ....41 A4
Poole BH15 ....202 C4
Churchfields SO45 ....151 A3
Churchfields Rd SO21 ....32 A4
Churchill Ave SO32 ....59 A4
Churchill Cl Alderholt SP6 ..92 C1
Titchfield P014 ....129 B2
Churchill Cres BH12 ....203 B2
Churchill Ct Cosham P06 ..158 C4
New Milton BH25 ....195 A1
Waterlooville P08 ....112 A4
Churchill Dr P010 ....136 C3
Churchill Dro BH21 ....91 B1
Churchill Gdns BH12 ....203 B3
Churchill Ho SO18 ....104 B1
Churchill Mews P012 ......181 A1
Churchill Rd
Bournemouth BH1 ....205 B3
Poole BH12 ....203 B1
Wimborne Minst BH21 .....163 C4
Churchill Sq P04 ....183 A1
Churchill Yard Ind Est
P07 ....111 C2
Churchmoor Rd BH21 ......164 A4
Churchward Gdns SO30 ....81 B1
Cinderford Cl 2 P06 ....133 A1
Cinnamon La 8 SO15 ....102 C1
Cinnamon La 10 SO15 .....202 C1
Circle The
8 Bournemouth BH9 ....190 B2
Poole BH15 ....214 C1
Portsmouth P05 ....182 B1
Wickham P017 ....108 A4
Circular Rd P01 ....182 B1
Cirrus Gdns SO31 ....127 C4
City Bldgs P01 ....215 B1
City Bsns Ctr SO23 ....11 A4
City Commerce Ctr 20
SO14 ....103 A1
City Ind Pk SO15 ....102 C1
City of Portsmouth Boys Sch
P01 ....111 C1
City of Portsmouth Girls' Sch
P01 ....111 C1
City of Toronto Homes
SO16 ....101 C
City Rd SO23 ....10 C
Civic Centre Rd
Havant P09 ....135 C
Southampton SO14 ....102 C
Clacton Rd P06 ....133 B
Claire Ct BH23 ....209 A
Claire Gdns P08 ....88 C
Clamp Gn 4 SO21 ....56 C
Clandon Dr SO50 ....55 C
Clanfield Cl SO53 ....55 B
Clanfield Dr SO53 ....55 B
Clanfield Ho 7 P01 ....215 C
Clanfield Jun Sch P08 ....88 A
Clanfield Rd SO18 ....104 B
Clanfield Way SO53 ....55 B
Clanwilliam Rd P013 ....179 C
Clare Cl P014 ....129 B
Clare Gdns
Blackfield SO45 ....177 C
Petersfield GU31 ....41 B
Clare Lodge Cl BH23 ......180 C
Claremont Ave BH9 ....190 A
Claremont Cl 1 SO50 ....56 A
Claremont Cres SO15 ......102 A
Claremont Gdns P07 ....134 C
Claremont Rd
Bournemouth BH9 ....190 A
Portsmouth P01 ....215 C
Southampton SO15 ....102 A
Clarence Espl P05 ....182 B
Clarence Ho 5 SO14 ....103 B
Clarence Par P05 ....182 B
Clarence Park Rd BH7 .....206 A

Clarence Rd
Gosport PO12 ....181 B3
Lyndhurst SO43 ....121 C3
3 Poole BH14 ....203 A2
Portsmouth PO5 ......182 B1
Clarence St PO1 .....215 B4
Clarendon Cl
Broadstone BH18 ......187 A2
10 Romsey SO51 ....28 A1
Clarendon Cres PO14 ...128 C3
Clarendon Ct
Bournemouth BH2 .....204 B1
9 Portsmouth PO5 ....182 B1
Clarendon Pk SO41 ...197 B1
Clarendon Pl PO1 ....215 C4
Clarendon Rd
Bournemouth BH4 .....204 B2
Broadstone BH18 ......186 C2
Christchurch BH23 .....207 A4
10 Havant PO9 ....215 C2
Portsmouth PO5 ......182 B1
Southampton SO16 ...102 A4
Clarendon St PO1 ....215 C4
Clark's Cl BH24 ....141 A4
Clarke's Rd PO1 ......182 C3
Claude Ashby Cl SO18 ...79 C2
Claudeen Cl SO18 .....79 C3
Claudeen Ct SO19 ....104 C3
Claudia Ct PO12 ......180 C3
Claudia Cl SO53 ....55 C4
Claudius Gdns SO53 ...55 C4
Clausen Way SO41 ....197 B1
Clausentum Cl SO53 ..55 C4
Clausentum Rd
Southampton SO14 ...103 A4
Winchester SO23 ......10 C3
Clave Cl PO13 ....179 C1
Claxton St PO1 ....215 C3
Clay Hill SO43 ....122 A2
Clay St SP5 ....24 A2
Claybank Rd PO3 .....158 A1
Claybank Spur PO3 ...158 A1
Claydon Ave PO4 ....183 A2
Clayfields Sports Ctr
SO45 ....125 B2
Clayford Ave BH22 ...165 A4
Clayford Cl BH17 .....187 B1
Clayhall Rd PO12 .....181 A1
Clayhill SO32 ....83 B2
Claylake Dr SO31 .....115 A3
Claylands Rd SO32 ...83 A4
Claylands Rd SO32 ...83 A4
Claylands Road Ind Est
SO32 ....83 A4
Claypit La SO17 ....80 B1
Claypits La SO45 .....125 B2
Cleasby Cl SO16 ......101 C4
Cleasby Grange **20** BH5 ...205 C2
Clease Way SO21 .....31 B4
Clee Ave PO14 ....154 B4
Cleethorpes Rd SO19 ...104 A2
Cleeve Cl PO6 ....133 A1
Cleeves Cl BH17 .....188 B1
Cleeves The SO40 ....100 B3
Clegg Rd PO4 ....183 A2
Clem's Way SO51 .....5 A1
Clematis Cl BH23 .....208 B4
Clement Atlee Way PO6 ...157 A4
Clement Mews BH4 ...204 A2
Cleric Ct PO14 ....129 B2
Cleveland Cl BH25 ....209 B4
Cleveland Ct
Bournemouth BH2 .....204 B1
7 Southampton SO18 ...80 A1
Cleveland Dr
Fareham PO14 ....154 B4
Hythe SO45 ....125 B1
Cleveland Gdns BH1 ...205 B3
Cleveland Rd
Bournemouth BH1 .....205 B3
Gosport PO12 ....181 A1
Portsmouth PO5 ......215 D2
Southampton SO18 ...79 C1
Clevelands Cl SO53 ...30 A1
Clewers Hill SO32 .....83 B2
Clewers La SO32 ......83 C2
Cliff Cres BH25 ....209 C4
Cliff Dr
Christchurch BH23 .....208 B3
Poole BH13 ....214 C3
Cliff Ho **10** BH6 ......206 C2
Cliff Rd
Milford on Sea SO41 ...211 A2
Southampton SO15 ...102 B3
Stubbington PO14 .....153 C1
Cliff Terr BH25 ....209 C3
Cliff The SO19 ....103 B2
Cliff Way SO21 ....31 B4
Cliffdale Prim Sch PO14 ...157 C1
Cliffe Ave SO31 ......127 C2
Cliffe Rd BH25 ....209 C4
Clifford Dibben Mews **1**
SO14 ....103 A4
Clifford Pl SO50 ......57 B1
Clifford Rd BH9 ......190 A1
Clifford St **12** SO14 ...103 A3
Clifford Cres PO7 .....111 A2
Clifton Cl
13 Bournemouth BH5 ...205 C2
19 New Milton BH25 ....195 A1
18 Southampton SO15 ...102 A4
Clifton Gdns
Ferndown BH22 ....165 B2
6 Southampton SO15 ...104 B4
West End SO18 ....80 B1
Clifton Hill SO22 .....10 C4
Clifton Lodge SO15 ...102 A4

Clifton Lodge No 1 **32**
SO22 ....10 C4
Clifton Lodge No 2 **33**
SO22 ....10 C4
Clifton Rd
Bournemouth BH6 ......206 B2
Lee-on-the-Solent PO13 ...180 A2
Poole BH14 ....203 C1
22 Portsmouth PO5 ....182 B1
Southampton SO15 ...102 A4
Winchester SO22 ......10 C4
Clifton St Gosport PO12 ...180 C3
Portsmouth PO1 ......215 D4
Clifton Terr
22 Portsmouth PO5 ....182 B1
Winchester SO23 ......10 C4
Clingan Rd BH6 ......206 B4
Clinton Cl BH23 ......194 A1
Clinton Rd
Lymington SO41 ......197 C3
Waterlooville PO7 .....111 B1
Clipper Cl SO31 ......128 C1
Clitherow Cotts SO42 ...148 C1
Clive Cl **19** BH4 ......204 B2
Clive Ct PO6 ....156 B4
Clive Rd
Bournemouth BH9 .....189 C1
Christchurch BH23 .....193 C1
Portsmouth PO1 ......182 C3
Waterlooville PO7 .....165 B4
Clock Ho **10** PO7 ....134 C4
Clock St PO1 ....182 A3
Clocktower Dr PO4 ...183 A1
Cloisters The
Christchurch BH23 .....207 A3
Fareham PO15 ....130 B1
Lymington SO41 ......197 C2
Ringwood BH24 ....141 B3
Romsey SO51 ....52 C4
Close Bellfield The
PO14 ....153 C4
Close The
Barton on Sea BH25 ...210 A4
Broadstone BH18 ......186 C2
Colden Common SO21 ...31 B1
Cosham PO6 ....158 A4
Fordingbridge SP6 .....94 B4
Hamble-le-Rice SO31 ...128 A2
Hedge End SO30 ......105 A3
Holbury SO45 ....125 B3
Langrish GU32 ....39 B2
Portchester PO16 .....156 B4
Redlynch SP5 ....47 B4
Ringwood BH24 ....140 C4
Southampton SO18 ...104 B4
St Leonards, Avon Castle
BH24 ....140 B2
St Leonards, St Ives BH24 ...140 A2
Sway SO41 ....172 A1
Whitbury SP6 ....45 A2
Closewood Rd PO7 ...111 A1
Clough La BH24 ......142 C2
Clough's Rd BH24 ....141 A4
Clovelly Rd
Emsworth PO10 ....160 C4
North Hayling PO11 ...160 B2
Portsmouth PO4 ......183 A2
Southampton SO14 ...103 A3
Southbourne PO10 ....137 B1
Clover Cl
Christchurch BH23 .....208 A4
Gosport PO13 ....155 A2
Locks Heath SO31 .....128 C1
Clover Ct
New Milton BH25 ......195 B2
Waterlooville PO7 .....135 A3
Clover Dr BH17 ....186 C1
Clover Nooke SO15 ...101 B4
Clover Way
Hedge End SO30 ......105 A3
Romsey SO51 ....53 B4
Clovers The BH12 ....204 A4
Clowes Ave BH6 ......207 A2
Clump Hill BH21 ......114 A1
Cluster Ind Est PO4 ...183 A3
Clyde Cl PO12 ....180 C3
Clyde Ho **10** SO14 ...103 B3
Clyde Rd Gosport PO12 ...180 C3
Poole BH17 ....187 A1
Clydebank Rd PO2 ....182 B4
Clydesdale Rd BH21 ...129 A4
Clydesdale Way SO40 ...100 A4
Coach Hill PO14 ......153 C4
Coach Hill Cl SO53 ...55 A4
Coach Hill La SO23 ...142 C3
Coach House Pl BH1 ...205 A3
Coach Rd SO31 ......127 C2
Coach Rd The
East Tytherley SP5 ....4 B4
West Tytherley SP5 ...4 B4
Coach-House Mews
PO4 ....183 A3
Coachmans Copse SO18 ...80 A1
Coachmans Halt PO7 ...86 B1
Coal Park La SO31 ....128 B4
Coalville Rd SO19 ....104 A2
Coastguard Cl PO12 ...180 C1
Coastguard Cotts
Exbury SO45 ....178 A1
Havant PO9 ....159 C3
Lymington SO41 ......198 A1
Coastguard Way BH23 ...207 C3
Coat Gdns SO45 ......125 B4
Coates Rd SO19 ......104 B2
Coates Way PO7 .....134 C3
Cobalt Ct PO13 ......180 B3
Cobb's Rd BH21 ......163 C3

Cobbett Cl SO22 ....10 B3
Cobbett Ct SO18 ......103 C4
Cobbett Ct **15** SO18 ...103 C4
Cobbett Rd SO18 .....103 C4
Cobbett Way SO30 ...105 C4
Coblers Cnr SO41 ....173 A2
Cobblewood PO10 ...136 C2
Cobbs La BH15 ....202 C3
Cobden Ave
Portsmouth PO3 ......183 A4
Southampton SO18 ...103 C4
Cobden Cres SO18 ...103 C4
Cobden Ct SO18 .....103 C4
Cobden Gdns SO18 ...79 C1
Cobden Hts SO18 .....79 C1
Cobden Marine Ct SO18 ...103 B4
Cobden Rise SO18 ....79 C1
Cobden St PO12 ......181 A3
Cobham Gr PO15 .....129 C3
Cobham Rd
Bournemouth BH9 .....190 A2
Ferndown BH21 ....165 A4
Cobham Way BH21 ...163 C1
Coblands Ave SO40 ...100 B4
Coburg Ho **6** SO14 ...103 B3
Coburg St
Portsmouth PO1 ......215 C4
Southampton SO14 ...103 B3
Cochrane Cl PO13 ....180 B3
Cochrane Ho **18** PO1 ...182 A3
Cockerell Cl
Locks Heath PO15 .....129 B3
Oakley BH21 ....163 C1
Cockleshell Cl SO31 ...128 C3
Cockleshell Gdns PO4 ...183 B2
Cockydown La SO40 ...100 B3
Cockshott La GU32 ...19 B1
Codogan Ct **14** BH1 ...205 A2
Cogdean Cl BH21 .....186 C4
Cogdean Way BH21 ...186 C4
Cogdeane Rd BH17 ...187 B1
Coghlan Cl PO16 .....131 A1
Coker Cl SO22 ....10 C4
Colborne Ave BH21 ...163 C3
Colborne Cl SO41 ....197 C3
Colbourne Cl
Bransgore BH23 ....193 A4
Poole BH15 ....202 B1
Colbourne Ct **6** SO23 ...2 A2
Colburn Cl SO16 ......77 C3
Colbury Gr PO9 ....135 B2
Colchester Ave SO50 ...56 C2
Cold East Cl SO31 ....128 C3
Cold Harbour Cl PO17 ...107 C2
Coldeast Hospl SO31 ...128 C2
Coldeast Way SO31 ...128 C3
Colden Common Prim Sch
SO21 ....56 C4
Coldharbour Farm Rd
PO14 ....136 C1
Coldharbour La SO16,
SO51 ....77 A4
Coldhill La PO8 ....111 C4
Cole Hill SO32 ....85 B3
Cole's La SP5 ....48 C3
Colebrook Ave
Portsmouth PO3 ......183 A4
Southampton SO15 ...78 B1
Colebrook Pl SO23 ...11 A4
Colebrook St SO23 ...11 A4
Colehill Cres BH9 ....190 A2
Colehill Fst Sch BH21 ...164 A4
Colehill La BH21 .....163 C4
Coleman Rd BH11 ....189 A2
Coleman St SO14 ....103 B4
Colemore Rd BH7 ....206 B4
Colemore Sq PO9 ....135 C2
Colenso Rd PO16 ....131 A1
Coleridge Cl SO18 ...128 B1
Coleridge Gdns PO8 ...111 C2
Coleridge Ct SO19 ...104 B3
Coleridge Gn BH23 ...207 C4
Coleridge Rd PO6 ....132 C1
Coles Ave BH15 .....201 C1
Coles Cl SO21 ....32 A4
Coles Gdns BH15 ....201 C1
Coles Mede SO21 ....31 A2
Colesbourne Rd PO6 ...133 A1
Coleson Rd SO18 ....103 C4
Coleville Ave SO45 ...151 A2
Colin Cl BH21 ....186 B3
Colinton Ave PO16 ...131 A1
Coll of Air Traffic Control
BH23 ....190 C4
Collard Way **4** GU33 ...20 C2
College Cl
Hamble-le-Rice SO31 ...127 C1
Rowland's Castle PO9 ...113 B1
College Keep SO14 ...103 B4
College Pl SO15 ......102 C4
College Rd **16** PO1 ...182 A3
College Pl **8** SO15 ...102 C4
College St
Petersfield GU31, GU32 ...40 C2
Portsmouth PO1 ......182 A3
Southampton SO19 ...103 C1
Winchester SO23 ......11 A3
College Wlk SO23 ....11 A3
Collett Cl SO30 ....81 A1
Colley Cl SO23 ....2 A2

Collier Cl SO17 ....103 B4
Collingbourne Ave BH6 ...206 B4
Collingbourne Dr SO53 ...55 A3
Collington Cres PO6 ...133 A1
Collingwood Ho PO15 ...130 B1
Collingwood Rd
Portsmouth PO1 ......182 B1
West Moors BH21 .....138 C3
Collingwood Ret Pk
PO14 ....155 A3
Collingworth Rise SO31 ...129 A4
Collins Cl SO53 ....54 C3
Collins Ho SO53 ......55 B3
Collis La ....
Ringwood BH24 ....141 A4
South Harting GU31 ...66 C4
Collins Rd BH24 .....183 A1
Collins' La SO21 .....30 B4
Collis Rd SO19 ....183 A1
Collwood Cl BH15 ....202 B4
Collyers Rd SO42 ....172 C4
Colman Ct BH1 ....205 B2
Colne Ave SO16 ......77 B1
Colne Ct SO16 ....77 C1
Colonnade Cl BH23 ...193 A1
Colonnade Rd BH5 ...206 A3
Colonnade Rd W **4**
BH5 ....206 A3
Colonnade The SO19 ...103 B2
Colpoy St PO5 ....215 A2
Colson Cl SO23 ....11 A4
Colson Rd SO23 ......11 A4
Colt Cl Rownhams SO16 ...77 C3
Wimborne Minst BH21 ...164 A3
Colton Copse SO53 ...54 C3
Colts Rd SO16 ....77 C4
Coltsfoot Cl SO30 ....105 A4
Coltsfoot Dr
Locks Heath SO31 .....128 C1
15 Waterlooville PO7 ...134 C4
Coltsfoot Wlk SO51 ...28 B1
Coltsmead PO6 ....156 C4
Columbia Rd BH10 ...189 B1
Columbia Trees La
BH10 ....189 B1
Columbian Way BH10 ...189 B1
Colvedene Cl SO21 ...31 C1
Colville Cl BH5 ......206 A3
Colville Dr SO32 ......83 B4
Colville Rd
6 Bournemouth BH5 ...206 A3
Cosham PO6 ....158 A4
Colvin Gdns SO53 ....55 A4
Colwell Cl SO16 ......101 B4
Colwell Rd PO6 ......157 C4
Combe Down SO31 ...101 C4
Combe Rd GU33 ......21 A1
Comber Rd **5** BH9 ...190 A2
Comet Way BH23 ....208 A3
Comfrey Cl Horndean PO8 ...88 B1
Romsey SO51 ....28 C2
Comines Way SO30 ...104 C4
Comley Hill PO9 ......136 B3
Comley Rd BH9 ......189 C1
Commercial Pl PO1 ...215 B4
Commercial Rd
Bournemouth BH2 .....204 C2
Poole BH14 ....203 A2
Portsmouth PO1 ......215 C3
Southampton SO15 ...102 C3
Totton SO40 ....101 A4
Commercial St SO18 ...104 A4
Commodore Ct **10** SO14 ...103 A2
Common Barn La PO13 ...179 C2
Common Cl SO53 .....55 B4
Common Gdns SO53 ...55 B4
Common Hill Rd SO51 ...28 B3
Common La
Southwick PO17 ......132 C4
Titchfield PO14 ....153 C4
Common Rd
Chandler's Ford SO53 ...55 B4
Westbourne PO10 .....137 C3
Whiteparish SP5 ......24 A1
Commonside PO10 ...137 A3
Commons Rd BH22 ...139 A1
Compass Cl
Gosport PO13 ....180 B3
Southampton SO19 ...104 A2
Compass Point
Fareham PO16 ....155 A4
Hamble-le-Rice SO31 ...127 C1
Compass Rd PO6 .....157 B4
Compton & Up Marden CE
Prim Sch PO18 ....90 C3
Compton Acres Gdns *
BH13 ....214 C4
Compton All Saints CE Prim
Sch SO21 ....31 B4
Compton Ave BH14 ...203 B1
Compton Beeches
BH24 ....140 A3
Compton Cl
Eastleigh SO50 ....55 C3
Havant PO9 ....135 C2
22 Lee-on-the-Solent
PO13 ....179 C1
Verwood BH31 ....114 C3
Winchester SO22 ......10 A2
Compton Cres BH22 ...139 A1
Compton Ct
4 Havant PO9 ....135 C1
Poole BH14 ....203 B2
8 Portsmouth BH14 ...203 B1
Compton Gdns SO53 ...54 B4
Compton Ho **4** SO18 ...102 A4
Compton Rd
New Milton BH25 ......195 A1

Compton Rd continued
Portsmouth PO2 ......157 C2
Totton SO40 ....101 A4
Winchester SO23 ......10 C4
Compton St SO21 .....31 B4
Compton Way SO22 ...10 A2
Compton Wlk **8** SO14 ...103 A3
Compton's Dr SO51 ...50 A3
Conan Rd PO12 ......157 C2
Concorde Cl PO15 ....129 B3
Concorde Way PO15 ...129 B3
Condor Ave PO6 .....155 C4
Condor Cl
Southampton SO19 ...103 B2
Three Legged Cross BH21 ...139 A3
Coney Gn SO23 ....2 A1
Conference Dr SO31 ...129 A2
Conference Pl **11** SO41 ...197 C1
Conford Ct PO7 ......135 B3
Congleton Cl SO43 ...98 B2
Conifer Ave BH14 ....203 A1
Conifer Cl
Christchurch BH23 .....191 B2
Ferndown BH22 ....165 C1
Hythe SO45 ....125 C2
St Leonards BH08 .....139 B2
Waterlooville PO8 .....112 A3
Winchester SO22 ......1 C1
Conifer Cres SO41 ...197 A2
Conifer Gr PO13 .....155 B2
Conifer Mews PO16 ...132 B1
Conifer Rd SO16 .....78 A2
Conigar Rd PO10 .....136 C2
Coniston Ave
Bournemouth BH11 ...188 C3
Portsmouth PO3 ......183 A4
Coniston Cl SO31 ....113 A3
Coniston Gdns SO30 ...105 A3
Coniston Ho **10** PO6 ...133 A1
Coniston Rd
Eastleigh SO50 ....55 C1
Ringwood BH24 ....141 A3
Southampton SO16 ...101 B4
Coniston Wlk PO14 ...154 C4
Connaught Cl BH25 ...194 C1
Connaught Cres PO12 ...203 C3
Connaught Dr PO16 ...156 C4
Connaught Hall SO18 ...79 B2
Connaught La PO6 ...156 C4
Connaught Pl **5** PO9 ...136 A1
Connaught Rd
Bournemouth BH6 .....206 A3
Poole BH12 ....203 C3
Portsmouth PO2 ......157 B1
Cornell Rd BH15 ......202 B3
Connemara Cres PO15 ...129 A4
Connigar Cl PO13 ....180 B3
Conqueror Way PO14 ...179 B3
Conrad Gdns PO15 ...129 B4
Conservatory The **48**
SO23 ....11 A4
Consort Cl Eastleigh SO50 ...56 A3
Poole BH12 ....203 B3
Consort Ho **9** PO1 ...182 B4
Consort Rd SO50 .....56 A3
Constable Cl
Gosport PO12 ....181 B1
Southampton SO19 ...104 B1
Constables Gate **22** SO22 ...10 C4
Constantine Ave SO53 ...55 C3
Constantine Cl SO53 ...55 C3
Constitution Hill Gdns
BH14 ....203 A3
Constitution Hill Rd
BH14 ....203 A3
Consulate Ho **22** SO14 ...103 A2
Convent Cl PO9 ......160 C4
Convent La PO10 ....160 C4
Conway Cl
Chandler's Ford SO53 ...55 C4
New Milton BH25 ......195 A2
Conway Ct **20** BH25 ...195 A2
Conways Dr BH14 ....203 A2
Cook Cl BH24 ....141 B4
Cook Row BH21 ......163 C3
Cook St SO14 ....103 A2
Cooke Gdns BH12 ...203 C3
Cooke Rd BH12 ......203 C3
Cooks La Awbridge SO51 ...27 A2
Lockerley SO51 ....25 C4
Southbourne PO10 ...137 A3
Totton SO40 ....76 B1
Cooley Ho PO13 .....155 A3
Coolhurst Rd BH14 ...214 B4
Coombe Ave BH10 ...189 C2
Coombe Farm Ave
PO16 ....155 A4
Coombe Gdns BH10 ...189 C1
Coombe La SO41 .....196 B4
Coombe Rd
East Meon GU32 ......63 C3
Gosport PO12 ....181 A4
Coombe Road Terr GU32 ...63 A4
Coombedale SO31 ...129 A1
Coombe Cl PO8 ......112 A3
Cooper Dean Dr BH8 ...190 C1
Cooper Dean Rdbt BH7,
BH8 ....191 A1
Cooper Gr PO16 .....156 B3
Cooper Rd Ashurst SO40 ...100 B2
Portsmouth PO3 ......183 A4
Cooper's Cl
West End SO18 ....80 B1
West Wellow SO51 ...51 A1
Cooper's La SO19 ....103 B2
Coopers Cl SO14 ....103 A2

Coopers La BH31 ....114 C4
Copeland Dr BH14 ....203 A1
Copeland Rd SO16 ....77 B1
Copenhagen Twrs 5 SO19 ....126 C4
Copinger Cl SO40 ....100 B3
Copnor Bridge Bsns Ctr PO3 ....183 A4
Copnor Inf & Jun Sch PO3 ....158 A1
Copnor Rd PO3 ....157 C2
Copper Beech Cl BH12 ..204 A2
Copper Beech Dr PO6 ..158 C4
Copper Beech Gdns BH10 ....189 B1
Copper Beeches SO45 ..150 C1
Copper St 5 PO5 ....215 A1
Coppercourt Leaze 5 BH21 ....163 B2
Copperfield Ho 21 PO1 ..182 B4
Copperfield Rd SO16 ....79 A3
Copperfields SO40 ....100 A4
Coppers Cl SP6 ....93 A3
Coppice Ave BH22 ....165 A4
Coppice Cl
New Milton BH25 ....195 B2
St Leonards BH24 ....139 C2
Winchester SO22 ....1 B1
Coppice Hill SO32 ....83 B4
Coppice Rd SO40 ....76 B1
Coppice The
Brockenhurst SO42 ....145 B1
Christchurch BH23 ....208 A3
Gosport PO13 ....155 B1
Waterlooville PO8 ....112 A3
Coppice View BH10 ....189 C2
Coppice Way PO15 ....130 B2
Coppins Gr PO16 ....156 B3
Copse Ave BH25 ....195 A1
Copse Cl Liss GU33 ....21 A2
North Baddesley SO52 ....53 C2
Otterbourne SO21 ....31 B2
Petersfield GU31 ....41 B2
Poole BH14 ....202 C2
Totton SO40 ....100 C3
Waterlooville PO7 ....134 B1
Copse Cvn Pk The SO40 ..99 B3
Copse La Chilworth SO16 ..54 C1
Gosport PO13 ....155 B1
Hamble-le-Rice SO31 ....127 C1
North Hayling PO11 ....160 A1
Copse Rd Burley BH24 ...142 C1
New Milton BH25 ....195 A1
Southampton SO18 ....80 A1
Verwood BH31 ....114 C3
Copse The
Chandler's Ford SO53 ....55 C3
Fareham PO15 ....130 B2
Romsey SO51 ....28 B1
Copse View SO19 ....104 C3
Copse Way BH23 ....208 C4
Copsewood Ave BH8 ....190 C1
Copsewood Rd
Ashurst SO40 ....100 B2
Hythe SO45 ....125 C2
Southampton SO18 ....79 C1
Copsey Cl PO6 ....158 B4
Copsey Gr PO6 ....158 B4
Copthorne Cotts SO45 ..151 B2
Copthorne La SO45 ....151 A2
Copythorn Rd PO2 ....157 C1
Copythorne CE Inf Sch SO40 ....75 A1
Copythorne Cl BH8 ....190 B1
Copythorne Cres SO40 ..75 B2
Coracle Cl SO31 ....128 C1
Coral Cl PO16 ....156 B3
Coral Ct Gosport PO13 ..180 B3
2 Poole BH12 ....204 A2
Coralin Gr PO7 ....112 A1
Coram Cl 3 SO23 ....2 A1
Corbar Rd BH23 ....206 C4
Corbett Rd PO7 ....134 B3
Corbiere Ave BH12 ....188 B1
Corbiere Cl SO16 ....77 C2
Corbin Ave BH22 ....166 A3
Corbin Ct SO41 ....197 A1
Corbin Rd SO41 ....197 A1
Corbould Rd SO45 ....149 C4
Corby Cres PO3 ....158 A2
Cordelia Cl SO45 ....125 B2
Corfe Cl PO14 ....179 A3
Corfe Halt Cl BH21 ....162 C1
Corfe Hills Sch BH18 ....186 C3
Corfe Lodge Rd BH18, BH21 ....186 B2
Corfe Mews BH15 ....202 B2
Corfe View Rd
Corfe Mullen BH21 ....186 B3
Poole BH14 ....203 B2
Corfe Way BH18 ....186 C2
Corfu BH13 ....214 C3
Corhampton Cres PO9 ..135 B2
Corhampton Ho 11 PO1 .215 C4
Corhampton La
Droxford SO32 ....60 B3
Meonstoke SO32 ....61 A3
Corhampton Rd BH6 ....206 B3
Coriander Dr SO40 ....100 B4
Coriander Way PO15 ....129 B4
Corinna Gdns SO45 ....125 B2
Corinthian Rd SO53 ....55 C4
Cork La SO40 ....101 C1
Cormorant Cl PO16 ....155 C4
Cormorant Dr SO45 ....126 B1
Cormorant Wlk PO13 ...155 A1
Corn Mkt SO51 ....52 C4
Cornaway La PO16 ....156 A4
Cornbrook Gr PO7 ....112 B1
Cornel Rd SO19 ....103 C3
Cornelia Cres BH12 ....204 A3
Cornelius Dr PO7 ....112 A1
Corner Mead PO7 ....110 C2
Cornerways Ct 7 BH25 .195 A1
Cornes Cl SO22 ....10 B4
Cornfield PO16 ....131 A2
Cornfield Cl SO53 ....54 C3
Cornfield Rd PO13 ....179 C1
Cornflower Cl SO31 ....128 C2
Cornflower Dr BH23 ....208 B4
Cornford Way BH23 ....208 B4
Cornforth Rd SO40 ....76 B1
Cornish Gdns BH10 ....189 B1
Cornpits La SP6 ....68 B2
Cornwall Cl 4 SO18 ....80 A1
Cornwall Cres SO18 ....79 C1
Cornwall Rd
Chandler's Ford SO53 ....55 B2
Portsmouth PO1 ....182 C3
Southampton SO18 ....79 C1
Cornwallis Cres PO1 ....215 C4
Cornwallis Ho PO1 ....215 B4
Cornwallis Rd SO41 ....211 A2
Cornwell Cl
Gosport PO13 ....180 B4
Portsmouth PO2 ....157 A1
Coronado Rd PO12 ....181 A4
Coronation Ave
Bournemouth BH9 ....189 C1
Upton BH16 ....201 A4
Coronation Cl BH31 ....114 C4
Coronation Eventide Homes 4 PO2 ....157 C2
Coronation Homes SO18 ....104 B4
Coronation Par SO31 ...127 C2
Coronation Rd
South Hayling PO11 ....185 C1
Swanmore SO32 ....84 A3
Verwood BH31 ....114 C4
Waterlooville PO7 ....134 C4
Coronation Terr SP6 ....69 A1
Corporation Rd BH1 ....205 B3
Corpus Christi RC Prim Sch
Bournemouth BH5 ....206 A3
Portsmouth PO2 ....157 B1
Corsair Dr SO45 ....125 B2
Corscombe Cl BH17 ....187 C1
Cort Way PO15 ....130 B2
Cortina Way SO30 ....105 B3
Cortry Cl BH12 ....204 A4
Corvette Ave SO31 ....128 C1
Cosford Cl SO50 ....57 A1
Cosham Park Ave PO6 ..157 C4
Cosham Sta PO6 ....157 C4
Cossack Gn 6 SO14 ....103 A2
Cossack La 20 SO23 ....11 A4
Cossack Lane Ho 23 SO23 ....11 A4
Cosworth Dr SO45 ....125 B2
Cotes Ave BH14 ....203 A3
Cotes Ct BH14 ....203 A3
Cotlands Rd BH1 ....205 A2
Cotsalls SO50 ....57 B1
Cotswold Cl Havant PO9 .135 C3
Hythe SO45 ....125 B2
Verwood BH31 ....114 C3
Cotswold Ct
6 Christchurch BH23 ....207 C4
12 Southampton SO17 ....79 A1
Cotswold Ho 3 PO6 ....157 B4
Cotswold Rd SO16 ....101 C4
Cotswold Wlk 17 PO14 ..154 C4
Cott La BH24 ....143 A1
Cott St SO32 ....84 B2
Cott Street La SO32 ....84 C2
Cottage Cl PO7 ....110 C2
Cottage Gdns BH12 ....203 B3
Cottage Gr Gosport PO12 .181 A3
Portsmouth PO5 ....215 B2
Cottage Grove Prim Sch PO5 ....215 B1
Cottage La GU32 ....19 C2
Cottage Mews SP6 ....69 C1
Cottage View PO1 ....215 C3
Cottagers La SO41 ....196 A2
Cottages The SP6 ....94 A2
Cotteridge Ho 1 PO1 ..215 C2
Cottes Way PO14 ....179 A3
Cottesway E PO14 ....179 A3
Cotton Cl
Bishopstoke SO50 ....56 C2
Corfe Mullen BH18 ....186 C3
Cotton Dr PO10 ....136 C2
Cotwell Ave PO8 ....112 A2
Coulmere Rd PO12 ....181 A3
Coulsdon Rd SO30 ....105 B3
Coultas Rd SO53 ....30 C1
Council Hos
Lockerley SO51 ....26 A3
Sopley BH23 ....167 C1
Countess Cl BH21 ....187 C4
Countess Gdns BH7 ....205 C4
Country View
Stubbington PO14 ....154 A2
West Wellow SO51 ....50 C2
County Gdns PO14 ....154 B4
Course Park Cres PO14 .129 B1
Court Barn Cl PO13 ....179 C2
Court Barn La PO13 ....179 C2
Court Cl
12 Christchurch BH23 ....207 C4
Cosham PO6 ....158 A4
Court Cl *continued*
Lymington SO41 ....197 B1
Southampton SO18 ....104 A3
Totton SO40 ....76 B1
Court Cotts SO41 ....197 B1
Court Hill SP6 ....68 C3
Court House Cl 4 SO45 .126 A2
Court La PO6 ....158 A4
Court Lane Inf Sch PO6 .158 A4
Court Lane Jun Sch PO6 ....158 A4
Court Mead PO6 ....158 A4
Court Rd
Bournemouth BH9 ....190 A1
Kings Worthy SO23 ....2 B3
Lee-on-the-Solent PO13 ...179 C2
Southampton SO15 ....102 C4
Court Royal Mews SO15 .102 C4
Courtenay Dr BH21 ....163 B3
Courtenay Pl SO41 ....197 C2
Courtenay Rd
Poole BH14 ....203 A2
Winchester SO23 ....2 A2
Courthill Fst Sch BH14 ..203 B2
Courthill Rd BH14 ....203 B2
Courtier Cl SO45 ....125 B2
Courtland Gdns SO16 ....79 A3
Courtlands SO41 ....197 C2
Courtlands Terr PO8 ....112 A2
Courtleigh Manor 6 BH5 ....205 B2
Courtmount Gr PO6 ....158 A4
Courtnay Cl PO15 ....129 B2
Courtney Pl BH21 ....186 B3
Courtyard Cl SO42 ....145 C1
Courtyard Mews SO42 ..145 C1
Courtyard The
Christchurch BH23 ....207 B3
14 Petersfield GU31 ....40 C2
Poole BH12 ....188 B1
7 Romsey SO51 ....52 C4
Cousins Gr PO4 ....182 C1
Cove Rd BH10 ....189 B1
Covena Rd BH6 ....206 C3
Coventry Cl BH21 ....186 B2
Coventry Cres BH17 ....187 A1
Coventry Ct
Gosport PO13 ....180 B3
7 Winchester SO23 ....2 A1
Coventry Rd SO15 ....102 C3
Coverack Way PO6 ....157 A4
Covert Gr PO7 ....135 A3
Covert The SO51 ....53 A3
Covindale Ho 8 PO4 ....183 A2
Covington Rd PO10 ....137 A3
Cow La Cosham PO6 ....157 B4
Portchester PO16 ....156 B4
Cowan Rd PO7 ....134 B3
Coward Rd PO12 ....180 C1
Cowdray Cl
Bishopstoke SO50 ....56 C1
Southampton SO16 ....78 A2
Cowdray Ho PO1 ....215 C3
Cowdray Pk PO14 ....179 A3
Cowdrey Gdns BH8 ....190 C1
Cowdrys Field 2 BH21 ..163 A3
Cowell Dr BH7 ....206 A4
Cowes La SO31 ....152 B3
Cowgrove Rd BH21 ....162 C3
Cowleas Cl SO51 ....26 C3
Cowleas Cotts SO51 ....26 C3
Cowley Cl SO16 ....77 C1
Cowley Rd
Lymington SO41 ....197 B2
Poole BH17 ....202 B4
Cowleys Rd BH23 ....192 B1
Cowper Ave BH25 ....195 A1
Cowper Rd
Bournemouth BH9 ....189 C1
Portsmouth PO1 ....182 C4
Southampton SO19 ....104 B3
Cowpitts La BH24 ....117 B1
Cowplain Sch PO8 ....111 C1
Cowslip Cl Gosport PO13 .155 B1
Locks Heath SO31 ....128 C1
Cowslip Rd BH18 ....186 C1
Cowslip Way SO51 ....28 B1
Cox Ave BH9 ....190 A2
Cox Cl BH9 ....190 A2
Cox Dale PO14 ....129 B1
Cox Row SO53 ....55 B2
Cox's Dr SO19 ....104 A1
Cox's La SO19 ....103 B2
Coxes Mdw GU32 ....40 C3
Coxford Cl SO16 ....78 A1
Coxford Dro SO16 ....78 A2
Coxford Rd SO16 ....78 A2
Coxs Hill SO21 ....32 A4
Coxstone La 2 BH24 ....141 A3
Coy Pond Rd BH12 ....204 A3
Cozens Cl SO19 ....103 C1
Crab Orchard Way BH21 ....114 C1
Crabapple Cl SO40 ....100 B4
Crabbe Ct PO5 ....215 B2
Crabbs Way SO40 ....100 A4
Crabbswood La SO41 ....195 C4
Crabden La PO8 ....88 C1
Crableck La SO31 ....128 B3
Crabthorne Farm La PO14 ....154 A2
Crabton Close Rd BH5 ..205 C2
Crabtree SO16 ....77 C1
Crabtree Cl BH23 ....192 B1
Crabwood Cl SO16 ....77 C1
Crabwood Ct PO9 ....135 B4
Crabwood Dr SO30 ....80 C1
Crabwood Rd SO16 ....77 C1
Cracknore Hard SO40 ...102 A1
Cracknore Hard La SO40 ....102 A1
Cracknore Rd SO15 ....102 B3
Craddock Ho
13 Portsmouth PO1 ....182 A3
2 Winchester SO23 ....11 B4
Craigmoor Ave BH8 ....190 C1
Craigmoor Cl BH8 ....190 C1
Craigmoor Way BH8 ....190 C1
Craigside Rd BH24 ....139 B2
Craigwell Rd PO7 ....134 B2
Craigwood Dr BH22 ....165 C2
Crampmoor La SO51 ....28 C1
Cranberry Cl SO40 ....101 C1
Cranborne Cres BH12 ...203 C4
Cranborne Ct
Bournemouth BH9 ....205 A4
14 Bournemouth, Westbourne BH4 ....204 B2
Cranborne Gdns SO53 ....30 A1
Cranborne Pl BH25 ....194 C2
Cranborne Rd
Alderholt SP6, BH21 ....92 A3
Bournemouth BH2 ....204 C1
Cosham PO6 ....134 A1
Wimborne Minst BH21 ....163 B4
Cranborne Wlk PO14 ....154 C4
Cranbourne Cl SO15 ....78 B1
Cranbourne Ct BH17 ....188 A1
Cranbourne Dr SO21 ....31 A2
Cranbourne Pk SO30 ....105 B2
Cranbourne Rd PO12 ....181 B2
Cranbrook Mews BH12 ..203 A3
Cranbrook Rd BH12 ....203 A3
Cranbury Ave SO14 ....103 A3
Cranbury Cl Downton SP5 .46 C3
Otterbourne SO21 ....31 A2
Cranbury Ct SO19 ....103 C2
Cranbury Gdns SO31 ....104 C1
Cranbury Pl SO14 ....103 A3
Cranbury Rd
Eastleigh SO50 ....56 A1
Southampton SO19 ....103 C2
Cranbury Terr 4 SO14 ..103 A3
Cranbury The 3 SO14 ..103 A3
Cranbury Twrs 6 SO14 ..103 A3
Crane Cl Gosport PO13 ..155 A1
Verwood BH31 ....114 C3
Crane Dr BH31 ....114 C4
Crane Way BH21 ....139 A3
Cranemoor Ave BH23 ....193 C1
Cranemoor Cl BH23 ....193 C1
Cranemoor Gdns BH23 ..193 C1
Cranes Mews BH15 ....202 B2
Craneswater Ave PO4 ...182 C1
Craneswater Gate 4 PO4 ....182 C1
Craneswater Jun Sch PO4 ....182 C1
Craneswater Mews 5 PO4 ....182 C1
Craneswater Pk PO4 ....182 C1
Cranfield Ave BH21 ....163 B3
Cranford Gdns SO53 ....55 A4
Cranford Ho 5 SO17 ....79 A1
Cranford Rd GU32 ....40 B1
Cranford Way SO17 ....79 A1
Cranleigh Ave PO1 ....182 C3
Cranleigh Cl BH6 ....206 C3
Cranleigh Ct BH6 ....206 C3
Cranleigh Gdns BH6 ....206 C3
Cranleigh Ho
Hedge End SO30 ....81 B2
Southampton SO17 ....103 A4
Cranleigh Paddock SO43 ....121 C3
Cranleigh Rd
Bournemouth BH6 ....206 C3
Hedge End SO30 ....105 B3
Portchester PO16 ....156 A4
Portsmouth PO1 ....182 C3
Cranmer Dr SO16 ....77 B3
Cranmer Rd BH9 ....204 C4
Cranmore SO31 ....127 B4
Cransley Ct BH4 ....204 B1
Cranstock Gr BH8 ....190 C1
Cranwell Cl
Bournemouth BH11 ....188 C2
Bransgore BH23 ....169 A1
Cranwell Ct SO16 ....77 C3
Cranworth Rd SO22 ....1 C1
Crasswell St PO1 ....215 C4
Craven Ct PO15 ....130 C2
Craven Rd SO53 ....55 B3
Craven St 18 SO14 ....103 A3
Crawford Cl SO16 ....77 B3
Crawford Dr PO16 ....130 C2
Crawley Ave PO9 ....136 A3
Crawley Hill SO51 ....50 C1
Crawshaw Rd BH14 ....203 A1
Crawte Ave SO45 ....150 B1
Crawters La 24 GU31 ....40 C2
Cray Ho PO12 ....181 B2
Creasey Rd BH11 ....189 A3
Credenhill Rd PO6 ....133 B1
Creech Rd BH12 ....203 B3
Creech View PO7 ....110 C2
Creech Wood Forest Wlk* PO7 ....110 B2
Creedy Gdns SO18 ....80 A2
Creek End PO10 ....160 C4
Creek Rd Gosport PO12 ..181 B2
South Hayling PO11 ....185 B1
Creekmoor La BH17 ....202 A4
Creighton Rd SO15 ....101 C3
Cremorne Pl 10 GU32 ....40 C2
Cremyll Cl PO14 ....179 B3
Crescent Cl SO22 ....10 A2
Crescent Cotts SO45 ....177 A3
Crescent Ct BH25 ....209 C4
Crescent Dr BH25 ....209 C4
Crescent Ho 2 SO50 ....56 A2
Crescent Prim Sch SO50 .56 A2
Crescent Rd
Bournemouth BH2 ....204 C2
Fareham PO16 ....131 A1
Gosport PO12 ....181 A1
Locks Heath SO31 ....128 C1
North Baddesley SO52 ....53 C3
Poole BH14 ....203 C2
Verwood BH31 ....115 A3
Wimborne Minst BH21 ....163 B2
Crescent The
Barton on Sea BH25 ....209 B4
3 Bournemouth BH7 ....205 C2
Eastleigh SO50 ....56 A2
Exbury SO45 ....177 A3
Marchwood SO40 ....101 C1
Netley SO31 ....127 B3
Netley Marsh SO40 ....99 C2
Romsey SO51 ....53 A4
Southampton SO19 ....104 A1
Southbourne PO10 ....161 B4
Twyford SO21 ....32 A3
Upham SO32 ....58 B1
Waterlooville PO7 ....134 B2
Crescent Wlk BH22 ....165 C1
Cressey Rd SO51 ....52 C4
Cressy Rd PO2 ....182 B4
Crest Cl PO16 ....131 B1
Crest Rd BH12 ....203 B3
Crest The PO7 ....134 B1
Crest Way SO19 ....104 B2
Cresta Ct 8 PO4 ....182 C1
Cresta Gdns BH22 ....165 C1
Crestland Cl PO8 ....112 A2
Crestwood Com Sch SO50 ....55 C3
Crete Cotts SO45 ....125 C1
Crete La SO45 ....125 C1
Crete Rd SO45 ....125 C1
Cribb Cl BH17 ....202 C4
Crichel Mount Rd BH14 .214 B4
Crichel Rd BH9 ....205 A4
Crichton Ho 11 SO31 ....127 A3
Cricket Cl BH23 ....207 C3
Cricket Dr PO8 ....112 A3
Cricklemede SO32 ....83 B4
Cricklewood Cl SO32 ....83 B4
Crigdon Cl SO16 ....101 C4
Crimea Rd BH9 ....204 C4
Cringle Ave BH6 ....207 A2
Crinoline Gdns PO4 ....183 A1
Cripple Gate La
Beaulieu SO42 ....175 B3
East Boldre SO42 ....175 B3
Cripstead La SO23 ....10 C3
Crispen Cl BH23 ....208 C4
Crispin Cl Fair Oak SO50 ..81 B3
Locks Heath SO31 ....129 A2
Crisspyn Cl PO8 ....112 A3
Criterion Arc 39 BH1 ...204 C2
Crittall Cl SO41 ....172 B1
Crockford Cl BH25 ....195 A3
Crockford Rd PO10 ....137 A2
Croft Cl BH21 ....186 B4
Croft Hts SP5 ....24 A2
Croft La PO11 ....159 C1
Croft Rd
Bournemouth BH9 ....189 C1
Bransgore BH23 ....193 A3
Christchurch BH23 ....207 C4
Poole BH12 ....203 A3
Portsmouth PO2 ....157 B1
Ringwood BH24 ....117 B1
Croft The
Chandler's Ford SO53 ....55 B2
Croucheston SP5 ....22 A4
Stubbington PO14 ....154 B2
Totton SO40 ....76 B1
Croftlands Ave PO14 ....154 B2
Crofton Anne Dale Jun Sch PO14 ....179 B3
Crofton Ave PO13 ....179 B2
Crofton Cl
Christchurch BH23 ....191 C1
Southampton SO17 ....79 A1
Waterlooville PO7 ....134 B3
Crofton Ct PO14 ....179 B3
Crofton Hammond Jun & Inf Schs PO14 ....179 B3
Crofton La PO14 ....179 A3
Crofton Rd
Portsmouth, Milton PO4 ...183 A3
Portsmouth, North End PO2 ....157 C1
Crofton Sch PO14 ....179 C3
Crofton Way
Locks Heath SO31 ....128 B1
Swanmore SO32 ....84 A3
Cromalt Cl SO45 ....125 B1
Cromarty Ave PO4 ....183 A2
Cromarty Cl PO14 ....154 A2
Cromarty Rd SO16 ....77 C3
Crombie Cl PO8 ....111 C2
Cromer Gdns BH12 ....203 C3
Cromer Rd
Bournemouth BH8 ....205 B4
Cosham PO6 ....133 C1
Poole BH12 ....203 C3
Southampton SO16 ....77 B1
Cromhall Cl PO14 ....154 B4
Crompton Way PO15 ....129 B3
Cromwell Pl 9 BH5 ....206 A3

Cromwell Rd
Bournemouth BH5 ....206 A3
Poole BH12 ....203 B3
Portsmouth PO4 ....183 A1
Southampton SO15 ....102 C4
16 Wimborne Minster BH21 .163 B2
Winchester SO22 ....10 C3
Crondall Ave PO9 ....135 C3
Crood Cl 7 PO16 ....131 B1
Crooked Hays Cl SO40 ...101 C1
Crooked Walk La PO17 ...132 C2
Crookham Cl PO9 ....135 B2
Crookham Rd SO19 ....126 C4
Crookhorn Com Sch The
PO7 ....134 C2
Crookhorn La
Soberton SO32 ....85 B4
Waterlooville PO7 ....134 C2
Crosby Rd BH4 ....204 B1
Crosfield Cl SO51 ....51 A1
Cross House Ctr SO14 ...103 B2
Cross Keys Pas 25 SO23 ..11 A1
Cross La
Bishop's Waltham SO32 ...59 A1
Waterlooville PO8 ....112 A3
Cross Lanes BH24 ....117 B4
Cross Rd
Christchurch BH23 ....191 B1
Compton(Hants) SO21 ....31 B3
Newport PO30 ....135 C1
Cross Ways BH23 ....169 B3
Crossbill Cl PO8 ....112 A4
Crossfell Wlk PO14 ....154 C4
Crosshouse Rd SO14 .....103 B2
Crossland Cl PO12 ....181 B2
Crossland Dr PO9 ....136 A2
Crossley Ct 6 SO15 .....102 B3
Crossmead Ave BH25 ....195 A1
Crossway The PO16 ......156 B4
Crossways SO41 ....196 B1
Crossways Cl SP5 ....46 C4
Crossways The
Denmead PO7 ....111 A4
Gosport PO12 ....181 A3
Upton BH16 ....201 B4
Crosswell Cl SO19 ....104 B3
Crouch La PO8 ....112 A4
Croucher's Croft SO22 ...1 B1
Crow Arch La BH24 ......141 A3
Crow Arch Lane Ind Est
BH24 ....141 A3
Crow Cotts BH24 ....141 B2
Crow Hill Top BH24 ......142 A2
Crow La BH24 ....141 B3
Crowder Terr PO12 ......10 C4
Crowders Gn 1 SO21 ....56 C4
Crowe Hill Ct 2 BH15 ...202 C2
Crown Cl Poole BH23 ....203 B3
Waterlooville PO7 ....134 C2
Crown Ct
Portsmouth PO1 ....215 C4
8 Wimborne Minster BH21 .163 A3
Crown Mead BH21 ....163 B2
Crown Mews 10 PO12 ...181 B2
Crown St
Portsmouth PO1 ....215 C4
Southampton SO15 ......102 A4
Crown Wlk 3 BH7 ....205 C2
Crows Nest La SO32 .....81 C1
Crowsbury Cl PO10 ......136 C2
Crowsport SO31 ....128 A2
Crowther Cl SO19 ....104 B2
Croydon Cl SO16 ....78 A2
Crummock Rd SO53 .....55 A4
Crusader Ct PO12 ....181 B4
Crusader Rd
Bournemouth BH11 ......188 B2
Hedge End SO30 ....105 B3
Crusader Way SO53 .....54 C3
Cruse Cl SO41 ....172 A1
Cruxton Farm Ctyd
BH21 ....163 B1
Crystal Way PO7 ....135 A4
Cucklington Gdns BH9 ...190 A2
Cuckmere La SO16 ......101 B4
Cuckoo Bush La SO53 ...55 B4
Cuckoo Hill Rly★ SP6 ...94 B1
Cuckoo Hill Way BH21 ...169 B1
Cuckoo La
22 Southampton SO14 ...102 C2
Stubbington PO14 ....154 C1
Cuckoo Rd BH12 ....203 A4
Cudnell Ave BH11 ....189 A3
Cudworth Mead SO30 ...81 B1
Cuffnells Cl BH24 ....117 A4
Cul-de-sac BH25 ....209 A4
Culford Ave SO40 ....100 C3
Culford Cl BH24 ....190 C1
Culford Cl 11 BH8 ......205 A3
Culford Way SO40 ......100 C3
Cull Cl BH12 ....204 B4
Cull La BH25 ....195 A3
Culliford Cres BH17 .....187 C1
Culloden Cl PO15 ....130 C1
Culloden Rd PO14 ......154 C3
Cullwood La BH25 ......195 B3
Culver SO31 ....127 B4

Culver Cl SO16 ....77 B1
Culver Dr PO11 ....185 B1
Culver Mews SO23 ......11 A4
Culver Rd
New Milton BH25 ....194 C1
Portsmouth PO4 ....183 A1
35 Winchester SO23 ....11 A1
Culverhayes Pl BH21 ...163 A3
Culverhayes Rd BH21 ..163 A3
Culverin Sq PO3 ....158 A2
Culverlands Cl SO32 ....107 C4
Culverley Cl SO42 ......145 C1
Culverwell Gdns 28 SO23 .10 C4
Culvery Gdns SO18 .....80 A1
Cumber Rd SO31 ....128 C2
Cumberland Ave
Chandler's Ford SO53 ...55 C3
Emsworth PO10 ....136 C2
Cumberland Bsns Ctr
PO1 ....215 C3
Cumberland Cl SO53 ....55 C3
Cumberland Ho PO1 ....182 A4
Cumberland House Natural
History Mus★ PO5 .....182 C1
Cumberland Inf Sch
PO4 ....183 A2
Cumberland Pl SO15 ...102 C3
Cumberland Rd PO1 ....215 D3
Cumberland St
Portsmouth PO1 ....182 A3
Southampton SO14 .....103 A2
Cumberland Way SO15 .125 B2
Cumbrian Way SO16 ...101 C4
Cummins Gn SO31 .....105 A1
Cunard Ave SO15 ......205 A2
Cunard Ave SO15 ......102 B4
Cunard Rd SO14 ....103 A1
Cundell Way SO23 .....2 A4
Cunningham Ave SO32 ..83 A4
Cunningham Cl
Bournemouth BH11 .....189 A2
Christchurch BH23 .....208 A3
Portsmouth PO2 ....157 B2
Ringwood BH24 ....141 B4
Cunningham Cres
Bournemouth BH11 .....189 A2
Southampton SO19 ....104 A2
Cunningham Ct
New Milton BH25 ......194 C2
1 Portsmouth PO5 ....182 B1
Cunningham Dr
Gosport PO13 ....155 B2
Locks Heath SO31 .....129 A2
Cunningham Gdns
SO31 ....127 C4
Cunningham Pl BH11 ..189 A2
Cunningham Rd
Horndean PO8 ....112 B4
Waterlooville PO7 .....134 B3
Cupernham Cl SO51 ...28 A1
Cupernham Inf Sch SO51 .28 A1
Cupernham Jun Sch
SO51 ....28 A1
Cupernham La SO51 ...28 A1
Curdridge Cl 13 PO9 ..136 A3
Curdridge La SO32 .....83 B2
Curdridge Prim Sch
SO32 ....106 B4
Curlew Cl
Emsworth PO10 ....160 C4
Ferndown BH22 ....165 A4
16 Hythe SO45 ....126 A1
Southampton SO16 ....78 A3
Curlew Dr Hythe SO45 .126 A1
Portchester PO16 .....154 B1
Curlew Gdns PO8 ......112 C2
Curlew Path 7 PO4 ...183 A3
Curlew Rd
Bournemouth BH8 .....190 B1
Christchurch BH23 ....208 A3
Curlew Sq SO50 ......55 C1
Curlew Wlk
Gosport PO13 ....155 A2
Hythe SO45 ....126 A1
Curlews The BH31 ....115 A3
Curlieu Rd BH15 .....202 B3
Curtis Mead PO7 .....157 C2
Curtis Rd PO3 ....203 B3
Curtiss Gdns PO12 ...180 C2
Curve The Gosport PO13 .155 A1
Horndean PO8 ....111 C3
Curzon Ct
32 Bournemouth BH4 .204 B2
Southampton SO16 ...78 B2
Curzon Howe Rd PO1 .182 A3
Curzon Pl SO41 ......197 B1
Curzon Rd
Bournemouth BH1 ....205 B3
Poole BH14 ....203 A2
Curzon Way BH23 ....208 A4
Custards Rd SO43 ....121 C3
Custards The SO43 ...122 A3
Cut Throat La
Droxford SO32 ....61 A1
Swanmore SO32 .....84 B3
Cuthbush La
Southampton SO18 ...104 A4
West End SO18 ......80 A2
Cuthbert Rd PO1 .....182 C3
Cuthburga Rd BH21 ...163 B2
Cuthbury Cl BH21 ....163 A2
Cuthbury Gdns BH21 .163 A2
Cutler Cl
New Milton BH25 ....195 B2
Poole BH12 ....204 B4
Cutlers La PO14 .....154 B2

Cutlers Pl BH21 ....164 A3
Cutter Ave SO31 ......128 C1
Cutts Arch Droxford SO32 .85 A3
Soberton SO32 ....85 A3
Cygnet Ct PO16 ....155 C4
Cygnet Ho PO12 ......181 A4
Cygnet Rd PO6 ....158 C4
Cygnus Gdns SO45 ...125 B2
Cynthia Cl BH12 .....203 B1
Cynthia Ho BH12 ....203 A4
Cynthia Rd BH12 ....203 A4
Cypress Ave SO19 ...103 C3
Cypress Cres PO8 ...112 A3
Cypress Gdns
Botley SO30 ....106 A4
Totton SO40 ....100 B4
Cypress Gr SO41 ....211 B4
Cyprus Rd
Portsmouth PO2 .....182 C4
Titchfield PO14 .....129 B1
Cyril Rd BH8 ....205 B3

D

D Ave SO45 ....150 C3
D-Day Mus★ PO5 ...182 B1
Dacombe Cl BH16 ...201 B4
Dacombe Dr BH16 ...201 B4
Dacres Wlk 3 SO41 .211 B3
Daffodil Rd SO16 ....79 B2
Daggons Rd SP6 ....92 B3
Dahlia Rd SO17 .....79 A2
Daintree Cl SO19 ...104 B2
Dairy Cl
Christchurch BH23 ...207 B4
Corfe Mullen BH21 ..186 A2
Dairy La SO31 ......77 A3
Dairymoor PO17 ....108 A2
Daisy Cl Gosport PO12 .181 A2
Locks Heath SO31 ..129 B2
Daisy Mead PO7 ...135 A4
Daisy Rd SO16 .....79 A2
Dakota Cl BH23 ....208 A4
Dale Cl Littleton SO22 ...1 A3
Dale Dr PO13 ......155 A3
Dale Park Ho 4 PO1 .215 B3
Dale Rd Hythe SO45 .125 C2
Poole BH15 ....202 A4
Southampton SO16 ...78 B1
Stubbington PO14 ...154 B2
Dale The PO7 ......134 B1
Dale Valley Cl SO16 .78 B1
Dale Valley Gdns SO16 .78 B1
Dale Valley Rd
Poole BH15 ....202 A4
Southampton SO16 ...78 B2
Dales Cl BH21 .....164 B3
Dales Dr BH21 .....164 A3
Dales La BH21 .....190 C4
Dales Way SO40 ...100 A4
Dalewood Ave BH11 .188 C3
Dalewood Rd PO15 .130 B1
Dalkeith Rd
Corfe Mullen BH21 ..186 B2
Poole BH13 ....204 A1
Dalling Rd BH12 ...204 A3
Dallington Cl PO14 .179 B3
Dalmally Gdns SO18 .103 C4
Dalmeny Rd BH6 ...207 A2
Dalrymple Rd 5 SO17 .2 A1
Damask Gdns PO7 .112 A1
Dame Elizabeth Kelly Ct 3
PO2 ....157 C2
Deacon Cres SO19 ..104 A3
Deacon Gdns SO19 ..104 A3
Deacon Rd
Bournemouth BH11 ..189 A3
Locks Heath SO31 ..129 A1
Southampton SO19 ..104 A3
Deacon Trad Est SO50 .56 B1
Deadman Hill SP6 ..71 B3
Deal Cl PO14 ......154 B2
Deal Rd PO6 ......133 C1
Dean Cl Hamworthy BH15 .201 C2
Winchester SO22 ..1 B1
Dandy's Ford La SO51 .25 C1
Danecourt Cl BH14 .202 C2
Danecourt Rd BH14 .202 C2
Danecrest Rd SO41 .195 C2
Danehurst Cl SO41 .211 A3
Danehurst New Rd
SO41 ....195 B4
Denmark Cl 4 SO23 .11 A4
Danes Cl BH25 ....209 A4
Danes Rd Awbridge SO51 .26 B2
Portchester PO16 ..132 A1
Danbury Cl PO9 ...135 C3
Danbury Gdns SO53 .55 A2
Dean La
Bishop's Waltham SO32 .59 C2
Rowland's Castle PO8 ..113 B3
Whiteparish SP5 .....24 A2
Winchester SO22 .....1 C1
Dean Park Cres BH1 .204 C2
Dean Park Rd BH1 ..204 C2
Dean Pk Cosham PO6 .157 C4
Fair Oak SO50 ......57 B1
West Dean SP5 .....3 A1
West Tytherley SP5 .3 C3
Dean Rd
Bishop's Waltham SO32 .59 C2
Southampton SO18 ..103 C4
Deacon Cl SO19 ....104 A3
Dansie Cl BH14 ....203 A2
Dapple PO15 ....130 A1
Darby's Cl BH15 ...202 A3

Darby's Cnr BH17 ...187 B1
Darby's La BH15 ...202 B3
Darby's La N BH17 .202 B4
Dark La Blackfield SO45 .150 C2
Bransgore BH23 ....194 A2
Cheriton SO24 .....14 B3
Darley Rd BH22 ....165 B2
Darlington Gdns SO15 .78 B1
Darrad's La Bransgore SO41 .194 C2
Darnan Ho 42 SO14 .103 A4
Darracott Rd BH5 ..206 A3
Darren Cl PO14 ....154 B2
Darren Ct 9 PO16 .131 A1
Darrian Ct BH16 ...201 A4
Dart Ho SO18 .....103 C4
Dart Rd SO18 .....80 A2
Dartington Rd SO50 .56 B3
Dartmouth Mews PO5 .215 A1
Dartmouth Rd PO3 .158 A2
Darvill Rd SO21 ...191 C1
Darwin Cl 4 BH12 .204 A2
Darwin Ho PO1 ...215 C4
Darwin Rd Eastleigh SO50 .56 A2
Southampton SO15 ..102 C4
Darwin Way PO13 ..180 B3
Daubeney Gdns 8 PO9 .135 B3
Daulston Rd PO1 ..182 C4
Davenport Cl
Gosport PO13 ......180 B3
Southampton SO16 ..201 B4
Daventry La PO3 ..158 B2
David Ct SO51 ....53 A3
David Hart Bsns Ctr SP5 .46 C4
David Way BH11 ..201 C1
David's La BH24 ..140 B3
Davidia Cl PO7 ...135 A3
Davidson Ct 27 PO1 .182 B3
Davis Cl PO13 ....180 B4
Davis Field BH25 ..194 C1
Davis Rd BH12 ...203 C3
Davis Way PO14 .155 A3
Daw La PO11 .....184 C4
Dawkins Bsns Ctr BH21 .201 B2
Dawkins Rd BH15 .201 B2
Dawkins Way BH25 .195 A1
Dawlish Ave SO15 .102 B4
Dawn Chorus BH14 .203 A2
Dawn Cl BH10 ...189 B1
Daws Ave BH11 ..189 A1
Dawson Rd SO19 ..104 B1
Day La PO8 ......111 C4
Day's Ct BH21 ...163 B2
Daylesford Cl BH14 .203 A1
Dayrell Cl SO40 ..76 A1
Dayshes Ct PO13 .155 A2
Daysdonbn Rd PO7 .134 B3
De Courtenai Cl BH11 .188 C3
De Grouchy La SO17 .79 A4
De Haviland Cl BH21 .163 C1
De Haviland Ho BH23 .208 A3
De Havilland Way BH23 .208 A3
De La Warr Rd SO41 .211 B2
De Lisle Cl PO7 ...134 B4
De Lisle Rd BH3 ...204 C4
De Lunn Bldgs 7 SO23 .11 A4
De Mauley Rd BH13 .214 C4
De Montfort Rd BH21 .163 B1
De Mowbray Way SO41 .197 B1
De Port Hts SO32 .83 B3
De Redvers Rd BH4 .203 B1
Deacon Cl SO19 ..104 A3

Deans Gate PO14 ...179 B3
Deans Gr BH21 ....163 B4
Deans The BH1 ....204 C2
Deanscroft Rd BH10 .189 C2
Deansfield Cl SO51 .53 A4
Deansleigh Rd BH7 .191 A1
Deanswood Dr PO7 .111 C1
Dear Hay La BH15 ..202 B1
Dearing Cl SO43 ...121 C2
Debney Lodge PO7 .134 C4
Decies Rd BH14 ...203 A3
Dee Cl SO53 ......55 A3
Dee Way BH15 ....202 A1
Deep Dell PO8 ...112 A3
Deepdene SO18 ...103 C4
Deepdene La BH11 .188 C3
Deeping Cl SO19 ..103 C1
Deeping Gate PO7 .135 A4
Deer Leap PO15 ...130 B3
Deer Park Cl BH25 .194 C2
Deer Park Farm Ind Est
SO50 ....57 C1
Deer Sanctuary★ BH24 .119 C3
Deerhurst Cl SO40 .100 B3
Deerhurst Ho 3 PO6 .133 A1
Deerleap Cl SO45 ..126 A2
Deerleap La SO40 ..100 B1
Deerleap Way
Hythe SO45 ......126 A2
New Milton BH25 ..195 A3
Defender Rd SO19 .103 B2
Defender Way SO19 .103 B2
Defoe Cl PO15 ....129 B4
Delamere Gdns BH10 .189 C2
Delamere Rd PO4 .182 C2
Delaval Ho 32 PO1 .182 A3
Delft Cl SO31 ....128 B4
Delft Gdns PO8 ..111 B1
Delft Mews BH23 .207 B3
Delhi Cl BH14 ...203 B2
Delhi Rd BH9 ....189 C1
Delilah Rd BH15 .201 B2
Delius Ave SO19 .104 B2
Delius Wlk SO19 .104 C3
Delkeith Ct BH22 .165 B2
Dell Cl Broadstone BH18 .186 C2
Fair Oak SO50 ....57 B1
Waterlooville PO7 .134 A4
Dell Cotts SO24 ..15 C1
Dell Piece E PO8 .112 B3
Dell Piece W PO8 .112 B3
Dell Quay Cl PO13 .155 A1
Dell Rd Southampton SO18 .79 C1
Winchester SO23 ..11 B3
Dell The
Barton on Sea BH25 .209 B4
Havant PO9 ....135 A1
Portchester PO16 ..131 A4
Delcrest Path PO6 .134 A1
Dellfield Cl 14 PO4 .133 A1
Delme Dr PO16 ...131 B1
Delme Dr PO16 ...131 B1
Delme Sq 28 PO16 .131 A1
Delph Rd BH21 ...187 B4
Delph Woods Woodland
Trail★ BH21 .....187 B4
Delphi Way PO7 .134 C1
Delta Bsns Pk PO16 .155 A4
Delta Cl BH23 ...208 A4
Dempsey Cl SO19 .104 B3
Denbigh Cl Eastleigh SO50 .55 C3
Totton SO40 .....100 B3
Denbigh Dr PO16 .130 B3
Denbigh Gdns SO16 .78 C2
Denby Rd BH15 ..202 C2
Dene Cl Chilworth SO16 .78 C4
Locks Heath SO31 .128 C2
Ringwood BH24 ..158 B4
Hollow PO6 ......158 B4
Dene Rd SO40 ...100 B1
Dene Way SO40 ..100 B1
Denecote Lo BH13 .214 D4
Deneside Copse SO41 .197 A1
Deneve Ave PO7 ..187 C1
Denewood Copse BH22 .138 B2
Denewood Rd PO4 .182 C2
Denewulf Cl 2 SO32 .83 B4
Denham Cl Poole BH17 .187 C2
Denham Ct SO23 ..2 A1
Denham Dr BH23 ..193 C1
Denham Fields SO50 .57 B2
Denham Gdns SO41 .127 A3
Denham's Cnr SO32 .81 B3
Denhill Cl PO11 ..184 C3
Denholm Cl BH24 .117 B1
Denison Rd BH17 .187 B1
Denmark La BH21 .202 B2
Denmark Rd
Bournemouth BH9 .189 C1
Poole BH15 ......202 B2
Denmark Terr BH1 .205 C4
Denmead PO25 ...195 B2
Denmead Ho 3 PO1 .215 C4
Denmead Inf Sch PO7 .111 A2
Denmead Jun Sch PO7 .111 A2
Dennet Ho SO23 ..2 B1
Dennetts La 19 BH15 .202 A1
Dennett Ho SO23 .104 A4
Denning Mews PO1 .215 B3

Dennis Rd BH21 ....186 B3
Dennis Way GU33 ....21 A2
Dennison Ct 8 SO15 ....102 A4
Dennistoun Ave BH23 ...207 C4
Denny Cl SO45 ....151 A2
Densome Cnr SP5 ....71 A3
Denville Ave PO16 ......156 B3
Denville Cl PO6 ....158 C4
Denvilles Cl PO9 ....136 A1
Denwood Rd BH4 ....204 A2
Denzil Ave Netley SO31 ..127 B3
Southampton SO14 ......103 A3
Depedene Cl SO45 ......150 B2
Derby Ct PO13 ....180 B3
Derby Ho 4 SO40 ....56 A1
Derby Rd
Bournemouth BH1 ....205 B2
Eastleigh SO50 ....55 C1
Portsmouth PO2 ....157 B1
Southampton SO14 ......103 A3
Dereham Way BH12 ......203 C3
Deridene Ct SO40 ......100 B3
Derlyn Rd PO16 ....131 A1
Derritt La BH23 ....192 B4
Derrybrian Gdns BH25 ...195 A1
Dersingham Cl PO6 .....133 C1
Derwent Cl
Bournemouth BH9 ....190 A1
Ferndown BH22 ....166 A3
Horndean PO8 ....88 B1
Stubbington PO14 ......154 B2
West End SO18 ....80 A1
Derwent Dr SO40 ....100 A4
Derwent Rd
Lee-on-the-Solent PO13 .179 C1
New Milton BH25 ....195 A3
Southampton SO16 ....77 C1
Derwentwater Rd BH21 ..163 B1
Desborough Cl 9 PO6 ..133 A1
Desborough Rd SO50 .....56 A1
Deveniish Rd SO22 ....1 B2
Devenish Rd BH23 ......207 A4
Deverell Pl PO7 ....134 B2
Devine Gdns 5 SO30 .....56 C1
Devon Cl SO53 ....55 B2
Devon Dr SO53 ....55 B2
Devon Rd
Christchurch BH23 .....206 C4
Poole BH15 ....202 C3
Portsmouth PO3 ....158 A2
Devonshire Ave PO4 ....183 A2
Devonshire Gdns
Burslendon SO31 ....105 A1
Hythe SO45 ....150 A4
Devonshire Inf Sch PO4 .182 C2
Devonshire Mans 10
SO15 ....102 C3
Devonshire Rd SO15 ....102 C3
Devonshire Sq PO4 .....182 C2
Devonshire Way PO14 ...154 B4
Dew La SO50 ....55 C2
Dewar Cl PO15 ....129 B3
Deweys La BH24 ....140 C4
Dewlands Pk BH31 ......114 B3
Dewlands Rd BH31 ......114 B3
Dewlands Way BH31 .....114 C3
Dewlish Cl BH17 ....188 A1
Dewsbury Ct 3 SO18 ....80 A1
Dhekelia Cl PO1 ....215 C4
Dial Cl BH23 ....169 B1
Diamond Cl SP6 ....93 C1
Diamond Ct
Fordingbridge SP6 ......93 C4
Waterlooville PO7 .....134 C4
Diamond St 52 PO5 .....215 A1
Diana Cl Gosport PO12 ..180 C2
Havant PO10 ....136 C2
Diana Ct BH23 ....209 A4
Diana Way BH21 ....156 C4
Dibben Wlk SO51 ....28 B1
Dibble Dr SO52 ....53 C2
Dibden Cl
Bournemouth BH8 ......190 B2
Havant PO9 ....135 B2
Dibden Lodge Cl SO45 ..125 C3
Dibles Rd SO31 ....128 C1
Dickens Cl PO2 ....182 B4
Dickens Dr PO15 ....106 B1
Dickens Rd BH6 ....206 B4
Dickson Pk PO17 ....108 A2
Didcot Rd Poole BH17 ..202 B4
Southampton SO15 ....78 B1
Dieppe Cres PO2 ....157 C2
Dieppe Gdns PO12 .....180 C2
Dight Rd PO12 ....181 B1
Diligence Cl SO31 .....105 A1
Dillington Ho 2 PO7 ...134 C4
Dilly Rd BH25 ....210 A4
Dimond Cl SO18 ....79 C1
Dimond Hill SO18 ....79 C1
Dimond Rd SO18 ....79 C1
Dingle Rd BH5 ....206 A2
Dingle Way SO31 ......128 B2
Dingley Rd BH15 ......202 B3
Dinham Ct BH25 ....195 B2
Dinham Rd BH25 ....195 B2
Dinsey Cl SO16 ....101 C4
Dipora Rd BH21 ....184 C4
Disa Ho SO15 ....102 C2
Discovery Ct PO14 .....154 B3
Disraeli Rd BH23 ......207 B3
Ditcham Cres PO9 .....135 C2
Ditcham Park Sch GU31 .98 C4
Ditchbury SO41 ....197 B3

Ditton Cl PO14 ....154 B2
Ditton Cotts SO42 .....148 C1
Dock La SO42 ....149 A1
Dock Mill Cotts 3 PO5 .182 B1
Dock Rd PO12 ....181 B2
Dockenfield Cl PO9 ....135 B2
Doctor's Hill SO51 ......26 A2
Doctors La GU32 ....37 B3
Dodds La SO32 ....84 B3
Dodgson Cl SP6 ....70 C4
Dodwell La SO31 ....105 A2
Doe Copse Way BH25 ...194 C2
Dogdean BH21 ....163 B4
Dogkennel La PO17 .....86 C2
Dogwood Dell 8 PO7 ...134 C3
Dogwood Rd BH18 ......186 C1
Dolbery Rd N BH12 .....188 B1
Dolbery Rd S BH12 .....188 B1
Dolphin Ave BH10 .....189 C3
Dolphin Cl 11 SO40 ....56 C1
Dolphin Cres PO12 .....181 B2
Dolphin Ct
7 Portsmouth PO5 .....182 C1
Stubbington PO14 .....154 A2
Dolphin Ctr BH15 .....202 B1
Dolphin Hill SO21 ......32 A3
Dolphin Rd BH25 ......210 A4
Dolphin Way PO12 .....181 B1
Dolton Rd SO16 ....77 C2
Dome Alley SO23 ....11 A4
Dominie Wlk 19 SO19 ..179 C1
Dominion Ctr BH11 ....188 C2
Dominion Rd BH11 .....188 C2
Dominy Cl SO45 ......126 A2
Domum Rd
Portsmouth PO2 ......157 C1
Winchester SO23 ....11 A3
Domvilles App PO2 ...157 C1
Donaldson Rd PO6 ....157 C3
Doncaster Rd SO50 .....80 A4
Donigers Cl SO32 ......84 A3
Donigers Dell SO32 ....84 A3
Donkey La SO30 ....106 A4
Donnelly Rd BH6 ......206 C3
Donnelly St PO12 ......181 A3
Donnington Ct 16 SO23 ..2 A1
Donnington Dr
Chandler's Ford SO53 ...55 A2
Christchurch BH23 .....208 A4
Donnington Gr SO17 ....79 B1
Donoughmore Rd 1
BH1 ....205 C2
Dorcas Cl 2 PO7 ......112 A1
Dorchester Cl SO15 ...102 C4
Dorchester Gdns BH15 .202 C3
Dorchester Mans BH1 ..205 B2
Dorchester Rd
Poole BH15 ....202 C3
Upton BH16 ....201 A4
Dore Ave PO16 ....132 B1
Dores La Braishfield SO51 ..29 A4
Hursley SO51 ....29 A4
Doric Cl SO53 ....55 C4
Dorking Cres PO6 .....157 C4
Dorland Gdns SO40 ....100 B3
Dorlands Rd PO8 ......112 B4
Dormers The BH25 ....194 C1
Dormington Rd PO6 ...133 B1
Dormy Cl SO31 ....128 B2
Dormy Way PO13 ......155 A4
Dornie Rd BH13 ......214 C4
Dornmere La PO7 .....135 A4
Dorothy Ct PO5 ....215 C1
Dorothy Dymond St
PO1 ....215 B3
Dorrick Ct 17 SO15 ...102 C4
Dorrien Rd PO12 .....181 A4
Dorrita Ave PO8 ......112 A2
Dorrita Cl PO4 ....182 C2
Dorrits The SO40 .....100 A4
Dorset Ave BH22 ......165 B2
Dorset Cl PO8 ....112 A3
Dorset Grange BH12 ..204 A3
Dorset Heavy Horse & Animal
Ctr* BH21 ....91 B1
Dorset Ho BH13 ....204 A1
Dorset Lake Ave BH14 .214 A4
Dorset Lake Manor
BH14 ....203 A1
Dorset Rd
Bournemouth BH4 .....204 B3
Chandler's Ford SO53 ..55 B2
Christchurch BH23 ....207 C4
Dorset St SO14 ....103 A4
Dorstone Rd PO6 .....133 B1
Dorval Ho 22 SO15 ...102 C4
Dorval Manor 24 SO15 .102 C4
Douglas Ave BH23 ....207 A3
Douglas Cl BH16 .....201 B4
Douglas Cres SO19 ...104 B3
Douglas Gdns
Havant PO9 ....136 A2
Poole BH12 ....203 C3
Douglas Mews
Bournemouth BH6 ....206 B3
Upton BH16 ....201 B4
Douglas Rd
Bournemouth BH6 ....206 C3
Poole BH12 ....203 C3
Doulton Gdns BH14 ...203 A1
Doussie Cl BH16 .....201 A4
Dove Cl PO8 ....111 C2
Dove Dale SO50 ....55 B1
Dove Gdns SO31 ......129 A3
Dove La SO51 ....29 A4

Dover Cl Poole BH13 ...204 A2
Stubbington PO14 .....154 A2
Dover Cr PO11 ....183 A4
Dover Rd Poole BH13 ..204 A2
Portsmouth PO3 ......183 A4
Dover St SO14 ....103 A4
Dovercourt Rd PO6 ...158 A3
Doveshill Cres BH10 ..189 B2
Doveshill Gdns BH10 ..189 B2
Doveshill Mobile Home Pk
BH10 ....189 B2
Doveys Cl BH24 ......143 A2
Dowds Cl SO30 ....105 A4
Dowell Ho PO4 ....183 A1
Dowlands Cl BH10 ....189 B2
Dowlands Rd BH10 ....189 B2
Down End PO6 ....134 B1
Down End Rd PO6 ....134 B1
Down Farm La SO22,SO23 ..1 C4
Down Farm Pl PO8 .....88 B1
Down Lodge Cl SP6 ....93 A3
Down Rd Horndean PO8 ..88 A1
Horndean PO8 ....88 B1
Down's Park Ave SO40 ..101 A3
Down's Park Cres SO40 .101 A3
Down's Park Rd SO40 ..101 A3
Downend Rd PO16 .....131 C1
Downey Cl BH11 ......188 C1
Downham Cl PO8 ......111 C2
Downhouse Rd PO8 .....88 A2
Downing Ct PO12 .....181 B1
Downland Cl
Botley SO30 ....105 C4
Locks Heath SO31 .....128 A2
Downland Pl SO30 ....105 A3
Downlands Cl SP5 ......46 C3
Downlands Pl BH17 ...202 C4
Downlands Rd SO22 ....10 A2
Downley Point PO9 ...136 A2
Downley Rd PO9 .....136 A2
Downs Cl PO7 ....134 C2
Downscroft Gdns SO30 .105 A4
Downside SO13 ....155 B1
Downside Ave SO19 ...104 A3
Downside Rd
Waterlooville PO7 ....134 B2
Winchester SO22 ....1 A1
Downsway The PO16 ..156 B4
Downton CE Prim Sch
SP5 ....46 C4
Downton Cl BH8 .....190 B2
Downton Hill SP5 ......47 B4
Downton Ho 2 PO6 ...157 B4
Downton La SO41 .....210 C4
Downton Sec Sch SP5 ..46 C4
Downview Rd SP6 ......43 A2
Downwood Cl
Fordingbridge SP6 .....69 B1
West Moors BH22 ......61 A1
Downwood Way PO8 ....88 B1
Doyle Ave PO2 ....157 C2
Doyle Cl PO2 ....157 C2
Doyle Ct
11 Portsmouth PO2 ..157 C2
Southampton SO19 ....103 C1
Doyle Ho PO9 ....135 A2
Doyne Rd BH14 ......203 C2
Dradfield La SO32 ....109 B4
Draffatts Ho SO15 ...102 B4
Dragon Est PO6 ......158 C4
Dragon La BH23 .....168 A4
Dragon St GU31,GU32 ..40 C2
Dragonfly Cl SO19 ....104 B2
Dragoon Way BH23 ...206 C4
Drake Cl
Christchurch BH23 ....207 C3
Locks Heath SO31 ....129 A3
Marchwood SO40 ......102 A1
New Milton BH25 .....194 C2
Ringwood BH24 ......117 B1
Drake Ct
Lee-on-the-Solent PO13 .179 B2
22 Poole BH15 ......202 B1
Drake Ho 4 PO1 .....182 A3
Drake Rd
Bishopstoke SO50 ......56 C2
Horndean PO8 ....88 A1
Lee-on-the-Solent PO13 .179 B2
Poole BH15 ....202 B1
Drakes Cl SO45 ......125 C1
Drakes La SO41 ......102 A2
Drakes Rd BH22 .....165 C2
Draper Rd
Bournemouth BH11 ..189 A2
Christchurch BH23 ...207 C4
Drapers Copse Cvn Site
SO45 ....125 B2
Draycote Rd PO8 ......88 B2
Draycott Rd PO7 .....189 B1
Drayton Cl 3 SO19 ...126 C4
Drayton La PO6 ......134 A1
Drayton Pl SO40 .....100 B4
Drayton Rd PO2 .....157 C1
Drayton St SO22 ....10 B4
Dreadnought Rd PO14 .130 A4
Dresden Dr PO8 ......111 C2
Dreswick Cl BH23 ...191 B2
Drew Cl BH12 ....204 B4
Drewitt Ind Est BH11 .188 C2
Drift Rd Clanfield PO8 ..88 B2
Fareham PO16 ....131 B1
Drift The PO9 ......113 A1
Driftwood Gdns
Portsmouth PO4 .....183 B1
Totton SO40 ....100 B3
Drill Shed Rd PO2 ...157 A1
Drinkwater Cl SO50 ...55 C2
Drive The Fareham PO16 .131 A1

Drive The continued
Gosport PO13 ....155 A1
Havant PO9 ....135 B1
Poole BH12 ....203 B3
Sherfield English SO51 ..25 A1
Southbourne PO10 ....161 B4
Totton SO40 ....100 C3
West End SO30 ....80 A2
West Wellow SO51 .....51 A1
Drove Cl SO21 ....31 C3
Drove Rd
Southampton SO19 ...104 A2
Southwick PO17 .....133 A2
Drove The
Blackfield SO45 ......150 C1
Durley SO32 ....82 B4
Fair Oak SO50 ....81 B3
Southampton SO18 ...104 A4
Swanmore SO32 ......84 B3
Totton SO40 ....76 A1
Twyford SO21 ....31 C3
West End SO30 ....80 C2
West Wellow SO51 .....50 C2
Droxford Cl PO12 .....180 C2
Droxford Jun Sch SO32 ..61 A1
Droxford Rd
Bournemouth BH6 ....206 A3
Swanmore SO32 ......84 B3
Druids Cl BH22 ......165 B1
Druitt Rd BH23 ......207 C4
Drum La GU32 ....40 C2
Drum Mead GU32 ......40 C2
Drummond Terr PO12 .181 B4
Drummond Ct SO22 ...10 C3
Drummond Ct
4 Eastleigh SO50 ......56 A3
8 Hythe SO45 ......126 A3
Southampton SO19 ...103 C2
Drummond Dr SO14 ..103 B4
Drummond Rd
Bournemouth BH1 ...205 B2
Hedge End SO30 ......81 B1
3 Hythe SO45 ......126 A2
Portsmouth PO1 .....215 C4
Drummond Way SO53 ..55 A4
Drury Rd BH4 ....204 A1
Dryden Ave PO6 .....132 C1
Dryden Cl Fareham PO16 .131 A1
St Leonards BH24 ...139 C3
Waterlooville PO7 ....134 C4
Dryden Pl 1 SO41 ...211 B3
Dryden Rd SO19 .....104 C3
Drysdale Mews PO4 ..183 A1
Duart Ct BH25 ....195 B2
Duck Island La 3 BH24 .119 A3
Duck La SH11 ....188 C2
Ducking Stool La BH23 .207 A3
Duckmead La GU33 ....21 A3
Duckworth Ho 25 PO1 .182 A3
Duddon Cl SO18 ....80 A1
Dudleston Heath Dr
PO8 ....112 A1
Dudley Ave
Fordingbridge SP6 ....69 C2
Hordle SO41 ....195 C2
Dudley Gdns BH10 ...189 B3
Dudley Pl BH10 .....195 A1
Dudley Rd
Bournemouth BH10 ..189 B3
Portsmouth PO3 .....183 A4
Dudley Terr GU33 .....21 A3
Dudmoor Farm Rd
BH23 ....191 C2
Dudmoor La BH23 ...191 C2
Dudsbury Ave
Ferndown BH22 .....165 B2
West Parley BH22 ...165 C2
Dudsbury Cres BH22 .165 C2
Dudsbury Ct 3 BH22 .207 C3
Dudsbury Gdns BH22 .189 C4
Dudsway Ct BH22 .....165 B3
Dudwell La PO10 ....137 C2
Dugald Drummond St
PO1 ....215 B3
Dugdell Cl BH22 .....165 C3
Duisbury Way PO5 ...182 A1
Duke Cres PO1 .....182 B4
Duke of Edinburgh Ho
PO1 ....182 A3
Duke St SO30 ....105 B3
Duke St SO14 ....103 A2
Duke Terr PO9 ......135 B3
Dukes Cl GU32 ....40 B2
Dukes Ct 4 SO32 .....83 B4
Dukes Dr BH11 ......188 C3
Dukes Mill Ctr 11 SO51 .52 C4
Dukes Rd Gosport PO12 .181 A4
Southampton SO14 ...103 A4
Dukes Wlk 14 SO41 ..211 A4
Dukes Wood Dr SO45 .126 A3
Dukesfield BH23 ....191 B1
Dulsie Rd BH3 ......204 B4
Dumbarton Cl PO2 ...182 B4
Dumbleton Cl SO19 ...104 C2
Dumbleton's Twrs SO19 .104 C2
Dummer Ct BH9 .....189 C3
Dummer Mews 23 SO23 ..2 A2
Dummer Rd SO22 .....10 A2
Dumpers Dro SO50 ....81 B3
Dumpton Sch BH21 ..163 B4
Dunbar Cl SO16 ......77 C3
Dunbar Cres BH23 ...193 C1
Dunbar Rd
Bournemouth BH3 ...204 C3
Portsmouth PO4 .....183 A2

Duncan Cl SO19 ....103 C1
Duncan Cooper Ho PO7 .134 B4
Duncan Ct SO19 ....104 B3
Duncan Rd
Locks Heath SO31 ....129 A3
New Milton BH25 ....195 B2
Portsmouth PO5 .....182 B1
Duncan Rd PO14 .....154 A4
Duncliff Rd BH6 .....207 A2
Duncombe Dr BH24 ..116 B2
Duncombe Rd SO32 ....63 B4
Duncton Rd PO8 ......88 B3
Duncton Way PO13 ...155 B2
Dundas Cl PO13 .....158 A1
Dundas La PO3 ......158 A1
Dundas Rd BH17 ....202 C4
Dundas Spur PO3 ...158 A1
Dundee Cl PO15 ....130 C2
Dundee Rd SO17 .....79 B1
Dundonald Cl
South Hayling PO11 ..185 A3
Southampton SO19 ...103 B1
Dundridge La SO32 ...60 B1
Dundry Way SO30 ...105 B4
Dune Crest BH13 ....214 B2
Dunedin Cl BH22 ...165 A2
Dunedin Dr BH22 ...165 A2
Dunedin Gdns BH22 .165 A2
Dunedin Gr BH23 ...208 B4
Dunfield Way SO45 .150 C1
Dunford Cl
Barton on Sea BH25 .209 C4
New Milton BH25 ...194 C1
Dunford Rd BH12 ...203 B3
Dunhurst (Bedales Jun Sch)
GU32 ....40 C3
Dunhurst Cl PO9 ....136 A2
Dunkeld Rd
Bournemouth BH3 ...204 C3
Gosport PO12 ......181 A4
Dunkirk Cl SO16 .....78 B2
Dunkirk Rd SO16 .....78 B2
Dunlin Cl
Christchurch BH23 ..208 A3
Portsmouth PO4 .....183 B3
Dunn Cl PO4 ....183 A2
Dunnings La SO52 ...53 C3
Dunnock Cl
Ferndown BH22 .....165 A4
Rowland's Castle PO9 .113 A1
Dunsbury Way PO9 ..135 C3
Dunsmore Cl PO5 ...215 B2
Dunstable Wlk PO14 .154 B4
Dunstans La BH15 ...203 A3
Dunster Cl SO16 .....78 B3
Dunvegan Dr SO16 ...78 B3
Dunvegan Rd SO16 ...78 B3
Dunvegan Way SO16 .78 B3
Dunyeats Rd BH18 ..187 A2
Dunyeats Robt BH18 .187 B3
Durban Cl SO51 ......28 A1
Durban Ct PO1 .....215 C4
Durban Ho PO1 ....215 C4
Durban Rd PO1 ....182 C4
Durdells Ave BH11 ..189 A3
Durdells Gdns BH11 .189 A3
Durford Ct PO9 .....135 B3
Durford Rd GU31 ....41 B2
Durham Gdns PO7 ..134 C3
Durham St Gosport PO12 .181 A3
Portsmouth PO1 ....215 B3
Durland Cl BH25 ...195 A1
Durley Ave PO8 ....111 C2
Durley Brook Rd
Durley SO32 ....81 C3
Durley SO32,SO50 ....82 A3
Durley CE Prim Sch
SO32 ....82 A3
Durley Chine Rd BH2 .204 B1
Durley Chine Rd BH2 .204 B1
Durley Chine Rd S BH2 .204 B1
Durley Cres SO40 ...100 B3
Durley Gdns BH2 ....204 B1
Durley Hall Rd SO32 ..58 B1
Durley Rd
Durley SO32 ....81 C3
Gosport PO12 ......181 A3
Durley Rd S PO12 ..204 B1
Durley St SO32 .....204 B1
Durlston Court Sch
BH25 ....210 A4
Durlston Cres BH23 .191 B2
Durlston Rd Poole BH14 .203 B1
Southampton SO16 ...77 B1
Durnford Rd SO14 ..103 A3
Durngate Pl SO23 ...11 A4
Durngate Terr 41 SO23 .11 A4
Durnstown SO41 ....172 B1
Durrant PRU PO9 ...136 A4
Durrant Rd
7 Bournemouth BH2 .204 C2
Poole BH14 ....203 B2
Durrant Way SO41 ..172 A1
Durrants Gdns PO9 ..136 A4
Durrants Rd PO9 ...136 A4
Durrington Pl BH7 ..206 A4
Durrington Rd BH7 ..206 A4
Dursley Cres PO6 ...157 B4
Durweston Dr BH9 ..190 A2
Dutton La SO50 ......56 A2
Dutton's Rd SO51 ....52 B4
Dyer Rd SO15 ......102 B4
Dymchurch Ho 3 PO6 .157 C4
Dymewood Rd BH21 .138 C4
Dymoke St PO10 ....136 C2
Dymott Cl SO15 ....102 B3
Dyneley Gn SO18 ....80 A1

Dyram Cl SO50 55 C3
Dysart Ave PO6 158 A4
Dyserth Cl SO19 104 A1
Dyson Dr SO23 2 A1

E

E Ave SO45 150 C3
Eadens La SO40 99 B4
Eagle Ave PO8 111 C2
Eagle Cl
Chandler's Ford SO53 55 A2
Portchester PO16 155 C4
Eagle Ct 12 SO23 10 C4
Eagle House Sch BH14 203 A2
Eagle Rd
Lee-on-the-Solent PO13 179 B2
Poole BH12 204 A2
Eaglhurst 5 BH12 204 A2
Eame's Cotts GU32 38 C1
Eames La GU33 19 C4
Earle Ho 3 SO23 11 B4
Earle Rd BH4 204 B1
Earley Ct SO41 197 C2
Earlham Dr BH14 203 B2
Earls Cl SO50 57 A1
Earls Rd Fareham PO16 155 A4
Southampton SO14 103 A4
Earlsdon St PO5 215 B2
Earlsdon Way BH23 208 C4
Earlsdown 47 SO23 11 A4
Earlswood Dr SP6 92 C3
Earlswood Pk BH25 195 B2
Earnley Rd PO11 185 C1
East Ave
Barton on Sea BH25 209 B4
Bournemouth BH3 204 B3
East Avenue Rdbt BH3 204 C3
East Bank Rd SO42 173 A4
East Bargate 7 SO14 103 A2
East Boldre Rd SO42 175 B3
East Borough BH21 163 A3
East Cams Cl PO16 131 C1
East Cl BH25 209 B4
East Cliff Way BH23 208 B4
East Cosham Rd PO6 158 A4
East Ct Cosham PO6 158 A4
Portsmouth PO1 182 C4
East Dean Rd SO51 4 C1
East Dr SO50 56 C2
East Field Cl PO10 137 C1
East Hill Lymington SO41 197 C2
Winchester SO23 11 A3
East Hill Cl PO16 131 B1
East Hill Dr GU33 21 A2
East Hoe Rd PO7 86 A2
East House Ave PO14 179 B3
East Howe La BH10 189 B2
East La SO41 196 C1
East Links SO53 55 B1
East Lodge
Fareham PO15 130 B1
7 Lee-on-the-Solent PO13 179 C1
East Lodge Pk PO6 158 C4
East Meon CE Prim Sch GU32 38 B1
East Meon Rd PO8 88 A3
East Overcliff Dr BH1 205 B2
East Park Terr SO14 103 A3
East Quay BH15 202 B1
East Quay Rd BH15 202 B1
East Rd Fawley SO45 150 B4
Southwick PO17 133 A3
East Shore Sch PO4 183 A3
East St Fareham PO16 131 B1
Hambledon PO7 86 B2
Havant PO9 135 C1
Poole BH15 202 B1
Portchester PO16 156 C4
Portsmouth PO1 182 A2
Southampton SO14 103 A2
Titchfield PO14 154 A4
Westbourne PO10 137 A2
Wimborne Minst BH21 163 B2
East Street Ctr 16 SO14 103 A2
East Surrey St PO1 215 B3
East View Rd BH24 141 A4
East View Terr 9 PO9 135 C1
East Way
Bournemouth BH8 190 B1
Corfe Mullen BH21 186 B3
East Woodhay Rd SO22 1 B2
Eastacre SO22 1 C1
Eastbourne Ave
Gosport PO12 180 C4
Southampton SO15 102 B4
Eastbourne Rd PO3 183 A4
Eastbrook Cl
Gosport PO12 180 C4
Locks Heath SO31 129 A3
Eastbrook Row BH21 163 B2
Eastbury Ct BH23 207 C2
Eastchurch Cl SO16 77 C2
Eastcliff Cl PO13 179 C2
Eastcot Cl SO45 150 B2
Eastcott Cl BH7 206 A4
Eastcroft Rd PO12 180 C3
Easter Rd BH9 190 A1
Eastern Ave PO4 183 A3
Eastern Ind Ctr PO6 158 B3
Eastern Par
Fareham PO16 155 A4
Portsmouth PO4 182 C1
Eastern Rd Fawley SO45 151 C1
Havant PO9 136 A1
Lymington SO41 197 B2
Eastern Rd *continued*
Portsmouth PO3, PO6 158 B2
Portsmouth, Whale Is PO2 157 A1
West End SO30 80 B1
Eastern Terr PO4 183 A1
Eastern Villas Rd PO4 182 B1
Eastern Way
Fareham PO16 131 B1
Milford on Sea SO41 211 C2
Eastfield Ave PO14 154 C4
Eastfield Ct BH24 141 B4
Eastfield La BH24 141 B4
Eastfield Rd
Portsmouth PO4 183 A2
Southampton SO17 103 B4
Eastfields PO5 215 C1
Eastgate St
Southampton SO14 103 A2
Winchester SO23 11 A4
Eastlake Ave BH12 203 B3
Eastlake Cl GU31 41 B2
Eastlake Hts PO4 183 B2
Eastlands BH25 195 A1
Eastleigh Coll SO50 56 A1
Eastleigh Coll of F Ed SO50 56 A1
Eastleigh Lakeside Rly* SO50 79 C4
Eastleigh Rd
Fair Oak SO50 57 B1
Havant PO9 136 B2
Eastleigh Sta SO50 56 A2
Eastleigh Town Mus* SO50 56 A1
Eastman Cl SP5 47 A3
Eastmeare Ct SO40 100 B3
Eastney Farm Rd PO4 183 B2
Eastney Rd PO4 183 A2
Eastney St PO4 183 A1
Eastoke Ave PO11 185 B1
Easton La SO21 2 C2
Easton Lane Bsns Ctr SO23 11 A4
Eastover Ct 10 PO9 135 B3
Eastville Rd SO50 57 B1
Eastways SO32 83 B4
Eastwood SO51 25 B1
Eastwood Ave BH22 165 C3
Eastwood Cl PO11 185 A3
Eastwood Rd 5 PO2 157 C2
Eastworth Rd BH31 114 C4
Eaton Rd BH13 204 A1
Ebblake Ent Pk BH31 115 B3
Ebblake Ind Est BH31 115 B2
Ebden Rd SO23 11 A4
Ebenezer La BH24 140 C4
Ebery Gr PO3 183 B4
Ebor Cl BH22 165 C1
Ebor Rd BH12 203 B3
Eccles Rd BH15 202 A1
Ecton La PO3 158 B2
Eddystone Rd SO40 76 B1
Edelvale Rd SO18 80 A1
Eden Ct 20 BH1 205 A2
Eden Gr BH21 163 B2
Eden Rd SO18 80 A1
Eden Rise PO16 155 A4
Eden St PO1 215 B4
Eden Terr 10 PO2 157 B1
Eden Wlk SO53 55 A3
Edenbridge Rd PO4 183 B3
Edenbridge Way SO31 128 C3
Edgar Cres PO16 156 B3
Edgar Rd SO23 10 C3
Edgar Villas SO23 10 C3
Edgarton Rd BH17 187 B2
Edgbaston Ho PO5 215 B2
Edgecombe Cres PO13 180 B4
Edgefield Gr PO7 112 B1
Edgehill Rd
Bournemouth BH9 189 C1
Southampton SO18 79 C1
Edgell Rd PO10 137 A2
Edgemoor Rd BH22 139 A1
Edgerly Gdns PO6 157 C3
Edgeware Rd PO4 183 A3
Edgewood Ct GU33 21 A1
Edifred Rd BH9 190 A2
Edinburgh Ct SO15 102 A3
Edinburgh Ho 8 SO22 10 C4
Edinburgh Rd PO1 215 A3
Edington Cl SO32 83 A4
Edington Rd SO23 2 A1
Edith Haisman Cl SO15 102 B3
Edmondsham Ho Gdns* BH21 91 A2
Edmondsham Rd BH31 114 C4
Edmonsham Ho 23 BH2 204 C2
Edmund Rd PO4 182 C2
Edmunds Cl
Barton on Sea BH25 195 A1
Hedge End SO30 105 B3
Edneys La PO7 111 A3
Edward Ave SO50 56 B2
Edward Cl SO45 150 C1
Edward Gdns PO9 135 B1
Edward Gr PO16 132 C1
Edward Rd
Bournemouth BH11 189 A2
Christchurch BH23 207 C4
Hythe SO45 126 A2
Poole BH14 203 B3
Southampton SO15 102 B4
Winchester SO23 10 C3
Edward Way Ct BH11 189 A2
Edward's Cl 29 PO6 133 A1
Edwards Cl SO41 197 A2
Edwin Jones Gn SO15 102 C4
Edwina Cl
North Baddesley SO52 54 A2
Ringwood BH24 117 B1
Southampton SO19 104 A3
Edwina Dr BH17 187 A1
Edwina Ho SO18 79 C2
Effingham Gdns SO19 104 B2
Efford Ct SO41 197 A1
Efford Farm Cotts SO41 197 A1
Efford Way SO41 197 A1
Egan Cl PO2 157 C2
Egbert Rd SO23 2 A1
Egdon Cl BH22 165 A2
Egdon Ct BH16 201 A4
Egdon Dr BH21 187 C4
Egerton Gdns BH8 205 B3
Egerton Rd BH8 205 B3
Eglantine Cl PO8 112 A2
Eglantine Wlk PO8 112 B2
Egmont Cl BH24 140 B1
Egmont Dr BH24 140 B1
Egmont Gdns BH24 140 B1
Egmont Rd BH16 201 A2
Eight Acres SO51 53 A4
Eileen Beard Ho 51 PO9 136 A3
Elaine Gdns PO8 112 A3
Elan Cl SO18 80 A1
Elcombes Cl SO43 121 C3
Elder Cl
Locks Heath SO31 128 C1
Marchwood SO40 102 A1
Winchester SO22 10 B2
Elder Gn SO21 57 A4
Elder Rd PO9 136 A2
Elderberry Cl
Clanfield PO8 88 B2
Fair Oak SO50 57 A1
Elderberry La BH23 207 C3
Elderberry Way PO8 112 B2
Elderfield Cl PO10 137 A2
Elderfield Rd PO9 135 B4
Eldon Ave BH25 209 C4
Eldon Cl BH25 209 C4
Eldon Ct 9 Poole BH14 203 A2
Portsmouth PO5 215 B2
Eldon Ho 22 SO14 103 A2
Eldon Pl BH4 204 A2
Eldon Rd
Bournemouth BH9 189 C1
Braishfield SO20, SO51 7 A3
King's Somborne SO20 7 A3
Eldon St PO5 215 B2
Eldridge Gdns SO51 52 C4
Eleanor Dr BH11 188 B3
Eleanor Gdns BH23 206 C4
Electron Way SO53 55 B3
Elettra Ave PO7 134 B4
Eleven Cross SP6 68 A3
Elfin Ct 11 SO17 103 A4
Elfin Dr BH22 165 B4
Elgar Cl Gosport PO12 181 A1
Portchester PO6 156 C4
Southampton SO19 104 B2
Elgar Ct SO41 197 C2
Elgar Rd
Bournemouth BH10 189 B2
Southampton SO19 104 B2
Elgar Wlk PO7 134 C3
Elgin Cl Fareham PO15 130 C1
Hythe SO45 126 A2
Elgin Rd
Bournemouth BH3,BH4 204 B3
Cosham PO6 157 C3
Poole BH14 203 B1
Southampton SO15 102 B3
Elijah Cl BH15 201 C1
Eling Cl SO22 1 B2
Eling Ct PO9 135 B3
Eling Hill SO40 101 A3
Eling Inf Sch SO40 101 A3
Eling La SO40 101 A3
Eling Tide Mill* SO40 101 A3
Eling View SO15 101 B4
Elingfield Ct SO40 101 A4
Eliot Ho
14 New Milton BH25 195 A1
Southampton SO17 79 B1
Elise Cl BH7 206 A4
Eliza Pl PO12 181 B3
Elizabeth Ave BH23 206 C4
Elizabeth Cl Downton SP5 46 B4
West End SO30 80 B1
Wickham PO17 107 C2
Elizabeth Cres SO41 196 A1
Elizabeth Ct
12 Bournemouth BH1 205 A2
6 Cosham PO6 157 C4
Eastleigh SO50 56 A2
Fareham PO14 154 C4
4 Gosport PO12 181 A3
11 New Milton BH25 195 A1
Southampton, Aldermoor SO16 78 A2
Southampton, Portswood SO17 79 B1
West End SO30 80 B1
Elizabeth Gdns
Christchurch BH23 208 B4
Hythe SO45 126 A1
Portsmouth PO4 182 C1
Elizabeth Ho SO40 76 B1
Elizabeth Rd Poole BH15 202 B2
Stubbington PO14 179 B3
Upton BH16 201 B4
Waterlooville PO7 134 C3
Wickham PO17 108 A2
Wimborne Minst BH21 163 B3
Elizabeth Way
Bishop's Waltham SO32 83 A4
Eastleigh SO50 56 A3
Elkhams Cl SO41 196 B1
Elkstone Rd PO6 133 A1
Ellachie Gdns PO12 181 A1
Ellachie Mews PO12 181 A1
Ellachie Rd PO12 181 A1
Elland Cl SO50 57 B1
Elldene Ct SO40 100 C3
Ellen Gdns SO53 55 A3
Ellen Wren Ho SO18 79 C2
Ellerslie Cl PO14 179 A3
Ellery Gr SO41 197 C3
Ellesfield Dr BH22 165 B1
Ellesmere Orch PO10 137 A3
Ellingham Cross BH24 116 C3
Ellingham Dr BH24 116 B3
Ellingham Dro BH24 117 A3
Ellingham Rd BH25 209 B4
Elliot Cl SO40 100 B4
Elliot Rd BH11 188 C2
Elliot Rise SO30 81 B1
Ellis Rd SO19 104 C3
Ellisfield Rd PO9 135 C2
Ellwood Ave SO19 104 C3
Ellwood Cl SO19 104 C3
Elm Ave
Christchurch BH23 191 C1
Lymington SO41 197 B1
New Milton BH25 195 A1
Elm Cl
South Hayling PO11 185 A2
Southampton SO16 78 C2
Elm Close Est PO11 184 C2
Elm Cotts 8 BH24 141 A4
Elm Cres Hythe SO45 150 A4
Upham SO32 58 C3
Elm Ct
Chandler's Ford SO53 30 B1
4 New Milton BH25 195 A1
Southampton, Sholing SO19 103 C2
29 Southampton, Westwood Pk SO17 79 A1
Winchester SO22 10 C4
Elm Gdns
Bournemouth BH4 204 B3
West End SO30 80 B2
Elm Gr Eastleigh SO50 55 C1
Gosport PO12 181 A3
Portsmouth PO5 215 B1
South Hayling PO11 185 A2
Elm La PO9 135 C1
Elm Lodge PO5 215 C1
Elm Park Rd PO9 135 C1
Elm Rd
Bishop's Waltham SO32 83 C4
Havant PO9 160 A4
Winchester SO22 10 C4
Elm St Portsmouth PO1 215 A1
Southampton SO14 103 A2
Elm Terr Liss GU33 20 C3
Southampton SO14 103 A2
Elm Tree Wlk BH22 189 C4
Elmdale GU31 41 A2
Elmdale Cl SO31 152 B4
Elmdale Gr SO51 51 A1
Elmers Way BH23 169 A1
Elmes Dr SO15 101 C4
Elmes Rd BH9 189 C1
Elmeswelle Rd PO8 112 A3
Elmfield Cl SP5 47 B3
Elmfield La SO45 178 C4
Elmgate Dr BH7 206 A4
Elmhurst Rd
Bournemouth BH11 189 A3
Fareham PO16 155 A4
Gosport PO12 181 B2
West Moors BH22 138 C1
Elmhurst Way BH22 138 C1
Elmleigh Rd PO9 135 C1
Elmore Ave PO13 180 A3
Elmore Cl PO13 179 C1
Elmore Dr BH24 139 C3
Elmore Rd PO13 179 C1
Elmrise Prim Sch BH11 189 A2
Elms Ave BH14 203 A1
Elms Cl Fordingbridge SP6 69 A1
Poole BH14 203 A1
Elms Rd PO16 155 A4
Elms Way BH6 206 C2
Elmsdown Ct BH24 140 C4
Elmsleigh Ct SO17 79 A2
Elmsleigh Gdns SO16 79 A2
Elmslie Gdns SO31 104 C1
Elmstead Rd BH13 214 C4
Elmtree Cl SO40 100 A1
Elmtree Gdns
2 Eastleigh SO50 56 A1
Romsey SO51 53 B3
Elmtree Rd PO6 158 C4
Elmwood Ave
Fordingbridge SP6 69 B1
Waterlooville PO7 134 C3
Elmwood Ct SO16 78 A1
Elmwood Lodge 2 PO16 131 A1
Elmwood Rd PO2 157 C2
Elmwood Way BH23 209 A4
Elphinstone Rd
Christchurch BH23 194 A1
Portsmouth PO5 182 B1
Elsfred Rd PO14 179 A3
Elson Inf Sch PO12 181 A4
Elson Jun Sch PO12 181 A4
Elson La PO12 181 A4
Elson Rd PO12 181 A4
Elstead Gdns PO7 134 B2
Elstree Rd SO19 103 C3
Eltham Cl BH7 206 A4
Elvin Cl SO41 195 C2
Elwell Gn PO11 184 C2
Elwyn Rd BH1 205 B3
Ely Ct PO13 180 B3
Elysium Ct BH22 165 C2
Emanuel St PO2 182 B4
Embankment Way BH24 141 A3
Embassy Ct PO4 215 D2
Emberley Cl BH22 166 A3
Embley Cl SO40 76 B1
Embley La SO51 51 C4
Embley Park Ind Est SO51 51 C4
Embley Park Jun Sch SO51 52 C4
Embley Park Sch SO51 51 C3
Embsay Rd SO31 128 B4
Emer Cl SO52 54 A3
Emerald Cl
Southampton SO19 104 A3
St Leonards BH24 139 C3
Waterlooville PO7 135 A4
Emerald Cres SO45 126 A2
Emerson Cl BH15 202 B1
Emerson Rd BH15 202 B1
Emily Cl BH23 192 A1
Emily Ct BH14 203 C3
Emily Davis Halls Of Residence 12 SO14 102 C3
Emmadale Ct 5 SO14 103 A3
Emmanuel CE Mid Sch BH31 114 C3
Emmanuel Cl PO14 129 B1
Emmett Rd SO16 77 C3
Emmons Cl SO31 128 A1
Empire Ct 13 PO9 135 C1
Empress Pk SO14 103 A4
Empress Rd
Lyndhurst SO43 121 C3
Southampton, Bevois Valley SO14 103 A4
Empshott Rd PO4 182 C2
Empson Wlk PO13 179 C2
Emsbrook Dr PO10 136 C1
Emsworth Common Rd PO9,PO10 136 C3
Emsworth House Cl PO10 136 C1
Emsworth Mus* PO10 160 C4
Emsworth Prim Sch PO10 136 C1
Emsworth Rd
Havant PO9 136 A1
Lymington SO41 197 C2
Portsmouth PO2 157 C1
Southampton SO15 102 A4
Thorney Island PO10 161 A1
Emsworth Sta PO10 136 C1
Encombe Cl BH12 203 C4
Endeavour Cl 17 SO15 102 A4
Endeavour Pk BH24 141 A3
Endeavour Rd PO12 181 B2
Endeavour Way SO45 126 A3
Enderleigh Ho PO9 135 C1
Enderwood Cl SO40 100 A4
Endfield Cl BH23 191 C1
Endfield Rd
Bournemouth BH9 190 A1
Christchurch BH23 191 C1
Endle St SO14 103 A2
Endofield Cl PO14 154 C3
Enfield Cres BH15 202 C3
Enfield Gr SO19 103 C2
Enfield Rd BH15 202 C3
Englands Way BH11 188 B2
Englefield Ct 4 SO31 127 A3
Englefield Rd SO18 103 B4
English Ct 16 SO51 52 C4
English Rd SO15 102 A4
Enmill La SO22 9 C3
Ennel Copse SO52 54 A2
Ennerdale Cl PO8 88 B1
Ennerdale Gdns SO18 80 A1
Ennerdale Rd
Southampton SO16 77 C1
Stubbington PO14 154 B2
Ensbury Ave BH10 189 B1
Ensbury Cl BH10 189 B1
Ensbury Ct BH10 189 C1
Ensbury Park Rd BH9 189 C1
Ensign Dr PO13 180 B3
Ensign Pk SO31 127 C1
Ensign Way SO31 127 C1
Enterprise Cl SO31 128 C1
Enterprise Ctr
Fareham PO14 155 A3
Portsmouth PO3 158 A2
Enterprise Ind Est PO8 112 B4
Enterprise Rd
Chilworth SO16 54 B1
Horndean PO8 112 B4
Enterprise Way
Hurn BH23 190 B4
Southampton SO14 103 A1
Eperston Rd PO8 112 A3
Epiphany CE Prim Sch BH9 190 A2
Epping Cl SO18 80 A1
Epsom Cl SO50 81 B4
Epsom Ct PO15 129 B4
Epworth Rd PO2 157 C1
Erasmus Pk SO23 2 B1

Eric Rd PO14 ....179 B3
Erica Cl
  Locks Heath SO31 ....128 C2
  Waterlooville PO8 .....112 A2
Erica Dr BH21 ....186 B3
Erica Way PO8 ....112 A2
Ericksen Rd BH11 ......189 B2
Erinbank Mans BH1 ....205 B2
Ernest Cl PO10 ....136 C1
Ernest Rd Havant PO9 ..135 B2
  Portsmouth PO1 ....182 C4
Erpingham Rd BH12 ....204 A3
Errington Rd 7 SO50 ...56 A1
Erskine Cl SO16 ....77 C3
Erskine Rd SO27 ....10 C4
Escombe Rd SO50 ....56 B2
Escur Cl PO22 ....157 C2
Esdaile La BH24 ....142 C2
Esher Gr PO7 ....111 B1
Eskdale Cl PO8 ....88 B1
Eskdale Ho 10 PO6 ....133 A1
Esmond Cl PO10 ....160 C4
Esmonde Cl PO13 ....179 C1
Esmonde Way BH17 ....202 C4
Esplanade Poole BH13 ..214 C4
  Portsmouth PO4 ....183 A1
Esplanade Gdns PO4 ...183 B1
Esplanade The PO12 ...181 C2
Essex Ave PO23 ....193 C2
Essex Gn SO53 ....55 B1
Essex Rd PO1 ....191 C2
Esslemont Rd PO4 .....182 C2
Estella Rd PO2 ....182 B4
Estridge Cl SO31 ......105 A1
Ethel Rd PO1 ....215 D4
Ethelbert Rd BH21 ....163 B2
Ethelburt Ave SO16 ....79 B3
Ethelred Gdns SO40 ...100 B3
Eton Ave SO16 ....214 B2
Eton Rd PO5 ....215 D2
Ettrick Rd BH13 ....204 A1
Eucalyptus Ave BH24 ..140 A1
European Way SO14 ....103 C1
Euryalus Rd PO14 ......155 A3
Euston Gr BH24 ....141 A3
Euston Rd PO4 ....183 A3
Eva Allaway Ct 26 PO1 .182 A3
Evans Cl
  Bournemouth BH11 ....188 C1
  Portsmouth PO2 ....157 A1
  St Leonards BH24 .....139 C3
Evans Rd PO4 ....183 A2
Evelegh Rd PO6 ....158 B4
Evelyn Cl SO22 ....10 A3
Evelyn Cres SO15 .....102 B4
Evelyn Mews 1 BH9 ...189 C1
Evelyn Rd BH9 ....190 A1
Evening Glade PO22 ...157 C1
Eventide Homes BH8 ..190 C1
Everdene Cl BH22 .....165 B1
Everdon La PO3 ....158 B2
Everest Rd BH23 ......207 C4
Everglades Ave PO8 ...111 C2
Everglades Cl BH22 ...165 B4
Evergreen Cl
  Marchwood SO40 .....101 C1
  Three Legged Cross BH21 .138 C4
  Waterlooville PO7 ....134 B4
Evergreens
  St Leonards BH24 .....139 C3
  Totton SO40 ....101 A3
Evering Ave BH12 .....188 B1
Evering Gdns BH12 ...188 B1
Everlea Cl SO41 ....196 C1
Everon Gdns BH25 ....195 A1
Evershot Rd BH8 ......190 C1
Eversleigh Rd BH21 ...204 B1
Eversley Cres PO9 ....135 C2
Eversley Pl SO22 ....10 B3
Everton Rd SO41 ......196 A1
Evesham Cl
  Bournemouth BH7 ....206 A4
  Southampton SO16 .....79 A3
Evesham Ct BH13 .....204 A1
Ewart Cl SO45 ....126 A3
Ewart Rd PO1 ....182 C4
Ewell Way SO40 ....76 B1
Ewhurst Cl PO9 ....135 B2
Exbourne Manor BH1 ..205 B2
Exbury Cl SO50 ....56 A1
Exbury Dr BH11 ....188 C3
Exbury Gdns* SO45 ...177 A3
Exbury Rd
  Blackfield SO45 ......150 C1
  Havant PO9 ....136 B2
Excellent Rd PO14 ....154 C3
Excelsior Rd PO14 ....203 B2
Exchange Rd PO1 .....215 A3
Exeter Cl Eastleigh SO50 ..155 C3
  Emsworth PO10 ......136 C1
  Locks Heath SO31 ....128 C1
  Southampton SO18 .....80 A1
Exeter Cres BH2 ....204 C2
Exeter Ct
  10 Christchurch BH23 ..209 A4
  Gosport PO13 ....180 B3
Exeter La BH2 ....204 C1
Exeter Park Mans BH2 .204 C1
Exeter Park Rd BH2 ...204 C1
Exeter Rd
  Bournemouth BH2 ....204 C2
  Portsmouth PO4 ......182 C1
  Southampton SO18 ...104 A4

Exford Ave SO18 ......104 B4
Exford Dr SO18 ....104 B4
Exleigh Cl SO18 ......104 A3
Exmoor Cl
  Swanwick PO15 ....79 B1
  Totton SO40 ....100 A4
Exmoor Rd SO14 ......103 A3
Exmouth Gdns SO50 ...81 B4
Exmouth Rd
  Gosport PO12 ....181 A4
  Portsmouth PO5 ......182 B1
Exmouth St SO14 .....103 A3
Explosion Mus of Naval
  Firepower* PO12 ......181 B4
Exton Gdns PO16 .....132 B1
Exton Rd
  Bournemouth BH6 ....206 B4
  Havant PO9 ....136 A3
Eyebright Cl SO50 .....81 B3
Eyeworth Wlk SO45 ..125 B2
Eynham Ave SO19 ....104 B3
Eynham Cl SO19 ......104 B3
Eynon Mews BH24 ....140 C3
Eyre Cl SO40 ....100 B3

F

F Ave SO45 ....150 C3
Faber Cl PO9 ....136 A2
Faber Mews SO51 ......53 A4
Fabers Yd 10 SO22 .....10 C4
Fabian Cl PO7 ....102 A4
Factory Rd Eastleigh SO50 .56 A1
  Upton BH16 ....201 B3
Fair Field SO51 ....28 A1
Fair Isle SO19 ....104 A3
Fair Isle Cl PO14 .....154 A2
Fair La SO21 ....11 C4
Fair Lea BH2 ....204 C1
Fair Oak Ct
  6 Fair Oak SO50 ......57 B1
  Gosport PO12 ....180 B2
Fair Oak Dr PO9 .....135 C2
Fair Oak Inf Sch SO50 ..57 B1
Fair Oak Jun Sch SO50 .57 B1
Fair Oak Rd SO50 .....57 B1
Fairacre Rise PO14 ...154 A4
Fairacre Wlk PO14 ...154 A4
Fairbairn Wlk SO53 ....54 C3
Fairbourne Cl PO8 ....111 C1
Fairclose Dr SO22 ......1 A3
Faircourt 18 BH25 ....195 A2
Faircross Cl SO45 ....150 B2
Fairdown Cl SO23 ......11 B4
Fairfax Cl SO22 ....10 A3
Fairfax Dr SO19 ......104 C3
Fairfax Mews SO19 ...104 C3
Fairfield
  Christchurch BH23 ....207 A4
  Denmead PO7 ....110 C3
Fairfield Ave PO14 ...154 C4
Fairfield Cl
  Christchurch BH23 ....207 A4
  Emsworth PO10 ......136 C1
  Hythe SO45 ....125 C2
  Lymington SO41 .....197 C2
  Wimborne Minst BH21 .163 C3
Fairfield Inf Sch PO9 .136 A1
Fairfield Rd
  Barton on Sea BH25 ..209 C4
  Compton(Hants) SO21 ..31 B3
  Havant PO9 ....135 C1
  Wimborne Minst BH21 .163 C3
  Winchester SO21 ....1 C1
Fairfield Sq PO6 ......157 C4
Fairgate Ctr The SP6 ...70 A2
Fairhavon Ct 12 BH5 .205 C2
Fairholme Cl PO12 ....181 A4
Fairlea Dr BH22 ......165 C2
Fairisle Inf Sch SO16 ...77 C2
Fairisle Jun Sch SO16 ..77 C2
Fairisle Rd SO16 ......77 C2
Fairlands Montessori Sch
  SO32 ....107 C4
Fairlawn Cl SO16 ......77 B4
Fairlawn Ho 27 SO22 ..10 C4
Fairlea Grange 3 SO16 .78 C2
Fairlea Rd
  Ensworth PO10 ......136 C2
  Lymington SO41 .....197 C3
Fairlead Dr PO13 .....180 B3
Fairlie BH24 ....117 B1
Fairlie Cl SO30 ....81 B2
Fairlie Pk PO14 ......203 C4
Fairlight La SO41 ....195 B4
Fairmead Ct PO11 ....184 C2
Fairmead Way SO40 ..100 C3
Fairmead Wlk PO8 ...112 A2
Fairmile Par BH23 ...191 C1
Fairmile Rd BH23 ....191 C1
Fairoak Rd
  Bishopstoke SO50 .....57 A1
  Fair Oak SO50 ....57 A1
Fairthorn Ct 1 BH2 ..204 C2
Fairthorne Gdns PO12 .181 B2
Fairview 1 Hythe SO45 .126 A2
  Romsey SO51 ....53 A4
Fairview Cres BH18 ..187 A3
Fairview Ct PO12 .....180 C2
Fairview Dr
  Broadstone BH18 ....187 A3
  Hythe SO45 ....126 A2
  Romsey SO51 ....28 A1
Fairview Par 1 SO45 ..126 A1
Fairview Pk BH14 ....203 B2
Fairview Rd BH18 ....187 A3
Fairwater Dr SO31 ...155 A1
Fairway Ave PO14 ...214 B4

Fairway Bsns Ctr PO3 .158 B1
Fairway Dr BH23 .....206 C3
Fairway Gdns SO16 ...77 C3
Fairway Rd SO45 .....125 C2
Fairway The
  Barton on Sea BH25 ..210 A4
  Gosport PO13 ....155 B1
  Locks Heath SO31 ....128 C1
  Portchester PO16 .....156 B4
  Rowland's Castle PO9 .113 B1
  Fairys BH22 ....165 C2
Fairwinds BH12 ......204 A2
Fairwood Rd BH31 ...145 A3
Fairy Cross Way PO8 .112 A1
Falaise Rd SO16 ....78 B2
Falcon Cl PO16 ....155 C4
Falcon Dr BH23 ......207 B4
Falcon Fields SO45 ..151 A2
Falcon Gn PO6 ....158 C4
Falcon Rd PO8 ....112 A4
Falcon Sq SO45 ......151 A2
Falcon View SO22 .....10 B2
Falcon Way SO32 ......81 C1
Falconer Ct SO45 ....150 B3
Falconer Dr BH15 ....201 C2
Falconwood Cl SP6 ...69 B1
Falcott Cl SO53 ....55 B2
Falkland Rd
  Chandler's Ford SO53 .55 B2
  Southampton SO15 ...102 A4
Falkland Sq 2 BH15 ..202 B1
Falklands Cl PO13 ...179 C2
Falklands Rd 8 PO2 ..157 C2
Fallow Field SO50 ....10 B2
Fallows The BH25 ....195 A3
Falstaff Way SO40 ...100 C3
Fancy Rd BH12 ....203 A4
Fanshawe St SO14 ...103 A3
Far Ends 16 BH14 ....203 A2
Far Meadow Way PO10 .160 A4
Farcroft Rd BH12 ....203 A3
Farcroft Rd BH12 ....203 A3
Fareham Coll PO14 ..130 C1
Fareham Hts PO16 ...131 B2
Fareham Ind Pk PO16 .131 B2
Fareham Park Rd PO15 .130 B2
Fareham Rd
  Gosport PO13 ....155 B2
  Southwick PO17 .....132 C3
  Wickham PO17 ......108 A2
Fareham Sta PO15 ...130 C1
Faringdon Rd 15 SO23 ..2 C1
Faringdon Rd SO18 ..104 B4
Farleigh Cl PO9 ......135 B3
Farley Cl Fair Oak SO50 .57 B1
  Winchester SO22 .....10 C1
Farley Ct SO15 ....78 B1
Farley La SO51 ....7 C1
Farley Mount Nature
  Reserve* SO21 ....10 C1
Farley Mount Rd SO21 ..9 A2
Farlington Ave PO6 ..134 B1
Farlington Marshes (Nature
  Reserve)* PO6 ......158 C2
Farlington Rd PO2 ...157 C1
Farm Cl
  Hamble-le-Rice SO31 ..128 A1
  Ringwood BH24 ......141 A4
Farm Edge Rd PO14 ..179 B3
Farm House Ct PO14 ..154 B3
Farm La
  Christchurch BH23 ....208 A3
  Southbourne PO18 ...161 C4
Farm La (N) PO25 ....210 A4
Farm La S BH25 ......210 A4
Farm Lane Cl PO7 ...134 B3
Farm Rd
  Titchfield PO14,PO15 ..129 C1
  West Moors BH22 ....138 B1
Farm View PO10 ......136 C2
Farm View Ave PO8 ...88 A3
Farmdene Cl BH23 ...208 B4
Farmers Wlk
  Hordle SO41 ....211 B4
  1 Wimborne Minst BH21 .163 A3
Farmery Cl SO18 ....79 B2
Farmhouse Way PO8 .112 A3
Farmlea Rd PO6 ......157 A4
Farmside Gdns PO3 ..157 C2
Farnham Rd Liss SO33 .20 C2
  Poole BH12 ....204 A4
  Steep SO21 ....41 A4
Farnleys Mead SO41 .197 C1
Faroes Cl PO14 ......154 A2
Farrant Way PO16 ...155 B3
Farriers Cl BH21 .....164 A3
Farriers Way PO7 ....112 B1
Farriers Wlk PO12 ...181 B3
Farrington Rd PO9 ...136 A2
Farringford Rd SO19 .104 B3
Farrington BH4 ......204 C3
Farthing La PO1 ......182 A2
Farthings Gate PO7 ..134 C2
Farwell Cl BH23 .....192 B2
Farwell Rd BH12 ....188 B1
Fastnet Cl SO16 ....77 C3
Fastnet Ho 16 PO5 ...215 C2
Fastnet Way PO14 ...154 A2
Fathersfield SO42 ...145 C1
Fathoms Reach PO11 .184 C2
Faulston Cnrs SP5 ....22 B4
Faversham BH21 .....204 B1
Fawcett Rd
  Barton on Sea BH25 ..194 C1
  Portsmouth PO4 .....215 D2
Fawley Bsns Ctr SO45 .151 A2
Fawley By Pass SO45 .151 A2
Fawley Ct 12 PO9 ....136 A3
Fawley Gn BH8 ......190 B2

Fawley Inf Sch SO45 .151 A2
Fawley La Froxfield GU34 ..17 A2
  Owslebury SO21 ....33 A4
Fawley Rd Fawley SO45 .150 C2
  Hythe SO45 ....150 A4
  Portsmouth PO2 ......157 C3
  Southampton SO15 ...102 A4
Fawn Gdns BH25 ....194 C2
Fay Cl PO14 ....179 B3
Fayre La PO16 ....155 A4
Fayrewood Ct BH31 ..114 A4
Fearon Rd PO2 ......157 C1
Felix Rd PO12 ....181 A4
Fell Cl SO31 ....129 A2
Fell Dr PO13 ....179 C2
Felmer Dr SO23 ....2 B4
Feltham Cl SO51 ......53 B4
Felton Cres BH23 ....208 C4
Felton Ct BH14 ......202 C3
Felton Rd BH14 .....202 C3
Feltons Pl PO3 ......157 C3
Fen Ave PO16 ....157 A4
Fenleigh Cl BH25 ...195 A1
Fennel Gdns SO41 ...197 C3
Fennell Cl PO7 ......111 B1
Fenton Rd BH6 ......206 B3
Fenwick Cl BH8 .....205 A3
Fenwick Ct BH8 .....205 A3
Fenwick Hospl SO43 .121 C3
Fern Bank BH2 ......204 C2
Fern Barrow BH12 ..204 A4
Fern Cl Alderholt SP6 ..93 A3
  Burton BH23 ....192 A2
  Petersfield GU31 .....41 B2
Fern Cotts 2 PO16 ..131 B1
Fern Ct SO18 ....103 C4
Fern Dr PO9 ....136 A1
Fern Rd Hythe SO45 ..125 C2
  Southampton SO19 ...103 C1
Fern Way PO15 ......129 B2
Ferncroft Cl PO14 ...179 B3
Ferncroft Gdns BH10 ..189 B3
Ferncroft Rd BH10 ..189 B3
Ferndale Hedge End SO30 .105 B3
  Waterlooville PO7 ...135 A4
Ferndale Mews PO13 ..155 A2
Ferndale Rd
  Marchwood SO40 ....101 C1
  New Milton BH25 ....195 A3
Ferndene Way SO18 ..103 C4
Ferndown Ct SP6 ......69 B1
Ferndown Fst Sch BH22 .165 B3
Ferndown Ind Est BH21 .164 C4
Ferndown Rd
  BH22 ....165 B3
Ferndown Upper Sch
  BH22 ....165 B3
Ferneham Rd PO15 ..130 B1
Ferngate BH25 ....195 A2
Fernheath Cl BH11 ..189 A2
Fernheath Rd BH11 ..189 A2
Fernhill Cl BH17 .....188 A1
Fernhill Flats 12 BH2 .204 C2
Fernhill Gate BH25 ..195 A2
Fernhill La BH25 ....195 A2
Fernhills Rd SO45 ...126 A1
Fernhurst Cl PO11 ..184 C2
Fernhurst Jun Sch PO4 .182 C2
Fernhurst Rd PO4 ...182 C2
Fernie Cl PO14 ......179 A3
Fernlea Ave BH22 ...165 B2
Fernlea Cl
  Ferndown BH22 .....165 B2
  St Leonards BH24 ...139 C2
Fernlea Gdns
  Ferndown BH22 .....165 B2
  St Leonards BH24 ...139 C2
Fernside Cl
  Holbury SO45 ....150 B2
  Southampton SO16 ..101 C4
Fernside Ct BH15 ...202 C2
Fernside Rd
  Bournemouth BH9 ...204 C4
  Poole BH15 ....202 C2
  West Moors BH22 ...138 C1
Fernside Wlk SO50 ...57 C1
Fernway Cl PO21 ....164 A2
Fernwood Cl BH24 ..140 A3
Fernwood Cres SO18 .103 C4
Fernwood Ho BH25 ..195 B2
Ferny Crofts (Scout Ctr)
  SO42 ....148 A4
Ferny Way BH13 ....204 A1
Ferrybridge Gn 3 SO30 .105 B3
Ferrymans Quay SO31 .127 A3
Ferrypoint SO41 .....198 A2
Festing Gr PO4 ......183 A1
Festing Rd PO4 .....183 A2
Feversham Ave BH8 ..190 C1
Fey Rd PO12 ....181 B3
Fibbards Rd SO42 ...145 C1

Field Cl
  Compton (Hants) SO21 .31 B3
  Gosport PO13 ....155 A3
  Locks Heath SO31 ...129 A1
  Romsey SO51 ....53 A4
  Southampton SO16 ...79 B3
Field End SO23 ....2 B4
Field Pl
  Barton on Sea BH25 ..209 B4
  Verwood BH31 ......114 C4
Field View SO50 ......54 C3
Field Way
  Christchurch BH23 ...193 B1
  Compton (Hants) SO21 .31 B3
  Corfe Mullen BH21 ..186 C4
  Denmead PO7 ....110 C2
  Fordingbridge SP6 ...70 B1
Field Wlk SO41 ......197 B3
Fielden Cl SO52 ......53 C2
Fielder Dr PO14 .....155 A3
Fielders Ct PO7 .....154 B4
Fielders' Way SO51 ..51 A1
Fieldfare Cl PO8 ......88 B2
Fieldfare Ct SO40 ...100 B4
Fieldhouse Dr PO13 .179 C2
Fieldmore Rd PO12 ..181 A4
Fields Cl SO45 ......150 C1
Fields The BH11 ....114 C4
Fieldway BH24 ......141 A4
Fifth Ave Cosham PO6 ..157 C4
  Havant PO9 ....136 A1
Fifth St PO1 ....182 C3
Filmer Cl PO13 .....180 B4
Filmorehill La GU34 ..17 A2
Filton Cl SO40 ....76 B1
Filton Rd SO41 .....197 B2
Finch Ho PO4 ....183 A1
Finch Rd PO4 ....183 B2
Finch's La SO21 ......31 C3
Finchdean Rd
  Havant PO9 ....135 B2
  Rowland's Castle PO9 .113 B2
Finches The SO17 ....79 A1
Finchfield Ave BH11 .188 C3
Finchmead La SO22 ..42 A2
Finchwood Farm Ind Units
  PO11 ....160 A1
Findon Rd PO12 .....181 A4
Fineshade 7 BH13 ..214 C4
Finisterre Cl PO14 ..154 A2
Finlay Cl SO19 ......104 B2
Finnes Cl SO23 ......11 B4
Fir Ave BH25 ....195 A1
Fir Cl Lyndhurst SO43 .121 C2
  West Moors BH22 ...138 C2
Fir Copse Rd PO7 ...134 B2
Fir Croft Dr SO53 ....55 B3
Fir Rd SO40 ....100 A1
Fir Tree Cl Fair Oak SO50 ..81 B4
  St Leonards BH24 ...139 B1
Fir Tree Ct SO18 ...104 A4
Fir Tree Gdns PO8 ..112 C3
Fir Tree Gr SO45 ...150 A4
Fir Tree Hill SP6 .....93 A3
Fir Tree La BH23 ...193 B1
Fir Tree Rd Cadnam SO40 .99 A4
  South Hayling PO11 ..184 C2
Fir Vale Rd BH1 ....204 C2
Firbank Rd BH9 ....205 A4
Firecrest Cl SO16 ....78 A3
Firgrove Cl SO52 ....53 C2
Firgrove Cres PO3 ..157 C3
Firgrove Ct SO15 ...102 B4
Firgrove La PO17 ...108 C1
Firgrove Rd
  North Baddesley SO52 .54 A3
  Southampton SO15 ..102 B4
Firlands Rise PO9 ...135 C3
Firmain Rd BH12 ...188 B1
Firmount Cl SO41 ...196 C1
Firs Ave PO8 ....111 C1
Firs Cres SO23 ....2 A4
Firs Dr SO30 ....105 A3
Firs Glen Rd
  Bournemouth BH9 ...204 C4
  Verwood BH31 ......115 A2
  West Moors BH22 ...138 C1
Firs La BH14 ....214 A4
Firs The
  Bournemouth BH1, ...205 A2
  Chandler's Ford SO53 ..55 B2
  Gosport PO13 ....155 B1
Firshill BH23 ....208 C4
Firside Rd BH21 ....186 B2
First Ave Cosham PO6 ..157 C4
  Cosham, Farlington PO6 .158 C4
  Havant PO9 ....136 A1
  Horndean PO8 ....88 B2
  Southampton SO15 ..101 B4
  Southbourne PO10 ..161 B4
First Marine Ave BH25 .209 C4
First St PO14 ....156 C3
Firsway BH16 ....201 B4
Firtree Cres SO41 ..195 C2
Firtree La SO50 ......81 A4
Firtree Way SO19 ...104 A3
Fisgard Rd PO12 ....181 B4
Fisher Cl PO14 .....154 A2
Fisher Rd PO13 ....155 B2
Fisher's Rd SO40 ...101 A3
Fisherman's Ave BH5,
Fisherman's Wlk BH5 ..206 A2
Fishermans Rd BH15 .202 B1
Fishermans The PO10 .161 A4

Fishermans Wlk PO11 ...185 C1
Fishers Gr PO6 ...158 C4
Fishers Hill PO15 ...130 A1
Fishery La PO11 ...185 B1
Fishlake Mdws SO51 ...28 A1
Fitzgerald Cl PO15 ...129 B4
Fitzharrys Ave BH9 ...205 A4
Fitzherbert Rd PO4 ...158 B4
Fitzherbert Spur PO6 ...158 C4
Fitzherbert St PO1 ...215 B4
Fitzhugh Ho SO15 ...102 C3
Fitzhugh Pl SO15 ...102 C4
Fitzhugh St [15] SO23 ...102 C3
Fitzmaurice Rd BH23 ...206 C4
Fitzpain Cl PO6 ...165 B1
Fitzpain Rd BH22 ...165 B1
Fitzpatrick Ct PO6 ...133 B1
Fitzroy Cl SO16 ...78 C4
Fitzroy Wlk PO1 ...215 C4
Fitzwilliam Ave PO11 ...179 A3
Fitzwilliam Cl BH11 ...188 C3
Fitzworth Ave BH16 ...200 A2
Fitzwygram Cres PO9 ...135 C2
Five Bridges Rd SO23 ...10 C2
Five Elms Dr SO51 ...53 B3
Five Heads Rd PO8 ...112 B4
Five Post La PO12 ...181 A3
Fivefields Cl SO23 ...11 B3
Fivefields Rd SO23 ...11 B4
Flag Staff Gn PO12 ...181 B3
Flag Wlk PO8 ...111 C3
Flaghead Rd BH13 ...214 C3
Flaghead Chine Rd BH13 ...214 C3
Flambard Ave PO15 ...192 A1
Flambard Rd BH14 ...203 B2
Flamborough Cl SO16 ...77 B2
Flamingo Ct PO16 ...155 C4
Flamston St SP5 ...22 A4
Flanders Ho [1] PO14 ...154 C4
Flanders Ind Pk SO30 ...105 A4
Flanders Rd SO30 ...105 A4
Flathouse Rd PO1 ...182 B4
Flaxfields End SP6 ...69 C1
Flazen Cl BH11 ...188 B2
Fleet Cl PO13 ...155 B1
Fleet End Bottom SO31 ...152 C4
Fleet End Rd SO31 ...152 C4
Fleet St SO21 ...31 A1
Fleet's Cnr BH17 ...202 A1
Fleetend Cl PO9 ...135 C3
Fleetpoint Bsns Ctr BH17 ...202 A3
Fleets East BH15 ...202 A3
Fleets La BH15 ...202 B3
Fleetsbridge Bsns Ctr BH17 ...202 A3
Fleetwood Ct BH15 ...202 B4
Fleming Ave SO52 ...54 A2
Fleming Cl PO15 ...129 B2
Fleming Ct
  North Baddesley SO52 ...54 A2
  Romsey SO51 ...103 B1
Fleming Pl
  Colden Common SO21 ...31 C1
  [4] Romsey SO51 ...52 C4
Fleming Rd SO17 ...79 B2
Fletcher Cl
  Bournemouth BH10 ...189 B2
  Hythe SO45 ...125 B2
Fletcher Rd BH10 ...189 B2
Fletchwood La SO40 ...100 A2
Fletchwood Rd SO40 ...100 A2
Fleuret Cl SO45 ...126 A1
Flexford Cl SO53 ...30 A1
Flexford Gdns PO9 ...136 A2
Flexford La SO51 ...196 B3
Flexford Rd SO52,SO53 ...54 C4
Flinders Ct PO4 ...183 A1
Flint Cl SO19 ...104 C2
Flint St PO5 ...215 A1
Floating Bridge Rd SO14 ...103 B2
Floral Farm BH21 ...164 A1
Florence Cl SO51 ...51 A1
Florence Ct [3] SO18 ...103 C4
Florence Rd
  Bournemouth BH5 ...205 C2
  Poole BH14 ...203 B2
  Portsmouth PO5 ...182 B1
  Southampton SO19 ...103 B1
Florentine Way PO7 ...135 A4
Florins The
  Locks Heath PO14 ...129 A1
  Waterlooville PO7 ...134 C2
Floristan Gdns BH25 ...195 B2
Flower Bldgs [6] PO13 ...179 C1
Flower Ct [10] BH12 ...163 B2
Flowerdown Cl SO40 ...100 B4
Flowerdown Cvn Pk SO22 ...1 B3
Flowerdown Ho SO22 ...1 B3
Flowers Cl SO51 ...127 C2
Flowers La SO51 ...50 B2
Flum' E Rd SO40 ...155 B3
Flushards SO41 ...197 C2
Flying Bull Cl [3] PO2 ...182 B4
Flying Bull La PO2 ...182 B4
Flying Bull Jun Sch PO2 ...182 B4
Foldscape Cl SO43 ...121 C3
Foley Ho PO1 ...215 B4
Folkestone Rd PO3 ...183 A4
Folly Farm La BH24 ...140 B3
Folly Field SO32 ...83 B4
Folly La GU32 ...40 C2

Font Cl PO14 ...129 B2
Fontley Rd PO15 ...130 A3
Fontmell Cl BH18 ...187 B2
Fontwell Cl SO40 ...76 B1
Fontwell Gdns SO50 ...81 B4
Fontwell Mews [10] PO7 ...112 A1
Fontwell Rd PO5 ...182 B1
Foord Cl SO30 ...105 A3
Football Gn SO43 ...98 B2
Footner Cl SO51 ...28 B1
Footners La BH23 ...192 B1
Forbes Cl SO16 ...77 C3
Forbes Rd SO23 ...2 A4
Forbury Rd [2] PO1 ...215 C2
Ford Ave SO53 ...55 B2
Ford Cl BH22 ...165 C4
Ford La SP6 ...166 A4
Ford Rd PO12 ...180 C3
Fordingbridge Bsns Pk SP6 ...69 B1
Fordingbridge Hospl SP6 ...69 C1
Fordingbridge Inf Sch SP6 ...69 C2
Fordingbridge Jun Sch SP6 ...69 C2
Fordingbridge Rd
  Aldershot SP6 ...93 A4
  Portsmouth PO4 ...183 A2
Fordington Ave SO22 ...10 C4
Fordington Rd [3] SO22 ...10 C4
Foreland Cl PO14 ...129 C1
Foreland Ct PO11 ...185 B1
Foreland Rd BH16 ...201 B2
Forelle Ct BH31 ...115 B2
Foremans Cotts PO12 ...181 C1
Foreshore N S045 ...151 A3
Foreshore S S045 ...151 A3
Forest Ave PO8 ...112 A2
Forest Cl
  Chandler's Ford SO53 ...55 B4
  Christchurch BH23 ...193 B1
  North Baddesley SO52 ...55 A3
  Verwood BH31 ...115 B2
  Waterlooville PO8 ...111 C2
Forest Cnr GU33 ...21 A4
Forest Ct
  Fordingbridge SP6 ...69 C1
  New Milton BH25 ...195 A1
Forest Edge SO45 ...151 A2
Forest Edge Cl
  St Leonards BH24 ...139 B3
  Sway SO41 ...172 A2
Forest Edge Dr BH24 ...139 B3
Forest Edge Rd BH24 ...141 C3
Forest End SO40 ...100 C4
Forest End PO7 ...134 B4
Forest Front SO45 ...125 B3
Forest Gate SO45 ...177 C4
Forest Gate Gdns SO41 ...197 B1
Forest Gdns
  Lyndhurst SO43 ...121 C3
  Waltham Chase SO32 ...83 C2
Forest Glade Cl SO42 ...145 B1
Forest Hall SO42 ...146 A1
Forest Hill Way SO45 ...125 C1
Forest Hills Dr BH24 ...141 B3
Forest Hills Dr SO18 ...79 C2
Forest La
  Fawley PO17 ...131 A4
  Holbury SO45 ...150 A3
  Ringwood BH24 ...141 C3
  Verwood BH31 ...114 C4
Forest Links Rd BH24 ...141 B3
Forest Mdw SO45 ...150 A4
Forest Mead PO7 ...110 C2
Forest Oak Dr BH25 ...195 A3
Forest Park Rd SO42 ...145 C1
Forest Pines BH25 ...195 A2
Forest Rd
  Bransgore BH23 ...169 C2
  Burley BH24 ...142 C3
  Chandler's Ford SO53 ...55 B4
  Denmead PO7 ...110 B2
  Liss GU33 ...21 A3
  Nomansland SP5 ...73 B4
  Poole BH15 ...204 A1
  Waltham Chase SO32 ...83 C2
  West Moors BH22 ...138 C2
  Woodgreen SP6 ...47 C2
Forest Rise
  Christchurch BH23 ...193 B1
  Liss GU33 ...21 A3
Forest View
  Brockenhurst SO42 ...145 B1
  New Milton BH25 ...194 B3
  [4] Southampton SO14 ...102 C2
Forest View Cl BH9 ...190 A1
Forest View Dr BH21 ...163 A3
Forest View Rd BH9 ...190 A1
Forest Walks (Rhinefield)* SO42 ...145 A1
Forest Way
  Christchurch BH23 ...193 B1
  Ferndown BH21 ...165 A3
  Gosport PO13 ...155 C1
  Hordle SO41 ...196 B1
  Totton SO40 ...100 B3
Forest Wlks (Blackwater)* GU32 ...144 C3
Forester Rd SO23 ...85 A1
Foresters Gate SO45 ...177 B4
Foresters Pk SO23 ...2 A2
Foresters Rd SO41 ...150 C1
Forestlake Ave PO4 ...141 B3
Forestside Ave PO9 ...136 A3
Forestside Gdns BH24 ...117 B1

Forestside The BH31 ...115 B3
Forge Cl SO31 ...105 A1
Forge La SO45 ...151 A2
Forge Rd SO45 ...177 C4
Forneth Gdns PO15 ...154 A4
Forres Sandle Manor SP6 ...69 B1
Forster Rd SO14 ...103 A4
Forsyth Gdns BH10 ...189 B1
Forsythia Cl Havant PO9 ...136 A2
  Hedge End SO30 ...105 A4
Forsythia Pl SO19 ...103 C4
Fort Brockhurst* PO12 ...155 C1
Fort Cumberland Pl BH15 ...201 B1
Fort Cumberland Rd PO4 ...183 B2
Fort Fareham Ind Est PO4 ...183 B2
Fort Fareham Ind Est PO14 ...155 A3
Fort Fareham Rd PO14 ...154 C3
Fort Nelson* PO16 ...132 A2
Fort Nelson Mus* PO17 ...132 A2
Fort Rd Gosport PO12 ...181 A1
  Southampton SO19 ...103 C2
Fort Wallington Ind Est PO16 ...131 B1
Fort Widley Married Quarters PO6 ...133 C1
Fortescue Rd
  Bournemouth BH3 ...205 A3
  Poole BH12 ...204 B1
Forth Cl
  North Baddesley SO53 ...55 A3
  Stubbington SO41 ...154 A2
Forth Ho [11] SO14 ...103 B3
Forties Cl PO14 ...154 B1
Fortin Rd Gosport PO12 ...181 A3
  Portsmouth PO1 ...182 C3
Fortune Cl SO53 ...55 B3
Fortune Ho PO12 ...181 A3
Fortune Way SO53 ...55 B3
Forum The [8] PO9 ...135 C1
Forward Dr SO41 ...197 B1
Foster Cl PO14 ...154 B2
Foster Rd Gosport PO12 ...181 A2
  Portsmouth PO1 ...182 C4
Founders Way PO13 ...155 B1
Foundry Cres SO31 ...127 C4
Foundry Ct [28] PO1 ...182 A4
Foundry La SO15 ...102 A4
Foundry Lane Prim Sch SO15 ...102 A4
Fountain Ct
  [4] Colden Common SO21 ...31 C1
  Poole BH15 ...203 C4
Fountain St PO1 ...215 B3
Fountain Way PO16 ...131 B2
Fountains Pk SO31 ...127 A4
Four Acre SO30 ...106 A3
Four Cnrs PO9 ...68 A2
Four Marks Gn [5] PO9 ...136 A3
Four Wells Rd BH21 ...164 A4
Fourposts Hill [12] SO15 ...102 C3
Fourshells Cl SO45 ...150 C1
Fourth Ave Cosham PO6 ...157 C4
  Havant PO9 ...135 C2
Fourth St PO1 ...182 C3
Fowey Cl SO53 ...55 A3
Fowey PO12 ...181 C3
Fowey The SO45 ...150 C1
Fowlers Rd SO30 ...105 A4
Fowlers Wlk SO16 ...54 B1
Fox Cl SO50 ...56 C1
Fox Field SO41 ...196 B1
Fox La PO4 SO41 ...197 B1
Fox's Wlk SO45 ...177 C4
Foxbury Cl SO45 ...126 A1
Foxbury Gr PO16 ...156 A4
Foxbury La Gosport PO13 ...155 B2
  Westbourne PO10 ...137 B2
Foxbury Rd BH24 ...166 C4
Foxcombe SO32 ...84 A3
Foxcote Gdns SO45 ...194 C2
Foxcote Ho PO6 ...132 C1
Foxcott Cl SO19 ...129 C2
Foxcroft Dr
  Holbury SO45 ...150 A2
  Wimborne Minst BH21 ...164 A3
Foxes Cl Verwood BH31 ...114 C3
  Waterlooville PO7 ...134 C3
Foxes La SO51 ...50 C3
Foxglade SO45 ...177 C4
Foxglove Cl BH23 ...208 B4
Foxglove Pl BH25 ...195 B2
Foxgloves Fareham PO16 ...131 B2
  Upton BH16 ...201 A4
Foxgloves The SO30 ...105 B3
Foxhayes La SO45 ...177 C4
Foxhills Ashurst SO40 ...100 B2
  Verwood BH31 ...115 A3
Foxhills Cl SO40 ...100 B2
Foxhills Inf Sch SO40 ...100 B2
Foxhills Jun Sch SO40 ...100 B2
Foxlands SO45 ...177 C4
Foxlease Terr SO43 ...121 C2

Foxley Dr PO3 ...158 A2
Foxtail Dr SO45 ...125 C1
Foxwood Ave BH23 ...207 C3
Foxy Paddock SO45 ...177 C4
Foy Gdns SO31 ...128 B1
Foyes Ct SO15 ...102 B3
Foyle Rd SO23 ...55 A3
Frampton Cl
  [4] Colden Common SO21 ...31 C1
  New Milton BH25 ...195 B3
Frampton Pl BH24 ...141 A4
Frampton Rd BH9 ...205 A4
Frampton Way
  Kings Worthy SO23 ...2 B4
  Totton SO40 ...100 C3
Frances Ct [16] BH23 ...209 A4
Frances Rd
  Bournemouth BH1 ...205 B2
  Waterlooville PO7 ...134 B2
Francesca Cl BH23 ...207 C4
Francesca Grange [18] BH23 ...207 C4
Francesca Lo [11] BH23 ...207 C4
Francis Ave
  Bournemouth BH11 ...188 B2
  Portsmouth PO4 ...182 C2
Francis Avenue Ind Est BH11 ...188 B2
Francis Cl PO13 ...180 A3
Francis Pl PO14 ...179 B3
Francis Rd Horndean PO8 ...88 B2
  Poole BH12 ...204 B2
Franconia Dr SO16 ...77 A2
Frank Judd Ct [33] PO1 ...182 A3
Frank Miles Ho [1] PO5 ...215 B2
Frank Wareham Cottage Homes The BH1 ...190 A2
Frankland Cres PO12 ...181 A1
Frankland Terr [3] PO10 ...161 A4
Franklin Rd
  Bournemouth BH9 ...190 A2
  Gosport PO13 ...180 A4
  New Milton BH25 ...195 B2
  Twyford SO21 ...32 A4
Franklyn Ave SO19 ...104 A2
Franklyn Cl BH16 ...201 A4
Franks Way BH12 ...206 B2
Frankston Rd BH6 ...206 B2
Frarydene PO10 ...161 B4
Fraser Cl SO16 ...77 C3
Fraser Ct BH25 ...194 C2
Fraser Gdns PO10 ...137 C1
Fraser Rd Gosport PO13 ...180 A2
  Havant PO9 ...135 B1
  Kings Worthy SO23 ...2 B4
  Poole BH12 ...203 C4
Fratton Park (Portsmouth FC) PO4 ...183 A3
Fratton Rd PO1 ...215 D4
Fratton Sta PO1 ...182 C3
Frattton Ind Est PO4 ...183 A3
Frayslea [4] SO45 ...126 A1
Freda Rd BH23 ...206 C3
Freda Routh Gdns [12] SO31 ...128 A4
Frederica Rd BH9 ...204 C4
Frederick St
  Portsmouth PO1 ...215 B4
  Southampton SO14 ...103 A4
Free St SO32 ...83 B4
Freedom Cl SO45 ...126 A2
Freefolk Gn [11] PO9 ...136 A3
Freegrounds Ave SO30 ...105 B3
Freegrounds Ct [1] SO30 ...105 B3
Freegrounds Inf Sch SO30 ...105 B3
Freegrounds Jun Sch SO30 ...105 B3
Freegrounds Rd SO30 ...105 B3
Freemans Cl SO30 ...105 B3
Freemans La BH24 ...164 A3
Freemantle Bsns Ctr [12] SO15 ...102 B3
Freemantle CE Inf Sch SO15 ...102 C3
Freemantle Cl SO19 ...103 C3
Freemantle Common Rd SO19 ...103 C3
Freestone Rd [8] PO5 ...182 B1
Fremington Ct [10] BH25 ...195 A2
French Rd BH17 ...187 A1
French St
  Portsmouth PO1 ...182 A2
  Southampton SO14 ...102 C2
French's Farm Rd BH16 ...201 A4
Frenches Cl SO51 ...51 B4
Frenchmans Rd GU32 ...40 C2
Frensham Cl
  Bournemouth BH9 ...189 C2
  Hedge End SO30 ...105 B3
Frensham Ct PO6 ...158 A4
Frensham Rd Portsmouth PO4 ...182 C2
Freshfield Gdns PO7 ...134 C4
Freshfield Rd SO15 ...102 B4
Freshfield Sq SO15 ...102 A4

Freshwater Ct
  Chandler's Ford SO53 ...30 C1
  [3] Lee-on-the-Solent PO13 ...179 C1
Freshwater Dr BH15 ...201 B2
Freshwater Rd
  Christchurch BH23 ...208 B3
  Cosham PO6 ...157 C4
Frewen Liby PO1 ...182 A2
Friars Croft SO40 ...76 B1
Friars Gate BH23 ...208 B3
Friars Pond Rd PO15 ...130 B1
Friars Rd
  Eastleigh SO50 ...55 C1
  Southampton SO18 ...79 B2
Friars Wlk BH25 ...210 A4
Friarscroft SO31 ...127 A4
Friarsgate SO23 ...11 A4
Friary Cl [5] PO5 ...182 B1
Friary The [5] PO5 ...182 B1
Friday's Ct BH24 ...140 C4
Friendly Societies' Homes PO4 ...183 A2
Friendship Ho PO15 ...215 B1
Frimstone Rd SO23 ...11 B4
Frinton Ct [6] BH14 ...203 A2
Frith La PO7 ...108 A4
Frith Lane End PO17 ...108 A4
Frith Rd SO40 ...100 B4
Fritham Gdns BH8 ...190 B2
Fritham Rd SO18 ...104 B1
Frobisher Ave BH12 ...188 C1
Frobisher Cl
  Christchurch BH23 ...207 C3
  Gosport PO13 ...180 B3
  Ringwood BH24 ...117 B1
Frobisher Ct SO40 ...102 A2
Frobisher Gdns
  [7] Emsworth PO10 ...160 C4
  Southampton SO19 ...104 B2
Frobisher Gr PO16 ...156 B4
Frobisher Ho [9] PO1 ...182 A3
Frobisher Ind Cntr SO51 ...27 C1
Froddington Rd PO1 ...215 C2
Frog La SP6 ...93 C4
Froghall SO45 ...126 A1
Frogham Gn PO9 ...135 B3
Frogham Hill SP6 ...94 B3
Frogmore PO1 ...154 B4
Frogmore La
  Nursling SO16 ...77 B2
  Waterlooville PO8 ...112 A3
Frogmore Rd PO4 ...183 A3
Frome Cl SO40 ...102 A1
Fromond Ct SO40 ...197 C3
Fromond Rd SO22 ...1 B2
Front Lawn Inf Sch PO9 ...135 C3
Front Lawn Jun Sch PO9 ...135 C3
Frost La SO45 ...126 A1
Frost Rd BH11 ...188 C2
Frosthole Cl PO15 ...130 C2
Frosthole Cres PO15 ...130 B2
Froud Way BH21 ...186 B2
Froude Ave PO12 ...181 B1
Froude Rd PO12 ...181 B1
Froxfield CE Inf Sch GU32 ...18 C1
Froxfield Cl SO22 ...1 B1
Froxfield Gdns PO16 ...132 B1
Froxfield Ho PO1 ...215 C3
Froxfield Rd PO9 ...136 A3
Froyle Ct [8] PO9 ...136 A3
Fry Cl Blackfield SO45 ...150 C1
  Hamble-le-Rice SO31 ...128 A2
Fryer Cl BH11 ...189 A3
Fryern Arc SO53 ...55 C4
Fryern Cl SO53 ...55 C3
Fryern Court Rd SP6 ...69 C3
Fryern Inf Sch SO53 ...55 C3
Fryern Jun Sch SO53 ...55 C3
Fryers Cl SO23 ...2 B4
Fryers Copse BH21 ...164 B3
Fryers Rd BH21 ...138 B4
Frys La SO41 ...196 B1
Fuchsia Gdns SO16 ...78 B1
Fulflood Ct [2] SO22 ...102 C3
Fulflood Rd PO9 ...135 C3
Fullegar Cotts SO32 ...84 A3
Fullerton Cl SO19 ...104 A2
Fulmar Cl
  Fareham PO16 ...136 C2
  Southampton SO19 ...104 A3
Fulmar Dr SO45 ...126 A1
Fulmar Rd BH23 ...206 A3
Fulmar Wlk PO8 ...111 C2
Fulwood Ave BH11 ...188 C3
Funtington Rd PO2 ...182 C4
Funtley Ct PO16 ...130 C2
Funtley Hill PO16 ...130 C2
Funtley La PO17 ...130 C3
Funtley Rd PO15,PO17 ...130 C3
Furdies PO7 ...110 C2
Furley Cl SO23 ...11 A4
Furlong Mews BH24 ...140 C4
Furlong The BH24 ...140 C4
Furlong Ho [3] BH24 ...140 C4
Furneaux Gdns PO16 ...131 A2
Furnell Rd BH15 ...202 B1
Furness Rd [10] PO5 ...182 B1
Furniss Way PO11 ...184 B2

Furnston Gr PO10 137 C1
Fury Way PO14 154 A2
Furze Cl SO19 104 A3
Furze Croft BH25 195 A1
Furze Hall PO16 131 A2
Furze Hill Dr BH14 203 B1
Furze La PO4 183 B2
Furze Rd SO19 104 A3
Furze Way PO8 112 A2
Furzebrook Cl BH17 187 C2
Furzedale Gdns SO45 126 A1
Furzedale Pk SO45 126 A1
Furzedown Cotts SO20 7 A4
Furzedown Cres [54] PO9 136 A3
Furzedown Ho SO20 7 A3
Furzedown Mews [13] SO45 126 A1
Furzedown Rd
King's Somborne SO20 7 A4
Southampton SO17 79 A1
Furzehall Ave PO16 131 A2
Furzehill BH21 163 B4
Furzelands Rd BH21 138 C4
Furzeley Rd PO7 110 C1
Furzey Ave SO45 126 A1
Furzey Cl SO45 150 C1
Furzey Gdns* SO43 98 A2
Furzey La SO42 148 A1
Furzey Rd BH16 201 A3
Furzley Ct PO9 135 B3
Furzley La SO43 74 B3
Furzley Rd SO40, SO43 74 C2
Furzy Whistlers Cl BH23 169 A1
Fushia Cl PO9 136 B2
Futcher Sch PO6 158 B4
Fyeford Cl SO16 77 C3
Fyfield Cl PO15 129 B4
Fyning St PO1 215 C4

G

G Ave SO45 150 C3
Gable Mews PO11 185 A2
Gables Ct SO16 78 C3
Gage Cl SO40 102 A1
Gain's Rd PO4 182 C1
Gainsborough Ave BH25 195 A3
Gainsborough Cl SO19 104 B1
Gainsborough Ct
[11] Bournemouth BH5 206 A3
Lymington SO41 197 B1
North Baddesley SO52 54 A2
Gainsborough Mews PO14 153 C4
Gainsborough Rd
Bournemouth BH7 205 C4
St Leonards BH24 139 C3
Gainsford Rd SO19 103 C3
Galaxie Rd PO8 112 A2
Gale Moor Ave PO12 180 B2
Galleon Cl SO31 128 C1
Gallia Ct SO17 78 C1
Gallop Way BH12 204 B4
Gallops The PO14 129 B1
Galloway Rd BH15 201 B2
Gallows Dr BH22 165 C1
Galsworthy Rd SO40 100 B4
Galt Rd PO6 158 B4
Galton Ave BH23 206 C3
Gamble Cl SO19 103 C2
Gamble Rd PO2 182 B4
Gamblins La SO32 107 C4
Gang Warily Recn Ctr SO45 150 C2
Ganger Farm La SO51 28 B1
Ganger Rd SO51 28 B1
Gannet Cl Hythe SO45 126 A1
Southampton SO16 78 A3
Gannets The PO14 154 A2
Gar St SO22 10 C4
Garage Cotts [2] GU32 40 C2
Garbett Rd SO23 11 B4
Garden City SO45 125 A3
Garden Cl
Lyndhurst SO43 121 C3
New Milton BH25 195 A1
South Hayling PO11 184 C2
Garden Court Cotts BH22 138 B2
Garden Ct
Bournemouth BH1 205 B3
Portchester PO16 156 B4
Garden Downton Moot* SP5 47 A4
Garden Ho [17] BH1 205 A2
Garden La
Portsmouth PO5 215 B1
St Leonards BH24 139 C2
[22] Winchester SO23 11 A4
Garden Mews SO31 128 B1
Garden Rd BH24 142 C2
Garden Terr [5] PO5 182 B1
Garden Wlk BH22 165 C4
Gardeners Cotts BH24 141 A2
Gardeners La
Awbridge SO51 52 A2
Romsey SO51 52 A2
Gardenia Dr PO15 129 C2
Gardens Cres BH14 214 A4
Gardens Ct [7] BH15 202 C2
Gardens Rd BH14 214 A4
Gardens The
Hambledon PO7 86 B2
Havant PO9 136 A1
Gardiner Cl SO40 102 A1
Gardner Ct BH23 206 C4
Gardner Rd
Christchurch BH23 206 C4
Ringwood BH24 141 A3
Titchfield PO14 153 C4
Garendon Ct SP6 69 C1
Garfield Ave BH1 205 B3
Garfield Cl SO32 83 B4
Garfield Rd
Bishop's Waltham SO32 83 B4
[5] Netley SO31 127 A3
Portsmouth PO2 182 B4
Southampton SO19 103 C4
Garland Ave PO10 136 C2
Garland Ct [12] PO12 181 A3
Garland Rd BH15 202 B2
Garland Way SO40 100 A4
Garnett Cl PO14 154 B2
Garnier Pk PO17 108 A2
Garnier Rd SO23 11 A3
Garnier St PO1 215 D3
Garnock Rd SO19 103 B1
Garratt Cl SO30 81 B1
Garrett Cl SO19 104 A1
Garrick Gdns SO19 104 A1
Garrick Ho [11] PO2 157 C2
Garrison Hill SO32 61 A1
Garrow Dr SO41 197 C3
Garsdale Cl BH11 189 A3
Garsons Rd PO10 161 B4
Garston Cl GU32 63 B4
Garstons Cl PO14 153 C4
Garstons Rd PO14 153 C4
Garth Cl BH24 139 B2
Garth Rd BH9 190 A1
Garton Rd SO19 103 B2
Gashouse Hill SO31 127 B3
Gaston Gdns SO51 52 C4
Gatcombe SO31 127 B4
Gatcombe Ave PO3 158 A1
Gatcombe Dr PO2 157 C2
Gatcombe Gdns
Fareham PO14 154 A4
West End SO18 80 A1
Gatcombe Park Inf Sch PO2 157 C2
Gate House Rd PO16 156 A4
Gatehouse The
[12] Southampton SO18 103 C4
West End SO30 80 B1
Gatekeeper Cl [10] SO23 11 B4
Gateway The BH13 203 C2
Gatwick Cl SO16 78 A2
Gaulter Cl PO9 136 A2
Gavan St SO19 104 B3
Gawn Pl PO12 181 B1
Gayda Ho PO12 180 C3
Gaydon Rise BH11 188 C2
Gaylyn Way PO14 154 A4
Gaza Ave SO42 175 B3
Gaza Ho PO15 130 B2
Gazelle Cl PO13 180 B3
Gazing La SO51 50 C2
Gazings The SO51 50 C2
Geddes Way GU31 41 B2
Gemini Cl SO16 77 C2
General Johnson Ct [6] SO22 10 B3
Geneva Ave BH6 206 B3
Genoa Cl SO41 197 B1
Genoa Ho PO6 157 A4
Gento Cl SO30 105 C3
Geoffrey Ave PO7 134 A1
Geoffrey Cres PO16 155 A3
George Byng Way PO2 182 B4
George Ct The [19] PO1 182 A2
George Curl Way SO18 79 C3
George Eyston Dr SO22 10 B3
George Rd SO41 211 B3
George Rdbt The BH15 202 B2
George St Eastleigh SO50 56 A2
Gosport PO12 181 B3
Portsmouth PO1, PO2 182 C4
Georges Mews BH21 186 B4
Georgia Cl PO13 179 C2
Georgian Cl BH24 141 A4
Georgian Way BH10 189 C2
Georgina Cl BH12 204 B4
Georgina Talbot Ho BH12 204 A4
Gerald Rd BH3 205 A3
Gerard Cres SO19 104 B3
Gerard Ho [6] PO2 157 C2
Germaine Cl BH23 208 C4
Gervis Cres BH14 203 A2
Gervis Pl BH2 204 C2
Gervis Rd BH1 205 A2
Gibbs Rd SO14 102 C3
Gibraltar Cl PO15 130 B1
Gibraltar Rd
Gosport PO14 154 C3
Portsmouth PO4 183 B2
Gibson Cl
Lee-on-the-Solent PO13 179 C2
Swanwick PO15 129 C3
Gibson Rd BH17 202 C4
Giddylake BH21 163 B3
Gifford Cl PO15 130 C2
Gilbert Cl Alderholt SP6 93 A3
Gosport PO13 180 B4
Lymington SO41 197 B1
Gilbert Ct [5] BH23 207 A4
Gilbert Mead PO11 184 C2
Gilbert Rd BH1 205 B3
Gilbert Way PO7 134 C3
Gilbury Cl SO18 79 C2
Gilchrist Gdns SO31 152 B4
Giles Cl Fareham PO16 131 A2
Gosport PO12 181 A3
Hedge End SO30 81 B1
Giles La SP5 50 A2
Gilkicker Rd PO12 181 B1
Gillam Rd BH10 189 B3
Gillcrest PO14 129 B2
Gillett Rd BH12 204 B4
Gillies The [17] PO16 131 A1
Gillingham Cl
Bournemouth BH9 190 B2
Kings Worthy SO23 2 B4
Gillingham Rd SO41 211 B2
Gillion Ct [2] BH23 207 C3
Gillman Rd PO6 134 C1
Gilpin Cl Boldre SO41 173 C1
Southampton SO19 104 C3
Gilpin Hill SO41 172 A1
Gins La SO42 176 C1
Girton Cl PO14 129 B1
Gitsham Gdns PO7 134 B2
Gladdis Rd BH11 188 C2
Glade The
Blackfield SO45 177 C4
Chandler's Ford SO53 30 C1
Fareham PO15 130 B2
South Hayling PO11 185 B1
St Leonards BH24 139 C3
Waterlooville PO7 135 A4
Gladelands Cl BH18 186 C2
Gladelands Mobile Home Pk BH22 165 C4
Gladelands Way BH18 186 C2
Glades The SO31 129 A2
Gladstone Cl BH23 207 B3
Gladstone Gdns PO16 156 B4
Gladstone Pl [4] PO2 182 B4
Gladstone Rd
Bournemouth BH7 205 C3
Gosport PO12 181 A4
Poole BH12 203 B3
Southampton SO19 104 A3
Gladstone Rd E BH7 205 C3
Gladstone Rd W BH1 205 C3
Gladstone St SO23 10 C4
Gladys Ave
Portsmouth PO2 157 B1
Waterlooville PO8 112 A2
Glamis Ave BH10 189 C3
Glamis Cl PO7 135 A4
Glamis Ct PO14 154 B2
Glamorgan Rd PO8 88 A2
Glasgow Rd PO4 183 A2
Glasslaw Rd SO18 104 A4
Glasspool PO7 110 C3
Gleadowe Ave BH23 206 C3
Glebe Cl PO11 184 C3
Glebe Cnr PO17 108 A2
Glebe Ct Botley SO30 106 A4
Fair Oak SO50 57 B1
Southampton SO17 79 A1
Glebe Dr PO13 155 B1
Glebe La SP5 49 B2
Glebe Mdw SP5 4 A1
Glebe Park Ave PO9 135 A1
Glebe Rd GU31 65 B3
Glebe The PO14 179 B3
Glebefield Gdns [1] PO6 157 C4
Glebefields [6] SO41 211 B3
Glen Cl BH25 209 B4
Glen Dale PO9 113 B1
Glen Eyre Cl SO16 79 A2
Glen Eyre Dr SO16 79 A3
Glen Eyre Hall SO16 79 A3
Glen Eyre Rd SO16 78 C3
Glen Eyre Way SO16 79 A2
Glen Fern Rd BH1 205 A2
Glen Ho PO12 180 C2
Glen Rd
Bournemouth BH5 205 C2
Locks Heath SO31 128 C3
Poole BH14 203 A2
Southampton SO19 103 B1
Swanwick SO31 128 C4
Glen Spey BH25 195 B1
Glen The Gosport PO13 155 C1
Poole BH12 203 B3
Poole, Canford Cliffs BH13 214 C4
Glenair Ave BH14 203 A2
Glenair Cres BH14 203 A2
Glenair Rd BH14 203 A2
Glenavon BH25 195 B1
Glenavon Rd BH23 193 C1
Glenbrook Wlk PO14 154 B4
Glencarron Way [11] SO16 78 C2
Glencoe Rd
Bournemouth BH7 205 C4
Poole BH12 203 B3
Portsmouth PO1 182 C4
Glencoyne Gdns SO16 77 C1
Glenda Cl SO31 152 B4
Glendale
Locks Heath SO31 129 A1
Swanmore SO32 84 A2
Glendale Ave BH22 165 C3
Glendale Cl
Christchurch BH23 191 B2
Wimborne Minst BH21 163 B3
Glendale Ct BH23 191 B2
Glendale Rd BH6 207 A2
Glendon Ave BH10 189 B3
Glendowan Rd SO53 55 A4
Glendrive BH25 209 B4
Gleneagles BH23 206 C3
Gleneagles Ave BH14 203 B1
Gleneagles Cl BH22 165 C3
Gleneagles Dr PO7 112 A1
Glenelg PO15 130 C1
Glenesha Gdns PO15 130 B1
Glenferness Ave BH3, BH4 204 B3
Glenfield Ave SO18 103 C4
Glenfield Cres SO18 103 C4
Glenfield Inf Sch SO18 103 C4
Glenfield Way SO18 103 C4
Glengariff Rd BH14 203 B2
Glengarry BH25 195 B1
Glengarry Way BH23 208 B3
Glenhurst Sch PO9 136 A1
Glenives Cl BH24 140 A2
Glenlea Cl SO30 80 B1
Glenlea Dr SO30 80 B1
Glenleigh Ave [19] PO6 157 C4
Glenleigh Ct [18] PO6 157 C4
Glenleigh Pk PO9 136 A1
Glenmeadows Dr BH10 189 A3
Glenmoor (Girls) Sch BH10 189 B1
Glenmoor Cl BH10 189 B1
Glenmoor Rd
Bournemouth BH9 204 C4
Ferndown BH22 165 B2
Glenmore Ct SO17 103 A4
Glenmount Dr BH14 203 A2
Glenn Rd SO30 80 B1
Glenroyd Gdns BH6 206 C2
Glenside
Barton on Sea BH25 209 A4
Hythe SO45 125 C2
Glenside Ave SO19 104 B2
Glenthorne Cl PO14 179 B3
Glenthorne Mdw GU32 38 C1
Glenthorne Rd PO3 158 A1
Glenville Cl BH23 194 A1
Glenville Gdns BH10 189 B1
Glenville Rd
Bournemouth BH10 189 B1
Christchurch BH23 194 A1
Glenwood Ave SO16 79 A3
Glenwood Cl BH22 138 C1
Glenwood Ct SO50 57 C1
Glenwood Gdns PO8 111 C2
Glenwood La BH22 138 C1
Glenwood Rd
Southbourne PO10 137 C1
Verwood BH31 114 C3
West Moors BH22 138 C1
Glenwood Sch PO10 136 C1
Glenwood Way BH22 138 C1
Glidden Cl PO1 215 C3
Glidden La PO7 86 C2
Glissons BH22 165 A1
Globe La BH15 202 B1
Gloster Ct PO14 129 B3
Gloucester Cl GU32 40 B2
Gloucester Ct [8] GU32 40 C2
Gloucester Ho [1] PO12 181 B2
Gloucester Pl PO5 215 B1
Gloucester Rd
Bournemouth BH7 205 C3
Poole BH12 203 C3
Portsmouth PO1 182 A3
Waterlooville PO7 134 C3
Gloucester Terr PO5 215 B1
Gloucester View PO5 215 B2
Glyn Dr PO14 179 B3
Glyn Jones Cl SO45 150 C1
Glyn Way PO14 179 B3
Glynville Cl BH21 164 A4
Glynville Ct BH21 164 A4
Glynville Rd BH21 164 A4
Goathorn Cl BH16 201 B2
Goathouse La PO17 109 A2
Goddard Cl SO51 50 C2
Godfrey Olson Ho [3] SO50 56 A2
Godfrey Pink Way SO32 83 B4
Godiva Lawn PO4 183 B2
Godmanston Cl BH17 188 A1
Godshill Cl BH8 190 B2
Godson Ho [24] SO23 11 A4
Godwin Cl
Emsworth PO10 136 C2
Winchester SO22 1 B1
Godwin Cres PO8 88 B2
Godwins Field SO21 31 B4
Godwit Cl PO12 181 A4
Godwit Rd PO4 183 B3
Gofton Ave PO6 158 A4
Goggs La SP5 47 C3
Gold Mead Cl [3] SO41 197 C1
Gold Oak SP6 91 C4
Gold St PO5 215 A1
Goldcrest Cl
Horndean PO8 112 A4
Portchester PO16 155 C4
Goldcrest Gdns SO16 78 A3
Goldcrest La SO40 100 B4
Golden Cres SO41 196 B1
Golden Ct SO30 80 C2
Golden Gates BH13 214 A2
Golden Gr SO14 103 A3
Golden Hind Pk SO45 125 C1
Golden Sands BH13 214 A2
Goldenleas Ct BH11 188 B2
Goldenleas Dr BH11 188 B2
Goldfinch Cl BH25 194 C1
Goldfinch La PO13 179 C2
Goldfinch Rd BH17 201 C4
Goldring Cl PO11 185 A2
Goldsmith Ave PO4 182 C2
Goldsmith Cl SO40 100 B4
Goldsmith Inf Sch PO4 182 C2
Goldsmith Rd SO50 55 C1
Goldsmiths Ct SO14 103 A2
Goldwire Dr SO53 54 C3
Golf Course Rd SO16 78 C3
Golf Links Rd
Broadstone BH18 187 A3
Ferndown BH22 165 C2
Goliath Rd BH15 201 B1
Gomer Ct PO12 180 C2
Gomer Inf Sch PO12 180 C2
Gomer Jun Sch PO12 180 C2
Gomer La PO12 180 C2
Good Acre Dr SO53 54 C3
Good Rd BH12 203 B4
Goodens The SO24 14 B3
Goodison Cl SO50 57 A1
Goodlands Vale SO30 105 A4
Goodsell Cl PO14 179 A3
Goodwin Cl SO16 77 B1
Goodwood Cl
Gosport PO12 181 A4
Titchfield PO14 129 B1
Waterlooville PO8 112 A1
Goodwood Ct PO10 161 C4
Goodwood Gdns SO40 100 B4
Goodwood Rd
Eastleigh SO50 55 C2
Gosport PO12 181 A4
Portsmouth PO5 215 D1
Gooseberry La BH24 140 C4
Gordleton Ind Pk SO41 196 C3
Gordon Ave
Southampton SO14 103 A4
Winchester SO23 11 B3
Gordon Bldgs SO15 102 B4
Gordon Ct BH4 204 B2
Gordon Mount BH23 209 A4
Gordon Rd
Bournemouth BH1 205 B2
Chandler's Ford SO53 30 B1
Christchurch BH23 209 A4
Curdridge SO32 83 A1
Fareham PO16 131 A1
Gosport PO12 181 A2
Hermitage PO10 161 A4
Lymington SO41 197 B2
Poole BH12 204 A3
Portsmouth PO1 182 A2
Waterlooville PO7 134 B3
Wimborne Minst BH21 163 C2
Winchester SO23 11 A4
Gordon Rd S BH12 204 A3
Gordon Terr SO19 104 A1
Gordon Way BH23 192 B1
Gore Grange BH25 194 C1
Gore Rd BH25 194 C1
Gore Rd Ind Est BH25 194 C1
Gorey Ave BH12 188 B1
Goring Ave PO8 88 B2
Goring Field SO22 1 B1
Gorleston Rd BH12 203 C3
Gorley Cross SP6 94 A2
Gorley Ct PO9 135 B3
Gorley Lynch SP6 94 B2
Gorley Rd BH24 117 B1
Gorran Ave PO13 155 B1
Gorse Cl
Locks Heath SO31 128 C1
New Milton BH25 195 B2
St Leonards BH24 139 B2
Gorse Down SO21 33 A2
Gorse Hill Cl BH15 202 C3
Gorse Hill Cres BH15 202 C3
Gorse Hill Rd BH15 202 C3
Gorse Knoll Dr BH31 114 C4
Gorse La BH16 201 B4
Gorse Rd
Corfe Mullen BH21 186 B3
Petersfield GU31 41 B2
Gorsecliff Ct [7] BH5 205 B2
Gorsecliff Rd BH10 189 B1
Gorsefield Rd BH25 195 A2
Gorseland Ct BH22 165 C2
Gorselands Rd SO18 80 A1
Gorselands Way PO13 180 B4
Gorseway PO11 184 B2
Gorseway The PO11 184 B2
Gort Cres SO19 104 A2
Gort Rd
Bournemouth BH11 189 A2
Poole BH17 187 A1
Gosling Cl BH17 202 C4
Gosport Ho [48] PO9 136 A3
Gosport La SO43 122 A2
Gosport Mus* PO12 181 B2
Gosport Rd
Fareham PO16 155 A4
Lee-on-the-Solent PO13 179 C1
Stubbington PO14 179 C3
Gosport Sh Prec [23] PO12 181 B2
Gosport St SO41 197 C2
Gough Cres BH17 187 A1
Gover Rd SO16 101 B4
Grace Dieu Gdns SO31 104 C1
Grace La SP6 70 C4
Gracefields PO15 154 A4
Graddidge Way SO40 100 B3
Graemar La SO51 25 B1
Grafton Cl
Bournemouth BH3 205 A4
Christchurch BH23 207 B3
Gosport PO12 181 B4
Grafton Gdns
Lymington SO41 197 B1
Southampton SO16 78 B3
Grafton Rd
Bournemouth BH3 205 A3

Grafton Rd continued
Winchester SO23 ......10 C3
Grafton St PO2 ......182 B4
Graham Ct SO10 ......104 A3
Graham Ho [4] SO14 ..103 B3
Graham Norris Bsns Ctr The
SO45 ......150 C1
Graham Rd
Gosport PO12 ......181 A4
Portsmouth PO4 ......182 C2
Southampton SO14 ......103 A3
Graham St SO14 ......103 B3
Grainger Gdns SO19 ..104 B2
Grammar School La
BH21 ......163 A2
Granada Cl PO8 ......112 A2
Granada Rd
Hedge End SO30 ......105 A3
Portsmouth PO4 ......182 C1
Granary Mews BH24 ..140 C4
Granary The BH24 ....140 C4
Granby Gr SO17 ......79 A2
Granby Rd BH9 ......190 A2
Grand 206 B2
Grand Division Row [11]
PO4 ......183 A2
Grand Par
[20] Poole BH15 ......202 A1
Portsmouth PO1 ......182 A2
Southampton SO15 ...185 A1
Grange Cl Gosport PO12 180 C3
Havant PO9 ......136 A1
Hordle SO41 ......211 C4
Southampton SO18 ....79 C2
Winchester SO23 ......10 C2
Grange Cotts SO30 ..105 C4
Grange Cres PO12 ....180 C3
Grange Ct
[10] Bournemouth BH1 ..205 A2
Netley SO31 ......127 A4
Grange Dr SO30 ......105 B4
Grange Gdns BH12 ...203 C4
Grange Inf Sch PO13 .180 B4
Grange Jun Sch PO13 .180 B4
Grange La SO41 ......180 B4
Grange Mews SO51 ...28 B1
Grange Park Mobile Homes
SO30 ......81 B1
Grange Rd
Bournemouth BH6 ....206 B2
Broadstone BH18 .....187 A2
Christchurch BH23 ...208 A4
Gosport PO13 ......180 B3
Hedge End SO30 ......105 B4
Netley SO31 ......127 A4
Petersfield GU32 ....40 C1
Portsmouth PO2 ......157 B1
[11] Southampton SO16 ...78 A1
St Leonards BH24 ....139 C1
Grange Road Bsns Ctr
BH23 ......208 A4
Grange Sch The BH23 207 C4
Grange The Hordle SO41 211 C4
[10] Southampton SO16 ...78 A1
Grangewood Ct SO50 ..57 A1
Grangewood Gdns SO50 57 A1
Grangewood Hall BH21 163 B3
Grant Rd PO6 ......158 B4
Grant's Ave BH1 ......205 B3
Grantham Ave SO31 ..127 C2
Grantham Ct [3] SO50 ..56 A1
Grantham Rd
Bournemouth BH1 ....205 C3
Eastleigh SO50 ......56 A1
Southampton SO19 ...104 B4
Grantley Rd [8] BH5 ..205 C2
Grants Cl BH1 ......205 C3
Granville Cl PO9 ......136 A1
Granville Pl
[2] Bournemouth BH1 ..204 C2
Winchester SO23 ......11 A3
Granville Rd
Bournemouth BH5 ....206 A3
Poole BH12 ......203 A3
Granville St SO14 ....103 A2
Grasdean Cl [8] SO18 ..80 A1
Grasmere SO50 ......55 C1
Grasmere Cl
Christchurch BH23 ...191 B2
West End SO18 ......80 A1
Grasmere Ct SO16 ....77 C1
Grasmere Gdns BH25 195 A3
Grasmere Ho [18] PO6 .133 A1
Grasmere Rd
Bournemouth BH5 ....206 A2
Poole BH13 ......214 A2
Grasmere Way PO14 ..154 B2
Grasmere Way PO7 ...112 B1
Grassymead PO14 ....129 B2
Grateley Cl [8] SO19 ..126 C4
Grateley Cres PO9 ...135 B2
Gravel Ct SP5 ......46 C4
Gravel Hill
Broadstone BH18 .....187 B3
Swanmore SO32 ......44 B2
Gravel La BH24 ......140 C4
Gray Cl Locks Heath SO41 128 C1
Poole BH17 ......202 C4
Gray's Yd [25] BH15 ..202 B1
Graycot Cl BH10 ......189 B3
Grayland Cl PO11 ....184 C2
Grays Ave SO45 ......126 A2
Grays Cl
Colden Common SO21 ..56 C4
Gosport PO12 ......180 C2
Romsey SO51 ......53 A4
Grays Ct PO1 ......182 A2

Grayshott Cl SO22 ......1 B2
Grayshott Rd
Gosport PO12 ......180 C2
Portsmouth PO4 ......182 C2
Great Cops Cl BH22 ..165 C2
Great Copse Dr PO9 ..135 C3
Great Elms Cl SO45 ..150 A2
Great Field Rd SO22 ....1 B2
Great Gays PO14 ......179 A3
Great Hanger GU31 ...41 A2
Great Mead
Denmead PO7 ......111 A2
Lyndhurst SO43 ......121 C2
Great Minster St [4] SO23 .11 A4
Great Posbrook Cotts
PO14 ......129 C2
Great Southsea St PO5 .215 B1
Great Well Dr SO51 ....53 A4
Greatbridge Rd SO51 ..27 C1
Greatfield Way PO9 ...113 A2
Greatwood Cl SO45 ..126 A1
Greaves Cl BH10 ......189 B2
Grebe Cl
Broadstone BH17 .....201 C4
Christchurch BH23 ...208 A3
Milford on Sea SO41 ..211 C2
Portchester PO16 ....155 C4
Waterlooville PO8 ....111 C2
Westbourne PO10 ....137 A2
Green Acres BH23 ....207 C4
Green Acres Cl BH24 140 B3
Green Bottom SO41 ..164 A4
Green Cl [11] Hythe SO45 .126 A2
Kings Worthy SO23 ......2 A3
Netley Marsh SO40 ..100 C1
Poole BH15 ......202 B1
Whiteparish SP5 ......24 A2
Green Cres PO13 .....155 B1
Green Cr SP6 ......93 A3
Green Farm Gdns PO3 157 C2
Green Gdns BH15 ....202 B1
Green Hollow Cl PO16 130 C2
Green Jacket Cl SO22 .10 C3
Green La Ampfield SO51 ..29 A1
Barton on Sea BH25 ..210 A4
Bishop's Waltham SO32 ..83 B4
Blackfield SO45 ......177 C4
Bournemouth BH10 ..189 B2
Bursledon SO31 ......104 C1
Chilworth SO16 ......54 C1
Clanfield PO8 ......88 B3
Denmead PO7 ......110 C2
Downton SP5 ......46 C4
Ferndown BH22 ......165 A1
Fordingbridge SP6 ....69 C1
Froxfield Green GU32 ..18 C3
Gosport PO12 ......181 B4
Gosport, Alverstoke PO12 .181 A2
Hamble-le-Rice SO31 ..128 A1
Hambledon PO7 ......90 A2
Locks Heath SO31 ...128 C1
New Milton BH25 ....194 C4
Ower SO40 ......76 A2
Portsmouth PO3 ......158 A2
Ringwood BH24 ......141 A4
Ringwood, Upper Kingston
BH24 ......141 B2
Soberton PO7 ......86 B4
South Hayling PO11 ..184 C2
Southampton SO16 ....77 C1
Swanmore SO32 ......84 B4
Swanwick SO31 ......106 A1
Swanwick, Lwr Swanwick
SO31 ......128 B4
Whitsbury SP6 ......69 B4
Green Loaning [8] BH23 .207 C3
Green Park Cl SO23 ....2 A1
Green Park Rd SO16 ..101 C4
Green Pk BH1 ......205 B2
Green Pond Cnr [9] PO9 .136 A1
Green Pond La SO51 ..29 B2
Green Rd
Bournemouth BH9 ....205 A4
Gosport PO12 ......181 A4
Poole BH15 ......202 B1
Portsmouth PO5 ......215 B2
Stubbington PO14 ....154 B2
Green The Liss GU33 ..20 C3
Locks Heath SO31 ...128 C3
Romsey SO51 ......28 B1
Rowland's Castle PO9 .138 C4
Whiteparish SP5 ......24 A2
Green Wlk PO15 ......130 C2
Green's Cl SO50 ......57 A1
Greenacre BH1 ......205 A4
Greenacre Cl BH16 ...201 B3
Greenacre Gdns PO7 .134 B2
Greenacres Downton SP5 ..46 B4
Greenacres Dr SO21 ..31 B2
Greenacres Specl Sch
SO22 ......1 C1
Greenaway La
Locks Heath SO31 ...128 B1
Locks Heath SO31 ...128 C1
Greenbank Cres SO16 ..78 C3
Greenbanks Cl SO41 ..138 C4
Greenbanks Gdns PO16 .131 B1
Greenclose La PO11 ..163 B2
Greendale
Chandler's Ford SO53 ..55 C3
Fareham PO15 ......130 B2
Greendale The PO15 ..130 B2
Greenfield Cres PO8 ..112 B2
Greenfield Gdns BH25 .210 A4
Greenfield Rd BH15 ..202 C4
Greenfield Rise 112 A2

Greenfields Liss GU33 ..21 A2
Poole BH12 ......203 C4
Greenfields Ave SO40 ..76 C1
Greenfields Cl SO40 ....76 C1
Greenfinch Cl
Broadstone BH17 .....186 C1
Eastleigh SO50 ......55 B1
Greenfinch Wlk BH24 141 B3
Greenhayes BH18 .....187 B1
Greenhays Rise BH21 .163 B3
Greenhill Ave SO22 ....10 C4
Greenhill Cl
Wimborne Minst BH21 .163 B3
Winchester SO22 ......10 C4
Greenhill La
Rownhams SO16 ......77 C4
Wimborne Minst BH21 .163 B3
Greenhill Rd
Wimborne Minst BH21 .163 B3
Winchester SO22 ......10 B4
Greenhill Terr SO22 ...10 C4
Greenlea Cl PO7 ......134 A1
Greenlea Cres SO16 ..79 B3
Greenlea Rd PO12 ....180 C4
Greenleaf Ave SO16 ..196 B1
Greens Cl SO32 ......83 A4
Greens Meade SP5 ....47 B3
Greenside Cl BH25 ...210 A3
Greensleeves Ave BH18 187 A3
Greensome Dr BH22 ..165 C3
Greenway GU32 ......38 C1
Greenway Cl SO41 ....197 B2
Greenway Cres BH16 .201 A4
Greenway La GU31 ...65 B3
Greenway Rd PO10 ...181 A3
Greenway The PO10 ..136 C2
Greenways
Chandler's Ford SO53 ..55 C3
Christchurch BH23 ...208 C4
Southampton, Sea SO41 ..211 B3
Southampton SO15 ....79 B3
Swanmore SO32 ......84 A3
Greenways Ave BH8 ..190 B2
Greenways Dr PO12 ..165 C2
Greenways Rd SO42 ..146 A1
Greenwich The
Blackfield SO45 ......150 C1
Southampton SO14 ..103 A2
Greenwood Ave
Cosham PO6 ......157 B4
Ferndown BH22 ......165 C3
Poole BH14 ......214 B4
Rownhams SO16 ......77 B3
Greenwood Cl
Eastleigh SO50 ......55 C1
Fareham PO16 ......131 A2
Romsey SO51 ......53 A4
Greenwood Copse
BH24 ......140 A2
Greenwood La SO32 ..82 A4
Greenwood Rd BH9 ..204 C4
Greenwood Way BH24 .140 A2
Greenwoods [22] BH25 .195 A1
Greetham St PO1 ....215 B3
Gregory Gdns SO40 ..76 B1
Gregory La SO21 ......82 B3
Gregson Ave PO13 ...155 B2
Gregson Cl PO13 .....155 B2
Grenadier Cl SO41 ...129 A1
Grendon Cl SO16 .....79 B2
Grenehurst Way GU31 .40 C2
Grenfell Rd BH9 ......189 C2
Grenfield Ct PO10 ...136 C2
Grenville Cl BH24 ...117 B1
Grenville Ct
[4] Bournemouth BH4 ..204 B2
[4] Poole BH15 ......202 B1
Southampton, SO15 ..102 C4
Southampton, Bitterne Pk
SO18 ......79 C2
Grenville Gdns SO45 .126 A1
Grenville Ho [22] PO1 .182 A3
Grenville Rd
Portsmouth PO5 ......215 D1
Wimborne Minst BH21 .163 B2
Gresham Rd BH9 .....189 C1
Gresley Gdns SO30 ...81 B1
Greville Gn PO10 ....136 C2
Greville Rd SO15 .....102 B4
Grevillea Ave PO15 ..129 C2
Greycot Cl PO11 ......138 C4
Greyfriars [3] SO23 ...11 A4
Greyfriars Ct PO5 ....215 B1
Greyfriars Rd PO15 ..130 B1
Greyhound Cl SO30 ...81 A2
Greylaytes SO31 .....104 B3
Greys Farm Cl SO24 ..14 B2
Greyshott Ave PO14 ..154 B4
Greystoke Ave BH11 ..188 C3
Greywell Ave SO16 ...78 B2
Greywell Ct SO16 .....78 B2
Greywell Sq PO9 .....135 C3
Griffen Cl [3] SO50 ..56 C1
Griffin Ct
Southampton SO17 ...103 B4
[11] Wimborne Minst PO10 .76 C1
Griffin Ind Pk SO40 ..76 C1
Griffin Wlk PO13 .....180 B3
Griffiths Gdns BH10 ..189 A3
Grindle Cl PO16 ......155 A1
Grinds Cl SO21 ......31 C4
Gritanwood Rd PO4 ..183 A2
Grosvenor Ct [10] BH1 .205 A2
Grosvenor Cl
Southampton SO17 ....79 B1
St Leonards BH24 ....139 B3

Grosvenor Ct
[2] Bournemouth BH1 ..205 B2
Christchurch BH23 ...209 A4
Cosham PO6 ......158 C4
Romsey SO51 ......53 B4
[7] Southampton SO17 ..79 B1
Stubbington PO14 ....179 B3
Grosvenor Dr SO23 .....2 A1
Grosvenor Gdns
Bournemouth BH1 ....205 C2
Southampton SO17 ....79 B1
West End SO30 ......104 B4
Grosvenor Ho [4] PO5 .215 B2
Grosvenor Lodge [5]
SO17 ......79 B1
Grosvenor Mews
Gosport PO12 ......181 B3
Lymington SO41 ......197 B3
Southampton SO17 ....79 B1
Grosvenor Rd
Bournemouth BH4 ....204 B2
Chandler's Ford SO53 ..30 C1
Southampton SO17 ....79 B1
Grosvenor Sq SO15 ..102 C3
Grosvenor St PO5 ....215 B2
Grove Ave Gosport PO12 .181 B3
Portchester PO16 ....156 B3
Grove Bldgs [6] PO12 .181 B2
Grove [4] PO9 ......135 C1
Grove Gdns SO19 ....104 A1
Grove Ho
Poole BH15 ......215 D1
Portsmouth PO5 ......215 C1
Grove La SP5 ......47 C4
Grove Mans [2] BH1 ..205 A2
Grove Mews SO19 ....104 A1
Grove Pastures SO41 .197 C2
Grove Pl Lymington SO41 .197 C2
Southampton SO19 ..104 A1
Grove Rd
Barton on Sea BH25 ..210 A4
Bournemouth BH1 ....205 A2
Compton (Hants) SO21 ..31 B3
Cosham PO6 ......158 B4
Fareham PO16 ......131 A1
Gosport PO12 ......181 A4
Havant PO9 ......135 C1
Lee-on-the-Solent PO13 .179 C1
Lymington SO41 ......197 C2
Portsmouth PO5 ......215 B3
Southampton SO15 ..102 A4
Wimborne Minst BH21 .163 B2
Grove Rd E PO5 ......215 B3
Grove Rd N PO5 ......215 B3
Grove Rd S PO5 ......215 B1
Grove Rd W BH23 ....206 C4
Grove St SO14 ......103 A2
Grove The
Bournemouth BH9 ....189 C2
Bursledon SO31 ......105 A1
Christchurch BH23 ...191 C1
Ferndown BH22 ......165 B2
Netley SO31 ......127 B4
Southampton SO19 ..104 A1
Verwood BH31 ......115 A3
Westbourne PO10 ....137 A2
Grovehurst SO31 .....129 A1
Grovelands Rd SO22 ....1 A1
Groveley Rd
Bournemouth BH4 ....204 A1
Christchurch BH23 ...207 C3
Groveley Way SO51 ...28 C1
Groves Down SO51 ...50 C2
Grower Gdns BH11 ...189 A2
Grundles GU31 ......41 A2
Gruneisen Rd PO2 ...157 B1
Guardhouse Rd PO1 ..182 A4
Guardian Ct [3] SO17 ..79 A1
Guardroom Rd PO2 ..157 A1
Gudge Heath La
PO15 ......130 C1
Guelders The PO7 ....134 C2
Guernsey Cl SO16 ....77 C2
Guernsey Rd BH12 ..188 B1
Guessens La PO14 ...153 C4
Guest Ave BH12 ......204 A3
Guest Cl BH12 ......204 A3
Guest Rd
Bishopstoke SO50 ....56 B2
Upton BH16 ......201 A4
Guildford Cl PO10 ...137 C1
Guildford Ct
Bournemouth BH4 ....204 B2
Gosport PO13 ......180 B3
Guildford Dr SO53 .....55 A2
Guildford Rd PO1 ....182 C3
Guildford St [30] SO14 ..103 B3
Guildhall Ct [3] BH15 .202 A1
Guildhall Sq PO1 ....215 B3
Guildhall Wlk PO1 ...215 B3
Guildhill Rd BH6 .....206 C2
Guillemot Cl SO45 ...126 A1
Guillemot Gdns PO13 .155 B1
Guili Cl PO13 ......155 A1
Gulliver Cl BH14 .....214 B4
Gulliver Cl [1] BH21 ..163 B3
Gulls The SO40 ......101 C1
Gullycroft Mead SO30 .105 A4
Gunners Bldgs PO3 ..157 C2
Gunners Pk SO32 ....83 C4
Gunners Row PO4 ...183 A1
Gunners Way PO12 ..155 C1
Gunstore Rd PO3 ....158 A2
Gunville Cres BH9 ...190 A2
Gunwharf Rd PO1 ...182 A2

Gurjun Cl BH16 ......201 A4
Gurkha Mus The* SO23 .10 C1
Gurnard Rd PO6 .....157 C4
Gurnays Mead SO41 ..50 C2
Gurney Rd
Corfe Mullen BH21 ...186 C3
Portsmouth PO4 ......183 A4
Southampton SO15 ..102 B4
Gussage Rd BH12 ...203 C4
Gutner La PO11 ......160 B1
Guy's Cl BH24 ......141 A3
Gwatkin Cl PO9 ......135 B2
Gwen-Rhian Ct [10] SO15 .102 C4
Gwenlyn Rd BH16 ...201 B3
Gwynne Rd BH12 ...203 C3
Gypsy La BH24 ......141 A4

H

H Ave SO45 ......150 C3
Ha'penny Dell PO7 ...134 C2
Haarlem Mews BH23 .207 B4
Hack Dr SO21 ......56 C4
Hackett Way PO14 ..155 A3
Hacketts La SO32 ....60 C1
Hackleys La SO51 ....51 A3
Hackups La SO51 ......6 B1
Hackworth Gdns SO30 .81 B2
Hadden Rd BH8 ......205 B4
Haddon Cl PO15 .....134 C2
Haddon Dr SO50 ......56 A3
Haddons Dr BH21 ....138 B4
Hadleigh Gdns SO50 ..56 A3
Hadleigh Rd [6] PO6 .157 B4
Hadley Field SO45 ...150 B3
Hadley Way BH18 ...186 C2
Hadow Rd BH10 ......189 B2
Hadrian Cl BH21 .....165 B1
Hadrian Way
Chilworth SO16 ......78 C4
Corfe Mullen BH21 ...186 C4
Hadrians Cl SO33 ....55 C3
Haflinger Dr PO15 ...129 A4
Haglane Copse SO41 .197 B1
Hahnemann Rd BH2 ..204 C1
Haig Ave BH13 ......203 C1
Haig Ct [2] PO2 ......157 C2
Haig Rd SO50 ......57 A1
Haileybury Gdns SO30 ..81 B1
Hainault Dr BH31 ....115 A3
Haking Rd BH23 .....207 B4
Halcyon Ct BH15 ....202 B3
Halden Cl [2] SO51 ...28 A1
Hale Ave BH25 ......195 A1
Hale Ct PO1 ......182 A2
Hale Gdns BH25 .....195 A1
Hale La SP6 ......47 A2
Hale Prim Sch SP6 ....47 B2
Hale Rd N PO1 ......215 C4
Hale St S PO1 ......215 C4
Hales Dr SO30 ......105 A3
Halesowen Ho [4] PO5 .215 A2
Halewood Way PO14 .206 C4
Half Moon St [2] PO1 .182 A3
Halfpenny La PO1 ....182 A2
Halfway Rd SO45 ....155 C1
Halifax Ct SO30 ......80 B1
Halifax Rise PO7 ....134 C4
Halifax Way PO3 .....208 A4
Hall Cl SO32 ......83 B4
Hall Ct SO32 ......83 B4
Hall Lands La SO50 ....57 B1
Hall of Aviation (Mus)*
SO14 ......103 A2
Hall Rd BH11 ......188 C2
Hall Way The SO22 .....1 A3
Hallett Cl SO18 ......80 A1
Hallett Rd PO9 ......136 A1
Halletts Cl PO14 ....154 B2
Halliards The PO16 ..155 A4
Halliday Cl PO12 ....181 A3
Halliday Cres PO4 ...183 B2
Halliday Ho PO4 .....183 A1
Hallowell Ho PO1 ...215 B4
Halsey Cl PO12 ......180 C2
Halstead Rd Cosham PO6 .158 B4
Southampton SO18 ....79 C1
Halstock Cres PO6 ..157 B4
Halter Path BH15 ...201 C2
Halter Rise BH21 ....164 B3
Halterworth Com Prim Sch
SO51 ......53 B4
Halterworth La SO51 ..53 B4
Halton Cl BH23 ......193 A4
Haltons Cl SO40 ......76 B1
Halyard Cl PO13 .....155 A1
Halyards SO31 ......128 A2
Ham La Ferndown BH21 .164 C2
Gosport PO12 ......156 A1
Horndean PO8 ......112 A4
Southbourne PO10 ...161 B4
Hambert Way SO40 ..100 C3
Hamble Cl SO31 .....128 B1
Hamble Court Bsns Pk
SO31 ......127 C2
Hamble Ct
Chandler's Ford SO53 ..55 B3
Gosport PO12 ......154 A2
[3] Waterlooville PO8 ..111 C2
Hamble Ho PO16 ....155 A4
Hamble House Gdns
SO31 ......128 A1

Hamble La
Burgledon SO31 ....127 C4
Hamble-le-Rice SO31 ....127 C1
Southampton SO31 ....104 C1
Waterlooville PO7 ....134 C3
Hamble Manor SO31 .....128 A1
Hamble Prim Sch SO31 ..127 C2
Hamble Rd Gosport PO12 188 C2
Poole BH15 ....203 A3
Hamble Sec Sch SO31 ...127 C3
Hamble Springs SO32 ....83 B4
Hamble Sta SO31 ....127 C3
Hamblecliff Ho SO31 .....127 B2
Hambledon Cl SO22 ....1 B2
Hambledon Gdns BH6 ...206 B3
Hambledon Inf Sch PO7 ..86 B2
Hambledon La PO7,SO32 ..85 C2
Hambledon Par PO7 .....111 B1
Hambledon Rd
Clanfield PO8 ....88 A3
Denmead PO7 ....111 A2
Hambledon PO7 ....110 B4
Waterlooville PO7 ....111 A2
Hambleside Ct SO31 ....127 C1
Hambleton Rd BH7 ......206 A4
Hamblewood SO30 ......106 A3
Hamblewood Ct SO30 ...106 A3
Hambrook Rd **1** PO12 ...181 A3
Hambrook St PO5 ....215 A1
Hamdown Cres SO51 .....51 A1
Hameldon Cl SO16 ......101 C4
Hamfield Dr PO14 ....184 C2
Hamilton Cl
Bournemouth BH1 ....205 B3
Christchurch BH23 ......207 C2
Hamworthy BH15 ....201 C1
Havant PO9 ....159 C4
Hamilton Cres BH15 ....201 C1
Hamilton Ct
10 Bournemouth BH8 ....205 A3
Milford on Sea SO41 ....211 B2
11 Portsmouth PO5 ......182 B1
23 Southampton SO17 ....79 A1
1 Wimborne Minst BH21 163 A3
Hamilton Gr PO13 ......155 A1
Hamilton Ho PO1 ....215 D4
Hamilton Mews
12 Hythe SO45 ....126 A1
Lymington SO41 ....197 C2
Hamilton Pk SP5 ....47 A4
Hamilton Rd
Bishopstoke SO50 ....56 B2
Bournemouth BH1 ....205 B2
Corfe Mullen BH21 .....186 C3
Hamworthy BH15 ....201 C1
Hythe SO45 ....150 A4
Portchester PO16 ....155 C4
Portsmouth PO5 ....182 B1
Hamilton Way BH25 ....194 C1
Hamlet Ct SO45 ....151 A2
Hamlet Way PO12 ......156 A1
Hammond Cl PO1 ....189 A2
Hammond Ho PO12 .....156 A1
Hammond Ind Pk PO14 .179 B3
Hammond Rd PO15 .....130 C1
Hammond's Gr SO40 ....100 B4
Hammonds Cl SO40 .....100 C4
Hammonds La SO40 .....100 C4
Hammonds Way SO40 ...100 C4
Hampage Gn PO9 ....135 B4
Hampden La BH6 ....206 A3
Hampshire CE Fst Sch
  BH21 ....164 C2
Hampshire Cl PO1 ......191 C1
Hampshire Corporate Pk
  SO53 ....55 A1
Hampshire County Cricket
  Ground* SO30 ....80 C1
Hampshire Ct
20 Bournemouth BH1 ....204 C2
Chandler's Ford SO53 ....55 B2
Hampshire Ctr The BH8 .190 C1
Hampshire Hatches La
  BH24 ....141 A2
Hampshire Ho **22** BH24 ..204 C2
Hampshire St PO1 ......182 C4
Hampshire Terr PO1 ....215 A2
Hampton Cl
Blackfield SO45 ....177 C4
Waterlooville PO7 ....135 A4
Hampton Dr BH24 ......117 A1
Hampton Gdns SO45 ....177 C4
Hampton Gr PO15 ......130 A1
Hampton Hill SO32 ......84 A3
Hampton La
Blackfield SO45 ....150 C1
Winchester SO22 ....1 B1
Hampton Twr **25** SO19 ..126 C4
Hamptworth Rd SP5 .....88 B2
Hamtun Cres SO40 ......76 C1
Hamtun Gdns SO40 ......76 C1
Hamtun Rd SO19 ....104 B2
Hamtun St **26** SO14 ....102 C2
Hamworthy Fst Sch
  BH15 ....201 C1
Hamworthy Sta BH16 ...201 B2
Hanbidge Cres PO13 ....155 B2
Hanbidge Wlk PO13 ....155 B2
Handel La SO15 ....102 C3
Handel Terr SO15 ....102 C3
Handford PI **21** SO15 ...102 C3
Handley Ct BH24 ....140 C4
Handley Lodge BH12 ...203 C4

Handley Rd PO12 ....180 C3
Handsworth Ho PO5 ....215 C2
Handy Villas **1** SO23 ...11 A4
Hanger Way GU31 ....41 A2
Hangers The SO32 ....59 C1
Hanham Ct BH12 ....204 A4
Hanham Rd
Corfe Mullen BH21 .....186 B3
Wimborne Minst BH21 ..163 B3
Hankinson Rd BH9 .....205 A4
Hanley Rd SO15 ....102 B4
Hann Rd SO16 ....77 C3
Hannah Gdns PO7 ......134 C4
Hannah Way SO41 ......196 C3
Hannay Rise SO19 ......104 B3
Hannington PI BH7 .....206 A3
Hannington Rd
Bournemouth BH7 ......206 A3
Havant PO9 ....135 B4
Hanns Way SO50 ....56 A1
Hanover Bldgs SO14 ...103 A2
Hanover Cotts SO32 .....36 C2
Hanover Ct
5 Hythe SO45 ....126 A2
7 Portsmouth PO1 ....182 A2
Hanover Gdns PO16 ....131 A2
Hanover Gn BH17 ......202 C4
Hanover Ho
Gosport PO13 ....155 A3
Poole BH15 ....202 B2
Totton SO40 ....101 A4
Hanover Lodge SO23 ...10 C3
Hanover St PO1 ....182 A3
Hanoverian Way PO15 .129 B4
Hanway Rd PO1, PO2 ..182 C4
Harbeck Rd BH8 ....190 B2
Harborough Rd SO15 ..102 C3
Harbour Cl BH13 ....214 B3
Harbour Cres BH23 ....207 C3
Harbour Ct
Barton on Sea BH25 ...209 C4
Christchurch BH23 .....207 C3
Poole BH13 ....214 C3
Harbour Hill Cres BH15 202 C3
Harbour Hill Rd BH15 ..202 C3
Harbour Hospl The
  BH15 ....202 B2
Harbour Lights BH15 ...202 C2
Harbour Prospect SO23 102 C2
Harbour Prospect BH14 .214 B4
Harbour Rd
Bournemouth BH6 ......207 A2
Gosport PO11 ....181 C3
South Hayling PO11 ....181 C2
Harbour Twr PO12 .....181 C2
Harbour View PO16 ....156 B3
Harbour View Cl BH14 .203 A3
Harbour View Ct BH23 .203 A2
Harbour View Rd BH14 .203 A2
Harbour Watch BH14 ...214 B4
Harbour Way
Emsworth PO10 ....161 A4
Portsmouth PO2 ....157 B1
Harbour Wlk PO1 ......182 A2
Harbourne Gdns SO18 ..80 A1
Harbourside PO9 ....159 C3
Harbridge Ct PO9 ......135 B4
Harbridge Dro BH24 ....93 B2
Harcombe Cl BH17 .....187 C2
Harcourt Mews **1** BH6 .206 A3
Harcourt Rd
Bournemouth BH5 .....206 A3
Fareham PO14 ....154 A4
Gosport PO12 ....181 A2
Portsmouth PO1 ....182 C4
Southampton SO18 ....103 C4
Hard The Gosport PO12 181 B3
Portsmouth PO1 ....182 A3
Harding Ho PO12 ......180 C3
Harding Rd PO12 ......180 C3
Hardley Ind Est SO45 ..150 A4
Hardley La SO45 ......150 A4
Hardley Rdbt SO45 ....150 A3
Hardley Sch & Sixth Form
  SO45 ....150 A4
Hardman Ct PO12 .....158 A2
Hardwick Rd SO33 ......55 B3
Hardwicke Cl SO16 .....77 C1
Hardwicke Way SO31 ..127 C2
Hardy Cl
Locks Heath SO31 ......129 A2
New Milton BH25 ......194 C2
Southampton SO15 ....102 A3
West Moors BH22 ......138 C1
Hardy Cres BH21 ......163 B2
Hardy Dr SO45 ....126 A1
Hardy Rd Cosham PO6 .158 C4
Eastleigh SO50 ....56 A1
Poole BH14 ....203 B2
West Moors BH22 .....138 C1
Hare La Aldershot BH21 ..91 C3
Hordle SO41 ....195 C2
New Milton BH25 ......195 C2
Harebell Cl PO16 ......131 B2
Harefield Ct SO51 ....50 A4
Harefield Inf Sch SO18 104 A4
Harefield Jun Sch SO18 104 A4
Harefield Rd SO17 ......79 B2
Hares Gn BH7 ....206 A4
Harestock Ct SO22 ......1 B3
Harestock Cnr SO22 ....1 B3
Harestock Prim Sch SO22 ..1 B2
Harestock Rd
Havant PO9 ....135 B2
Winchester SO22 ....1 B2
Harewood Ave BH7 ....206 A3
Harewood Cl SO50 .....56 A3

Harewood Cres BH7 ....205 C4
Harewood Gdns BH7 ...205 C4
Harewood PI BH7 ......205 C4
Harewood PI SO41 .....212 A2
Harford Cl SO41 ....197 B1
Harford Rd BH12 ......203 B4
Harkness Dr PO7 ......135 A4
Harkwood Dr BH15 ....201 C2
Harland Cres SO15 ......78 B1
Harland Rd BH6 ....207 A2
Harlaxton Cl SO40 ......55 C3
Harlequin Gr PO15 ....130 C1
Harleston Rd PO6 .....133 B1
Harleston Villas 17
  BH21 ....163 B2
Harley Ct SO31 ....128 B1
Harley Wlk PO1 ....215 C4
Harlyn Rd SO16 ....77 C1
Harman Rd PO13 ......155 B2
Harness Cl BH21 ......164 A3
Harold Cl SO40 ....100 B3
Harold Rd
Portsmouth PO4 ....182 C2
South Hayling PO11 ...185 A1
Southampton SO15 ....102 B4
Stubbington PO14 .....154 B2
Westbourne PO10 ......137 A2
Harold Terr PO10 ......161 A3
Harpway La BH23 .....192 B3
Harrage The SO51 ......52 C4
Harrier Cl Horndean PO8 112 A4
Lee-on-the-Solent PO13 .179 C1
Southampton SO16 .....78 A3
Harrier Dr BH21 ....163 B1
Harrier Gn SO45 ......150 A3
Harrier Way
Holbury SO45 ....150 A3
Peterstield GU31 ....41 A3
Harriers Cl BH23 ......208 B4
Harriet Cl PO14 ....179 A3
Harrington Ct BH23 ...208 C4
Harris Ave SO30 ......105 A4
Harris Rd PO13 ....155 B2
Harris Way BH25 ......195 A3
Harrison Ave BH1 .....205 B3
Harrison Cl BH23 .....192 B2
Harrison Ho **12** PO12 .157 B1
Harrison Prim Sch
  PO16 ....131 A1
Harrison Rd
Fareham PO16 ....131 A1
Southampton SO17 .....79 B2
Harrison Way BH22 ...138 C2
Harrison's Cut SO14 ...103 A2
Harrow Cl BH23 ....193 A4
Harrow Down SO22 ......1 A3
Harrow La SO22 ....40 C3
Harrow Rd
Bransgore BH23 ......193 A3
Portsmouth PO5 ......215 D2
Harrowgate La PO7,PO8 .87 A1
Harry Barrow Cl 1
  BH24 ....141 A3
Harry Law Hall PO1 ...215 B3
Hart Cl BH25 ....194 C2
Hart St SO19 ....103 C2
Hart Hill SO45 ....126 B1
Hart Plain Ave PO8 ....111 C1
Hart Plain Jun & Inf Sch
  PO7,PO8 ....111 C1
Hartford Ho PO1 ......215 A1
Harthill Dro SP5 ....47 C3
Harting Ct PO8 ....88 B2
Harting Gdns PO12 .....41 A2
Harting Gdns PO16 ...132 B1
Harting Rd BH6 ....206 B4
Hartington Rd
Gosport PO12 ....180 C3
Southampton SO14 ....103 B4
Hartland Ct PO10 ......137 B1
Hartland's Rd PO16 ...131 A1
Hartley Ave SO17 ......79 A2
Hartley Cl
Bishopstoke SO50 ......57 A1
Hythe SO45 ....126 A1
Hartley Ct **6** SO17 ...103 A4
Hartley Grange SO16 ...79 A2
Hartley Rd
Bishopstoke SO50 ......57 A1
Gosport PO12 ....157 C2
Hartley Wlk **8** SO50 ..126 A1
Hartnell Ct BH21 ......186 B3
Harts Farm Way PO9 .159 B4
Hartsgrove Ave SO45 .150 C1
Hartsgrove Cl SO45 ...150 C1
Hartwell Rd PO3 ......158 A2
Hartwood Gdns PO8 ..111 C1
Harvest Cl SO22 ....10 B2
Harvest Rd
Chandler's Ford SO53 ..54 C3
Denmead PO7 ....110 C2
Harvester Dr PO15 ....130 A1
Harvester Way SO41 ..197 B3
Harvestgate Wlk 6
  PO9 ....135 B3
Harvesting La GU32,PO8 .64 B3
Harvey Brown Ho PO11 185 A3
Harvey Cres SO31 .....128 B2
Harvey Ct SO45 ....150 C1
Harvey Gdns SO45 ....126 A2
Harvey Ho PO4 ....183 A1

Harwell Rd BH17 ......202 B4
Harwich Rd PO6 ......133 B1
Harwood Cl
Gosport PO13 ....155 B2
Totton SO40 ....100 B4
Harwood Gdns PO5 ...194 C2
Harwood PI SO23 ....2 B4
Harwood Rd PO13 ....155 B1
Haselbury Rd SO40 ...100 C4
Haselfoot Gdns SO30 .104 C4
Haselworth Dr PO12 ..181 A1
Haselworth Prim Sch
  PO12 ....181 A2
Haskells Cl SO43 .....121 C2
Haskells Rd BH12 ....203 A4
Haslar Cres PO7 ......111 B1
Haslar Marina PO12 ..181 C2
Haslar Rd PO12 ....181 B1
Haslar Terr PO12 .....181 B1
Haslegrave Ho **2** PO22 182 B4
Haslemere Ave BH23 .209 A4
Haslemere Gdns PO11 185 C1
Haslemere PI BH23 ..209 A4
Haslemere Rd
Portsmouth PO4 ......182 C2
Southbourne PO10 ....137 B1
Hasler Rd BH17 ......187 B1
Haslop Rd BH21 ......164 A4
Hassocks The **3** PO7 135 A4
Hastings Ave PO12 ...180 C4
Hastings Ho **3** PO2 ..157 B1
Hastings Rd
Bournemouth BH8 ....190 C1
Poole BH17 ....187 A1
Hatch Ct PO9 ....135 B4
Hatch La GU33 ....21 B2
Hatch Mead SO30 ......80 B1
Hatch Pond Rd BH17 .202 B4
Hatches La SO21 ....33 A3
Hatchet Cl SP6 ....47 B2
Hatchet La
Beaulieu SO42 ....175 B4
East Boldre SO42 .....175 B4
Hatchley La SO21 ......58 A3
Hatchmore Rd PO7 ...135 C4
Hatfield Ct PO4 ....206 A4
Hatfield Rd **7** PO4 ...183 A2
Hathaway Cl SO50 .....56 A2
Hathaway Gdns PO7 ..112 A4
Hathaway Rd BH6 ....206 B2
Hathenden Ave BH14 .202 C3
Hatherell Cl SO30 ......80 B1
Hatherley Cres PO16 .156 A4
Hatherley Rd PO16 ...156 A4
Hatherley Mans 4
  SO15 ....102 B4
Hatherley Rd
Cosham PO6 ....133 A1
Winchester SO22 ......1 C1
Hatt La SO51 ....5 C1
Hatton Rd SO16 ....100 B4
Havant Bsns Ctr PO9 .135 C2
Havant Coll PO9 ......135 C1
Havant Education PRU
  PO8 ....111 C1
Havant Farm Cl PO9 .135 C2
Havant Mus & Arts Ctr*
  PO9 ....136 A1
Havant Rd Cosham PO6 158 B4
Emsworth PO10 ....160 B3
Horndean PO8 ....112 B3
North Hayling PO11 ...159 C1
Portsmouth PO2 ......182 C4
Havant St PO1 ....182 A3
Havant Sta PO9 ......135 C1
Havant War Meml Hospl
  PO9 ....135 C1
Havant-by-pass PO9 ..160 A4
Havelock Cl SO41 .....128 B1
Havelock Mans PO5 ..215 D2
Havelock Rd
Locks Heath SO31 ....128 B1
Poole BH12 ....204 A3
Portsmouth PO5 .....215 C2
Southampton SO14 ...102 C3
Havelock Way SO23 ..193 B1
Haven Cres SO31 .....154 C1
Haven Ct
1 Milford on Sea SO41 211 B2
Poole BH13 ....214 A2
Haven Gdns BH25 ....195 A1
Haven Rd
Corfe Mullen BH21 ...186 B3
Poole BH13 ....214 C4
South Hayling PO11 ..185 C1
Haven The Eastleigh SO50 56 A3
Gosport PO12 ....181 A1
Locks Heath SO31 ....129 A2
Portsmouth PO4 ......183 A3
Southampton SO19 ...103 C2
Havendale SO30 ......105 B3
Havenhurst BH13 ....214 C3
Havenstone Way SO18 ..79 B2
Haviland Mews BH7 ..205 C3
Haviland Rd
Bournemouth BH1, BH7 .205 C3
Ferndown BH21 ......165 A4
Haviland Rd E BH7 ...205 C3
Haviland Rd W **5** BH7 205 C3
Havisham Rd PO2 ....182 B4
Haviland Rd W BH7 ..205 C3
Hawden Rd BH11 .....189 A1
Hawfinch Cl SO16 ......78 A3
Hawk Cl
Stubbington PO14 ....179 A3
Wimborne Minst BH21 164 A4

Hawkchurch Gdns
  BH17 ....187 C1
Hawke St PO1 ....182 A3
Hawker Cl BH21 ......162 A4
Hawkeswood Rd SO18 103 B4
Hawkewood Ave PO7 .111 B1
Hawkhill SO45 ....125 B2
Hawkhurst Cl SO19 ...104 A4
Hawkins Cl BH24 .....117 B1
Hawkins Ct SO40 .....101 C2
Hawkins Rd
Gosport PO13 ....155 B1
Poole BH15 ....188 C1
Hawkley Gn SO19 ....104 A4
Hawkley Rd Hawkley GU33 .20 B3
Liss GU33 ....20 B3
Hawks Mead GU33 ...20 C3
Hawkswell PO16 ....155 B1
Hawkwell Rd BH15 ...205 C2
Hawkwood Rd BH5 ...206 A2
Hawley Cl PO9 ....135 C3
Haworth Cl BH23 ....192 A1
Hawstead Gn PO9 ...135 B3
Hawthorn Cl SO16 ....77 C1
Hawthorn Cr
Colden Common SO21 ..57 A4
1 Fair Oak SO50 ......57 B1
Hedge End SO30 ......105 B3
New Milton BH25 .....195 B2
Hawthorn Cres PO6 ..158 A3
Hawthorn Ct **22** BH31 ...41 B2
Hawthorn Dr
Broadstone BH17 .....186 C1
Sway SO41 ....172 A1
Hawthorn La SO31 ...128 C3
Hawthorn Rd
Bournemouth BH9 ....204 C4
Burton BH23 ....192 C2
Denmead PO7 ....110 C2
Horndean PO8 ....86 A4
Hythe SO45 ....125 C2
Southampton SO17 ....79 C2
Hawthorn Wlk **20** PO13 179 C1
Hawthorne Rd PO11 .185 A2
Hawthorne Rd W SO40 100 B4
Hawthorns The
Bishop's Waltham SO32 ..83 A4
Christchurch BH23 ...207 C3
Eastleigh SO50 ....55 C1
Marchwood SO40 ....102 A1
Hawthorns The Urban
  **Wildlife Ctr* SO15 ..102 C4
Hayburn Rd SO16 .....77 B1
Hayden Ct SO41 ......197 C2
Haydens Cl SO41 .....197 C2
Haydn Cl SO23 ....2 A4
Haydock Cl SO40 ....100 B4
Haydock Mews **8** PO7 112 A1
Haydon Rd BH13 .....204 A1
Hayes Ave BH7 ......205 C3
Hayes Cl Fareham PO15 130 B2
Wimborne Minst BH21 .164 A3
Hayes La BH21 ....164 A3
Hayes Mead SO45 ....150 A3
Hayes Terr PO12 .....181 A3
Hayeswood Fst Sch
  BH21 ....164 A3
Hayeswood Rd BH21 .164 A3
Hayle Rd SO18 ....80 A1
Hayley Cl SO45 ....149 C4
Hayling Ave PO3 .....183 A4
Hayling Cl Fareham PO14 154 B4
Gosport PO12 ....181 B4
Hayling Sch The PO11 .185 A3
Haymoor Mid Sch BH17 187 C1
Haymoor Rd BH15 ...203 A4
Haynes Ave BH15 ....202 B2
Haynes Way SO45 ...125 C3
Hays Cotts GU32 ......40 B4
Haysoms Cl BH25 ...195 A1
Hayter Gdns SO51 ....53 A4
Hayters Way SP6 .....93 A3
Hayton Ct SO40 ......100 C4
Hayward Bsns Ctr PO9 136 A2
Hayward Cl SO40 ....100 B4
Hayward Cres BH31 ..114 C3
Hayward Ct SO45 ....150 B2
Hayward Way BH31 ..114 C3
Haywards Ct **11** PO11 182 A2
Haywards Farm Cl
  BH31 ....114 C3
Haywards La BH21 ...186 B4
Hazel Cl Alderholt SP6 ..93 A3
Chandler's Ford SO53 ..30 B1
Christchurch BH23 ...193 B1
Colden Common SO21 ..32 A1
Hazel Ct
Bournemouth BH9 ....190 B2
22 New Milton BH25 ..195 A1
Portsmouth PO4 .....182 C2
Hazel Dr BH22 ....165 B4
Hazel Farm Rd SO40 .100 B4
Hazel Gr Ashurst SO40 ..99 C2
Clanfield PO8 ....88 B3
Locks Heath SO31 ...129 A1
Winchester SO22 .....10 B3
Hazel Rd Clanfield PO8 .163 B3
Lymington SO41 ......197 A2
Southampton SO19 ...103 B2
Hazel Wood Inf Sch
  SO40 ....100 B4
Hazelbank Cl GU31 ....41 A2
Hazeldale Villas 6
  SO41 ....126 A3
Hazeldean Ct PO9 ....113 A1
Hazeldean Dr PO9 ...113 A1
Hazeldene BH18 ......187 A2
Hazeldown Rd SO16 ..77 C3
Hazeleigh Ave SO19 ..103 C1
Hazeley Cotts SO21 ..32 B4

Hazeley Gn P09 .....136 A3
Hazeley Rd S021 .....32 B3
Hazelholt Dr P09 .....135 B2
Hazel Ave BH10 .....189 A1
Hazelton Cl BH7 .....206 A4
Hazelwood P014 .....154 A3
Hazelwood Ave
　Havant P09 .....135 A2
　New Milton BH25 .....194 C2
Hazelwood Dr BH31 .....115 A2
Hazelwood Rd S018 .....80 A1
Hazlebury Rd BH17 .....202 A4
Hazlemere Dr P04 .....139 C2
Hazleton Way P08 .....112 A2
Head Down S031 .....41 A2
Head's La BH10 .....189 C3
Headbourne Worthy Ho
　S023 .....2 A3
Headland Dr S031 .....129 A2
Headlands Bsns Pk
　BH24 .....117 A1
Headlands The SP5 .....46 C4
Headless Cross BH10 .....189 B3
Headley Cl P013 .....179 C1
Headley Rd
　Bournemouth BH10 .....189 A1
　Gosport P012 .....181 A4
Heads Farm Cl BH10 .....189 C3
Headswell Ave BH10 .....189 C2
Headswell Cres BH10 .....189 C2
Headswell Gdns BH10 .....189 C2
Heanor Cl BH10 .....189 B1
Hearne Gdns S032 .....84 A1
Hearts of Oak Mews
　S041 .....197 B2
Heath Ave BH15 .....202 B3
Heath Cl Fair Oak S050 .....57 B1
　Horndean P08 .....112 A4
　Wimborne Minst BH21 .....164 A4
Heath Ct GU31 .....40 C1
Heath Farm Cl BH22 .....165 B2
Heath Farm Rd BH22 .....165 B2
Heath Farm Way BH22 .....165 B2
Heath Gdns S031 .....127 B4
Heath House Cl S030 .....105 A2
Heath House Gdns
　S030 .....105 A2
Heath La S030 .....105 B2
Heath La S042 .....175 B4
Heath Lawns P015 .....130 B1
Heath Lodge GU31 .....40 C1
Heath Rd
　Christchurch BH23 .....194 A1
　Hordle S041 .....195 C2
　Locks Heath S031 .....129 A2
　North Baddesley S052 .....54 A2
　Petersfield GU31 .....41 A2
　Soberton S032 .....85 A1
　Southampton S019 .....104 A3
　St Leonards BH24 .....139 B2
Heath Rd E GU31 .....41 A1
Heath Rd N S031 .....128 C2
　St Leonards BH24 .....139 B2
Heath Rd S S031 .....128 C2
Heath Rd W GU31 .....41 A1
Heath The P07 .....111 A2
Heathcote Pl S021 .....30 A4
Heathcote Rd
　Bournemouth BH5 .....205 C2
　Chandler's Ford S053 .....55 B3
　Portsmouth P02 .....157 C1
Heathen St S032 .....82 A2
Heather Chase S050 .....57 A1
Heather Cl
　Bournemouth BH8 .....190 B2
　Christchurch BH23 .....194 A1
　Corfe Mullen BH21 .....186 C3
　Gosport P013 .....155 A1
　Hordle S041 .....196 A2
　St Leonards BH24 .....139 C1
　Totton S040 .....100 C4
　Waterlooville P07 .....134 C3
Heather Ct S018 .....104 B4
Heather Dell BH16 .....201 A3
Heather De P012 .....165 B4
Heather Gdns P015 .....130 B2
Heather Lo **B** BH25 .....195 A2
Heather Rd
　Blackfield S045 .....150 C1
　Bournemouth BH9 .....189 B2
　Petersfield GU31 .....41 B2
Heather View Rd BH12 .....203 C4
Heather Way BH24 .....165 B4
Heatherbank Rd BH4 .....204 B2
Heatherbrae Gdns S052 .....53 C2
Heatherbrae La BH16 .....201 A3
Heatherdeane Rd S017 .....79 A1
Heatherdene Rd S053 .....30 C1
Heatherdown Rd GU31 .....139 A1
Heatherdown Way
　BH22 .....139 A1
Heatherfield GU31 .....65 B3
Heatherlands Fst Sch
　BH12 .....203 C3
Heatherlands Rd S016 .....78 C4
Heatherlands Rise
　BH12 .....203 B3
Heatherlea Rd BH6 .....206 B2
Heatherley Ct P05 .....215 C1
Heatherstone Ave S045 .....126 C1
Heatherton Mews P010 .....136 C1
Heatherview Cl S052 .....53 C3
Heathfield S045 .....125 C1
Heathfield Ave
　Fareham P015 .....130 B1
　Poole BH15 .....204 A4
Heathfield Cl
　Chandler's Ford S053 .....30 B1
　Southampton S019 .....104 A2
Heathfield Ho BH23 .....169 C1

Heathfield Jun Sch
　S019 .....104 B1
Heathfield Rd
　Chandler's Ford S053 .....30 B1
　Petersfield GU31 .....41 B2
　Portsmouth P02 .....157 B1
　Southampton S019 .....104 B2
　West Moors BH22 .....139 A1
Heathfield Specl Sch
　P014 .....154 B4
Heathfield Way BH22 .....138 C1
Heathlands Ave BH22 .....165 B1
Heathlands Cl
　Burton BH23 .....192 B2
　Chandler's Ford S053 .....55 B4
　Verwood BH31 .....115 A3
Heathlands Prim Sch
　BH11 .....189 A2
Heathlands Rd S053 .....55 B4
Heathwood Ave BH25 .....209 C4
Heathwood Rd BH9 .....204 C4
Heathy Cl BH25 .....209 C4
Heaton Rd
　Bournemouth BH10 .....189 A1
　Gosport P012 .....181 A4
Heavytree Rd BH14 .....203 A2
Hebrides Cl P014 .....154 A2
Heckfield Cl **20** P09 .....136 A3
Heckford La BH15 .....202 B2
Heckford Rd
　Corfe Mullen BH21 .....186 B3
　Poole BH15 .....202 B2
Hector Cl P07 .....134 C1
Hector Rd P014 .....155 A3
Hedera Rd S031 .....128 C2
Hedge End Bsns Ctr
　S030 .....81 A1
Hedge End Sta S030 .....81 B2
Hedge End Wlk **7** P09 .....136 A3
Hedgerley BH25 .....210 A4
Hedgerow Cl S016 .....77 C4
Hedgerow Dr S018 .....80 A1
Hedgerow Gdns P010 .....136 C2
Hedley Cl S045 .....150 C1
Hedley Gdns S030 .....81 A2
Heidelberg Rd P04 .....182 C2
Heights App BH16 .....201 B4
Heights Rd BH16 .....201 B4
Heights The
　Fareham P016 .....131 B1
　Hedge End S030 .....105 A3
Helena Rd P04 .....182 C1
Helford Gdns S018 .....80 A1
Helic Rd **2** BH21 .....163 B3
Hellyer Rd P04 .....183 A2
Helm Cl P013 .....180 B3
Helsby Cl P014 .....154 C4
Helsted Cl P012 .....180 C2
Helston Dr P010 .....136 C2
Helston Rd P06 .....132 C1
Helvellyn Rd S016 .....101 C4
Helyar Rd BH8 .....190 C1
Hemdean Gdns S030 .....80 B1
Hemlock Rd P08 .....111 C2
Hemlock Way S053 .....54 C3
Hemming Cl S040 .....100 C3
Hemmingway Gdns
　P015 .....129 B4
Hempland La GU34 .....17 B2
Hempsted Rd P06 .....133 A1
Hemsley Wlk P08 .....112 A2
Henbest Cl BH21 .....164 B3
Henbury Cl
　Corfe Mullen BH21 .....186 B3
　Poole BH17 .....188 A1
Henbury Rise BH21 .....186 B3
Henbury View Fst Sch
　BH21 .....186 B3
Henbury View Rd BH21 .....186 B3
Henchard Cl BH22 .....165 B1
Henderson Rd P04 .....183 B2
Hendford Gdns BH10 .....189 B1
Hendford Rd BH10 .....189 B1
Hendy Cl P05 .....215 B1
Hengist Rd BH1 .....205 B2
Hengistbury Head Nature
　Reserve* BH6 .....207 C1
Hengistbury Head Nature
　Trail* BH6 .....207 B2
Hengistbury Rd
　Barton on Sea BH25 .....209 C4
　Bournemouth BH6 .....207 A2
Henley Ct S041 .....211 C2
Henley Gdns
　Bournemouth BH7 .....206 A4
　Fareham P015 .....130 B2
Henley Rd P04 .....182 C2
Henning's Park Rd
　BH15 .....202 C3
Henry Beaufort Sec Sch
　S022 .....1 C2
Henry Cort Com Sch
　P015 .....130 A2
Henry Cort Dr P015 .....130 B2
Henry St
　Bishopstoke S050 .....56 B2
　Southampton S015 .....102 B4
Henry St
　9 Bournemouth P012 .....181 B2
　Southampton S015 .....102 C3
Henstead Ct S015 .....102 C3
Henstead Rd S015 .....102 C3
Hensting La
　Colden Common S021,S050 .....32 C1
　Owslebury S021 .....58 C1
Henty Rd S016 .....102 A4
Henville Cl P013 .....180 B4

Henville Rd **6** BH8 .....205 B3
Henwood Down GU31 .....41 A2
Hepworth Cl S019 .....104 B1
Herald Ind Est S030 .....81 A1
Herald Rd S030 .....81 A1
Herbert Ave BH12 .....203 B4
Herbert Cl BH12 .....203 B4
Herbert Rd
　Bournemouth BH4 .....204 A1
　Gosport P012 .....180 C3
　New Milton BH25 .....195 A2
　Poole BH13 .....204 A1
　Portsmouth P04 .....182 C1
　Redlynch SP5 .....47 B3
Herbert St P01 .....182 B4
Herbert Walker Ave
　S015 .....102 B2
Herberton Rd BH6 .....206 B3
Hercules Rd BH15 .....201 B2
Hercules St BH12 .....182 B4
Hereford Ct
　Gosport P013 .....180 B3
　Portsmouth P05 .....215 C1
Hereford Rd P05 .....215 C1
Hereward Cl S051 .....53 A4
Heritage Ct BH13 .....214 C4
Heritage Ctr* S031 .....127 B2
Heritage Gdns P016 .....156 A4
Heritage Way P012 .....181 B4
Herm Rd BH12 .....188 B1
Hermes Ct P012 .....181 B4
Hermes Rd P013 .....179 B2
Hermitage Cl
　Bishop's Waltham S032 .....83 A4
　Havant P09 .....135 C2
　Three Legged Cross BH21 .....138 C4
Hermitage Gdns P07 .....134 C4
Hermitage Rd BH14 .....203 A3
Hermitage The BH14 .....203 A2
Hern La SP6 .....94 A3
Herne Jun Sch GU31 .....41 A2
Herne Rd Cosham P06 .....157 C4
Heron Cl Portsmouth P04 .....183 A3
　Sway S041 .....172 A1
Heron Court Rd BH3,
　BH9 .....205 A4
Heron La S051 .....27 B3
Heron Quay P010 .....161 A4
Heron Sq S051 .....53 C1
Heron Way P013 .....155 A2
Herons Cl P014 .....154 B2
Herons Ct P011 .....185 A3
Heronswood S040 .....76 B1
Herrick Cl S019 .....104 B2
Herriot Cl P08 .....112 A3
Herriot Ho P08 .....112 A1
Herstone Cl BH17 .....187 C1
Hertford Cl **8** BH23 .....209 A4
Hertford Pl P01 .....182 B4
Hertsfield P014 .....129 B2
Hesketh Cl BH24 .....140 A3
Hesketh Ho **8** S015 .....102 B3
Hessian Cl BH21 .....191 B2
Hester Rd P04 .....183 A2
Hestia Cl S051 .....53 B4
Heston Way P012 .....138 B2
Heston Wlk P012 .....180 C2
Hetherington Gdns P06 .....133 C4
Hewett Ho P04 .....112 A3
Hewett Rd P014 .....153 C4
Hewett Rd
　Portsmouth P02 .....157 C1
　Titchfield P014 .....153 B3
Hewetts Rise S031 .....152 B4
Hewitt Cl P012 .....181 A4
Hewitt Rd BH15 .....201 C2
Hewitt's Rd S015 .....102 B3
Heyes Dr S019 .....104 B2
Heysham Rd
　Broadstone BH18 .....187 A2
　Southampton S015 .....102 A4
Heyshott Gdns P08 .....88 B2
Heyshott Rd P04 .....182 C2
Heyward Rd P04 .....182 C2
Heywood Gdns BH10 .....135 B3
Heywood Gr S019 .....104 C3
Hibberd Way BH10 .....189 B1
Hibbs Cl BH16 .....201 B4
Hickes Cl BH11 .....188 C2
Hickory Cl BH16 .....201 A4
Hickory Dr S022 .....1 B2
High Barn Cotts S032 .....36 C2
High Brow BH22 .....165 B3
High Cross S032 .....18 C1
High Cross La GU32 .....18 B1
High Ct P04 .....183 A2
High Dr P013 .....155 B3
High Firs Gdns S051 .....53 B4
High Firs Rd Romsey S051 .....53 B4
　Southampton S019 .....104 B3
High Howe Cl BH11 .....188 C2
High Howe Gdns BH11 .....188 C2
High Howe La BH11 .....188 C2
High Lawn Way P09 .....135 C3
High Marryats BH25 .....210 A4
High Mdw S019 .....104 B3
High Mead
　Fareham P015 .....130 C2
　Ferndown BH22 .....165 A1
High Mead La BH21 .....165 A1
High Oaks Cl S031 .....129 A2
High Oaks Gdns BH21 .....186 C2
High Park Rd BH18 .....186 C2

High Pines BH23 .....208 A2
High Point S018 .....103 C4
High Rd S016 .....79 B2
High Ridge Cres BH25 .....195 B1
High St Beaulieu S042 .....148 C1
　Bishop's Waltham S032 .....83 B4
　Botley S030 .....106 A4
　Buriton GU31 .....65 B3
　Burslodon S031 .....128 A4
　Christchurch BH23 .....207 A3
　Cosham P06 .....157 C4
　Damerham SP6 .....68 B3
　Downton SP5 .....47 A4
　Droxford S032 .....37 C4
　East Meon GU32 .....38 C1
　Eastleigh S050 .....56 A1
　Emsworth P010 .....160 C4
　Fareham P016 .....131 B1
　Fordingbridge SP6 .....69 C1
　Gosport P012 .....181 B2
　Hamble-le-Rice S031 .....128 A1
　Hambledon P07 .....86 B2
　Hythe S045 .....126 A3
　Lee-on-the-Solent P013 .....179 C1
　Lymington S041 .....197 C2
　Lyndhurst S043 .....121 C3
　Meonstoke S032 .....61 B2
　Milford on Sea S041 .....211 B2
　Petersfield GU32 .....40 C2
　Poole BH15 .....202 B2
　Portsmouth P01 .....182 A2
　Ringwood BH24 .....140 C4
　Sheffield S032 .....107 C4
　Soberton S032 .....85 A2
　Southwick P017 .....132 C3
　St Leonards BH24 .....139 C3
　Titchfield P014 .....153 A2
　Totton S040 .....101 A4
　Twyford S021 .....32 A4
　West End S030 .....80 B1
　West Moors GU32 .....37 B3
　Wimborne Minst BH21 .....163 A2
　Winchester S023 .....11 A4
　Woodgreen SP6 .....70 C4
High Sch N BH15 .....202 B2
High Town Hill BH24 .....141 C4
High Trees Fair Oak S050 .....57 C1
　Poole BH13 .....214 C4
　Waterlooville P07 .....134 B4
High Trees Dr S022 .....1 C1
High Trees Wlk BH22 .....165 B4
High View P016 .....132 B1
High View Way S018 .....103 C4
High Walls P010 .....161 A4
High Wlk BH18 .....186 C2
High Wlk P015 .....130 C2
Highbank Ave P07 .....134 B2
Highbank Gdns BH6 .....206 A3
Highbridge Rd
　Colden Common, Highbridge
　S050,S021 .....56 B4
　Colden Common, Twyford Moors
　S021 .....31 C1
Highbury Bldgs P06 .....157 C3
Highbury Cl Fair Oak S050 .....57 B1
　New Milton BH25 .....195 A1
Highbury Coll P06 .....158 A3
Highbury Gr P06 .....158 A3
Highbury Prim Sch P06 .....158 A3
Highbury St **5** P01 .....182 A2
Highbury Way P06 .....157 C3
Highclere Ave P06 .....135 C2
Highclere Rd S016 .....78 B2
Highclere Way S053 .....55 A2
Highcliff Ave S014 .....103 A4
Highcliffe Castle*
　BH23 .....208 C4
Highcliffe Cnr BH23 .....209 A4
Highcliffe Dr S050 .....56 A4
Highcliffe Jun Sch
　BH23 .....193 C1
Highcliffe Rd
　Christchurch BH23 .....208 B4
　Gosport P012 .....180 C4
　Winchester S023 .....11 A3
Highcliffe Sch BH23 .....193 B1
Highcroft Ind Est P08 .....112 B4
Highcroft La P08 .....112 B4
Highcrown Mews S017 .....79 A1
Highcrown St S017 .....79 A1
Higher Blandford Rd
　BH18,BH21 .....186 C3
Higher Merley La BH21 .....186 C4
Highfield Lymington S041 .....197 B2
　Twyford S021 .....32 A3
Highfield Ave
　Fareham P014 .....154 C4
　Lymington S041 .....197 B2
　Ringwood BH24 .....141 A4
　Southampton S016,S017 .....78 C2
　Twyford S021 .....32 A3
　Waterlooville P07 .....111 C1
Highfield Campus (Univ of
　Southampton) S017 .....79 A2
Highfield CE Inf Sch
　S017 .....79 A1
Highfield CE Prim Sch
　S017 .....79 A1
Highfield Cl
　Chandler's Ford S053 .....55 C3
　Corfe Mullen BH21 .....186 C3
　Southampton S017 .....79 A1
　Sway S041 .....172 A1
　Waterlooville P07 .....111 C1
Highfield Cres S017 .....79 A1

Highfield Ct S021 .....83 A4
Highfield Dr BH24 .....141 A4
Highfield Gdns Liss GU33 .....21 A2
　Sway S041 .....172 A1
Highfield Hall S017 .....79 A1
Highfield Ho **8** BH4 .....204 A1
Highfield La Redlynch SP5 .....47 B3
　Southampton S017 .....79 A1
Highfield Lodge **3** S017 .....79 A1
Highfield Par P07 .....112 A1
Highfield Rd
　Bournemouth BH9 .....189 C1
　Chandler's Ford S053 .....55 C3
　Corfe Mullen BH21 .....186 C3
　Gosport P012 .....180 C3
　Lymington S041 .....197 B2
　Portsmouth P01 .....215 C3
　Portsmouth P011 .....215 C3
　Ringwood BH24 .....141 A4
　West Moors BH22 .....138 C2
Highfield Terr **4** S022 .....10 C4
Highfields S031 .....128 C1
Highgate Rd P03 .....158 A1
Highgrove Ind Pk P03 .....158 A2
Highgrove Rd P03 .....183 A3
Highland Ave P03 .....194 A1
Highland Cl P010 .....160 C4
Highland Rd
　Emsworth P010 .....136 C1
　Poole BH14 .....203 A2
　Portsmouth P04 .....183 A2
　Wimborne Minst BH21 .....163 B3
Highland St P04 .....182 C2
Highland Terr P04 .....182 C2
Highland View Cl BH21 .....163 B3
Highlands Cl Hythe S045 .....126 A3
　North Baddesley S052 .....53 C3
Highlands Cres BH10 .....189 B2
Highlands Ho S019 .....103 B2
Highlands Rd
　Barton on Sea BH25 .....210 A4
　Cosham P06 .....158 A4
　Fareham P015,P016 .....130 B2
Highlands Way
　Hythe S045 .....125 C1
　Whiteparish SP5 .....24 A2
Highmoor Cl
　Corfe Mullen BH21 .....186 B3
　Poole BH14 .....203 A2
Highmoor Rd
　Bournemouth BH11 .....189 A1
　Corfe Mullen BH21 .....186 B3
　Poole BH14 .....203 B2
Highmount Cl S023 .....11 B4
Highnam Gdns S031 .....128 C2
Hightown Gdns BH24 .....141 B3
Hightown Ind Est BH24 .....141 C3
Hightown Prim Sch
　S019 .....104 C2
Hightown Rd BH24 .....141 A3
Hightown Twrs S019 .....104 C2
Hightrees Ave BH8 .....190 C1
Highview Cl BH12 .....191 C2
Highview Gdns BH12 .....203 B4
Highways Rd S021 .....31 B3
Highwood Cl SP6 .....92 B3
Highwood La
　North Baddesley S051 .....53 B4
　Ringwood BH24 .....117 C2
Highwood Lawn P09 .....135 B4
Highwood PR1V S042 .....172 C4
Highwood Rd
　Brockenhurst S042 .....172 C4
　Gosport P013 .....180 B4
　Poole BH14 .....203 C2
Higworth La P011 .....184 C3
Hilary Ave P06 .....158 A4
Hilary Cl P013 .....122 A2
Hilary Ct P013 .....180 B3
Hilda Ct **8** S015 .....102 C4
Hilda Gdns P07 .....111 A2
Hilda Pl **2** S014 .....103 B3
Hilden Cl P011 .....184 C2
Hilden Way S022 .....1 A3
Hill Brow Rd GU33 .....21 A1
Hill Cl BH23 .....193 A4
　Fair Oak S050 .....57 B3
Hill Close Est SP6 .....70 C4
Hill Croft P015 .....129 C2
Hill Dr P015 .....130 B2
Hill Farm Rd S015 .....102 C4
Hill Grove S032 .....84 B3
Hill Head Rd P014 .....179 A3
Hill House Sch S041 .....172 B3
Hill Houses La S024 .....14 A3
Hill La **B** Bransgore BH23 .....193 A4
　Burton BH23 .....192 C1
　Colden Common S021 .....31 C1
　Southampton S015 .....78 C1
Hill Park Rd
　Fareham P015 .....130 B2
　Gosport P012 .....180 C4
Hill Pl S031 .....128 A4
Hill Rd P016 .....132 B1
Hill Rise Meonstoke S032 .....61 B2
　Poole BH15 .....202 B1
Hill St Over S040 .....76 B3
Hill Terr S050 .....57 B3
Hill Top S022 .....1 B3

Hill View GU32 ... 38 B1
Hill View Prim Sch BH10 ... 189 C2
Hill View Rd
Braishfield SO51 ... 28 B3
Ferndown BH22 ... 165 B4
Michelmersh SO51 ... 27 B4
Portchester PO16 ... 132 B1
Hill Way BH24 ... 139 C3
Hill Wlk PO15 ... 130 B2
Hillary Cl PO16 ... 130 C1
Hillary Rd BH23 ... 207 C4
Hillborough Cres 2 PO5 ... 215 C1
Hillborough Ct 1 PO5 ... 215 C1
Hillbourne Fst & Mid Schs BH17 ... 187 A1
Hillbourne Rd BH17 ... 187 A1
Hillbrow Cl
Fareham PO15 ... 130 B2
Rowland's Castle PO9 ... 113 A1
Hillbrow Rd BH6 ... 206 A3
Hillbury Pk SP6 ... 93 A3
Hillbury Rd SP6 ... 93 A3
Hillcrest Ave
Chandler's Ford SO53 ... 55 C3
Ferndown BH22 ... 165 B4
Hillcrest Cl
Bournemouth BH9 ... 190 A2
North Baddesley SO52 ... 53 C3
Hillcrest Dr SO53 ... 55 B3
Hillcrest Gdns SO32 ... 83 B2
Hillcrest Hospl BH10 ... 189 B1
Hillcrest Rd
Bournemouth BH9 ... 190 A2
Corfe Mullen BH21 ... 186 B3
Hillcroft SP5 ... 47 B3
Hilldene Way SO30 ... 80 C1
Hillditch SO41 ... 197 B3
Hilldown Rd SO17 ... 79 A1
Hilldowns Ave PO2 ... 157 B1
Hillers Wlk 16 PO13 ... 179 C1
Hillgrove Rd SO18 ... 79 C2
Hillier Way SO23 ... 2 A1
Hillman Rd BH14 ... 203 B3
Hillmead Gdns PO9 ... 135 A1
Hillmeadow BH31 ... 115 A2
Hillside Curdridge SO32 ... 106 C4
Littleton SO22 ... 1 B3
Hillside Ave Romsey SO51 ... 53 A4
Southampton SO18 ... 79 C1
Waterlooville PO7 ... 134 A1
Hillside Cl
Chandler's Ford SO53 ... 55 B3
Horndean PO8 ... 88 B2
West Dean SP5 ... 3 B1
Winchester SO22 ... 1 B1
Hillside Cres PO6 ... 132 C1
Hillside Dr BH23 ... 191 B2
Hillside First Sch BH31 ... 114 C4
Hillside Gdns BH21 ... 186 B2
Hillside Ind Est PO8 ... 112 B4
Hillside Mews BH21 ... 186 B2
Hillside Rd
Corfe Mullen BH21 ... 186 B3
Lymington SO41 ... 197 B2
Poole BH12 ... 188 C1
Verwood BH31 ... 114 C4
Winchester SO22 ... 1 B1
Woodlands BH21 ... 114 A3
Hillside Wlk BH21 ... 114 A3
Hillsley Rd PO6 ... 132 C1
Hillson Dr PO15 ... 130 B2
Hillson Ho PO15 ... 130 B2
Hillsons Rd SO30 ... 106 A4
Hilltop Cl BH22 ... 165 A4
Hilltop Cres PO6 ... 134 B1
Hilltop Dr SO19 ... 104 B2
Hilltop Gdns PO8 ... 88 B2
Hilltop Rd
Corfe Mullen BH21 ... 186 C3
Ferndown BH22 ... 165 A4
Hillview PO8 ... 112 B3
Hillview Rd
Bournemouth BH10 ... 189 B2
Hythe SO45 ... 125 C2
Hillway The
Chandler's Ford SO53 ... 55 B4
Portchester PO16 ... 156 B4
Hilly Cl SO21 ... 33 A2
Hillyfields SO16 ... 77 B2
Hilsea Cres PO2 ... 157 C3
Hilsea Mkt PO2 ... 157 C3
Hilsea Sta PO3 ... 158 A2
Hiltingbury Cl SO53 ... 30 B1
Hiltingbury Ct SO53 ... 30 A1
Hiltingbury Inf Sch SO53 ... 30 B1
Hiltingbury Jun Sch SO53 ... 30 B1
Hiltingbury Rd
Chandler's Ford SO53 ... 30 B1
53 Havant PO9 ... 136 A3
Hiltom Rd BH24 ... 141 A4
Hilton Cl BH15 ... 203 A3
Hilton Rd Gosport PO12 ... 181 B2
Hedge End SO30 ... 105 B4
New Milton BH25 ... 195 A2
Hinchcliffe Cl BH15 ... 201 C1
Hinchcliffe Rd BH15 ... 201 C1
Hinkler Ct SO19 ... 104 B2
Hinkler Rd SO19 ... 104 C3
Hinton Admiral Mews BH23 ... 193 C1
Hinton Admiral Sta BH23 ... 193 C1
Hinton Ampner Ho* SO24 ... 14 C2
Hinton Cl PO9 ... 135 B2
Hinton Cres SO19 ... 104 C2
Hinton Hill SO24 ... 14 C2
Hinton Ho 1 PO7 ... 134 C4
Hinton Manor La PO8 ... 87 C1
Hinton Rd BH1 ... 204 C2
Hinton Wood BH1 ... 205 A1
Hinton Wood Ave BH23 ... 193 C1
Hintonwood La BH23 ... 193 C1
Hipley Rd PO9 ... 136 A2
Hirst Rd SO45 ... 126 A2
Hispano Ave PO15 ... 129 B4
Hither Gn PO10 ... 137 C1
Hitherwood Cl 14 PO7 ... 112 A1
Hive Gdns BH13 ... 214 B3
Hives Way SO41 ... 197 B3
HMS Victory* PO1 ... 181 C3
HMS Warrior* PO1 ... 181 C3
Hoad's Hill PO17 ... 108 A1
Hoadlands GU31 ... 41 A2
Hobart Dr SO45 ... 126 A2
Hobart Rd BH25 ... 194 C1
Hobb La SO30 ... 105 B3
Hobbs Ct PO12 ... 181 C2
Hobbs Pass PO12 ... 181 C2
Hobbs Pk BH24 ... 139 C2
Hobbs Rd BH12 ... 203 B4
Hobby Cl PO3 ... 158 A2
Hobson Way SO45 ... 150 B2
Hoburne Ct BH23 ... 193 B1
Hoburne Gdns BH23 ... 193 B1
Hoburne La BH23 ... 208 B4
Hockham Ct PO9 ... 135 B4
Hockley Cl 7 PO6 ... 157 B4
Hockley Cotts
Cheriton SO24 ... 13 C2
Twyford SO21 ... 32 A4
Hockley Link SO21 ... 10 C1
Hocombe Dr SO53 ... 30 A1
Hocombe Park Cl SO53 ... 30 A1
Hocombe Rd SO53 ... 30 B1
Hocombe Wood Rd SO53 ... 30 A1
Hodder Cl SO53 ... 55 A3
Hodges Cl Havant PO9 ... 136 A2
Poole BH17 ... 202 C4
Hoe La SO52 ... 53 B2
Hoe Rd SO32 ... 83 C4
Hoe St PO7 ... 109 C4
Hoe The PO13 ... 155 C1
Hoeford Cl PO16 ... 155 A3
Hogarth Cl
7 Romsey SO51 ... 28 A1
Southampton SO19 ... 104 B1
Hogarth Way BH8 ... 191 A1
Hoggarth Cl GU32 ... 41 A2
Hogs Lodge La PO8 ... 88 C4
Hogue Ave BH10 ... 189 B3
Hogwood La SO30 ... 80 C3
Holbeach Cl PO6 ... 133 C1
Holbein Lodge SO41 ... 198 A2
Holbrook Pl 6 SO51 ... 52 C4
Holbrook Prim Sch PO13 ... 155 B2
Holbrook Rd
Fareham PO16 ... 155 A4
Portsmouth PO1 ... 215 C3
Holbury Cl BH8 ... 190 C2
Holbury Ct 25 PO9 ... 136 A3
Holbury Dro SO45 ... 150 B2
Holbury Inf Sch SO45 ... 150 B2
Holbury Jun Sch SO45 ... 150 B2
Holbury La
East Tytherley SO51 ... 4 B2
Lockerley SO51 ... 4 B2
Holcombe Rd BH16 ... 201 A3
Holcot La PO3 ... 158 B2
Holcroft Rd SO19 ... 104 C3
Holdaway Cl SO23 ... 2 B4
Holden La SO24 ... 34 C4
Holdenbury Ct PO3 ... 158 B2
Holdenhurst Ave BH7 ... 206 B4
Holdenhurst Cl PO8 ... 88 B1
Holdenhurst Rd
Bournemouth BH8 ... 205 B3
Bournemouth, Holdenhurst BH8 ... 191 A2
Hole La Curdridge SO32 ... 83 A1
Soberton PO7 ... 110 A4
Holes Bay North Rdbt BH17 ... 202 A3
Holes Bay Rd BH15 ... 202 A2
Holes Bay Rdbt BH15 ... 202 A3
Holes Cl SO41 ... 195 C2
Holkham Cl SO16 ... 77 C2
Hollam Cl PO14 ... 154 A4
Hollam Cres PO14 ... 154 A4
Hollam Dr PO14 ... 154 A4
Hollam Rd PO4 ... 183 A2
Holland Cl SO53 ... 55 A2
Holland Pk SO31 ... 128 C2
Holland Pl Gosport PO13 ... 155 B1
Southampton SO16 ... 78 A1
Holland Rd
Portsmouth PO5 ... 215 D2
Southampton SO19 ... 103 B1
Totton SO40 ... 100 B4
Holland Way BH18 ... 186 C3
Hollands Cl SO22 ... 1 A3
Hollands Wood Dr BH25 ... 195 A3
Hollies Cl SO41 ... 172 A1
Hollies The SO51 ... 50 C2
Hollingbourne Cl SO18 ... 103 B4
Hollman Dr SO51 ... 52 B4
Hollow La PO11 ... 184 C2
Holloway Ave BH11 ... 188 C3
Holly Cl Hythe SO45 ... 150 A4
Locks Heath SO31 ... 128 C2
St Leonards BH24 ... 139 B2
Upton BH16 ... 201 A4
Holly Ct BH15 ... 202 B2
Holly Dell SO16 ... 78 C3
Holly Dr PO7 ... 135 A3
Holly Gdns Burton BH23 ... 192 B1
Milford on Sea SO41 ... 211 B3
West End SO30 ... 80 B2
Holly Gr Fareham PO16 ... 130 C2
Verwood BH31 ... 114 C3
Holly Green Rise BH11 ... 188 C2
Holly Hatch Rd SO40 ... 100 C3
Holly Hedge La BH17 ... 202 B4
Holly Hill SO16 ... 78 C3
Holly Hill Cl SO16 ... 78 C3
Holly Hill La SO31 ... 128 B3
Holly Hill Mans SO31 ... 128 C2
Holly Hill Woodland Pk* SO31 ... 128 B2
Holly Ho SO19 ... 103 C1
Holly La Boldre SO41 ... 174 A1
Christchurch BH23 ... 194 B1
New Milton BH25 ... 195 B2
Holly Lo 13 BH12 ... 204 A2
Holly Lodge
Chandler's Ford SO53 ... 55 B2
Southampton SO17 ... 79 A1
Holly Oak Ct SO16 ... 78 A2
Holly Oak Rd SO16 ... 78 A2
Holly Rd Ashurst SO40 ... 100 A1
Blackfield SO45 ... 177 C4
Holly St PO12 ... 181 B2
Hollybank PO13 ... 179 C1
Hollybank Cl
12 Hythe SO45 ... 126 A2
Waterlooville PO8 ... 112 B3
Hollybank Cres SO45 ... 125 C2
Hollybank La PO10 ... 136 C2
Hollybank Rd SO45 ... 125 C2
Hollybrook Ave SO16 ... 78 B2
Hollybrook Cl SO16 ... 78 A1
Hollybrook Gdns SO31 ... 129 A3
Hollybrook Inf Sch SO16 ... 78 B2
Hollybrook Jun Sch SO16 ... 78 B2
Hollybrook Rd SO16 ... 78 B1
Hollydene SO45 ... 126 A2
Hollywell Dr PO6 ... 157 A4
Hollywood Cl SO52 ... 53 C2
Hollywood Ct SO41 ... 197 B3
Hollywood La SO41 ... 197 B3
Holm Cl BH24 ... 117 B1
Holm Ct PO11 ... 184 C1
Holm Hill La BH23 ... 194 A4
Holm Oak Cl Littleton SO22 ... 1 A3
Verwood BH31 ... 114 C4
Holman Cl PO8 ... 112 A1
Holmbush Ct PO5 ... 215 B1
Holmdale Rd PO12 ... 180 C4
Holme Cl SO41 ... 197 B1
Holme Rd BH23 ... 209 A4
Holmes Cl 8 SO31 ... 127 A3
Holmesland Dr SO30 ... 105 C4
Holmesland La SO30 ... 105 C4
Holmesland Wlk SO30 ... 105 C4
Holmfield SO43 ... 122 A3
Holmfield Ave
Bournemouth BH7 ... 206 B4
Fareham PO14 ... 154 C4
Holmgrove PO14 ... 129 B2
Holmhurst Ave BH23 ... 193 C1
Holmsley Cl
Lymington SO41 ... 197 A1
Southampton SO18 ... 104 B4
Holmsley Ct SO40 ... 100 A4
Holmsley Pass BH24 ... 170 B4
Holmsley Rd BH25 ... 170 C1
Holmwood Garth BH24 ... 141 B3
Holne Ct PO4 ... 183 B2
Holnest Rd BH17 ... 187 B1
Holst Way PO7 ... 134 C3
Holt Cl PO17 ... 107 C2
Holt Ct SO19 ... 126 C4
Holt Down GU31 ... 41 A2
Holt Gdns PO9 ... 113 A2
Holt Rd Poole BH12 ... 203 C3
Southampton SO15 ... 102 C3
Verwood BH21 ... 138 B4
Holt View 9 SO50 ... 56 C1
Holworth Cl BH11 ... 188 C2
Holy Family RC Prim Sch SO16 ... 77 B1
Holy Rood Est SO14 ... 103 A2
Holyborne Rd SO51 ... 53 A4
Holybourne Rd PO9 ... 135 C2
Holyrood Ave SO17 ... 79 A1
Holyrood Cl
Broadstone BH17 ... 202 A4
4 Waterlooville PO7 ... 135 A4
Holyrood Ho 12 SO14 ... 103 A2
Holywell Cl BH17 ... 187 B2
Home Farm Bsns Ctr SP5 ... 4 C3
Home Farm Cl SO45 ... 126 A2
Home Farm La SO45 ... 177 C3
Home Farm Office Village PO16 ... 155 B4
Home Farm Rd BH31 ... 114 C3
Home Farm Way BH31 ... 114 C3
Home Field Dr SO16 ... 77 B3
Home Mead PO7 ... 110 C2
Home Rd BH11 ... 189 A3
Home Rule Rd SO31 ... 129 A2
Home Way GU31 ... 41 B2
Homeborough Ho 7 SO45 ... 126 A3
Homebridge Ho SP6 ... 69 C1
Homedale Ho BH2 ... 204 C3
Homedene Ho BH15 ... 202 B2
Homefayre Ho 19 PO16 ... 131 A1
Homefield SO51 ... 28 A1
Homefield Cotts GU33 ... 20 C3
Homefield Ho 13 BH25 ... 195 A1
Homefield Ind Prep Sch BH6 ... 206 C3
Homefield Ind Senior Sch BH23 ... 192 B3
Homefield Rd
Cosham PO6 ... 158 B4
Westbourne PO10 ... 137 A2
Homefield Way PO8 ... 88 A3
Homeforde Ho SO42 ... 146 A1
Homefort Ho 2 PO12 ... 181 A2
Homegrange Ho 15 SO41 ... 211 B2
Homegrove Ho PO5 ... 215 C1
Homeheights 23 PO5 ... 182 B1
Homelake Ho BH14 ... 203 A2
Homelands Est BH23 ... 206 C3
Homelands Ho BH22 ... 165 B3
Homeleigh Ho 5 BH8 ... 205 A3
Homemead Ho SO51 ... 52 C3
Homemill Ho 5 BH25 ... 195 A2
Homeoaks Ho BH2 ... 204 C3
Homepoint Ho SO18 ... 104 A4
Homer Cl Gosport PO13 ... 180 A4
Waterlooville PO8 ... 111 C1
Homer Mobile Home Pk SO45 ... 177 C3
Homerise Ho 1 SO23 ... 11 A4
Homerose Ho PO5 ... 215 B2
Homeryde Ho 11 PO13 ... 179 C1
Homesea Ho PO5 ... 215 B2
Homeside Rd BH9 ... 190 A1
Homespinney Ho SO18 ... 79 B1
Homestour Ho 1 BH23 ... 207 A3
Hometide Ho 13 PO13 ... 179 C1
Homeview Ho BH15 ... 202 B2
Homewater Ho 7 PO7 ... 134 C4
Homeway Cotts SO40 ... 101 A3
Homewell PO9 ... 135 C1
Homewood Cl BH25 ... 195 B2
Homewood Ho SO41 ... 197 B1
Honey La Burley BH24 ... 142 C1
Fareham PO15 ... 130 B3
Honeybourne Cres BH6 ... 207 A2
Honeycritch La GU32 ... 19 B2
Honeysuckle Cl
Gosport PO13 ... 155 A2
Locks Heath SO31 ... 129 A3
Winchester SO22 ... 10 C2
Honeysuckle Ct
Locks Heath SO31 ... 129 A3
5 Southampton SO18 ... 104 A4
Waterlooville PO7 ... 135 A3
Honeysuckle Gdns SO41 ... 196 B1
Honeysuckle La BH17 ... 186 C1
Honeysuckle Rd SO16 ... 79 A2
Honeysuckle Way
Christchurch BH23 ... 208 A4
North Baddesley SO53 ... 55 A3
Honeywood Cl
Portsmouth PO3 ... 157 C2
Totton SO40 ... 76 B1
Honeywood Ho BH14 ... 214 B4
Honister Cl SO16 ... 101 C4
Hood Cl
Bournemouth BH10 ... 189 A1
Locks Heath SO31 ... 129 A2
Hood Cres BH10 ... 189 A1
Hood Rd SO18 ... 104 A4
Hook Cl SO51 ... 30 A1
Hook Cotts SO31 ... 152 C4
Hook Cres SO51 ... 30 A1
Hook La PO14,SO31 ... 153 A4
Hook Park Rd SO31 ... 152 C3
Hook Rd Ampfield SO51 ... 29 C1
Chandler's Ford SO51 ... 29 C1
Hook Water Cl SO53 ... 30 A1
Hook Water Rd SO53 ... 30 A1
Hook with Warsash CE Prim Sch SO31 ... 152 B4
Hook's Farm Way PO9 ... 135 B2
Hook's La PO9 ... 135 B2
Hooke Cl BH17 ... 188 A1
Hookpit Farm La SO23 ... 2 A4
Hookwood La SO51 ... 29 C1
Hop Cl BH16 ... 201 A4
Hope Lodge Sch SO18 ... 103 C4
Hope Rd SO30 ... 80 C1
Hope St PO1 ... 215 B4
Hopfield Cl PO7 ... 134 C4
Hopfield Ho PO7 ... 134 C3
Hopfield Mews PO7 ... 134 C3
Hopkins Cl
Bournemouth BH8 ... 191 A1
Portchester PO6 ... 156 C4
Hopkins Ct PO4 ... 183 A1
Horace Rd 10 BH5 ... 205 C2
Horder Cl SO16 ... 78 C2
Hordle CE Prim Sch SO41 ... 196 A2
Hordle Ho Sch SO41 ... 210 C3
Hordle La SO41 ... 196 A1
Hordle Rd PO9 ... 135 B2
Hordle Walhampton Sch SO41 ... 198 A3
Horlock Rd SO42 ... 146 A1
Hornbeam Cl 9 SO30 ... 105 B3
Hornbeam Gdns SO30 ... 80 B2
Hornbeam Rd
Chandler's Ford SO53 ... 54 C3
Havant PO9 ... 136 A2
Hornbeam Way BH21 ... 163 C3
Hornby Cl SO31 ... 152 B4
Hornchurch Rd SO16 ... 77 C3
Horndean CE Jun Sch PO8 ... 112 B4
Horndean Com Sch PO8 ... 112 A4
Horndean Ho 6 PO1 ... 215 C4
Horndean Inf Sch PO8 ... 112 B4
Horndean Prec PO8 ... 112 B4
Horndean Rd
Emsworth PO10 ... 136 C2
Horndean PO8 ... 112 C4
Hornet Cl Fareham PO15 ... 130 B1
Gosport PO12 ... 181 B2
Hornet Rd Gosport PO14 ... 154 C3
Thorney Island PO10 ... 161 A2
Horning Rd BH12 ... 203 C3
Horns Dro SO16 ... 77 C3
Horns Hill Nursling SO16 ... 77 B3
Soberton SO32 ... 85 A1
Horns Hill Cl SO16 ... 77 B3
Horsa Cl BH6 ... 206 C2
Horsa Ct BH6 ... 206 C2
Horsa Rd BH6 ... 206 C2
Horse Sands Cl PO4 ... 183 B2
Horsea La PO2 ... 157 C2
Horsea Rd PO2 ... 157 C3
Horsebridge Rd PO9 ... 136 A2
Horsebridge Way SO16 ... 77 C3
Horsecroft 2 SO51 ... 52 C4
Horsefair Ct SO51 ... 52 C4
Horsefair Mews SO51 ... 52 C4
Horsefair The SO51 ... 52 C4
Horsehoe Bridge SO14 ... 103 B4
Horsepost La PO7,PO8 ... 87 A1
Horseshoe Cl
Titchfield PO14 ... 129 B1
Wimborne Minst BH21 ... 164 A3
Horseshoe Ct
4 Bournemouth BH1 ... 204 C2
Downton SP5 ... 46 C4
Horseshoe Dr
Romsey SO51 ... 28 A1
Totton SO40 ... 76 A1
Horseshoe Lodge SO31 ... 128 C1
Horseshoe The BH13 ... 214 B2
Horsham Ave BH10 ... 189 B3
Horton Cl BH9 ... 190 B2
Horton Rd Gosport PO13 ... 155 B2
St Leonards BH24 ... 139 C3
Verwood BH21 ... 114 A1
Horton Way
Bishopstoke SO50 ... 56 C1
Verwood BH31 ... 114 B3
Hosier's La 23 BH15 ... 202 A1
Hosker Rd BH5 ... 206 A3
Hospital La PO16 ... 156 C3
Hospital Rd SO32,PO17 ... 108 A4
Hotspur Cl SO45 ... 125 C3
Houchin St SO32 ... 83 B4
Houghton Cl 1 PO9 ... 136 A3
Houlton Rd BH15 ... 202 C2
Hound Cl SO31 ... 127 B3
Hound Manor SO31 ... 127 C3
Hound Rd SO31 ... 127 B3
Hound Road Gdns SO31 ... 127 B3
Hound Way SO31 ... 127 B3
Hounds Way BH21 ... 164 A3
Houndwell Pl SO14 ... 103 A2
Hounsdown Ave SO40 ... 100 C3
Hounsdown Cl SO40 ... 100 C3
Hounsdown Sec Sch SO40 ... 100 C2
Hounslow Cl BH15 ... 201 C1
House Farm Rd PO12 ... 180 C2
Hove Ct PO13 ... 179 C1
Hoveton Gr SO53 ... 55 A4
Howard Cl Burley BH24 ... 143 A2
Chandler's Ford SO53 ... 55 B2
Christchurch BH23 ... 207 C3
Fair Oak SO50 ... 57 B1
Southampton SO18 ... 79 C2
Howard Oliver Ho SO45 ... 126 A2
Howard Rd
Bournemouth BH8 ... 205 B4
Portsmouth PO2 ... 157 C2
Southampton SO15 ... 102 B3
Verwood BH31 ... 114 C3
Howard's Gr SO15 ... 102 B4
Howards Mead SO41 ... 197 A1
Howe Cl
Christchurch BH23 ... 207 C3
New Milton BH25 ... 194 C2
Howe La BH31 ... 114 C3
Howe Rd PO13 ... 180 B3
Howell Ho BH21 ... 163 C4
Howerts Cl SO31 ... 152 B4
Howeth Cl BH10 ... 189 B2
Howeth Rd BH10 ... 189 B2
Howlett Cl SO41 ... 197 B2
Howton Cl BH10 ... 189 B3
Howton Rd BH10 ... 189 B3
Hoxley Rd BH10 ... 189 B2
Hoyal Rd BH15 ... 201 B2
Hoylake Cl PO13 ... 155 B1
Hoylake Rd PO6 ... 134 B1
Hoyle Cl SO32 ... 58 B2
Hoylecroft Cl PO15 ... 130 C2
Hubert Rd SO23 ... 10 C2
Hudson Cl Gosport PO13 ... 180 B3
Poole BH12 ... 188 B1
Ringwood BH24 ... 141 B4
Hudson Ct SO40 ... 100 B3
Hudson Davies Cl SO41 ... 173 C1
Hudson Rd PO5 ... 215 C2
Hughes Bsns Ctr BH23 ... 208 A4
Hughes Cl SO45 ... 150 C1
Hulbert Jun Sch PO7 ... 134 C3

Hulbert Rd Havant PO9 135 A2
Waterlooville PO7 134 C4
Hull Cres BH11 188 C2
Hull Rd BH11 188 C2
Hull Way BH11 188 C2
Hulles Way SO52 53 C2
Hulse Lodge 4 SO15 102 C4
Hulse Rd SO15 102 C4
Hulton Cl SO19 103 B1
Humber Cl PO14 154 A2
Humber Gdns SO31 105 A1
Humber Rd BH22 166 A3
Hummicks The SO42 176 B4
Hundred Acres PO17 108 C2
Hundred Acres Rd
PO17 108 C2
Hundred La SO41 198 A4
Hundred The
Fordingbridge SP6 69 C1
Romsey SO51 52 C4
Waterlooville PO7 111 B1
Hunger Hill BH15 202 B1
Hungerfield Cl BH23 169 A1
Hungerford SO31 128 A4
Hungerford Hill SP6 94 B3
Hungerford Rd BH8 190 B2
Hunt Ave SO31 127 B3
Hunt Rd
Christchurch BH23 207 C4
Poole BH15 202 C2
Hunter Cl
Christchurch BH23 208 A4
Gosport PO13 180 B4
Holbury SO45 150 A3
Wimborne Minst BH21 164 B3
Hunter Ct 13 SO16 78 A1
Hunter Rd
Portsmouth PO4 183 A2
Thorney Island PO10 161 A2
Hunters Chase SO32 84 B2
Hunters Cl BH31 115 B3
Hunters Cres SO51 28 B1
Hunters Ct SO31 105 A2
Hunters Hill SO40 100 B2
Hunters Lodge PO15 130 B1
Hunters Ride PO7 134 C3
Hunters Way SO50 57 A1
Huntfield Rd BH9 190 A1
Huntingdon Cl
Titchfield PO14 129 B1
Totton SO40 76 C1
Huntingdon Dr BH21 163 C1
Huntingdon Gdns
Christchurch BH23 192 A1
Horton Heath SO50 81 B4
Huntley Cl 30 PO6 133 A1
Huntly Rd BH3 204 B4
Huntly Way SO18 103 C4
Hunton Cl SO16 78 B2
Hunts Pond Rd SO31,
PO14 129 B2
Huntsbottom La GU33 21 A2
Huntsman Cl PO8 111 C3
Huntvale Rd BH9 190 A2
Hurdle Way SO21 31 B4
Hurdles Mead 17 SO41 211 B2
Hurdles The
Christchurch BH23 206 C4
Titchfield PO14 129 B1
Hurlingham Gdns SO16 79 A3
Hurn Cl BH24 140 B3
Hurn Court La BH23 190 C3
Hurn Ct
Bournemouth BH8 191 A2
15 Havant PO9 136 A3
Hurn La BH24 140 B3
Hurn Rd
Christchurch BH23 191 B2
St Leonards BH24 140 B2
Hurn Way BH23 191 B1
Hurricane Dr SO16 77 C3
Hursley Cl BH7 206 B4
Hursley Ct SO53 30 A1
Hursley Dr SO45 177 C4
Hursley Park Rd
Hursley SO21 30 A3
Hursley SO21 30 A4
Hursley Rd
Chandler's Ford SO53 55 B4
Havant PO9 135 B3
Hurst Castle* SO41 212 B1
Hurst Cl
Barton on Sea BH25 209 B4
Chandler's Ford SO53 55 A2
Christchurch BH23 194 B1
Stubbington PO14 179 A3
Totton SO40 100 C4
Hurst Ct
6 Christchurch BH23 209 A4
5 Milford on Sea SO41 211 B2
Hurst Gn PO13 155 A1
Hurst Green Cl
Southampton SO19 104 A1
Waterlooville PO8 112 A1
Hurst Hill BH14 214 B4
Hurst La
Colden Common SO21 58 A4
Froxfield GU34 18 A2
Hurst Rd
Milford on Sea SO41 211 C2
Ringwood BH24 117 A1
Hurstbourne Ave BH23 193 C1
Hurstbourne Cl PO9 135 B3
Hurstbourne Pl SO19 126 C4
Hurstdene Rd BH8 190 B1
Hurstly La SO41 173 A2
Hurstville Dr PO7 134 C4
Hurstwood Ave PO10 137 C1
Hussar Cl BH23 206 C4
Hussar Ct PO7 111 B1
Hussey Cl 2 SO23 2 A1
Hutfield Ct 8 PO12 181 A3
Hutwood Rd SO16 79 A4
Huxley Cl SO31 129 A1
Huxley Ct SO45 125 B1
Hyacinth Cl BH17 186 C1
Hyde Abbey Rd SO23 11 A4
Hyde CE Prim Sch SP6 94 B3
Hyde Church La SO23 2 A1
Hyde Church Path 24
SO23 2 A1
Hyde Cl Southampton SO15 78 B1
Sway SO41 172 A1
Totton SO40 100 A4
Winchester SO23 1 C1
Hyde Gate SO23 2 A1
Hyde House Gdns 22 SO23 2 A1
Hyde La Downton SP5 46 B4
Fordingbridge SP6 94 B3
Hyde Lodge SO22 1 C1
Hyde Park Ho PO1 215 B2
Hyde Park Rd PO1 215 B3
Hyde Rd BH10 189 B3
Hyde St Portsmouth PO5 215 B2
Winchester SO23 2 A1
Hyde The BH25 194 C2
Hyden Cross GU32 63 C1
Hyden Farm La PO8 87 B4
Hyden Wood GU32 63 C1
Hylton Rd GU32 40 C2
Hyman Way SO40 100 C4
Hynes Ct 19 SO17 103 A4
Hynesbury Rd BH23 208 B4
Hyssop Cl PO15 129 B4
Hythe By Pass SO45 149 C4
Hythe Bypass SO45 150 A4
Hythe Hospl SO45 126 A1
Hythe Prim Sch SO45 126 A2
Hythe Rd Cosham PO6 157 C4
Marchwood SO40 124 C4
Poole BH15 203 A4

I

Ibbertson Cl BH8 190 C1
Ibbertson Rd BH8 190 C1
Ibbertson Way BH8 190 C1
Ibbett Rd BH10 189 B2
Ibbotson Way SO40 100 B3
Ibsen Cl PO15 129 B4
Ibsley Cl BH8 205 B3
Ibsley Dro BH24 94 A1
Ibsley Gr PO9 135 B2
Icarus Pl PO7 134 C1
Iddesleigh Rd BH3 205 A3
Ideal Park Homes SO50 56 C3
Idsworth Cl PO8 112 C3
Idsworth Ho PO1 215 B4
Idsworth Rd
Portsmouth PO3 183 A4
Waterlooville PO8 112 A1
Iford Bridge Home Pk
BH6 206 B4
Iford Cl BH6 206 C3
Iford Ct 18 PO9 136 A3
Iford Gdns BH7 206 B4
Iford La BH6 206 C3
Ilex Cres SO31 128 C2
Ilex Wlk PO11 185 B1
Imber Dr BH23 208 C4
Imber Rd SO23 11 B4
Imber Way SO19 104 B2
Imbre Ct BH13 214 C4
Imperial Ave SO15 102 A4
Imperial Ct 4 BH13 214 C4
Imperial Pk SO14 103 A4
Imperial Rd SO14 103 A4
Imperial Way SO15 102 B3
Implacable Rd PO13 179 C2
Ingarth 8 BH6 206 C2
Ingle Glen SO45 126 A1
Ingle Gn SO40 76 A1
Ingledene Cl
Gosport PO12 181 A2
Havant PO9 135 B1
Inglegreen Cl BH25 194 C1
Inglesham Way BH15 201 C2
Ingleside SO31 127 B4
Ingleside Cl PO14 154 A4
Ingleton Rd SO16 77 B1
Inglewood Ave BH8 190 C1
Inglewood Dr BH25 195 A1
Inglewood Gdns SO50 57 B2
Inglis Rd PO5 215 D1
Ingoldfield La
PO17&SO32 109 B4
Ingram Ct SO17 103 B4
Ingram Wlk 13 BH21 163 B2
Ingworth Rd BH12 204 A3
Inhams La PO7 110 B3
Inhurst Ave PO7 135 A4
Inhurst Rd PO2 157 C1
Inkerman Rd SO19 103 B2
Inkpen Wlk PO9 135 B4
Inlands Rd PO18 161 C4
Inmans La GU32 41 A3
Insley Cres BH18 186 C3
International Pk SO18 79 C3
International Way SO19 126 C4
Inveravon BH23 207 C2
Inverclyde Ho BH14 203 A2
Inverclyde Rd BH14 203 B2
Invergordon Ave PO6 158 A4
Inverkip Cl PO13 179 C2
Inverleigh Rd BH6 206 B3
Inverness Ave PO15 130 C2
Inverness Rd
Gosport PO12 181 A3
Poole BH13 214 C4
Portsmouth PO1 182 C4
Inwood Rd GU33 21 A2
Ionic Cl SO53 55 C4
IOW Ferry Terminal
SO14 102 C1
Iping Ave PO9 135 C2
Ipley Way SO45 126 A1
Ipswich Rd BH4 204 A2
Ireland Way PO7 134 C3
Iris Rd Bournemouth BH9 189 C1
Southampton SO16 79 A2
Iron Mill Cl PO15 130 B2
Ironbridge Cres SO31 129 A3
Ironbridge La PO4 183 B2
Ironmill La PO15 130 A3
Ironside Ct 12 SO14 102 C2
Irvine Cl PO16 131 A2
Irvine Way BH23 207 C4
Irving Rd
Bournemouth BH6 206 B3
Southampton SO16 77 C1
Irwell Cl SO53 55 A3
Irwin Hts PO12 181 A4
Isaacs Cl BH12 204 A4
Isambard Brunel Jun Sch
PO2 182 C4
Isambard Brunel Rd
PO1 215 B3
Isis Cl SO16 101 C4
Island Cl PO11 160 A2
Island Point SO41 197 C2
Island View SO41 172 A2
Island View Ave BH23 208 A3
Island View Cl SO41 211 C2
Island View Rd BH25 209 B4
Island View Terr PO2 157 B1
Island View Wlk PO16 132 B1
Islay Gdns PO6 133 C1
Itchen Ave SO50 56 C1
Itchen Cl Petersfield GU31 40 C1
West Wellow SO51 50 B2
Itchen Coll SO19 104 A3
Itchen Ct
4 Waterlooville PO8 111 C2
40 Winchester SO23 11 A4
Itchen Rd PO9 136 A3
Itchen Valley Ctry Pk
SO30 80 B3
Itchen View SO18 79 C2
Itchenor Rd PO11 185 C1
Itchenside Cl SO18 79 C2
Itchin Cl SO40 100 B3
Ithica Cl PO11 185 A2
Ivamy Pl BH11 188 C1
Ivanhoe Rd SO15 78 B1
Ivor Cl SO45 150 B2
Ivor Rd
Corfe Mullen BH21 186 B2
Poole BH15 202 A1
Ivy Cl St Leonards BH24 139 B2
Totton SO40 76 C1
Winchester SO22 10 C3
Ivy Cotts SO21 31 A1
Ivy Ct Southampton SO16 78 B2
Waterlooville PO7 134 B2
Ivy Dene SO19 104 B2
Ivy Ho 2 PO12 181 B2
Ivy La Portsmouth PO1 182 A3
Ringwood BH24 117 A2
West End SO18 80 B1
Ivy Orch PO8 88 A3
Ivy Rd Oakley BH21 187 B4
Southampton SO17 103 B4
Ivydene Gdns PO8 112 A2
Ivyhouse La GU32 18 C2
Iwerne Cl BH9 190 A2

J

J Ave SO45 151 A3
Jacaranda Cl PO15 129 C2
Jack Cl SO53 54 C3
Jack Cockerill Way 14
PO5 182 B1
Jackdaw Cl PO8 111 C2
Jackdaw Rise SO50 55 B1
Jackie Wigg Gdns SO40 101 A4
Jacklin Ct BH18 187 A3
Jackman's Hill SO21 33 A3
Jackmans Cl SO19 103 B2
Jackson Cl PO6 158 B3
Jackson Gdns BH12 203 B3
Jackson Rd BH12 203 B3
Jacmar Ct 8 BH25 195 A1
Jacob's Gutter La SO40 101 A2
Jacob's St PO1 215 B4
Jacobean Cl BH23 194 A1
Jacobs Cl Clanfield PO8 88 B3
Romsey SO51 53 A4
Jacobs Rd BH15 201 C1
Jacobs Wlk SO40 100 C3
Jacomb Pl PO13 155 B1
Jacqueline Ave PO7 134 B2
Jacqueline Rd BH12 203 B4
Jade Ct Gosport PO13 180 B3
6 Waterlooville PO7 134 C4
Jago Rd PO1 181 C3
Jamaica Pl PO12 181 B2
James Butcher Ct 12
PO5 182 B1
James Callaghan Dr
Cosham PO6 133 A1
Portchester PO17 132 C1
James Cl Gosport PO13 155 B2
South Hayling PO11 184 C2
James Copse Rd PO8 111 C3
James Ct SO51 53 A3
James Grieve Ave SO31 129 A1
James Howell Ct PO7 110 C2
James Rd Gosport PO13 155 B2
Havant PO9 135 C1
Poole BH12 204 A3
James St SO14 103 A2
Jameson Rd
Bournemouth BH9 189 C1
Southampton SO19 103 C2
Jamica Rd PO12 181 B3
Janaway Gdns SO17 103 B4
Janes Cl SO45 177 C4
Janred Ct BH25 209 C4
Janson Rd SO15 102 B4
Japonica Way PO9 136 B2
Jarndyce Wlk PO2 182 B4
Jarvis Fields SO31 128 A4
Jasmine Ct
Gosport PO13 180 B3
Lymington SO41 197 C2
Jasmine Gr PO7 135 A3
Jasmine Rd SO30 105 A4
Jasmine Way PO8 88 B3
Jasmine Wlk 5 PO14 154 C4
Jasmond Rd PO6 157 C3
Jason Pl PO7 134 C1
Jason Way PO12 180 C4
Jaundrells Cl BH25 195 B2
Java Dr PO15 129 B4
Javelin Rd PO10 161 A2
Jay Cl Horndean PO8 112 A4
Stubbington PO14 154 A3
Jay's Ct BH23 209 A4
Jealous La SO41 173 A1
Jefferson Ave BH1 205 B3
Jeffries Cl SO16 77 C3
Jellicoe Ave PO12 180 C2
Jellicoe Cl BH14 202 C3
Jellicoe Dr BH23 207 C3
Jellicoe Ho 8 PO1 215 C4
Jenkins Cl SO30 106 A4
Jenkins Gr PO3 183 A4
Jenner Way SO51 53 B4
Jennings Rd Poole BH14 203 B1
Totton SO40 101 A4
Jensen Ct SO15 102 C4
Jephcote Rd BH11 188 C2
Jermyns La SO51 28 C2
Jerome Ct SO19 104 B3
Jerram Cl PO12 180 C2
Jerrett's La SO16 77 B2
Jersey Cl Poole BH12 188 B1
Southampton SO16 77 C2
Stubbington PO14 179 B3
Jersey Rd Poole BH12 188 B1
Portsmouth PO2 182 C4
Jervis Court La SO32 84 A4
Jervis Dr PO12 181 A3
Jervis Rd PO2 157 B1
Jesmond Ave BH23 208 C4
Jesmond Gr SO31 129 A1
Jessamine Rd SO16 78 A1
Jessica Ave BH31 114 B4
Jessica Cl 4 PO7 112 A1
Jessie Rd Gosport PO12 181 A2
Havant PO9 135 B2
Portsmouth PO4 182 C2
Jessie Terr 23 SO14 103 A2
Jessop Cl
Bournemouth BH10 189 C2
Hythe SO45 125 C3
Jessop Rd BH21 164 A3
Jessop Wlk SO45 125 C3
Jessopp Ho 6 BH21 163 B3
Jetty Rd SO45 151 A3
Jewell Rd BH8 191 A1
Jewry St SO23 11 A4
Jex Blake Cl SO16 78 A2
Jimmy Brown Ave BH22 138 C3
Jinny La SO51 27 C3
Joanna Cl SP5 46 B4
Jockey La SO50 56 C3
Jodrell Cl PO8 112 B4
Joe Bigwood Cl SO16 77 B3
John Bunyan Cl PO15 129 B4
John Darling Mall 4
SO50 56 A2
John King Shipyard
PO10 161 A4
John St SO14 103 A2
John's Rd SO19 103 B2
Johns Rd PO16 155 A4
Johnson Rd BH21 165 A4
Johnson St 2 SO14 103 A2
Johnson View PO15 129 C3
Johnston Rd BH15 202 B4
Johnstone Rd BH23 207 C3
Jolliffe Ave BH15 202 B2
Jolliffe Ct 16 GU32 40 C2
Jolliffe Rd BH15 202 B2
Jonas Nichols Sq SO14 103 A2
Jonathan Cl SO41 197 C3
Jonathan Rd PO15 130 C1
Jones La SO45 126 A3
Jopps Cnr BH23 192 B2
Jordan Ho SO15 102 B3
Jordans La Boldre SO41 198 A4
Sway SO41 172 B1
Joseph Nye Ct 30 PO1 182 A3
Joseph St 8 PO12 181 B2
Joshua Cl BH15 201 C1
Josian Wlk 12 SO14 103 A3
Joslin Block PO12 181 B3
Jowitt Dr BH25 194 C1
Joyce Dickson Cl BH24 141 A3
Joys La SO41 198 C4
Joys Rd BH21 138 C4
Jubilee Ave PO6 156 C4
Jubilee Bsns Ctr PO7 134 C4
Jubilee Cl
Corfe Mullen BH21 186 C4
Eastleigh SO50 55 C1
Fordingbridge SP6 69 B1
Ringwood BH24 141 B4
Jubilee Cres BH12 203 B3
Jubilee Ct Fareham PO14 155 A4
Sway SO41 172 A1
Jubilee Gdns
Bournemouth BH10 189 B1
Southampton SO18 104 A4
Jubilee Ho PO10 136 C1
Jubilee Rd
Corfe Mullen BH21 186 C4
Fordingbridge SP6 69 B1
Gosport PO12 181 A3
Poole BH12 203 B3
Portchester PO16 156 B4
Portsmouth PO4 182 C2
Romsey SO51 52 C4
Waterlooville PO7 111 C1
Jubilee Terr
Portsmouth PO5 215 A1
Westbourne PO10 137 A2
Julia Cl BH23 208 C4
Julian Cl SO16 78 C3
Julian Ct 1 SO18 79 C1
Julian Rd SO19 104 A2
Julian's Rd BH21 163 A2
Julie Ave PO15 130 C1
Juliet Ct PO7 135 A4
Julius Cl SO53 55 C3
Julyan Ave BH12 204 A4
Jumar Cl SO31 152 B4
Jumpers Ave BH23 206 C4
Jumpers Rd BH23 206 C4
Junction Rd
Bournemouth BH9 204 C4
Hamworthy BH16 201 B2
Totton SO40 101 A4
Juniper Cl
Ferndown BH22 165 B4
Lymington SO41 197 A1
North Baddesley SO52 53 C3
Three Legged Cross BH21 138 C4
Winchester SO22 10 B3
Juniper Ct 17 SO18 103 C4
Juniper Flats BH23 206 C4
Juniper Rd Horndean PO8 88 B1
Southampton SO18 103 C4
Juniper Sq PO9 159 C4
Jupiter Cl SO16 77 C2
Jupiter Ct PO1 182 A2
Jupiter Way BH21 186 C4
Jura Cl PO6 133 C1
Jurd Way SO31 104 C1
Jurds Lake Way SO19 103 C1
Justin Cl PO14 154 C4
Justin Gdns BH10 189 C2
Justine Ct 4 SO18 104 A4
Justinian Cl SO53 55 C4
Jute Cl PO16 132 A1
Jutland Cl PO15 129 A4
Juventu Cl PO9 136 A2

K

Kamptee Copse BH25 195 A3
Kanes Hill SO19 104 C3
Kanes Hill Prim Sch
SO19 104 C3
Kangaw Pl BH15 201 B1
Karen Ave PO6 158 B3
Kassassin St PO4 183 A1
Kassel Cl PO7 135 A4
Katherine Chance Cl
BH23 192 B2
Kathleen Rd SO19 104 A2
Katrina Gdns PO11 185 A3
Katrine Cres SO53 55 A4
Katterns Cl BH23 191 C1
Kay Cl BH23 207 C3
Kayak Cl SO31 128 C1
Kayleigh Cl SO40 100 B3
Kealy Rd PO12 181 A3
Kearsney Ave PO2 157 C2
Keast Wlk PO13 155 B2
Keats Ave
Milford on Sea SO41 211 B3
Portchester PO16 132 C1
Keats Cl Swanwick PO15 106 A1
Waterlooville PO8 111 C2
Winchester SO22 10 B2
Keats Ho Havant PO9 135 C2
17 New Milton BH25 195 A1
Keats Rd SO19 104 B3
Keble Cl
Chandler's Ford SO53 55 B2
Hursley SO21 30 A4
Keble Meml CE Prim Sch
SO21 30 A3
Keble Rd SO53 55 B2
Keble St SO22 10 B3
Keeble Cl BH10 189 B3
Keeble Cres BH10 189 B3
Keeble Rd BH10 189 B3
Keel Cl Gosport PO13 180 B3
Portsmouth PO3 158 B2
Keelan Ct PO5 182 B1

Keep The P016 . . . . .156 C4
Keepers Cl SO53 . . . . .55 A3
Keepers La
  Ferndown BH21 . . . . . . .164 C2
  Mottisfont SO51 . . . . .5 B1
Kefford Cl P08 . . . . .22 A1
Keighley Ave BH18 . . . . . .186 C1
Keith Cl P012 . . . . .181 A3
Keith Rd BH3 . . . . .204 B4
Kelburn Cl SO53 . . . . .55 A4
Kellaway Rd BH17 . . . . . . .202 C4
Kellett Rd SO15 . . . . .102 C4
Kelly Cl BH17 . . . . .202 C4
Kelly Ct
  10 Fareham P016 . . . . . .131 A1
  Southampton SO16 . . . . . .78 B3
  2 Southampton, Bitterne
    SO18 . . . . .103 C4
Kelly Ho SO18 . . . . .79 C2
Kelly Rd P07 . . . . .134 C3
Kelmscott Gdns SO25 . . . .30 A1
Kelsall Gdns BH25 . . . . . .195 A2
Kelsey Ave P010 . . . . .137 C1
Kelsey Cl Liss GU33 . . . . . .21 A3
  Locks Heath P014 . . . . . .129 A1
Kelsey Head P06 . . . . .157 A4
Kelston Cl
  1 Southampton SO15 . . .102 A4
  Southampton SO15 . . . . .102 A4
Kelvin Cl SO45 . . . . .126 A2
Kelvin Gr Netley SO31 . . . .127 B3
  Portchester P016 . . . . . .156 B4
Kelvin Rd SO50 . . . . .55 C1
Kemp Rd BH9 . . . . .204 C4
Kemp Welch Ct BH12 . . . .204 A4
Kemps Quay Ind Pk
  SO18 . . . . .103 B4
Kempton Ct P015 . . . . . . .129 B4
Kempton Pk **6** P07 . . . . .112 A1
Kemshott Ct P09 . . . . .135 B3
Ken Berry Ct P09 . . . . . . .136 A3
Ken Rd BH6 . . . . .206 C2
Kench The P011 . . . . .183 C2
Kendal Ave
  Portsmouth P03 . . . . . . .158 A1
  Southampton SO16 . . . . .101 B4
Kendal Cl
  Chandler's Ford SO53 . . . .55 C4
  Waterlooville P08 . . . . . .112 A2
Kendal Ct SO16 . . . . .77 B1
Kenilworth Cl
  1 Christchurch BH23 . . .207 A4
  1 Poole BH13 . . . . . . .214 C4
  B Winchester SO23 . . . .2 A1
Kenilworth Dr SO53 . . . . . .55 C4
Kenilworth Gdns SO30 . . . .80 C1
Kenilworth Ho **10** SO14 . .103 B3
Kenilworth Rd
  Portsmouth P05 . . . . . . .182 B1
  Southampton SO15 . . . . .102 C3
Kenmore Cl SO40 . . . . . . .100 C3
Kennard Ct BH25 . . . . .194 C2
Kennard Rd BH25 . . . . . . .194 C2
Kennart Rd BH17 . . . . .202 A4
Kennedy Ave P015 . . . . . .130 C2
Kennedy Cl P07 . . . . .134 C2
Kennedy Cres P012 . . . . . .180 C1
Kennedy Rd SO16 . . . . .77 C2
Kennel La SO22 . . . . .1 B2
Kennet Cl Gosport P012 . .181 A1
  Romsey SO51 . . . . .53 B4
  West End SO18 . . . . .80 A2
Kennet Rd
  Petersfield GU31 . . . . . . .40 C1
  Romsey SO51 . . . . .53 B4
Kenneth Ct **15** BH23 . . .209 A4
Kennington La SO40 . . . . . .99 A4
Kennington Rd BH17 . . . .202 B4
Kensington Cl SO50 . . . . . .56 B3
Kensington Ct **3** SO17 . . .79 B1
Kensington Ct P04 . . . . . .182 B4
Kensington Fields SO45 . .125 B1
Kensington Gdns P014 . . .129 B1
Kensington Pk SO41 . . . . .211 B2
Kensington Rd
  Gosport P012 . . . . .181 B2
  Portsmouth P02 . . . . . . .157 C1
Kenson Gdns SO19 . . . . . .104 A2
Kent Gdns SO40 . . . . .100 B3
Kent Gr P016 . . . . .156 B3
Kent Ho
  12 Bournemouth BH4 . .204 B2
  2 Southampton SO14 . .103 B3
Kent La BH24 . . . . .93 B1
Kent Rd
  Chandler's Ford SO53 . . . .55 B2
  Gosport P013 . . . . .155 A2
  Poole BH12 . . . . .203 C3
  Portsmouth P05 . . . . . . .215 B1
  Southampton SO17 . . . . .79 B1
Kent St Portsmouth P01 . .182 A3
  Southampton SO14 . . . . .103 B3
Kentidge Rd P07 . . . . .134 B3
Kentish Rd SO15 . . . . .102 B4
Kenwood Rd P016 . . . . . . .156 B3
Kenwyn Cl SO18 . . . . .80 A1
Kenya Rd P016 . . . . .156 C4
Kenyon Cl BH15 . . . . .202 C4
Kenyon Rd Poole BH15 . . .202 C4
  Portsmouth P02 . . . . . . .157 C1
Keppel Cl BH24 . . . . .141 A4
Kerley Rd BH12 . . . . .204 C1

Kern Cl SO16 . . . . .77 C2
Kerrfield SO22 . . . . .10 B4
Kerrfield Mews SO22 . . . . .10 B4
Kerrigan Ct SO17 . . . . . . .103 A4
Kerry Cl
  Chandler's Ford SO53 . . . .55 B3
  Lymington SO41 . . . . . . .197 B2
Kerry Gdns SP6 . . . . .69 A1
Kersley Gdns SO19 . . . . . .104 A2
Kesteven Way SO18 . . . . .104 A4
Kestrel Cl
  Bishop's Waltham SO32 . .83 A4
  Botley SO32 . . . . .81 C1
  Clanfield P08 . . . . .88 B2
  Ferndown BH22 . . . . . . .165 A4
  Marchwood SO40 . . . . . .101 C1
  Southampton SO16 . . . . .78 A3
  Stubbington P014 . . . . . .154 A2
  Upton BH16 . . . . .201 A4
  Winchester SO22 . . . . . . .10 B2
Kestrel Ct BH24 . . . . .141 A4
Kestrel Dr BH23 . . . . .208 A3
Kestrel Pl P06 . . . . .158 C4
Kestrel Rd Eastleigh SO50 . .55 C1
  Portsmouth P03 . . . . . . .158 A2
Kestrel Way SP6 . . . . .93 A3
Keswick Ave P03 . . . . .183 A4
Keswick Ct BH25 . . . . .195 A3
Keswick Rd
  Bournemouth BH5 . . . . . .206 A2
  New Milton BH25 . . . . . .195 A3
  Southampton SO19 . . . . .103 B1
Keswick Way BH31 . . . . . .114 C3
Kettering Terr P02 . . . . . .182 B4
Keverstone Ct BH1 . . . . . .205 B2
Kevlyn Cres SO31 . . . . . . .104 C1
Kew La SO31 . . . . .128 A4
Kewlake La SO40 . . . . .74 B1
Key La **21** BH25 . . . . . . .202 A1
Keydell Ave P08 . . . . .112 A3
Keydell Cl P08 . . . . .112 A3
Keyes Cl
  Christchurch BH23 . . . . .207 C3
  Gosport P013 . . . . .155 B2
  Poole BH12 . . . . .203 C4
Keyes Ct **4** P05 . . . . . . .215 C1
Keyes Rd P013 . . . . .155 B2
Keyhaven Ct P013 . . . . . . .155 A1
Keyhaven Dr P09 . . . . . . .135 B3
Keyhaven Rd SO41 . . . . . .211 C2
Keynsham Rd SO19 . . . . . .104 A4
Keysworth Ave BH25 . . . .209 C4
Keysworth Rd BH16 . . . . .201 B2
Khandala Gdns P07 . . . . .134 C2
Khartoum Rd SO17 . . . . . . .79 A1
Khyber Rd BH12 . . . . .203 B3
Kidmore La P07 . . . . .110 C3
Kielder Cl SO53 . . . . .55 A4
Kielder Gr **2** P013 . . . . .155 B1
Kilbride **1** BH12 . . . . . . .204 A2
Kilbride Path **8** P02 . . . .182 B4
Kilford Ct SO30 . . . . .106 A3
Kilham La SO22 . . . . .10 A3
Killarney Cl SO19 . . . . . . .104 C2
Killock **8** BH13 . . . . .214 C4
Kilmarnock Rd BH9 . . . . . .189 C1
Kilmeston Cl P09 . . . . . . .135 C3
Kilmeston Rd
  Cheriton SO24 . . . . .14 B2
  Kilmeston SO24 . . . . .14 B1
Kilmington Way BH23 . . . .208 A4
Kilmiston Dr P016 . . . . . . .132 B1
Kilmiston Rd P011 . . . . . . .182 C4
Kiln Acre P016 . . . . .131 A2
Kiln Cl Corfe Mullen BH21 .186 B2
  Hythe SO45 . . . . .125 C2
Kiln Field GU33 . . . . .20 C3
Kiln Gn SO21 . . . . .57 A4
Kiln Hill SO32 . . . . .109 A4
Kiln La Braishfield SO51 . . .28 B3
  Buriton GU31 . . . . .65 B3
  Otterbourne SO21 . . . . . .31 B1
  Redlynch SP5 . . . . .47 C4
  Southwick P017 . . . . . . .109 B2
Kiln Rd Fareham P016 . . . .131 A2
  Portsmouth P03 . . . . . . .158 A1
Kiln Way BH31 . . . . .115 B2
Kilnside P07 . . . . .110 C2
Kilnyard Cl SO40 . . . . .76 B1
Kilpatrick Cl **5** P02 . . . .182 B4
Kilwich Way P016 . . . . . . .156 A3
Kimball Rd BH11 . . . . .188 C2
Kimberley Cl
  Christchurch BH23 . . . . .206 C4
  Fair Oak SO50 . . . . .57 B1
Kimberley Ct SO19 . . . . . .103 C1
Kimberley Rd
  Bournemouth BH6 . . . . . .206 B3
  Poole BH14 . . . . .203 A2
  Portsmouth P04 . . . . . . .183 A1
Kimbers GU32 . . . . .40 C2
Kimbridge Cnr SO51 . . . . .27 A4
Kimbridge Cres P09 . . . . .136 A3
Kimbridge La SO51 . . . . . .26 C1
Kimmeridge Ave BH12 . . .203 B4
Kimpton Cl P010 . . . . .179 C1
Kimpton Ct **11** P09 . . . .136 A3
Kineton Rd SO15 . . . . .78 C1
King Albert Ct P01 . . . . . .215 C4
King Albert St P01 . . . . . .215 C4
King Alfred Pl SO23 . . . . . . .2 A1
King Alfred Terr **9** SO23 . .2 A1
King Alfred's Coll SO22 . . .10 C4
King Arthur's Ct P06 . . . . .158 B4
King Charles St **9** P01 . .182 A2
King Cl P01 BH24 . . . . .141 A4
King Cote Villas **1** P05 . .182 C1

King Cup Ave SO31 . . . . . .128 C2
King Edward Ave
  Bournemouth BH9 . . . . . .190 A1
  Southampton SO16 . . . . .102 A4
King Edward Ct BH9 . . . . .189 C1
King Edward Pk (Cvn Pk)
  SO53 . . . . .55 A4
King Edward VI Sch
  SO15 . . . . .102 C4
King Edward's Cres
  P02 . . . . .157 B1
King Fisher Way BH21 . . . .208 A3
King George Ave
  Bournemouth BH9 . . . . . .189 C1
  Petersfield GU32 . . . . . . .40 C2
King George Mews **7**
  GU32 . . . . .40 C2
King George Mobile Home Pk
  BH25 . . . . .194 C1
King George Rd P016 . . . .156 B4
King George's Ave
  SO15 . . . . .101 C4
King Harold Ct SO23 . . . . .10 C3
King Henry I St P01 . . . . . .215 A3
King John Ave
  Bournemouth BH11 . . . . .188 B3
  Portchester P016 . . . . . .156 A4
King John Cl BH11 . . . . . .188 B3
King La GU32 . . . . .39 C4
King Richard 1 Rd P01 . . .182 A2
King Richard Cl P06 . . . . .157 B4
King Richard Dr BH11 . . . .188 B3
King Richard I Rd P01 . . . .215 A3
King Richard Sch P06 . . . .156 C4
King St Emsworth P010 . .160 A4
  Gosport P012 . . . . .181 B3
  Portsmouth P05 . . . . . . .215 B2
  Southampton SO14 . . . . .103 A2
  Westbourne P010 . . . . . .137 A2
  Wimborne Minst BH21 . . .163 A2
King William St P01 . . . . .182 A3
King's Arms La BH24 . . . . .140 C4
King's Arms Row BH24 . . .140 C4
King's Ave BH23 . . . . .206 C3
King's Cl SO53 . . . . .55 B4
King's Copse Rd SO45 . . .177 B4
King's Cres BH14 . . . . . . .203 C1
King's Croft La P09 . . . . . .135 B1
King's Ho **12** SO14 . . . .103 A2
King's La GU32 . . . . .18 B2
King's Park Athletic Ctr*
  BH7 . . . . .205 C3
King's Park Dr BH7 . . . . . .205 C3
King's Park Rd
  Bournemouth BH7 . . . . . .205 C3
  Southampton SO15 . . . . .103 A3
King's Park Sch BH7 . . . . .205 C3
King's Rd
  Bournemouth BH3 . . . . . .205 A4
  Emsworth P010 . . . . . . .160 C4
  Fareham P016 . . . . .131 A1
  Lee-on-the-Solent P013 .179 C2
  Portsmouth P05 . . . . . . .215 B1
  Winchester SO22 . . . . . . .10 B3
King's Saltern Rd SO41 . . .198 A1
King's Sch Prim The
  SO30 . . . . .80 C2
King's Terr
  1 Emsworth P010 . . . .160 C4
  Portsmouth P01 . . . . . . .215 A1
Kingcup Cl BH18 . . . . .186 C1
Kingdom Cl P015 . . . . .129 B3
Kingfisher Cl
  Bournemouth BH6 . . . . . .206 C3
  Hamble-le-Rice SO31 . . . .128 A2
  Rowland's Castle P09 . . .113 A1
  South Hayling P011 . . . . .185 B4
  Waterlooville P08 . . . . . .111 C2
  West Moors BH22 . . . . . .138 C1
Kingfisher Copse SO31 . . .129 A2
Kingfisher Ct
  18 Havant P09 . . . . . .136 A1
  Poole BH15 . . . . .202 B4
  1 Southampton SO17 . .79 A1
Kingfisher Dr P010 . . . . . .137 A2
Kingfisher Park Homes **17**
  BH10 . . . . .189 C2
Kingfisher Rd SO50 . . . . . .55 C1
Kingfisher Way
  Marchwood SO40 . . . . . .101 C1
  Ringwood BH24 . . . . . . .117 A1
  Romsey SO51 . . . . .52 C4
Kingfishers
  9 Christchurch BH23 . . .207 A3
  Portchester P016 . . . . . .155 C4
Kingfishers The BH11 . . . .188 C2
Kingham Heath Ind Est
  BH11 . . . . .188 C2
Kingland Cres BH15 . . . . .202 B1
Kingland Rd BH15 . . . . . . .202 B1
Kings Ave
  Hamble-le-Rice SO31 . . . .127 C2
  Poole BH14 . . . . .203 B1
  Winchester SO22 . . . . . . .10 B3
Kings Bench Alley P01 . . .182 A3
Kings Cl Lymington SO41 . .197 B2
  Lyndhurst SO43 . . . . . . .121 C3
  Rowland's Castle P09 . . .113 A1
  Twyford SO21 . . . . .32 A4
  West Moors BH22 . . . . . .138 C1
Kings Copse Ave SO30 . . .105 B3
Kings Copse Prim Sch
  SO30 . . . . .105 B3
Kings Copse Rd SO30 . . . .105 B3
Kings Court Sch P08 . . . . .88 A1
Kings Cres SO41 . . . . .197 B2
Kings Ct SP6 . . . . .69 C1

Kings Field SO31 . . . . .105 A1
Kings Field Gdns SO31 . . .105 A1
Kings Head Yd **32** SO23 . .11 A4
Kings Huts SO41 . . . . .197 A2
Kings La Chilcomb SO21 . .11 C3
  Sway SO41 . . . . .196 C4
Kings Mede P08 . . . . .112 A3
Kings Mews P05 . . . . .182 B1
Kings Park Com Hospl
  BH7 . . . . .205 C3
Kings Rd
  Chandler's Ford SO53 . . . .55 B3
  Gosport P012 . . . . .181 A3
  Lymington SO41 . . . . . . .197 B2
  New Milton BH25 . . . . . .195 B2
  Petersfield GU32 . . . . . . .40 B2
  South Hayling P011 . . . . .185 A3
Kings Ride SO45 . . . . .177 C4
Kings Row **7** SO22 . . . . .10 C4
Kings Royal Hussars Mus
  The * SO23 . . . . .10 C4
Kings Sch The SO50 . . . . . .57 A1
Kings Somborne Rd SO51 . .7 B1
Kings Way P01 . . . . .113 A1
Kings Worthy Prim Sch
  SO23 . . . . .2 A4
Kings' Sch SO22 . . . . .10 A4
Kingsbere Ave BH10 . . . . .189 A1
Kingsbere Gdns BH23 . . . .209 A4
Kingsbere Rd BH15 . . . . . .202 A2
Kingsbridge Rd BH14 . . . .203 B2
Kingsbury Ct P08 . . . . .88 A3
Kingsbury Rd SO14 . . . . . .103 A4
Kingsbury's La BH24 . . . . .140 C4
Kingsclere Ave
  Havant P09 . . . . .135 B3
  Southampton SO19 . . . . .126 C4
Kingsclere Cl SO19 . . . . . .103 C1
Kingscote Ho **7** P06 . . .132 C1
Kingscote Rd
  Cosham P06 . . . . .132 C1
  Waterlooville P08 . . . . . .111 B2
Kingscroft Ct P09 . . . . . . .135 B1
Kingsdale SO23 . . . . .10 C4
Kingsdown Cl SO45 . . . . . .125 A2
Kingsdown Pl **1** P01 . . . .182 A3
Kingsdown Way SO18 . . . .80 A1
Kingsey Ave P010 . . . . . . .160 A3
Kingsfernsden La GU32 . . .41 A3
Kingsfield
  Lymington SO41 . . . . . . .198 A1
  Ringwood BH24 . . . . . . .141 A4
Kingsfold Ave SO18 . . . . . .79 C2
Kingsford Cl SP5 . . . . .47 B3
Kingsgate Rd SO23 . . . . . . .10 C3
Kingsgate St SO23 . . . . . . .11 A3
Kingsland Cl P06 . . . . .133 B1
Kingsland Ct Poole BH13 . .214 C4
  4 Southampton SO14 . .103 A2
Kingsland Rd **10** SO14 . .103 A3
Kingsland Sq **13** SO14 . .103 A2
Kingsleigh Fst Sch
  BH10 . . . . .189 B2
Kingsleigh Jun Sch
  BH10 . . . . .189 B2
Kingsleigh Sec Sch
  BH10 . . . . .189 B2
Kingsley Ave BH6 . . . . . . .207 A2
Kingsley Cl BH6 . . . . .207 A2
Kingsley Gdns SO40 . . . . .100 A4
Kingsley Gn P09 . . . . .135 C3
Kingsley Pl SO22 . . . . .10 C3
Kingsley Rd
  Gosport P012 . . . . .180 C4
  Portsmouth P04 . . . . . . .183 B2
  Southampton SO15 . . . . .102 A4
Kingsmead P017 . . . . .108 B4
Kingsmead Ave P014 . . . .179 A3
Kingsmead Ct
  10 Southampton SO15 . .78 A1
  6 Wimborne Minst BH21 .163 A3
Kingsmill Cl P012 . . . . . . .180 C2
Kingsmill Rd BH17 . . . . . .202 C4
Kingston SO31 . . . . .127 B4
Kingston Cres P02 . . . . . . .182 B4
Kingston Cross P02 . . . . . .182 B4
Kingston Ct SO16 . . . . .77 C1
Kingston Gdns P015 . . . . .130 B2
Kingston Lacy Ho (NT)*
  BH21 . . . . .162 A4
Kingston Pk SO41 . . . . . . .197 B1
Kingston Rd
  Gosport P012 . . . . .180 C3
  Poole BH15 . . . . .202 B2
  Portsmouth P01, P02 . . .182 C4
  Southampton SO15 . . . . .102 B3
Kingsway
  Chandler's Ford SO53 . . . .55 C4
  Ferndown BH22 . . . . . . .165 A4
  North Hayling P011 . . . . .160 A2
  Southampton SO14 . . . . .103 A2
Kingsway Cl SO53 . . . . . . .55 C4
Kingsway Ct SO23 . . . . .2 C4
Kingsway Gdns SO53 . . . . .55 C4
Kingsway The P06 . . . . . . .156 B4
Kingswell Cl BH10 . . . . . .189 B1
Kingswell Gdns BH10 . . . .189 A1
Kingswell Path P01 . . . . . .215 B4
Kingswell Rd BH10 . . . . . .189 B1
Kingswell St P01 . . . . .215 B4
Kingswood
  Bournemouth BH4 . . . . . .204 B1
  Marchwood SO40 . . . . . .102 A1
Kingsworthy Rd P09 . . . . .135 C2
Kinloss Cl SO16 . . . . .78 A3
Kinnell Cl P010 . . . . .160 C4

Kinross Cres P06 . . . . .158 A4
Kinross Rd
  Bournemouth BH3 . . . . . .204 C3
  Totton SO40 . . . . .100 C3
Kinsbourne Ave BH10 . . . .189 B1
Kinsbourne Cl SO19 . . . . .104 C3
Kinsbourne Rise SO19 . . .104 C3
Kinsbourne Way SO19 . . .104 C3
Kinsford Ct SO42 . . . . .145 C1
Kinson Ave BH15 . . . . . . .203 A4
Kinson Gr BH10 . . . . .189 B3
Kinson Park Rd BH10 . . . .189 B3
Kinson Pottery Ind Est
  BH4 . . . . .201 A3
Kinson Prim Sch BH11 . . .189 A3
Kinson Rd BH10 . . . . .189 B2
Kinterbury Ct P017 . . . . . .103 A4
Kintyre Rd P06 . . . . .133 C1
Kinver Cl SO51 . . . . .28 A1
Kiosks The **26** BH15 . . .202 B1
Kipling Bldgs **18** P02 . .157 C2
Kipling Cl P015 . . . . .106 B1
Kipling Cl SO19 . . . . .103 C1
Kipling Rd Eastleigh SO50 . .55 C2
  Poole BH14 . . . . .203 A3
  Portsmouth P02 . . . . . . .157 C2
Kirby Cl BH15 . . . . .202 C3
Kirby Ct **4** P02 . . . . .157 C1
Kirby Rd P02 . . . . .157 C1
Kirby Way BH6 . . . . .206 B2
Kirk Gdns SO40 . . . . .100 C3
Kirkham Ave BH23 . . . . . .192 B2
Kirkstall Rd P04 . . . . .182 C1
Kirkway BH18 . . . . .187 A2
Kirn Cl P013 . . . . .155 B2
Kirton Rd P06 . . . . .158 B4
Kitchener Cres BH17 . . . . .187 A1
Kitchener Rd SO17 . . . . . . .79 B1
Kitchers Cl SO41 . . . . .172 A1
Kite Cl P08 . . . . .111 C2
Kites Croft Cl P014 . . . . . .129 B1
Kitnocks Hill SO32 . . . . . .106 C4
Kitscroft Rd BH10 . . . . . . .189 B3
Kitt's La SO24 . . . . .16 B1
Kittiwake Cl
  Bournemouth BH6 . . . . . .206 C3
  Gosport P013 . . . . .155 A1
Kitwalls La SO41 . . . . .211 B3
Kitwood Gr **45** P09 . . . .136 A3
Kivernell Pl **1** SO41 . . . .211 B2
Kivernell Rd SO41 . . . . . . .211 B2
Kiwi Cl BH15 . . . . .202 C2
Kleves Ct SO19 . . . . .104 A3
Knapp Cl BH23 . . . . .207 A4
Knapp La SO51 . . . . .29 B2
Knapp Mill Ave BH23 . . . .207 A4
Knapps Hard GU32 . . . . . .37 A3
Knatchbull Cl SO51 . . . . . .52 C4
Knellers La SO40 . . . . .100 B2
Knight Cl SO23 . . . . .2 A1
Knighton Crest P04 . . . . . .196 C1
Knighton Ct P08 . . . . .112 B4
Knighton Heath Cl
  BH11 . . . . .188 C2
Knighton Heath Rd
  BH11 . . . . .188 C2
Knighton La BH21 . . . . . . .188 B4
Knighton Pk BH25 . . . . . .209 C4
Knighton Rd SO19 . . . . . .103 C2
Knights Bank Rd P014 . . .153 C1
Knights Cl SO31 . . . . .128 C1
Knights Rd BH11 . . . . .188 B3
Knightsbridge Cl BH4 . . . .204 C1
Knightstone Ct **12** P02 . .157 C2
Knightstone Gr BH22 . . . .138 B1
Knightstone Grange **2**
  SO45 . . . . .126 A1
Knightwood Ave
  Havant P09 . . . . .136 A3
  Lyndhurst SO43 . . . . . . .121 C3
Knightwood Cl
  Ashurst SO40 . . . . .100 A1
  Christchurch BH23 . . . . .208 A4
  Lyndhurst SO43 . . . . . . .121 C3
Knightwood Oak*
  SO43 . . . . .120 C1
Knightwood Prim Sch
  SO53 . . . . .54 C4
Knightwood Rd
  Chandler's Ford SO52 . . . .55 A3
  Hythe SO45 . . . . .126 A2
  North Baddesley SO52 . . .55 A3
Knobcrook Rd BH21 . . . . .163 A3
Knole Ct **5** BH1 . . . . . . .205 B2
Knole Gdns BH1 . . . . .205 B2
Knole Rd BH1 . . . . .205 B2
Knoll Gdns*
  Ferndown BH21 . . . . . . .164 C2
  St Leonards BH24 . . . . . .139 C2
Knoll La BH21 . . . . .186 A4
Knoll Manor P04 . . . . .204 C3
Knotgrass Rd SO31 . . . . . .128 C1
Knowland Dr SO41 . . . . . .211 B3
Knowle Hill SO50 . . . . .56 A4
Knowle Hospl P017 . . . . . .130 C4
Knowle La SO50 . . . . .57 C1
Knowle Rd SO42 . . . . .145 C1
Knowles Cl
  Christchurch BH23 . . . . .207 C4
  Southampton SO16 . . . . .77 B3
Knowles Mdw GU33 . . . . . .21 A1
Knowlton Gdns BH9 . . . . .190 A2
Knowlton Rd BH17 . . . . . .202 C4
Knowsley Cres P06 . . . . . .158 A4
Knowsley Rd P06 . . . . .157 C4
Knox Rd Havant P09 . . . . .135 B1
  Portsmouth P02 . . . . . . .157 B1
Knyght Cl SO51 . . . . .53 A3

Knyveton Ho BH11 .....205 A2
Knyveton Rd BH1 .....205 B2
Kootenay Ave SO18 .....104 C4
Kooyong Cl SO51 .....51 A1
Kynegils Rd SO22 .....1 C1
Kynon Cl PO12 .....181 B4
Kyrchil La BH21 .....163 C3
Kyrchil Way BH21 .....163 C4
Kytes La SO32 .....82 B3

L

Labrador Dr BH15 .....202 B1
Laburnham Dr SO23 .....2 A4
Laburnum Ave PO6 .....158 B4
Laburnum Cl
  Ferndown BH22 .....165 A3
  North Baddesley SO52 .....54 A3
  Verwood BH31 .....115 B3
Laburnum Cres SO45 .....150 A4
Laburnum Ct SO19 .....103 B2
Laburnum Dr SO41 .....211 C4
Laburnum Gr
  Eastleigh SO50 .....56 A2
  Portsmouth PO2 .....157 C1
  South Hayling PO11 .....185 A2
Laburnum Ho
  [8] Bournemouth BH10 .....189 C2
  Hedge End SO30 .....105 B3
Laburnum Rd
  Fareham PO16 .....155 A3
  Hedge End SO30 .....105 B3
  Southampton SO16 .....79 B2
  Waterlooville PO7 .....134 B3
Lacey Cres BH15 .....203 A3
Lackford Ave SO40 .....100 C3
Lacon Cl SO18 .....103 C4
Lacy Cl BH21 .....163 B3
Lacy Dr BH21 .....163 B3
Ladram Rd PO12 .....180 C2
Lady Betty's Dr PO15 .....129 C3
Ladybridge Rd PO7 .....134 B2
Ladycross Rd SO45 .....126 A1
Ladysmith Rd BH23 .....207 C4
Ladysmith Terr SO32 .....83 B4
Ladywood SO51 .....55 C3
Ladywood Ho PO1 .....215 B2
Lagado Cl BH14 .....214 B4
Lagland St [2] BH15 .....202 B1
Lagland St BH15 .....202 B1
Lagoon Cl BH14 .....214 A4
Lagoon Rd BH14 .....214 A4
Laidlaw Cl BH12 .....204 A4
Lake Ave BH15 .....201 B1
Lake Cres BH15 .....201 C2
Lake Ct BH15 .....201 B1
Lake Farm Cl SO30 .....105 B4
Lake Grove Rd BH25 .....195 A2
Lake Ho SO15 .....102 B3
Lake Rd
  Bournemouth BH11 .....189 A3
  Chandler's Ford SO53 .....55 C4
  Curdridge SO32 .....106 C4
  Hamworthy BH15 .....201 C1
  Portsmouth PO1 .....215 C4
  Southampton SO19 .....103 B1
  Verwood BH31 .....115 A3
Lake View Manor BH25 .....195 A2
Lakeland Gdns SO40 .....101 C1
Lakelands Dr SO15 .....102 B3
Lakes The SO32 .....84 A2
Lakeside Fareham PO17 .....130 C3
  Lee-on-the-Solent PO13 .....179 C1
  Ower SO51 .....75 B3
  Ringwood BH24 .....141 B3
Lakeside Ave
  Portsmouth PO3 .....183 A4
  Rownhams SO16 .....77 C3
Lakeside Ctry Pk* SO50 .....79 C4
Lakeside Gdns PO9 .....136 A1
Lakeside Pines BH25 .....195 A2
Lakeside Rd BH13 .....204 A1
Lakesmere Rd PO8 .....112 B3
Lakeview Dr BH24 .....141 B3
Lakewood Cl SO53 .....55 B4
Lakewood Rd
  Ashurst SO40 .....100 B2
  Chandler's Ford SO53 .....30 C1
  Christchurch BH23 .....193 C1
Lamberhurst Cl SO19 .....127 A4
Lambert Cl PO7 .....134 C3
Lambourn Cl PO14 .....154 B4
Lambourn Sq SO53 .....55 A3
Lambourne Cl SO45 .....125 C1
Lambourne Dr SO31 .....129 A2
Lambourne Ho SO30 .....105 A3
Lambourne Rd SO18 .....80 A1
Lambs Cl BH17 .....187 B1
Lambs Lease GU33 .....21 A2
Lambsgreen La BH21 .....162 C1
Lammas Rd SO45 .....126 A1
Lampeter Ave PO6 .....158 A4
Lampton Gdns BH9 .....189 C1
Lamward Mans [30] SO43 .....103 A4
Lancaster Cl
  Burslesdon SO31 .....105 A1
  Christchurch BH23 .....208 B4
  Corfe Mullen BH18 .....186 C3
  Lee-on-the-Solent PO13 .....180 A2
  Portchester PO16 .....132 A1
Lancaster Ct SO30 .....80 B1
Lancaster Dr
  Corfe Mullen BH18 .....186 C3
  Verwood BH31 .....114 C3
Lancaster Rd
  Ferndown BH22 .....165 A4
  Southampton SO16 .....77 C2

Lancaster Way PO7 .....134 C3
Lance's Hill SO18 .....103 C4
Lancer Cl BH23 .....206 C4
Lander Cl BH15 .....202 B1
Landford CE Prim Sch
  SP5 .....49 B2
Landford Common Farm
  SP5 .....49 C1
Landford Gdns BH8 .....190 B1
Landford Way BH8 .....190 B1
Landguard Rd
  Portsmouth PO4 .....183 A2
  Southampton SO15 .....102 B3
Landon Rd PO13 .....180 B4
Landport St
  Portsmouth PO1 .....215 C4
  Portsmouth, Southsea
  PO5 .....215 A2
Landport Terr PO1 .....215 A2
Landport View PO1 .....215 B4
Lands End Rd SO31 .....128 B4
Landsdowne St PO5 .....215 A2
Landseer Rd
  [13] Bournemouth BH4 .....204 B2
  Southampton SO19 .....104 B2
Lane End SO24 .....17 B4
Lane End Cotts SP5 .....49 B2
Lane End Dr PO10 .....160 C4
Lane The
  [4] Bournemouth BH4 .....205 B3
  Fawley SO45 .....151 A2
  Gosport PO12 .....181 A1
  Portsmouth PO4 .....182 C1
Lanehays Rd SO45 .....125 C2
Lanes End PO14 .....179 B3
Lanes The BH25 .....195 A3
Lanesbridge Cl SO40 .....99 C3
Langbar Cl SO19 .....103 C3
Langbrook Cl PO9 .....159 C4
Langdale Ave PO6 .....158 A4
Langdale Cl SO16 .....101 C4
Langdon Cl BH14 .....203 B2
Langdon Rd BH14 .....203 B2
Langdown Firs SO45 .....126 A2
Langdown Inf Sch SO45 .....126 A1
Langdown Jun Sch
  SO45 .....126 A2
Langdown Lawn SO45 .....126 A2
Langdown Lawn Cl
  SO45 .....126 A1
Langford La SP5 .....47 C4
Langford Rd PO1 .....182 C4
Langham Cl SO52 .....53 C2
Langham Ct BH23 .....191 C1
Langley Chase BH24 .....140 A3
Langley Gdn SP6 .....70 A2
Langley Lodge Gdns
  SO45 .....177 C4
Langley Rd
  Christchurch BH23 .....193 C1
  Poole BH14 .....203 C2
  Southampton PO2 .....182 C4
  Southampton SO15 .....102 A3
Langrish Cl BH23 .....193 C1
Langrish Hill GU32 .....39 B2
Langrish Inf Sch SO23 .....40 A2
Langrish Prim Sch GU32 .....40 A2
Langrish Rd SO16 .....78 A2
Langside Ave PO14 .....204 A4
Langside Sch BH12 .....204 A4
Langstone Ave PO9 .....159 C4
Langstone High St PO9 .....159 C4
Langstone Ho
  [11] Havant PO9 .....136 C4
  Havant PO9 .....136 A2
Langstone Inf Sch PO9 .....183 A4
Langstone Jun Sch PO3 .....183 A4
Langstone Marina Hts
  PO4 .....183 B2
Langstone Rd
  Havant PO9 .....159 C4
  Portsmouth PO3 .....183 A3
Langstone Wlk
  Fareham PO14 .....154 B4
  Gosport PO13 .....155 A1
Langton Cl
  Barton on Sea BH25 .....210 A4
  Winchester SO22 .....1 C1
Langton Dene [27] BH4 .....204 B2
Langton Farm Gdns
  PO1 .....182 C4
Langton Rd
  Bishop's Waltham SO32 .....83 B4
  Bournemouth BH7 .....205 C3
Lanham La SO22 .....1 A1
Lankhills Rd SO23 .....2 A3
Lankhills Sch SO22 .....2 C1
Lansdell Ct [5] BH15 .....202 C2
Lansdown Ave PO16 .....156 B3
Lansdown Terr PO10 .....137 A3
Lansdowne Ave
  Waterlooville PO7 .....134 A1
  Winchester SO23 .....10 C3
Lansdowne Cl [3] SO51 .....52 C4
Lansdowne Cres BH1 .....205 A2
Lansdowne Ct
  Romsey SO51 .....52 C4
  [3] Winchester SO23 .....10 C3
Lansdowne Gdns
  Bournemouth BH1 .....205 A2
  Romsey SO51 .....52 C4
Lansdowne Hill [9]
  SO14 .....102 C2
Lansdowne Ho
  [13] Bournemouth BH1 .....205 A2
  [3] Gosport PO12 .....181 A3

Lansdowne Rd
  Bournemouth BH1 .....205 A3
  Southampton SO15 .....102 A4
Lansdowne The BH1 .....205 A2
Lantana PO7 .....134 C3
Lantern Ct SO23 .....10 C3
Lanyard Dr PO13 .....180 B3
Lapthorn Cl PO13 .....155 A2
Lapwing Cl
  Gosport PO12 .....181 A4
  Horndean PO8 .....112 A4
  Portsmouth PO4 .....183 B3
Lapwing Gn SO40 .....100 B4
Lapwing Gr PO16 .....155 C4
Lapwing Rd BH21 .....164 A4
Lara Cl BH8 .....190 B2
Larch Ave SO45 .....150 B3
Larch Cl
  Broadstone BH17 .....186 C1
  Hordle SO41 .....195 C2
  Kings Worthy SO23 .....2 A4
  Lee-on-the-Solent PO13 .....180 A3
  St Leonards BH24 .....140 A2
  West End SO30 .....80 B1
Larch Ct PO1 .....215 C4
Larch Rd SO16 .....78 A2
Larch Row SP6 .....70 B1
Larch Way
  Burslesdon SO31 .....127 C4
Larch Wood Cl SO45 .....126 A1
Larchdale Cl SO32 .....152 B4
Larches Gdns PO15 .....130 B1
Larchwood Ave PO9 .....135 A2
Larchwood Rd SO40 .....100 B3
Larcombe Rd GU32 .....40 B1
Larg Dr SO22 .....1 B2
Lark Hill Rise SO22 .....10 B2
Lark Rd
  Christchurch BH23 .....208 A3
  Eastleigh SO50 .....55 B1
  Lark Way PO10 .....137 B2
Larkhill Rd PO3 .....157 C2
Larkin Cl BH22 .....165 A4
Larks Rise BH22 .....165 A4
Larksfield Ave BH9 .....190 B2
Larkshill Cl BH25 .....195 A2
Larkspur Chase SO19 .....104 C3
Larkspur Cl
  Locks Heath SO31 .....128 C1
  Swanmore SO32 .....84 A3
Larkspur Dr
  Chandler's Ford SO53 .....54 C3
  Marchwood SO40 .....124 C4
Larkspur Gdns
  [7] Hedge End SO30 .....105 B3
  Hollbury SO45 .....150 A2
Larkwhistle Wk PO9 .....135 B4
Lascelles Ct [1] BH7 .....206 A3
Lascelles Rd BH7 .....206 A3
Laser Cl SO31 .....128 C2
Lasham Gn [9] PO9 .....136 A3
Lasham Ho SO16 .....102 A4
Lasham Wlk PO14 .....154 B4
Lashley Mdw PO7 .....86 B2
Latch Farm Ave BH23 .....207 A4
Latchmore Dr SO45 .....125 B2
Latchmore Forest Gr
  PO8 .....112 A2
Latchmore Gdns PO8 .....111 C2
Latelie Cl SO31 .....128 C3
Latham Cl SO50 .....57 A1
Latham Ct SO15 .....102 A4
Latham Rd Fair Oak SO31 .....57 A1
  Romsey SO51 .....53 A4
Latimer Ct
  Portsmouth PO3 .....158 A2
  [3] Southampton SO17 .....79 A1
Latimer Gate [2] SO14 .....103 A2
Latimer Rd BH9 .....204 C4
Latimer St Romsey SO51 .....52 C4
  Southampton SO14 .....103 A2
Latimers Cl BH23 .....193 C1
Lauder Cl PO10 .....137 C1
Launcelyn Cl SO52 .....53 C2
Launceston Cl PO12 .....181 B4
Launceston Dr SO50 .....55 C2
Laundry La SO41 .....211 C2
Laundry Rd SO16 .....78 A1
Laurel Cl
  Christchurch BH23 .....193 B1
  Corfe Mullen BH21 .....186 B4
  Gosport PO12 .....181 B4
  Hordle SO41 .....195 C2
  Hythe SO45 .....125 C2
  Locks Heath SO31 .....129 A2
  Southampton SO19 .....103 B2
  St Leonards BH24 .....139 C2
Laurel Dr BH18 .....187 A2
Laurel Gdns
  Broadstone BH18 .....187 B2
  Locks Heath SO31 .....129 A2
Laurel La BH24 .....139 C2
Laurel Rd
  Locks Heath SO31 .....129 A2
  Waterlooville PO8 .....112 B2
Laurels The
  Brockenhurst SO42 .....172 C4
  Ferndown BH22 .....165 B4
Lauren Mews PO11 .....184 C1
Laurence Ct [2] SO50 .....57 B1
Laurence Gn PO10 .....136 C2
Laurence Mews SO51 .....52 C4
Lauriston Dr SO53 .....30 A1
Laurus Cl PO7 .....135 A3
Laurus Wlk [10] PO13 .....179 C1
Lavant Cl PO8 .....112 A1
Lavant Ct [3] GU32 .....40 C2

Lavant Dr PO9 .....136 A2
Lavant St GU32 .....40 C2
Lavender Cl
  Southampton SO19 .....103 C3
  Verwood BH31 .....115 B3
Lavender Rd
  Bournemouth BH8 .....190 B2
  Hordle SO41 .....195 C2
  Waterlooville PO7 .....135 A3
Lavender Villas [1]
  BH23 .....209 A4
Lavender Way BH13 .....186 B2
Laverock Lea PO16 .....132 B1
Laverstoke Cl SO16 .....77 C3
Laverstone Ct [3] BH5 .....206 C2
Lavey's La PO15 .....130 A3
Lavington Gdns SO52 .....53 C2
Lavinia Rd Gosport PO12 .....181 A3
  Poole BH12 .....203 B4
Lawford Rd BH9 .....190 A2
Lawford Way SO40 .....100 C4
Lawn Cl Gosport PO12 .....180 B4
  Milford on Sea SO41 .....211 C2
Lawn Ct SO17 .....103 A4
Lawn Dr SO31 .....129 A1
Lawn Ho [6] SO23 .....11 A4
Lawn Rd Eastleigh SO50 .....56 A3
  Littleton SO22 .....1 B2
  Lymington SO41 .....197 A2
Lawn St SO23 .....11 A4
Lawn View BH25 .....194 B3
Lawns Cl BH21 .....164 B3
Lawns Rd BH21 .....164 B3
Lawns The BH23 .....209 A4
Lawnside Rd SO15 .....102 A4
Lawnswood SO50 .....57 B1
Lawnswood Cl PO8 .....111 C1
Lawrence Ave PO8 .....111 C1
Lawrence Cl
  Bournemouth BH8 .....205 B3
  Southampton SO19 .....103 C1
Lawrence Dr BH13 .....203 C1
Lawrence Ho SO16 .....102 A4
Lawrence Ho [8] SO45 .....126 A2
Lawrence La SP6 .....94 A2
Lawrence Mans PO5 .....215 D1
Lawrence Rd
  Fareham PO15 .....130 C1
  Portsmouth PO5 .....215 D1
  Ringwood BH24 .....117 B1
Lawrence Sq [20] PO12 .....181 B2
Lawrence Wlk BH11 .....180 B3
Lawson Cl SO31 .....128 B4
Lawson Ct [3] SO16 .....78 A1
Lawson Rd Poole BH12 .....203 A3
  Portsmouth PO5 .....215 D2
Laxton Cl
  Locks Heath SO31 .....129 A2
  Southampton SO19 .....104 A1
Lay Gdn BH21 .....163 B1
Laymoor La BH21 .....164 B3
Layton Cl BH12 .....203 B3
Layton Rd Gosport PO13 .....155 B2
Lazy Acre PO10 .....161 B4
Le Patourel Cl BH23 .....207 B4
Lea Rd SO45 .....177 C4
Lea The BH31 .....115 A3
Lea Way BH11 .....188 C3
Lea-Oak Gdns PO15 .....130 B2
Leabrook SO31 .....129 A3
Leacock Cl SO32 .....84 A3
Leafy La PO15 .....129 C3
Lealand Gr PO6 .....158 B4
Lealand Rd PO6 .....158 B4
Leamington Cres PO13 .....179 C1
Leamington Ho [9] PO5 .....215 B2
Leamington Rd BH9 .....205 A4
Leander Cl SO50 .....56 A3
Leander Dr PO12 .....181 B4
Leaphill Rd BH7 .....206 A3
Lear Rd PO12 .....181 A3
Learoyd Rd BH17 .....202 C4
Leaside Way SO16 .....79 B3
Leatherhead Gdns SO30 .....80 B1
Leaway The PO16 .....156 B4
Lebanon Rd SO15 .....101 B4
Lechlade Gdns
  Bournemouth BH7 .....206 A4
  Portsmouth PO15 .....130 C2
Leckford Cl
  Portchester PO16 .....132 A1
  Southampton SO18 .....104 B4
Leckford Rd PO9 .....136 A3
Ledbury Rd
  Christchurch BH23 .....207 C3
  Cosham PO6 .....133 B1
Lederle La PO13 .....155 B3
Ledgard Cl BH14 .....203 A2
Lee Church La SO51 .....76 C4
Lee Cl BH22 .....165 B2
Lee Dro SO51 .....53 A1
Lee La SO51 .....77 A4
Lee Rd PO12 .....181 A3
Lee-on-the-Solent Inf Sch
  PO13 .....179 C1
Lee-on-the-Solent Jun Sch
  PO13 .....179 C1
Leedam Rd BH10 .....189 B2
Leelands SO41 .....197 B1
Leep La PO12 .....181 A1
Lees Cl BH23 .....191 B2
Lees La PO12 .....181 A3
Lees La N PO12 .....181 A3
Leesland CE Inf Sch
  PO12 .....181 A2

Leesland CE Jun Sch
  PO12 .....181 A2
Leesland Rd PO12 .....181 A3
Leeson Dr BH22 .....165 A4
Leeson Rd BH7 .....205 C4
Legg La BH21 .....163 B2
Legion Cl
  Hamworthy BH15 .....201 C1
  Southampton SO16 .....79 B2
Legion La SO23 .....2 B4
Legion Rd BH
  Hamworthy BH15 .....201 C1
  South Hayling PO11 .....185 A2
Leicester Ct PO13 .....180 B3
Leicester Rd Poole BH13 .....203 C2
  Southampton SO15 .....78 B1
Leigh Cl BH22 .....165 A4
Leigh Comm BH21 .....163 C3
Leigh Ct SO50 .....55 C2
Leigh Gdns BH21 .....163 B2
Leigh House Hospl
  Chandler's Ford SO53 .....55 B4
  Winchester SO21 .....11 C4
Leigh La BH21 .....163 C3
Leigh Mans [10] SO17 .....79 A1
Leigh Rd
  Eastleigh SO50, SO53 .....55 C2
  Fareham PO16 .....131 A1
  Havant PO9 .....135 C1
  New Milton BH25 .....195 A2
  Southampton SO17 .....79 A1
  Wimborne Minst BH21 .....163 C2
Leigham Vale Rd BH6 .....206 B2
Leighton Ave [7] SO15 .....102 A4
Leighton Rd SO19 .....103 C2
Leisure The PO13 .....155 B2
Leith Ave PO16 .....132 C1
Lemon Rd SO15 .....102 A4
Lendorber Ave PO6 .....158 A4
Lennox Cl
  Chandler's Ford SO53 .....55 C4
  Gosport PO12 .....181 B1
  Southampton SO16 .....77 C3
Lennox Rd N PO5 .....182 B1
Lennox Rd S PO5 .....182 B1
Lensyd Gdns PO8 .....111 C3
Lent Hill Ct [3] SO22 .....10 B3
Lentham Cl BH17 .....187 B1
Lentune Way SO41 .....197 B1
Leofric Ct PO4 .....183 B2
Leominster Rd PO6 .....133 A1
Leonard Rd PO12 .....181 B3
Leonards Ct SO16 .....101 B4
Leopold Dr SO32 .....83 A4
Leopold St PO4 .....182 C1
Lepe Ctry Pk* SO45 .....178 A1
Lepe Rd SO45 .....177 C2
Leroux Cl SO15 .....102 C3
Lerryn Rd PO13 .....155 B1
Leslie Loader Ct SO50 .....56 A2
Leslie Loader Ho SO19 .....103 C3
Leslie Rd
  Bournemouth BH9 .....204 C4
  Poole BH14 .....203 A2
Lester Ave PO9 .....135 B1
Lester Rd PO12 .....180 C3
Lester Sq BH23 .....143 B2
Leven Ave BH4 .....204 B3
Leven Cl
  Bournemouth BH4 .....204 B3
  North Baddesley SO52 .....55 A4
Leventhorpe Ct PO12 .....181 B2
Leveson Cl PO12 .....181 C2
Levet's La [3] BH15 .....202 A1
Leviathan Cl PO14 .....179 B3
Lewens Cl BH21 .....163 B2
Lewens La BH21 .....163 B2
Lewes Cl SO50 .....56 A3
Lewesdon Dr BH18 .....186 C2
Lewin Cl SO21 .....56 C4
Lewins Wlk SO31 .....104 C1
Lewis Cl SO45 .....125 B1
Lewis Ho [8] SO14 .....103 A3
Lewis Rd PO10 .....137 A2
Lewis Silkin Way SO16 .....78 A2
Lewry Cl SO30 .....105 B4
Lexby Rd SO40 .....101 A3
Lexden Gdns PO11 .....184 C2
Leybourne Ave
  Bournemouth BH10 .....189 B2
  Southampton SO18 .....104 A4
Leybourne Cl BH10 .....189 B3
Leydene Ave BH8 .....190 C1
Leydene Cl BH8 .....190 C1
Leydene Pk GU32 .....63 C2
Leyland Cl PO12 .....181 A2
Leyland Rd BH12 .....188 C1
Leyside BH23 .....207 C3
Leyton Conyers [10]
  BH1 .....214 C4
Liam Cl PO9 .....103 B3
Liberty Cl BH21 .....139 A3
Liberty Ct BH23 .....206 C4
Liberty Rd PO17 .....109 A4
Liberty Row SO31 .....128 A1
Library Mews BH12 .....203 B3
Library Rd
  Ferndown BH22 .....189 C1
  Ferndown BH22 .....165 B3
  Poole BH12 .....203 B3
  Totton SO40 .....101 A4
Lichen Way SO40 .....101 C1
Lichfield Ct PO13 .....180 B3

Lichfield Dr PO12 ......181 B4
Lichfield Rd
Locks Heath PO14 ......129 B2
Portsmouth PO3 ......183 A3
Liddel Way SO53 ......55 A3
Liddiards Way PO7 ......134 C2
Lidgate Gdns PO4 ......183 A1
Liederbach Dr BH31 ......115 B2
Lightfoot Lawn PO4 ......183 B2
Lightning Cl SO45 ......150 C1
Lilac Cl Havant PO9 ......136 B2
Ringwood BH24 ......141 A4
Lilac Rd SO16 ......79 A2
Lilies The SO50 ......81 B4
Lilley Cl SO40 ......101 C1
Lilliput CE Fst Sch
BH14 ......214 B4
Lilliput Ct BH14 ......203 A2
Lilliput Rd BH14 ......214 B4
Lily Ave PO7 ......134 A1
Limberline Rd PO3 ......158 A2
Limberline Spur PO3 ......158 A3
Lime Ave SO19 ......104 A3
Lime Cl
Colden Common SO21 ......57 A4
Hythe SO45 ......125 C1
Poole BH15 ......202 C3
Southampton SO19 ......104 A3
Lime Gdns SO30 ......80 B2
Lime Gr Cosham PO6 ......133 A1
Hordle SO41 ......211 B4
South Hayling PO11 ......184 B2
Lime Kiln La SO45 ......150 A3
Lime Kiln Lane Mobile Home
Pk SO45 ......150 A3
Lime St SO14 ......103 A2
Lime Tree Cl SP6 ......92 C3
Lime Tree Ho SO41 ......197 C2
Lime Wlk Botley SO30 ......105 C4
Hythe SO45 ......125 C1
Limekiln La
Bishop's Waltham SO32 ......59 C2
East Meon GU32 ......64 B3
Limes Cl GU33 ......20 C2
Limes The Gosport PO13 ......155 B1
Havant PO9 ......159 C4
Marchwood SO40 ......102 A1
Waterlooville PO7 ......134 B2
Limetree Wlk PO8 ......11 B4
Limited Rd BH9 ......190 A1
Lin Brook Dr BH24 ......117 B1
Linacre Rd SO19 ......104 B3
Linbrook Ct BH24 ......117 A1
Lincoln Ave
Bournemouth BH1 ......205 B3
Christchurch BH23 ......191 C1
Lincoln Cl
Locks Heath PO14 ......129 B2
Romsey SO51 ......28 A1
Lincoln Ct Gosport PO13 ......180 B3
Southampton SO15 ......78 C1
West End SO30 ......80 B1
Lincoln Rd Poole BH12 ......203 B4
Portsmouth PO1 ......182 C3
Lincoln Rise PO8 ......112 A2
Lincolns Rise SO50 ......31 A1
Lind Cl PO7 ......134 C2
Lind Rd PO12 ......181 B1
Linda Gr PO8 ......111 C2
Linda Rd SO45 ......151 A2
Lindbergh Cl PO13 ......180 B3
Lindbergh Rd BH21 ......165 A4
Lindbergh Rise PO15 ......129 C3
Linden Cl Ferndown BH22 ......165 B1
Waltham Chase SO32 ......83 C2
Linden Ct
Locks Heath SO31 ......129 B2
Ringwood BH24 ......140 C4
[10] Romsey SO51 ......54 C2
West End SO18 ......80 A2
Linden Dr GU33 ......20 C2
Linden Gdns
Hedge End SO30 ......105 B3
Ringwood BH24 ......140 C4
Linden Gr
Chandler's Ford SO53 ......55 B4
Gosport PO12 ......181 A2
South Hayling PO11 ......185 A2
Linden Lea PO16 ......132 B1
Linden Rd
Bournemouth BH9 ......190 A2
Ferndown BH22 ......165 B1
Poole BH12 ......203 B3
Romsey SO51 ......52 C4
Southampton SO16 ......78 A2
Linden Way Havant PO9 ......135 C2
Lymington SO41 ......197 B2
Waterlooville PO8 ......112 B3
Linden Wlk SO52 ......53 C3
Lindens Cl PO10 ......138 C1
Lindens The BH23 ......192 B2
Lindisfarne Cl PO6 ......158 A4
Lindley Ave PO4 ......183 A1
Lindsay Ho **[5]** PO5 ......182 B1
Lindsay Manor **[16]** BH12 ......204 A2
Lindsay Pk **[6]** BH13 ......204 A2
Lindsay Rd Poole BH13 ......204 A2
Southampton SO19 ......104 C3
Lindum Ct **[3]** BH2 ......204 A2
Lindvray SO31 ......129 A3
Liners Ind Est SO15 ......102 B3
Lineside BH23 ......207 B4
Linford Cl BH25 ......195 A2
Linford Cres SO16 ......78 B2
Linford Ct Fair Oak SO50 ......57 B1

Linford Ct continued
Havant PO9 ......135 B4
Linford Ho BH24 ......117 C2
Linford Rd BH24 ......117 B1
Ling Dale SO16 ......78 C4
Ling Rd BH12 ......188 A1
Lingdale Pl **[3]** SO17 ......103 A4
Lingdale Rd BH6 ......206 B3
Lingfield Ct **[20]** PO1 ......182 A2
Lingfield Gdns SO18 ......79 C1
Lingfield Grange BH4 ......204 A2
Lingwood Ave BH23 ......207 C3
Lingwood Cl SO16 ......78 C4
Lingwood Wlk SO16 ......78 C4
Linhorns La BH25 ......195 A3
Link Rd Ringwood BH24 ......141 B4
Southampton SO16 ......77 C2
Link Rise BH21 ......186 C3
Link The PO7 ......112 A1
Link Way PO14 ......129 A4
Linkenholt Way PO9 ......135 B2
Linklater Path PO1 ......182 B4
Links Cl PO9 ......113 A1
Links Dr BH23 ......191 B1
Links La
Rowland's Castle PO9 ......113 A1
South Hayling PO11 ......184 B2
Links Rd Poole BH14 ......203 B1
Winchester SO22 ......1 B1
Links The PO13 ......155 B1
Links View Ave BH14 ......203 C1
Links View Way SO16 ......78 C3
Linkside Ave BH8 ......205 C4
Linmead Dr BH11 ......189 A3
Linnet Cl Petersfield GU31 ......41 B1
Ringwood BH24 ......141 B3
Waterlooville PO8 ......111 C2
Linnet Ct Gosport PO12 ......180 C3
New Milton BH25 ......194 C2
Linnet Rd BH17 ......201 C4
Linnet Sq SO50 ......55 B1
Linnets The
Portchester PO16 ......155 C4
Totton SO40 ......100 B4
Linnies La SO41 ......196 A4
Linthorpe Rd BH15 ......202 C2
Linwood Cl SO45 ......126 A1
Linwood Mix Sch BH9 ......205 A4
Linwood Rd BH9 ......205 A4
Lion Brewery The **[24]**
PO2 ......182 B4
Lion Ho PO17 ......108 A2
Lion Rd PO1 ......181 C4
Lion St PO1 ......182 A3
Lion Terr PO1 ......182 A3
Lionheart Cl BH11 ......188 B3
Lionheart Way SO31 ......105 A1
Lions Hall **[38]** SO22 ......10 C4
Lions La BH24 ......139 B3
Lions Wood BH24 ......139 C2
Liphook Ho **[9]** PO9 ......136 A3
Lipizzaner Fields SO31 ......129 A4
Lippen La SO32 ......36 C2
Lisbon Rd SO15 ......102 B3
Lisle Cl Lymington SO41 ......197 B2
Winchester SO22 ......10 A2
Lisle Court Rd SO41 ......198 B2
Lisle Ct SO22 ......10 C3
Lisle Way PO10 ......136 C2
Liss Inf & Jun Schs GU33 ......21 A2
Liss Rd PO4 ......182 C2
Liss GU33 ......20 C2
Litchfield Cres SO18 ......79 C1
Litchfield Rd
Southampton SO18 ......79 C1
Winchester SO22 ......1 B1
Litchford Rd BH25 ......195 B2
Lith Ave PO8 ......112 B4
Little Abshot Rd PO14 ......153 A4
Little Anglesey PO12 ......181 A1
Little Anglesey Rd
PO12 ......181 A1
Little Arthur St PO2 ......182 C4
Little Ashton La SO32 ......59 C2
Little Barn Pl GU33 ......21 A2
Little Barrs Dr BH25 ......195 A2
Little Barrs BH13 ......214 C3
Little Gays PO14 ......179 A3
Little George St PO1 ......182 C4
Little Gr PO12 ......181 A1
Little Green Orch PO12 ......181 A1
Little Hambrook St **[6]**
PO5 ......215 A1
Little Holbury Park Mobile
Home Pk SO45 ......150 A3
Little Hyden La PO8 ......88 A4
Little Kimble Wlk **[3]**
SO30 ......105 B3
Little La PO12 ......181 A1
Little Lance's Hill SO19 ......103 C3
Little Lonnen BH21 ......163 C4
Little Mead PO7 ......111 A2
Little Minster St SO23 ......11 A4
Little Oak Rd SO16 ......78 C2
Little Park Cl SO30 ......105 A3

Little Park Farm Rd
PO15 ......129 B3
Little Park Mans PO17 ......107 C2
Little Quob La SO30 ......80 C1
Little Reynolds SO40 ......100 B3
Little Shore La SO32 ......83 B4
Little Southsea St PO5 ......215 A1
Little Toller SO16 ......78 C4
Little Woodfalls Dr SP5 ......47 B2
Little Woodham La
PO13 ......180 B3
Littlecroft Ave BH9 ......190 A2
Littledown Ave BH7 ......205 C4
Littledown Dr BH7 ......205 C4
Littlefield Cres SO53 ......54 C3
Littlegreen Ave PO9 ......136 A2
Littlegreen Sch PO18 ......90 C2
Littlemead Cl BH17 ......202 A4
Littlemeads SO51 ......52 B4
Littlemill La SP6 ......68 B3
Littlemoor Ave BH11 ......188 B2
Littlepark Ave PO9 ......135 A2
Littleton Gr PO9 ......135 C2
Littleton La SO21 ......1 A3
Littleton Rd SO22 ......1 A2
Littlewood SO11 ......50 C2
Littlewood Gdns
Locks Heath SO31 ......128 C2
West End SO30 ......80 B1
Liverpool Ct PO13 ......180 B3
Liverpool Rd
Gosport PO14 ......154 C3
Portsmouth PO1 ......182 C3
Liverpool St SO14 ......103 A4
Livesay Gdns PO1 ......182 C3
Livingston Rd BH12 ......203 B3
Livingstone Ct PO13 ......180 B3
Livingstone Rd
Bournemouth BH5 ......206 A3
Christchurch BH23 ......207 B4
Portsmouth PO5 ......215 C1
Southampton SO14 ......103 A4
Wimborne Minst BH21 ......163 C2
Llewellin Cl BH16 ......201 B4
Llewellin Ct BH16 ......201 B4
Lloyd Ave SO40 ......101 C1
Loaders Cl BH9 ......205 A4
Loane Rd SO19 ......103 C2
Lobelia Rd SO16 ......79 A2
Locarno Rd PO3 ......158 A1
Loch Rd BH14 ......203 C3
Lock App PO6 ......157 A4
Lock View PO6 ......157 A4
Lock's Cotts SO45 ......125 B3
Locke Rd SO30 ......105 B4
Lockerley Cl SO41 ......197 C1
Lockerley Cres SO16 ......77 C1
Lockerley Endowed CE Prim
Sch SO51 ......5 A1
Lockerley Rd PO9 ......136 A2
Lockerly Ct SO15 ......102 C4
Lockhams Rd SO32 ......106 C4
Locks Heath Cl SO31 ......129 A2
Locks Heath Jun & Inf Schs
SO31 ......129 A1
Locks Rd SO31 ......129 B1
Locksheath Cl **[6]** PO9 ......135 B3
Locksheath Park Rd
SO31 ......129 A1
Locksley Dr BH23 ......165 B2
Locksley Rd SO50 ......55 C1
Locksway Rd PO4 ......183 B2
Lockswood Keep SO31 ......129 A2
Lockswood Rd SO31 ......128 C2
Lockyer Cl GU32 ......41 A3
Lockyer's Mid Sch BH21 ......186 B4
Lockyer's Rd BH21 ......186 C4
Lockyers Dr BH22 ......165 C3
Lode Hill SP5 ......47 A4
Loders Cl BH17 ......187 B2
Lodge Ave PO6 ......158 A4
Lodge Cl BH14 ......203 C2
Lodge Ct BH14 ......203 C2
Lodge Dro SP5 ......47 B2
Lodge Gdns PO12 ......181 A2
Lodge Hill PO17 ......109 A3
Lodge Rd
Christchurch BH23 ......206 C4
Havant PO9 ......135 A1
Locks Heath SO31 ......129 A2
Lymington SO41 ......197 A2
Southampton SO14 ......103 A4
Lodge The
Bournemouth BH2 ......204 C2
Christchurch BH23 ......165 A2
Waterlooville PO7 ......135 A3
Lodge Vale SO51 ......51 A1
Lodgebury Cl PO10 ......161 C4
Lodsworth Cl PO8 ......88 B2
Lodsworth Ho PO1 ......182 C4
Loewy Cres BH12 ......188 B1
Lofting Cl **[1]** SO50 ......56 C1
Logan Cl SO16 ......77 C3
Lomax Cl SO30 ......81 B1
Lombard Ave BH6 ......206 B3
Lombard Ct **[9]** PO1 ......182 A2
Lombard St PO1 ......182 A2
Lombardy Cl
Gosport PO13 ......155 C1
Lombardy Rise PO7 ......113 A3
Lomond Ave PO7 ......134 C4
Lomer La BH24 ......93 B2
Lomond Cl PO2 ......182 C4
Londesborough Rd PO4 ......182 C2
London Ave PO2 ......157 B1
London Ct PO12 ......181 A1

London La BH23 ......167 C1
London Rd Clanfield PO8 ......88 B2
Cosham PO7 ......134 B2
Hill Brow GU33 ......21 A1
Horndean PO8 ......88 B2
Kings Worthy SO23 ......2 A3
Petersfield GU31 ......41 A3
Portsmouth PO2 ......157 C2
Southampton SO15 ......103 A3
Steep GU31 ......41 B3
Waterlooville PO7, PO6 ......134 B2
London Tavern Cvn Pk The
BH24 ......141 B4
Lone Barn La SO22 ......60 C4
Lone Pine Dr BH22 ......165 C2
Lone Pine Way BH22 ......165 C1
Lone Valley PO7 ......134 B2
Long Acre Ct PO1 ......182 C4
Long Beech Dr SO40 ......100 B3
Long Cl Downton SP5 ......46 C4
Winchester SO23 ......10 C3
Long Copse SO45 ......150 C2
Long Copse Ct PO10 ......136 C2
Long Copse La PO10 ......137 A2
Long Curtain Rd PO5 ......182 A1
Long Down GU31 ......41 A2
Long Dr Gosport PO13 ......155 B1
West End SO30 ......80 C1
Long La Bursledon SO31 ......105 A1
Holbury SO45 ......150 C2
Marchwood SO40 ......101 B3
Ringwood BH24 ......141 A2
Wimborne Minst BH21 ......163 C4
Long Lane Cl SO45 ......150 B2
Long Priors GU32 ......37 A3
Long Rd
Bournemouth BH10 ......189 B3
Petersfield GU32 ......41 A3
Soberton SO32 ......85 B3
Long Water Dr PO12 ......181 B1
Long Wlk
Portsmouth PO1 ......182 B4
Winchester SO21 ......2 C1
Longacre Cl GU33 ......21 A2
Longacre Dr BH22 ......165 B2
Longacres PO14 ......129 B2
Longbarrow Cl BH8 ......191 A1
Longbridge Cl SO40 ......76 B1
Longbridge Ho SO40 ......76 B1
Longbridge Ho **[7]** PO5 ......215 B2
Longbridge Ind Pk
SO14 ......103 B2
Longclose Rd SO30 ......105 B4
Longcroft PO9 ......135 C1
Longden Cl **[1]** PO6 ......133 A1
**Longdown Dairy Farm*
SO40 ......100 B1
Longespee Rd BH21 ......187 C4
Longfield Ave PO14 ......154 C4
Longfield Cl PO14 ......183 B3
Longfield Dr
Bournemouth BH11 ......189 A3
Ferndown BH22 ......189 C4
Longfield Rd
Emsworth PO10 ......136 C2
Fair Oak SO50 ......57 B1
Hordle SO41 ......196 A1
Winchester SO23 ......11 B4
Longfleet CE Comb Sch
BH15 ......202 B2
Longfleet Rd BH15 ......202 C2
Longford Pl SO41 ......197 B1
Longhouse Gn **[9]** SO23 ......11 B4
Longlands Rd PO10 ......161 B4
Longleat Gdns
New Milton BH25 ......194 C2
Southampton SO16 ......78 A2
Longmead Cl GU32 ......20 C2
Longmead Ave SO50 ......56 B2
Longmead Ct PO9 ......159 C4
Longmead Gdns PO9 ......159 C4
Longmead Rd
Burley BH24 ......142 C2
[1] Southampton SO18 ......80 A1
Longmeadow Gdns
SO45 ......125 C1
Longmeadow La BH17 ......201 C4
Longmore Ave SO19 ......103 B1
Longmore Cres SO19 ......103 B1
Longmynd Dr PO14 ......154 B4
Longridge Rd SO30 ......105 B3
Longs La PO14 ......154 B2
Longshore Way PO4 ......183 B2
Longspee Sch BH17 ......202 B4
Longstaff Gdns PO16 ......130 C2
Longstock Cl SO19 ......127 A4
Longstock Cres SO40 ......100 C4
Longstock Rd PO9 ......136 A3
Longwood Ave PO8 ......112 A2
Longwood Dean La SO32,
SO23 ......34 A3
Longwood Rd SO21 ......33 B3
Longworth Rd SO45 ......125 C1
Lonnen Rd BH21 ......164 A4
Lonnen Wood Cl BH21 ......164 A4
Lonsdale Ave
Cosham PO6 ......158 A4
Portchester PO16 ......156 B3
Lonsdale Rd BH3 ......204 C3
Loosehanger SP5 ......47 C2
Loperwood SO40 ......76 A1
Loperwood La Ower SO40 ......76 A2
Totton SO40 ......76 B3
Loraine Ave BH23 ......209 B4
Lord Cl BH17 ......202 C4
Lord Montgomery Way **[1]**
PO1 ......215 A2

Lord Mountbatten Cl
SO18 ......79 C2
Lord Wilson Sch SO31 ......128 C2
Lord's Hill Ctr **[5]** SO16 ......77 C2
Lord's Hill Ctr W SO16 ......77 C2
Lord's Hill Way SO16 ......78 A3
Lordington Cl PO6 ......158 A4
Lords Cl PO1 ......215 C4
Lords St PO1 ......215 C4
Lordswood SO50 ......56 C4
Lordswood Cl SO16 ......78 B2
Lordswood Gdns SO16 ......78 B2
Lordswood Inf Sch SO16 ......78 B2
Lordswood Jun Sch SO16 ......78 B2
Loreille Gdns SO16 ......77 C4
Loring Ho **[7]** PO2 ......157 C2
Lorne Park Rd BH1 ......205 A2
Lorne Pl SO18 ......104 A4
Lorne Rd PO5 ......215 C4
Lortemore Pl **[8]** SO51 ......52 C4
Loughwood Cl SO50 ......56 A3
Louis Flagg Ho **[2]** PO5 ......215 B2
Lovage Gdns SO40 ......100 B4
Lovage Way PO8 ......88 B1
Lovatt Gr PO15 ......130 B2
Love La
Milford on Sea SO41 ......211 B3
Petersfield GU31 ......41 A2
Romsey SO51 ......52 C4
Twyford SO21 ......32 A3
Upham SO24,SO32 ......35 A2
Woodgreen SP6 ......70 C4
Lovedean La
Horndean PO8 ......111 C3
Waterlooville PO8 ......111 C3
Lovedon La SO23 ......2 B4
Lovett Rd PO3 ......158 A2
Lovett Wlk SO22 ......1 B2
Lowcay Rd PO5 ......182 C1
Lowden Cl SO22 ......10 B2
Lower Alfred St **[10]**
SO14 ......103 A3
Lower Ashley Rd PO5 ......195 B1
Lower Banister St **[7]**
SO15 ......102 C3
Lower Bartons SP6 ......69 C1
Lower Baybridge La
SO21 ......33 B1
Lower Bellfield PO14 ......153 C4
Lower Bere Wood PO7 ......134 C4
Lower Blandford Rd
BH18 ......187 A2
Lower Brook St SO23 ......11 A4
Lower Brookfield Rd
PO1 ......182 C3
Lower Brownhill Rd
SO16 ......77 B2
Lower Buckland Rd
SO41 ......197 B3
Lower Canal Wlk SO14 ......103 A2
Lower Chase Rd SO32 ......83 C2
Lower Church Path
PO1 ......215 B3
Lower Church Rd PO14 ......129 B2
Lower Common La
BH21 ......139 A4
Lower Common Rd SO51 ......50 C2
Lower Crabbick La PO7 ......110 A1
Lower Densome Wood
SP6 ......70 C4
Lower Derby Rd PO2 ......157 B1
Lower Drayton La PO6 ......158 A4
Lower Duncan Rd SO31 ......129 A3
Lower Farlington Rd
PO6 ......158 C4
Lower Farm La SO51 ......29 A2
Lower Forbury Rd PO5 ......215 B2
Lower Golf Links Rd
BH18 ......187 A3
Lower Gr Rd PO5 ......45 A1
Lower Grove Rd PO9 ......160 A4
Lower Heyshott GU31 ......41 A2
Lower La SO32 ......83 B4
Lower Lamborough La
SO24 ......14 B3
Lower Mead GU31 ......41 A2
Lower Mead End Rd
SO41 ......171 C1
Lower Moors Rd SO21 ......31 C1
Lower Mortimer Rd
SO19 ......103 B2
Lower Mullin's La SO45 ......125 C2
Lower New Rd SO30 ......80 B1
Lower Northam Rd
SO30 ......105 B4
Lower Pennington La
SO41 ......212 B4
Lower Quay PO16 ......155 A4
Lower Quay Cl PO16 ......155 A4
Lower Quay Rd PO16 ......155 A4
Lower Rd PO9 ......135 B1
Lower Sandy Down La
SO41 ......173 B2
Lower Spinney SO31 ......152 B4
Lower St SO51 ......28 A4
Lower St Helens Rd
SO30 ......105 B3
Lower Stanmore La
SO23 ......10 C3
Lower Swanwick Rd
SO31 ......128 A4
Lower Vicarage Rd
SO19 ......103 B2
Lower Wardown GU31 ......41 A2
Lower William St SO14 ......103 B3
Lower William St Ind Est
SO14 ......103 B3

Lower Wingfield St
PO1 ....215 C4
Lower Woodside SO41 .....212 C4
Lower York St SO14 ....103 B3
Lowesmore St BH14 ....203 B2
Lowestoft Rd PO6 ....133 B1
Loweswater Rd PO PO6 ...133 A1
Lowford Will SO31 ....104 C1
Lowland Rd PO7 ....110 C2
Lowry Gdns SO19 ....104 B1
Lowther Gdns 3 BH8 .....205 B3
Lowther Rd BH8 ....205 A3
Loxwood Rd PO8 ....111 C3
Luard Ct 7 PO9 ....136 A1
Lucas Cl SO16 ....77 C3
Lucas Rd Poole BH15 .....202 A1
Poole, Upper Parkstone
BH12 ....203 B3
Luccombe Pl SO16 ....78 B1
Luccombe Rd SO16 ....78 B1

Lucerne Ave
Bournemouth BH6 ....206 B3
Waterlooville PO7 ....111 B1
Lucerne Gdns SO30 ......105 A4
Lucerne Rd SO41 ....211 B2
Luckham Cl BH9 ....190 A1
Luckham Gdns BH9 ....190 B1
Luckham Pl BH9 ....190 A1
Luckham Rd BH9 ....190 A1
Luckham Rd E BH9 ....190 A1
Lucknow St PO1 ....215 D3
Lucky La SO41 ....174 A1
Ludcombe PO7 ....110 C2
Ludlow Inf Sch SO19 .....103 C2
Ludlow Jun Sch SO19 ....103 C2
Ludlow Rd Cosham PO6 ...133 B1
Southampton SO19 ....103 C2
Ludwell's La SO32 ....83 C2
Lugano Cl PO7 ....111 B1
Lukes Cl SO31 ....128 A1
Lukin Dr SO16 ....77 B3
Lulworth Ave SO16 ....201 C1
Lulworth Bsns Ctr SO40 ..76 C1

Lulworth Cl
Chandler's Ford SO53 .....55 A2
Hamworthy BH15 ....201 C1
South Hayling PO11 ......185 A3
Southampton SO16 ....201 C1
Lulworth Cres BH23 ......205 C1
Lulworth Gn SO16 ....77 C1
Lulworth Rd PO13 ....179 C1
Lumby Dr BH24 ....141 A4
Lumby Drive Cvn Pk 3
BH24 ....141 A4
Lumley Gdns PO10 ......161 A4
Lumley Rd PO10 ....137 A1
Lumley Terr PO10 ....137 A1
Lumsden Ave SO15 ....102 B4
Lumsden Mans 3 SO15 ..102 B4
Lumsden Rd PO4 ....183 B2
Lundy Cl SO16 ....77 C3
Lundy Wlk PO14 ....154 A2
Lunedale Rd SO45 ....149 C4
Lupin Rd SO16 ....79 B3
Luscombe Rd BH14 ......203 B1
Luther Rd BH9 ....204 C4
Lutman St PO10 ....136 C2
Luton Rd SO19 ....104 A2
Luxton Cl SO30 ....105 C4
Luzborough La SO51 ......53 B3
Lyburn Cl SO16 ....78 B2
Lyburn Ct SO16 ....78 B2
Lyburn Ho SP5 ....73 A4
Lych Gate Ct BH24 ......141 A3
Lychgate Dr PO8 ....112 A4
Lychgate Gn PO14 ....154 B3
Lydden Ct 1 PO13 ....155 B1
Lydford Gdns BH11 ......189 A1
Lydford Rd BH11 ....189 A1
Lydgate SO40 ....100 C4
Lydgate Cl SO19 ....104 B2
Lydgate Gn SO19 ....104 B2
Lydgate Rd SO19 ....104 B2
Lydgate The SO41 ....211 A3
Lydiard Cl SO50 ....56 A3
Lydlinch Cl BH22 ....165 B1
Lydlynch Inf Sch SO40 ...100 C4
Lydlynch Rd SO40 ....100 C4
Lydney Cl PO6 ....157 B4
Lydney Rd BH11 ....189 C3
Lydwell Cl BH11 ....188 C3
Lyell Rd BH12 ....203 B3
Lymbourn Rd PO9 ....136 A1
Lyme Cl SO50 ....55 C3
Lyme Cres BH23 ....208 C4
Lymefields SO41 ....211 C3
Lymer La SO16 ....77 B3
Lymer Villas SO16 ....77 B3

Lymington Cath Sch
SO41 ....197 C2
Lymington CE Inf Sch
SO41 ....197 B2
Lymington Hospl SO41 ...197 C2
Lymington Infmy & Day Hospl
SO41 ....197 C2
Lymington Jun Sch
SO41 ....197 B2
Lymington Pier Sta
SO41 ....198 A2

Lymington Rd
Barton on Sea BH25 ......195 B1
Brockenhurst SO42 ......146 A1
Christchurch BH23 ....208 C4
East Boldre SO41 ....199 A4
Milford on Sea SO41 .....211 C3
Lymington Town Sta
SO41 ....197 C2

Lymington Vineyard*
SO41 ....197 A1
Lymore La SO41 ....211 C3
Lymore Valley SO41 .....211 C3
Lynch Cl SO22 ....1 C1
Lynch La GU32 ....37 B2
Lyndale Cl SO41 ....211 C1
Lyndale Rd SO31 ....129 B2
Lynden Cl PO14 ....154 A4
Lynden Gate SO19 ....104 A2
Lyndhurst CE Inf Sch
SO43 ....121 C3
Lyndhurst Cl
South Hayling PO11 ......185 A2
Winchester SO22 ....1 B2
Lyndhurst Hill SO40 ......98 C4
Lyndhurst Ho PO9 ....135 C3
Lyndhurst Jun Sch PO2 ..157 C1
Lyndhurst Rd
Ashurst SO40 ....100 A1
Bransgore BH23 ....193 B3
Brockenhurst SO42 ......146 A1
Burley BH24 ....143 B3
Burton BH23 ....193 B3
Cadnam SO40 ....98 C4
Christchurch BH23 ....193 B1
Gosport PO12 ....181 A2
Landford SP5 ....49 B2
Portsmouth PO2 ....157 C1
Lyndock Cl SO19 ....103 C1
Lyndock Pl SO19 ....103 C1
Lyndum Cl GU32 ....40 C2
Lyne PF PO8 ....112 A3
Lyne's La PO14 ....140 C4
Lynford Ave SO22 ....1 C1
Lynford Way SO22 ....1 C1
Lynn Cl SO18 ....80 A2
Lynn Rd Poole BH17 .....187 C1
Portsmouth PO2 ....182 C4
Lynric Cl BH25 ....210 A4
Lynton Cres BH23 ....191 B2
Lynton Cl SO40 ....100 C3
Lynton Gdns PO16 ......130 C2
Lynton Gr PO3 ....183 A4

Lynton Rd
Hedge End SO30 ....105 B4
Petersfield GU32 ....40 C2
Lynwood Ave PO8 ....111 B2
Lynwood Ct BH24 ......165 B4
Lynwood Ct
Lymington SO41 ....197 B2
Winchester SO22 ....1 C1
Lyon Ave BH25 ....195 A2
Lyon Rd BH12 ....188 C1
Lyon St SO14 ....103 A3
Lysander Cl SO19 ....104 B4
Lysander Dr PO8 ....108 A4
Lysander Ct PO3 ....182 A2
Lysander Way PO7 ......135 B4
Lyse Ct GU33 ....20 C2
Lysses PO16 ....131 B1
Lyster Rd SP6 ....79 B3
Lystra Rd BH9 ....190 A2
Lytchett Dr BH18 ....187 A2
Lytchett Way BH16 ......201 A3
Lytteltane Rd SO41 .....197 B1

Lytham Rd
Broadstone BH18 ....187 A2
Southampton SO18 ....80 A1
Lytton Cl
Bournemouth BH1 ....205 B3
Hythe SO45 ....126 A1

M

Mabey Ave BH10 ....189 B1
Mabey Cl PO12 ....181 B1
Mablethorpe Rd PO6 ....133 C1
Macandrew Rd BH13 ....214 C4
Macarthur Cres SO18 ...104 A4
Macaulay Ave PO6 ......132 C1
Mafeking Rd PO4 ....158 C2
Macklin Ho 54 SO22 .....10 C4
Maclaren Rd BH9 ....189 C2
Maclean Rd BH11 ....188 C2
Macnaghten Rd SO18 ...103 B4
Maddison Ct SO41 ....180 C2
Maddison St 5 SO14 ....102 C2
Maddoford La SO32 ......82 A1
Maddoxford Way SO32 ...81 C1

Madeira Rd
Bournemouth BH1 ....205 A2
Poole BH14 ....203 B3
Portsmouth PO2 ....157 C2
Madeline Cl BH12 ....203 A4
Madeline Cres BH12 ....203 A4
Madeline Rd GU31 ....40 C2
Madison Ave BH1 ....205 B3
Madison Cl SO19 ....180 C4
Madison Ct 10 PO16 ....131 B1
Madrisa Ct SO41 ....197 C2
Mafeking Rd PO4 ....158 C2
Maffey Cct SO30 ....106 A4
Mag's Barrow BH22 .....165 C1
Magazine La SO40 ......102 A2
Magdala Rd Cosham PO6 .157 C4
South Hayling PO11 ......185 A4
Magdalen Cl 3 BH2 ....205 A2
Magdalen Hill SO23 ......11 A4
Magdalen La BH23 ......208 C4
Magdalen Mews 48 SO23 .11 A4
Magdalen Rd SO19 ......103 C2
Magdalene Way PO14 ...129 B1
Magennis Cl PO13 ......180 B4

Magenta Ct PO13 ....180 B3
Magna Cl 2 BH11 ......188 C3
Magna Gdns BH11 ......188 C3
Magna Rd BH11 ....188 B4

Magnolia Cl
Bournemouth BH6 ....207 A3
Fareham PO14 ....154 C4
Hythe SO45 ....125 B2
Verwood BH31 ....115 B2
Magnolia Gn SO41 ......211 C3
Magnolia Rd SO19 ......103 C3
Magnolia Terr PO7 .....134 C3
Magnolia Way PO14 ....112 B2
Magpie Cl
Bournemouth BH8 ....190 B2
Fareham PO16 ....131 C1
Magpie Cotts PO8 ......113 B2
Magpie Dr SO40 ....100 B4
Magpie Gdns SO40 .....104 B2
Magpie Gr BH25 ....194 C1
Lee-on-the-Solent PO13 ..155 C1
Magpie Rd PO8 ....113 B3
Magpie Wlk PO8 ....111 B2
Maiden La SO41 ....197 C1
Maidford Gr PO3 ....158 B2
Maidment Cl BH11 ......188 C2
Maidstone Cres PO6 ....133 C1
Main Dr PO17 ....133 A3
Main Rd
Colden Common SO21 ....32 A1
Compton(Hants) SO21 ....31 B2
East Boldre SO41,SO42 ...199 A4
Fawley SO45 ....150 B3
Gosport PO13 ....155 B3
Hermitage PO10,PO18 ...161 B4
Hythe SO45 ....125 B2
Littleton SO22 ....1 A3
Marchwood SO40 ....101 C1
Otterbourne SO21 ....31 A2
Owslebury SO21 ....33 A2
Portsmouth PO1 ....157 C4
Southbourne PO10,PO18 .161 B4
Totton SO40 ....100 C2
Boldre SO41 ....198 A4

Mainline Bsns Ctr GU33 .20 C2
Mainsail Dr PO16 ....155 A4
Mainstream SO45 ....52 B3
Mainstream Ct SO50 .....56 B2
Maisemore Gdns PO10 ..160 B4
Maitland Cres PO1 ......182 B4
Maitland Ct SO41 ....197 B2
Maitland St PO1 ....182 B4
Maitlands The BH2 ......204 B1
Maizemore Wlk 21
PO13 ....179 C1
Majestic Rd SO16 ....77 A2
Major Ct PO12 ....181 A4
Majoram Way PO15 .....129 B4
Majorca Mans 11 BH2 ..204 C2
Malan Cl BH17 ....202 C4

Malcolm Cl
Chandler's Ford SO53 ....30 C1
Locks Heath SO31 ......129 A2
Malcolm Rd SO53 ....30 C1
Malcomb Cl BH6 ....207 A2
Malcroft Mews SO40 ...102 A1
Maldon Cl SO50 ....56 B2
Maldon Rd
5 Cosham PO6 ....157 B4
Southampton SO18 .....103 C2
Malibres Rd SO53 ....55 C4
Malin Cl
Southampton SO16 ....77 C2
Stubbington PO14 ......154 A2
Malins Rd PO2 ....182 B4
Mall The Burley BH24 ...143 A2
Chandler's Ford SO53 ....55 C4
Portsmouth PO2 ....157 B1
Mallard Bldgs 3 BH25 ..195 A2
Mallard Cl
Bishop's Waltham SO32 ...83 A4
Bournemouth BH8 ....190 B1
Christchurch BH23 ......193 A4
Horde SO41 ....196 A2
Romsey SO51 ....52 C4
Mallard Gdns
Gosport PO13 ....155 A1
Hedge End SO30 ....81 B1
Mallard Rd
Bournemouth BH8 ....190 B1
Locks Heath SO31 ......129 B2
Ringwood BH24 ....140 C4
Rowland's Castle PO9 ...113 A1
Wimborne Minst BH21 ..164 A4
Mallard Way PO10 ......137 B2
Mallards Rd SO31 ......127 C4
Mallards The
Fareham PO16 ....131 A2
Havant PO9 ....135 C3
Mallett Cl SO30 ....81 C1
Mallory Cl BH23 ....207 C4
Mallory Cres PO16 ......131 A2
Mallow Cl
Broadstone BH18 ....186 C2
Christchurch BH23 ......208 B4
5 Fareham PO15 ....130 C4
Locks Heath SO31 ......128 C1
Waterlooville PO7 ......134 C3
Mallow Rd SO30 ....105 A4
Mallows The BH25 ......195 B2
Malmesbury Cl SO50 .....57 B1
Malmesbury Ct BH8 .....205 B3
Malmesbury Gdns SO22 ..1 B1
Malmesbury Park Pl 7
BH8 ....205 A3
Malmesbury Park Prim Sch
BH8 ....205 A3

Malmesbury Park Rd
BH8 ....205 A3
Malmesbury Pl SO15 ....102 B4
Malmesbury Rd
Romsey SO51 ....52 C4
Southampton SO15 .....102 B4
St Leonards BH24 ......139 C2
Southampton SO15 .....102 B4
Maloney Mews PO1 .....185 C1
Maloren Way BH22 .....139 A1
Malory Cl SO19 ....104 B3
Malt La SO32 ....83 B4
Malta Rd PO2 ....182 C4
Malthouse BH25 ....202 B1
Malthouse Cl
Romsey SO51 ....52 C4
Winchester SO21 ....2 C2
Malthouse Cotts SO51 ...77 A4
Malthouse Gdns SO41 ...101 C1
Malthouse La PO14 .....131 A1
Malthouse Rd PO2 ......182 B4
Maltings The
Bournemouth BH11 .....188 C3
Fareham PO16 ....131 B1
Petersfield GU31 ....40 C2
Malus Cl PO14 ....154 C4
Malvern Ave PO14 .....154 C4
Malvern Bsns Ctr SO16 ..78 B1
Malvern Cl
Bishop's Waltham SO32 ..83 B4
Bournemouth BH9 ......190 A2
Malvern Ct
4 Bournemouth BH9 ...190 A1
2 Christchurch BH23 ...207 C4
Malvern Dr SO45 ....125 B2
Malvern Gdns SO30 .....81 B1
Malvern Mews PO1 .....136 C1
Malvern Rd
Bournemouth BH9 ......190 A1
Gosport PO12 ....180 C3
Hill Brow GU33 ....21 A1
Portsmouth PO5 ....182 B1
Southampton SO16 ......78 B1
Malvern Terr SO14 ......78 B1
Malwood Ave SO16 ......78 B2
Malwood Cl PO9 ....136 A3
Malwood Gdns SO40 ...100 B4
Malwood Rd SO45 ......126 A2
Malwood Rd W SO45 ..125 C2
Manaton Way SO30 .....81 A1
Manchester Ct PO13 ...180 B3
Manchester Rd
1 Netley SO31 ....127 A3
Southampton PO2 ....182 C3
Sway SO41 ....172 A2
Manchester Terr PO10 ..137 A2
Mancroft Ave PO14 ....179 B3
Mandalay Dr BH11 .....114 C3
Mandale Cl BH11 ....189 A2
Mandale Rd BH11 ......188 C2
Mandarin Way PO15 ...102 C3
Mandela Way SO15 ....102 C3
Manderley SO41 ....211 C2
Manley Rd SO31 ....104 A4
Manners La PO4 ....182 C2
Manners Rd PO4 ....182 C2
Manning Ave BH23 .....193 B1
Manning's Heath Rd
PO12 ....188 A1
Manning's Heath Rdbt
BH17 ....188 A1
Mannings Heath Works
SO31 ....188 A1
Mannington Pl 18 BH2 ..204 C2
Mannington Way PO7 ..138 B1
Manns Cl SO18 ....80 B1
Mannyngham Way SO51 .27 B4
Manor Ave BH12 ....188 A1
Manor Cl 4 Burseldon SO31 .104 C1
Ferndown BH22 ....165 C3
Fordingbridge SP6 ....69 C1
10 Havant PO9 ....135 C1
Milford on Sea SO41 ....211 B3
Wickham PO17 ....108 A2
41 Winchester SO23 .....11 A4
Manor Cres
Burseldon SO31 ....104 C1
Hedge End SO30 ....81 B1
Manor Ct Havant PO9 ...135 B1
Locks Heath PO15 ......129 B2
Ringwood BH24 ....140 C4
Verwood BH31 ....114 C3
Manor Farm Cl
4 Bishopstoke SO50 ....56 C1
New Milton BH25 ....194 C1
Manor Farm Ctry Pk*
SO31 ....105 B2
Manor Farm Gr SO21 ....31 C3
Manor Farm Gr 3 SO50 ..56 C1
Manor Farm La SO21 ....31 C3
Manor Farm Mus*
SO30 ....105 C2
Manor Farm Rd
Bournemouth BH10 .....189 B4
Fordingbridge SP6 ....69 B1
Southampton SO18 ......79 B1
Manor Farmyard BH8 ...191 A2
Manor Flats SO21 ......31 C3
Manor Gdns
Ringwood BH24 ....140 C4
Southbourne PO10 .....137 B1
1 Verwood BH31 ....114 C3
Manor House Ave SO15 .101 C3
Manor Inf Sch
Holbury SO45 ....150 A2
Portsmouth PO1 ....182 C4

Low – Mar 245

Manor La BH31 ....114 C3
Manor Lodge Rd PO9 ...113 A1
Manor Park Ave PO3 ...183 A4
Manor Park Rd 14 SO18 .103 C4
Manor Pk PO15 ....202 A3
Manor Rd
Bishopstoke SO50 ....56 C1
Bournemouth BH1 ......205 B2
Chilworth SO16 ....54 B1
Christchurch BH23 ......207 A3
Durley SO32 ....82 B4
East Tytherley SP5 ....4 C4
Holbury SO45 ....150 B2
Hythe SO45 ....125 A2
Milford on Sea SO41 ....211 B3
New Milton BH25 ....195 A2
North Hayling PO11 .....184 C3
Portsmouth PO1 ....182 C4
Ringwood BH24 ....140 C4
Southbourne PO10 .....137 B1
Twyford SO21 ....31 C3
Verwood BH31 ....114 C3
Manor Rd N SO19 ....103 C2
Manor Rd S SO19 ......103 C2
Manor Terr
Burseldon SO31 ....104 C1
Durley SO32 ....82 C4
Manor Villas PO17 .....108 A2
Manor Way
Lee-on-the-Solent PO13 ..179 C1
Lee-on-the-Solent PO13 ..179 C2
South Hayling PO11 ....185 A1
Southbourne PO10 .....137 B1
Verwood BH31 ....114 C4
Whites Way SO40 ......101 A4
Mansard Ct BH13 ......214 A2
Mansbridge Prim Sch
SO18 ....79 C2

Mansbridge Rd
Eastleigh SO50 ....56 A1
Southampton SO18 ......79 C2
Mansel Cl BH12 ....204 B4
Mansel Ct SO16 ....77 C1
Mansel Inf Sch SO16 ....77 B1
Mansel Jun Sch SO16 ...77 B1
Mansel Rd E SO16 ......77 C1
Mansel Rd W SO16 .....77 B1
Mansell Cl SO45 ....125 C1
Mansergh Wlk SO40 ...100 A4
Mansfield Ave BH14 ....203 B2
Mansfield Cl
Ferndown BH22 ....165 B1
Poole BH14 ....203 B2
Mansfield Rd
Bournemouth BH9 ......189 C2
Gosport PO13 ....180 B4
Poole BH14 ....203 B2
Ringwood BH24 ....140 C4
Mansion Ct 2 PO4 .....182 C1
Mansion Rd
Portsmouth PO4 ....182 C1
Southampton SO15 .....102 B3
Manston Ct SO16 ....77 C2
Mansvid Ave PO6 ....158 A4
Mantle Cl PO12 ....181 A4
Mantle Sq PO2 ....157 A1
Manton Cl BH15 ....201 C2
Manton Rd PO1 ....201 C2

Maple Cl
Barton on Sea BH25 ....210 A4
Burseldon SO31 ....127 C4
Christchurch BH23 ......208 C4
Emsworth PO10 ....136 C1
Fareham PO15 ....130 B1
Lee-on-the-Solent PO13 ..179 C1
Romsey SO51 ....52 B3
Maple Cres PO8 ....88 B3
Maple Ct SO19 ....103 C1
Maple Dr Denmead PO7 ..111 A2
Ferndown BH22 ....165 B4
Kings Worthy SO23 ....2 A4
Maple Gdns SO40 ......100 B3
Maple Ho SO16 ....78 C4
Maple Lo BH16 ....201 B4
Maple Rd
Bournemouth BH6 ......204 C4
Hythe SO45 ....150 A4
Poole BH15 ....202 B2
Portsmouth PO5 ....182 B1
Southampton SO18 .....103 C4
Maple Sq SO50 ....55 C3
Maple Wood PO9 ....135 A1
Mapleleaf Gdns 1 SO50 .56 A1
Maples The SO53 ....55 B4
Mapleton Rd SO30 .....105 B3
Mapperley Ave PO8 ....112 A2
Maplewood Cl SO40 ....100 B3
Mapperton Cl BH17 ....187 C1
Marabout Cl BH23 .....207 B4
Maralyn Ave PO7 ......134 C3
Marathon Pl SO50 ....57 A1
Marazan Rd PO3 ....158 A1
Marbrearn Cl SP6 ....69 B1
Marchesi Ct PO14 .....154 B2
Marchwood By Pass
Marchwood SO40 ......124 C4
Totton SO40 ....101 A2
Marchwood CE Inf Sch
SO40 ....124 C4
Marchwood Ct PO12 ...180 B2
Marchwood Ind Pk
SO40 ....102 A2

Marchwood Jun Sch
SO40 ....101 C1
Marchwood Rd
Bournemouth BH10 ....189 B2
Havant PO9 ....135 C3
Southampton SO15 ....102 A3
Totton SO40 ....101 B2
Marchwood Terr SO40 ....101 C1
Marcus Cl SO50 ....57 A1
Mardale Rd SO16 ....101 B4
Mardale Wlk SO16 ....101 B4
Marden Paddock SO42 ....145 C1
Marden Way GU31 ....41 A2
Mardon Cl SO18 ....79 C3
Mare La SO21 ....32 C3
Margam Ave SO19 ....103 C3
Margards La BH31 ....114 C3
Margaret Cl PO7 ....111 B1
Margarita Rd PO15 ....130 C1
Margate Rd PO5 ....215 C2
Margery's Ct 20 PO1 ....182 A3
Marian Cl BH21 ....186 B2
Marian Rd BH21 ....186 B2
Marianne Cl SO15 ....101 C3
Marianne Rd Poole BH12 ....204 B4
Wimborne Minst BH21 ....164 A4
Marie Ave SP5 ....46 B4
Marie Cl BH12 ....203 B4
Marie Ct 5 PO7 ....134 C4
Marie Rd SO19 ....104 B2
Marigold Cl PO15 ....130 C1
Marina Bldgs 3 PO12 ....181 A2
Marina Cl PO10 ....161 A4
Marina Ct
21 Bournemouth BH5 ....205 C2
Christchurch BH23 ....209 A4
Marina Dr
Hamble-le-Rice SO31 ....128 A1
Poole BH14 ....203 A1
Marina Gr
Portchester PO16 ....156 B3
Portsmouth PO3 ....183 A4
Marina Keep PO6 ....157 A3
Marina The BH5 ....205 C2
Marina Twrs 24 BH5 ....205 C2
Marina View
6 Christchurch BH23 ....207 A3
Netley SO31 ....126 C4
Marine Cotts 14 PO12 ....181 A3
Marine Ct
Barton on Sea BH25 ....209 B4
Portsmouth PO4 ....183 A1
Marine Dr BH25 ....209 C4
Marine Dr E BH25 ....210 A3
Marine Drive W BH25 ....209 C4
Marine Par SO14 ....103 A2
Marine Parade E PO13 ....179 C1
Marine Parade W PO13 ....179 B1
Marine Rd BH6 ....206 B2
Marine Wlk PO11 ....185 B2
Mariner's Cl SO31 ....128 A2
Mariners Ct
Christchurch BH23 ....208 A3
Lymington SO41 ....197 C1
Mariners Mews 7
SO45 ....126 A2
Mariners Way
Gosport PO12 ....181 B2
Locks Heath SO31 ....128 B1
Mariners Wlk PO4 ....183 A3
Marion Ct BH23 ....207 A4
Marion Rd PO4 ....182 C1
Maritime Ave SO40 ....102 A2
Maritime Mus* SO14 ....102 C2
Maritime Way SO14 ....103 A1
Maritime Wlk SO14 ....103 A1
Marjoram Cres PO8 ....112 A2
Mark Anthony Ct PO11 ....184 C2
Mark Cl Portsmouth PO3 ....157 C2
Southampton SO15 ....102 A4
Mark Ct PO7 ....134 C4
Mark Way SO51 ....4 B2
Mark's La BH25 ....195 A3
Mark's Rd PO14 ....179 C3
Markall Cl SO24 ....14 B3
Marken Cl SO31 ....128 C2
Market Bldgs SO16 ....79 B2
Market Cl BH15 ....202 B1
Market La SO23 ....11 A4
Market Par PO9 ....135 C1
Market Pl
Fordingbridge SP6 ....69 C1
Ringwood BH24 ....140 C4
Romsey SO51 ....52 C4
10 Southampton SO14 ....103 A2
Market St Eastleigh SO50 ....56 A1
Poole BH15 ....202 A1
Winchester SO23 ....11 A4
Market Way BH21 ....163 B2
Marketway PO1 ....215 B4
Markham Ave BH10 ....189 B4
Markham Cl BH10 ....189 B3
Markham Rd BH9 ....205 A4
Marks Rd BH9 ....189 C2
Marks Terr SO32 ....83 A4
Marks Tey Rd PO14 ....154 B3
Markway Cl PO10 ....136 B1
Marlands Lawn PO9 ....135 B3
Marlands The (Sh Ctr)
SO14 ....102 C2
Marlborough Cl PO7 ....134 B3
Marlborough Ct
21 Bournemouth BH4 ....204 B2
Chandler's Ford SO53 ....55 A2
Hythe SO45 ....125 C1
Marlborough Ct *continued*
7 Poole BH12 ....204 A2
3 Wimborne Minst BH21 ....163 B3
Marlborough Gdns SO30 ....81 B2
Marlborough Gr PO16 ....156 B4
Marlborough Ho SO15 ....102 C4
Marlborough Mans 2
BH7 ....206 A3
Marlborough Pk PO9 ....136 B2
Marlborough Pl
Lymington SO41 ....197 B3
Wimborne Minst BH21 ....163 B3
Marlborough Rd
Bournemouth BH4 ....204 B2
Chandler's Ford SO53 ....30 C1
Gosport PO12 ....180 C3
Poole BH14 ....203 B2
Southampton SO15 ....102 A4
Marlborough Row PO1 ....182 A3
Marldell Cl PO9 ....136 A3
Marler Ho BH4 ....204 A2
Marles Cl PO13 ....180 B4
Marley Ave BH25 ....194 C2
Marley Cl BH25 ....194 C2
Marley Mount SO41 ....171 C1
Marlhill Cl SO18 ....79 C1
Marlin Cl PO13 ....180 B3
Marline Rd BH12 ....203 B3
Marlott Rd BH15 ....202 B3
Marlow Cl PO15 ....130 C2
Marlow Dr BH23 ....191 C2
Marlow Rd SO32 ....83 A4
Marlowe Ct
Southampton SO19 ....103 C1
Waterlooville PO7 ....111 B1
Marlpit Dr BH23 ....194 A1
Marlpit La BH25 ....195 A4
Marls Rd SO30 ....105 C3
Marmion Ave PO5 ....182 B1
Marmion Gn BH23 ....207 C4
Marmion Rd PO5 ....182 B1
Marne Ho 9 PO14 ....154 C4
Marne Rd SO18 ....104 A4
Marnhull Rd BH15 ....202 B2
Marpet Cl BH11 ....188 C3
Marples Way PO9 ....135 B1
Marquis Way BH11 ....188 B3
Marram Cl SO41 ....197 C3
Marrelswood Gdns PO7 ....134 B2
Marryat Ct
Christchurch BH23 ....209 A4
New Milton BH25 ....194 C2
Marryat Rd BH25 ....194 C2
Marsden Rd PO6 ....157 A4
Marsh Cl PO6 ....158 B3
Marsh Gdns SO30 ....81 B1
Marsh Ho 20 SO14 ....103 A2
Marsh La Breamore SP6 ....70 A4
Christchurch BH23 ....191 C1
Fawley SO45 ....151 A2
Lymington SO41 ....197 C3
Southampton SO14 ....103 A2
Upton BH16 ....201 A4
Marsh Par 1 SO45 ....126 A2
Marsh The SO45 ....126 A2
Marshal Rd BH17 ....187 A1
Marshall Pl 9 SO16 ....78 C2
Marshall Rd PO11 ....185 B1
Marshfield BH21 ....163 C4
Marshfield Cl SO40 ....101 B1
Marshfield Ho PO6 ....158 B4
Marshlands Cl BH23 ....207 B3
Marshlands Rd PO6 ....158 B4
Marshlands Spur PO6 ....158 C4
Marshwood Ave
Poole BH17 ....187 C2
Waterlooville PO7 ....135 A4
Marston Cl BH25 ....195 A3
Marston Gate 5 SO23 ....11 A4
Marston Gr BH23 ....193 C1
Marston La PO3 ....158 A2
Marston Rd
New Milton BH25 ....195 A3
2 Poole BH15 ....202 A1
Southampton SO19 ....104 C3
Martello Cl PO12 ....180 B2
Martello Ho 10 BH13 ....214 C4
Martello Pk BH13 ....214 C4
Martello Rd BH13 ....203 C1
Martello Rd S BH13 ....214 C4
Martello Twrs BH13 ....214 C4
Martells Ct 1 PO1 ....182 A2
Martells The BH25 ....210 A4
Martin Ave
Denmead PO7 ....111 A2
Stubbington PO14 ....179 B3
Martin Cl
Broadstone BH17 ....201 C4
Lee-on-the-Solent PO13 ....179 C2
Swanmore SO32 ....84 A2
Martin Down National Nature
Reserve* SP5,SP6 ....42 B2
Martin Kemp-Welch Sch The
BH12 ....203 B4
Martin Rd Havant PO9 ....136 A2
Portsmouth PO3 ....183 A4
Stubbington PO14 ....179 B3
Martin St SO32 ....83 A4
Martin's Rd SO42 ....146 A1
Martindale Ave BH21 ....164 A3
Martindale Terr SO16 ....101 C4
Martingale Cl BH16 ....201 B4
Martins Cl BH22 ....165 C4
Martins Dr BH22 ....165 C4
Martins Fields SO21 ....10 B1
Martins Hill Cl BH23 ....192 B1
Martins Hill La BH23 ....192 B1
Martins Rise SP5 ....24 A2
Martins The SO50 ....57 B1
Martins Way BH22 ....165 C4
Martley Gdns SO30 ....81 B1
Marvic Ct PO9 ....135 C3
Marvin Cl SO30 ....105 C4
Marvin Way
Hedge End SO30 ....105 B4
Southampton SO18 ....104 B3
Marwell Cl BH7 ....206 A4
Marwell Zoological Pk*
SO21 ....57 C4
Mary La BH22 ....138 B1
Mary Mitchell Cl BH24 ....140 C4
Mary Rose* PO1 ....181 C3
Mary Rose Cl PO15 ....130 C2
Mary Rose St The PO1 ....215 B3
Marybridge Cl SO40 ....100 C3
Marycourt Sch PO12 ....181 A1
Maryfield SO14 ....103 A2
Maryland Cl SO18 ....79 C2
Maryland Ct 3 SO41 ....211 A2
Maryland Gdns SO41 ....211 A2
Maryland Rd BH16 ....201 B2
Masefield Ave PO6 ....132 C1
Masefield Cl SO50 ....55 C2
Masefield Cres PO8 ....111 C2
Masefield Gr SO19 ....104 B3
Mason Moor Prim Sch
SO16 ....101 C4
Masseys La SO42 ....175 B4
Masten Cres PO13 ....180 B4
Masters Ct BH4 ....204 B2
Masterson Cl BH23 ....207 B4
Matapan Rd PO2 ....157 C2
Matchams Cl BH24 ....167 A4
Matchams La BH23 ....167 A2
Matheson Rd SO16 ....78 A3
Matilda Pl 3 SO23 ....11 A4
Matley Gdns SO40 ....100 A4
Matlock Rd BH22 ....165 B2
Matthews Cl PO9 ....135 B2
Matthews La SO42 ....175 B3
Maturin Cl SO41 ....197 B2
Maundeville Cres BH23 ....206 B4
Maundville Rd BH23 ....206 C4
Maunsell Way SO30 ....81 B1
Maureen Cl BH12 ....203 A4
Maurepas Way PO7 ....134 C4
Mauretania Ho 13 SO14 ....103 B3
Mauretania Rd SO16 ....77 A2
Maurice Rd
Bournemouth BH8 ....205 B4
Portsmouth PO4 ....183 B2
Maury's La SO51 ....50 B2
Mavis Cres PO9 ....135 C1
Mavis Rd BH9 ....190 A1
Maxstoke Cl PO1 ....215 C3
Maxwell Rd
Bournemouth BH9 ....205 A4
Broadstone BH18 ....186 C2
Poole BH13 ....214 C4
Portsmouth PO4 ....183 A2
Southampton SO19 ....104 A2
May Ave SO41 ....197 B3
May Bush La SO32 ....85 A1
May Cl SO45 ....150 B2
May Copse SO45 ....150 B2
May Cres SO45 ....150 B2
May Gdns
Bournemouth BH11 ....188 C2
Christchurch BH23 ....194 A1
May La SO41 ....174 A1
May Rd SO15 ....102 B4
May Tree Cl SO22 ....10 B2
May's La PO14 ....154 B2
Maybray King Way
SO18 ....104 A4
Maybush Ct 2 SO16 ....78 A1
Maybush Rd SO16 ....77 C1
Maycroft Ct 3 SO15 ....102 C4
Maydman Sq PO3 ....183 A3
Mayfair BH4 ....204 B1
Mayfair Ct SO30 ....106 A4
Mayfair Gdns
Bournemouth BH11 ....189 A2
Southampton SO15 ....102 C4
Mayfield PO13 ....179 C1
Mayfield Ave Poole BH14 ....203 C2
Totton SO40 ....100 C4
Mayfield Cl
Ferndown BH22 ....165 B3
Stubbington PO14 ....154 B2
Mayfield Dr BH22 ....165 B3
Mayfield Rd
Bournemouth BH9 ....190 A1
Fordingbridge SP6 ....69 B1
Gosport PO12 ....181 B2
Portsmouth PO2 ....157 C1
Southampton SO17 ....79 B2
Mayfield Sch PO2 ....157 C1
Mayfield Way BH22 ....165 B3
Mayflower Cl
Chandler's Ford SO53 ....55 A3
Lymington SO41 ....198 A1
Stubbington PO14 ....179 B3
Mayflower Ct 14 SO15 ....102 C4
Mayflower Dr PO4 ....183 B3
Mayflower Rd SO15 ....102 A4
Mayflowers The SO17 ....79 A2
Mayfly Cl SP6 ....69 C1
Mayford Rd BH12 ....204 A3
Mayhall Rd PO3 ....158 A1
Mayhill La SO32 ....84 C4
Maylands Ave PO4 ....183 A3
Maylands Rd PO9 ....135 A1
Mayles Cl PO17 ....108 A2
Mayles La PO17 ....107 C1
Mayles Rd PO4 ....183 A3
Maylings Farm Rd PO16 ....130 C2
Maynard Cl PO13 ....155 B2
Maynard Pl PO8 ....112 A4
Maynard Rd SO40 ....100 C4
Mayo Cl PO1 ....182 B4
Maypole Villas SO50 ....56 A4
Mayridge PO14 ....129 B2
Mays Firs SP6 ....47 C1
Maytree Cl Fair Oak SO50 ....57 B1
Locks Heath SO31 ....129 A2
Maytree Gdns PO8 ....111 C2
Maytree Inf Sch SO14 ....103 A3
Maytree Rd
Chandler's Ford SO53 ....30 B1
16 Fareham PO16 ....131 A1
Southampton SO19 ....104 A3
Waterlooville PO8 ....111 C2
Mayvale Cl SO40 ....101 C1
Mayville High Sch PO5 ....182 B1
Mc William Rd 2 BH9 ....190 A1
McIntyre Rd BH23 ....191 A4
McKinley Rd BH4 ....204 B1
McWilliam Cl BH12 ....204 B4
Meacher Cl SO40 ....100 C4
Mead Cl
Broadstone BH18 ....187 A1
Romsey SO51 ....53 A4
Mead Cres SO18 ....79 B2
Mead Ct
Chandler's Ford SO53 ....55 B3
Southampton SO16 ....78 A2
Mead End Rd
Denmead PO7 ....111 A2
Sway SO41 ....171 C1
Mead Rd
Chandler's Ford SO53 ....55 B3
Lymington SO41 ....197 A1
Winchester SO23 ....10 C2
Mead The Gosport PO13 ....155 A2
Hythe SO45 ....125 C2
Liss GU33 ....20 C2
Petersfield GU32 ....40 B1
Mead Way PO16 ....131 A2
Meadbrook Gdns SO53 ....55 B3
Meadcrest Wood SO42 ....145 B1
Meadcroft Cl SO31 ....152 B4
Meadend Cl PO9 ....136 A3
Meadow Ave
Fordingbridge SP6 ....69 C1
Locks Heath SO31 ....129 A2
Meadow Cl
Bransgore BH23 ....193 A4
Burley BH24 ....142 C1
Ferndown BH22 ....165 B1
Fordingbridge SP6 ....69 C1
North Baddesley SO52 ....54 A2
North Hayling PO11 ....159 C2
Ringwood BH24 ....141 A4
Sopley BH23 ....192 A4
Totton SO40 ....100 C3
Waltham Chase SO32 ....83 C2
West End SO30 ....80 C1
Meadow Court Cl BH9 ....190 A2
Meadow Croft Cl SO21 ....31 B2
Meadow Ct
6 Bournemouth BH9 ....190 A2
2 Emsworth PO10 ....160 C4
Fordingbridge SP6 ....69 C1
Whiteparish SP5 ....24 B2
15 Wimborne Minst BH21 ....163 B2
Meadow Edge PO7 ....134 A1
Meadow Farm La BH21 ....186 B4
Meadow Gdns SO32 ....83 C2
Meadow Gr
Chandler's Ford SO53 ....55 B2
Verwood BH31 ....115 A3
Meadow La Burton BH23 ....192 B1
Hamble-le-Rice SO31 ....128 A1
Meadow Rd
Lymington SO41 ....197 B1
New Milton BH25 ....195 A2
Ringwood BH24 ....141 A4
Meadow Rise
Corfe Mullen BH18 ....186 C3
Waterlooville PO8 ....112 A2
Meadow St PO5 ....215 A2
Meadow Terr 12 PO16 ....131 A1
Meadow The
Denmead PO7 ....110 C2
Romsey SO51 ....28 A1
Meadow View Rd BH11 ....188 C2
Meadow Way
Barton on Sea BH25 ....210 A4
Fawley SO45 ....151 A2
Ringwood BH24 ....141 A4
Verwood BH31 ....115 A3
Winchester SO22 ....10 B2
Meadow Wlk
Gosport PO13 ....155 A3
1 Liss GU33 ....20 C2
Portsmouth PO1 ....215 B4
Meadowbank BH16 ....201 B4
Meadowbank Rd PO15 ....130 B1
Meadowhead Rd SO16 ....78 C2
Meadowland
Christchurch BH23 ....207 C3
Kings Worthy SO23 ....2 A4
Meadowlands
Havant PO9 ....136 A1
Lymington SO41 ....197 B2
Ringwood BH24 ....141 A2
Rowland's Castle PO9 ....113 B2
Meadowlands Jun & Inf Schs
PO8 ....111 C3
Meadowmead Ave
SO15 ....102 A4
Meadows Cl BH16 ....201 B4
Meadows Dr BH16 ....201 B4
Meadows The
Fareham PO16 ....131 B2
Lyndhurst SO43 ....122 A2
Waterlooville PO7 ....134 B4
Meadowside Cl SO18 ....79 C2
Meadowsweet PO7 ....112 A1
Meadowsweet Rd BH17 ....201 C4
Meadowsweet Way
Cosham PO6 ....133 B1
Fair Oak SO50 ....81 B3
Meads The
North Baddesley SO53 ....55 A3
Romsey SO51 ....52 B4
Meadway The BH23 ....193 B1
Mears Rd SO50 ....57 B1
Meath Cl PO11 ....185 B1
Medina Cl SO53 ....55 C3
Medina Ct PO13 ....179 B2
Medina Ho 10 PO16 ....155 A4
Medina Prim Sch PO6 ....157 C4
Medina Rd Cosham PO6 ....157 C4
Southampton SO15 ....78 A1
Medina Way BH23 ....208 B3
Medlar Cl Burton BH23 ....192 B1
8 Hedge End SO30 ....105 B3
Medley Pl 18 SO15 ....102 A4
Medlicott Way SO32 ....84 A2
Medstead Rd PO9 ....135 C2
Medwall Gr SO19 ....104 B3
Medway Dr SO53 ....55 A4
Medway Rd BH22 ....166 A3
Meerut Rd SO42 ....145 C1
Meeting House La
BH24 ....140 C4
Megan Ct 20 PO6 ....157 C4
Megan Rd SO30 ....80 B1
Megana Way SO51 ....28 B3
Meggeson Ave SO18 ....80 A1
Melboure Rd BH23 ....191 C1
Melbourne Gdns 6
SO30 ....105 B3
Melbourne Ho PO1 ....215 B3
Melbourne Pl PO5 ....215 B2
Melbourne Rd
Bournemouth BH8 ....205 B3
5 Hedge End SO30 ....105 B3
Melbourne St SO14 ....103 A2
Melbury Ave BH12 ....203 C4
Melbury Cl
Ferndown BH22 ....165 B2
Lymington SO41 ....197 B2
Melbury Ct 19 SO17 ....79 A1
Melchet Cl SO51 ....25 A1
Melchet Rd SO18 ....104 B4
Melford Ct BH1 ....205 A2
Melick Cl SO40 ....101 C1
Mellor Cl 4 PO6 ....157 B4
Mellstock Rd BH15 ....202 B3
Melrose Cl PO4 ....183 A2
Melrose Ct
New Milton SO40 ....195 B2
Totton SO40 ....76 B1
Melrose Gdns PO12 ....180 C4
Melrose Rd SO15 ....78 B1
Melton Ct BH13 ....203 C2
Melverley Gdns BH21 ....163 B3
Melville Cl SO16 ....78 B3
Melville Rd
Bournemouth BH9 ....204 C4
Gosport PO12 ....181 A4
Portsmouth PO4 ....183 B2
Melvin Jones Ho PO14 ....154 B2
Mendip Cl
New Milton BH25 ....195 B1
Verwood BH31 ....114 C3
Mendip Ct 4 BH23 ....207 C4
Mendip Gdns SO45 ....125 B1
Mendip Rd
Southampton SO16 ....101 C4
Verwood BH31 ....114 C3
Mendips Rd PO14 ....154 C4
Mendips Wlk PO14 ....154 B4
Mengham Ave PO11 ....185 A1
Mengham Ct PO11 ....185 A2
Mengham Inf Sch PO11 ....185 A2
Mengham Jun Sch
PO11 ....185 A2
Mengham La PO11 ....185 A2
Mengham Rd PO11 ....185 A2
Menin Ho PO15 ....130 B1
Menslands La
Hambledon PO7 ....86 A1
Soberton PO7 ....109 C4
Mentone Rd 2 BH14 ....203 A2
Menzies Cl SO16 ....77 C3
Meon Cl Clanfield PO8 ....88 B2
Gosport PO13 ....155 A1
Petersfield GU32 ....40 C2
Romsey SO51 ....53 B4
Meon Cres SO53 ....55 B3
Meon Ct SO18 ....104 B4
Meon Gdns SO32 ....84 A3
Meon Ho 8 PO16 ....155 A4
Meon Jun & Inf Schs
PO4 ....183 A2
Meon Rd
Bournemouth BH7 ....206 A4
Portsmouth PO4 ....183 A3
Romsey SO51 ....53 B4
Meoncross Sch PO14 ....154 B2
Meonstoke CE Sch SO32 ....61 B2
Meonwara Cres GU32 ....37 B3
Mercer Way SO51 ....53 A4
Merchants Pl 17 SO23 ....11 A4
Merchants Wlk 21 SO14 ....102 C2
Merchistoun Rd PO7 ....112 B4
Mercury Cl SO16 ....77 C2
Mercury Gdns SO31 ....128 A2

Mercury Pl PO7 . . . . .134 C1
Merdon Ave SO53 . . . . .55 B4
Merdon Cl SO53 . . . . .55 B4
Merdon Ct SO53 . . . . .55 B4
Merdon Jun Sch SO53 . . . .55 B4
Mere Croft PO15 . . . . .129 C2
Meredith Cl BH23 . . . . .207 B4
Meredith Gdns SO40 . . . . .100 B3
Meredith Inf Sch PO2 . . . .182 C4
Meredith Lodge 7 PO7 .135 C4
Meredith Rd PO2 . . . . .157 C2
Meredith Twrs SO19 . . . . .104 C2
Merdun Cl SO21 . . . . .30 A4
Merepond La GU34 . . . . . . .17 C2
Merganser Cl PO12 . . . . . .181 A4
Meriden Cl BH13 . . . . .214 C4
Meriden Ct SO22 . . . . .2 A1
Meriden Rd PO5 . . . . .215 A2
Meridian Ctr 12 PO9 . . . .135 C1
Meridians The BH23 . . . . .206 C3
Merino Way BH22 . . . . . . .138 C1
Merleoak Cl PO4 . . . . .204 C2
Merlewood Ct 16 BH25 .195 A2
Merley Dr BH23 . . . . .209 A4
Merley Fst Sch BH21 . . . .163 B1
Merley Gdns BH21 . . . . . .163 C1
Merley Ho BH21 . . . . .163 A1
Merley House La BH21 . .163 B1
Merley House Mus*
  BH21 . . . . .163 A1
Merley La BH21 . . . . .163 C1
Merley Park Rd
  Corfe Mullen BH21 . . . . .186 C4
  Wimborne Minst BH21 . .163 B1
Merley Ways BH21 . . . . . .163 B1
Merlin Cl
  Bishop's Waltham SO32 . . .83 A4
  Ringwood BH24 . . . . .141 B3
Merlin Dr PO3 . . . . .158 A2
Merlin Way
  Chandler's Ford SO53 . . . .54 C4
  Christchurch BH23 . . . . . .208 A3
Mermaid Ct 22 BH5 . . . .205 C2
Mermaid Ct SO14 . . . . . . .154 C3
Mermaid Way SO14 . . . . .103 A1
Merrick Way SO53 . . . . . . .55 A4
Merridale Rd SO19 . . . . . .103 C3
Merriefield Ave BH18 . . . .187 A3
Merriefield Cl BH18 . . . . .187 A3
Merriefield Dr BH18 . . . . .187 A3
Merrieleas Cl SO53 . . . . . . .55 B4
Merrieleas Dr SO53 . . . . . .55 B4
Merriemeade Cl 2
  SO45 . . . . .125 C1
Merriemeade Par 1
  SO45 . . . . .125 C1
Merrifield BH21 . . . . .163 C4
Merritown La BH23 . . . . . .190 B4
Merritt Ct SO53 . . . . .55 B2
Merrivale Ave BH6 . . . . . .206 C3
Merrivale Cl SO45 . . . . . . .125 C2
Merrivale Ct PO10 . . . . . . .137 B1
Merrivale Rd PO2 . . . . . . .157 C2
Merrow Ave BH12 . . . . . . .204 A4
Merrow Chase 1 BH13 .214 C4
Merrow Cl PO16 . . . . .156 A4
Merry Gdns SO52 . . . . .54 A3
Merryfield PO14 . . . . .129 B2
Merryfield Ave PO9 . . . . .135 B3
Merryfield Cl
  Bransgore BH23 . . . . .193 A4
  Verwood BH31 . . . . .114 C3
Merryfield Ct BH10 . . . . . .189 B2
Merryfield La BH10 . . . . . .189 B2
Merryoak Gn SO19 . . . . . .103 C3
Merryoak Rd SO19 . . . . . .103 C3
Merrytree Cl SO51 . . . . . . .50 C2
Merryweather Est 8
  BH24 . . . . .141 B4
Mersea Gdns SO19 . . . . . .104 A2
Mersham Gdns SO18 . . . .104 A4
Merstone Rd PO13 . . . . . . .155 B1
Merthyr Ave PO6 . . . . .158 A4
Merton Ave PO16 . . . . . . .156 B3
Merton Cl PO16 . . . . .69 C2
Merton Cres PO16 . . . . . . .156 B3
Merton Ct
  8 Christchurch BH23 . . . .209 A4
  3 Poole BH15 . . . . .202 C2
  2 Portsmouth PO5 . . . . .215 C1
Merton Gr BH24 . . . . .140 C4
Merton Rd
  Portsmouth PO5 . . . . .215 C1
  Southampton SO17 . . . . . .79 A2
Merville Gdns BH9 . . . . . .204 C4
Meryl Rd PO4 . . . . .183 B2
Mesh Pond SP5 . . . . .46 B4
Mesh Rd SO51 . . . . .6 A1
Metcalfe Ave PO14 . . . . . .154 B2
Meteor Rd PO10 . . . . .161 A2
Methuen Cl 2 BH8 . . . . . .205 B3
Methuen Rd
  Bournemouth BH8 . . . . . .205 A3
  Poole BH17 . . . . .187 A1
  Portsmouth PO4 . . . . . . .183 A2
Methuen St SO14 . . . . . . .103 A4
Metuchen Way SO30 . . . .105 B2
Mews Cl SO21 . . . . .31 A2
Mews La SO22 . . . . .10 C4
Mews The
  Blackfield SO45 . . . . .177 C4
  Bournemouth BH2 . . . . . .204 B2
  Chandler's Ford SO53 . . . .55 B2

Mews The continued
  Gosport PO12 . . . . .181 C2
  Havant PO9 . . . . .135 C2
  Petersfield GU31 . . . . .41 A2
  Rownhams SO16 . . . . .77 C3
Mewsey Ct PO9 . . . . .135 B4
Mey Cl PO7 . . . . .135 A4
Meynell Cl SO50 . . . . .55 C2
Meyrick Cl BH23 . . . . .193 A4
Meyrick Ho 19 PO2 . . . . .157 B1
Meyrick Park Cres BH3 .204 C3
Meyrick Park Mans 5
  BH2 . . . . .204 C2
Meyrick Rd
  Bournemouth BH1 . . . . . .205 A2
  Havant PO9 . . . . .135 B1
  Portsmouth PO2 . . . . . . .157 B1
Micawber Ho 16 PO1 . . .182 B4
Michael Crook Cl PO4 . . .135 B2
Michael's Way SO45 . . . . .125 C2
Michaels Way SO50 . . . . . .57 B1
Michelgrove Rd BH5 . . . .205 C2
Michelmersh Cl SO16 . . . .77 C3
Michelmersh Gn BH8 . . . .190 B1
Michigan Way SO40 . . . . .100 A4
Micklemarsh Cl SO32 . . . .61 A1
Midanbury Cres SO18 . . . .79 C1
Midanbury Ct 10 SO18 .103 C4
Midanbury La SO18 . . . . .103 C4
Midanbury Wlk 1 SO18 .103 C4
Midas Cl PO13 . . . . .134 C2
Middle Brook BH11 . . . . .189 A3
Middle Brook St SO23 . . . .11 A4
Middle Common Rd
  SO41 . . . . .197 A2
Middle Ct PO1 . . . . .182 C4
Middle La BH24 . . . . .141 A4
Middle Mdw GU33 . . . . . . .21 A2
Middle Mead PO14 . . . . . .154 A4
Middle Park Way PO9 . . .135 B3
Middle Rd
  Bournemouth BH10 . . . . .189 B3
  Lymington SO41 . . . . .197 B2
  New Milton SO41 . . . . . . .195 C4
  North Baddesley SO52 . . . .54 A2
  Poole BH15 . . . . .202 C3
  Southampton SO19 . . . . .104 A2
  Sway SO41 . . . . .172 A1
  Sway, Tiptoe SO41 . . . . . .195 C4
  Winchester SO22 . . . . . . .10 C4
Middle St
  Portsmouth PO5 . . . . . . .215 B2
  Southampton SO14 . . . . .103 A4
Middlebere Cres BH16 . . .201 B2
Middlebridge St SO51 . . . .52 C3
Middlebrook 3 SO32 . . . .83 B4
Middlecroft La PO12 . . . . .180 C3
Middlehill Dr BH11 . . . . . .164 B3
Middlehill Rd BH21 . . . . . .164 A3
Middlesex Rd PO4 . . . . . . .183 A2
Middleton Cl
  Fareham PO14 . . . . .154 C4
  Southampton SO18 . . . . . .80 A1
Middleton Rd
  Bournemouth BH9 . . . . . .189 C1
  Ringwood BH24 . . . . .141 A4
Middleton Rise PO8 . . . . . .88 B2
Middleton Wlk 10 PO14 .154 C4
Midfield Cl PO14 . . . . .154 C4
Midhurst Ho PO10 . . . . . .215 C4
Midland Rd BH9 . . . . .189 C1
Midlands Est SO30 . . . . . . .80 B1
Midlington Hill SO32 . . . . .85 A4
Midlington Ho SO32 . . . . . .85 A4
Midlington Rd SO32 . . . . . .85 A4
Midway SO45 . . . . .125 C2
Midway Path BH13 . . . . . .214 B2
Midway Rd PO2 . . . . .157 C3
Midways PO14 . . . . .179 B3
Midwood Ave BH8 . . . . . .190 C1
Milbeck Cl PO8 . . . . .112 A2
Milborne Cres SO18 . . . . .203 C4
Milburn Rd BH4 . . . . .204 B2
Milburn Rd BH4 . . . . .204 A2
Milburns The SO51 . . . . . . .27 B4
Milbury Cres SO18 . . . . . .104 A3
Milbury Ho PO6 . . . . .133 A1
Mildmay Ct SO22 . . . . .10 B3
Mildmay St SO22 . . . . .10 B3
Mile End Rd PO2 . . . . .182 B4
Milebush Rd PO4 . . . . . . .183 B3
Miles Ct PO11 . . . . .185 B1
Miles La SP5 . . . . .24 B3
Milestone Rd BH15 . . . . . .202 B3
Milford Cl PO9 . . . . .135 B2
  West Moors BH22 . . . . . .138 C1
Milford Cres SO41 . . . . . . .211 C2
Milford Ct Gosport PO12 .180 B2
  Milford on Sea SO41 . . . .211 C2
  6 Portsmouth PO4 . . . . .183 A2
Milford Dr BH11 . . . . .188 C3
Milford Gdns SO53 . . . . . . .55 C3
Milford Ho SO41 . . . . .211 C3
Milford on Sea Prim Sch
  SO41 . . . . .211 C3
Milford Rd
  Barton on Sea BH25 . . . . .210 A4
  Lymington SO41 . . . . . . .197 B3
  Portsmouth PO6 . . . . .157 C1
  Milford Trad Est SO41 . . .211 C2
Military Rd
  Fareham PO16 . . . . .131 B1
  Gosport PO12 . . . . .181 A1
  Gosport, Brockhurst PO13 .180 C3
  Gosport, Clayhall PO12 . .181 B1
  Portsmouth, Hilsea PO3 . .157 C3

Military Rd continued
  Portsmouth, Landport PO1 .182 A4
Milkwood Ct SO40 . . . . . . .100 B4
Milky Down Back La
  BH24 . . . . .141 C4
Mill Cl Denmead PO7 . . . .111 A2
  North Hayling PO11 . . . . .159 C1
  Nursling SO16 . . . . .77 B1
Mill Ct Fordingbridge SP6 . .69 C1
  4 Southampton SO17 . . . .79 B1
Mill End Damerham SP6 . . .68 B2
  Hermitage PO10 . . . . . . .161 A4
Mill Gate Ho 17 PO1 . . . .182 A3
Mill Hill SO30 . . . . .106 A3
Mill Hill SO14 . . . . .203 A2
Mill House Bsns Ctr
  SO19 . . . . .103 B2
Mill House Cir SO40 . . . . .101 A4
Mill House Lodge SO40 . . .56 B2
Mill La Boldre SO41 . . . . . .198 C3
  Brockbridge SO42 . . . . . . .61 B1
  Burley BH24 . . . . .143 B2
  Christchurch BH23 . . . . . .209 A4
  Crouchend SP5 . . . . .22 B4
  Droxford SO32 . . . . .61 A1
  Durley SO32 . . . . .82 B2
  Gosport PO12 . . . . .181 A2
  Havant PO9 . . . . .159 C3
  Havant, Bedhampton PO9 .135 B1
  Hawkley GU33 . . . . .19 C4
  Hermitage PO10 . . . . . . .137 A1
  Hurn BH23 . . . . .191 A3
  Kings Worthy SO21 . . . . . . .2 B3
  Lymington SO41 . . . . . . .197 C2
  Minstead SO43 . . . . .98 C1
  Nursling SO16 . . . . .76 C2
  Petersfield GU32 . . . . .41 A3
  Poole BH14 . . . . .203 A2
  Portsmouth PO1 . . . . . . .182 B4
  Romsey SO51 . . . . .52 B4
  Sherfield English SO51 . . . .25 C1
  Southwick PO7 . . . . .133 C2
  Steep Marsh GU32 . . . . . .40 C4
  Sway SO41 . . . . .196 C4
  Titchfield PO15 . . . . .130 A1
  Westbourne PO10 . . . . . .137 A1
  Wickham PO17 . . . . .108 A3
  Wimborne Minst BH21 . .163 A3
  Mill Mdw SO41 . . . . .211 B3
Mill Pond Rd PO12 . . . . . .181 A3
Mill Pond The SO45 . . . . .150 A3
Mill Quay PO10 . . . . .161 A4
Mill Race View SP5 . . . . . . .46 C4
Mill Rd
  Christchurch BH23 . . . . . .207 A4
  Denmead PO7 . . . . .111 A2
  Fareham PO16 . . . . .155 A2
  Gosport PO12 . . . . .181 A3
  Liss GU33 . . . . .21 A3
  Southampton SO15 . . . . .102 A4
  Totton SO40 . . . . .101 A4
  Waterlville PO7 . . . . .134 C3
Mill Rd N BH8 . . . . .190 B2
Mill Rd S BH8 . . . . .190 B1
Mill Rise SO51 . . . . .5 B1
Mill Rythe Inf Sch PO11 .185 A3
Mill Rythe Jun Sch
  PO11 . . . . .185 A3
Mill Rythe La PO11 . . . . . .185 A4
Mill St Broadstone BH21 . .162 A1
  Eastleigh SO50 . . . . .56 A2
  Titchfield PO14 . . . . .154 A4
Mill Way SO40 . . . . .100 C3
Millais Rd SO23 . . . . .11 A3
Milland Rd SO23 . . . . .11 A3
Millbank Ho
  4 Southampton SO14 . . .103 B3
  5 Wimborne Minst BH21 .163 B3
Millbank St SO14 . . . . .103 B3
Millbridge Gdns SO19 . . . .104 A2
Millbrook Cl
  Chandler's Ford SO53 . . . .55 A3
  Liss GU33 . . . . .21 A2
Millbrook Com Sch SO16 . .77 C2
Millbrook Dr PO9 . . . . . . .136 A3
Millbrook Flyover SO15 . .101 C4
Millbrook Point Rd
  SO15 . . . . .101 B4
Millbrook Rd E SO15 . . . .102 B3
Millbrook Rd W SO15 . . .102 A3
Millbrook Sta SO15 . . . . .102 A3
Millbrook Trad Est
  SO15 . . . . .101 B4
Millcourt 6 SO50 . . . . .57 B1
Millennium Cl 11 PO7 . . .134 C3
Miller Dr PO15 . . . . .129 C1
Miller Dr PO16 . . . . .130 C1
Miller Rd BH23 . . . . .207 B4
Miller's Pond Gdns
  SO19 . . . . .103 C2
Millers La SO32 . . . . .9 C2
Millers Quay Ho 2
  PO16 . . . . .155 A4
Millers Way SO45 . . . . . . .125 C1
Millfield
  Broadstone BH17 . . . . . .202 A4
  New Milton BH25 . . . . . .195 A4
Millhams Cl BH10 . . . . . . .189 A3
Millhams Dr BH10 . . . . . . .189 A3
Millhams Rd BH10 . . . . . .189 A3
Millhams St BH23 . . . . . . .207 A3
Millhams St N BH23 . . . . .207 A3
Milliken Cl SO45 . . . . .150 C1
Mills Rd PO2 . . . . .157 B1
Mills The BH12 . . . . .203 C4

Millstream Cl
  Broadstone BH17 . . . . . .202 A4
  Wimborne Minst BH21 . .163 B2
Millstream Rise SO51 . . . . .52 B4
Millstream Trad Est
  BH24 . . . . .141 A3
Millverton Ct 8 SO18 . . .104 A4
Millvina Cl SO40 . . . . .99 C2
Millway SO32 . . . . .82 A3
Millyford Cl BH25 . . . . . . .209 B4
Milman Ct SO45 . . . . .125 B1
Milne Rd BH17 . . . . .187 A1
Milner Ct SO15 . . . . .102 B4
Milner Pl SO22 . . . . .10 C3
Milner Rd BH4 . . . . .204 B1
Milnthorpe La SO22 . . . . . .10 C4
Milton Cl BH14 . . . . .203 B2
Milton Ct Ferndown BH22 .165 B3
  Portsmouth PO4 . . . . . . .183 A3
Milton Gr
  Locks Heath SO31 . . . . . .129 A1
  5 Waterlooville PO7 . . . .135 A4
Milton Par PO7 . . . . .135 A4
Milton Park Ave 3 PO4 .183 A2
Milton Park Jun & Inf Schs
  PO4 . . . . .183 A2
Milton Rd
  Bournemouth BH8 . . . . . .205 A3
  Eastleigh SO50 . . . . .56 A3
  Poole BH14 . . . . .203 B2
  Portsmouth PO3,PO4 . . . .183 A3
  Southampton SO15 . . . . .102 C3
  Waterlooville PO7,PO8 . .111 C1
  Wimborne Minst BH21 . .163 B3
Milton Villas BH8 . . . . . . .205 A3
Milton's Sch PO3 . . . . . . .183 A3
Milverton Cl
  Christchurch BH23 . . . . . .193 C1
  Totton SO40 . . . . .101 A3
Milverton Ho PO5 . . . . . . .215 B2
Milverton Rd
  Totton SO40 . . . . .101 A3
  Winchester SO22 . . . . . . .10 C4
Milvil Ct 5 PO13 . . . . . . .179 C1
Milvil Rd PO13 . . . . .179 C1
Mimosa Ave BH21 . . . . . . .158 C4
Mimosa Cl PO15 . . . . .129 C2
Mimosa Dr SO50 . . . . .57 C1
Mincingfield La SO32 . . . . .82 B3
Mincingfield Terr SO32 . . .82 B3
Minden Ho
  Fareham PO14 . . . . .154 C4
  Romsey SO51 . . . . .53 A4
Minden Way SO22 . . . . . . .10 B3
Minerva Cl PO7 . . . . .134 C1
Minerva Cres SO14 . . . . . .103 A1
Minerva Dr PO12 . . . . .181 B4
Minley Ct 32 PO9 . . . . . . .136 A3
Minnitt Rd PO12 . . . . .181 C2
Minstead Ave SO18 . . . . . .104 B4
Minstead Cl 4 SO17 . . . .103 A4
Minstead Rd
  Bournemouth BH9 . . . . . .189 B2
  Portsmouth PO4 . . . . . . .183 B3
Minstead Rural Studies Ctr
  SO43 . . . . .98 A1
Minster Cl PO15 . . . . .130 B1
Minster Ct 1 SO15 . . . . .102 B3
Minster La 10 SO23 . . . . . .11 A4
Minster Pk BH21 . . . . .138 C3
Minster The* BH21 . . . . . .163 A2
Minster View BH21 . . . . . .163 B3
Minster Way BH16 . . . . . .201 A4
Mint Rd GU33 . . . . .21 A3
Mint The GU31,GU32 . . . . .40 C1
Minter's Lepe PO7 . . . . . . .134 C2
Minters Cl SO50 . . . . .56 B3
Minterne Grange BH14 . .214 B4
Minterne Rd
  4 Bournemouth BH9 . . . .190 A1
  Christchurch BH23 . . . . . .207 C3
  Poole BH14 . . . . .214 B4
Minton Mews PO4 . . . . . . .204 C3
Mintys Hill SP6 . . . . .68 C4
Mintys Yd 4 BH24 . . . . . .141 A3
Mirror Cl SO31 . . . . .128 C1
Misselbrook Mead 6
  SO45 . . . . .98 A1
Missenden Acres SO30 . .105 B4
Missenden Pl 8 SO50 . . . .56 A1
Mission La PO8 . . . . .112 A2
Mission Rd BH14 . . . . .187 A1
Misslebrook La SO52,
  SO52 . . . . .54 B2
Mistletoe Gdns SO31 . . . .128 C3
Mitchell Cl
  Barton on Sea BH25 . . . . .210 A4
  Christchurch BH23 . . . . . .207 B4
Mitchell Dr SO50 . . . . .57 B2
Mitchell Point SO31 . . . . .127 C1
Mitchell Rd
  Eastleigh SO50 . . . . .56 A1
  Ferndown BH21 . . . . .165 A4
  Poole BH17 . . . . .187 C1
Mitchell Way
  Eastleigh SO18 . . . . .79 C3
  Southampton SO18 . . . . . .80 A3
Mitchells Cl Redlynch SP5 . .47 B3
  Romsey SO51 . . . . .52 C4
Mitre Copse SO50 . . . . . . .56 C1
Mitre Ct 18 PO14 . . . . . . .154 C4
Mizen Ho PO6 . . . . .157 A4
Mizen Way PO13 . . . . .180 B3
Mizoah Villa SO32 . . . . . . .83 C2
Moat Cl SO45 . . . . .150 A2

Moat Ct
  Bournemouth BH4 . . . . . .204 B3
  Gosport PO12 . . . . .180 B2
Moat Hill SO18 . . . . .79 C2
Moat Hill SO18 . . . . .80 B2
Moat La BH25 . . . . .209 C4
Moat Wlk PO12 . . . . .180 B2
Mockbeggar La BH24 . . . .117 A4
Moffat Rd BH23 . . . . .207 B4
Moggs Mead GU31 . . . . . . .41 A2
Mole Hill PO7 . . . . .134 C3
Molefields SO41 . . . . .211 C3
Molesworth Rd PO12 . . . .181 B2
Molison Rise PO15 . . . . . .129 B3
Molyneux Rd BH25 . . . . . .195 B2
Momford Rd SO22 . . . . . . .10 A2
Mon Cres SO18 . . . . .104 B4
Monaco Ct BH9 . . . . .205 A4
Monarch Cl
  Locks Heath SO31 . . . . . .129 A1
  5 Waterlooville PO7 . . . .135 A4
Monarch Way
  West End SO30 . . . . .80 C1
  Winchester SO22 . . . . . . .10 B3
Monastery Rd SO18 . . . . .103 C4
Monckton Rd
  Gosport PO12 . . . . .181 A1
  Portsmouth PO3 . . . . . . .158 A1
Moneyfield Ave PO3 . . . . .158 A1
Moneyfield La PO3 . . . . . .158 A1
Moneyfield Sch BH21 . . . .115 A3
Monk's Hill PO10 . . . . . . .137 A3
Monks Brook Cl SO50 . . . .55 C1
Monks Brook Ind Pk
  SO53 . . . . .55 A3
Monks Cl BH22 . . . . .166 A4
Monks Ct 10 SO41 . . . . . .197 C1
Monks Hill PO13 . . . . .179 B2
Monks Orch GU32 . . . . . . .40 C3
Monks Pk SO40 . . . . .100 B3
Monks Rd Netley SO31 . . .127 A3
  Winchester SO23 . . . . .2 A1
Monks Way
  Bournemouth BH11 . . . . .188 B3
  Eastleigh SO50 . . . . .55 C1
  Stubbington SO18 . . . . . . .79 A2
  Stubbington PO14 . . . . . .179 A2
Monks Wlk SO45 . . . . .149 C4
Monks Wood GU32 . . . . . . .40 C3
Monks Way SO16 . . . . .79 A3
Monkshood Cl BH23 . . . . .193 A1
Monkswell Grn BH23 . . . .207 B3
Monkton Cl BH22 . . . . . . .165 B3
Monkton Ho PO12 . . . . . . .181 A1
Monkton La SO40 . . . . . . .100 B3
Monkwood Cl PO9 . . . . . .135 B3
Monkworthy Dr BH24 . . . .139 C3
Monmouth Cl
  North Baddesley SO53 . . . .55 A3
  Verwood BH31 . . . . .115 A2
Monmouth Ct
  Lymington SO41 . . . . . . .197 C2
  Ringwood BH24 . . . . .140 C4
Monmouth Dr BH31 . . . . .115 A2
Monmouth Gdns SO40 . . .100 B3
Monmouth Rd PO2 . . . . . .157 B1
Monmouth Sq SO22 . . . . . .10 A3
Monnow Gdns SO18 . . . . . .80 A1
Monroe Cl PO12 . . . . .180 C2
Mons The 11 SO23 . . . . . . .10 B4
Monsal Ave BH22 . . . . . . .165 B2
Montacute Sch BH17 . . . .187 B1
Montacute Way BH21 . . . .187 C4
Montagu Cl PO12 . . . . . . .181 B4
Montagu Pk BH23 . . . . . . .209 B4
Montagu Rd BH23 . . . . . . .209 A4
Montague Cl SO19 . . . . . .104 B2
Montague Ct SO19 . . . . . .104 B2
Montague Rd SO45 . . . . . .149 C4
Montague Gdns GU31 . . . .41 B2
Montague Rd
  Bishopstoke SO50 . . . . . . .56 B2
  Bournemouth BH5 . . . . . .206 A2
  Portsmouth PO2 . . . . . . .157 C1
Montague Wallis Ct 31
  PO1 . . . . .182 A3
Montana Ct PO7 . . . . .135 A3
Montefiore Ho SO18 . . . . . .79 B2
Monterey Dr Havant PO9 .136 A2
  Hordle SO41 . . . . .195 C2
  Locks Heath SO31 . . . . . .129 A1
Montfort Cl SO51 . . . . .53 B4
Montfort Coll SO51 . . . . . . .53 B4
Montfort Hts SO51 . . . . . . .53 B4
Montfort Rd SO51 . . . . .53 B4
Montgomerie Rd PO5 . . . .215 C2
Montgomery Ave
  Bournemouth BH11 . . . . .189 A2
  Totton SO40 . . . . .100 B4
Montgomery Cl SO22 . . . . .10 B4
Montgomery Rd
  Portsmouth PO3 . . . . . . .155 B2
  Havant PO9 . . . . .136 A1
  Southampton SO18 . . . . .104 A4
Montgomery Way SO53 . . .55 A2
Montgomery Wlk PO7 . . .134 B3
Montpelier Cl SO31 . . . . .129 B2
Montrose Ave PO16 . . . . .132 C1
Montrose Cl
  Hedge End SO30 . . . . . . .105 C3
  2 Verwood BH31 . . . . . .114 C3
Montrose Dr BH10 . . . . . .189 A1
Montserrat Rd PO13 . . . . .179 C1
Monument Cl SO14 . . . . . .103 A1

Monument La
Boldre SO41 ....198 A3
Southwick PO17 ....132 B2
Walderton PO18 ....137 C4
Monxton Gn 10 PO9 ...136 A3
Moody Rd PO14 ....179 B3
Moody's Hill SP5 ....3 B1
Moon Cl SO40 ....101 C1
Moonhills La SO42 ......149 A1
Moonrakers BH13 ....214 C4
Moonrakers Way BH23 ..193 C1
Moonscross Ave SO40 ..100 C2
Moor La SP5 ....48 B4
Moor Pk PO7 ....112 A1
Moor Rd BH18 ....187 A3
Moor View Rd BH15 ....202 C4
Morcroft Ave BH23 .....192 B1
Moordown Cl BH9 ....190 A2
**Moordown St John's CE Prim
  Sch** BH9 ....189 C1
Moore Ave BH11 ....189 A2
Moore Cl BH25 ....194 C1
Moore Cres SO31 ....127 B4
Moore Gdns PO12 ......180 C2
Moorfield Gr BH9 ....189 C1
Moorgreen Rd BH23 ....214 C4
Moorgreen Hospl SO30 ..80 C1

Moorgreen Rd
Havant PO9 ....136 A3
West End SO30 ....80 C1
Moorhaven BH22 ....165 B3
Moorhead Ct SO14 .....103 B1
Moorhill Gdns SO18 ....104 C4
Moorhill Rd Burley BH24 .143 A1
West End SO30 ....104 B4
Moorings Cl BH12 ......163 B2
Moorings SO11 ....201 C1
Moorings The
7 Christchurch BH23 ....207 A3
Fareham PO16 ....155 A4
Moorings Way PO4 .....183 B3
Moorings Way Inf Sch
PO4 ....183 B3
Moorland Ave BH25 ....209 C4
Moorland Cl Hythe SO45 .125 B2
Locks Heath SO31 ....129 A2
Moorland Cres BH16 ....201 A4
Moorland Gate BH24 ...141 A3
Moorland Par BH16 .....201 A4
Moorland Rd
Bournemouth BH1 ....205 B2
Portsmouth PO1 ....182 A3
Moorland Way BH16 ....201 A4
Moorlands Cl SO42 .....145 B1
Moorlands Coll BH23 ...192 A3
Moorlands Cres SO18 ...104 A4
Moorlands Inf Sch SO18 .80 A1
Moorlands Rd
Swanmore SO32 ....84 A4
Verwood BH31 ....114 C4
West Moors BH22 ....138 C2
Moorlands Rise BH22 ...138 C2
Moorlea 10 BH8 ....205 A3
Moors Cl
Colden Common SO21 .....31 C1
Hurn BH23 ....191 A4
**Moors Valley Ctry Park
  Visitor Ctr* BH24** 139 B4
Moors Valley Ctry Pk
St Leonards BH24 ....139 B4
* Verwood BH24 ....115 C1
Moors Valley Rly*
BH24 ....115 B1
Moorside Cl BH11 ......189 A2
Moorside Rd
Bournemouth BH11 ....189 A2
Corfe Mullen BH21 ....186 B3
West Moors BH22 ....138 C1
Winchester SO23 ....2 B3
Moortown Ave PO6 .....134 B1
Moortown Dr BH21 .....188 A4
Moortown La BH24 .....141 A3
Moortown La BH24 .....141 B2
Moorvale Rd BH9 ....190 A1
Moot Cl SP5 ....47 A4
Moot Gdns SP5 ....46 C3
Moot La SP5 ....46 C3
Mopley SO45 ....177 C4
Mopley Cl SO45 ....177 C4
Morant Cl 14 BH25 ....195 A2
Morant Rd BH24 ....117 A1
Moraunt Ct PO12 ......181 B4
Moraunt Dr PO16 ......156 A3
Moray Ct 14 BH21 .....163 A3
Mordaunt Rd SO14 .....103 A4
Morden Ave BH22 ......165 B2
Morden Rd BH9 ....189 C1
Morecombe Ct 4 BH25 .215 C2
Moreland Rd PO12 .....181 A3
Morelands Ct PO7 ......134 C2
Morelands Prim Sch
PO7 ....134 C1
Morelands Rd PO7 .....134 C2
Moresby Ct 21 PO11 ...131 A1
Morestead Rd
Winchester SO21 ....11 C2
Winchester SO21 ....11 A2
Moreton Rd BH9 ....190 A2
Morgan Le Fay Dr SO53 .54 C4
Morgan Rd
Hedge End SO30 ....105 B3
Portsmouth PO4 ....183 B2
Morgan's La SP5 ....42 A1
**Morgan's Vale & Woodfall's
  Prim Sch** SP5 ....47 B4

Morgans Dr PO14 ......154 B3
Morgans Rise Rd SP5 ....47 B4
Morgans Vale Rd SP5 ....47 B3
Moriconium Quay BH15 .201 B1
Morington Ct 8 BH8 ...205 A3
Morland Rd SO15 ....78 B1
Morley Cl
Bournemouth BH5 ....206 A3
Burton BH23 ....192 B2
Southampton SO19 ....103 C3
Morley Cres PO8 ....112 A2
Morley Dr SO32 ....83 B4
Morley Rd
Bournemouth BH5 ....206 A3
Portsmouth PO4 ....183 A1
Morley Way BH22 ......165 C2
Morleys La SO51 ....29 B2
Morningside Ave PO16 ..132 C1
Mornington Dr SO22 .....1 B1
Mornish Rd BH13 ....203 C1
Morpeth Ave SO40 .....100 C4
Morris Cl Gosport PO13 .155 A3
Southampton SO18 ....125 B2
Morris Rd Poole BH17 ..202 B4
Southampton SO15 ....102 C3
Morrison Ave BH12 .....203 C3
Morse Cl SO31 ....127 A3
Morshead Cres PO16 ...130 C2
Mortimer Cl
Christchurch BH23 ....208 A3
Kings Worthy SO23 ....2 A3
9 Netley SO31 ....127 A3
Totton SO40 ....76 B1
Mortimer Lawn PO9 ....135 B4
Mortimer Rd
Botley SO30 ....106 A3
Bournemouth BH8 ....190 A1
Cosham PO6 ....133 B1
Southampton SO19 ....103 C2
Mortimer Way SO52 .....53 C2
Mortimer's Ind Units
SO51 ....75 C3
Mortimers La 10 SO50 ..57 B1
Mortimers La SO32 .....58 A2
Mortimore Rd PO12 ....180 C3
Mosaic Cl SO19 ....104 C2
Mosdell Rd PO10 ....161 C4
Mosedale Wlk SO14 ....101 C4
Moselle Cl SO15 ....102 B3
Moss Cl GU33 ....21 A2
Moss Dr SO40 ....101 C1
Moss Rd SO23 ....11 A4
Mossleigh Ave SO16 ....77 C3
Mossley Ave BH12 .....189 A1
Motcombe Rd BH13 ....204 A1
Mottisfont Abbey (NT)*
SO51 ....5 C1
Mottisfont Abbey Gdns*
SO51 ....5 C1
Mottisfont Cl SO15 .....102 A3
Mottisfont Rd SO50 .....56 A2
Moulin Ave PO5 ....182 C1
Mound Cl PO12 ....181 A2
Mount Ave BH25 ....195 A1
Mount Cl
New Milton BH25 ....195 A1
Winchester SO22 ....1 B2
Mount Dr
Chandler's Ford SO53 ....55 C2
Fareham PO15 ....134 A4
Mount Grace Dr BH14 ..214 B4
Mount Heatherbank 30
BH1 ....204 C2
Mount Hospl The SO50 ..56 B3
Mount House Cl 8
SO45 ....126 A3
Mount La SO51 ....25 C4
Mount Pleasant
Christchurch BH23 ....208 A3
Denmead PO7 ....110 C1
Kings Worthy SO23 ....2 B3
7 Ringwood BH24 ....141 A4
Romsey SO51 ....52 C3
Mount Pleasant Dr BH8 .190 C1
Mount Pleasant Ind Pk
SO14 ....103 A4
Mount Pleasant Jun Sch
SO14 ....103 A4
Mount Pleasant La
Lymington SO41 ....197 A4
Sway SO41 ....197 B4
Mount Pleasant Rd
Gosport PO12 ....181 A2
Southampton SO14 ......103 A3
Mount Rd
Bournemouth BH11 ....189 A2
Poole BH14 ....203 A3
Mount Temple SO51 .....53 A4
Mount The Gosport PO13 .155 C1
Ringwood BH24 ....141 B4
5 Southampton, Bassett
SO16 ....78 C2
6 Southampton, Shirley
SO16 ....78 A1
Mount View SO50 ....56 A2
Mount View Rd SO22 ....10 A2
Mountain Ash Cl SO18 ..104 B4
Mountbatten Ave SO51 ..52 C4
Mountbatten Bsns Ctr
SO15 ....102 B3
Mountbatten Bsns Pk
PO6 ....158 B3
Mountbatten Cl
Christchurch BH23 ....208 A3
Gosport PO13 ....155 B2
Mountbatten Ct
New Milton BH25 ....194 C2
Winchester SO22 ....1 C2

Mountbatten Dr
Ferndown BH22 ....165 B3
Waterlooville PO7 ....134 B3
Mountbatten Gdns BH6 .190 C1
Mountbatten Pl SO23 .....2 B4
Mountbatten Rd
Eastleigh SO50 ....56 A3
Poole BH13 ....204 A1
Totton SO40 ....100 B4
Mountbatten Sch The
SO51 ....53 B3
Mountbatten Sq PO4 ...183 A1
Mountbatten Way
Portsmouth PO1 ....215 A4
Southampton SO15 ....102 B3
Mountfield SO45 ....125 C2
Mountjoy Cl BH21 ......163 C1
Mountview Ave PO16 ...132 C1
Mountwood Rd PO10 ...137 B1
Mousehole La
Hythe SO45 ....126 A2
Southampton SO18 ....103 C4
Mousehole Rd PO6 .....132 C1
Mowbray Rd SO19 .....104 A2
Moxhams SP6 ....69 C1
Moyles Court Sch BH24 .117 B3
Mt Pleasant Dr BH23 ...169 B1
Mt Pleasant Rd BH15 ...202 B2
Muccleshell Cl PO9 .....136 A2
Muddyford Rd SP5 ....47 B4
Mude Gdns BH23 ....208 A3
Mudeford BH23 ....208 A3
Mudeford Cty Inf Sch
BH23 ....207 C3
Mudeford Cty Jun Sch
BH23 ....207 C3
Mudeford Green Cl
BH23 ....207 C3
Mudeford La BH23 .....207 C3
Muir Ho SO45 ....125 C1
Muira Est SO14 ....103 B3
Mulberry Ave
Cosham PO6 ....158 A4
Stubbington PO14 ....179 B3
Mulberry Cl PO12 ......181 A2
Mulberry Ct 4 BH23 ...207 A4
Mulberry Gdns SP6 .....93 C4
Mulberry Gr SO41 ......211 B4
Mulberry La
Cosham PO6 ....158 A4
Locks Heath SO31 ....128 C3
Mulberry Mews SP6 ....93 C4
Mulberry Rd SO40 .....101 C1
Mulberry Wlk SO15 .....102 B4
Mullen Cl SO19 ....103 C2
Mullins Cl BH12 ....204 B4
Mullion Cl PO6 ....157 A4
Mumby Rd PO12 ....181 B3
Mundays Row PO8 ......88 B1
Munro Cres SO15 ......101 C4
Munster Rd Poole BH14 .203 B2
Portsmouth PO2 ....157 B1
Murefield Rd PO1 ....215 C3
Muriel Rd PO7 ....134 C4
Murley Rd BH9 ....205 A4
Murray Cl Fareham PO15 .130 C1
Southampton SO19 ....104 C3
Murray Cotts SO32 .....107 B4
Murray Rd PO8 ....112 A3
Murray's La PO1 ....181 C3
Murrills Est PO16 ......156 C4
Mus of Childhood*
BH8 ....205 C3
Mus of Electricity*
BH23 ....207 A4
Muscliff Prim Sch BH9 ..190 B2
Muscliffe Ct 27 PO9 ...136 A3
Muscliffe La BH9 ....190 A3
Muscliffe Rd BH9 ....189 C1
Museum of Archaeology*
SO14 ....103 A1
Museum Rd PO1 ....182 A2
Mussett Cl SO40 ....100 C4
Mustang Ave PO15 ....129 B4
My Lords La PO11 .....185 A2
Myers Cl SO32 ....84 A3
Myrtle Ave
Portchester PO16 ....156 B4
Totton SO40 ....100 B3
Myrtle Cl Gosport PO13 .155 A2
Hordle SO41 ....195 C2
Myrtle Gr PO3 ....183 A4
Myrtle Rd
Bournemouth BH8 ....205 B3
Southampton SO16 ....78 A2
Myvern Cl SO45 ....150 B2

N

Nada Rd BH23 ....193 B1
Nailsworth Rd PO6 .....133 A1
Nairn Cl BH3 ....204 C4
Nairn Rd
Bournemouth BH3 ....204 C3
Poole BH13 ....214 C4
Naish Cl PO9 ....135 B4
Naish Dr PO12 ....156 A1
Naish Holiday Village*
BH25 ....209 A4
Namu Rd BH9 ....189 C1
Nancy Rd PO1 ....215 D3
Nansen Ave BH15 ......202 B3
Napier Cl PO13 ....180 B3
Napier Cres PO15 ......130 B1
Napier Rd
Hamworthy BH15 ....201 B2

Napier Rd continued
Horndean PO8 ....112 B3
Portsmouth PO5 ....182 B1
Southampton SO19 ......104 C3
Narrow La
Ringwood BH24 ....117 B1
11 Romsey SO51 ....52 C4
Narvik Rd PO2 ....157 B2
Naseby Cl 5 PO6 ....133 A1
Naseby Rd BH9 ....190 A1
Nash Cl SO45 ....125 B1
Nash Ct SO45 ....125 B1
Nashe Cl PO15 ....130 B2
Nashe Ho PO15 ....130 B2
Nashe Way PO15 ......130 B2
Nasmith Cl PO12 ......180 B2
Nat Gonella Sq 4 PO12 .181 B2
Nat Motor Mus The*
SO42 ....148 C1
Nations Hill SO23 ....2 B3
Navarac Ct BH14 ......203 B2
Navigator's Way SO30 ..105 B4
Navy Rd PO1 ....182 A3
Nea Cl BH23 ....208 B4
Nea Dr BH24 ....116 A3
Nea Rd BH23 ....208 C4
Neacroft Cl BH25 ......209 B4
Neath Way SO53 ....55 A3
Needles Cl 11 SO41 ....211 B2
Needles Ho 7 PO16 ....155 A4
Needles Point SO41 ....211 B2
Neelands Gr PO6 ....156 C4
Neighbourhood Ctr
BH17 ....187 C1
Neilson Cl SO53 ....55 B4
Nelson Ave
Portchester PO16 ....156 A4
Portsmouth PO2 ....157 B1
Nelson Cl Holbury SO45 .150 B2
New Milton BH25 ......194 C2
Romsey SO51 ....52 C4
Nelson Cres PO8 ....112 B4
Nelson Ct Fareham PO16 .154 C3
12 Hythe SO45 ....126 A1
10 Poole BH15 ....202 B1
Nelson Dr BH23 ....207 D3
Nelson Ho PO12 ....181 B2
Nelson Ind Pk SO30 .....81 A1
Nelson Pl PO16 ....132 B1
Nelson Pl SO41 ....197 C2
Nelson Rd
Bishopstoke SO50 ....56 B2
Bournemouth BH4 ....204 A2
Gosport PO12 ....181 A2
Poole BH12 ....204 A2
Portsmouth PO5 ....182 B3
Southampton SO15 ......102 B3
Winchester SO23 ....11 B3
Nelson's Gdns SO30 .....81 B2
Nepean Cl PO12 ....181 A1
Neptune Ct
Portsmouth PO1 ....182 A2
Southampton SO16 ....77 C2
Neptune Ho 4 PO6 ....157 C4
Neptune Rd
Fareham PO15 ....130 B1
Gosport PO12 ....154 C3
Neptune Way SO14 ....103 A1
Nerissa Cl 2 PO7 ......135 A4
Nerquis Cl SO51 ....53 A4
Nesbitt Cl PO13 ....155 A2
Nessus St PO2 ....157 B1
Nest Bsns Pk PO9 .....136 A2
Nethercliffe Sch SO22 ...1 C1
Netherfield Cl PO9 .....136 A1
Netherhall Gdns BH4 ...204 B2
Netherhill La SO32 ......82 A1
Netherton Rd PO12 ....180 C4
Netherwood Pl BH23 ...163 A3
Netley Abbey Inf Sch
SO31 ....127 A4
Netley Abbey Jun Sch
SO31 ....127 A4
Netley Cl
Chandler's Ford SO53 ....55 A2
Poole BH15 ....203 A4
Netley Cliff SO31 ....127 A3
Netley Court Sch SO31 .127 A3
Netley Firs Cl SO19 ....104 C2
Netley Firs Rd SO30 ....105 A3
Netley Hill Est SO30 ...104 C2
Netley Lodge Cl SO31 ..127 B3
Netley Marsh CE Inf Sch
SO40 ....100 A4
Netley Rd
21 Portsmouth PO5 .....182 B1
Titchfield PO14 ....129 B1
Netley St SO31 ....182 B1
Netley Terr 22 PO5 ....182 B1
Nettlecombe Ave PO4 ..182 C1
Nettlestone SO31 ....127 B4
Nettlestone Rd PO4 ....183 A1
Nettleton Cl BH17 .....202 C4
Netton Cl SP5 ....22 A4
Netton St SP5 ....22 A4
Neva Rd SO18 ....103 C4
Neville Ave PO16 ......156 B3
Neville Ct PO12 ....181 A2
Neville Gdns PO10 .....136 C2
Neville Lovett Com Sch
PO14 ....154 C4
Neville Rd PO3 ....183 A4
Neville Shute Rd PO3 ...158 B2
New Borough Rd BH21 .162 C3
New Brighton Rd PO10 .136 C1
New Cliff Ho SO19 .....103 C1

New Cliffe Gdns SO30 ..105 A3
**New Coll (Univ of
  Southampton)** SO15 ...102 C2
New Cotts Ashurst SO40 .123 C4
Boldre SO41 ....199 A3
Exbury SO45 ....177 A3
Fareham PO16 ....155 A4
Ferndown BH21 ....164 C1
Nursling SO16 ....77 B1
New Ct BH24 ....140 C4
New Cut PO11 ....159 C2
New Down La PO6,PO7 .134 A1
New Fields Bsns Pk
BH17 ....202 B4
New Forest Dr SO42 ...145 B1
New Forest Ent Ctr
SO40 ....100 C3
**New Forest Mus & Visitor
  Ctr* SO43** 122 A3
**New Forest Otter, Owl &
  Wildlife Pk* SO40** 123 C4
New Forest Owl Sanctuary*
BH24 ....141 B3
New Forest Reptiliary*
SO43 ....121 A2
New Hall SO23 ....11 A3
New Harbour Rd BH15 .202 A1
New Harbour Rd S
BH15 ....213 A4
New Harbour Rd W
BH15 ....202 A1
New Inn Cotts SO42 ...175 B3
New Inn La Cadnam SO40 .99 A3
East Boldre SO42 ....175 B3
New Inn Rd SO40 ....99 A4
New La Havant PO9 .....136 A2
Milford on Sea SO41 ....211 C2
New Marsh Ho 8 SO45 .126 A2
New Merrifield BH21 ...163 C4
New Milton Inf Sch
BH25 ....195 A1
New Milton Jun Sch
BH25 ....195 A1
New Milton Sta BH25 ..195 A2
New Orch BH15 ....202 A1
New Par
Bournemouth BH10 ......189 C2
Portchester PO16 ....156 B4
New Park Rd BH6 ......206 B2
New Quay Rd BH15 ....202 A1
New Rd Ashurst SO40 ..100 B1
Bishop's Waltham SO32 ..59 B1
Blackfield SO45 ....150 C1
Bournemouth BH10 ......189 C3
Clanfield PO8 ....88 B3
Colden Common SO21 ...31 C1
Fair Oak SO50 ....57 A1
Fareham PO16 ....131 A1
Ferndown BH22 ....165 C2
Havant PO9 ....135 C1
Holbury SO45 ....150 B4
Horndean PO8 ....116 C3
Hythe, Hardley SO45 ....150 A4
Ibsley BH24 ....117 A4
Landford SP5 ....49 C1
Littleton SO22 ....1 A3
Locks Heath SO31 ....152 C4
Meonstoke SO32 ....61 B2
Michelmersh SO51 ....27 B4
Milford on Sea SO41 ....212 A2
Netley SO31 ....127 A3
Poole BH12 ....203 B3
Portsmouth PO2 ....182 C4
Ringwood BH24 ....141 A2
Rockbourne SP6 ....44 C1
Romsey SO51 ....53 A4
Southampton SO14 ......103 A1
Southbourne PO10 ......161 C4
Swanmore SO32 ....84 A3
Swanwick SO31 ....128 C4
Westbourne PO10 ....137 A2
Woodlands BH21 ....114 A3
New Rd E PO2 ....182 C4
New St Lymington SO41 .197 C2
9 Poole BH15 ....202 A1
New Street Mews SO41 .197 C2
New Town PO16 ....156 B4
New Valley Rd SO41 ....211 B3
Newbarn La PO18 ......137 C4
Newbarn Rd PO9 ......135 B2
Newbolt Cl PO8 ....111 C2
Newbolt Rd
22 Cosham PO6 ....133 A1
Portchester PO16 ....132 C1
Newbridge SO31 ....127 B3
Newbridge Jun Sch
PO1 ....182 C4
Newbridge Rd SO40 ....75 A1
Newbridge Way SO41 ..197 A4
Newbroke Rd PO13 ....180 C4
Newburgh St SO23 ......10 C4
Newbury Cl SO50 ....57 A1
Newbury Dr BH10 ......189 B3
Newbury Pl SO31 ......128 C3
Newbury Rd SO15 ......78 B3
Newcombe Rd
Bournemouth BH6 ....206 C3
Southampton SO15 ......102 C3
West Moors BH22 ....138 B1
Newcomen Ct 8 PO2 ...157 B1
Newcomen Rd BH23 ...207 A4
Newcroft Gdns BH23 ...207 A4
Newenham Rd SO41 ...197 C1
Newfield Rd GU33 ......21 A2

Newfoundland Dr BH15 .202 B1
Newfoundland Drive Rdbt
  BH15 ....202 B1
Newgate La PO14 ....155 A2
Newgate Lane Ind Est
  PO14 ....155 A3
Newland Ave PO12 ...181 A2
Newlands PO15 ....130 B1
Newlands Ave SO15 ..102 B4
Newlands Cl
  Blackfield SO45 ....150 C1
  Chandler's Ford SO53 ..54 C3
Newlands Copse SO45 .150 C1
Newlands Inf Sch SO16 ..77 C1
Newlands Jun Sch SO16 .77 C1
Newlands La PO7 ....134 A3
Newlands Manor SO41 .211 B4
Newlands Rd
  Blackfield SO45 ....150 C1
  Bournemouth BH7 ...206 A3
  Christchurch BH23 ..207 C4
  New Milton BH25 ...195 A1
Newlands Way BH17 ..79 B1
Newlyn Way Poole BH12 .203 C4
  Portsmouth PO6 ....157 A4
Newlyn Wlk SO51 ...28 A1
Newman St SO16 ....102 A4
Newman's La PO17 ..138 B2
Newmans Cl BH22 ...138 C3
Newmans Hill PO17 ..84 B1
Newmarket Cl SO50 ..81 B4
Newmer Ct 4 PO9 ...135 B3
Newmorton Rd BH9 ..190 A2
Newney Cl PO2 .....157 C2
Newnham Cir PO9 ...136 A3
Newport Cl SO53 ...55 A2
Newport La SO53 ...28 B3
Newport Rd PO12 ...180 C3
Newstead Rd BH6 ...206 B2
Newton Bglws SP5 ..24 A2
Newton CE Prim Sch
  PO12 ....181 B3
Newton Cl
  Stubbington PO14 ...154 B2
  Whiteparish SP5 ....54 C2
Newton La Romsey SO51 .52 C3
  Whiteparish SP5 ....24 A2
Newton Morrell BH14 .203 B2
Newton Pl PO17 ....179 C2
Newton Rd
  Barton on Sea BH25 .210 A4
  Poole BH13 ....214 C4
  Southampton SO18 ..79 C1
  Twyford SO21 ......32 A4
Newtown Bsns Ctr
  BH12 ....203 A4
Newtown Cl SO31 ...128 B1
Newtown La
  Corfe Mullen BH21 .186 B4
  Ibsley SP6,BH24 ...94 B1
  South Hayling PO11 .184 C2
  Verwood BH31 .....115 A3
Newtown Rd
  Eastleigh SO50 ....56 A2
  Locks Heath SO31 .152 B4
  Sherfield English SO51 .26 A2
  Southampton SO19 .104 A4
  Verwood BH31 .....115 A3
Newtown Soberton Inf Sch
  PO17 ....109 B3
Nichol Rd SO53 ....30 B1
Nicholas Cl BH23 ..194 A1
Nicholas Cres PO15 .130 C1
Nicholas Ct
  10 Lee-on-the-Solent
  PO13 ....179 C1
Nicholas Gdns PO8 .189 B1
Nicholas Rd SO45 ..177 C4
Nichole Cl BH12 ...203 A4
Nicholl Pl PO13 ...155 B1
Nicholson Cl PO12 .142 A1
Nicholson Ct PO17 .202 C4
Nicholson Gdns 1 PO1 .215 C3
Nicholson Way PO9 .135 C2
Nicholson Wlk SO16 .77 B3
Nickel St 4 PO5 ...215 A1
Nickleby Gdns SO40 .100 A4
Nickleby Ho 10 PO1 .182 B4
Nickleby Rd PO8 ...88 A3
Nickson Cl SO53 ...55 A4
Nightingale Ave SO50 .55 B1
Nightingale Cl
  Bursledon SO31 ...127 C4
  Gosport PO12 .....180 C3
  Romsey SO51 ......53 A4
  Rowland's Castle PO9 .113 A3
  Verwood BH31 ....115 A3
  West Wellow SO51 .50 B2
  Winchester SO23 ..10 B3
Nightingale Cres SO32 .107 C4
Nightingale Dr SO40 .100 B4
Nightingale Gr SO15 .102 B4
Nightingale La 4 BH15 .202 B1
Nightingale Mews
  Locks Heath SO31 .129 A2
  Netley SO31 ......127 B3
Nightingale Pk 8 PO7 .136 A1
Nightingale Prim Sch
  SO50 ....55 B1
Nightingale Rd
  Petersfield GU32 ..40 B1

Nightingale Rd continued
  Portsmouth PO5 ....182 A1
  Southampton SO15 ..102 B4
Nightingale Wlk SO31 .127 B2
Nightingale Ct 9
  SO15 ....102 B3
Nightjar Cl
  Broadstone BH17 ...201 C4
  Waterlooville PO8 ..112 A3
Nile Rd SO17 ......79 A1
Nile St PO10 ......160 C4
Nimrod Dr PO13 ....180 B3
Nimrod Way BH21 ...164 C3
Nine Acres GU32 ...20 A1
Nine Elms La PO17 .131 C2
Ninian Cl SO30 ....57 B1
Ninian Park Rd PO3 .158 A1
Niton Cl PO13 .....155 B1
Niton Rd PO13 .....155 B1
Noads Cl SO45 .....125 C1
Noads Way SO45 ...125 C1
Noadswood Sch
  SO45 ....125 C1
Nob's Crook SO21 ..57 A4
Nobbs La PO1 ......182 A2
Nobes Ave PO13 ...155 B2
Nobes Cl PO13 ....155 B1
Noble Cl BH11 .....188 C1
Noble Rd SO30 ....105 B3
Noel Cl SO42 .....146 A1
Noel Rd BH10 .....189 A1
Noel The BH25 ....195 B2
Nomansland & Hamptworth
  CE Sch SP5 ....73 B4
Nook The Eastleigh SO50 .56 A3
  Gosport PO13 .....155 C1
Noon Gdns BH31 ...115 A3
Noon Hill Dr BH31 .115 A3
Noon Hill Rd BH31 .115 A3
Norbury Cl SO53 ..55 A4
Norbury Gdns SO31 .127 C1
Norcliffe Cl BH10 .189 A2
Norcliffe Rd SO17 .103 A4
Norcroft Ct SO15 ..78 B1
Nordik Gdns SO30 .105 B3
Nore Cres PO10 ...136 B1
Nore Farm Ave PO10 .136 B1
Norevil Rd GU32 ..40 B2
Norfolk Ave PO3 ..191 C1
Norfolk Cres PO11 .184 C1
Norfolk Cl SO53 ..55 B2
Norfolk Ho 4 PO9 .136 A1
Norfolk Mews PO11 .184 C1
Norfolk Rd Gosport PO12 .180 C4
  Portsmouth PO1 ..215 C4
Norfolk St PO5 ...215 B2
Norgett Way PO16 .156 A4
Norham Ave SO16 .78 B1
Norham Cl SO16 ..78 B1
Norland Rd PO4 ..215 C1
Norlands Dr SO21 .31 B2
Norley Cl PO9 ...135 C3
Norleywood BH23 .208 C4
Norleywood Rd SO41 .198 C4
Norman Ave PO13 .204 A3
Norman Cl BH8 ..190 C4
Norman Ct 11 PO4 .182 C1
Norman Gdns
  Hedge End SO30 .105 A3
  Poole BH12 ......204 A3
Norman Ho 10 SO14 .103 B3
Norman Rd
  Blackfield SO45 .177 C4
  Gosport PO12 ...181 A3
  Portsmouth PO4 .182 C2
  South Hayling PO11 .185 A3
  Southampton SO15 .102 B3
  Winchester SO23 .10 C3
Norman Way PO9 .135 B1
Normandy Cl
  Rownhams SO16 .77 C3
  Sway SO41 ......172 A1
Normandy Ct
  Locks Heath SO31 .128 B1
  Wickham PO17 ...108 A2
Normandy Dr BH23 .207 A4
Normandy Gdns PO12 .180 C2
Normandy Ho SO51 .53 A4
Normandy La SO41 .197 C1
Normandy Rd PO2 .157 C2
Normandy Way
  Fordingbridge SP6 .69 C1
  Hamworthy BH15 .201 B1
  Marchwood SO40 .102 A1
Normanhurst Ave BH8 .190 C1
Normans SO23 ....10 C3
Normanton Cl BH23 .191 C1
Norris Cl Romsey SO51 .28 B1
  St Leonards BH24 .139 C2
Norris Gdns Havant PO10 .160 A4
  New Milton BH25 .195 A1
Norris Hill SO18 ..79 C3
Norris Ct PO12 ...182 C4
Norrish Rd BH12 .203 B3
Norset Rd PO15 ..130 B1
North Ave
  Bournemouth BH10 .189 B3
  Portsmouth PO2 ..157 C3
North Baddesley Inf Sch
  SO52 ....54 A2
North Baddesley Jun Sch
  SO52 ....54 A2
North Battery Rd PO2 .157 A1
North Bay PO11 ...161 A2
North Block SO15 .102 B3
North Cl Gosport PO12 .180 C2
  Havant PO9 ......160 A4
  Lymington SO41 ..197 C2
  Romsey SO51 .....28 B1

North Common La
  Landford SP5 .....49 A3
  Sway SO41 ....196 C4
North Cres PO11 ..185 A2
North Cross St PO12 .181 B2
North Ct PO1 .....182 C4
North Cl PO13 ....104 B3
North East Rd SO19 .104 A2
North End Ave PO2 .157 B1
North End Cl SO53 .55 B2
North End Farm Cotts
  SO24 ....14 B4
North End Cr PO2 .157 B1
North End La SP6,BH24 .93 B2
North Fields Cotts .32 A4
North Front 16 SO14 .103 A3
North Greenlands SO41 .197 B1
North Head SO41 ..211 A3
North Hill Cl SO22 .1 C1
North Hill Ct SO22 .1 C1
North La Beaulieu SO42 .148 C3
  Burton GU31 .....65 C3
  Clanfield PO8 ....88 B4
  East Meon PO8 ...64 B1
  Nomansland SP5 .73 B4
  West Tytherley SP5 .44 A1
North Lodge Rd BH14 .203 C2
North Millers Dale SO53 .55 A4
North Park Bsns Ctr
  PO17 ....130 B4
North Poulner Rd BH24 .117 A1
North Rd
  Bournemouth BH7 .205 C3
  Brockenhurst SO42 .146 A1
  Horndean PO8 ...88 B1
  Hythe SO45 ......125 C3
  Kings Worthy SO23 .2 A4
  Petersfield GU32 .40 C2
  Poole BH14 ......203 A2
  Southampton SO17 .103 B4
North Rd E PO17 ..133 A3
North Rd W PO17 .133 A3
North Shore Rd PO11 .184 B2
North St Emsworth PO10 .136 C1
  Gosport PO12 ....181 B2
  Havant PO9 ......135 B1
  Havant, Bedhampton PO9 .135 B1
  Lymington SO41 ..197 B1
  Poole BH15 ......202 B1
  Portsmouth PO1 .215 C4
  Portsmouth, Portsea PO1 .182 A3
  Westbourne PO10 .137 A2
North Street Arc 11
  ....135 C1
North Stroud La SO32 .39 C2
North Trestle Rd SO45 .151 B3
North View SO22 .100 C4
North Wallington PO16 .131 B1
North Walls SO23 .11 A4
North Way Gosport PO13 .155 B2
  Havant PO9 ......135 C1
North Weirs SO42 .145 B1
North Wlk BH2 ...203 A3

Northern Rd
  Cosham PO6 ......157 C4
  Fawley SO45 .....151 C1
Northern Way PO1 .181 C4
Northerwood Ave SO43 .121 C3
Northerwood Cl SO52 .53 C2
Northey Rd BH6 ...206 C3
Northfield Ave PO14 .154 C4
Northfield Cl
  Bishop's Waltham SO32 .59 A1
  Horndean PO8 ....88 B1
Northfield Pk PO16 .132 A1
Northfield Rd
  Milford on Sea SO41 .211 C2
  Ringwood BH24 ...117 A1
  Southampton SO18 .79 C1
Northfields Farm La
  PO17 ....108 A3
Northgate Ave PO2 .182 C4
Northgate Chambers 9
  SO23 ....11 A4
Northlands Cl SO40 .100 B4
Northlands Dr SO23 .2 A1
Northlands Gdns SO15 .102 C4
Northlands Rd
  Eastleigh SO50 ..56 A2
  Romsey SO51 .....53 B3
  Southampton SO15,SO40 .102 C4
  Totton SO40 .....100 C4
Northleigh Cnr SO18 .79 C3
Northleigh La BH21 .163 C3
Northmead Dr BH17 .201 C4
Northmere Dr PO12 .203 C4
Northmere Rd BH12 .203 C4
Northmore Cl SO31 .129 A3
Northmore Rd SO31 .129 A3
Northney La PO11 .160 B2
Northney Rd PO11 .160 B2
Northolt Gdns SO16 .78 A3
Northover BH3 ....204 C3
Northover La SO41 .195 C4
Northover Rd
  Lymington SO41 ..197 A2
  Portsmouth PO3 ..183 A4
Northumberland Ct
  BH24 ....140 C4
Northumberland Rd
  Portsmouth PO5 ..215 D3
  Southampton SO14 .103 A3
Northways PO14 ...179 B3
Northwood Cl SO16 .79 A3
Northwood La PO11 .160 A1
Northwood Rd PO2 .157 C3
Northwood Sq 8 PO16 .131 A1
Northwt Rd BH5 ..205 A3
Norton Cl
  Christchurch BH23 .207 B4
  Southampton SO19 .103 C2
  Stubbington SO31 .127 C4
  Waterlooville PO7 .132 C3
  Waterlooville PO7 .134 B4
Norton Dr PO16 ...131 A2
Norton Rd
  Bournemouth BH9 .204 C4
  Cosham PO6 ......133 B1
Norway Cl 3 BH9 .189 C1
Norway Rd PO3 ...158 A2
Norwich Ave BH2 ..204 B2
Norwich Ave W BH2 .204 A2
Norwich Cl SO31 .128 C2
Norwich Ct 12 BH2 .204 B2
Norwich Mans 4 BH2 .204 B2
Norwich Pl PO13 .179 C2
Norwich Rd
  Bournemouth BH2 .204 C2
  Cosham PO6 ......133 B1
Norwood Pl BH5 ..206 A3
Norwood Prim Sch SO30 .56 A2
Nottingham Pl PO13 .179 C2
Nouale La BH24 ...141 B4
Novello Gdns PO7 .134 C3
Noyce Dr SO50 ...57 B1
Noyce Gdns BH8 ..191 A1
Nuffield Hospl BH5 .205 C2
Nuffield Ind Est BH17 .202 B4
Nuffield Rd BH17 .202 B4
Nugent Rd BH6 ...207 A2
Nunns Pk SP5 ....24 A2
Nuns Rd SO23 ....2 A1
Nurse's Path SO21 .32 A3
Nursery Cl
  Emsworth PO10 ..136 C2
  Gosport PO13 ....155 A2
Nursery Field GU33 .20 C2
Nursery Gdns
  Chandler's Ford SO53 .55 B2
  Romsey SO51 .....53 A4
  Southampton SO19 .104 A3
  Waterlooville PO8 .112 A2
  Winchester SO23 .10 B4
Nursery Gr SO30 .105 B3
Nursery La PO14 .179 B3
Nursery Rd
  Bournemouth BH9 .190 A2
  Havant PO9 ......135 B1
  Ringwood BH24 ..141 A3
  Southampton SO18 .79 B1

Nutbourne Pk PO18 .161 C4
Nutbourne Rd
  Cosham PO6 ......158 B4
  South Hayling PO11 .185 C1
Nutburn Rd SO52 ..54 A3
Nutfield Ct SO16 ..77 C2
Nutfield Pl PO1 ...215 C4
Nutfield Rd SO16 ..77 B3
Nuthatch Cl
  Broadstone BH17 .201 C4
  Ferndown BH22 ..165 A4
  Rowland's Castle PO9 .113 A1
Nuthatch Cl BH11 .188 C2
Nutley Rd PO9 ...135 B3
Nutley Way BH11 .188 C2
Nutsey Ave SO40 .76 B1
Nutsey Cl SO40 ..76 C2
Nutsey La SO40 ..76 C1
Nutshalling Ave SO16 .77 C3
Nutshalling Cl SO40 .76 B3
Nutwick Rd PO9 ..136 A2
Nutwood Way SO40 .76 C1
Nyewood Ave PO16 .132 B1
Nyria Way PO12 ..181 B2

O

O' Jays Ind Pk PO3 .158 A1
O'Connell Rd SO50 .55 C1
Oak Ave BH23 ....206 B4
Oak Cl Corfe Mullen BH21 .186 B3
  Fareham BH22 ...165 C1
  Hythe SO45 .....125 C1
  Lyndhurst SO43 ..121 C2
  Southampton SO15 .103 B3
  Upham SO32 .....58 C3
  Waterlooville PO8 .111 C1
Oak Coppice Cl SO50 .57 A1
Oak Ct Fareham PO15 .130 B1
  Lymington SO41 ..197 B3
Oak Dr SO50 .....57 B1
Oak Gdns SO41 ..211 B4
Oak Green Way SO18 .104 A4
Oak La BH24 .....141 A4
Oak Lodge 4 PO2 .157 B1
Oak Lodge Specl Sch
  ....125 B2
Oak Meadow CE Prim Sch
  SO31 ....105 B2
Oak Mews BH12 ..203 B3
Oak Park Dr PO9 .156 A4
Oak Park Ind Est PO6 .157 B4
Oak Rd Alderholt SP6 .92 C3
  Bishop's Waltham SO32 .83 C4
  Bournemouth BH8 .205 B3
  Bursledon SO31 ..127 C4
  Clanfield PO8 ...88 B3
  Fareham PO15 ...125 C1
  New Milton BH25 .195 B2
  Southampton SO19 .103 C3
  Upton BH16 .....201 B3
Oak St PO12 .....181 B2
Oak Tree Cl SO21 .56 C4
Oak Tree Dr
  Emsworth PO10 ..136 C2
  Liss GU33 ....21 A2
Oak Tree Gdns SO30 .105 A3
Oak Tree Rd SO18 .79 C1
Oak Tree Way SO50 .56 A3
Oak Vale SO30 ...80 A2
Oak Wlk SO50 ...57 B1
Oakapple Gdns PO6 .158 C4
Oakbank Rd
  Bishopstoke SO50 .56 B2
  Southampton SO19 .103 C2
Oakcroft La PO14 .154 B3
Oakdale Rd BH15 .202 C3
Oakdale South Road Mid Sch
  BH15 ....202 B3
Oakdene Gosport PO13 .155 B1
  8 Southampton SO17 .79 B2
  Totton SO40 ....100 B4
Oakdene Cl BH21 .163 B3
Oakdene Gdns 3 SO50 .57 B1
Oakdown Rd PO14 .154 B2
Oakenbrow Hythe SO45 .125 B3
  Sway SO41 ......172 A1
Oakes The PO14 ..154 A2
Oakfield Ct 32 PO9 .136 A3
Oakfield Prim Sch SO40 .76 C2
Oakfield Rd Cadnam SO40 .99 A4
  Poole BH15 ......202 B3
  Totton SO40 ....100 C4
Oakfields SO50 ..56 A4
Oakford Ct BH8 ..190 B2
Oakgrove Rd SO50 .56 C1
Oakgrove Rd SO50 .56 C1
Oakham Grange BH22 .165 C3
Oakhall SO31 ....105 A1
Oakhill Cl
  Bursledon SO31 ..105 A1
  Chandler's Ford SO53 .55 C3
Oakhill Cr SO53 ..55 C3
Oakhill Terr SO31 .105 A1
Oakhurst Cl Netley SO31 .127 B3
  West Moors BH22 .138 B3
Oakhurst Dr PO7 .134 A4
Oakhurst Fst Sch BH22 .138 C1
Oakhurst Gdns PO7 .134 A4
Oakhurst La GU33 .21 A1
Oakhurst Rd
  Southampton SO17 .79 A2
  West Moors BH22 .138 C1

Oakhurst Way SO31 ....127 B3
Oakland Dr SO40 ....101 C1
Oakland Wlk BH22 ....165 C1
Oaklands
  Chandler's Ford SO53 ....30 A1
  Lymington SO41 ....197 C1
  Waterlooville PO7 ....135 A3
Oaklands Ave SO40 ....100 C4
Oaklands Cl
  Fordingbridge SP6 ....69 C1
  Verwood BH31 ....114 C3
  Winchester SO22 ....10 B3
Oaklands Com Sch SO16 ....77 C2
Oaklands Gdns PO14 ....129 B1
Oaklands Gr PO8 ....111 C2
Oaklands Ho ☑ PO6 ....132 C1
Oaklands RC Comp Sch
  PO7 ....134 C3
Oaklands Inf Sch
  Petersfield GU32 ....40 C2
Oaklands The SO53 ....55 B2
Oaklands Way
  Hythe SO45 ....125 B1
  Southampton SO16 ....78 C2
  Titchfield PO14 ....129 B1
Oaklea Cl SO40 ....124 C4
Oakleigh Cres SO40 ....100 C3
Oakleigh Dr SP5 ....73 B4
Oakleigh Gdns SO51 ....53 A4
Oakleigh Way BH23 ....208 C4
Oakley Cl SO45 ....150 B2
Oakley Gdns BH16 ....201 A4
Oakley Hill BH21 ....163 B1
Oakley Ho
  Portsmouth PO5 ....215 B1
  ⑪ Southampton, Banister's Pk
  SO15 ....102 C4
  ⑱ Southampton, Shirley
  SO16 ....102 A4
Oakley La BH21 ....163 C1
Oakley Rd Havant PO9 ....135 B3
  Mottisfont SO51 ....5 C2
  Southampton SO16 ....102 A4
  Wimborne Minst BH21 ....163 B1
Oakley Straight BH21 ....163 C1
Oakmead Coll of Tech
  BH11 ....188 C2
Oakmead Gdns BH11 ....188 C2
Oakmead Rd BH17 ....201 C4
Oakmeadow Cl PO10 ....137 A2
Oakmount Ave
  Chandler's Ford SO53 ....55 B2
  Southampton SO17 ....79 A1
  Totton SO40 ....100 C4
Oakmount Dr PO8 ....111 C1
Oakmount Mans SO17 ....78 C1
Oakmount Rd SO53 ....55 C3
Oakridge Rd SO15 ....101 B4
Oaks Coppice PO8 ....112 A3
Oaks Dr BH24 ....139 B2
Oaks Mead BH31 ....115 A3
Oaks The Burslodon SO31 ....127 C4
  Southampton SO19 ....103 C3
  Verwood BH31 ....114 C4
  Waterlooville PO8 ....112 A1
Oakshott Dr PO9 ....136 A3
Oakthorn Cl PO13 ....180 B3
Oaktree Cl
  Milford on Sea SO41 ....211 B2
  Southampton SO16 ....78 C2
Oaktree Cvn Pk SO30 ....80 B2
Oaktree Pear BH21 ....169 A1
Oaktree Rd PO10 ....183 A3
Oakville Mans ⑪ SO15 ....102 C2
Oakwood BH3 ....204 C4
Oakwood Ave
  Havant PO9 ....135 A2
  New Milton BH25 ....195 B2
  Otterbourne SO21 ....31 B2
Oakwood Cl
  Bournemouth BH9 ....190 A1
  Chandler's Ford SO53 ....30 B1
  Locks Heath SO31 ....152 B4
  Otterbourne SO21 ....31 B2
  Romsey SO51 ....28 B1
Oakwood Ct
  Chandler's Ford SO53 ....30 B1
  New Milton BH25 ....195 A2
  West End SO30 ....80 C1
Oakwood Ctr The PO9 ....136 A2
Oakwood Dr SO16 ....78 B3
Oakwood Ho SO21 ....31 B2
Oakwood Jun Sch SO16 ....78 A3
Oakwood Lodge SO21 ....31 B2
Oakwood Rd
  Bournemouth BH9 ....190 A1
  Chandler's Ford SO53 ....55 B4
  Christchurch BH23 ....193 C1
  Portsmouth PO2 ....157 C2
  South Hayling PO11 ....184 C2
Oakwood Way SO31 ....128 A2
Oasis Mews BH16 ....201 A4
Oasis The ⑪ BH12 ....204 A2
Oates Rd BH9 ....189 C1
Oatfield Gdns SO40 ....76 B1
Oatlands SO51 ....52 C4
Oatlands Cl SO32 ....81 C1
Oatlands Rd SO32 ....81 C1
Oban Rd BH3 ....204 C4
Obelisk Ct SO19 ....103 B1
Obelisk Rd SO19 ....103 C1
Ober Rd SO42 ....145 C1
Oberfield Rd SO42 ....145 B1

Oberland Ct SO41 ....197 B2
Oberon Cl PO7 ....135 A4
Occupation La PO14 ....153 C4
Ocean Cl PO15 ....130 B1
Ocean Ct PO11 ....184 C2
Ocean Hts ☑ BH5 ....205 C2
Ocean Pk PO3 ....158 A1
Ocean Rd Gosport PO14 ....154 C3
  Southampton SO14 ....103 A1
  Ocean Way SO14 ....103 A1
Ockendon Cl PO5 ....215 B2
Ocknell Gr SO45 ....125 B2
Octavia Gdns SO31 ....55 C4
Octavia Hill SO22 ....10 B3
Octavia Rd SO18 ....79 C2
Octavius Ct ⑱ PO7 ....112 A1
Odell Cl PO16 ....130 C2
Odeon Bldgs ⑩ PO6 ....157 C4
Odiham Cl
  Chandler's Ford SO53 ....55 A2
  Southampton SO16 ....77 C2
Oelander Cl SO31 ....129 A3
Oglander Rd SO23 ....2 A1
Ogle Rd SO14 ....102 C2
OK Mobile Home Pk
  BH23 ....208 A4
Okeford Rd BH18 ....187 B2
Okement Cl SO18 ....80 A1
Old Agwi Rd SO45 ....151 B3
Old Barn Cl
  Christchurch BH23 ....191 B1
  Ringwood BH24 ....141 B4
Old Barn Cres PO7 ....86 B1
Old Barn Farm Rd BH21 ....139 A3
Old Barn Gdns PO8 ....111 C3
Old Barn Rd BH23 ....191 B1
Old Bound Rd BH16 ....201 B3
Old Brickyard Rd SP6 ....69 A1
Old Bridge Cl SO31 ....128 A4
Old Bridge House Rd
  SO31 ....128 A4
Old Bridge Rd
  Bournemouth BH6 ....206 B4
  Portsmouth PO4 ....182 C1
Old Canal ⑤ PO4 ....183 A2
Old Christchurch La ⑱
  BH1 ....204 C2
Old Christchurch Rd
  Bournemouth BH1,BH2 ....204 C2
  Hordle SO41 ....196 B1
Old Coastguard Rd
  BH13 ....214 A2
Old Comm SO31 ....129 A2
Old Commercial Rd
  PO1 ....182 B4
Old Common Gdns
  SO31 ....129 A2
Old Copse Rd PO9 ....136 A2
Old Cottage Cl SO51 ....50 C2
Old Court Mews BH14 ....203 A2
Old Courts The SO16 ....77 A3
Old Cracknore Cl SO40 ....102 A1
Old Cricket Mews SO15 ....102 C4
Old Farm Cl BH24 ....117 B1
Old Farm Copse SO51 ....50 C2
Old Farm Dr SO18 ....79 C2
Old Farm La
  Stubbington PO14 ....179 B3
  Westbourne PO10 ....137 B2
Old Farm Rd BH15 ....202 C3
Old Farm Way PO6 ....158 C4
Old Farm Wlk SO41 ....197 C3
Old Farmhouse Mews
  SO41 ....197 C3
Old Forge Cl SP6 ....92 C3
Old Forge Ct SO41 ....197 B1
Old Forge Ho PO13 ....183 A4
Old Forge The SO32 ....107 B4
Old Garden Cl SO31 ....129 B1
Old Gdns SO22 ....1 C1
Old Generator Ho The
  BH12 ....204 A3
Old Gosport Rd PO16 ....155 A4
Old Granary The SP5 ....46 C4
Old Ham La BH21 ....164 B2
Old Highway Mews
  BH21 ....163 B2
Old Hillside Rd SO22 ....1 B1
Old Infirmary Rd PO1 ....182 A2
Old Ivy La SO18 ....80 A3
Old Kennels Cl SO22 ....10 A2
Old Kennels La SO22 ....10 A2
Old Kiln Rd BH16 ....201 B3
Old Lifeboat House (Mus)*
  BH15 ....202 B1
Old Litten La GU32 ....19 B2
Old London Rd PO2 ....157 C2
Old Lyndhurst Rd SO40 ....98 C4
Old Magazine Cl SO40 ....101 C1
Old Maltings The SO41 ....197 B2
Old Manor Cl BH21 ....163 B2
Old Manor Farm PO9 ....135 A1
Old Manor Way PO6 ....158 A4
Old Market Rd BH21 ....186 A4
Old Mill Ho BH24 ....140 C3
Old Mill La
  Hambledon PO8 ....87 B2
  Petersfield GU31 ....41 A3
Old Mill Way SO16 ....78 A1
Old Milton Gn BH25 ....194 C1
Old Milton Rd BH25 ....195 A1
Old Mulberry Cl BH10 ....189 A1
Old Orch BH15 ....202 B2
Old Orchards SO41 ....197 C1
Old Parsonage Ct SO21 ....31 B2
Old Pines Cl BH22 ....165 C2
Old Priory Cl SO31 ....128 A1
Old Priory Rd BH6 ....206 C2

Old Rd Gosport PO12 ....181 B2
  Romsey SO51 ....53 A4
  Southampton SO14 ....103 A1
  Wimborne Minst BH21 ....163 A3
Old Rectory Cl
  Corfe Mullen BH21 ....186 B4
  Westbourne PO10 ....137 A2
Old Rectory Ct SO40 ....101 A3
Old Rectory Gdns SO21 ....32 A3
Old Rectory La SO21 ....32 A3
Old Rectory Rd PO6 ....158 B4
Old Redbridge Rd SO15 ....101 B4
Old Reservoir Rd PO6 ....158 B4
Old River PO7 ....110 C2
Old Road The PO6 ....157 C3
Old Romsey Rd SO40 ....98 C4
Old Rope Wlk The BH15 ....201 C1
Old Ropewalk BH15 ....202 A1
Old Salisbury La SO51 ....27 A1
Old Salisbury Rd SO51 ....75 C4
Old Sandpit La BH16 ....186 A1
Old Sawmill Cl BH31 ....114 B4
Old School Cl
  Ferndown BH22 ....165 B3
  Holbury SO45 ....150 A3
  Netley SO31 ....127 B4
  Poole BH14 ....203 A2
Old School Dr PO11 ....185 A1
Old School Gdns SO30 ....80 C1
Old School Rd GU33 ....20 C2
Old Shambleburst La
  SO30 ....81 B1
Old Spring La SO32 ....84 A3
Old St PO14 ....154 A2
Old St John's Mews
  BH9 ....189 C2
Old Stacks Gdns BH24 ....141 B3
Old Star Pl ⑳ PO1 ....182 A3
Old Station App SO23 ....11 A4
Old Swanwick La SO31 ....128 B4
Old Timbers PO11 ....184 C2
Old Town Mews ⑤
  BH15 ....202 B1
Old Turnpike PO16 ....131 A2
Old Turnpike Bsns Pk
  PO16 ....131 A1
Old Van Diemans Rd
  PO7 ....134 B3
Old Vicarage Cl BH10 ....189 C3
Old Vicarage La SO41 ....196 B4
Old Vineries The SP6 ....69 B1
Old Wareham Rd
  Corfe Mullen BH21 ....186 A2
  Poole BH12 ....203 A4
Old Well Cl The SO19 ....104 A4
Old Winchester Hill La
  Warnford SO32,GU32 ....37 A1
  West Meon GU32 ....37 B1
Old Winchester Hill Nature
  Reserve* SO32 ....62 B3
Old Winchester Hill Nature
  Trail* GU32 ....62 B3
Old Wymering La PO6 ....157 C4
Oldbarn Cl SO40 ....76 B1
Oldbury Cl SO16 ....77 B1
Oldbury Ho ⑱ PO5 ....215 B2
Oldbury Way PO14 ....154 B4
Oldenburg SO21 ....31 B2
Oldgate Gdns ⑧ PO2 ....157 C2
Oleander Dr SO40 ....100 A4
Olinda St PO1 ....182 B4
Olive Cres PO16 ....156 B3
Olive Ct PO2 ....182 C4
Olive Rd SO16 ....78 A2
Oliver Rd Lymington SO41 ....197 B2
  Portsmouth PO4 ....183 A2
Oliver's Battery Cres
  SO22 ....10 A2
Oliver's Battery Gdns
  SO22 ....10 A2
Oliver's Battery Prim Sch
  SO22 ....10 A2
Oliver's Battery Rd N
  SO22 ....10 A2
Oliver's Battery Rd S
  SO22 ....10 A2
Olivers Cl SO40 ....100 A4
Olivers Rd BH21 ....164 A3
Olivers Way BH21 ....164 A3
Olivia Cl ⑨ PO7 ....112 A1
Olympic Way SO19 ....104 A3
Omdurman Ct ⑳ SO17 ....79 A1
Omdurman Rd SO17 ....79 A1
Omega Ho PO1 ....215 C3
Omega St PO1 ....215 C3
Onibury Cl SO18 ....80 A1
Onibury Rd SO18 ....80 A1
Onslow Gdns BH21 ....163 B3
Onslow Ho BH21 ....163 B3
Onslow Rd
  Portsmouth PO5 ....182 B1
  Southampton SO14 ....103 B3
Ophir Gdns ⑱ BH8 ....205 B3
Ophir Rd
  Bournemouth BH8 ....205 A3
  Portsmouth PO2 ....157 C2
Oracle Dr PO7 ....134 C2
Orange Gr PO13 ....155 B1
Orange Row PO10 ....160 C4
Oratory Gdns BH13 ....214 C4
Orchard Ave
  Bishopstoke SO50 ....56 C1
  Southampton SO19 ....202 C1
Orchard Bglws PO7 ....109 A1
Orchard Cl
  Christchurch BH23 ....207 A3
  Colden Common SO21 ....53 C4

Orchard Cl continued
  Corfe Mullen BH21 ....186 B4
  Edmondsham BH21 ....91 A2
  Fawley SO45 ....151 A2
  Ferndown BH22 ....165 C2
  Fordingbridge SP6 ....69 C1
  Gosport PO12 ....156 A1
  Horndean PO8 ....112 B3
  North Baddesley SO52 ....54 B4
  Ringwood BH24 ....141 A4
  South Hayling PO11 ....184 C1
  Totton SO40 ....100 C3
Orchard Ct Cadnam SO40 ....98 C4
  Hedge End SO30 ....105 C4
  ⑩ New Milton BH25 ....195 A3
  Verwood BH31 ....115 A2
Orchard Cvn Pk The
  SO40 ....99 B3
Orchard Gdns SP6 ....69 C1
Orchard Gr
  New Milton BH25 ....195 A1
  Portchester PO16 ....156 A4
  Waterlooville PO8 ....111 C2
Orchard Ho ⑱ SO14 ....103 A2
Orchard Inf Sch SO45 ....125 C2
Orchard Jun Sch SO45 ....125 C2
Orchard La
  Corfe Mullen BH21 ....186 B4
  Hermitage PO10 ....161 A4
  Romsey SO51 ....52 C4
  Southampton SO14 ....103 A2
Orchard Lea Inf Sch
  PO15 ....130 C2
Orchard Lea Jun Sch
  PO15 ....130 C2
Orchard Leigh ⑥ BH25 ....195 A3
Orchard Mead ⑱ BH24 ....141 A4
Orchard Mews ⑳ BH21 ....207 A3
Orchard Mount ⑳ BH24 ....141 A4
Orchard Pl SO14 ....103 A2
Orchard Rd Fair Oak SO50 ....57 B1
  Gosport PO12 ....181 B3
  Havant PO9 ....159 C4
  Locks Heath SO31 ....128 C1
  Portsmouth PO4 ....182 C2
  Redlynch SP5 ....42 B2
  South Hayling PO11 ....185 A1
Orchard St BH2 ....204 C2
Orchard The
  Bournemouth BH11 ....188 B3
  Bransgore BH23 ....193 B4
  Chilworth SO16 ....54 C1
  Cosham PO6 ....157 C4
  Denmead PO7 ....110 C2
  Milford on Sea SO41 ....211 B2
  Southampton SO16 ....79 A3
Orchard Way SO45 ....125 C1
Orchard Wlk
  ⑳ Bournemouth PO4 ....204 C2
  Winchester SO22 ....1 B1
  Southampton SO30 ....84 B2
Orchards Way
  Southampton SO17 ....79 A1
  West End SO30 ....80 B1
Orcheston Rd BH8 ....205 B3
Orchid Way BH23 ....207 B4
Ordnance Ct PO3 ....158 A3
Ordnance Rd
  Gosport PO12 ....181 B2
  Southampton SO15 ....103 A3
Ordnance Row PO1 ....182 A3
Ordnance Way SO40 ....102 A2
Oregon Cl SO19 ....104 A2
Orestes Gate BH23 ....208 A3
Orford Cl BH23 ....191 B2
Orford Ct ⑰ PO6 ....157 C4
Oriana Way SO16 ....77 A2
Oriel Dr PO14 ....129 A1
Oriel Rd PO2 ....157 B1
Orient Dr SO22 ....1 B1
Orion Cl
  Southampton SO16 ....77 C2
  Stubbington PO14 ....179 B3
Orion Ind Ctr SO18 ....79 C3
Orkney Cl SO16 ....77 C2
Orkney Rd PO6 ....133 C1
Ormesby Dr SO53 ....30 A1
Ormond Cl SO50 ....57 A1
Ormonde Rd BH13 ....204 A1
Ormsby Rd PO5 ....215 B1
Orpen Rd SO19 ....104 B2
Orpine Cl PO15 ....129 C2
Orsmond Cl PO7 ....134 C3
Orwell Cl SO16 ....77 C1
Orwell Cres PO14 ....129 B1
Orwell Rd GU31 ....40 C1
Osborn Cl PO15 ....158 A2
Osborn Mall Rd PO16 ....131 B1
Osborn Rd PO16 ....131 A1
Osborn Sq ⑤ PO16 ....131 B1
Osborne Cl Netley SO31 ....127 B3
  ⑨ Waterlooville PO7 ....135 A4
Osborne Dr
  Chandler's Ford SO53 ....55 C3
Osborne Gdns
  Fair Oak SO50 ....57 C1
  Southampton SO17 ....79 B1
Osborne Ho
  Southampton SO14 ....103 A2
  West Wellow SO51 ....50 C2
Osborne Rd
  Bournemouth BH9 ....190 A2
  Lee-on-the-Solent PO13 ....179 C1
  Locks Heath SO31 ....152 B4
  New Milton BH25 ....195 A3

Osborne Rd continued
  Petersfield GU32 ....40 C2
  Poole BH14 ....203 A2
  Portsmouth PO5 ....182 B1
  Totton SO40 ....101 A4
  Wimborne Minst BH21 ....163 B2
Osborne Rd N SO17 ....79 B1
Osborne Rd S
  Fareham PO16 ....131 A1
  Southampton SO17 ....103 B4
Osborne View Rd PO14 ....179 A3
Osbourne Ho ⑤ BH25 ....195 A2
Osbourne Rd PO12 ....181 B3
Osier Cl PO2 ....157 B2
Osier Rd GU31 ....40 B1
Oslands La SO31 ....128 B4
Oslo Twrs ⑤ SO19 ....126 C3
Osprey Cl
  Christchurch BH23 ....208 A3
  Cosham PO6 ....158 C4
  Marchwood SO40 ....101 C1
  Southampton SO16 ....78 A3
Osprey Ct PO16 ....155 C4
Osprey Dr PO11 ....185 A2
Osprey Gdns PO13 ....179 C1
Osprey Quay PO10 ....161 A4
Ossemsley Manor Ho
  BH23 ....194 B3
Ossemsley South Dr
  BH25 ....194 C4
Osterley Cl SO30 ....105 C3
Osterly Rd SO19 ....103 C3
Oswald Cl BH9 ....189 C1
Oswald Rd BH9 ....189 C1
Othello Dr PO7 ....135 A4
Otter Cl Bishopstoke SO50 ....57 A1
  Gosport PO13 ....180 B3
  Upton BH16 ....201 A3
  Verwood BH31 ....115 A3
Otter Rd BH15 ....202 C3
Otterbourne CE Prim Sch
  SO21 ....31 A1
Otterbourne Cres PO9 ....135 B2
Otterbourne Hill SO21 ....31 B2
Otterbourne Ho SO21 ....31 A1
Otterbourne House Gdns
  SO21 ....31 A1
Otterbourne Rd SO21 ....31 B3
Otters Wlk BH25 ....195 B3
Ouse Cl SO53 ....55 A4
Outer Circ SO16 ....78 A2
Outlands La SO30 ....106 B4
Outram Rd PO5 ....215 C1
Outwick Cross SP6 ....69 C4
Oval Gdns PO12 ....180 C2
Oval Rd SO51 ....5 A1
Oval The GU33 ....20 C2
Over Links Dr BH14 ....203 B1
Overbrook SO45 ....125 C2
Overbrook Way SO52 ....53 C3
Overbury Rd BH14 ....203 B2
Overcliff Rise SO16 ....78 C2
Overcliffe Mans BH1 ....205 B2
Overcombe Cl BH17 ....187 C1
Overdell Ct ⑳ SO15 ....102 C4
Overmead Cl SO41 ....211 B2
Overton Cres PO9 ....135 B3
Overton Rd PO10 ....137 C1
Oviat Cl SO40 ....100 A4
Ovington Ave BH7 ....206 B4
Ovington Ct SO18 ....104 B4
Ovington Gdns BH7 ....206 B4
Ovington Rd SO50 ....56 A1
Owen Cl PO13 ....180 B4
Owen Rd SO50 ....55 C1
Owen St PO4 ....183 A1
Owen's La SO42 ....121 C1
Owers La SO45 ....178 C4
Owls Rd
  Bournemouth BH5 ....205 C2
  Verwood BH31 ....115 A3
Owslebury Bottom SO21 ....33 A3
Owslebury Gr PO9 ....135 C3
Owslebury Prim Sch
  SO21 ....33 A3
Oxburgh Cl SO50 ....55 C3
Oxenwood Gn ⑦ PO9 ....135 B3
Oxey Cl BH25 ....195 A1
Oxford Ave
  Bournemouth BH6 ....206 A3
  Southampton SO14 ....103 A3
Oxford La PO16 ....131 A1
Oxford La
  Bournemouth BH11 ....189 A3
  Swanmore SO32 ....84 C4
Oxford Rd
  Bournemouth BH1 ....205 A2
  Gosport PO12 ....180 C3
  Portsmouth PO5 ....215 D1
  Southampton SO14 ....103 A4
Oxford St SO14 ....103 A2
Oxford Terr SO41 ....172 A1
Oxlease Cl SO51 ....28 B1
Oxleys Cl PO14 ....154 A4
Oxted Cl ⑥ PO4 ....183 A3
Oyster Cl PO13 ....179 B2
Oyster Est The PO6 ....158 B3
Oyster Mews
  ⑤ Emsworth PO10 ....160 C4
  ⑱ Emsworth PO10 ....182 A2
Oyster Quay PO6 ....157 A4
Oyster St PO1 ....182 A2
Ozier Rd SO18 ....80 A1

Pacific Cl SO14 ....103 B1
Packridge La SO51,SO52 ...53 C1
Padbury Cl PO2 ....157 C2
Paddington Cl BH11 ......188 B2
Paddington Ct BH11 ......188 B2
Paddington Rd PO2 ....157 C1
Paddock Cl
 Ferndown BH11 ....165 A3
 St Leonards BH24 ....139 C2
Paddock Ct PO7 ....110 C2
Paddock Gdns SO41 ....197 B3
Paddock Gr BH31 ....115 A3
Paddock The
 Brockenhurst SO42 ....145 C1
 Eastleigh SO50 ....56 A3
 Fordingbridge SP6 ....94 C3
 Gosport PO12 ....181 A2
 Kings Worthy SO23 ....2 B3
 Stubbington PO14 ....154 B2
 Totton SO40 ....76 B1
Paddock Way GU32 ....40 B1
Paddock Wlk PO6 ....157 A4
Paddocks Cl BH12 ....203 A4
Paddocks The
 Bournemouth BH10 ......189 B2
 Fawley SO45 ....151 A2
Padfield Cl BH6 ....206 C3
Padget Rd BH24 ....117 B1
Padnell Ave PO8 ....112 A1
Padnell Inf Sch PO8 .....112 A2
Padnell Jun Sch PO8 .....112 A2
Padnell Pl PO8 ....112 A1
Padnell Rd PO8 ....112 A2
Padstow Pr SP6 ....93 C4
Padwell Rd SO14 ....103 A4
Padwick Ave PO6 ....158 A4
Padwick Ct PO11 ....184 C2
Paffard Cl PO13 ....180 B4
Page La SO45 ....150 B1
Pages La SO42 ....175 B3
Paget Cl BH21 ....164 A4
Paget Rd
 Bournemouth BH11 ......189 A2
 Gosport PO12 ....181 A1
Paget St SO14 ....103 A2
Pagham Cl PO10 ....161 A4
Pagham Gdns PO11 ....185 C1
Paignton Ave PO3 ....183 A4
Paignton Rd SO16 ....77 C1
Paimpol Pl SO51 ....52 C3
Pain's Rd PO5 ....215 C2
Painswick Cl
 Cosham PO6 ....157 B4
 Locks Heath SO31 ....128 C3
Painter Cl PO3 ....158 A2
Painters Field SO23 ......10 C2
Paisley Rd BH6 ....206 B3
Palace Ho* SO42 ....148 C1
Palace La SO42 ....148 C1
Palace Mews SO42 ....83 B4
Palfrey Rd BH10 ....189 B3
Paling Bsns Pk SO30 .....105 A2
Palk Rd PO9 ....135 B1
Pallant Gdns PO16 ....131 B1
Pallant The PO9 ....135 C1
Pallet Cl SO21 ....56 C4
Pallot Cl SO31 ....104 C1
Palm Cl 10 PO5 ....182 B1
Palm Hall Cl SO23 ....11 B4
Palm Rd SO16 ....78 A2
Palma Ct BH23 ....209 A4
Palmer Pl BH25 ....195 A2
Palmer Rd BH15 ....202 B3
Palmers Ford Rd PO10 ...136 C1
Palmers Cl SO50 ....57 B1
Palmerston Ave
 Christchurch BH23 ....207 B3
 Fareham PO16 ....131 A1
Palmerston Bsns Pk
 PO14 ....155 A4
Palmerston Ct BH16 .....201 B4
 SO23 ....10 C3
Palmerston Dr PO14 .....155 A4
Palmerston Mans
 PO5 ....182 B1
Palmerston Rd
 Bournemouth BH1 ....205 C3
 Poole BH14 ....206 C4
 Portsmouth PO5 ....182 B1
 South Hayling PO11 .....185 A2
 Southampton SO14 ......103 A2
 Upton BH16 ....201 B4
Palmerston Road Prec 28
 PO5 ....182 B1
Palmerston St SO51 ....52 C4
Palmerston Way PO12 ....180 C1
Palmyra Rd PO12 ....181 A4
Palomino Dr PO15 ....129 A4
Pamphill CE Fst Sch
 BH21 ....162 C3
Pamplyn Cl SO41 ....197 B2
Pan St PO1 ....215 B4
Pangbourne Ave PO6 .....158 A4
Pangbourne Cl SO19 .....104 A2
Pannall Rd PO12 ....181 A4
Panorama Ct 2 PO13 .....179 C1
Panorama Rd BH13 ....214 A2
Pans Cnr BH21 ....165 C2
Pansy Rd SO16 ....79 A2
Pantheon Rd SO53 ....155 C4
Pantiles The SP6 ....69 B1
Panton Cl PO10 ....136 C2
Panwell Rd SO18 ....104 A4
Parade Ct PO7 ....157 C3

Parade The
 Barton on Sea BH25 .....194 C1
 5 Bournemouth BH6 .....206 C2
 Cadnam SO40 ....98 C4
 Gosport PO13 ....155 A2
 New Milton BH25 ....195 B2
 Poole BH17 ....187 A1
 Portsmouth PO1 ....182 A3
Paradise La
 Bishop's Waltham SO32 ...83 C3
 Netley Marsh SO40 ....99 B3
 Portchester PO16 ....131 C1
 Westbourne PO10 ....137 A2
Paradise St
 10 Poole BH15 ....202 A1
 Portsmouth PO1 ....215 B4
Parchment St SO23 ......11 A4
Parchment The PO9 ......135 C1
Pardoe Cl SO30 ....105 B3
Pardys Hill BH21 ....186 B4
Parham Cl BH25 ....194 C2
Parham Dr SO50 ....55 C2
Parham Rd
 Bournemouth BH10 ......189 B1
 Gosport PO12 ....181 B3
Parish Ct SO41 ....197 C2
Parish Rd BH15 ....202 C2
Park Ave
 Bournemouth BH10 ......189 B3
 Lymington SO41 ....197 B2
 Waterlooville PO7 ......186 A3
 Winchester SO23 ....11 A4
Park Cl
 Brockenhurst SO42 ......146 A1
 Burton BH23 ....209 A2
 Gosport PO12 ....180 C3
 Hythe SO45 ....126 A2
 Lyndhurst SO43 ....122 A2
 Marchwood SO40 ....101 B1
 Milford on Sea SO41 ....211 C2
 New Milton BH25 ....195 B3
 Winchester SO23 ....2 A1
Park Com Sch PO9 ....135 B3
Park Cotts PO17 ....108 A2
Park Court Flats 3
 SO15 ....102 B3
Park Cres PO10 ....136 B1
Park Dr
 14 Milford on Sea SO41 ..211 B2
 North Baddesley SO51 ....53 B3
 12 Petersfield GU31 .....40 C2
 Portsmouth PO5 ....215 B1
 11 Winchester SO23 .....2 A1
Park Dr BH31 ....114 C4
Park Farm Ave PO15 .....130 B2
Park Farm Cl PO15 ......130 B2
Park Farm Rd PO17 ......134 B2
Park Gate Bsns Ctr
 SO31 ....129 A3
Park Gate Mews 14
 BH2 ....204 C2
Park Gate Prim Sch
 SO31 ....129 A2
Park Gdns SO30 ....207 C4
Park Glen SO31 ....129 B2
Park Gr PO6 ....157 C4
Park Hill Cl SO45 ....150 B2
Park Ho
 22 Portsmouth PO5 .....182 B1
 Winchester SO22 ....11 A4
Park Homer Dr BH21 ....164 A3
Park Homer Rd BH21 ....163 C3
Park House Farm Way
 PO9 ....135 B3
Park House Prim Sch
 PO9 ....135 A3
Park La Alderholt SP6 ....92 C3
 Beaulieu SO41 ....200 A4
 Bournemouth BH9 ....189 C2
 Cosham PO6 ....158 A4
 Droxford SO32 ....61 A1
 Havant PO21 ....135 B4
 Havant PO9 ....135 B2
 Holbury SO45 ....150 A2
 Kings Worthy SO21 ......2 B3
 Marchwood SO40 ....101 B1
 Milford on Sea SO41 ....211 B2
 Otterbourne SO21 ....31 A1
 Rowland's Castle PO10 ..137 B4
 Stubbington PO14 ......154 B2
 Swanmore SO32 ....84 C1
 Twyford SO21 ....32 A3
 Waterlooville PO8 ......112 A1
 Wimborne Minst BH21 ..163 B2
Park Lane Rd BH15 ......202 C1
Park Mans 3 PO6 ....158 A4
Park Par PO9 ....135 C2
Park Pl PI BH14 ....202 C2
Park Rd
 Barton on Sea BH25 ....194 C1
 Bishop's Waltham SO32 ..83 A4
 Bournemouth BH8 ....205 A4
 Chandler's Ford SO53 ....55 B4
 Denmead PO7 ....110 C3
 Fordingbridge SP6 ....69 C1
 Gosport PO12 ....181 A2
 Lymington SO41 ....197 B2
 Milford on Sea SO41 ....211 C2
 New Milton BH25 ....195 B3
 4 Petersfield GU31 ......40 C2
 Poole BH14 ....202 C2
 Portsmouth PO1 ....182 C4
 South Hayling PO11 ....184 B2
 Southampton SO15 .....102 B3
 Southbourne PO10 ......137 B1
 Waterlooville PO8 ......134 B2
 Winchester SO22,SO23 ...1 C1

Park Rd N PO9 ....135 C1
Park Rd S PO9 ....135 C1
Park Royal 17 PO2 ......157 C2
Park St Gosport PO12 ...181 A3
 Portsmouth PO5 ....215 A2
 Southampton SO15,SO16 .102 A4
Park Terr 10 PO12 ......181 B2
Park The
 Barton on Sea BH25 .....209 B4
 Droxford SO32 ....61 A1
 3 Bfield Wlk 20 PO9 ....136 A3
Park View Botley SO30 ...106 A4
 Compton (Hants) SO21 ..31 C3
 Hedge End SO30 ....105 A4
 Lockerley SO21 ....4 C2
 New Milton BH25 ....195 A1
 Otterbourne SO21 ....31 A1
 5 Poole BH15 ....202 C2
 Portsmouth PO2 ....157 B2
 Rowland's Castle PO9 ...136 A4
Park View Mews BH25 ...195 A1
Park Villas SO32 ....61 A1
Park Vista GU32 ....38 B1
Park Way Fair Oak SO50 ..57 C1
 Havant PO9 ....135 C1
 West Moors BH22 ....138 C1
Park Wlk Fareham PO15 .130 B2
 Southampton SO14 .....103 A3
Parker Cl PO12 ....156 A1
Parker Gdns PO7 ....134 B1
Parker Rd BH9 ....204 C4
Parkers Cl BH24 ....117 B1
Parkfield Ho 11 PO6 ....132 C1
Parkland BH31 ....115 B2
Parkland Dr BH25 ......209 C4
Parkland Pl
 New Milton BH25 ....195 A1
 18 Southampton SO17 ..103 A4
Parklands
 Locks Heath SO31 ......129 A2
 6 Southampton SO18 ...79 C1
 Totton SO40 ....101 A4
Parklands Ave PO8 ......112 A3
Parklands Bsns Pk PO7 .110 C2
Parklands The
 Chandler's Ford SO53 ....55 B4
 Gosport PO12 ....181 A3
Parkside
 Christchurch BH23 ......193 B1
 Havant PO9 ....135 B1
 Ringwood BH24 ....141 A3
 Totton SO40 ....100 C3
Parkside Ave SO16 ......101 B4
Parkside Gdns
 Bournemouth BH10 .....189 C1
 Winchester SO22 ....1 B1
Parkside Rd BH14 ......203 B2
Parkside The SO15 ......102 A4
Parkstone Ave
 Poole BH14 ....203 B2
 Portsmouth PO4 ....182 C1
Parkstone Gram Sch
 BH14 ....187 A1
Parkstone Hts
 Poole BH14 ....202 C3
 Poole BH14 ....203 A3
Parkstone Rd BH15 .....202 C2
Parkstone Sta BH14 ....203 A2
Parkview BH2 ....204 C2
Parkville Rd SO16 ....79 B2
Parkway PO15 ....129 C4
Parkway Dr BH8 ....205 C4
Parkway Gdns SO53 .....55 B4
Parkway The
 Gosport PO12 ....155 A1
 Southampton SO16 ......79 A3
Parkwood Cl SO30 ......105 B4
Parkwood Ctr PO7 ......134 C4
Parkwood La 12 BH5 ....206 A3
Parkwood Rd
 Bournemouth BH5 ......206 A2
 Wimborne Minst BH21 ..163 B2
Parley Cl BH22 ....165 B1
Parley Cross BH22 ......189 C4
Parley Fst Sch BH22 ....165 B2
Parley La BH23 ....190 B4
Parley Rd BH9 ....190 A1
Parliament Pl SO22 .....10 B2
Parmiter Dr BH21 ......163 C2
Parmiter Ho 2 SO23 ....11 A4
Parmiter Rd BH21 ......163 C2
Parmiter Way BH21 ....163 C2
Parnholt Rd SO51 ....55 C1
Parnholt Rd SO50 ....55 C1
Parr Ho 8 BH14 ....203 A2
Parr Rd 8 BH14 ....203 A2
Parr St BH14 ....203 A2
Parry Cl PO6 ....156 C4
Parsonage Barn La
 BH24 ....141 A4
Parsonage Cl
 Fordingbridge SP6 ....69 C1
 Petersfield GU32 ....41 A3
Parsonage Ct 3 BH8 ....205 A3
Parsonage La SO32 ......82 A3
Parsonage Park Dr SP6 ..69 C1
Parsonage Rd
 Bournemouth BH1 ......205 A2
 Southampton SO14 .....103 B3
 West Wellow SO51 ......50 B2
Parsons Cl PO13 ....157 C2
Partridge Cl
 Christchurch BH23 ......208 A3
 Portchester PO16 ......131 C4
Partridge Down SO22 ....10 A2
Partridge Dr BH14 ......203 B1
Partridge Gdns PO8 .....111 B2
Partridge Gn SO45 .....195 A3
Partridge Hill SP5 ......50 A2

Partridge Rd
 Brockenhurst SO42 .....172 C4
 Hythe SO45 ....125 C1
Partridge Wlk BH14 ....203 A1
Partry Cl SO53 ....55 B4
Pascoe Cl BH14 ....203 A2
Passage La SO31 ....128 A1
Passfield Ave SO50 ......55 C1
Passfield Cl SO50 ....55 C1
Passingham Wlk PO8 ....112 A2
Pastures The
 Cheriton SO24 ....14 B3
 Denmead PO7 ....110 C2
Pat Bear Cl SO15 ......101 B4
Patchins Rd BH16 ......201 A2
Patchins The BH14 .....214 B4
Pathway Dr PO14 ......154 B4
Paternoster Ho 17 SO23 .11 A4
Paternoster Row 28
 SO23 ....11 A4
Patricia Cl SO30 ....80 B1
Patricia Dr SO30 ....105 B4
Patrick Howard- Dobson Ct
 8 PO8 ....111 C2
Patrick's Cl GU33 ....21 A2
Patrick's Copse Rd GU33 .21 A2
Paulet Cl SO18 ....80 A1
Paulet Lecave Ave SO16 .77 C3
Paulet Pl SO22 ....10 C3
Pauletts La SO40 ....76 A2
Pauls La SO41 ....196 C4
Paulsgrove Ent Ctr PO6 .157 B4
Paulsgrove Ind Ctr PO6 .157 A4
Paulsgrove Prim Sch
 PO6 ....157 B4
Paulsgrove Rd PO2 .....182 C4
Paulson Cl SO53 ....55 B4
Paultons Pk* SO51 ......75 B3
Pauncefoot Hill SO51 ...52 B3
Pauncefote Rd PO4 .....206 A3
Pauntley Rd BH23 ......207 C3
Pavan Gdns BH10 ....189 B1
Pavilion Cl SO40 ....81 B4
Pavilion Ct 20 SO15 ....102 C2
Pavilion Rd SO30 ......105 B4
Paxton Cl SO30 ....105 B3
Paxton Rd PO14 ....155 A4
Payne Cl BH22 ....138 C3
Payne's La SO50 ....57 B2
Payne's Rd SO15 ......102 B3
Paynes Hay Rd SO51 ....28 B4
Peace Cl BH23 ....193 A4
Peach Rd SO16 ....78 A2
Peacock Cl PO16 ......155 C4
Peacock La PO1 ....182 A2
Peacock Pl 8 SO23 ......11 B4
Peak Cl SO16 ....101 C4
Peak Dr PO14 ....154 B4
Peak La
 Bishop's Waltham SO32 ..59 A2
 Fareham PO14 ....154 B4
Peak Rd PO8 ....88 A3
Peak The PO9 ....113 B1
Peake New Rd SO32 .....61 C4
Peakfield PO7 ....110 C2
Peaksham Gdns SP6 .....69 C1
Pear Cl BH12 ....204 B2
Pear Tree Cl
 Aldershot SP6 ....92 C3
 Botley SO30 ....81 C1
 Bransgore BH23 ....193 A4
Pear Tree Dr SP5 ....73 B4
Pearce Ave BH14 ......203 A1
Pearce Cl PO12 ....181 B3
Pearce Gdns BH14 .....203 A1
Pearce Rd BH16 ....201 A3
Pearce-Smith Cl BH25 ..209 C4
Pearl Gdns BH10 ......189 B2
Pearl Rd BH10 ....189 B2
Pearman Ct 8 SO41 ....197 C1
Pearman Ct SO41 ......197 B1
Pearson Ave BH14 .....203 A1
Pearson Gdns BH10 ....189 B3
Peartree Cl
 Southampton SO19 ....103 B2
 Stubbington PO14 .....154 B2
 West Wellow SO51 .....50 B2
Peartree Ct
 5 Lymington SO41 .....197 C1
 Southampton SO19 ....103 B2
Peartree Rd Hythe SO45 .125 C1
 Southampton SO19 ....103 B2
Pebble Cl PO11 ....185 A1
Pebble Ct
 Marchwood SO40 ......101 C1
 South Hayling PO11 ...185 B1
Pebmarsh Rd 8 PO6 ....156 B4
Pedham Cl PO4 ....183 A2
Pedlars Wlk BH24 .....140 C4
Pedula Way SO50 ....56 C3
Peeks Mews BH4 ......206 C3
Peel Cl Poole BH12 .....203 B3
 Romsey SO51 ....52 B3
Peel Common Jun & Inf Sch
 PO13 ....155 A1
Peel Pl PO7 ....215 B2
Peel Rd PO12 ....181 B2
Peel St SO14 ....103 B3
Pegwell Hill SO31 ......105 A2
Pegasus Ave SO31 ......128 C1
Pegasus Cl Gosport PO13 180 B3
 Hamble-le-Rice SO31 ...127 C1
Southampton SO16 ......77 C2

Pegasus Ct
 Bournemouth BH1 ......205 A3
 8 New Milton BH25 ....195 A2
Pegasus Lodge BH22 ....165 B3
Peggotty Ho 10 PO1 ....182 B4
Pegham Ind Pk PO15 ....130 A3
Pelham Cl BH23 ....207 B3
Pelham Rd Gosport PO12 181 A3
 Portsmouth PO5 ....215 B1
Pelham Terr 2 PO10 ....161 A4
Pelican Cl PO15 ....130 B1
Pelican Ct SO21 ....30 A4
Pelican Mead BH24 .....141 B3
Pelican Rd PO14 ....154 C3
Pembers Cl SO50 ....57 B1
Pemberton Rd SO43 ....122 A3
Pembrey Cl SO16 ....78 A3
Pembridge Rd SP6 ....70 A1
Pembroke Cl
 Eastleigh SO50 ....55 C3
 Portsmouth PO1 ......182 A2
 Romsey SO51 ....52 C4
 Totton SO40 ....101 A4
Pembroke Cres PO14 ...179 A3
Pembroke Ct
 11 Christchurch BH23 ..209 A4
 5 Gosport PO13 ....155 B1
 Southampton SO17 .....79 A1
Pembroke Rd
 Bournemouth BH4 .....204 A1
 Poole BH12 ....203 B4
 Portsmouth PO1 ......182 A2
 Southampton SO15 ....102 B4
Pembury Rd Havant PO9 160 A4
 Stubbington PO14 .....154 B2
Pemerton Rd SO22 ....1 B2
Penarth Ave PO6 ......158 A4
Pencraig BH13 ....204 A2
Pendennis Rd PO6 .....132 C1
Pendle Cl SO16 ....101 C4
Pendle Gn SO51 ....4 C1
Pendleton Gdns SO45 ..150 C1
Penelope Ct 23 BH23 ...209 A4
Penelope Gdns SO31 ...104 C1
Penfords Paddock 8
 SO32 ....83 B4
Pengelly Ave PO14 .....189 C3
Penhale Gdns PO14 ....129 A1
Penhale Inf Sch PO4 ...182 C3
Penhale Rd PO1 ....182 C3
Penhale Way SO40 .....100 C3
Penhurst Rd PO9 ......135 A1
Peninsula Rd SO22 .....10 C4
Peninsula Sq SO22 .....10 C4
Penistone Cl SO19 .....104 A1
Penjar Ave PO7 ....134 B2
Penk Ridge PO9 ....158 C4
Penn Cl BH25 ....194 C1
Penn Ct BH22 ....138 B1
Penn Hill Ave BH14 ....203 B2
Penn Way PO12 ....180 C2
Pennant Hills PO9 .....135 A1
Pennant Pk PO16 ......131 B2
Pennant Rd BH23 ......207 C4
Pennard Way SO53 ......55 A2
Penner Rd PO9 ....135 B4
Pennerley Ct PO9 ......135 B4
Pennine Cl 6 BH23 .....207 C4
Pennine Gdns SO45 ....125 B1
Pennine Ho SO16 ......101 C4
Pennine Rd SO16 ......101 C4
Pennine Way
 Chandler's Ford SO53 ...55 B2
 Lee-on-the-Solent PO13 .180 A2
 Verwood BH31 ....114 C3
Pennine Wlk PO14 .....179 A3
Pennington CE Jun Sch
 SO41 ....197 B2
Pennington Cl
 Colden Common SO21 ...56 C4
 Lymington SO41 ....197 B1
 West Moors BH22 .....138 B1
Pennington Cres BH22 .138 B1
Pennington Cross SO41 .197 B1
Pennington Inf Sch
 SO41 ....197 B2
Pennington Oval SO41 .197 A1
Pennington Rd BH22 ...138 B1
Pennington Way PO15 .130 B2
Penns Rd GU32 ....40 C2
Penny Hedge BH25 .....210 A4
Penny La
 6 Bournemouth BH7 ...205 C2
 Hermitage PO10 ....161 A4
Penny Pl PO7 ....134 C2
Penny St PO1 ....182 A2
Penny's Cl SP6 ....69 C2
Penny's Cnr SO41 .....195 C2
Penny's Cres SP6 ....69 C2
Penny's La SP6 ....69 B2
Penny's Wlk BH22 ......165 B3
Pennycress SO31 ......128 C1
Pennys La SP6 ....69 C2
Penrose Gdns BH25 ....195 C2
Penrhyn Ave PO6 ......158 A4
Penrhyn Ct SO50 ....55 C3
Penrith Cl BH31 ....114 C3
Penrith Rd BH5 ....206 A2
Penrose Cl PO1 ....157 B1
Penrose Rd PO12 ......165 B3
Penshurst Way SO50 ....56 A3
Pentagon The SO45 ....151 A1
Pentere Rd PO8 ....112 A3

Pentire Ave SO15 . . . . .78 B1
Pentire Way SO15 . . . . .78 B1
Pentland Cl SO45 . . . . . . .125 B1
Pentland Rise PO10 . . . . . .132 B1
Penton Ct PO9 . . . . .136 A3
Penton Pl B SO23 . . . . .11 A3
Penton Rd SO21 . . . . .32 A4
Pentons Hill SP6 . . . . .94 B3
Pentridge Way SO40 . . . . .100 C3
Penwood Gn 24 PO9 . . . . .136 A3
Peper Harow PO8 . . . . . . .112 A3
Peppard Cl SO18 . . . . . . .104 B3
Peppercorn Way SO30 . . . .81 B2
Pepys Ave SO19 . . . . .104 B3
Pepys Ct Gosport PO12 . . .181 A1
Portsmouth PO4 . . . . .182 C2
Percival Rd PO2 . . . . .182 C4
Percivale Rd SO53 . . . . . . .54 C2
Percy Chandler St PO1 . . .215 C4
Percy Cl SO45 . . . . .125 C3
Percy Rd
 Bournemouth BH5 . . . . . .205 C2
 Gosport PO12 . . . . .181 B2
 Portsmouth PO4 . . . . . . .182 C2
 Southampton SO16 . . . . .102 A4
Peregrine Cl SO40 . . . . . .100 B3
Peregrine Rd BH23 . . . . . .208 A3
Peregrines Par PO16 . . . . .155 C4
Pergin Cres SO42 . . . . . . .202 A4
Pergin Way BH17 . . . . . . .202 A4
Pern Dr SO30 . . . . .106 A4
Peronne Cl PO3 . . . . .157 C3
Peronne Rd PO3 . . . . .157 C3
Perran Rd SO16 . . . . .77 B1
Perry Gdns BH15 . . . . . . .202 B1
Perry's Ct SO40 . . . . .102 A1
Perryfield Gdns BH7 . . . . .206 A4
Perrywood Cl SO45 . . . . . .150 B2
Perrywood Gdns SO40 . . .100 A4
Perseus Pl PO7 . . . . .134 C2
Perseus Terr PO1 . . . . . . .182 A2
Pershore Cl SO31 . . . . . . .129 A2
Persian Dr PO15 . . . . .129 A4
Persley Rd BH10 . . . . .189 C2
Perth Cl SO31 . . . . .191 C1
Perth Ho PO1 . . . . .215 C3
Perth Rd Gosport PO13 . . .155 B2
 Portsmouth PO4 . . . . . . .183 A2
Pervin Rd PO6 . . . . .157 C4
Pestell La SO32 . . . . .85 B2
Peter Ashley Activity Ctr
 PO6 . . . . .134 B1
Peter Ashley Rd PO6 . . . . .134 B1
Peter Grant Way BH22 . . .165 B3
Peter Symonds' Coll SO22 . .1 C1
Peterborough Ct PO13 . . .180 B3
Peterborough Rd
 Cosham PO6 . . . . .133 C1
 Southampton SO14 . . . . .103 A4
Peters Cl
 Locks Heath SO31 . . . . . .128 C2
 Upton BH16 . . . . .201 B3
Peters Rd
 Ferndown BH22 . . . . . . .165 C2
 Locks Heath SO31 . . . . . .128 C2
Peterscroft Ave SO40 . . . .100 A1
Petersfield Buss Pk
 GU32 . . . . .40 B2
Petersfield Ho PO1 . . . . . .215 C4
Petersfield Hospl GU32 . . .40 C2
Petersfield Inf Sch GU32 . .40 C2
Petersfield Rd BH7 . . . . . .206 A4
Petersfield Rd
 Bournemouth BH7 . . . . . .206 A4
 Buriton GU31 . . . . .65 B3
 Cheriton SO24 . . . . .14 B2
 Clanfield PO8 . . . . .88 B4
 Havant PO9 . . . . .136 A3
 Winchester SO21, SO23 . . .11 B4
Petersfield Sch The
 GU32 . . . . .40 C1
Petersfield Sta GU32 . . . . .40 C2
Petersgate Inf Sch PO8 . . .88 B2
Petit Rd BH9 . . . . .190 A2
Petrel Wlk PO13 . . . . .155 A1
Petrie Rd PO13 . . . . .179 C1
Petticoat La SP5 . . . . .47 C4
Pettinger Gdns SO17 . . . .103 B4
Petty Cl SO51 . . . . .53 A3
Pettycot Cres PO13 . . . . .155 A2
Petworth Gdns
 Eastleigh SO50 . . . . .56 A3
 Southampton SO16 . . . . . .78 B3
Petworth Rd PO3 . . . . . . .183 A3
Pevensey Cl PO16 . . . . . . .166 A3
Peveril Cl SO32 . . . . .166 A3
Peverell Rd BH16 . . . . . . .201 A2
Peverells Rd SO53 . . . . . . .55 C4
Peverells Wood Ave
 SO53 . . . . .55 C4
Peverells Wood Cl SO53 . .55 C3
Peveril Rd BH24 . . . . .139 C3
Peveril Rd SO19 . . . . .103 C2
Pewsey Pl SO15 . . . . .78 B1
Phelipps Rd PO21 . . . . . . .186 C3
Philip Rd PO7 . . . . .134 C2
Philimore Rd SO16 . . . . . . .79 B2
Phillips Cl SO16 . . . . .77 C3
Philpott Dr SO40 . . . . . . .101 C1
Phoenix Bldgs PO3 . . . . . .158 A1
Phoenix Cl SO31 . . . . .105 A1
Phoenix Pk SO50 . . . . .56 B1
Phoenix Pupil Referral Unit
 SO45 . . . . .149 C4

Phoenix Sq PO2 . . . . .157 C2
Phoenix Way PO13 . . . . . .155 B1
Phyldon Cl BH12 . . . . . . .203 A3
Phyldon Rd BH12 . . . . . . .203 A3
Pickard Rd BH22 . . . . . . .165 C4
Pickering Cl BH18 . . . . . . .187 A1
Picket Cl SP6 . . . . .69 C2
Pickford Rd BH11 . . . . . . .189 C1
Pickwick Cl SO40 . . . . . . .100 A4
Pickwick Ho 18 PO1 . . . . .182 B4
Picton Ho 10 PO5 . . . . . . .215 B2
Pier Head Rd PO2 . . . . . . .157 A1
Pier Rd PO1 . . . . .182 A2
Pier St PO13 . . . . .179 C1
Pig Shoot La BH23 . . . . . .190 C3
Pigeon House La PO7 . . . .133 B2
Pikes Hill SO43 . . . . .121 C3
Pikes Hill Ave SO43 . . . . .121 C3
Pilbrow Ct PO12 . . . . .180 C2
Pilchards Ave SO50 . . . . . .57 A2
Pilford Heath Rd BH21 . . .164 A4
Pilgrim Park Homes 1
 BH24 . . . . .117 A1
Pilgrim Pl SO18 . . . . .79 C2
Pilgrim's Cl BH25 . . . . . . .195 B2
Pilgrims Gate SO22 . . . . . . .1 C1
Pilgrims Sch The SO23 . . . .11 A4
Pilgrims Way
 Broadstone BH17 . . . . . . .202 A4
 Stubbington PO14 . . . . . .179 A3
Pill Hill SP5 . . . . .74 A2
Pilley Bailey SO41 . . . . . .174 A1
Pilley Gn SO41 . . . . .174 A1
Pilley Hill SO41 . . . . .173 C1
Pilley St SO41 . . . . .174 A1
Pilning Cl PO14 . . . . .154 B4
Pilot Hight Rd BH11 . . . . .189 A2
Pilsdon Dr BH17 . . . . .187 C2
Pimpern Cl BH17 . . . . .187 C1
Pimpernel Cl SO31 . . . . . .128 C1
Pine Ave
 Bournemouth BH6 . . . . . .206 B2
 Poole BH12 . . . . .203 C3
Pine Cl Ashurst SO40 . . . .100 B2
 Barton on Sea BH25 . . . .209 C4
 Ferndown BH22 . . . . . . .165 B4
 Hythe SO45 . . . . .125 C1
 Landford SP5 . . . . .49 B1
 North Baddesley SO52 . . .53 C3
 Winchester SO22 . . . . . . .10 A2
Pine Cotts GU33 . . . . .21 A4
Pine Cres
 Chandler's Ford SO53 . . . .30 B1
 Christchurch BH23 . . . . . .208 C4
Pine Ct PO10 . . . . .136 C2
Pine Dr Clanfield PO8 . . . . .88 B3
 Poole BH13 . . . . .203 C2
 Southampton SO18 . . . . .104 B4
 St Leonards BH24 . . . . . .139 C2
Pine Dr E SO18 . . . . .104 C4
Pine Glen Ave BH22 . . . . .165 B4
Pine Gr PO9 . . . . .136 A1
Pine Grange 4 BH1 . . . . .205 A2
Pine Ho New Milton BH25 .195 A2
 Southampton SO16 . . . . . .78 C4
Pine Lo 16 BH13 . . . . .214 C4
Pine Manor Rd BH24 . . . .139 B3
Pine Manns 3 BH1 . . . . . .205 B2
Pine Park Mans 18
 BH13 . . . . .204 A2
Pine Rd Aldershot SP6 . . . .92 C3
 Bishop's Waltham SO32 . . .83 B4
 Bournemouth BH9 . . . . . .205 A4
 Broadstone BH12 . . . . . . .162 C1
 Chandler's Ford SO53 . . . .55 B4
 Romsey SO51 . . . . .53 B3
Pine Tree Cl BH21 . . . . . . .163 B3
Pine Tree Gdns PO8 . . . . .162 A4
Pine Tree Glen BH4 . . . . . .204 B2
Pine Trees Cl PO14 . . . . . .154 B4
Pine Vale Cres BH10 . . . . .189 C2
Pine View Cl Redlynch SP5 .97 B3
 Upton BH16 . . . . .201 B3
Pine View Rd BH31 . . . . . .114 B4
Pine Way SO16 . . . . .78 B4
Pine Wlk Chilworth SO16 . .78 C4
 Liss GU33 . . . . .21 A3
 Locks Heath SO31 . . . . . .129 A3
 Verwood BH31 . . . . .115 A3
 West Moors BH22 . . . . . .138 C2
Pinebeach Ct BH13 . . . . . .214 C4
Pinecliff Rd BH13 . . . . . . .214 C4
Pinecliffe Ave BH6 . . . . . .206 B2
Pinecliffe Rd BH25 . . . . . .209 B4
Pinefield Rd SO18 . . . . . . .79 C1
Pinegrove Rd SO19 . . . . . .103 C2
Pinehill Ct BH24 . . . . .117 A2
Pinehurst
 10 Milford on Sea SO41 . .211 B2
 13 Southampton SO17 . . .79 A1
Pinehurst Ave BH23 . . . . .207 C3
Pinehurst Cl PO7 . . . . . . .112 B1
Pinehurst Rd
 Southampton SO16 . . . . . .78 C4
 West Moors BH22 . . . . . .138 C1
Pinelands Cl SO16 . . . . . . .78 B2
Pinelands Rd SO16 . . . . . . .78 B2
Pines The
 Fordingbridge SP6 . . . . . . .70 B1
 Poole BH13 . . . . .204 A1
 Portchester PO16 . . . . . .132 A1
 Southampton SO16 . . . . . .78 A2
Pineside BH9 . . . . .205 A4
Pinesprings Dr BH18 . . . .186 C1
Pinetops Cl SO41 . . . . . . .197 A2
Pinetree Wlk BH17 . . . . . .201 C4

Pineview Cl SO31 . . . . . . .105 A1
Pinewood Gosport PO13 . .155 C1
 Southampton SO16 . . . . . .78 C3
Pinewood Ave
 Bournemouth BH10 . . . . .189 B3
 Havant PO9 . . . . .135 A2
Pinewood Cl
 Bournemouth BH10 . . . . .189 B3
 Christchurch BH23 . . . . . .194 A1
 Romsey SO51 . . . . .28 B1
 Stubbington PO14 . . . . . .154 B4
 Upton BH16 . . . . .201 A4
Pinewood Cres SO45 . . . . .126 A1
Pinewood Dr SO45 . . . . . .126 A1
Pinewood Gdns BH22 . . . .165 B4
Pinewood Lodge 6
 PO16 . . . . .131 A1
Pinewood Pk SO19 . . . . . .104 C3
Pinewood Rd
 Christchurch BH23 . . . . . .193 C1
 Ferndown BH22 . . . . . . .165 A4
 New Milton BH25 . . . . . . .195 C2
 Poole BH13 . . . . .204 A1
 St Leonards BH24 . . . . . .139 C2
 Upton BH16 . . . . .201 A4
Pink End BH22 . . . . .165 C2
Pink Rd PO4 . . . . .183 A2
Pinkney La SO43 . . . . . . .121 C2
Pinks Hill PO16 . . . . .131 B1
Pinsley Dr PO17 . . . . .133 A3
Pinto Cl PO15 . . . . .129 B4
Pipers Ash 8 BH24 . . . . . .117 A1
Pipers Cl SO40 . . . . .100 B3
Pipers Dr BH23 . . . . .208 A4
Pipers Mead PO8 . . . . .88 A3
Pipers Wood Ind Est
 PO7 . . . . .134 B4
Piping Cl SO21 . . . . .56 C4
Piping Gn B SO21 . . . . . . .56 C4
Piping Rd SO21 . . . . .56 C4
Pipit Cl Gosport PO12 . . . .181 A4
 Waterlooville PO8 . . . . . .112 A3
Pippin Cl
 Christchurch BH23 . . . . . .191 C1
 6 Lymington SO41 . . . . . .197 C1
Pirelli St SO15 . . . . .102 C2
Pirrie Cl SO15 . . . . .78 B3
Pit Hill La PO7 . . . . .86 C1
Pitcairn Mews PO4 . . . . . .183 A1
Pitchponds Rd SO31 . . . . .152 B4
Pitcot La SO21 . . . . .33 A2
Pitcroft La GU31 . . . . .65 C3
Pitcroft Rd PO2 . . . . .157 B1
Pitmore Cl SO50 . . . . .56 A4
Pitmore La SO41 . . . . .172 B1
Pitmore Rd SO50 . . . . .56 A4
Pitmore Sch SO53 . . . . . . .55 C4
Pitreavie Rd PO6 . . . . . . .157 C3
Pitt Rd SO15 . . . . .102 B3
Pitt Rdbt SO22 . . . . .10 A3
Pitter Cl SO22 . . . . .1 A3
Pittmore Rd BH23 . . . . . . .192 B1
Pitts Deep La SO41 . . . . . .199 B2
Pitt PH25 . . . . .195 B1
Pitwines Cl BH15 . . . . . . .202 B1
Pitymoor La PO17 . . . . . . .133 A2
Place Cres PO7 . . . . .134 C3
Place House Cl SO31 . . . . .130 B1
Place La SO21 . . . . .31 C4
Plaitford Gr PO9 . . . . .135 B3
Plaitford Wlk SO16 . . . . . . .77 C1
Plant Park Rd BH24 . . . . . .140 B1
Plantaganet Cres BH11 . . .188 B3
Plantation SO41 . . . . .211 C4
Plantation Ct
 Lymington SO41 . . . . . . .197 B2
 Poole BH17 . . . . .187 B1
Plantation Dr
 Christchurch BH23 . . . . . .194 A1
 Marchwood SO40 . . . . . .101 C1
Plantation Rd
 Hill Brow GU33 . . . . .21 A1
 Poole BH17 . . . . .187 B1
 West Wellow SO51 . . . . . .74 B4
Plantation The SO32 . . . . .82 C1
Plants Cl SO51 . . . . .51 A1
Plassey Cres BH10 . . . . . .189 B3
Platform Rd SO14 . . . . . . .103 A1
Platoff Rd SO41 . . . . .212 C4
Player Cl SP6 . . . . .69 C2
Players Cres SO40 . . . . . . .100 C3
Playfair Rd PO5 . . . . .215 C2
Playfields Dr BH12 . . . . . .203 C3
Plaza Mews 15 SO51 . . . . .52 C4
Pleasance Way BH25 . . . . .194 C2
Pleasant La PO10 . . . . . . .161 B1
Pleasant Rd PO4 . . . . .183 A2
Plecy Cl BH22 . . . . .165 B1
Plemont Cl BH12 . . . . .188 C1
Pless Rd SO41 . . . . .211 B2
Plough La SO32 . . . . .85 B1
Plough Way SO22 . . . . . . .10 B1
Plover Cl
 Southampton SO16 . . . . . .78 A3
 Stubbington SO16 . . . . . .179 A3
Plover Dr SO41 . . . . .211 C2
Plover Rd SO40 . . . . .100 B4
Plover Reach PO4 . . . . . . .183 A3
Plovers Down SO22 . . . . . .10 A2
Plovers Rd PO8 . . . . .112 A4
PLPH Rd SO45 . . . . .151 A3
Plumer Rd BH17 . . . . .187 A1
Plumley Wlk PO9 . . . . . . .135 B4
Plumpton Gdns PO3 . . . . .158 A2
Plumpton Gr 7 PO7 . . . . .112 A1
Plymouth Dr PO14 . . . . . .154 A2
Plymouth St PO1 . . . . .215 B2
Pococks La GU33 . . . . .19 C4

Poets Way SO22 . . . . .10 B4
Poinsettia Cl PO15 . . . . . .129 C2
Pointout Cl SO16 . . . . .78 C2
Pointout Rd SO16 . . . . .78 C2
Pokesdown Com Prim Sch
 BH5 . . . . .206 A3
Pokesdown Sta BH7 . . . . .206 A3
Poles La Hursley SO21 . . . .30 B3
 Lymington SO41 . . . . . . .197 C1
 Otterbourne SO21 . . . . . . .31 A3
Police Station La SO32 . . . .61 A1
Police Training Ctr
 SO31 . . . . .127 B2
Pollards Moor Rd SO40 . . .75 A1
Pollesden Cl SO03 . . . . . . .106 A3
Polygon Ct SO15 . . . . . . .102 C3
Polygon Special Sch The
 SO15 . . . . .102 C3
Polygon The SO15 . . . . . .102 C3
Pomona Cl BH22 . . . . .165 B3
Pompey's Cnr BH21 . . . . . .165 A2
Pompey's La BH22 . . . . . . .165 A1
Pond Cl Marchwood SO40 .101 C1
 New Milton BH25 . . . . . . .195 A2
Pond Cotts GU32 . . . . .39 B1
Pond La P08 . . . . .88 A2
Pond Piece PO7 . . . . .110 C2
Pond Rd SO31 . . . . .128 C3
Pondhead Cl SO45 . . . . . .150 B2
Pondside Flats SO42 . . . . .148 C1
Pondside La SO32 . . . . . . .83 B4
Ponsonby Ho PO5 . . . . . . .215 B2
Ponsonby Rd BH14 . . . . . .203 B2
Pony Dr BH16 . . . . .201 B4
Pook La Fareham PO17 . . .131 B2
 Havant PO9 . . . . .160 A4
Pooksgreen SO40 . . . . . . .100 B1
Pool La Babb BH11 . . . . . .188 C2
 Southampton SO19 . . . . .103 C2
 Upton BH16, BH17 . . . . . .201 B4
 Wimborne Minst BH21 . . .163 B2
Poole Gr BH15 . . . . .202 B2
Poole Hill BH2 . . . . .204 C2
Poole Hospl BH15 . . . . . . .202 B2
Poole La BH11 . . . . .189 A3
Poole Rd
 Bournemouth BH2,BH4 . . .204 B2
 Poole BH12 . . . . .204 A2
 Southampton SO19 . . . . .103 C2
 Upton BH16, BH17 . . . . . .201 B4
 Wimborne Minst BH21 . . .163 B2
Poole Sta BH15 . . . . .202 B2
Popes La Totton SO40 . . . .100 C4
 Upham SO32 . . . . .58 B2
Popes Rd BH15 . . . . .202 B3
Popham Ct PO9 . . . . .135 B3
Poplar Cl
 Bransgore BH23 . . . . .193 B4
 Christchurch BH23 . . . . . .209 A4
 6 Poole BH15 . . . . .202 B3
 Wimborne Minst BH21 . . .163 B2
Poplar Cres BH24 . . . . . . .141 A4
Poplar Gr PO11 . . . . .185 A2
Poplar La BH23 . . . . .193 B4
Poplar Rd
 New Milton BH25 . . . . . . .195 B2
 Southampton SO19 . . . . .103 C3
Poplar Way
 Hedge End SO30 . . . . . . .105 B3
 North Baddesley SO52 . . .53 C3
 Ringwood BH24 . . . . .141 A4
Poplars The SO32 . . . . . . .83 C2
Poppy Cl
 Christchurch BH23 . . . . . .208 B4
 Southampton SO31 . . . . .128 C1
Poppy Rd SO16 . . . . .79 B3
Poppyfields SO53 . . . . .55 A3
Porchester Cl 17 BH1 . . . .205 A3
Porchester Pl BH8 . . . . . . .205 A3
Porchester Rd
 Bournemouth BH8 . . . . . .205 A3
 Southampton SO19 . . . . .103 C2
Porlock Rd SO16 . . . . .77 B1
Port La Hursley SO21 . . . . .30 B4
 Winchester SO22 . . . . . . .10 A4
Port Royal St PO1 . . . . . . .215 C3
Port Way PO6 . . . . .157 A4
Portal Rd
 Bishopstoke SO50 . . . . . . .56 B2
 Southampton SO19 . . . . .104 A2
 Totton SO40 . . . . .100 B4
 Winchester SO23 . . . . . . .11 A3
Portarlington Cl BH4 . . . . .204 B1
Portarlington Rd BH4 . . . .204 B1
Portchester Boys Sch
 BH7 . . . . .206 A4
Portchester Castle*
 PO16 . . . . .156 C3
Portchester Com Sch
 PO16 . . . . .156 C3
Portchester Hts PO16 . . . .132 B1
Portchester La PO17 . . . . .132 B2
Portchester Rd
 Portchester PO16 . . . . . .156 A4
 Portsmouth PO2 . . . . . . .182 C4
Portchester Rise SO50 . . . .56 A4
Portchester Sta PO16 . . . .156 B4
Portcreek Cotts PO6 . . . . .158 A3
Portelet Cl BH12 . . . . .188 B1
Portelet Ho SO16 . . . . .77 C3
Portelet Pl SO30 . . . . .105 B3
Porter Rd BH17 . . . . .202 A4
Porter's La SO14 . . . . .102 C2

Porters La BH21 . . . . .164 B3
Portersbridge St SO51 . . . .52 C4
Portesham Gdns BH9 . . . .190 A2
Portesham Way BH17 . . . .187 C2
Porteus Cres SO33 . . . . . . .55 C3
Portfield Cl BH23 . . . . . . .207 A4
Portfield Rd
 Christchurch BH23 . . . . . .207 A4
 Portsmouth PO3 . . . . . . .158 A2
Portfield Sch
 Christchurch BH23 . . . . . .207 A4
 Portsmouth PO3 . . . . . . .207 A4
Portiere Ho BH11 . . . . . . .188 C2
Portland Bldgs 5 PO12 . . .181 B2
Portland Dr PO12 . . . . . . .180 B2
Portland Ho 20 PO12 . . . .181 B2
Portland Pl BH2 . . . . .204 C2
Portland Rd
 Bournemouth BH9 . . . . . .205 A4
 Portsmouth PO5 . . . . . . .182 B1
 Waterlooville PO7 . . . . . .134 C4
Portland Sq 8 GU33 . . . . .20 C2
Portland St
 Fareham PO16 . . . . .131 A1
 Portsmouth PO1 . . . . . . .182 A3
 Southampton SO14 . . . . .102 C2
Portland Terr
 21 Portsmouth PO5 . . . . .182 B1
 Southampton SO14 . . . . .102 C2
Portland's Cl GU32 . . . . . . .41 A3
Portman Cres BH5 . . . . . .206 A2
Portman Pl BH7 . . . . .205 C3
Portman Terr 2 BH5 . . . . .206 A2
Portman Terr BH5 . . . . . . .206 A2
Portmore Cl BH18 . . . . . . .187 B3
Portobello Gr PO16 . . . . . .132 C1
Portsdown Ave PO6 . . . . . .158 B4
Portsdown Hill Rd
 Havant PO9 . . . . .135 A1
 Portchester PO17 . . . . . .132 B1
Portsdown Prim Sch
 PO6 . . . . .157 C4
Portsdown Rd PO16 . . . . . .156 C4
Portside Cl SO40 . . . . .102 A2
Portsmouth & Southsea Sta
 PO1 . . . . .215 B3
Portsmouth Cath (CE)
 PO1 . . . . .182 A3
Portsmouth Cath(RC)
 PO1 . . . . .182 A2
Portsmouth City Mus & Art
 Gallery* PO1 . . . . .182 A2
Portsmouth Coll PO3 . . . .183 B4
Portsmouth Gram Sch
 PO1 . . . . .182 A2
Portsmouth Harbour Sta
 PO1 . . . . .181 C3
Portsmouth High Sch for
 Girls PO5 . . . . .215 A1
Portsmouth High Sch for
 Girls(Juns) PO5 . . . . . . .182 B1
Portsmouth Print Workshop
 PO1 . . . . .182 A2
Portsmouth RC Cath*
 PO1 . . . . .215 A4
Portsmouth Rd
 Bursledon SO31 . . . . . . .105 A1
 Colden Common SO50,
 SO21 . . . . .57 B3
 Horndean PO8 . . . . .112 A3
 Lee-on-the-Solent PO13 . .180 A2
 Southampton SO19,SO31 .104 B1
Portsmouth Sea Life Ctr*
 PO5 . . . . .215 A1
Portsview Ave PO16 . . . . .156 C4
Portsview Gdns PO16 . . . .132 B1
Portswood Ave SO17 . . . . .103 A4
Portswood Ctr 22 SO17 . . .79 B1
Portswood Dr 2 BH9 . . . . .190 A2
Portswood Pk SO17 . . . . .103 A4
Portswood Prim Sch
 SO17 . . . . .79 B1
Portswood Rd
 Havant PO9 . . . . .135 B3
 Portsmouth PO2 . . . . . . .157 C3
 Southampton SO17 . . . . . .79 B1
Portuguese Fireplace*
 SO43 . . . . .120 C2
Portview Rd SO18 . . . . . . .79 C1
Portway Cl SO18 . . . . .104 A4
Posbrook La PO14 . . . . . . .153 C3
Posbrooke Rd PO4 . . . . . .183 A2
Post Office Bldgs BH9 . . . .204 C4
Post Office La
 41 Chandlers Ford SO53 . .202 B1
 St Leonards BH24 . . . . . .140 A3
Post Office Rd
 Bournemouth BH1 . . . . . .204 C2
 Waterlooville PO7 . . . . . .134 B3
Postern Cl PO16 . . . . .156 B4
Postern Ct 18 SO14 . . . . .102 C2
Potash Terr PO9 . . . . .135 C1
Potterdale Ho 17 PO6 . . . .133 A1
Potteries The PO16 . . . . . .131 A2
Potterne Way GU32 . . . . . .41 B3
Potterne Wood Cl BH31 . . .115 B2
Potters Ave PO10 . . . . . . .162 A1
Potters Field GU33 . . . . . . .21 A2
Potters Heron Cl SO51 . . . .29 C2
Potters Heron La SO51 . . . .29 C2
Potters Hill BH14 . . . . . . .203 B1
Pottery Junc BH14 . . . . . .203 B1
Pottery Rd BH14 . . . . .203 A1
Poulner Cl SO19 . . . . .104 A1
Poulner Ct PO9 . . . . .135 B3
Poulner Inf & Jun Schs
 BH24 . . . . .117 B1

Poulner Mobile Home Pk BH24 .....117 B1
Poulner Pk BH24 .....117 B1
Pound Cl Gosport PO13 .....180 B4
Poole BH15 .....202 C3
Ringwood BH24 .....141 A4
Pound Cotts SO32 .....61 B3
Pound Ct SO18 .....104 A4
Pound Gate Dr PO14 .....153 B4
Pound Hill SO51 .....50 B3
Pound La Ampfield SO51 .....29 A1
Ashurst SO40 .....100 C2
Burley BH24 .....142 C1
Cadnam SO40 .....75 B1
3 Damerham SP6 .....68 A3
Sherfield English SO51 .....25 C1
Pound Lea PO11 .....185 A3
Pound Rd
Bursledon SO31 .....104 C1
Kings Worthy SO23 .....2 B1
Lymington SO41 .....197 A1
Pound St SO18 .....104 A4
Pound Tree Rd SO14 .....103 A2
Poundbury Ct SO21 .....129 A3
Pounds Terr PO1 .....182 B3
Powell Cres SO40 .....100 C3
Powell Rd BH14 .....203 A2
Powell Sq 5 PO1 .....182 A3
Power Rd PO1 .....182 C3
Powerscourt Rd
Barton on Sea BH25 .....209 C4
Portsmouth PO2 .....182 C4
Pownall Cres PO1 .....182 A2
Powis Cl BH23 .....195 A2
Powlett Rd SO41 .....197 C2
Poynor Cl PO16 .....131 A1
Poynings Pl PO1 .....182 A2
Precinct The
Holbury SO45 .....150 B2
10 Waterlooville PO7 .....134 C4
Precosa Rd SO30 .....105 C3
Prelate Way PO14 .....129 B1
Premier Ctr The SO51 .....53 B3
Premier Par SO18 .....79 C2
Premier Way SO51 .....53 A3
Preshaw Cl SO18 .....78 B2
Preshaw Est SO32 .....35 A2
Presseys Cnr SP6 .....93 A4
Preston Cl BH16 .....201 B4
Preston Rd BH23 .....192 B2
Preston Rd Poole BH15 .....202 B3
Portsmouth PO2 .....182 C4
Preston Way BH23 .....208 B4
Prestwood Cl BH10 .....194 C1
Prestwood Rd SO30 .....105 B3
Pretoria Rd
Hedge End SO30 .....105 A3
Portsmouth PO4 .....182 C2
Prettyjohn Ho PO4 .....183 A1
Pricketts Hill PO17 .....108 A3
Prideaux - Brune Ave PO13 .....155 B2
Priest Croft SO45 .....150 C1
Priest Croft Dr SO45 .....150 C1
Priest La BH23 .....192 A4
Priest's House Mus & Gdns* BH21 .....163 A2
Priestfields PO14 .....129 B1
Priestlands SO51 .....52 C4
Priestlands Cl SO40 .....100 A3
Priestlands La SO41 .....197 B2
Priestlands Pl SO41 .....197 B2
Priestlands Rd SO41 .....197 B1
Priestley Cl SO40 .....100 B4
Priestley Rd SO19 .....104 B4
Primate Cl PO18 .....129 B1
Primrose
Chandler's Ford SO53 .....54 C2
Redlynch SP5 .....47 B3
Hedge End SO30 .....105 B3
Primrose Ct PO7 .....135 A3
Primrose La Rake GU33 .....21 B2
Redlynch SP5 .....47 B3
Primrose Rd SO16 .....79 B2
Primrose Terr SO31 .....59 B1
Primrose Way
Christchurch BH23 .....208 B4
Locks Heath SO31 .....128 C1
Romsey SO51 .....28 B1
Prince Albert Rd PO4 .....183 A2
Prince Alfred St PO12 .....181 A2
Prince George St PO1 .....182 A3
Prince George's St PO9 .....135 C1
Prince of Wales Ave SO15 .....105 A4
Prince of Wales Cl 6 PO7 .....135 A4
Prince of Wales Rd
Bournemouth BH4 .....204 B2
3 Gosport PO12 .....181 B2
Prince Rd Gosport PO14 .....154 C3
Rownhams SO16 .....77 C3
Prince Regent Ct PO15 .....215 B2
Prince William Ct 8 SO50 .....56 C1
Prince's Bldgs 18 SO23 .....11 A4
Prince's Mead Sch SO23 .....2 C3
Prince's Rd SO51 .....52 C4

Prince's St
Portsmouth PO1 .....182 B4
Southampton SO14 .....103 B3
Princes Cl
Bishop's Waltham SO32 .....83 A4
Ferndown BH22 .....165 B3
Redhych SP5 .....47 C4
Princes Cotts GU32 .....63 B4
Princes Cres SO43 .....122 A3
Princes Ct
Lyndhurst SO43 .....122 A3
6 Poole BH12 .....204 A2
2 Southampton SO14 .....103 B3
Princes Dr PO7 .....112 A1
Princes Hill SP5 .....47 C4
Princes Ho
Portsmouth PO5 .....215 A1
3 Southampton SO14 .....103 B3
Princes Pl SO22 .....10 C1
Princes Rd
Petersfield GU32 .....40 B2
Southampton SO15 .....102 B3
Princess Anne Hospl SO16 .....78 A2
Princess Ave BH23 .....207 A3
Princess Cl SO30 .....80 C1
Princess Ct 10 SO23 .....11 A4
Princess Gdns PO8 .....112 B4
Princess Rd
Ashurst SO40 .....100 A1
Bournemouth BH4 .....204 A2
Poole BH12 .....204 A2
Pringles Cl BH22 .....165 C3
Pringles Dr BH22 .....165 C3
Prinstead Cl 7 SO23 .....11 A3
Prinsted Cres PO6 .....158 B4
Prinsted La PO10 .....161 B4
Prinsted Wlk PO14 .....154 B4
Printers Row 11 SO20 .....10 C4
Priors Barton SO23 .....10 C3
Priors Cl
Christchurch BH23 .....208 B4
Southampton PO10 .....137 C1
Priors Dean Rd SO22 .....1 B2
Priors Hill La SO31 .....127 C4
Priors Leaze La PO18 .....137 C1
Priors Rd PO14 .....154 B4
Priors Way SO22 .....10 A2
Priors Wlk BH21 .....163 A3
Priorsdean Ave PO3 .....183 A3
Priorsdean Cres PO9 .....135 B2
Priory Ave SO17 .....79 B1
Priory CE Prim Sch The BH23 .....207 A3
Priory Cl
Bishop's Waltham SO32 .....83 A4
Portchester PO16 .....156 C4
Portsmouth PO5 .....215 D2
Priory Gdns
Portchester PO16 .....156 B4
Waterlooville PO7 .....111 C1
West Moors BH22 .....166 A4
12 Winchester SO23 .....11 A4
Priory Ho
Christchurch BH23 .....207 B3
18 Southampton SO14 .....103 A3
Priory Inf Sch PO7 .....208 A4
Priory Quay BH23 .....207 B3
Priory Rd
Bournemouth BH2 .....204 C1
Eastleigh SO50 .....55 C1
Fareham PO15 .....130 B1
Gosport PO12 .....181 A4
Netley SO31 .....127 A3
Portsmouth PO4 .....183 A1
Southampton SO17 .....103 B4
West Moors BH22 .....166 A4
Priory Sch SO32 .....83 A4
Priory Sec Sch PO5 .....215 D2
Priory View Ct 8 BH23 .....207 A3
Priory View Pl 9 BH9 .....190 A2
Priory View Rd
Bournemouth BH9 .....190 A2
Burton BH23 .....192 B1
Private Rd SO41 .....197 C2
Privet Rd BH9 .....204 C4
Privett Ho PO1 .....182 A3
Privett Pl PO12 .....180 C2
Privett Rd Fareham PO15 .....130 B1
Froxfield Green GU32 .....18 C1
Gosport PO12, PO13 .....180 C2
Waterlooville PO7 .....134 B2
Prochurch Rd PO8 .....112 A2
Proctor Cl SO19 .....104 B3
Proctor Dr SO52 .....53 C2
Proctor La PO1 .....182 C3
Promenade PO8 .....208 A3
Promenade Ct 4 PO13 .....179 C1
Promenade The
Emsworth PO10 .....160 C4
Hythe SO45 .....126 A3
20 Portsmouth PO7 .....157 B1
Prospect La PO9 .....136 A3
Prospect Pl
Chandler's Ford SO50 .....55 B3
Hythe SO45 .....126 A3
Prospect Rd PO1 .....182 B4
Prosperous St 14 BH15 .....202 B1
Protea Gdns PO14 .....130 A1
Provene Cl GU32 .....83 C2
Provene Gdns SO32 .....83 C2
Providence Ct 8 PO1 .....182 B4
Providence Hill SO31 .....105 A1
Provost St SP6 .....69 C1

Pruetts La GU33 .....20 C1
Prunus Cl
Ferndown BH22 .....165 A4
Southampton SO16 .....78 B3
Prunus Dr BH22 .....165 A4
Pudbrook Ho SO30 .....106 A4
Puddlebrooke Gdns SO30 .....105 A4
Pudding La SO23 .....2 A3
Puddletown Cres BH17 .....187 C1
Puffin Cl BH23 .....78 A3
Puffin Cres PO14 .....154 A2
Puffin Gdns PO13 .....155 A2
Puffin Wlk PO8 .....111 B2
Pug's Hole 4 A3
Pulens Cres GU31 .....41 B2
Pulens La GU31 .....41 A2
Pullman Ct BH22 .....138 B1
Pullman Way BH24 .....141 A3
Pump La Gosport PO13 .....155 B1
Waterlooville PO8 .....112 A3
Pundle Green Est SO40 .....99 A3
Punsholt La SO24 .....16 C3
Purbeck Ave BH15 .....201 C1
Purbeck Cl BH16 .....201 A4
Purbeck Ct
Bournemouth BH5 .....206 A2
8 Christchurch BH23 .....207 C4
Purbeck Dr
Fareham PO14 .....154 B4
Verwood BH31 .....114 C3
Purbeck Gdns BH14 .....202 C3
Purbeck Hts BH14 .....203 A3
Purbeck Rd
Barton on Sea BH25 .....209 B4
Bournemouth BH4 .....204 C1
Purbeck St PO1 .....182 A3
Purbeck Way PO16 .....156 B4
Purbeck Wlk PO14 .....154 B4
Purbrook Chase Prec PO7 .....134 C2
Purbrook Cl SO16 .....78 B2
Purbrook Gdns PO7 .....134 B3
Purbrook Heath Rd PO7 .....134 A3
Purbrook Ho PO7 .....134 A3
Purbrook Inf Sch PO7 .....134 B3
Purbrook Jun Sch PO7 .....134 B3
Purbrook Park Sch PO7 .....134 B3
Purbrook Rd PO1 .....182 C3
Purbrook Way PO7,PO9 .....135 B2
Purcell Cl PO7 .....134 C3
Purcell Rd SO19 .....104 B2
Purchase Rd BH11 .....204 B4
Purewell BH23 .....207 C3
Purewell Cl BH23 .....207 C3
Purewell Cross Rd BH23 .....207 B4
Purewell Cross Rd BH23 .....207 C4
Purewell Ct 11 BH23 .....207 C4
Purkiss Cl SO53 .....55 B4
Purley Way SO51 .....50 A2
Purrocks The GU32 .....40 C1
Purvis Gdns SO19 .....104 A1
Pussex La BH23 .....191 A4
Putmans La GU31 .....66 C4
Pycroft Cl
North Hayling PO11 .....160 B2
Southampton SO19 .....104 A3
Pye Cl BH21 .....186 C4
Pye Cnr BH21 .....163 A2
Pye La Alderholt BH21 .....91 C3
Wimborne Minst BH21 .....163 A2
Pye St PO1 .....182 C3
Pylands La SO31 .....105 A2
Pyle Cl PO8 .....112 A2
Pylewell Rd SO45 .....126 A2
Pyramid Ctr PO3 .....158 A2
Pyramids L Ctr The PO5 .....182 B1
Pyrford Cl BH9 .....190 A4
Pyrford Gdns 1 SO41 .....197 C1
Pyrford Mews SO41 .....197 C1
Pytchley Cl PO14 .....179 A3

Q
Quadra Point PO3 .....158 A2
Quadrangle The
Eastleigh SO50 .....56 A2
North Baddesley SO51 .....53 B3
Quadrant SP6 .....93 C4
Quail Way PO8 .....101 A2
Quaker Ct BH24 .....140 C4
Quantock Cl 7 BH23 .....207 C4
Quantock Rd SO16 .....101 C4
Quantocks The SO45 .....125 B1
Quarely Rd PO9 .....135 B3
Quarr Ho SO41 .....172 A2
Quarry Chase 2 BH4 .....204 B2
Quarry Cl BH21 .....164 A4
Quarry Rd
Wimborne Minst BH21 .....164 A4
Winchester SO23 .....11 B4
Quarterdeck Ave PO2 .....157 A1
Quarterjack Mews 1 BH21 .....163 B2
Quartremaine Rd PO3 .....158 A2
Quay 2000 SO14 .....103 B4
Quay Haven SO31 .....128 B4
Quay Hill SO41 .....197 C2
Quay La Gosport PO12 .....181 C2
Gosport, Elson PO12 .....156 A1
Quay Point 19 Poole BH15 .....202 B1

Quay Point continued
Portsmouth PO6 .....157 B4
Quay Rd
Christchurch BH23 .....207 A3
Lymington SO41 .....197 C2
Quay St 5 Fareham PO16 .....131 B1
Fareham PO16 .....155 B4
Lymington SO41 .....197 C2
Quay The
Hamble-le-Rice SO31 .....128 A1
Poole BH15 .....202 B2
Quayle Dr BH11 .....188 C3
Quayside SO30 .....106 A3
Quayside Commerce Ctr 1 PO16 .....155 B4
Quayside Rd
Fawley SO45 .....151 C1
Southampton SO18 .....103 B4
Quayside Wlk SO40 .....101 C2
Quebec Gdns SO31 .....104 C1
Queen Alexandra Hospl PO6 .....157 C4
Queen Anne Dr BH21 .....187 C4
Queen Anne's Dr PO9 .....135 B1
Queen Elizabeth Ave SO41 .....197 B2
Queen Elizabeth Ct
Southampton SO17 .....79 B2
Wimborne Minst BH21 .....163 A2
Queen Elizabeth Ctry Pk* PO8 .....64 C2
Queen Elizabeth's Sch BH21 .....162 C3
Queen Katherine Rd SO41 .....197 C2
Queen Mary Ave BH9 .....189 C1
Queen Mary Rd PO16 .....156 B4
Queen Rd PO14 .....154 C3
Queen St Emsworth PO10 .....161 A4
Lymington SO41 .....197 B2
Portsmouth PO1 .....182 A3
Twyford SO21 .....11 B1
Woodgreen SP6 .....47 A1
Queen's Cl BH23 .....207 A3
Queen's Cres PO5 .....215 B1
Queen's Ct SO15 .....102 C3
Queen's Gdns SO14 .....103 A2
Queen's Gr PO5 .....215 B1
Queen's Inclosure Prim Sch PO8 .....112 A1
Queen's Par
Lyndhurst SO43 .....121 C3
8 Waterlooville PO7 .....134 C4
Queen's Park Ave BH8 .....205 B4
Queen's Park Gdns BH8 .....205 B4
Queen's Park Rd BH8 .....205 B4
Queen's Park South Dr BH8 .....205 B3
Queen's Park West Dr BH8 .....205 B4
Queen's Pl PO5 .....215 B1
Queen's Rd
Bournemouth BH4 .....204 B2
Chandler's Ford SO53 .....30 B1
Christchurch BH23 .....207 C3
Corfe Mullen BH21 .....186 B3
Fareham PO16 .....131 A1
Gosport PO12 .....181 A4
Locks Heath SO31 .....129 B4
Portsmouth, Buckland PO2 .....182 C4
Southampton SO15 .....102 C3
Waterlooville PO7 .....111 C1
Winchester SO22 .....10 B4
Queen's Terr PO5 .....215 B1
Queen's Terr SO14 .....103 A2
Queen's Way SO15 .....215 B1
Queen's Wlk 3 Hythe SO45 .....126 A2
Lee-on-the-Solent PO13 .....179 C1
West Moors BH22 .....138 B1
Queens Cl
Horndean PO8 .....112 A4
Stubbington PO14 .....154 B4
Queens Ct
Bournemouth BH4 .....204 B2
New Milton BH25 .....195 B2
20 Winchester SO23 .....10 C4
Queens Gdns
Bournemouth BH4 .....204 B2
Fordingbridge SP6 .....69 C1
Queens Gr
New Milton BH25 .....195 B2
Waterlooville PO7 .....134 B3
Queens Ho 15 SO14 .....103 A2
Queens Keep 17 PO5 .....182 B1
Queens Mead SO22 .....10 B3
Queens Par PO2 .....180 C2
Queens Rd
Ferndown BH22 .....165 B4
Lee-on-the-Solent PO13 .....179 C1
Netley SO31 .....127 A3
Petersfield GU32 .....40 C2
Queens Ride SO52 .....53 C2
Queens View SO31 .....127 A3
Queens Way BH24 .....141 A4
Queensbury Mans 7 BH1 .....205 A2
Queensland Rd BH9 .....206 A3
Queensmead 4 BH23 .....163 B3
Queenstown Rd SO15 .....102 B3
Queensway
New Milton BH25 .....194 C2
North Hayling PO11 .....160 A2
Southampton SO14 .....103 A2
Queensway The PO16 .....156 A4

Queenswood Ave BH8 .....190 C1
Queenswood Dr BH22 .....165 B4
Querida Cl SO31 .....128 C1
Quilter Cl SO19 .....104 B2
Quince La SO41 .....163 C3
Quinton Cl
Christchurch BH23 .....208 C4
Portsmouth PO1 .....215 C2
Quintrell Ave PO16 .....156 A4
Quob Farm Cl SO30 .....80 C2
Quob La SO30 .....80 C2
Quomp The BH24 .....141 A4

R
R L Stevenson Ave BH4 .....204 A2
Racecourse View SO43 .....121 C3
Rachel Cl Fair Oak SO50 .....57 A1
Poole BH12 .....203 B4
Rachel Madocks Sch PO8 .....111 B2
Racton Ave PO6 .....158 A4
Racton Rd PO10 .....136 C2
Radcliffe Ct 10 SO14 .....103 A3
Radcliffe Rd SO14 .....103 B3
Radclyffe Rd PO16 .....131 B1
Radipole Rd BH17 .....188 A1
Radleigh Gdns SO40 .....100 A4
Radley Cl SO30 .....81 B1
Radnor St PO5 .....215 B2
Radstock Rd SO19 .....103 C2
Radway Cres SO15 .....102 B4
Radway Rd SO15 .....78 C1
Raebarn Cl SO24 .....14 B3
Raeburn Dr SO30 .....105 B4
Raglan Cl SO53 .....55 A2
Raglan Ct
3 Eastleigh SO50 .....56 A3
Gosport PO12 .....181 A2
Locks Heath SO31 .....129 A3
Raglan Gdns BH11 .....189 A1
Raglan St PO1 .....215 C3
Raglan Terr PO10 .....137 A1
Ragmore La GU32 .....18 C3
Rails La PO11 .....185 B1
Railway Cotts
Southampton SO15 .....101 B4
West Meon GU32 .....37 B2
West Tisted GU34 .....17 B3
Railway Flats PO1 .....182 C3
Railway Terr SO42 .....172 C4
Railway Triangle Ind Est PO6 .....158 A3
Railway View PO1 .....215 C3
Railway View Rd SO17 .....103 B4
Rainbow Pl SO15 .....102 B3
Rake Bsns Pk GU33 .....21 C2
Rake CE Prim Sch GU33 .....21 C3
Rake Rd GU33 .....21 A2
Raleigh Cl
Christchurch BH23 .....207 C3
New Milton BH25 .....194 C3
Ringwood BH24 .....141 B4
Raleigh Ho 22 PO1 .....182 A3
Raleigh Rd BH12 .....188 C1
Raleigh Wlk PO11 .....180 B3
Raley Rd SO31 .....129 A1
Ralph La SO51 .....28 A1
Ralph Rd BH21 .....165 A1
Ramalley La SO53 .....55 A4
Rambler Dr PO13 .....180 B3
Ramblers Way PO7 .....112 B1
Ramillies Ho
1 Fareham PO14 .....154 C4
2 Gosport PO12 .....181 B2
Rampart Gdns PO3 .....157 C3
Rampart Rd SO18 .....103 B4
Rampart Row PO12 .....181 C1
Ramparts The SO41 .....197 B3
Rams Wlk GU32 .....40 C2
Ramsay Pl PO13 .....155 B1
Ramsay Rd SO23 .....2 B4
Ramsdale Ave PO9 .....135 B3
Ramsdean Rd GU32 .....39 C1
Ramsey Ct BH25 .....194 C2
Ramshill GU31 .....41 A2
Rances Way SO22 .....10 C3
Randall Cl SO40 .....76 B1
Randall Rd SO53 .....30 B1
Randall's La PO14 .....154 A4
Randolph Rd
2 Bournemouth BH1 .....205 C2
Poole BH15 .....203 B3
Portsmouth PO2 .....157 C1
Randolph St PO2 .....157 C1
Ranelagh Ct
Christchurch BH23 .....208 C4
5 Southampton SO17 .....103 A4
Ranelagh Gdns SO13 .....102 C4
Ranelagh Rd
Christchurch BH23 .....208 C4
Havant PO9 .....135 B1
Portsmouth PO2 .....157 B1
Winchester SO23 .....11 A2
Range Gdns SO19 .....104 A2
Range Gn PO2 .....157 B2
Ranger Cl SO42 .....172 B2
Rannoch Cl PO15 .....130 C2
Ranmore La PO14 .....153 C4
Ranvilles Jun & Inf Schs PO14 .....154 B4
Ranvilles La PO14 .....154 A4

Rapson Cl PO6 . . . . .133 B1
Raeridge La SO32 . . . . .83 C4
Ratcliffe Rd
  Hedge End SO30 . . . . .105 B4
  Hythe SO45 . . . . .125 C1
Rattigan Gdns PO15 . . . . . .129 B4
Ravana Ct 2 BH8 . . . . .205 A3
Raven Cl PO13 . . . . .180 B3
Raven Croft PO5 . . . . .215 B1
Raven Rd SO14 . . . . .103 A3
Raven Sq SO50 . . . . .55 B1
Raven Way BH23 . . . . .208 A3
Ravens Cl PO14 . . . . .179 B3
Ravens Way SO41 . . . . .211 B2
Ravenscourt Rd
  Bournemouth BH6 . . . . .206 B3
  Lymington SO41 . . . . .197 B1
Ravenscroft Cl SO31 . . . . . .104 C1
Ravenscroft Way SO32 . . . . . .81 C1
Ravensdale Cl BH12 . . . . . . .203 B3
Ravenshall BH2 . . . . .204 B1
Ravenswood PO14 . . . . .129 B2
Ravenswood Gdns 6
  PO5 . . . . .182 B1
Ravine Cl BH13 . . . . .214 C4
Ravine Gdns 5 BH13 . . . . . .214 C4
Ravine Rd
  Bournemouth BH5 . . . . .206 A2
  Poole BH13 . . . . .214 C4
Raymond Cl
  Holbury SO45 . . . . .150 B2
  Verwood BH31 . . . . .115 A3
  West End SO30 . . . . .80 C2
Raymond Rd
  Portchester PO6 . . . . .132 C1
  Southampton SO15 . . . . . . .102 B4
Rayners Dr BH12 . . . . .202 B3
Rayners Gdns SO16 . . . . .79 B2
Raynes Rd PO13 . . . . .180 A2
Reading Room La SO32 . . . .106 B4
Readon Cl GU31 . . . . .41 A2
Readon Ho GU31 . . . . .41 A2
Rebbeck Rd BH7 . . . . .206 A3
Recess The SO50 . . . . .56 A3
Record Rd PO10 . . . . .136 C1
Recreation Cotts SO51 . . . . . .50 C2
Recreation Rd BH12 . . . . . . .203 C3
Rectory Ave BH21 . . . . .162 B1
Rectory Cl Gosport PO12 . . .181 A1
  Stubbington PO14 . . . . .154 B2
Rectory Ct SO30 . . . . .105 C4
Rectory Hill SP5 . . . . .2 B2
Rectory La Breamore SP6 . . . .46 A1
  Meonstoke SO32 . . . . .61 B3
Rectory Rd Havant PO9 . . . .159 C4
  Poole BH15 . . . . .202 B3
Red Barn Ave PO16 . . . . . . .132 B1
Red Barn Com Prim Sch
  PO16 . . . . .156 B4
Red Barn La PO15,PO16 . . . .130 C2
Red Hill Cres SO10 . . . . .78 C2
Red Hill Way SO16 . . . . .78 C2
Red Horn Cl BH16 . . . . .201 B2
Red House Mews SO14 . . . . .197 C2
Red House Mews & Gdns*
  BH23 . . . . .207 A3
Red La
  Compton (Hants) SO21 . . . . .31 C4
  Corfe Mullen BH21 . . . . . . .186 A4
  Owslebury SO21 . . . . .58 A3
  West Tytherley SP5 . . . . .4 A4
Red Leaves SO32 . . . . .83 C1
Red Lodge SO53 . . . . .55 A2
  Red Lodge Sch SO16 . . . . . .78 C2
Red Oaks Cl BH22 . . . . .165 A4
Red Oaks Dr SO31 . . . . .129 A3
Red Roofs BH22 . . . . .165 C2
Redan Cl BH23 . . . . .208 C4
Redan The PO12 . . . . .181 B1
Redbreast Rd BH9 . . . . .190 A2
Redbreast Rd N BH9 . . . . . .190 A2
Redbridge Causeway
  SO15,SO40 . . . . .101 A4
Redbridge Com Sch
  SO16 . . . . .101 B4
Redbridge Flyover
  SO15 . . . . .101 B4
Redbridge Gr PO9 . . . . .135 B2
Redbridge Hill SO16 . . . . . . .77 C1
Redbridge La SO16 . . . . .77 B2
Redbridge Prim Sch
  SO16 . . . . .101 B4
Redbridge Rd SO15 . . . . . . .101 B4
  Redbridge Sta SO15 . . . . . .101 B4
Redbridge Twrs SO16 . . . . . .101 B4
Redbrook Cotts SP6 . . . . . . .94 A4
Redcar Ave PO3 . . . . .143 C3
Redcar St SO15 . . . . .102 A4
Redcliffe Cl BH23 . . . . .192 B2
Redcote Cl SO18 . . . . .104 A4
Redcotts La BH21 . . . . .163 A3
Redcotts Rd BH21 . . . . .163 A3
Redcourt 2 SO16 . . . . .78 C2
Redcroft La SO31 . . . . .105 A1
Redfords The SO40 . . . . .76 C1
Redhill SO16 . . . . .78 C2
Redhill Ave BH9,BH10 . . . . .189 C2
Redhill Cl
  Bournemouth BH10 . . . . . . .189 C2
  Southampton SO16 . . . . . . .78 C2
Redhill Cres BH9 . . . . .189 C2
Redhill Ct BH10 . . . . .189 C2
Redhill Dr BH10 . . . . .189 C2
Redhill Ho PO1 . . . . .215 C4

Redhill Park Homes 1
  BH10 . . . . .189 C2
Redhill Rd PO9 . . . . .113 A1
Redhill Rdbt BH10 . . . . .189 C2
Redhoave Rd BH17 . . . . . . .187 C1
Redhouse Park Gdns
  PO12 . . . . .180 C4
Redlands
  Christchurch BH23 . . . . . . .208 A4
  Poole BH12 . . . . .203 C3
Redlands Dr SO19 . . . . .103 C3
Redlands Gr PO4 . . . . .183 B2
Redlands La
  Emsworth PO10 . . . . .136 C2
  Fareham PO14,PO16 . . . . . .155 A4
Redlands Prim Sch
  PO16 . . . . .155 A4
Redlynch CE Prim Sch
  SP5 . . . . .48 A3
Redlynch Cl PO9 . . . . .136 A2
Redmans View BH31 . . . . . .114 C3
Redmoor Cl SO19 . . . . .103 C3
Rednal Ho PO1 . . . . .215 C3
Redoubt Ct PO14 . . . . .154 C3
Redrise Cl SO45 . . . . .150 B2
Redsails BH13 . . . . .214 A2
Redshank Cl BH17 . . . . .186 C1
Redshank Rd PO8 . . . . .112 A4
Redvers Cl SO41 . . . . .197 B1
Redvers Rd BH23 . . . . .207 C4
Redward Rd SO16 . . . . .77 C3
Redwing Ct PO4 . . . . .183 B3
Redwing Gdns SO40 . . . . . .100 B4
Redwing Rd PO8 . . . . .88 B2
Redwood Cl Hythe SO45 . . .125 B2
  Lymington SO41 . . . . .197 B3
  Ringwood BH24 . . . . .141 A4
  West End SO30 . . . . .80 C2
Redwood Ct 3 PO7 . . . . . . .134 C4
Redwood Dr
  Ferndown BH22 . . . . .165 B4
  Porchester PO16 . . . . .156 A4
Redwood Gdns SO40 . . . . . .100 B4
Redwood Gr PO9 . . . . .136 A2
Redwood Lodge 4
  PO16 . . . . .155 A4
Redwood Park Sch PO6 . . . .158 A3
Redwood Rd BH16 . . . . .201 A4
Redwood Way SO16 . . . . . . .79 A3
Reed Dr SO40 . . . . .101 C1
Reeder Cl SO6 . . . . .69 C1
Reedling Dr PO4 . . . . .183 B3
Reedmace Cl PO7 . . . . .135 A3
Reeds La GU33 . . . . .21 B3
Reeds Mdw GU32 . . . . .39 B2
Reeds Pl PO12 . . . . .181 A3
Reeds Rd PO12 . . . . .181 A4
Reeves Cl SO51 . . . . .50 C2
Reeves Way SO31 . . . . .104 C1
Regal Cl PO6 . . . . .157 C4
Regency Cres BH23 . . . . . . .206 C4
Regency Ct 7 PO12 . . . . . . .182 A2
Regency Gdns PO7 . . . . . . .134 B3
Regency Pl
  Fareham PO15 . . . . .130 C1
  Ringwood BH24 . . . . .141 A4
Regent Cl SO21 . . . . .31 B2
Regent Ct
  24 Southampton SO17 . . . . .79 A1
  17 Winchester SO23 . . . . . .2 A2
Regent Dr BH7 . . . . .205 C4
Regent Ho SO30 . . . . .105 A2
Regent Mews GU32 . . . . . . .40 B2
Regent Pl PO5 . . . . .215 A1
Regent Rd SO53 . . . . .55 B3
Regent St
  Portsmouth PO1 . . . . .182 B4
  Southampton SO14 . . . . . . .102 C2
Regent Way BH23 . . . . .207 A3
Regent's Gr 1 SO15 . . . . . . .102 A4
Regent's Park Gdns
  SO15 . . . . .102 A4
Regent's Park Rd SO15 . . . .102 A4
Regents Ct Havant PO9 . . . .159 C4
  6 Southampton SO16 . . . . . .102 A4
Regents Gate SO31 . . . . . . .128 C3
Regents Park Girls Sch
  SO16 . . . . .102 A4
Reginald Rd PO4 . . . . .183 A2
Reid St BH23 . . . . .207 A4
Reigate Ho PO1 . . . . .215 C4
Relay Rd PO7 . . . . .134 B4
Reldas The 8 PO1 . . . . .182 B2
Reliant Cl SO53 . . . . .55 A3
Rempstone Rd BH21 . . . . . .187 B4
Renault Dr BH18 . . . . .187 A1
Renda Rd SO45 . . . . .150 B2
Renny Rd PO1 . . . . .182 C3
Renouf Cl SO41 . . . . .197 B2
Renown Cl SO53 . . . . .55 A3
Renown Gdns PO8 . . . . .111 C3
Renown Ho 14 PO12 . . . . . .181 B2
Repton Cl PO12 . . . . .180 C2
Repton Gdns SO40 . . . . .81 B1
Reservoir La
  Hedge End SO30 . . . . .105 A3
  Petersfield GU32 . . . . .40 C3
Resolution Ho 18 PO12 . . . .181 B2
Rest-a-wyle Ave PO11 . . . . .185 A3
Restharrow BH1 . . . . .205 A2
Restynge Ho BH31 . . . . . . .114 C4
Retreat Rd BH21 . . . . .163 B2
Retreat The
  Eastleigh SO50 . . . . .56 A2
  Portsmouth PO5 . . . . .215 B1
  Totton SO40 . . . . .101 A3
Revenge Cl PO4 . . . . .183 B3
Revenge Ho 12 PO12 . . . . . .181 B2

Rewlands Dr SO22 . . . . .1 B2
Rex Est SO53 . . . . .55 B3
Reynard Ct BH15 . . . . .202 C2
Reynolds Ct SO51 . . . . .53 A3
Reynolds Dale SO40 . . . . . .100 B3
Reynolds Rd
  Fair Oak SO50 . . . . .57 B1
  Gosport PO12 . . . . .181 B1
  Southampton SO15 . . . . . . .102 B4
Rhinefield Cl
  Bishopstoke SO50 . . . . .56 C1
  Brockenhurst SO42 . . . . . . .145 C1
  Havant PO9 . . . . .135 C4
Rhinefield Ornamental Dr*
  SO42 . . . . .144 C3
Rhinefield Rd
  Brockenhurst SO42 . . . . . . .145 B1
  New Milton BH25 . . . . .170 C1
Rhiners Cl SO41 . . . . .172 A1
Rhyme Hall Mews SO45 . . .151 A2
Rhys Ct 3 PO4 . . . . .183 A2
Ribble Cl
  Broadstone BH18 . . . . .187 A1
  Chandler's Ford SO53 . . . . . .55 B3
Ribble Ct SO16 . . . . .77 C1
Ribbonwood Hts BH14 . . . . .203 A2
Ricardo Cres BH23 . . . . . . .208 A3
Rice Gdns BH16 . . . . .201 B2
Rice Terr BH16 . . . . .201 B2
Richard Cl SO45 . . . . .126 A1
Richard Gr PO12 . . . . .156 A1
Richard Moss Ho 8
  SO23 . . . . .11 A4
Richard Taunton Pl SO17 . . . .79 A1
Richards Cl
  Blackfield SO45 . . . . .150 C1
  Locks Heath SO31 . . . . .129 A2
Richards Ct 15 SO15 . . . . . . .78 A1
Richlans Rd SO30 . . . . .105 B3
Richmond Cl
  Chandler's Ford SO53 . . . . . .30 B1
  South Hayling PO11 . . . . . . .184 C2
  Totton SO40 . . . . .76 A1
Richmond Ct
  16 Bournemouth BH1 . . . . .205 A2
  12 Milford on Sea SO41 . . . .211 B2
  7 New Milton BH25 . . . . . . .195 A2
Richmond Dr PO11 . . . . . . .184 C2
Richmond Gdns
  Bournemouth BH1 . . . . .204 C2
  Southampton SO17 . . . . . . .79 C1
  Waterlooville PO7 . . . . .134 B3
Richmond Hall 6 SO17 . . . . .79 C1
Richmond Hill BH1,BH2 . . . .204 C2
Richmond Hill Dr BH2 . . . . .204 C2
Richmond Ho
  Portsmouth PO1 . . . . .182 A3
  18 Southampton SO15 . . . . .102 B3
  9 Winchester SO22 . . . . . . .10 C4
Richmond La SO51 . . . . .30 B1
Richmond Park Ave
  BH8 . . . . .205 B4
Richmond Park Cl BH8 . . . . .205 B3
Richmond Park Cres
  BH8 . . . . .205 B4
Richmond Park Rd BH8 . . . .205 B4
Richmond Pk SO21 . . . . .31 B2
Richmond Rd
  Gosport PO12 . . . . .181 B1
  Lee-on-the-Solent PO13 . . . .179 C1
  Poole BH14 . . . . .203 B2
  Portsmouth PO5 . . . . .182 B1
  Southampton SO15 . . . . . . .102 B3
  Wimborne Minst BH21 . . . . .164 B2
Richmond Rise
  Bournemouth BH8 . . . . .205 B3
  Porchester PO16 . . . . .132 B1
Richmond St SO14 . . . . .103 A2
Richmond Wood Rd
  BH8 . . . . .205 B4
Richville Rd SO16 . . . . .102 A4
Ridding Cl SO15 . . . . .78 B1
Riders Inf Sch PO9 . . . . . . .135 C3
Riders Jun Sch PO9 . . . . . . .135 C3
Riders La PO9 . . . . .135 C2
Rideway PO9 . . . . .135 B1
Ridge Cl PO8 . . . . .88 B2
Ridge Common La GU32 . . . .40 B3
Ridge La Botley SO30 . . . . . .106 B2
  Romsey SO51 . . . . .76 B4
Ridge The SP5 . . . . .47 B3
Ridge Top La GU32 . . . . .39 C3
Ridgefield Gdns BH23 . . . . .208 B4
Ridgemede Jun Sch
  SO32 . . . . .83 B4
Ridgemount Ave SO16 . . . . . .78 B3
Ridgemount Gdns BH15 . . . .201 C2
Ridgemount La SO16 . . . . . . .78 C3
Ridgeway
  Broadstone BH18 . . . . .187 A2
  Corfe Mullen BH21 . . . . . . .186 B4
  Ferndown BH22 . . . . .189 C4
  Winchester SO22 . . . . .10 B3
Ridgeway Cl
  Chandler's Ford SO53 . . . . . .55 C3
  Cosham PO6 . . . . .132 C1
  Fair Oak SO50 . . . . .57 B2
Ridgeway House Specl Sch
  SO19 . . . . .103 C3
Ridgeway La SO41 . . . . .197 B1
Ridgeway The PO16 . . . . . . .131 C1
Ridgeway Wlk SO53 . . . . . . .55 C3
Ridgewood Cl SO45 . . . . . . .125 B2
Ridings The Fair Oak SO50 . . .57 A1
  Liss GU33 . . . . .21 A2
  Poole BH12 . . . . .203 C2
  Waltham Chase SO32 . . . . . .83 C2

Ridley Cl SO45 . . . . .150 B2
Ridley Rd BH9 . . . . .204 C4
Ridout Cl BH10 . . . . .189 A1
Rigby Rd SO17 . . . . .103 A4
Riggs Gdns BH11 . . . . .188 C1
Rigler Rd BH15 . . . . .202 A1
Rimbury Way BH23 . . . . . . .207 A4
Rimington Gdns 1 SO51 . . . .28 A1
Rimington Rd PO8 . . . . .111 C2
Ring The SO16 . . . . .78 C4
Ringbury SO41 . . . . .197 B3
Ringlet Way 6 SO23 . . . . . . .11 B4
Ringwood CE Inf Sch
  BH24 . . . . .141 A4
Ringwood Dr SO52 . . . . .53 C3
Ringwood Ho PO9 . . . . .135 C3
Ringwood Jun Sch
  BH24 . . . . .141 A3
Ringwood Rd
  Alderholt SP6 . . . . .93 A2
  Bournemouth BH11 . . . . . . .188 C2
  Bransgore BH23 . . . . .193 B3
  Burley BH24 . . . . .142 C3
  Christchurch BH23 . . . . . . .194 A1
  Ferndown BH22 . . . . .165 B2
  Fordingbridge SP6 . . . . . . .94 B2
  Fordingbridge SP6 . . . . . . .94 B2
  Poole BH12,BH14 . . . . .203 A4
  Portsmouth PO4 . . . . .183 A2
  Sopley BH23 . . . . .192 A4
  St Leonards BH24 . . . . .139 B1
  Three Legged Cross BH22 . .138 C4
  Totton SO40 . . . . .100 B4
  Verwood BH31 . . . . .115 A3
Ringwood Ret Pk BH11 . . . .188 C2
Ringwood Sch BH24 . . . . . .141 A4
Ringwood Terr SO42 . . . . . .146 A1
Ringwood Trad Est
  BH24 . . . . .141 A3
Ringwood Waldorf Sch
  BH24 . . . . .141 A3
Ripley Gr PO3 . . . . .183 A4
Ripon Cl SO50 . . . . .81 B4
Ripon Gdns 11 PO7 . . . . . . .112 A1
Ripon Rd BH9 . . . . .190 A1
Ripplewood SO40 . . . . .102 A1
Ripstone Gdns SO17 . . . . . . .79 A2
Rise The
  Brockenhurst SO42 . . . . . . .145 C1
  Waterlooville PO7 . . . . .134 B1
Ritchie Cl PO11 . . . . .185 B3
Ritchie Ct SO19 . . . . .104 A2
Ritchie Pl PO22 . . . . .138 B2
Ritchie Rd BH11 . . . . .189 A2
Rival Moor Rd GU31 . . . . . . .41 B1
River Cl SO41 . . . . .197 C2
River Ct SO41 . . . . .197 C2
River Gdns SO41 . . . . .211 C2
River Gn SO31 . . . . .128 A1
River La PO15 . . . . .130 B3
River Mews SO40 . . . . .56 B2
  River Park L Ctr SO23 . . . . . .2 A1
River Pk BH6 . . . . .206 C3
River Rd SP6 . . . . .70 B1
River St PO10 . . . . .137 A2
River View Ho SO19 . . . . . . .103 B2
River View Rd SO18 . . . . . . .79 B1
River Way
  Christchurch BH23 . . . . . . .191 B1
  Havant PO9 . . . . .136 A2
River's St PO5 . . . . .215 C2
Riverbourne Cl SO18 . . . . . .103 B4
Riverdale Ave PO7 . . . . .135 A4
Riverdale Cl SP6 . . . . .69 C1
Riverdale Cotts PO6 . . . . . .131 B2
Riverdale La BH23 . . . . .207 A3
Riverdene Pl SO18 . . . . .103 B4
Riverhead Cl PO4 . . . . .183 A3
Riverlea Rd BH23 . . . . .207 A3
Rivermead Cl SO51 . . . . .52 B4
Rivermead Ct PO10 . . . . . . .137 A2
Rivermead Gdns BH23 . . . . .191 C1
Riverpark Ct SO18 . . . . .103 C4
Rivers Reach SO41 . . . . . . .197 C2
Riversdale 8 BH21 . . . . . . .163 B2
Riverside Cl SO19 . . . . .126 C4
Riverside Gdns 7 PO9 . . . . .135 C3
Riverside Rd BH6 . . . . .207 A3
Riverside
  Bishopstoke SO50 . . . . .56 B2
  4 Bournemouth BH10 . . . . .189 C2
  Ringwood BH24 . . . . .140 C3
Riverside Ave
  Bournemouth BH7 . . . . .191 B1
  Fareham PO16 . . . . .131 B2
  Riverside Bsns Pk SO41 . . .197 C2
Riverside Cl Cadnam SO40 . . .99 B3
  Liss GU33 . . . . .20 C2
Riverside Cotts SO21 . . . . . . .31 C3
Riverside Gdns SO41 . . . . . .52 C2
Riverside Ho 44 SO23 . . . . . .11 A4
Riverside Mews BH6 . . . . . .207 A3
Riverside Mews PO7 . . . . . . .108 A2
Riverside Pk BH23 . . . . .207 A3
Riverside Pk Ind Est
  BH21 . . . . .163 B2
Riverside Pl SP6 . . . . .70 C1
Riverside Rd
  Bournemouth BH6 . . . . .206 C3
  West Moors BH22 . . . . .138 B1
Riverside Sch PO7 . . . . .134 C2
Riverside Wlk GU31 . . . . . . .41 A2
Riverslea Mews BH23 . . . . .207 B3
Riversmeet Ct BH23 . . . . . . .207 B3
Riverview SO40 . . . . .100 C3

Riverview Terr SO31 . . . . . .128 B4
Riviera Ct
  3 Bournemouth BH2 . . . . . .204 B2
  3 Poole BH13 . . . . .214 C4
Riviera 22 BH1 . . . . .205 A2
RN Submarine Mus & HMS
  Alliance* PO12 . . . . .181 C2
Road View PO2 . . . . .182 B4
Roads Hill PO8 . . . . .88 A1
Robere Ho SO19 . . . . .103 B2
Robert Cecil Ave SO18 . . . . .79 C2
Robert Mack Ct 32 PO1 . . . .182 A3
Robert Whitworth Dr
  SO51 . . . . .27 C1
Roberts Cl Hordle SO41 . . . .196 C1
  Wickham PO17 . . . . .108 A2
Roberts La BH17 . . . . .187 C1
Roberts Rd
  Bournemouth BH7 . . . . .206 A3
  Gosport PO12 . . . . .180 C2
  Hythe SO45 . . . . .125 C2
  Poole BH17 . . . . .187 A1
  Southampton SO15 . . . . . . .102 C3
  Totton SO40 . . . . .100 C3
Robertshaw Ho SO43 . . . . .125 C1
Robertson Block PO12 . . . . .181 B3
Robin Cres BH25 . . . . .194 B3
Robin Ct SO15 . . . . .102 C4
Robin Gdns Totton SO40 . . .100 B4
  Waterlooville PO8 . . . . .111 B2
Robin Gr BH25 . . . . .194 B3
Robin Sq SO50 . . . . .55 B1
Robina Cl PO7 . . . . .135 A4
Robina Ct PO7 . . . . .135 A4
Robinia Gr SO16 . . . . .78 B3
Robins Cl PO14 . . . . .154 B2
Robins Ct 8 PO12 . . . . .163 B2
Robins Mdw PO14 . . . . .129 B1
Robins Way BH23 . . . . .208 A3
Robinson Cl PO16 . . . . .132 B1
Robinson Rd PO14 . . . . .179 A3
Robinson Way PO13 . . . . . .158 B2
Robinswood Dr BH22 . . . . . .165 B4
Robsall Cl BH12 . . . . .203 C4
Robville Ct BH6 . . . . .206 A3
Rochester Ct PO13 . . . . .180 B3
Rochester Rd
  Bournemouth BH11 . . . . . . .189 A2
  Portsmouth PO4 . . . . .182 C2
Rochester St SO14 . . . . .103 B3
Rochford Rd PO6 . . . . .157 B4
Rockall Cl SO17 . . . . .77 C3
Rockbourne Cl PO9 . . . . . . .135 B2
Rockbourne Gdns BH25 . . . .209 B4
Rockbourne La
  Damerham SP6 . . . . .68 B4
  Rockbourne SP6 . . . . .68 B4
Rockbourne Rd SO22 . . . . . . .1 B3
Rockbourne Roman Villa*
  SP6 . . . . .68 C4
Rockery Cl SO45 . . . . .125 B2
Rockford Cl BH6 . . . . .206 C2
Rockford Ho SO50 . . . . .57 A1
Rockingham Way PO16 . . . .156 A4
Rockleigh Dr SO40 . . . . . . .100 B3
Rockleigh Rd SO16 . . . . .78 B2
Rockley Rd BH15 . . . . .201 C1
Rockpit Cotts GU33 . . . . . . .21 A2
Rockram Cl SO40 . . . . .99 A4
Rockram Gdns SO45 . . . . . .125 B2
Rockrose Way PO6 . . . . .133 A1
Rockstone Ct 2 SO14 . . . . .103 A3
Rockstone La SO14 . . . . . . .103 A3
Rockstone Pl SO15 . . . . .102 C3
Rockville Dr PO7 . . . . .134 C4
Rodbard Ho SO31 . . . . .104 C1
Rodbourne Cl SO41 . . . . . . .211 B4
Rodfield La SO24 . . . . .7 B3
Rodleaze La SO41 . . . . .173 C1
Rodney Cl Gosport PO13 . . .180 B3
  Poole BH12 . . . . .204 A4
Rodney Ct
  Christchurch BH23 . . . . . . .208 A3
  Poole BH15 . . . . .202 B1
  Southampton SO19 . . . . . . .104 B2
Rodney Dr BH23 . . . . .207 C3
Rodney Ho PO7 PO12 . . . . .181 B2
Rodney Rd PO4 . . . . .183 A3
Rodney Way PO8 . . . . .112 A3
Rodway BH21 . . . . .163 B2
Rodwell Cl BH10 . . . . .189 B3
Roebuck Ave PO15 . . . . . . .130 B3
Roebuck Cl Cosham PO6 . . .157 C4
  New Milton BH25 . . . . .195 A2
Roebuck Dr PO12 . . . . .181 A4
Roeshot Cres BH23 . . . . . . .193 C1
Roeshot Hill BH23 . . . . .193 B1
Roewood Cl SO45 . . . . .150 B2
Roewood Rd SO45 . . . . .150 B2
Rogate Gdns PO16 . . . . .132 B1
Rogate Ho 1 PO1 . . . . .215 C4
Roger Penny Way
  Brook SO43 . . . . .73 B1
  Fordingbridge, Bramshaw
  SP6 . . . . .72 B3
  Fordingbridge, Godshill SP6 .71 A3
Rogers Cl
  Bishopstoke SO50 . . . . .56 C2
  Gosport PO12 . . . . .181 A3
Rogers Ho PO13 . . . . .179 C1
Rogers Rd SO50 . . . . .56 C2
Roker Way SO50 . . . . .57 A1
Roland Cl PO8 . . . . .112 A3
Rollestone Rd SO45 . . . . . . .150 B1
Rolls Dr BH6 . . . . .207 A2
Roman Cl SO53 . . . . .54 C4
Roman Ct PO10 . . . . .137 B1
Roman Dr SO16 . . . . .78 C4
Roman Gdns SO45 . . . . .125 B1

Roman Gn P07 ....110 C2
Roman Gr P016 ....156 B3
Roman Ho S018 ....103 B4
Roman Hts BH21 ....186 C4
Roman Mdw SP5 ....46 C4
Roman Quay SP6 ....69 C1
Roman Rd Chilworth S016 ....78 C4
Corfe Mullen BH18 ....186 C2
Havant P010 ....136 B1
Holbury S045 ....150 A3
Hythe S045 ....125 B1
Twyford S021 ....32 A3
Roman Row S032 ....83 B4
Roman Way Havant P09 ....135 C1
Hythe S045 ....125 B1
Pamphill BH21 ....162 B3
Romans' Rd ■ S023 ....11 A3
Romford Rd S031 ....152 B4
Romill Cl S030 ....80 A2
Romsey Cl BH10 ....189 C2
Romsey Rd BH10 ....189 C2
Romsey Abbey* S051 ....52 C4
Romsey Abbey CE Prim Sch
S051 ....52 C4
Romsey Ave
Portchester P016 ....156 A4
Portsmouth P03 ....183 A3
Romsey Cl S030 ....56 A2
Romsey Ct ᵈ S015 ....102 B3
Romsey Hospl S051 ....53 A4
Romsey Ind Est S051 ....52 C4
Romsey Inf Sch S051 ....52 C4
Romsey Jun Sch S051 ....53 A4
Romsey Lodge ᵈ S016 ....78 A1
Romsey Rd Cadnam S051 ....75 C3
Eastleigh S050 ....56 A2
Horndean P08 ....88 B1
King's Somborne S051 ....6 B4
Lyndhurst S043 ....121 C3
Ower S040,S051 ....75 B2
Southampton S016 ....77 C2
West Wellow S051 ....51 A2
Whiteparish SP5 ....24 C2
Winchester S022, S023 ....10 B3
Romsey Sch The S051 ....52 C4
Romsey Sta S051 ....52 C4
Romyns Ct P014 ....130 C1
Ronald Bowker Ct ᵈ
S022 ....10 C4
Ronald Pugh Ct S018 ....79 C2
Rook Hill BH23 ....208 B3
Rookcliff ᵈ S041 ....211 B2
Rookcliff Way S041 ....211 B2
Rookery Ave
Southampton S019 ....129 B4
Swanwick P015,S031 ....129 A4
Rookery Cotts SP5 ....3 B2
Rookery Gr P015 ....129 A4
Rookery La SP6 ....45 C1
Rookery The P010 ....137 A1
Rookes Cl P08 ....112 A3
Rookes La S041 ....197 B1
Rookes Mews S031 ....41 A2
Rookesbury Park Sch
P017 ....108 B2
Rooks Down Rd S022 ....10 B3
Rooksbridge S045 ....125 B2
Rooksbury Croft P09 ....136 A3
Rookway Gr P016 ....155 C4
Rookwood ᵈ S041 ....211 B2
Rookwood Cl S050 ....56 A3
Rookwood Gdns SP6 ....69 B1
Rookwood View P07 ....110 C3
Roosevelt Cres BH11 ....189 A3
Rope Wlk S041 ....173 B1
Rope Wlk S031 ....128 A1
Rope Wlk The ᵈ P016 ....155 A4
Ropers La BH16 ....201 B4
Ropewalk Ho ᵈ S023 ....11 A4
Ropley Cl S019 ....127 A4
Ropley Ct P017 ....184 C2
Ropley Rd
Bournemouth BH7 ....206 B4
ᵈ Havant P09 ....136 A3
Rosamund Ave BH21 ....163 C1
Roscrea Cl BH6 ....207 A2
Roscrea Dr BH6 ....207 A2
Rose Cl Hedge End S030 ....105 B4
Hythe S045 ....126 A1
Rose Cott P08 ....112 B4
Rose Cres SH15 ....202 C3
Rose Ct BH15 ....202 C2
Rose Gdn The BH23 ....191 B1
Rose Gdns BH9 ....190 A2
Rose Hill P08 ....112 A3
Rose Rd
Southampton S014 ....103 A4
Totton S040 ....101 A3
Rosebank Cl S016 ....77 C3
Rosebank Lodge S016 ....77 C3
Rosebay Cl S050 ....81 B3
Rosebay Ct ᵈ P07 ....134 C3
Rosebery Ave
Cosham P06 ....158 A4
Hythe S045 ....126 A1
Rosebery Cl BH11 ....115 B3
Rosebery Cres S050 ....56 A3
Rosebery Rd BH5 ....206 A3
Rosebrook Cl S018 ....103 C4
Rosebud Ave ᵈ BH9 ....190 A1
Rosecrae Cl BH25 ....194 C2
Rosedale Ave S051 ....53 A4
Rosedale Cl
ᵈ Christchurch BH23 ....207 C3
Titchfield P014 ....153 C4
Rosehill Cl BH23 ....169 A1
Rosehill Dr BH23 ....169 A1

Roseship Cl S050 ....57 A1
Roselands
Waterlooville P08 ....112 A3
West End S030 ....104 B4
Roselands Cl S050 ....57 A2
Roselands Gdns S017 ....79 A1
Roseleigh Dr S040 ....100 C3
Rosemary Ct ᵈ BH23 ....209 A4
Rosemary Gdns
Hedge End S030 ....105 B3
Poole BH12 ....203 A4
Swanwick P015 ....129 B4
Rosemary La ᵈ P011 ....182 A3
Rosemary Rd BH12 ....203 B4
Rosemary Way P08 ....112 A3
Rosemary Wlk ᵈ P013 ....179 C1
Rosemoor Gr S053 ....30 A1
Rosemount Rd BH4 ....204 A1
Rosendale Rd S053 ....55 B2
Rosery The P012 ....181 A1
Rosetta Rd P04 ....183 A2
Rosewall Rd S016 ....77 C2
Rosewarne Ct ᵈ S023 ....2 A1
Rosewood P013 ....155 C1
Rosewood Gdns
Clanfield P08 ....88 B3
Marchwood S040 ....102 A1
New Milton BH25 ....194 C2
Rosina Cl P07 ....135 A4
Roslin Gdns BH3 ....204 B4
Roslin Rd BH3 ....204 C4
Roslin Rd S BH3 ....204 C4
Roslyn Ho P05 ....215 B1
Rossan Ave S019 ....103 C2
Rosoman Rd S019 ....103 C2
Ross Gdns
Bournemouth BH11 ....188 B3
Southampton S016 ....78 A1
Ross Glades BH3 ....204 C3
Ross Mews ᵈ S031 ....127 A3
Ross Rd BH24 ....117 B1
Ross Way P013 ....179 C2
Rossan Ave S031 ....152 B4
Rossington Ave S018 ....103 C4
Rossington Way S018 ....103 C4
Rossiters La S040 ....99 C3
Rossiters Quay BH23 ....207 B3
Rossley Cl BH23 ....193 C1
Rosslyn Cl S052 ....54 A2
Rossmore Ctr ᵈ P04 ....203 A4
Rossmore Rd BH12 ....203 B4
Rostrevor La ᵈ P04 ....182 C3
Rostron Cl S018 ....80 A1
Rosyth Rd S018 ....103 C4
Rotary Cl BH21 ....163 A1
Rotary Ct S031 ....127 A3
Rotary Ho S015 ....102 B4
Rothbury Cl
Southampton S019 ....104 A2
Totton S040 ....76 B1
Rothbury Pk BH25 ....195 A1
Rother Cl Petersfield GU31 ....41 B2
West End S018 ....80 A1
Rother Dale S019 ....104 C2
Rother Ho GU33 ....20 C2
Rotherbank Farm La
GU33 ....21 A3
Rothercombe La GU32 ....40 A2
Rotherfield Rd
Bournemouth BH5 ....206 A2
Christchurch BH23 ....194 A1
Rotherley ᵈ GU32 ....40 C2
Rotherwick Cl P09 ....136 A3
Rothesay Dr BH23 ....208 C4
Rothesay Rd
Bournemouth BH4 ....204 B3
Gosport P012 ....181 A4
Rothsbury Dr S053 ....55 A3
Rothschild Cl S019 ....103 C1
Rothville Pl S053 ....30 A1
Rothwell Cl ᵈ P06 ....133 A1
Rotterdam Dr BH23 ....207 B4
Rotterdam Twrs ᵈ
S019 ....126 C4
Roughdown La S045 ....150 B1
Roumelia La BH5 ....206 A3
Roundabouts The GU33 ....21 A3
Roundcopse S045 ....125 B2
Roundhaye Rd BH11 ....188 C3
Roundhill Cl S018 ....80 A1
Roundhill Cross S06 ....45 C1
Roundhouse Ct P011 ....185 A1
Roundhouse Dr S040 ....100 A3
Roundhouse Mdw P010 ....161 A4
Roundway ᵈ S023 ....11 B4
Roundway P07 ....134 C4
Roundways BH11 ....188 C2
Routs Way S016 ....77 C4
Row The SP5 ....47 B4
Row Wood La P013 ....155 A1
Rowallan Ave P013 ....180 B4
Rowan Ave P013 ....179 C1
Rowan Cl
Bursledon S031 ....127 C4
Christchurch BH23 ....208 B4
Lee-on-the-Solent P013 ....179 C1
Romsey S051 ....53 B3
Southampton S016 ....78 A2
St Leonards BH24 ....139 B2
Swanmore S032 ....84 A2
Sway S041 ....172 A1
Totton S040 ....100 A3
Rowan Ct
Portsmouth P04 ....182 C2
Southampton S019 ....103 C2
Rowan Dr
Broadstone BH17 ....186 C1

Rowan Dr continued
Christchurch BH23 ....208 B4
Verwood BH31 ....115 A2
Rowan Gdns S030 ....105 B3
Rowan Tree Cl GU33 ....21 A3
Rowan Way
Fareham P014 ....154 B4
Havant P09 ....136 A2
Rowans Pk S041 ....197 B2
Rowans The S040 ....101 C1
Rowbarrow Cl BH17 ....187 C1
Rowborough Rd S018 ....103 C4
Rowbury Rd P09 ....135 B3
Rowden Cl S051 ....50 C1
Rowe Asheway S031 ....128 C2
Rowena Ct P05 ....215 C2
Rowena Rd BH6 ....206 C3
Rowes Alley P01 ....181 C2
Rowlands La S041 ....199 A4
Rowhay La S032 ....58 B3
Rowin Cl P011 ....185 B1
Rowland Ave BH15 ....202 C3
Rowland Rd
Fareham P015 ....130 C1
Portchester P016 ....132 C1
Rowlands Ave P07 ....111 C1
Rowlands Castle Rd
P08 ....112 C4
Rowlands Castle St John's CE
Prim Sch P09 ....136 A4
Rowlands Castle Sta
P09 ....113 B1
Rowlands Cl S053 ....55 A2
Rowlands Hill BH21 ....163 B3
Rowley Cl ᵈ S018 ....80 A1
Rowley Cl S030 ....105 C4
Rowley Cr S030 ....105 C4
Rowley Dr S030 ....105 C4
Rowlings Rd S022 ....1 B2
Rowner Cl P013 ....155 B1
Rowner Jun & Inf Schs
P013 ....155 B1
Rowner La Gosport P013 ....155 B1
Rowner, Gosport P013 ....180 B4
Rowner Rd Gosport P013 ....155 A1
Stubbington P013 ....155 A1
Rownhams CE Prim Sch
S016 ....77 C3
Rownhams Cl S016 ....77 C3
Rownhams La S016 ....77 C2
Rownhams La S052, S016 ....53 C1
Rownhams La S016 ....77 C4
Rownhams Rd
Bournemouth BH8 ....190 B2
Havant P09 ....135 B3
North Baddesley S052 ....54 A2
Southampton S016 ....77 C3
Rownhams Rd N S016 ....77 C3
Rownhams Way S016 ....77 C4
Roxan Ct ᵈ S015 ....102 C4
Roxburgh Ho S031 ....129 A2
Royal Arc ᵈ BH7 ....205 C2
Royal Bournemouth Gen
Hospl The BH7 ....191 A1
Royal Crescent Rd
S014 ....103 A2
Royal Ct
Chandler's Ford S053 ....55 B3
Fareham P016 ....155 A3
Royal Gate P04 ....183 A1
Royal Gdns P09 ....113 A1
Royal Hampshire Cty Hospl
S022 ....10 C4
Royal Hampshire Regiment
Mus* S023 ....10 C4
Royal London Pk S030 ....105 A4
Royal Marines Mus*
P04 ....183 A1
Royal Naval Cotts P017 ....132 C3
Royal Naval Hospl Haslar
P012 ....181 B1
Royal Naval Hospl Mus*
P04 ....181 C3
Royal Oak Rd BH10 ....189 B3
Royal South Hants Hospl
S014 ....103 A3
Royal Sovereign Ave
BH6 ....207 A2
Royal The P011 ....184 C1
Royal Victoria Ctry Pk*
S031 ....127 B2
Royal Victoria Hospl
BH4 ....204 B2
Royal Way P07 ....134 C4
Royden La S041 ....173 B2
Roydon Ct S022 ....10 C3
Royster Cl BH17 ....187 B1
Royston Ave S050 ....56 A3
Royston Cl S017 ....79 A4
Royston Ct S040 ....76 C1
Royston Dr BH21 ....163 B3
Royston Pl BH25 ....210 A4
Rozel Ct S016 ....77 C2
Rozel Manor BH13 ....204 A1
Rozelle Cl S022 ....1 A3
Rozelle Rd BH14 ....203 B2
Ruben Dr BH15 ....201 B1
Rubens Cl BH25 ....195 A2
Ruby Ct P07 ....134 C4
Rudd La S051 ....6 A1
Rudd La S051 ....27 C4
Rudgewick Cl P016 ....156 A4
Rudmore Ct ᵈ P02 ....157 B1
Rudmore Rd P02 ....182 B4
Rudmore Sq P02 ....182 B4
Ruffield Cl S022 ....1 B1

Rufford Cl S050 ....56 A3
Rufford Gdns BH6 ....206 C3
Rufus Cl
Chandler's Ford S053 ....55 C4
Rowhams S016 ....77 B3
Rufus Ct S043 ....122 A3
Rufus Gdns S040 ....100 B4
Rufus Stone* S043 ....98 A3
Rugby Rd Poole BH17 ....187 A1
Portsmouth P05 ....215 D2
Rumbridge Gdns S040 ....101 A4
Rumbridge St S040 ....101 A3
Runnymede
Fareham P015 ....130 B2
West End S030 ....80 B1
Runnymede Ave BH11 ....188 C3
Runway The BH23 ....203 C3
Runway The BH23 ....208 A4
Rushcombe Fst Sch
BH21 ....186 B3
Rushcombe Way BH21 ....186 C3
Rushes Farm GU32 ....40 C2
Rushes Rd GU32 ....40 C2
Rushes The S040 ....101 C1
Rushford Warren BH23 ....207 C2
Rushin Ho P016 ....156 B4
Rushington Ave S040 ....100 C3
Rushington Bsns Pk
S040 ....100 C3
Rushington La S040 ....100 C3
Rushmere Gate P07 ....86 B1
Rushmere La P017 ....110 C4
Rushmere Rd BH6 ....206 B4
Rushmere Wlk ᵈ P09 ....135 B3
Rushpole Ct S045 ....125 B2
Rushton Cres BH3 ....204 C3
Ruskin Ave BH9 ....190 A2
Ruskin Rd Eastleigh S050 ....56 A3
Rushmere Wlk P09 ....135 B3
Rusland Cl S053 ....55 A4
Russel Rd BH10 ....189 B3
Russell Bldgs P016 ....156 B4
Russell Churcher Ct
P012 ....180 C4
Russell Cl P013 ....179 C1
Russell Cotes Art Gall &
Mus* BH1 ....205 A1
Russell Cotes Rd BH1 ....205 A1
Russell Ct ᵈ BH25 ....195 A2
Russell Dr
Christchurch BH23 ....207 B3
Mottisfont S051 ....5 B1
Russell Gdns
Hamworthy BH16 ....201 B2
St Leonards BH24 ....140 A3
Russell Pl Fareham P016 ....131 A1
Southampton S017 ....79 A1
Russell Rd Havant P09 ....135 C1
Lee-on-the-Solent P013 ....179 C1
Winchester S023 ....2 A1
Russell St Gosport P012 ....181 A3
ᵈ Southampton S014 ....103 A2
Russell Way GU31 ....41 A1
Russet Cl Ferndown BH22 ....165 B3
ᵈ Lymington S041 ....197 C1
Russet Gdns P010 ....161 A4
Russet Ho S030 ....105 A3
Russett Cl S032 ....84 A2
Russett Dr BH24 ....141 A3
Rustan Cl Fair Oak S050 ....57 B1
Hedge End S030 ....105 A3
Rustington Ho P01 ....215 B3
Rutland Ct S018 ....104 A4
Rutland Gdns S031 ....105 A1
Rutland Manor ᵈ BH12 ....204 A2
Rutland Rd
Bournemouth BH9 ....204 B3
Christchurch BH23 ....191 C1
Rutland Way S018 ....80 A1
Ryall Rd BH17 ....187 B1
Ryan Cl BH22 ....165 B4
Ryan Gdns
Bournemouth BH11 ....189 A3
Fareham BH22 ....165 B4
Rydal Cl
Christchurch BH23 ....191 B2
ᵈ Cosham P06 ....133 A1
Rydal Ho ᵈ P06 ....133 A1
Rydal Rd BH12 ....203 C4
Ryde Pl P013 ....180 A2
Ryde Rd S014 ....103 A2
Ryde Terr S014 ....103 A2
Rye Cl S053 ....54 C3
Rye Dale S040 ....100 B2
Rye Paddock La S045 ....151 A2
Ryecroft Havant P09 ....136 A1
Titchfield P014 ....129 B1
Ryecroft Ave BH11 ....188 C3
Ryedown La S051 ....51 C2
Ryefield Cl GU31 ....41 B2
Ryefield Cotts GU31 ....41 C1
Rylands Cl S016 ....77 C2

S

Sabre Rd P010 ....161 A2
Sackville St P05 ....215 B2
Saddle Cl BH21 ....164 B3
Saddlers Cl S050 ....56 B3
Sadlers La S045 ....126 A1
Sadlers Wlk P010 ....161 A4
Saffron Ct
Bournemouth BH11 ....188 B2
Locks Heath S031 ....128 C1
ᵈ Southampton S014 ....103 A2
Saffron Dr BH23 ....208 A4

Saffron Way
Bournemouth BH11 ....188 B2
Swanwick P015 ....129 B4
Sage Cl P07 ....135 A3
Sages La GU34 ....23 C3
Sailors La S032 ....60 B4
Sainsbury Lodge P01 ....215 D3
Saints Cl BH21 ....138 C4
St Adlem's CE Comb Sch
BH12 ....204 A3
St Agatha's Rd S031 ....128 A2
St Agathas Way P01 ....215 B4
St Alban's Ave BH8 ....205 B4
St Alban's CE Prim Sch
P09 ....136 A2
St Alban's Cres BH8 ....205 A4
St Alban's Rd
Bournemouth BH8 ....205 A4
Havant P09 ....136 A2
Portsmouth P04 ....182 C2
Southampton S014 ....103 A3
St Albans Ct P013 ....180 B3
St Aldhelm's Cl BH14 ....203 C2
St Aldhelm's Rd BH13 ....203 C2
St Aldhelm's Rd BH13 ....203 C2
St Andrew Cl P08 ....88 B1
St Andrew's Bldgs S031 ....128 A2
St Andrew's Rd
Cosham P06 ....158 C4
Gosport P012 ....181 A2
Portsmouth P05 ....215 C2
South Hayling P011 ....185 A1
Southampton S014 ....103 A3
St Andrews BH23 ....207 A3
St Andrews Cl
Michelmersh S051 ....27 B3
North Baddesley S052 ....53 C3
St Andrews Gn S032 ....61 B3
St Andrews Ho BH17 ....103 A4
St Andrews Pk S050 ....81 B3
St Andrews Rd
Broadstone BH18 ....187 A3
Southampton S014 ....103 A3
St Ann's Cres P012 ....181 A3
St Ann's Rd P09 ....135 C1
St Ann's Hospl BH13 ....214 C3
St Ann's Rd P08 ....112 B4
St Anne's Ave BH6 ....206 C3
St Anne's Convent RC Girls
Sch S015 ....102 C4
St Anne's Gr P014 ....154 C4
St Anne's Rd
Portsmouth P04 ....182 C2
Southampton S019 ....103 C1
Upton BH16 ....201 A4
St Annes Cl S022 ....10 B2
St Annes Gdns S041 ....197 B2
St Annes Ho S051 ....52 C3
St Annes La S032 ....107 B2
St Annes Mews ᵈ S014 ....103 A4
St Anns Ct ᵈ S017 ....79 A1
St Anthony's RC Prim Sch
P014 ....129 B1
St Aubin's Rd BH24 ....204 C3
St Aubin's Ave S019 ....104 A3
St Aubin's Pk P011 ....184 B2
St Aubyns Ct BH15 ....202 A3
St Aubyns La BH24 ....117 C1
St Augustin's Rd BH2 ....204 C3
St Augustine Gdns S017 ....79 B1
St Augustine Rd P04 ....182 C2
St Austell Cl S050 ....56 C2
St Barbara Way P02 ....157 C2
St Barbe Cl S051 ....53 A3
St Barbe Mus* S041 ....197 C2
St Bartholomew's Gdns
P05 ....215 C1
St Bede CE Prim Sch
S023 ....11 A4
St Bede's Ct S023 ....2 A1
St Bernard Ho ᵈ S014 ....103 A3
St Birinus Rd SP5 ....47 B3
St Blaize Rd S051 ....53 B3
St Boniface Ct S052 ....54 A2
St Bonnet Dr S032 ....83 B4
St Brelade Pl S016 ....77 B2
St Brelades BH14 ....203 B1
St Brelades Ave P012 ....180 B3
St Catherine Hts S022 ....182 B1
St Catherine's Par BH23 ....191 C1
St Catherine's RC Prim Sch
BH21 ....164 A3
St Catherine's Rd
Bournemouth BH6 ....206 C2
South Hayling P011 ....184 B2
Southampton S018 ....79 C1
Winchester S023 ....11 B2
St Catherine's Way
S030 ....191 B2
St Catherines Rd BH21 ....163 B2
St Catherines Ct S011 ....184 B2
St Catherines Rd S050 ....56 B3
St Catherines View
S030 ....105 A3
St Catherines Way
Portchester P016 ....131 C1
Winchester S023, S021 ....11 B3
St Chads Ave P07 ....157 C1
St Christopher Ave
P016 ....131 B2
St Christopher's Rd
P09 ....135 B2
St Christophers Cl S052 ....54 A2
St Christophers Gdns ᵈ
P013 ....155 B1

St Christophers Hospl PO16 131 A2
St Christophers Sch SO18 103 C4
St Clair Rd BH13 214 C4
St Clares Ave PO9 135 B4
St Cleeves Way BH22 165 B2
St Clement & St John CE Inf Sch BH8 205 B3
St Clement St
21 Winchester SO22 10 C4
31 Winchester SO23 11 A4
St Clement's Gdns BH1 205 B3
St Clement's Rd BH8 205 B3
St Clements Cl SO51 52 C4
St Clements La BH15 202 A1
St Clements Rd BH15 203 A4
St Colman's Ave PO6 158 A4
St Cross Ct 4 SO23 10 C3
St Cross Hospl* SO23 10 C2
St Cross Mede SO23 10 C2
St Cross Rd SO22 10 C3
St Cuthberts Cl SO31 129 A2
St Cuthberts La SO31 129 A2
St Cyres Meml Cotts SO41 197 C3
St David's Cl SO40 76 B1
St David's Ct
3 Bournemouth BH1, 205 C3
Gosport PO13 180 B3
North Baddesley SO52 54 A2
St David's Rd
Clanfield PO8 88 B3
Portsmouth PO5 215 C2
Upton BH16 201 A4
St Davids Rd SO31 128 C2
St Denys 28 BH25 195 A1
St Denys Prim Sch SO17 79 B1
St Denys Rd SO17,SO18 79 B1
St Denys Wlk 13 PO9 135 B3
St Denys' Sta SO17 103 B4
St Edmondsbury Ct PO13 180 B3
St Edmund Cl PO14 129 A1
St Edmund's Rd SO16 102 A4
St Edmunds RC Sch PO1 215 C3
St Edward's RC/CE Sch BH15 202 C4
St Edward's Rd
Gosport PO12 181 A2
Portsmouth PO5 215 B1
St Edward's Sch SO51 25 A1
St Edward's Terr PO12 181 A3
St Edwards Rd SO31 127 A4
St Elizabeth's Ave SO18 104 A4
St Evox Cl SO16 77 C3
St Faith's CE Prim Sch SO22 10 C3
St Faith's Cl PO12 181 A3
St Faith's Rd
Portsmouth PO1 215 B4
Winchester SO22 10 C3
St Francis Ave SO18 104 A4
St Francis CE Prim Sch SO53 55 A3
St Francis Cl SO45 177 C4
St Francis Ct
Locks Heath PO14 129 B2
2 Portsmouth PO2 157 C2
St Francis Pl PO9 135 C2
St Francis Rd
Blackfield SO45 177 C4
Gosport PO12 181 B1
St Francis Specl Sch PO14 154 B4
St Gabriel's Rd SO18 104 A4
St George Cl SO31 104 C1
St George RC Sch (Boys) SO17 79 B3
St George's Almshos 11 BH15 202 A1
St George's Ave
Bournemouth BH8 205 B4
Havant PO9 136 A1
Poole BH12 203 A4
St George's Beneficial CE Prim Sch PO1 182 A3
St George's Bsns Ctr 28 PO1 182 A3
St George's Cl
Bournemouth BH8 205 B4
Christchurch BH23 208 B4
St George's Cotts SP6 47 B2
St George's Cres SP6 69 C1
St George's Ct
2 Bournemouth BH1, 205 C3
North Baddesley SO52 54 A2
7 Portsmouth PO5 215 A1
St George's Dr BH22 165 B2
St George's Ho 14 SO23 11 A4
St George's Rd
Cosham PO6 157 C4
Portsmouth PO1 182 A2
Portsmouth, Southsea PO4 183 A1
South Hayling PO11 184 B2
St George's Sq 7 SO32 83 B4
St George's St
Southampton SO14 103 A2
Winchester SO23 11 A4
St George's Way PO1 182 A3
St George's Wlk 11 PO7 134 C4
St Georges Cl BH23 193 A4
St Georges Cotts
Martin SP6 43 B2
Woodgreen SP6 70 C4
St Georges Ct 4 PO16 155 A4
St Georges Ho 22 SO17 103 A4
St Georges Ind Est PO4 183 A3
St Georges Mans 18 BH5 205 C2
St Georges Rd
Fordingbridge SP6 69 C1
Locks Heath SO31 128 C2
St Georges Sq PO1 182 A3
St Giles Cl SO23 11 A4
St Giles Hill SO23 11 A4
St Giles Way PO8 88 B1
St Helen's Cl PO4 182 C1
St Helen's Par PO4 182 C1
St Helen's Rd
Gosport PO12 180 C2
South Hayling PO11 184 B2
St Helena Gdns SO18 79 C2
St Helena Way PO16 156 B4
St Helens Mews 8 SO50 57 B1
St Helier Pl SO16 77 C2
St Helier Rd BH12 188 B1
St Hellen's Rd PO6 158 B4
St Hermans Mans PO11 185 B1
St Hermans Rd PO11 185 B1
St Hilda Ave PO8 88 B1
St Hubert Rd PO8 88 B1
St Ives End La BH24 140 A2
St Ives Fst Sch BH24 140 A3
St Ives Gdns BH2 204 C3
St Ives Park BH24 140 A3
St Ives Wood BH24 140 A3
St James CE Fst Sch SP6 93 A3
St James CE Prim Sch
Bournemouth BH7 206 A3
Emsworth PO10 136 C1
West End SO30 80 C1
St James Cl Clanfield PO8 88 B2
7 Poole BH15 202 A1
St James Ho 23 SO14 103 A2
St James Hospl PO4 183 B3
St James Pk (Cvn Pk) SO53 55 A4
St James Rd
Ferndown BH22 165 A3
Sway SO41 172 B1
West End SO30 80 B1
St James Way PO16 156 B4
St James' La SO22,SO23 10 C4
St James' Rd PO10 136 C1
St James' Terr SO23 10 C4
St James' Villas SO23 10 C4
St James's 20 BH5 205 C2
St James's Cl SO15 78 B1
St James's Park Rd SO16 78 B1
St James's Rd
Portsmouth PO5 215 B2
Southampton SO15 102 B4
St James's Sq BH5 206 A3
St James's St PO1 182 A3
St John the Baptist CE Prim Sch
Titchfield PO14 129 B1
Waltham Chase SO32 83 C1
St John's Ave PO7 134 C2
St John's Cl
Gosport PO12 181 A3
Wimborne Minst BH21 163 B2
St John's Coll PO5 215 C1
St John's Ct
4 Bournemouth BH1, 205 C3
North Baddesley SO52 54 A2
16 Portsmouth PO2 157 B1
St John's Ctr SO30 105 A3
St John's Gdns 3 BH9 189 C1
St John's Hill BH21 163 B3
St John's Hospital (Almshouses)(N) 27 SO23 11 A4
St John's Hospital (Almshouses)(S) 38 SO23 11 A4
St John's Rd
Bournemouth BH5 205 C2
Christchurch BH23 207 A3
Cosham PO6 158 A4
Eastleigh SO50 56 A2
Havant PO9 135 B2
Hedge End SO30 105 A3
Locks Heath SO31 129 A1
Poole BH15 202 B2
Southbourne PO10 137 B1
Winchester SO23 11 A4
St John's St Hythe SO45 126 A2
Winchester SO23 11 A4
St Johns CE Fst Sch BH21 163 B2
St Johns CE Prim Sch PO12 181 A4
St Johns Cl
Rownhams SO16 77 C4
South Hayling PO11 184 C1
St Johns Ct SO40 101 C1
St Johns Dr SO40 101 C1
St Johns Gdns SO51 52 C4
St Johns Glebe SO16 77 C3
St Johns Inf Sch SO14 102 C2
St Johns La SO32 107 C4
St Johns Mews SO31 129 B2
St Johns RC Prim Sch PO1 215 C3
St Johns Rd BH25 195 A4
St Johns Sq 13 PO12 181 A3
St Joseph Cl SO31 129 A2
St Joseph's Mews PO5 215 C1
St Joseph's RC Comb Sch BH12 203 C4
St Joseph's RC Prim Sch BH23 208 A4
St Jude's CE Prim Sch PO1 182 A2
St Jude's RC Prim Sch PO14 130 C1
St Judes Cl PO5 215 B1
St Julien's Hospl (Almhouses) SO14 103 A2
St Just Cl BH22 165 B2
St Katharine's CE Prim Sch BH6 207 A2
St Katherine's CE Prim Sch BH6 206 A2
St Kitts Ho 4 PO6 132 C1
St Lawrence Cl SO30 81 B1
St Lawrence Rd
Eastleigh SO50 56 A2
31 Southampton SO14 103 A2
St Ledger's Pl BH1 205 B3
St Ledger's Rd BH8 205 B3
St Leonard's Ave PO11 185 A2
St Leonard's Rd
Bournemouth BH8 205 A3
Winchester SO23 11 B3
St Leonards Cl PO15 129 C2
St Leonards Hospl BH24 139 B1
St Leonards Rd SO41 199 A4
St Leonards Way BH24 139 B2
St Lucia Ho 2 PO6 132 C1
St Luke's CE Prim Sch
Bournemouth BH9 204 C4
Sway SO41 172 A1
St Luke's CE Sec Sch PO1 215 B3
St Luke's Rd
Bournemouth BH3 204 C4
Gosport PO12 181 A3
St Lukes Cl SO30 81 B1
St Margaret's Almshouses BH21 163 A3
St Margaret's Ave BH23 207 A3
St Margaret's Cl SO18 104 A4
St Margaret's Cotts SO32 59 B1
St Margaret's Rd
Bishopstoke SO50 56 B2
Bournemouth BH10 189 B1
Poole BH15 202 B2
St Margarets BH2 204 C3
St Margarets Cl BH21 163 A3
St Margarets Hill BH21 163 A3
St Margarets Ho 6 SO16 102 C4
St Margarets La PO14 129 C1
St Margarets Rd PO11 185 A2
St Mark's CE Jun Sch SO15 102 B4
St Mark's CE Prim Sch BH10 189 B1
St Mark's Cl PO12 181 A1
St Mark's Pl PO12 181 A1
St Mark's Rd
Bournemouth BH11 189 A2
Gosport PO12 181 A1
Portsmouth PO2 157 B1
St Marks Cl SO53 30 C1
St Marks Ct 6 PO12 181 A3
St Marks Rd
Lymington SO41 197 A2
Southampton SO14 103 A3
St Martin Cl SO23 11 A4
St Martin's Cl
Bishopstoke SO50 56 B2
Southampton SO16 77 C2
St Martin's Ho 15 PO5 182 B1
St Martins Rd BH16 201 A4
St Martins Trad Pk SO23 11 A4
St Mary Gr SO41 196 A1
St Mary Magdalen Almshouses 50 SO23 11 A4
St Mary St
Southampton SO14 103 A2
Winchester SO22 10 B3
St Mary's SO51 52 C3
St Mary's Ave PO12 181 A1
St Mary's Church Cl SO18 79 B2
St Mary's Cl
Droxford SO32 61 A1
Kings Worthy SO21 2 B3
Redlynch SP5 47 C2
St Mary's Coll
Southampton SO18 103 C4
Winchester SO23 11 A3
St Mary's Ct BH6 206 C2
St Mary's Ho PO1 182 C3
St Mary's Hospl East Wing PO3 183 A3
St Mary's Hospl West Wing PO1 182 C3
St Mary's Maternity Hospl BH15 202 B2
St Mary's Mews BH22 165 B2
St Mary's Pl SO14 103 A2
St Mary's Prim Sch SO14 103 A2
St Mary's RC Prim Sch PO12 181 A3
St Mary's Rd
Bishopstoke SO50 56 B2
Bournemouth BH1 205 B3
Ferndown BH22 165 B3
Liss GU33 20 C2
Netley SO31 127 B3
Poole BH15 202 C2
St Mary's Rd *continued*
Portsmouth PO1 182 C3
South Hayling PO11 184 C2
Southampton SO14 103 A3
Stubbington PO14 154 B2
St Mary's Stad SO14 103 A3
St Mary's Terr SO21 32 A3
St Marys Cl BH23 193 B4
St Matthew's Rd PO6 157 C4
St Matthews Cl 22 SO14 103 A3
St Matthews Ct PO12 181 B3
St Matthews Rd SO22 1 B1
St Merrin's Cl BH10 189 B2
St Michael's 2 BH2 204 B2
St Michael's CE Mid Sch BH21 163 C4
St Michael's CE Prim Sch BH2 204 B2
St Michael's Ct 28 PO6 133 A1
St Michael's Gdns 26 SO22 10 C4
St Michael's Gr PO14 154 C4
St Michael's Ho 8 PO14 154 C4
St Michael's Mews 16 BH2 204 C2
St Michael's Pas SO23 11 A3
St Michael's Pl 18 BH2 204 C2
St Michael's Rd
Bournemouth BH2 204 C1
Havant PO9 135 B2
Portsmouth PO1 215 A2
Winchester SO22 10 C3
St Michael's Rdbt BH4 204 B2
St Michael's Sq 16 SO14 102 C2
St Michael's St 18 SO14 102 C2
St Michaels Cl
Blackfield SO45 150 C1
Hamworthy BH15 201 C1
Verwood BH31 114 C3
St Michaels Ct 1 BH6 206 B2
St Michaels Rd
Locks Heath SO31 129 A1
Totton SO40 100 C4
Verwood BH31 114 C2
St Michaels Way PO8 88 B1
St Monica Inf Sch SO19 104 A2
St Monica Jun Sch SO19 104 A2
St Monica Rd SO19 104 A2
St Nicholas Ave PO13 180 B4
St Nicholas Flats 18 PO2 157 B1
St Nicholas Rise SO23 2 A3
St Nicholas Row PO17 108 A2
St Nicholas St PO1 182 A2
St Nicholas' Rd PO9 135 B2
St Osmund's Rd BH14 203 B2
St Patrick's Ct SO52 54 A2
St Patrick's La GU33 21 B3
St Patrick's RC Prim Sch SO19 103 C2
St Paul's Hill SO22 10 C4
St Paul's La BH1 205 A2
St Paul's Pl BH1 205 A2
St Paul's Rd
Bournemouth BH1 205 A2
Locks Heath SO31 128 C3
Portsmouth PO5 215 A2
St Paul's Sq PO5 215 A2
St Pauls Pl 19 SO22 10 C4
St Pauls RC Prim Sch PO6 157 A4
St Peter St SO23 11 A4
St Peter's Ave PO11 160 B1
St Peter's Cres 36 BH1 204 C2
St Peter's Ct
17 Petersfield GU32 40 C2
7 Poole BH14 203 A2
St Peter's Gr PO5 215 C1
St Peter's RC Comp Sch BH6 206 C2
St Peter's RC Prim Sch SO22 10 A3
St Peter's RC Sch BH7 206 A4
St Peter's Rd
Bournemouth BH1 205 A2
Petersfield GU32 40 C2
Poole BH14 203 A2
St Peter's Rdbt BH1 205 A2
St Peter's Sq 6 PO10 160 C4
St Peter's St SO32 83 B4
St Peter's Wlk 38 BH1 204 C2
St Peters Cl SO32 106 B4
St Peters Ct
Bournemouth BH1 205 A2
4 Emsworth PO10 161 A4
St Peters RC Prim Sch PO7 134 C3
St Peters Rd PO11 160 B2
St Philip's Way SO18 104 A4
St Pirans Ave PO3 183 A4
St Quentin Ho 12 PO14 154 C4
St Richards Gdns PO7 134 B3
St Ronan's Ave PO4 182 C1
St Ronan's Rd PO4 182 C1
St Saviors Cl BH7 206 B4
St Sebastian Cres PO16 131 A2
St Simon Cl SO31 129 A2
St Simon's Rd PO5 182 B1
St Stephen's Ct 6 BH2 204 C2
St Stephen's Rd
Bournemouth BH2 204 C2
Portsmouth PO2 182 C4
Winchester SO22 1 B1
St Stephen's Way 27 BH2 204 C2
St Stephens La BH31 115 A4
St Swithun Cl SO32 83 A4
St Swithun St SO23 11 A4
St Swithun Wells (RC) Prim Sch SO53 55 C3
St Swithun's Cl SO51 28 B1
St Swithun's RC Prim Sch PO5 182 B1
St Swithun's Rd BH1 205 A2
St Swithun's Rd S BH1 205 A2
St Swithun's Sch SO21 11 B4
St Swithuns Ct 7 SO14 103 A3
St Swithuns Rd PO2 157 C1
St Theresas Cl PO9 135 B2
St Thomas Ave PO11 184 B2
St Thomas Cl PO16 131 B2
St Thomas Ct 7 SO50 57 B1
St Thomas Garnet's RC Sch BH5 206 A3
St Thomas Mews 22 SO23 10 C4
St Thomas More's RC Prim Sch PO9 135 B2
St Thomas Pk SO41 197 B2
St Thomas St SO22 10 C4
St Thomas's Cl BH10 189 C1
St Thomas's Ct 5 PO1 182 A2
St Thomas's Rd PO12 181 A4
St Thomas's St
Lymington SO41 197 C2
Portsmouth PO1 182 A2
St Tristan Cl SO31 129 A1
St Ursula Gr PO5 215 C1
St Valerie Rd
Bournemouth BH2 204 C3
Gosport PO12 181 A2
St Vigor Way
Colden Common SO21 31 C1
Colden Common SO21 57 A4
St Vincent Coll PO12 181 A3
St Vincent Cres PO8 112 A3
St Vincent L Ctr PO12 181 B3
St Vincent Rd
Gosport PO12 181 A3
Portsmouth PO5 182 B1
St Vincent St PO5 215 A2
St Walburga's RC Prim Sch BH9 190 A1
St Winifred's Rd
Bournemouth BH2 204 C3
Southampton SO16 78 B1
St Winifred's Sch SO17 79 A1
Salcombe Ave PO3 158 A1
Salcombe Cl SO53 55 A2
Salcombe Cres SO40 100 C3
Salcombe Rd
Southampton SO15 102 B4
Totton SO40 100 C3
Salcot Rd SO23 2 A1
Salem St SO15 78 B1
Salerno Dr PO12 180 C2
Salerno Ho
Fareham PO14 154 C4
Romsey SO51 53 A4
Salerno Pl BH15 201 B1
Salerno Rd
Portsmouth PO2 157 B2
Southampton SO16 78 B2
Salet Way PO7 112 A1
Salisbury Cl SO50 56 A2
Salisbury Ct 1 SO50 56 A2
Salisbury Rd
Awbridge SO51 52 A3
Bournemouth BH1 205 C2
Breamore SP6 70 A3
Burton BH23 192 B2
Cosham PO6 158 A4
Fordingbridge SP6 70 A1
Fordingbridge, Ibsley BH24 94 A1
Ower SO51 76 B2
Poole BH14 203 B3
Portsmouth PO4 182 C1
Ringwood BH24 116 C3
Sopley, Winkton BH23 192 A3
Southampton SO17 79 A2
Totton SO40 76 B2
West Wellow SO51 50 B2
West Wellow SO51 51 A1
Salisbury Road Arc SO40 100 C4
Salisbury St
Fordingbridge SP6 69 C1
6 Southampton SO15 102 C3
Salisbury Terr PO13 179 C1
Salmon Dr SO50 56 C1
Salt La SO32,SO24 34 C2
Salt Meat La PO12 181 B3
Salter Rd BH13 214 B2
Salterns Ave PO4 183 A3
Salterns Cl PO11 185 B2
Salterns Ct BH14 214 A4
Salterns Est PO16 155 A4
Salterns La
Bursledon SO31 128 A4
Fareham PO16 155 A4
South Hayling PO11 185 B2
Salterns Point BH14 214 A4
Salterns Quay BH14 214 A4
Salterns Rd Poole BH14 203 A2
Stubbington PO13,PO14 179 A2
Salterns Specl Sch SO40 101 A4
Salterns Way BH14 214 A4
Salters Acres SO22 1 B2
Salters La SO22 1 A1
Saltgrass La SO41 212 A2
Saltings Rd BH16 201 A3
Saltings The
Cosham PO6 158 C4

Saltings The continued
Havant PO9 ....159 C3
Saltmarsh La PO11 ....184 C3
Saltmarsh Rd SO14 ....103 A2
Saltmead SO17 ....79 B1
Salvia Cl PO17 ....135 A3
Salwey Rd SO30 ....105 B3
Samber Cl SO41 ....197 B2
Sammy Miller Motorcycle
  Mus★ BH25 ....194 C3
Sampan Cl SO31 ....128 C1
Samphire Cl SO41 ....197 C3
Samples Way BH17 ....202 C4
Sampson Rd
  Gosport PO14 ....154 C3
  Portsmouth PO1 ....181 C3
Samson Cl PO13 ....180 B4
Samson Rd BH15 ....201 B1
Samuel Rd PO1 ....182 C3
San Diego Rd PO12 ....181 A3
San Remo Twrs ⓦ BH5 ...205 C2
Sancreed Rd BH12 ....203 C4
Sancroft BH21 ....164 A1
Sand Cl SO51 ....50 C2
Sandbanks Bsns Ctr
  BH13 ....214 A2
Sandbanks Rd BH14 ......203 A1
Sandbourne Rd
  Bournemouth BH4 ....204 B1
  Poole BH15 ....202 B2
Sandcroft Cl PO12 ....180 C2
Sandecotes Rd BH14 .....203 B2
Sandell Ct SO16 ....79 A3
Sanderling Rd PO4 ....183 B3
Sanderlings BH24 ....141 B3
Sanderlings The PO11 ....185 A1
Sandford Rd PO12 ....180 B2
Sandford Gr BH9 ....190 B2
Sandford Way PO14 ......186 C1
Sandhill La PO13 ....180 A3
Sandhills Cl BH17 ....187 B1
Sandhurst Ct PO5 ....215 C1
Sandhurst Dr PO12 ....139 A4
Sandhurst Rd SO15 ......102 C3
Sandilands Way 🔟
  SO45 ....126 A1
Sandisplatt Rd SO41 .....154 B4
Sandle Copse SP6 ....69 A1
Sandleford Rd PO9 ....135 B4
Sandleheath Ind Est SP6 .69 A1
Sandleheath Rd SP6 ....92 C4
Sandown Cl
  Clanfield PO8 ....88 B3
  Totton SO40 ....100 B4
Sandmartin Cl BH25 .....209 C4
Sandown Cl PO12 ....180 B2
Sandown Rd
  Christchurch BH23 ....207 C3
  Cosham PO6 ....157 C4
  Southampton SO15 ....78 A1
Sandpiper Cl
  Broadstone BH17 ....186 C1
  Horndean PO8 ....112 A4
  Marchwood SO40 ....101 C1
Sandpiper Rd SO16 ....78 A3
Sandpipers PO6 ....158 C4
Sandpit La
  Beaulieu SO41 ....199 B3
  Poole BH15 ....202 B2
Sandport Gr PO16 ....156 A4
Sandringham Cl
  Bournemouth BH9 ....190 A2
  Chandler's Ford SO53 ....54 C2
Sandringham Ct
  Bournemouth BH8 ....205 B3
  Southampton, Millbrook
  SO15 ....102 A3
  🔟 Southampton, Westwood Pk
  SO17 ....79 A1
Sandringham Gdns BH9 ..190 A2
Sandringham La PO1 .....215 D3
Sandringham Rd
  Fareham PO14 ....154 B4
  Petersfield GU32 ....40 C2
  Poole BH14 ....203 B2
  Portsmouth PO1 ....215 D3
  Southampton SO18 ....79 C1
Sandsbury La GU32 ....40 B3
Sandy Beach Est PO11 ...185 C1
Sandy Brow PO7 ....134 B2
Sandy Cl Petersfield GU31 .41 B2
  Wimborne Minst BH21 ...164 A4
Sandy Down SO41 ....173 B2
Sandy La
  Abbotswood SO51 ....28 A2
  Bournemouth BH6 ....206 A3
  Christchurch BH23 ....191 C1
  Fair Oak SO50 ....57 B1
  Lymington SO41 ....197 C2
  North Baddesley SO52 ....54 A3
  Pamphill BH21 ....162 A3
  Rake GU33 ....21 C2
  Redlynch SP5 ....47 C4
  St Leonards BH24 ....140 A3
  Three Legged Cross BH21 .114 C1
  Titchfield PO14 ....196 A3
  Upton BH16 ....201 A3
  Verwood BH31 ....115 A3
  Waltham Chase SO32 ....83 B4
  Wimborne Minst BH21 ...164 A4
Sandy Mead Rd BH8 ......190 C1
Sandy Plot BH23 ....207 B4
Sandy Point Rd PO11 ....185 C1
Sandy Way BH10 ....189 C4
Sandycroft SO31 ....152 B4
Sandyfield Cres PO8 .....111 C2
Sandyhurst Cl BH17 .....187 B1
Sanross Cl PO14 ....179 A3

Santoy BH13 ....214 B3
Sapphire Ridge PO7 .....135 A4
Saracen Cl SO41 ....197 B1
Saracens Rd SO53 ....55 C4
Sarah Cl BH7 ....206 A4
Sarah Robinson Ho 🔟
  PO1 ....182 A3
Sarah Sands Cl BH23 ....207 B4
Sarisbury CE Jun Sch
  SO31 ....128 C3
Sarisbury Gate SO31 ....129 A3
Sarisbury Inf Sch SO31 .128 C2
Sark Rd BH12 ....203 B4
Sarnia Ct SO16 ....77 C2
Sarum Ave BH22 ....138 C2
Sarum Cl SO22 ....10 B4
Sarum Ct SO22 ....10 B4
Sarum St 🔟 BH15 ....202 A1
Sarum View SO22 ....10 A4
Sarum Wlk SO41 ....197 B3
Satchell La SO31 ....128 A2
Saturn Cl SO16 ....77 C2
Saulfland Dr BH23 ....208 B4
Saulfland Ho BH23 ....208 B4
Saulfland Pl BH23 ....208 B4
Saunders Ho PO6 ....132 C1
Saunders La SO51 ....26 C3
Saunders Mews PO4 .....183 A1
Savernake Cl
  Gosport PO13 ....155 B1
  🔊 Romsey SO51 ....28 A1
Saville Cl
  Bishopstoke SO50 ....56 B3
  Gosport PO12 ....180 C2
Saville Ct 🔟 BH21 ......163 B2
Saville Gdns PO16 ......131 A2
Savoy Bldgs 🔊 PO16 ....131 A1
Savoy Ho SO40 ....100 A4
Sawmills The SO32 ....82 A3
Sawyer Cl SO22 ....1 A1
Saxholm Cl SO16 ....78 C3
Saxholm Dale SO16 ......78 C3
Saxholm Way SO16 ......78 C3
Saxley Ct PO9 ....135 B3
Saxon Cl Horndean PO8 ..88 B2
  Locks Heath SO31 ......128 C1
  Portchester PO16 ....132 A1
Saxon Gdns SO30 ....105 A3
Saxon Ho 🔟 SO14 ....103 B3
Saxon Hts BH6 ....206 C3
Saxon King Gdns BH6 ...207 A2
Saxon Mdw SP5 ....46 C4
Saxon Rd SO41 ....197 B3
Saxon Rd Blackfield SO45 .150 C1
  Southampton SO15 ......102 B3
  Winchester SO23 ....2 A1
Saxon Shore Inf Sch
  PO6 ....156 C4
Saxon Sq Sh Ctr 🔟
  BH23 ....207 A3
Saxon Way Alderholt SP6 .93 A3
  Romsey SO51 ....53 A4
Saxonbury Rd BH6 ......206 C3
Saxonford Rd BH23 ......208 B4
Saxonhurst Cl BH10 ....189 C3
Saxonhurst Gdns BH10 .189 C2
Saxonhurst Rd BH10 ....189 C2
Saxton Cl 🔊 SO23 ....11 A4
Sayers Rd SO50 ....56 C2
Scafell Ave SO14 ....154 B4
Scallows La SO51 ....50 C3
Scantabout Ave SO53 ....55 C4
Scantabout Prim Sch
  SO53 ....55 C4
Scarf Rd BH17 ....202 C4
Scarff Ct PO11 ....185 A1
Scholars' Wlk PO6 ....158 B4
School Cl
  Chandler's Ford SO53 ....55 A3
  Verwood BH31 ....115 A4
School Hill SO32 ....85 B3
School La Boldre SO41 ...197 C4
  Bournemouth BH11 .....189 A3
  Bransgore BH23 ....169 C2
  Chandler's Ford SO53 ....55 A3
  Compton (Sussex) PO18 ...90 C1
  Denmead PO7 ....133 B3
  Emsworth PO10 ....160 C4
  Hamble-le-Rice SO31 ....128 A1
  Kings Worthy SO23 ......2 A3
  🔊 Lisss GU33 ....20 C2
  Lymington SO41 ....197 C2
  Michelmersh SO51 ....6 B1
  Milford on Sea SO41 ....211 C3
  Petersfield GU32 ....41 A3
  Poole BH15 ....202 B3
  Ringwood BH24 ....141 A4
  St Leonards BH24 ....140 A2
  Three Legged Cross BH21 .138 C4
  Westbourne PO10 ....137 A3
  Wimborne Minst BH21 ...163 A3
  Wimborne Minst BH21 ...163 A3
School Rd
  Bransgore BH23 ....169 C2
  Bursledon SO31 ....128 A4
  Fawley SO45 ....151 A2
  Gosport PO12 ....155 C1
  Havant PO9 ....135 C1
  Hythe SO45 ....126 A2
  Nomansland SP5 ....73 B4
  Redlynch SP5 ....48 A3

School Rd continued
  Romsey SO51 ....28 B1
  Totton SO40 ....101 A3
  Twyford SO21 ....31 C3
  West Wellow SO51 ....50 C1
  Whitchurch PO17 ....108 A2
Schooner Way
  Locks Heath SO31 ......128 C1
  Portsmouth PO4 ....183 B3
Schooners Cl PO13 ......179 C2
Scimitars The PO14 .....154 A2
Scivier's La SO32 ....58 B1
Scotland Cl SO30 ....57 C1
Scotney Ct 🔊 PO9 ......136 A3
Scott Cl
  Colden Common SO21 ....57 A4
  Poole BH12 ....188 C1
Scott Ho 🔊 PO2 ....157 B1
Scott Rd Eastleigh SO50 .55 C1
  Poole BH12 ....188 C1
  Portsmouth PO1 ....181 C3
  Portsmouth, Hilsea PO3 .157 C3
  Southampton SO19 ......103 C1
Scott's Gn BH23 ....207 C4
Scott-Paine Dr SO45 ....126 A2
Scotter Rd
  Bishopstoke SO50 ....56 B2
  Bournemouth BH7 ......206 A3
Scotter Sq SO50 ....56 B2
Scotts Hill La BH23 .....207 B4
Scratchface La
  Havant PO9 ....134 C2
  Waterlooville PO7 ....134 C2
Scullards La 🔟 SO14 ....102 C2
Sea Breeze Gdns PO4 ...183 B2
Sea Crest Rd PO13 ......179 C1
Sea Front PO11 ....184 C2
Sea Front Est PO11 .....185 A1
Sea Grove Ave PO11 ....185 A1
Sea Kings PO14 ....154 A2
Sea La SO41 ....179 B2
Sea Mill Gdns 🔊 PO1 ...182 A3
Sea Pines 🔊 SO41 ....211 B2
Sea Point 🔊 BH13 ......214 C4
Sea Rd
  Barton on Sea BH25 ....209 C4
  Bournemouth, Boscombe
    BH5, BH6 ....205 C2
  Bournemouth, Southbourne
    BH6 ....206 C2
  Milford on Sea SO41 ....211 C2
  Southampton SO19 ......103 B2
Sea View Cotts PO10 ....185 B3
Sea View Est SO31 ......127 A3
Sea View Rd
  Cosham PO6 ....134 B1
  Poole BH12 ....203 A3
  South Hayling PO11 ....185 B2
  Upton BH16 ....201 A4
Sea Vixen Ind Est BH23 .208 A4
Seabank Cl BH16 ....201 A4
Seabird Way PO16 ......155 A4
Seabourne Rd 🔟 BH5 ...206 A3
Seabourne Rd BH5 ......206 A3
Seacombe Gn SO16 ......77 B1
Seacombe Rd BH23 .....214 A2
Seacroft Ave BH25 .....209 C4
Seafarers Wlk PO11 ....185 C1
Seafield Cl BH25 ....209 C4
Seafield Dr BH6 ....206 C3
Seafield Park Rd PO14 .179 A3
Seafield Rd
  Barton on Sea BH25 ....209 C4
  Bournemouth BH6 ......206 B2
  Christchurch BH23 .....208 B4
  Portchester PO16 ......156 A4
  Portsmouth PO3 ....182 C4
  Southampton SO16 ......77 C2
Seafield Terr PO12 ......181 B2
Seafields PO10 ....160 C4
Seaford Cl SO31 ....104 C1
Seagarth Cl SO16 ....78 B2
Seagarth La SO16 ....78 B2
Seager's Ct PO1 ....181 C2
Seagrove Rd PO2 ....157 B1
Seagull Cl PO4 ....183 B3
Seagull Cr PO10 ....136 C1
Seagull La PO10 ....136 C1
Seagull Rd BH8 ....190 B1
Seagulls The PO13 ......180 A2
Seahorse Wlk PO12 .....181 B3
Sealark Rd PO12 ....181 B3
Seamans La SO43 ....98 B2
Seamead La BH4 ....179 B2
Seamoor La BH4 ....204 A2
Seamoor Rd BH4 ....204 A2
Searles Hill SO21 ....32 A3
Seathrift Cl PO13 ......179 C1
Seathwaite Ho 🔊 PO6 ..133 A1
Seaton Ave PO3 ....183 A4
Seaton Cl
  Christchurch BH23 .....209 A4
  Lymington SO41 ....197 C3
  Stubbington PO14 ......179 B3
  West End SO18 ....80 B1
Seaton Rd BH23 ....209 A4
Seatown Cl SH17 ....188 A1
Seaview Ave PO16 ......132 C1
Seaview Ct 🔊 Gosport PO12 .180 B2
  🔟 Lee-on-the-Solent
    PO13 ....179 C1
Seaview Rd
  Barton on Sea BH25 ....209 C4
  Christchurch BH23 .....194 B1
Seaward Ave BH25 .....209 C4
Seaward Gdns SO19 ....103 C2
Seaward Rd Hythe SO45 .126 A2

Seaward Rd continued
  Southampton SO19 ......103 C2
Seaward Twr PO12 ......181 C2
Seaway BH25 ....210 A4
Seaway Ave BH23 ......208 B4
Seaway Cres PO14 .....183 B2
Seaway Rd PO14 ....156 B3
Seawinds SO41 ....211 A3
Sebastian Gr PO7 ......135 A4
Second Ave Cosham PO6 .157 C4
  Cosham, Farlington PO6 .158 C4
  Emsworth PO9 ....136 A1
  Southampton SO15 .....101 B4
  Southbourne PO10 .....161 B4
Second Marine Ave
  BH25 ....210 A3
Second St SO45 ....150 C4
Sedberg Ho SO16 ....77 B1
Sedbergh Rd SO16 ......77 B1
Seddul-Bahr SO30 ......80 C3
Sedgefield Cl
  Porchester PO6 ....156 C4
  Totton SO40 ....100 B2
Sedgeley Gr PO12 .....181 A4
Sedgemead SO31 ....127 A3
Sedgemead Ct SO31 ....127 A3
Sedgewick Cl PO13 ....180 B4
Sedgewick Ct SO50 ....56 B2
Sedgewick Rd
  Bishopstoke SO50 ....56 B2
  Southampton SO19 ....104 B3
Sedgley Cl PO5 ....215 C2
Sedgley Rd BH9 ....190 A3
Seed Warehouse The 🔟
  BH15 ....202 B1
Segars La SO21 ....31 C3
Segensworth E Ind Est
  PO15 ....129 B3
Segensworth N Ind Est
  PO15 ....129 C3
Segensworth Rd PO15 ..129 C2
Segensworth W Ind Est
  PO15 ....129 B3
Selangor Ave SO16 .....136 B1
Selborne Ave
  Havant PO9 ....135 B3
  Southampton SO18 ....104 B4
Selborne Ct 🔟 SO51 ....28 A1
Selborne Pl SO22 ....10 B3
Selborne Rd SO40 .....100 B4
Selborne Wlk SO18 ....104 B4
Selbourne Dr SO50 .....56 B2
Selbourne Gdns PO12 ..180 C2
Selbourne Rd PO9 .....135 C1
Selbourne Terr PO1 ....215 D3
Selby Cl BH18 ....187 A2
Seldon Cl SO22 ....10 A2
Seldon Gr PO15 ....202 B2
Seldown Bridge BH15 ..202 B2
Seldown La BH15 ....202 B2
Seldown Rd BH15 ......202 B2
Sellrield Ave PO6 ......207 A2
Selfridge Ave BH6 .....207 A2
Selfridge Cl BH6 ....207 A2
Selhurst Ho PO1 ....215 C4
Selhurst Way SO50 .....57 B1
Seliot Cl BH15 ....202 B3
Selkirk Cl PO17 ....163 C1
Sellwood Rd SO31 ......127 B3
Sellwood Way BH25 ....209 B4
Selsdon Ave SO51 ......53 A4
Selsey Ave Gosport PO12 .181 A4
  Portsmouth PO4 ....183 A1
Selsey Cl
  South Hayling PO11 ....185 C1
  Southampton SO16 .....77 C1
Selsmore Ave PO11 ....185 B1
Selsmore Rd PO11 .....185 B1
Selwood Pk BH10 .....189 A4
Selworth La SO32 ......85 A2
Selworth Cl BH14 .....203 A1
Selwyn Ct 🔟 PO6 ......157 C4
Selwyn Gdns SO50 .....56 A3
Sengana Cl SO30 ......105 B3
Senlac Rd SO15 ....102 A3
Sennen Pl PO6 ....157 A4
Sentinel Cl BH15 ......202 C2
Sentinel Cl PO7 ....111 A4
Seps 4 Rd SO45 ....151 B2
September Cl SO30 .....80 B1
Serle Cl SO40 ....100 B3
Serle Gdns SO40 ......100 B3
Sermon Rd SO22 ....1 A1
Serpentine Rd
  Fareham PO16 ....131 A1
  Poole BH15 ....202 B2
  🔊 Portsmouth PO5 ....182 B1
  Waterlooville PO7 .....134 B1
Service Rd PO6 ....157 B4
Set Thorns Rd SO41 ...172 B1
Setley Gdns BH8 ......190 C2
Setters Cl SO21 ....56 C4
Settle Cl SO16 ....102 A4
Settlers Cl PO1 ....215 C3
Sevenoaks Dr BH7 .....206 A4
Sevenoaks Rd PO6 .....158 C4
Severn Cl Cosham PO6 .133 A1
  Portchester PO16 ......156 A4
Severn Rd
  Ferndown BH22 ....166 A3
  Southampton SO16 ....101 C4
Severn Way SO30 ......80 B1
Severn Ave BH6 ....206 B2
Seward Rd SO50 ....53 B4
Seymour Cl
  Chandler's Ford SO53 ...55 C3
  Portsmouth PO2 ....182 B4

Seymour Cl continued
  Totton SO40 ....76 B1
Seymour Ho SO16 ....78 B2
Seymour La SO52 ......53 C2
Seymour Rd
  Lee-on-the-Solent PO13 .180 A2
  Ringwood BH24 ....117 A1
  Southampton SO16 ......78 B2
Shackleton Ho 🔊 PO2 ..157 C1
Shackleton Rd PO13 ...180 B4
Shackleton Sq BH23 ...169 A1
Shadwell Ct 🔟 PO2 ....157 B1
Shadwell Rd PO2 ......157 B1
Shaftesbury Ave
  Chandler's Ford SO53 ...55 B2
  Southampton SO17 ......79 A1
  Waterlooville PO7 .....134 C2
Shaftesbury Ct BH22 ...138 C1
Shaftesbury Rd
  Gosport PO12 ....181 B2
  Poole BH15 ....202 B2
  West Moors BH22 .....138 C1
Shaftesbury St SP6 .....69 C1
Shaftsbury Rd
  Bournemouth BH8 .....205 B3
  Portsmouth PO5 ......182 B1
Shaggs Mdw SO43 .....122 A3
Shakespeare Ave SO17 .103 A4
Shakespeare Bsns Ctr
  SO50 ....56 A2
Shakespeare Dr SO40 ..76 B1
Shakespeare Gdns PO8 .111 C2
Shakespeare Jun Sch
  SO50 ....56 A3
Shakespeare Mews
  PO14 ....154 A4
Shakespeare Rd
  Bournemouth BH6 .....206 B4
  Eastleigh SO50 ....56 A2
  Portsmouth PO1 ....182 C4
  Wimborne Minst BH21 .163 B3
Shakespeare Road Inf Sch
  SO50 ....56 A3
Shalbourne Rd PO12 ...181 A4
Shalcombe SO31 ....127 A4
Shalden Cl SO16 ....78 B2
Shaldon Rd 🔊 PO9 ....136 A3
Shales Rd SO18 ....104 A1
Shallow La SO41 ......197 C4
Shallows The SP6 ......70 B4
Shamblehurst La N SO32 .81 B2
Shamblehurst La S SO30 .81 B1
Shamblehurst Prim Sch
  SO30 ....105 B4
Shamrock Cl PO12 .....181 B2
Shamrock Ct 🔟 BH21 .163 B2
Shamrock Quay SO14 ..103 B3
Shamrock Rd SO19 ....103 B3
Shamrock Villas 🔊 SO17 .79 B1
Shamrock Way SO45 ..126 A3
Shanklin Cres SO15 ....78 B1
Shanklin Rd
  Portsmouth PO4 ....182 C4
  Southampton SO15 .....78 B1
Shannon Cl PO15 ....130 B1
Shannon Ho 🔊 SO14 ..103 B3
Shannon Rd
  Gosport PO14 ....155 A3
  Stubbington PO14 ......154 A3
Shannon Way SO53 .....55 A3
Shapland Ave BH11 ....188 C3
Shappen Hill La BH24 ..142 C1
Shapton Cl SO45 ....150 C4
Shapwick Rd BH15 .....202 A1
Shard Cl BH31 ....114 B3
Sharlands Cl BH18 ....187 A2
Sharlands Rd PO14 ....155 A3
Sharon Ct PO12 ....181 B3
Sharon Rd SO30 ....80 B1
Sharp Rd BH12 ....204 A4
Sharp's Copse Inf Sch
  PO9 ....136 A3
Sharp's Copse Jun Sch
  PO9 ....136 A3
Sharp's Rd PO9 ....136 A3
Sharpness Cl PO14 ....154 B4
Sharps Cl PO3 ....158 A2
Sharvells Rd SO41 .....211 B3
Shavard La SO32 ......195 A3
Shaw Cl Totton SO40 ..100 B4
  West End SO18 ....80 A1
Shaw Rd BH24 ....117 B1
Shawcross Ind Pk PO3 .158 A3
Shawfield Rd PO9 .....160 A4
Shawford Cl
  🔊 Southampton SO16 ..78 C2
Shawford Gdns BH8 ...190 B1
Shawford Gr PO9 ......135 B3
Shawford Rd
  Bournemouth BH6 .....190 B2
  Twyford SO21 ....31 C3
Shawford Sta SO21 ....31 C2
Shear Hill GU31 ....41 A3
Sheardley La SO32 ......62 A1
Shearer Rd PO1 ....182 C4
Shears Brook Cl BH23 ..169 A1
Shears Rd SO50 ....56 C2
Shearwater Ave PO16 ..155 C4
Shearwater Cl PO13 ...185 B1
Shearwater Dr PO6 ....158 C4

Sheep Pond La S032 . . . . .61 A2
Sheep St GU32 . . . . .40 C2
Sheepwash La P07 . . . . .133 C4
Sheet Prim Sch GU32 . . . . . . .41 A3
Sheffield Cl S050 . . . . .56 B3
Sheffield Ct P013 . . . . .180 B3
Sheffield Rd P01 . . . . .215 D3
Sheiling Sch The BH24 . . . . .140 B3
Shelbourne Cl BH8 . . . . .205 A3
Shelbourne Rd BH8 . . . . . . .205 A3
Sheldrake Gdns
  Hordle S041 . . . . .196 A2
  Southampton S016 . . . . .78 A3
Sheldrake Rd BH23 . . . . . . .208 A3
Shelford Rd P04 . . . . .183 A3
Shell Bay Sailing Ctr★
  BH19 . . . . .214 A1
Shell Ct S040 . . . . .101 C1
Shellcroft S051 . . . . .152 B4
Shelley Ave P06 . . . . .132 C1
Shelley Cl
  Bournemouth BH1, ...205 C3
  Christchurch BH23 . . . . . . .208 B4
  St Leonards BH24 . . . . .139 C3
  Winchester S022 . . . . .10 B4
Shelley Ct
  Ferndown BH22 . . . . .165 B3
  Southampton S015 . . . . . . .102 C3
Shelley Gdns
  Bournemouth BH1, ...205 C3
  Waterlooville P08 . . . . .111 C2
Shelley Hamlets BH23 . . . .208 B4
Shelley Ho BH25 . . . . .195 A1
Shelley La S051 . . . . .75 C4
Shelley Park (Bournemouth
  & Poole Coll) BH5 . . . . . . .205 C2
Shelley Rd
  Bournemouth BH7 . . . . . . .205 C3
  Eastleigh S050 . . . . .57 C1
  Poole BH12 . . . . .203 B3
  Southampton S019 . . . . . . .104 C3
  Totton S040 . . . . .76 B1
Shelley Rd E BH7 . . . . .205 C3
Shelley Way S041 . . . . .211 B3
Shelton Rd BH6 . . . . .206 B3
Shenley Cl P015 . . . . .130 B1
Shenstone Ct BH25 . . . . . . .195 A1
Shepards Cl P014 . . . . .154 B4
Shepheard's Way P012 . . . .181 B1
Shepherd Cl BH23 . . . . .193 C1
Shepherds Cl
  Cadnam S040 . . . . .99 A3
  Winchester S022 . . . . .10 A2
Shepherds Down Specl Sch
  S021 . . . . .31 B3
Shepherds Hey Rd S040 . . . .76 A1
Shepherds Hill BH24 . . . . .116 B3
Shepherds La
  Compton (Hants) S021 . . . . . .31 B3
  Ibsley BH24 . . . . .116 B3
Shepherds Purse Cl
  S031 . . . . .128 C1
Shepherds Rd
  Cadnam S040 . . . . .99 B3
  Winchester S023 . . . . .11 B4
Shepherds Way
  Bournemouth BH7 . . . . . . .206 A4
  Nursling S016 . . . . .78 A3
Sheppard Cl P08 . . . . .112 A3
Sheppards Field ■
  BH21 . . . . .163 A2
Sherborn Cres BH17 . . . . . .188 A1
Sherborne Cl S050 . . . . .56 A3
Sherborne Dr BH22 . . . . . .165 B2
Sherborne House Sch
  S053 . . . . .155 B2
Sherborne Rd S017 . . . . .79 A2
Sherborne Way S030 . . . . . .105 B3
Sherbrooke Cl S023 . . . . .2 B4
Sherecroft Gdns S030 . . . . .106 A4
Sherfield Ave P09 . . . . .136 A3
Sherfield Cl BH8 . . . . .190 B1
Sherfield English La
  S051 . . . . .50 B3
Sherfield English Rd S51 . . .50 A2
Sherfield Ho ◼ S015 . . . . . .102 C4
Sheridan Cl
  Southampton S014 . . . . . . .104 B3
  Winchester S022 . . . . .10 B3
Sheridan Gdns
  Swanwick P015 . . . . .129 B4
  Totton S040 . . . . .100 B4
Sheringham Rd
  Cosham P06 . . . . .133 B1
  Poole BH12 . . . . .203 C3
Sherley Gn S031 . . . . .105 A1
Sherrin Cl BH15 . . . . .202 B3
Sherringham Cl S045 . . . . . .151 A2
Sherwin Wlk P012 . . . . .181 A2
Sherwood Ave
  Ferndown BH22 . . . . .165 B2
  Hedge End S030 . . . . .105 B2
  Poole BH14 . . . . .203 A2
Sherwood Cl Liss GU33 . . . . .21 A4
  ◼ Southampton S016 . . . . . .78 C2
Sherwood Dr BH31 . . . . . .115 A3
Sherwood Gdns S031 . . . . . .128 C2
Sherwood Rd
  Chandler's Ford S053 . . . . . .30 C1
  Gosport P012 . . . . .181 A2
Sherwood Way S045 . . . . . .127 C4
Shetland Cl Cosham P06 . . .133 C1
  Totton S040 . . . . .100 A4
Shetland Rise P015 . . . . . . .129 A4

Shetland View BH31 . . . . . .115 A3
Shillinglee P07 . . . . .134 C2
Shillingstone Dr BH9 . . . . .190 A2
Shillingstone Gdns
  BH12 . . . . .203 C4
Shilito Rd BH12 . . . . .203 C3
Shingle Bank Dr S041 . . . . .211 B2
Shinwell Ct 17 S015 . . . . . . .78 A1
Ship Leopard St 12 P01 . . .182 A3
Shipbuilding Rd P01 . . . . .181 C4
Shipcote La S032 . . . . .32 A4
Shipley Rd S021 . . . . .32 A4
Shipstal Cl BH16 . . . . .201 B2
Shipton Gn P09 . . . . .135 B3
Shipwrights Wlk S041 . . . .212 A2
Shire Cl Swanwick P015 . . .129 A4
  Waterlooville P07 . . . . .133 B2
Shires Cl BH24 . . . . .141 A2
Shires Copse BH6 . . . . .206 C2
Shires Mead BH31 . . . . .115 A3
Shires Wlk S040 . . . . .100 A4
Shirley Ave
  Portsmouth P04 . . . . .183 B2
  Southampton S015 . . . . . . .102 B4
Shirley Cl
  Bransgore BH23 . . . . .169 A1
  West Moors BH22 . . . . .138 C1
Shirley High St S015,
  S016 . . . . .102 A4
Shirley Inf Sch S015 . . . . . .102 B4
Shirley Park Rd S016 . . . . .102 A4
Shirley Rd
  Bournemouth BH9 . . . . . . .190 A1
  Poole BH12 . . . . .203 A3
  Portsmouth P05 . . . . .182 B3
  Southampton S015 . . . . . . .102 B4
  Upton BH16 . . . . .201 B4
Shirley Twrs S015 . . . . .102 B4
Shirley Warren Prim Sch
  S016 . . . . .78 A1
Shirrel Ct P012 . . . . .180 B2
Shoblands Way ◼
  S045 . . . . .126 A1
Shoe La Meonstoke S032 . . . .61 B3
  Upham S032 . . . . .59 C2
Sholing Ct P09 . . . . .135 B3
Sholing Girls Sch S019 . . . .104 A2
Sholing Inf Sch S019 . . . . . .104 A3
Sholing Jun Sch S019 . . . . .104 A3
Sholing Rd S019 . . . . .103 C2
Sholing Sta S019 . . . . .103 C1
Shoot Hill PO7&PO17 . . . . .109 B2
Shoot La P013 . . . . .180 A4
Shooters Hill Cl S019 . . . . .104 A2
Shop La S019,S031 . . . . .104 C1
Shore Ave
  Portsmouth P04 . . . . .183 A3
  Upton BH16 . . . . .201 B3
Shore Cl
  Milford on Sea S041 . . . . . .211 B2
  Fawley S045 . . . . .126 B3
Shore Cres S032 . . . . .83 B4
Shore Gdns BH16 . . . . .201 A3
Shore La
  Bishop's Waltham S032 . . . . .83 B4
  Upton BH16 . . . . .201 B3
Shore Rd Hythe S045 . . . . . .126 A2
  Locks Heath S031 . . . . .128 B1
  Poole BH13 . . . . .214 B3
Shoreacres BH13 . . . . .214 B2
Shorefield Cres S041 . . . . . .211 B3
Shorefield Cvn Pk S041 . . .211 A3
Shorefield Rd
  Marchwood S040 . . . . .101 C1
  Milford on Sea S041 . . . . . .211 A3
Shorefield Way S041 . . . . . .211 B3
Shorehaven P06 . . . . .156 C4
Shorewell S031 . . . . .127 B4
Shorewood Cl S031 . . . . . . .128 C1
Short Cl BH12 . . . . .204 A4
Short Hill Nomansland SP5 .73 A4
Short Rd P014 . . . . .179 A3
Short Row P01 . . . . .182 A3
Shorts Cl BH23 . . . . .192 B1
Shorts Rd S050 . . . . .57 B1
Shotterfield Terr GU33 . . . . .20 C2
Shotters Hill Cl S030 . . . . . .105 B3
Shotts La S041 . . . . .198 C2
Shottsford Rd BH15 . . . . . .202 B3
Shraveshill Cl S040 . . . . .76 B1
Shrub's Ave S041 . . . . .197 C2
Shrubbery Cl P016 . . . . .156 B4
Shrubbery The P012 . . . . . .180 C4
Shrubbs Hill Gdns S043 . . .121 C2
Shrubbs Hill Rd S043 . . . . .121 C2
Shrubland Cl S018 . . . . .104 A4
Sibland Cl P014 . . . . .154 B4
Siblings The S019 . . . . .104 C3
Sicily Ho 18 P014 . . . . .154 C4
Siddal Cl S019 . . . . .104 B2
Sidings The Downton SP5 . . .47 A4
  Netley S031 . . . . .105 A2
Sidlesham Cl P011 . . . . .185 C1
Sidmouth Ave P04 . . . . .183 A2
Sidney Gdns ◼ BH9 . . . . . .190 A2
Sidney Smith Ct BH17 . . . .187 C1
Silchester Cl BH12 . . . . . . .204 C3
Silchester Rd P03 . . . . .183 A4
Silhouette Ct P011 . . . . . . .185 B3
Silkin Gdns S040 . . . . .100 B3
Silkstead Ave P09 . . . . .135 C3
Silkstead La S021 . . . . .30 C4
Sillen La SP6 . . . . .43 A2
Silver Birch Ave P014 . . . . .154 C4
Silver Birch Cl Liss GU33 . . .21 A2

Silver Birch Cl *continued*
  Poole BH12 . . . . .204 A2
  Southampton S019 . . . . . . .104 B2
Silver Birches S031 . . . . . . .127 C4
Silver Business Pk BH23 . . .207 A4
Silver Hill S023 . . . . .11 A4
Silver St
  Christchurch BH23 . . . . . . .207 A3
  Hordle S041 . . . . .196 B3
  Lyndhurst S043 . . . . .121 B3
  ◼ Portsmouth P05 . . . . . . .182 C1
Silver Way BH23 . . . . .208 C4
Silverdale BH25 . . . . .210 A4
Silverdale Cl BH18 . . . . .186 C2
Silverdale Cres SP6 . . . . .43 A2
Silverdale Ct ◻ S015 . . . . . .102 C4
Silverdale Rd S015 . . . . . . .102 C4
Silverlock Cl ■ P02 . . . . . . .182 B4
Silverlock Pl P010 . . . . .137 A3
Silvers End BH31 . . . . .115 A3
Silvers Wood S040 . . . . .76 B2
Silversands Gdns P011 . . . .185 A1
Silverthorne Way P07 . . . . .134 B4
Silvertrees P010 . . . . .136 C1
Silverweed Cl S053 . . . . .54 C4
Silverweed Ct S031 . . . . . . .128 C1
Silverwood Cl
  Wimborne Minst BH21 . . . .163 B1
  Winchester S022 . . . . .10 B3
Silvester Rd P08 . . . . .111 C1
Silwood Cl S022 . . . . .1 B3
Simmonds Cl BH15 . . . . . . .202 B3
Simmonds Gn P011 . . . . . . .185 B2
Simmons Cl S030 . . . . .105 B4
Simnel St ◼ S014 . . . . .102 C2
Simon Ct S018 . . . . .104 C4
Simon Way S019 . . . . .104 C3
Simonds Ct ■ S023 . . . . .2 A1
Simpson Cl P016 . . . . .156 B4
Simpson Rd P02 . . . . .157 B1
Sinah La P011 . . . . .184 B2
Sinclair Ct ■ BH14 . . . . . . .203 A2
Sinclair Inf Sch S019 . . . . . .78 A3
Sinclair Jun Sch S019 . . . . . .78 A3
Sinclair Rd S019 . . . . .78 A3
Singleton Dr BH10 . . . . .189 B1
Singleton Gdns P08 . . . . . . .88 B2
Singleton Way S040 . . . . . . .100 A4
Sir Christopher Cl S045 . . . . .126 A2
Sir Christopher Ct ⑤
  S045 . . . . .126 A2
Sir Galahad Rd S053 . . . . .54 C3
Sir George's Rd S015 . . . . . .102 B3
Sir Harold Hillier Gardens &
  Arboretum★ S051 . . . . .28 B2
Sir Lancelot Cl S053 . . . . .54 C3
Sirdar Ho S017 . . . . .79 B2
Sirdar Rd S017 . . . . .79 B2
Sirius Ct P05 . . . . .182 C1
Siskin Cl
  Bishop's Waltham S032 . . . . .83 A4
  Ferndown BH22 . . . . .165 A4
  Southampton S016 . . . . . . .78 A3
Siskin Gr P07 . . . . .135 A3
Siskin Inf Sch P013 . . . . . . .180 B3
Siskin Jun Sch P013 . . . . . .180 B3
Siskin Rd P04 . . . . .183 B3
Sissinghurst Cl S019 . . . . . .104 A1
Sissinghurst Rd P016 . . . . .156 A4
Siverdale Dr P07 . . . . .111 B2
Siward Ho 22 GU32 . . . . .40 C2
Six Dials S014 . . . . .103 A3
Six Oaks Rd S052 . . . . .54 A2
Sixpenny Cl
  Locks Heath P014 . . . . .129 A1
  Poole BH12 . . . . .203 C4
Sixth Ave P06 . . . . .157 C4
Sizer Way S045 . . . . .125 B2
Skew Rd P017 . . . . .132 B1
Skinner St BH15 . . . . .202 B1
Skintle Gn ◼ S031 . . . . .56 C4
Skipper Cl S040 . . . . .102 A2
Skipper Way P013 . . . . .180 A3
Skipton Cl BH18 . . . . .187 A1
Skipton Rd S053 . . . . .55 B2
Sky End La S041 . . . . .196 A1
Skys Wood Rd S053 . . . . . . .54 C3
Slab La Redlynch SP5 . . . . . .47 B3
  West Wellow S051 . . . . .52 A1
Slade Cl S041 . . . . .196 A2
Slade's La BH10 . . . . .204 B4
Slades Farm Hostel
  BH11 . . . . .189 B1
Slades Farm Rd BH10 . . . . .189 B1
Slades Farm Specl Sch
  BH10 . . . . .189 B1
Slater Ave P015 . . . . .150 C1
Slater App P07 . . . . .135 A4
Slater Cl S040 . . . . .100 A4
Sleepbrook Cl BH31 . . . . . .114 C3
Sleepers Hill Ho S022 . . . . . .10 B3
Sleepers Hill Rd S022 . . . . . .10 B3
Sleepers Delle Gdns
  S022 . . . . .10 C3
Sleepers Hill Gdns S022 . . .10 B3
Sleight La BH21 . . . . .186 B4
Slepe Cres BH12 . . . . .203 C4
Slindon Ct P08 . . . . .88 B3
Slindon Gdns ◼ P09 . . . . . .135 C1
Slindon St P01 . . . . .215 B3
Slingsby Cl P01 . . . . .215 A1
Slip End BH23 . . . . .207 C4
Slip Way BH15 . . . . .202 A1
Slipper Rd P010 . . . . .161 A4
Slipway The P06 . . . . .157 A4

Sloane Ct S045 . . . . .150 B2
Sloane Pk S032 . . . . .107 B4
Sloane Stanley Ct P012 . . .181 A2
Slocum Ho 17 P012 . . . . . . .181 B2
Sloe Tree Cl P014 . . . . .129 B1
Slough La BH16 . . . . .201 A3
Smallcutts Ave P010 . . . . . .137 B1
Smeaton St 7 P02 . . . . .157 B1
Smeeton Rd S031 . . . . .179 C1
Smith Cl S045 . . . . .150 C1
Smith Gr S030 . . . . .106 B3
Smith La P010 . . . . .161 B3
Smith St P012 . . . . .181 A3
Smith's Field S051 . . . . .28 A1
Smithe Cl S050 . . . . .56 A2
Smithfield Pl BH9 . . . . .189 C1
Smiths La S032 . . . . .107 C4
Smithson Cl BH12 . . . . .204 B4
Smithy La BH25 . . . . .194 C3
Smithy The P07 . . . . .111 C2
Smugglers La BH21 . . . . . . .163 C4
Smugglers La N BH23 . . . . .193 C1
Smugglers La S BH23 . . . . .193 C1
Smugglers Reach BH23 . . . .208 A3
Smugglers Wood Rd
  BH23 . . . . .193 C1
Smythe Rd S019 . . . . .104 B2
Snailing La GU33 . . . . .20 B4
Snails La BH24 . . . . .117 A2
Snakemoor La S032 . . . . . . .81 C3
Snapdragon Cl S031 . . . . . .128 C1
Snape Cl P013 . . . . .180 B4
Snellgrove Cl S040 . . . . .76 B1
Snellgrove Pl S040 . . . . .76 B1
Snooks La S041 . . . . .198 A2
Snowberry Cres P09 . . . . . .136 B2
Snowdon Dr P014 . . . . .154 C4
Snowdon Rd BH4 . . . . .204 B2
Snowdrop Cl S031 . . . . .128 C1
Snowdrop Gdns BH23 . . . . .193 A1
Soake Rd P07 . . . . .111 A2
Soalwood La GU32 . . . . .39 C4
Soberton Ho
  Portsmouth P01 . . . . .215 C4
  ◼ Southampton S017 . . . . .79 A1
Soberton Rd
  Bournemouth BH8 . . . . . . .205 B3
  Havant P09 . . . . .135 C2
Soberton Twrs S032 . . . . . . .85 B3
Solar Ct BH13 . . . . .204 A1
Soldridge Cl ⑤ BH23 . . . . .136 A3
Solent Ave
  Lymington S041 . . . . .198 A2
  Southampton S019 . . . . . . .104 C3
Solent Bsns Ctr S015 . . . . .102 B3
Solent Bsns Pk P015 . . . . . .129 C4
Solent Cl
  Chandler's Ford S053 . . . . . .55 C3
  Lymington S041 . . . . .197 C2
Solent Ct
  ◻ Milford on Sea S041 . . . .211 B2
  Southampton S019 . . . . . . .103 C1
  Stubbington P014 . . . . .179 B3
Solent Ctr P015 . . . . .129 C4
Solent Dr
  Barton on Sea BH25 . . . . . .210 A4
  Hythe S045 . . . . .125 C2
  Locks Heath S031 . . . . .152 B3
  South Hayling P011 . . . . . .184 C1
Solent Gate
  Gosport P014 . . . . .155 A3
  ◼ Portsmouth P05 . . . . . . .182 B1
Solent Ho
  ◼ Fareham P016 . . . . .155 A4
  Havant P09 . . . . .136 A2
  Southampton S019 . . . . . . .104 C3
Solent Homes S031 . . . . . . .104 C3
Solent Hts
  12 Lee-on-the-Solent
  P013 . . . . .179 C1
Solent Inf Ctr S015 . . . . . . .102 B3
Solent Ind Est S030 . . . . . . .81 A1
Solent Inf Sch P06 . . . . . . .158 B3
Solent Lo ◼ BH25 . . . . .195 A1
Solent Mdws S031 . . . . . . .128 A1
Solent Pines ◼ S041 . . . . . .211 A2
Solent Rd
  Barton on Sea BH25 . . . . . .209 B4
  Bournemouth BH6 . . . . . . .207 A2
  Christchurch BH23 . . . . . . .194 A1
  Cosham P06 . . . . .158 B4
  Havant P09 . . . . .135 C1
  Hythe S045 . . . . .125 C2
  Stubbington P014 . . . . .179 A3
Solent View Boldre S041 . . .198 A2
  Bournemouth BH6 . . . . . . .207 A2
  Fawley S045 . . . . .151 A4
  Lee-on-the-Solent P013 . . .179 B2
Solent Village P015 . . . . . .129 C2
Solent Way
  Gosport P012 . . . . .180 C2
  Milford on Sea S041 . . . . . .211 C2
  Solihull Ho P05 . . . . .215 A2
Solly Cl BH12 . . . . .203 C4
Solomon Way BH15 . . . . . . .202 A1
Solomons La S032 . . . . .83 C1
Solona Cl S053 . . . . .54 C3
Solway Ho ◼ S014 . . . . . . .103 A3
Somborne Cl 12 S017 . . . . . .79 A1
Somborne Dr P09 . . . . .135 C3
Somborne Ho S019 . . . . . . .103 C1
Somerby Rd BH15 . . . . .202 B3
Somerford Ave BH23 . . . . . .208 A4
Somerford Bsns Pk
  BH23 . . . . .208 A4
Somerford Cl S019 . . . . . . .104 A3

Somerford Ct BH23 . . . . . . .208 C4
Somerford Cty Inf Sch
  BH23 . . . . .207 C4
Somerford Cty Jun Sch
  BH23 . . . . .207 C4
Somerford Rd BH23 . . . . . . .207 C3
Somerford Way BH23 . . . . . .207 C3
Somerley Rd BH9 . . . . .205 A4
Somerley View BH23 . . . . . .141 A4
Somers Cl S022 . . . . .10 B3
Somers Park Prim Sch
  P01 . . . . .215 C3
Somers Rd
  Portsmouth P01 . . . . .215 C2
  Portsmouth P05 . . . . .215 C3
Somers Rd N P01 . . . . .215 C2
Somerset Cres S053 . . . . .55 B2
Somerset Ct ◼ S015 . . . . . .102 B3
Somerset La S018 . . . . .104 B4
Somerset Rd
  Bournemouth BH7 . . . . . . .206 A3
  Christchurch BH23 . . . . . . .206 C4
  Portsmouth P05 . . . . .182 B1
  Southampton S017 . . . . .79 B1
Somerset Terr S015 . . . . . . .102 B3
Somerstown Flats P09 . . . .136 A1
Somerton Ave S018 . . . . . . .104 A4
Somerton Cl BH25 . . . . .195 B2
Somervell Cl P012 . . . . .181 A3
Somervell Dr P016 . . . . .131 A2
Somerville Ct BH25 . . . . . . .194 C2
Somerville Pl ◼ P02 . . . . . .157 B3
Somerville Rd
  Bournemouth BH1 . . . . . . .204 B2
  Kings Worthy S023 . . . . .2 B4
  Ringwood BH24 . . . . .141 B4
Somers Cl S019 . . . . .103 B2
Sommers Ct S019 . . . . .103 B2
Sonata Ho P06 . . . . .157 A4
Sonnet Way P07 . . . . .135 A4
Sonning Way BH8 . . . . .190 A1
Soper's La BH23 . . . . .207 A3
Sopers La BH17 . . . . .187 A3
Sopley Cl BH25 . . . . .209 B4
Sopley Ct ◼ P09 . . . . .136 A3
Sopley Farm Bldgs
  BH23 . . . . .192 A3
Sopley Prim Sch BH23 . . . . .168 B3
Sopwith Cl BH23 . . . . .208 A3
Sopwith Cres BH21 . . . . . . .163 C3
Sopwith Way S031 . . . . .128 A1
Sorrel Cl Romsey S051 . . . . .28 B1
  Waterlooville P07 . . . . .135 A3
Sorrel Dr BH23 . . . . .208 B4
Sorrel Gdns BH18 . . . . .186 C3
Sorrell Cl S031 . . . . .128 C1
Sorrell Ct BH23 . . . . .208 A4
Sorrell Way BH23 . . . . .208 A4
South Ave Fawley S045 . . . . .150 C2
  Holbury S045 . . . . .150 B3
  New Milton BH25 . . . . .195 A3
  Portsmouth P02 . . . . .157 C2
South Baddesley CE Prim Sch
  S041 . . . . .198 C3
South Baddesley Rd
  S041 . . . . .198 A2
South Bay P010 . . . . .161 A2
South Cl Gosport P012 . . . . .180 C2
  Havant P09 . . . . .160 A4
  Romsey S051 . . . . .28 B1
South Cliff Rd BH2 . . . . . . .204 C1
South Cross St P012 . . . . . .181 B2
South Ct S031 . . . . .127 C4
South Downs Coll P07 . . . . .135 A2
South Dr Awbridge S051 . . . .27 A2
  Littleton S022 . . . . .1 A2
South East Cres S019 . . . . . .104 A2
South East Rd S019 . . . . . . .104 A2
South End Cl S021 . . . . .30 A4
South Front
  ◼ Romsey S051 . . . . .52 C4
  Southampton S014 . . . . . . .103 A2
South Gr S041 . . . . .197 C2
South Hampshire Ind Pk
  S040 . . . . .76 B1
South Haven Cl BH16 . . . . .201 A2
  Aldershot SP6 . . . . .93 A3
  Droxford S032 . . . . .85 A4
  Southampton S016 . . . . .79 A2
South Kinson Dr BH11 . . . . .189 A2
South La Buriton GU31 . . . .65 B2
  Clanfield P08 . . . . .88 A3
  Downton SP5 . . . . .46 C4
  Horndean P08 . . . . .89 A2
  Nomansland SP5 . . . . .73 B4
  Southbourne P010 . . . . . . .137 C1
  Westbourne P010 . . . . .137 B2
South Lo BH13 . . . . .214 D4
South Lodge P015 . . . . .130 A1
South Mill Rd S015 . . . . . . .102 A4
South Millers Dale S053 . . .55 A4
South Normandy ■
  P01 . . . . .182 A2
South Par
  Portsmouth P05 . . . . .182 B1
  Totton S040 . . . . .100 C4
South Parade Pier★
  P04 . . . . .182 C1
South Park Rd S014 . . . . . . .204 A4
South Pl P013 . . . . .180 A2
South Rd
  Bournemouth BH1 . . . . . . .205 C3
  Corfe Mullen BH21 . . . . . . .186 C3
  Cosham P06 . . . . .158 B4
  Horndean P08 . . . . .88 B1
  Poole BH15 . . . . .202 B3
  Portsmouth P01 . . . . .182 C4
  Southampton S017 . . . . .79 C2
  South Hayling S011 . . . . . .184 C2

South Rd continued
Southwick PO17 ... 133 A3
South Road Comb Sch
BH15 ... 202 B1
South St Eastleigh SO50 ... 80 A4
Emsworth PO10 ... 160 C4
Gosport PO12 ... 181 B2
Havant PO9 ... 135 C1
Hythe SO45 ... 126 A2
Lymington SO41 ... 197 B1
Portsmouth PO5 ... 215 B1
Titchfield PO14 ... 153 C4
South Stoneham Ho
SO18 ... 79 B2
South Sway La SO41 ... 196 B4
South Terr PO1 ... 182 A3
South Trestle Rd SO45 ... 151 B3
South View
Bournemouth BH2 ... 204 C3
Winchester SO22 ... 10 C4
South View CI PO8 ... 112 A2
South View Park Homes
SO22 ... 10 B2
South View PI [17] BH2 ... 204 C2
South View Rd
Christchurch BH23 ... 207 A3
Southampton SO15 ... 102 B4
Winchester SO22 ... 10 A2
South Way PO15 ... 129 C2
South Weirs SO42 ... 172 B4
South Western Cres
BH14 ... 203 A1
Southampton Airport
Parkway Sta SO18 ... 79 C3
Southampton Central Sta
SO15 ... 102 C3
Southampton City Coll
SO14 ... 103 A2
Southampton Gen Hospl
SO16 ... 78 A1
Southampton Hill PO14 ... 153 C4
Southampton Ho [88]
PO9 ... 136 A3
Southampton Inst of H Ed
Marine Operations Ctr
SO40 ... 102 A1
Southampton Inst(City
Campus) SO14 ... 103 A3
Southampton International
Airport SO18 ... 79 C3
Southampton Oceanography
Ctr SO14 ... 103 A1
Southampton Rd
Brockenhurst SO41,SO42 ... 173 A2
Cadnam SO40 ... 98 C4
Cadnam, Bartley SO40 ... 99 A4
Cosham PO6 ... 157 B4
Eastleigh SO50 ... 56 A1
Fareham PO14 ... 154 A4
Fareham PO16 ... 131 A1
Fordingbridge SP6 ... 70 A1
Hythe SO45 ... 125 C2
Locks Heath SO31,PO14 ... 129 C4
Lymington SO41 ... 197 B3
Lyndhurst SO43 ... 122 A3
North Baddesley SO51 ... 53 A3
Ringwood BH24 ... 140 C4
Romsey SO51 ... 53 A3

Southern Oaks BH25 ... 194 C1
Southern Rd
Bournemouth BH6 ... 206 B2
Fawley SO45 ... 151 C1
Lymington SO41 ... 197 B2
Southampton SO15 ... 102 C2
West End SO30 ... 80 C1
Southernhay PO7 ... 110 C2
Southernhay Rd BH31 ... 115 A3
Southey Rd BH23 ... 207 C4
Southfield BH24 ... 141 A3
Southfield La BH24 ... 143 B1
Southfield Mews [6]
BH24 ... 141 A3
Southfield Wlk PO9 ... 135 B4
Southfields CI SO32 ... 83 B4
Southgate St SO23 ... 10 C4
Southgate Villas SO23 ... 10 C4
Southill Ave BH12 ... 203 B3
Southill Gdns BH9 ... 190 A1
Southill Rd
Bournemouth BH9 ... 190 A1
Poole BH12 ... 203 B3
Southlands Cosham PO6 ... 158 A4
Lymington SO41 ... 197 B1
Southlands Ave
Bournemouth BH6 ... 206 C2
Corfe Mullen BH21 ... 186 C3
Southlands CI BH21 ... 186 B3
Southlands Ct BH18 ... 187 A2
Southlands Sch SO41 ... 197 C4
Southlawns Wlk BH25 ... 194 C2
Southlea Ave BH6 ... 206 C2
Southleigh Gr PO11 ... 184 C2
Southleigh Rd PO9 ... 136 B2
Southmead Rd PO15 ... 130 C1
Southsea Ave SO22 ... 159 B4
Southsea Castle* PO5 ... 182 B1
Southsea Inf Sch PO4 ... 182 C1
Southsea Terr PO5 ... 215 A1
Southview SO32 ... 61 A1
Southville Rd BH5 ... 206 A4
Southwater [1] PO13 ... 179 C1
Southways PO14 ... 155 B2
Southwick Ave PO16 ... 132 C1
Southwick CI SO22 ... 1 A2
Southwick Ct PO14 ... 155 A3
Southwick Hill Rd PO6 ... 133 C1
Southwick Ho [5] PO1 ... 215 C4
Southwick PI BH6 ... 206 B4
Southwick Rd
Bournemouth BH6 ... 206 B3
Cosham PO7,PO17 ... 133 B1
Denmead PO7 ... 110 C2
Wickham PO17 ... 108 B2
Southwood Ave
Bournemouth BH6 ... 206 B2
Christchurch BH23 ... 194 A1
Southwood CI
Christchurch BH23 ... 194 A1
Ferndown BH22 ... 165 B3
Southwood Ct BH23 ... 194 A1
Southwood Gdns SO31 ... 128 C2
Southwood Rd
Portsmouth PO2 ... 157 C2
South Hayling PO11 ... 185 B1
Sovereign Bsns Ctr
BH15 ... 202 A3
Sovereign CI
Ashurst SO40 ... 100 B4
Bournemouth BH7 ... 205 C4
Portsmouth PO4 ... 183 B3
Sovereign Cres PO14 ... 129 A1
Sovereign Ct [20] SO17 ... 79 A1
Sovereign Ctr BH1 ... 205 C3
Sovereign Dr
Hedge End SO30 ... 105 B3
Portsmouth PO4 ... 183 B3
Sovereign La PO7 ... 134 C2
Sovereign Sq [6] BH7 ... 205 C2
Sovereign Way SO50 ... 55 C3
Soverign Dr SO30 ... 105 A3
Sowden CI SO30 ... 105 A4
Sowley La SO41 ... 199 B3
Spa Rd SO14 ... 102 C2
Spain Bldgs [18] GU32 ... 40 C2
Spain The GU32 ... 40 C2
Spalding Rd SO19 ... 104 C3
Spaniard's La SO51 ... 53 A2
Sparkford CI
Bournemouth BH7 ... 206 A4
Winchester SO22 ... 10 C3
Sparkford Rd SO22 ... 10 C4
Sparrow CI PO8 ... 111 C2
Sparrow Ct PO13 ... 179 C2
Sparrow Sq SO50 ... 55 B1
Sparrowgrove SO21 ... 31 B2
Sparrowhawk CI PO3 ... 158 A2
Sparsholt CI PO9 ... 135 A3
Sparsholt Rd
Southampton SO19 ... 126 C4
Winchester SO21,SO22 ... 9 B2
Spartan CI
Stubbington PO14 ... 154 B3
Thorney Island PO10 ... 161 A2
Spartina Dr SO41 ... 197 C3
Spear Rd SO14 ... 103 A4
Specks La PO4 ... 183 A3
Speedfields Pk PO14 ... 155 A3
Speedwell CI
Chandler's Ford SO53 ... 55 A3
Locks Heath SO31 ... 128 C1
Speedwell Dr BH23 ... 208 A4
Speggs Wlk [2] SO30 ... 105 B3
Speltham Hill PO7 ... 86 B1
Spencer CI PO11 ... 185 A2

Spencer Ct
[5] New Milton BH25 ... 195 A1
Stubbington PO14 ... 179 C3
Spencer Dr PO13 ... 179 C1
Spencer Gdns PO8 ... 111 C2
Spencer Rd
Bournemouth BH1 ... 205 B2
Eastleigh SO50 ... 55 C1
Emsworth PO10 ... 136 C2
New Milton BH25 ... 195 A1
Poole BH13 ... 214 C4
Portsmouth PO4 ... 182 C1
Southampton SO19 ... 104 B3
Spenlow CI PO2 ... 182 B4
Spenser CI SO31 ... 152 B4
Spetisbury CI BH9 ... 190 A2
Spice Quay [2] PO1 ... 182 A2
Spicer La BH1 ... 188 C3
Spicer St PO1 ... 215 B4
Spicer's Wlk SO40 ... 100 C3
Spicer's Way SO40 ... 100 C3
Spicers Ct [5] SO22 ... 10 C4
Spicewood PO15 ... 130 C1
Spinacre BH25 ... 210 A4
Spindle CI
Broadstone BH18 ... 186 C1
Spindle Warren PO9 ... 136 B2
Spindlewood CI
[26] Barton on Sea BH25 ... 195 A1
Southampton SO16 ... 79 A3
Spindlewood Way SO40 ... 124 C4
Spinnaker CI
Gosport PO13 ... 180 B4
South Hayling PO11 ... 184 C2
Spinnaker Dr PO2 ... 157 B2
Spinnaker Grange PO11 ... 160 B2
Spinnaker Ho PO6 ... 157 A4
Spinnaker View PO9 ... 135 A1
Spinners CI [2] SO41 ... 138 C1
Spinners Gdn* SO41 ... 173 C1
Spinney CI
St Leonards BH24 ... 139 B2
Waterlooville PO8 ... 111 C2
Spinney Dale SO45 ... 126 A1
Spinney The
Compton (Hants) SO21 ... 31 B4
Denmead PO7 ... 110 C2
Fair Oak SO50 ... 57 A1
Gosport PO13 ... 155 B1
Portchester PO16 ... 131 C1
Southampton SO16 ... 79 A3
St Leonards BH24 ... 139 C3
Totton SO40 ... 76 B1
Waterlooville PO8 ... 112 A3
Spinney Way BH25 ... 195 A3
Spinney Wlk SO18 ... 79 C2
Spinneys La BH22 ... 165 B3
Spinningfield Ho [4]
GU32 ... 40 C2
Spitfire Ct SO19 ... 103 B2
Spitfire End [8] SO23 ... 11 B4
Spitfire Link SO23 ... 11 B4
Spitfire Loop SO18 ... 80 A4
Spitfire Quay SO19 ... 103 B2
Spitfire Rdbt SO23 ... 11 B4
Spithead Way SO31 ... 127 C1
Spithead Ave PO12 ... 181 B1
Spithead Ho PO16 ... 155 A4
Spithead Hts PO4 ... 183 B2
Spittlefields BH24 ... 141 A4
Spouts La SO51 ... 50 B3
Spring CI Fair Oak SO50 ... 57 B1
Southampton SO19 ... 103 C2
Verwood BH31 ... 114 C3
Spring Cres SO17 ... 103 A4
Spring Ct Poole BH12 ... 203 B3
[7] Southampton SO15 ... 102 C3
Spring Firs SO19 ... 103 B3
Spring Garden La PO12 ... 181 B3
Spring Gdns
[1] Emsworth PO10 ... 161 A4
North Baddesley SO52 ... 54 A2
Poole BH12 ... 203 B3
Portsmouth PO1 ... 215 A4
Spring Gr SO31 ... 105 A1
Spring House CI SO21 ... 32 A1
Spring Rd
Bishopstoke SO50 ... 56 B2
Colden Common SO21 ... 31 C1
New Milton BH25 ... 195 B1
Swanmore SO32 ... 84 A3
Spring PI [5] SO51 ... 52 C4
Spring Rd
Hythe SO45 ... 126 A2
Locks Heath SO31 ... 128 C3
Lymington SO41 ... 198 A4
Southampton SO19 ... 104 A4
Spring St PO1 ... 215 B4
Spring The PO7 ... 110 C2
Spring Vale
Swanmore SO32 ... 84 A2
Waterlooville PO8 ... 112 A2
Spring Wlk PO1 ... 215 B4
Springbank Rd BH7 ... 205 C4
Springbourne Ct BH1 ... 205 B3
Springbourne Mews
BH1 ... 205 B3
Springcroft PO13 ... 155 A3
Springdale Ave BH18 ... 186 C3
Springdale Ct SO40 ... 100 C4
Springdale First Sch
BH18 ... 186 C2
Springdale Gr BH18 ... 186 C2
Springdale Rd BH18,
BH21 ... 186 C2

Springfield [2] GU33 ... 20 C2
Springfield Ave
Bournemouth BH6 ... 207 A2
Christchurch BH23 ... 191 B1
Holbury SO45 ... 150 B2
Springfield CI
Havant PO9 ... 135 A1
Lymington SO41 ... 198 A2
Verwood BH31 ... 114 C3
Wickham PO17 ... 108 A2
Springfield Cres
Poole BH14 ... 203 A2
Redlynch SP5 ... 47 B3
Springfield Ct SO19 ... 103 C1
Springfield Dr SO40 ... 100 C3
Springfield Gdns BH25 ... 195 B1
Springfield Gr SO45 ... 150 B2
Springfield Rd
Poole BH14 ... 203 A2
Verwood BH31 ... 114 C3
Springfield Sch PO6 ... 158 B4
Springfield Way PO14 ... 179 B3
Springfields CI [5] SO21 ... 31 C1
Springford CI SO16 ... 78 A2
Springford Cres SO16 ... 78 A2
Springford Gdns SO16 ... 78 A2
Springford Rd SO16 ... 78 A2
Springhill RC Prim Sch
SO15 ... 102 C3
Springhill Rd SO53 ... 55 B3
Springles La PO15 ... 130 A3
Springvale Ave
Bournemouth BH7 ... 206 A4
Kings Worthy SO23 ... 2 A3
Springvale Rd SO23 ... 2 A4
Springwater CI BH11 ... 189 A2
Springwater CI BH23 ... 207 B3
Springwater Dr BH23 ... 207 B3
Springwater Rd BH11 ... 189 A2
Springwood Ave PO7 ... 134 C3
Spruce Ave PO7 ... 135 A3
Spruce CI
Broadstone BH17 ... 186 C1
Locks Heath SO31 ... 152 B4
Spruce Dr
Southampton SO19 ... 104 C3
Totton SO40 ... 100 B2
Spruce Wlk [22] PO13 ... 179 C1
Spur CI BH21 ... 164 B3
Spur Hill Ave BH14 ... 203 B2
Spur Rd Cosham PO6 ... 157 C4
Poole BH14 ... 203 B2
Waterlooville PO7 ... 134 C4
Spur The Gosport PO12 ... 180 C1
Wickham PO17 ... 108 A2
Spurgeon Rd BH7 ... 206 A3
Spurlings Rd PO17 ... 131 B2
Spurlings Yd PO17 ... 131 B2
Square The
Bournemouth BH2 ... 204 C2
Compton (Sussex) PO18 ... 90 C1
Fawley SO45 ... 151 A2
Gosport PO12 ... 181 B4
Hamble-le-Rice SO31 ... 128 A1
Lymington SO41 ... 197 B2
Petersfield GU32 ... 40 C2
Sherfield English SO51 ... 26 A2
Southbourne PO10 ... 161 B4
Titchfield PO14 ... 153 C4
Westbourne PO10 ... 137 A2
Wickham PO17 ... 108 A2
Wimborne Minst BH21 ... 163 A3
Winchester SO23 ... 11 A4
Squires CI SP5 ... 46 C3
Squires Wlk SO19 ... 103 C1
Squirrel CI SO50 ... 56 C1
Squirrel Dr SO19 ... 104 A2
Squirrel Wlk BH31 ... 114 C3
Squirrel's CI BH23 ... 191 B1
Squirrels Wlk SO45 ... 125 C1
Stable CI PO14 ... 129 B1
Stable La [2] SO21 ... 40 C2
Stables The
Christchurch BH23 ... 206 C4
Locks Heath SO31 ... 129 A1
Stacey CI BH12 ... 203 B4
Stacey Ct PO9 ... 135 B4
Stacey Gdns BH8 ... 190 C1
Staff Rd SO51 ... 6 A1
Stafford Rd
Bournemouth BH1 ... 205 A2
Petersfield GU32 ... 40 C2
Portsmouth PO5 ... 215 C1
Southampton SO15 ... 102 B3
Stag Gates SO45 ... 150 C1
Stag Way PO15 ... 130 B3
Stagbrake CI SO45 ... 150 A2
Stags La SO21 ... 33 A3
Stagshorn Rd PO8 ... 112 B4
Stagswood BH31 ... 114 B3
Stainer CI SO19 ... 104 B2
Staith CI SO19 ... 104 B3
Stake's La SO21 ... 59 C4
Stakes Hill Inf Sch PO7 ... 134 C3
Stakes Hill Rd PO7 ... 134 C3
Stakes Rd PO7,PO8 ... 134 B3
Stakes Rd PO7 ... 134 B2
Stalbridge Dr BH22 ... 165 B2
Stalbridge Rd BH11 ... 202 A4
Stalham Rd BH12 ... 203 C3
Stallards La BH24 ... 140 C4
Stallards CI BH24 ... 140 C4
Stalybridge CI SO31 ... 129 A3
Stamford Ave PO11 ... 184 C2
Stamford Lodge PO11 ... 184 C2

Stamford Rd BH6 ... 206 B3
Stamford St PO1 ... 215 C4
Stamford Way SO50 ... 56 C1
Stampsey Ct [3] PO2 ... 157 B1
Stamshaw Ct [14] PO2 ... 157 B1
Stamshaw Inf Sch PO2 ... 157 B1
Stamshaw Jun Sch PO2 ... 157 B1
Stamshaw Rd PO2 ... 157 B1
Stanbridge Earls Sch
SO51 ... 27 A2
Stanbridge La SO51 ... 27 A2
Stanbridge Rd PO9 ... 136 A2
Standard Way PO16 ... 131 B3
Standen Rd SO16 ... 77 B3
Standford St SO14 ... 103 A2
Standing Hill SP5 ... 3 C4
Stanfield Ct BH12 ... 203 B4
Stanfield Rd
Bournemouth BH9 ... 204 C4
Ferndown BH22 ... 165 B3
Poole BH12 ... 203 B4
Stanford Ct PO6 ... 157 B4
Stanford CI
[9] Havant PO9 ... 136 A3
Southampton SO19 ... 104 B2
Stanford Rd SO41 ... 197 B2
Stanford Rise SO41 ... 172 A1
Stanhope Rd PO1 ... 215 B3
Stanier Way SO30 ... 81 B1
Staniforth Ct BH23 ... 207 B3
Stanley Ave PO3 ... 183 A4
Stanley CI
Crouchston SP5 ... 22 A4
Fareham PO15 ... 130 C1
Gosport PO12 ... 156 A1
Verwood BH31 ... 115 A3
Stanley Ct
Bournemouth BH1 ... 205 B3
Poole BH15 ... 202 B3
Stanley Green Cres
BH15 ... 202 B3
Stanley Green Fst Sch
BH15 ... 202 B3
Stanley Green Rd BH15 ... 202 B3
Stanley La PO5 ... 182 B1
Stanley Pearce Ho
BH17 ... 187 B1
Stanley Rd
Bournemouth BH1 ... 205 B3
Christchurch BH23 ... 209 A4
Emsworth PO10 ... 161 A4
Holbury SO45 ... 150 B2
Lymington SO41 ... 198 A1
Poole BH15 ... 202 B1
Portsmouth PO2 ... 157 B1
Southampton SO19 ... 79 B1
Stanley St PO5 ... 182 B1
Stanmore La SO22 ... 10 B3
Stanmore Prim Sch
SO22 ... 10 C3
Stannington CI BH25 ... 195 A1
Stannington Cres SO40 ... 100 C4
Stannington Way SO40 ... 100 C4
Stanpit BH23 ... 207 C3
Stanstead Rd SO50 ... 55 C2
Stansted CI PO9 ... 113 B1
Stansted Cres PO9 ... 136 A3
Stansted Ct PO9 ... 113 B1
Stansted Rd PO5 ... 215 C2
Stanswood Rd
Blackfield SO45 ... 178 B3
Havant PO9 ... 135 B3
Stanton Bldgs [20] SO15 ... 102 A4
Stanton Lacy [1] BH14 ... 214 C4
Stanton Rd
Bournemouth BH10 ... 189 B1
Petersfield GU32 ... 40 C2
Southampton SO15 ... 102 A4
Stanton Rd Ind Est
SO15 ... 102 A4
Stanton Road Ind Est [21]
SO15 ... 102 A4
Stapehill Cres BH21 ... 164 B3
Stapehill Mus & Gdns*
BH21 ... 164 C3
Staple Ash La GU32 ... 39 B4
Staple CI PO7 ... 111 B1
Staple Close La BH15 ... 202 B3
Staple Cross
Burton BH23 ... 207 C4
Christchurch BH23 ... 132 A4
Staple Gdns SO23 ... 10 C4
Staplecross La SO23 ... 207 B4
Stapleford Ave PO7 ... 132 C3
Stapleford CI SO51 ... 28 A1
Staplehurst CI SO19 ... 104 A1
Staplers Reach PO13 ... 155 A1
Stapleton Rd PO3 ... 183 A4
Staplewood La SO40 ... 124 B4
Star Cottage Gdn*
BH21 ... 162 B3
Star Cotts PO17 ... 108 A2
Star La BH24 ... 140 C4
Stares CI PO13 ... 180 B4
Stares Gdns PO7 ... 135 A4
Starlight Farm CI BH31 ... 115 A4
Starling Sq SO50 ... 55 B1
Station App
Broadstone BH18 ... 187 A2

Station App continued
Brockenhurst SO42 . . . . . . .146 A1
1 Portsmouth PO1 . . . . . . .182 A3
Station Cl PO17 . . . . .108 A2
Station Cotts SO42 . . . . . .123 B1
Station Hill
Burslecon SO31 . . . . .128 A4
Curdridge SO30 . . . . .106 B4
Eastleigh SO50 . . . . .56 A2
Winchester SO23 . . . . .10 C4
Station La SO53 . . . . .55 B3
Station Rd Alderholt SP6 . .92 C3
Bishop's Waltham SO32 . . . .83 B4
Burley BH24 . . . . .170 B4
Burslecon SO31 . . . . .128 A4
Christchurch BH23 . . . . . . .207 A4
Christchurch, Highcliffe
BH23 . . . . .193 C1
Cosham PO6 . . . . .158 B4
Fordingbridge SP6 . . . . .69 B1
Gosport PO12 . . . . .180 C4
Hamworthy BH15 . . . . .202 A1
Liss GU33 . . . . .20 C2
Locks Heath SO31 . . . . . . .129 C1
Netley SO31 . . . . .127 B3
New Milton BH25 . . . . . . .195 A1
Nursling SO16 . . . . .77 A3
Petersfield GU31, GU32 . . . .40 C2
Poole BH14 . . . . .203 A2
Portchester PO16 . . . . .156 B4
Portsmouth PO3 . . . . .183 A4
Romsey SO51 . . . . .52 C4
Soberton SO32 . . . . .85 B4
South Hayling PO11 . . . . . .184 C2
Southampton, Redbridge
SO15 . . . . .101 B4
Southampton, Sholing
SO19 . . . . .103 C2
Sway SO41 . . . . .172 A1
Verwood BH31 . . . . .45 C4
West Moon GU32 . . . . .37 B2
West Moors BH22 . . . . . . .138 B1
Wickham PO17 . . . . .108 A2
Wimborne Minst BH21 . . . .163 B2
Station Rd N SO40 . . . . . . .101 A4
Station Rd S SO40 . . . . . . .101 A4
Station St
Lymington SO41 . . . . .197 C2
Portsmouth PO1 . . . . .215 B3
Station Terr Twyford SO21 .31 C3
Wimborne Minst BH21 . . . .163 B2
Station Yd SP6 . . . . .92 C3
Staunton BH2 . . . . .204 C1
Staunton Ave PO11 . . . . . .184 A4
Staunton Ctry Pk* PO9 . . . .136 A4
Staunton Park Com Sch
PO9 . . . . .136 A4
Staunton Rd PO9 . . . . .135 C1
Staunton St PO1 . . . . .215 B4
Stead Cl PO11 . . . . .185 A2
Stedman Rd BH5 . . . . .206 A3
Steel St PO5 . . . . .215 A1
Steele Cl SO53 . . . . .55 B2
Steels Dro SP6 . . . . .70 C4
Steels La SO4 . . . . .68 B2
Steep CE Prim Sch GU32 . .40 C4
Steep Cl
Portchester PO16 . . . . .132 B1
Southampton SO18 . . . . . . .104 B4
Steepdene BH14 . . . . .203 A2
Steeple Cl BH17 . . . . .187 B2
Steeple Way PO14 . . . . . . .129 B2
Steepleton Rd BH18 . . . . . .187 B2
Steerforth Cl PO2 . . . . . . .182 B4
Stein Rd PO10 . . . . .137 B1
Steinbeck Cl PO15 . . . . . . .129 B4
Stella Ct
10 Christchurch BH23 . . .209 A4
Southampton SO16 . . . . . . .78 B2
Stem La BH25 . . . . .194 C2
Stenbury Way SO31 . . . . . .127 B4
Stenhurst Rd BH15 . . . . . .202 C3
Step Terr SO22 . . . . .10 C4
Stephen Cl PO8 . . . . .112 A1
Stephen Langton Dr
BH11 . . . . .188 B3
Stephen Lodge PO5 . . . . . .215 B1
Stephen Martin Gdns
SP6 . . . . .69 C1
Stephen Rd PO15 . . . . . . .130 C1
Stephens Ct SO51 . . . . .52 C3
Stephens Wlk BH24 . . . . . .140 C4
Stephenson Ct PO12 . . . . .181 A1
Stephenson Rd
Totton SO40 . . . . .76 B1
Locks Heath PO14,PO15 . .129 C1
Stephenson Way SO30 . . . .81 A2
Steplake La SO51 . . . . .25 B1
Steplake Rd SO51 . . . . .50 B4
Stepnell Reach BH16 . . . . .201 B3
Sterte Ave BH15 . . . . .202 A2
Sterte Ave W BH15 . . . . . .202 A2
Sterte Cl BH15 . . . . .202 B2
Sterte Ct BH15 . . . . .202 B2
Sterte St BH15 . . . . .202 B2
Sterte Espl BH15 . . . . .202 B2
Sterte Ind Est BH15 . . . . . .202 A2
Steuart Rd SO18 . . . . .103 B4
Stevens Ct BH14 . . . . .203 C2
Stevenson Rd BH6 . . . . . . .207 A2
Stevensons Cl **3** BH21 . . .163 B2
Stevenson Rd SO18 . . . . . .104 B4
Stewart Cl **6** BH8 . . . . . . .205 B3
Stewart Ho SO53 . . . . .30 B1
Stewart Pl PO1 . . . . .182 C4

Stewart Rd BH8 . . . . .205 A3
Stewarts Gn PO7 . . . . .86 B2
Stewarts Way BH22 . . . . . .165 C4
Stibbs Way BH23 . . . . .169 B1
Stillmore Rd BH11 . . . . . . .188 B2
Stinchar Dr SO53 . . . . .55 A3
Stinsford Cl BH9 . . . . .190 A2
Stinsford La BH17 . . . . . . .202 B4
Stinsford Rd BH17 . . . . . . .187 B1
Stirling Ave PO7 . . . . .134 C4
Stirling Cl
New Milton BH25 . . . . .195 A2
Totton SO40 . . . . .77 A1
Stirling Cres
Hedge End SO30 . . . . .81 B1
Totton SO40 . . . . .101 A4
Stirling Ct
Bournemouth BH4 . . . . . . .204 B1
Fareham PO15 . . . . .130 C2
21 New Milton BH25 . . . .195 A2
Stirling Rd BH3 . . . . .204 C4
Stirling St PO2 . . . . .182 B4
Stirling Way BH23 . . . . . . .208 A3
Stirling Wlk SO51 . . . . .52 C4
Stirrup Cl Upton BH16 . . . .201 B4
Wimborne Minst BH21 . . . .164 B3
Stoborough Dr BH18 . . . . . .187 A1
Stock La SP5 . . . . .61 A3
Stock's Cross SO43 . . . . . . .73 C2
Stock's La SO42 . . . . .61 C3
Stockbridge Cl
Havant PO9 . . . . .136 A3
Poole BH17 . . . . .188 A1
Stockbridge Rd SO21,
SO22, SO23 . . . . .1 B1
Stocker Pl PO13 . . . . .155 B1
Stockers Ave SO22 . . . . .1 B1
Stockheath La PO9 . . . . . . .135 C2
Stockheath Rd PO9 . . . . . .135 C2
Stockheath Way PO9 . . . . .135 C2
Stockley Cl SO45 . . . . .150 B2
Stockton Cl SO30 . . . . .105 B4
Stoddart Ave SO19 . . . . . .103 C3
Stodham La GU33 . . . . .20 C1
Stoke Common Rd SO50 . .56 C3
Stoke Gdns PO12 . . . . .181 B2
Stoke Hts SO50 . . . . .57 A2
Stoke Park Dr SO50 . . . . . . .56 B2
Stoke Park Ind Est SO50 . .56 C1
Stoke Park Jun Sch
SO50 . . . . .56 C1
Stoke Park Rd SO50 . . . . . .56 B2
Stoke Rd Gosport PO12 . . .181 B2
Southampton SO16 . . . . . . .78 A1
Winchester SO23 . . . . .2 A2
Stoke Wood Cl SO50 . . . . . .57 A1
Stoke Wood Rd BH3 . . . . . .204 C3
Stokes Ave BH15 . . . . .202 B2
Stokes Bay Rd PO12 . . . . .180 C1
Stokesay Cl SO45 . . . . .150 A4
Stone Gdns BH8 . . . . .191 A1
Stone La
5 Gosport PO12 . . . . .181 A2
Wimborne Minst BH21 . . . .163 A3
Stone Lane Ind Est
BH21 . . . . .163 A3
Stone Sq PO9 . . . . .135 C2
Stone St PO5 . . . . .215 A1
Stone Terr SO21 . . . . .31 A1
Stonechat Cl
Ferndown BH22 . . . . .165 A4
Petersfield GU31 . . . . .41 B1
Stonechat Ct BH23 . . . . . .207 C4
Stonechat Dr SO40 . . . . . .100 B4
Stonechat Rd PO8 . . . . . . .112 A4
Stonecrop Cl BH18 . . . . . .186 C1
Stoneham Cemetery Rd
SO18 . . . . .79 C2
Stoneham Cl
Petersfield GU32 . . . . .40 B2
Southampton SO16 . . . . . . .79 B3
Stoneham Ct SO16 . . . . . . .79 A3
Stoneham Gdns SO31 . . . .104 C1
Stoneham La
Chilworth SO50 . . . . .79 C4
Southampton SO16 . . . . . . .79 B3
Stoneham Pk GU32 . . . . . . .40 B2
Stoneham Way SO16,
SO18 . . . . .79 C3
Stonehills SO45 . . . . .151 B2
Stoneleigh **18** BH13 . . . . . .214 C4
Stoneleigh Ave SO41 . . . . .195 C2
Stoneleigh Cl PO16 . . . . . .156 A4
Stoner Hill Rd GU32 . . . . . .19 A1
Stoners Ct PO13 . . . . .155 A2
Stoney La SO22 . . . . .1 B3
Stony La Burton BH23 . . . .192 B1
Friefield Green GU32 . . . . . .18 C1
Portsmouth PO1 . . . . .182 A3
Stony La S BH23 . . . . .207 B3
Stonymoor Cl SO45 . . . . . .150 B2
Stopples La SO41 . . . . .195 C2
Storrington Rd PO8 . . . . . . .88 B3
Story La BH18 . . . . .187 A2
Stour Cl Ferndown BH21 . .164 B2
Petersfield GU31 . . . . .40 C1
West End SO18 . . . . .80 A2
West Wellow SO51 . . . . .50 B2
Stour Pk BH10 . . . . .189 C3
Stour Rd
Bournemouth BH8 . . . . . . .205 B3
Christchurch BH23 . . . . . . .207 A3
Stour View Gdns BH21 . . .162 C1
Stour Way BH23 . . . . .191 B1

Stour Wlk
Bournemouth BH8 . . . . . . .190 B2
11 Wimborne Minst BH21 .163 B2
Stourbank Rd BH23 . . . . . .207 A3
Stourcliffe Ave BH6 . . . . . .206 B2
Stourcroft Dr BH23 . . . . . .191 C1
Stourfield Fst & Jun Schs
BH6 . . . . .206 B3
Stourfield Rd BH5 . . . . . . .206 A2
Stourpaine Rd BH17 . . . . .187 A1
Stourton Cl **17** BH8 . . . . . .190 B2
Stourvale Ave BH23 . . . . . .206 B4
Stourvale Gdns SO53 . . . . . .55 B3
Stourvale Pl **10** BH5 . . . . . .206 A3
Stourvale Rd BH5,BH6 . . . .206 A3
Stourwood Ave BH6 . . . . . .206 B2
Stourwood Mans **4**
BH6 . . . . .206 B2
Stourwood Rd BH6 . . . . . . .206 B2
Stouts La BH23 . . . . .169 A1
Stow Cres PO15 . . . . .130 B1
Stowe Cl SO30 . . . . .81 B1
Stowe Rd PO4 . . . . .183 A2
Stradbrook PO13 . . . . .155 A1
Stragwyne Cl SO52 . . . . . . .53 C3
Straight Mile The SO51 . . .28 C1
Strand SO14 . . . . .103 A2
Strand St BH15 . . . . .202 B1
Strand The PO11 . . . . .185 B1
Stratfield Dr SO53 . . . . .30 A1
Stratfield Gdns PO9 . . . . . .135 B4
Stratfield Pk PO7 . . . . .134 B2
Stratfield Pl **10** BH25 . . . .194 C2
Stratford Ct **3** SO23 . . . . . .2 A1
Stratford Ho PO5 . . . . .215 B2
Stratford Pl
Eastleigh SO50 . . . . .56 A2
Lymington SO41 . . . . .197 B3
Stratford Rd PO7 . . . . .135 A4
Strathmore Dr BH31 . . . . . .115 A3
Strathmore Rd
Bournemouth BH9 . . . . . . .190 A2
Gosport PO12 . . . . .181 B2
Stratton Cl PO6 . . . . .157 B4
Stratton Rd
Bournemouth BH9 . . . . . . .190 B2
Southampton SO15 . . . . . . .78 B1
Winchester SO23 . . . . .11 B4
Strawberry Fields
East Boldre SO42 . . . . .175 B3
Hedge End SO30 . . . . .105 A3
Strawberry Hill SO31 . . . .128 C2
Strawberry Mead SO50 . . .57 A1
Streamleaze PO14 . . . . . . .129 B1
Street End SO52 . . . . .54 A3
Street The SP5 . . . . .24 A2
Streets La BH24 . . . . .141 B2
Strete Mount **10** BH23 . . .207 A4
Stretton Ct BH14 . . . . .203 A2
Stride Ave PO3 . . . . .183 A3
Strides La BH24 . . . . .140 C4
Strides Way SO40 . . . . . . .100 A4
Strode Gdns BH24 . . . . . . .140 A3
Strode Rd PO2 . . . . .157 B1
Strongs Cl SO51 . . . . .53 A4
Stroud Cl BH21 . . . . .164 A3
Stroud End GU32 . . . . .40 A2
Stroud Gdns BH23 . . . . . . .207 B4
Stroud Green La PO14 . . . .154 B3
Stroud La BH21 . . . . .207 C3
Stroud Park Ave BH23 . . . .207 C3
Stroud Sch SO51 . . . . .53 C4
Strouden Ave BH8 . . . . . . .205 B4
Strouden Court Prec
PO9 . . . . .135 B4
Strouden Ct PO9 . . . . .135 B4
Strouden Rd BH9 . . . . .190 A1
Stroudley Ave PO6 . . . . . . .158 B3
Stroudley Way SO30 . . . . . .81 B1
Stroudwood Rd
Fair Oak SO32 . . . . .58 A2
Havant PO9 . . . . .136 A2
Struan Cl BH24 . . . . .139 C3
Struan Dr BH24 . . . . .140 A3
Struan Dr BH24 . . . . .140 A3
Struan Gdns BH24 . . . . . . .139 C3
Stuart Bridgewater Ho
SO18 . . . . .104 A4
Stuart Cl
Stubbington PO14 . . . . . . .179 B3
Upton BH16 . . . . .201 A4
Stuart Cres SO22 . . . . .10 C3
Stuart Ct **7** PO6 . . . . .157 C4
Stuart Rd BH23 . . . . .209 A4
Stubbermere PO10 . . . . . . .136 C4
Stubbington Ave PO2 . . . . .157 C1
Stubbington Gn PO14 . . . .179 B3
Stubbington La PO14 . . . . .179 B3
Stubbington Study Ctr
PO14 . . . . .179 B2
Stubbs Dro SO30 . . . . .57 B1
Stubbs Rd SO19 . . . . .104 B1
Stuckton Rd SP6 . . . . .94 A4
Student Village BH12 . . . . .204 B4
Studland Cl SO16 . . . . .77 B1
Studland Dr SO41 . . . . . . .211 B3
Studland Rd
Bournemouth BH4 . . . . . . .204 B1
Lee-on-the-Solent PO13 . .179 C2
Southampton SO16 . . . . . . .77 B1
Studley Ave SO45 . . . . . . .150 B2
Studley Ct BH23 . . . . .209 B4
Studley Ct BH25 . . . . .209 B4
Sturminster Ho **4** SO16 . . .78 A1
Sturminster Rd BH9 . . . . . .190 A2
Styles The SP5 . . . . .22 B4
Sudbury Rd PO6 . . . . .157 B4

Suetts La SO32 . . . . .83 C4
Suffolk Ave
Christchurch BH23 . . . . . . .191 C1
Southampton SO15 . . . . . . .102 B4
Suffolk Cl
Chandler's Ford SO53 . . . . .55 B1
Wimborne Minst BH21 . . . .164 B3
Suffolk Dr
Chandler's Ford SO53 . . . . .55 B1
Swanwick SO15 . . . . .129 A4
Suffolk Gn SO53 . . . . .55 B1
Suffolk Rd
Bournemouth BH2 . . . . . . .204 B2
Bournemouth BH2 . . . . . . .204 C2
Portsmouth PO4 . . . . .183 A2
Suffolk Rd S BH2 . . . . .204 B2
Sullivan Cl PO6 . . . . .158 C4
Sullivan Rd SO19 . . . . .104 B2
Sullivan Way PO7 . . . . .134 C3
Sultan Rd
Emsworth PO10 . . . . .136 C1
Portsmouth PO1, PO2 . . . .182 B4
Sumar Cl PO14 . . . . .154 B3
Summer Field Cl BH21 . . . .164 A2
Summer Flds BH31 . . . . . .114 C2
Summerbee Comp Sch
BH8 . . . . .190 B1
Summerbee First Sch
BH8 . . . . .190 B1
Summerbee Jun Sch
BH8 . . . . .190 B1
Summercroft Way
BH22 . . . . .19 A2
Summerfield Cl BH23 . . . . .192 B1
Summerfield Ct PO13 . . . . .155 B3
Summerfield Gdns SO16 . . .79 B3
Summerfields
Bournemouth BH7 . . . . . . .205 C4
Locks Heath SO31 . . . . . . .129 A1
Summerhill Rd PO8 . . . . . .112 A2
Summerlands Rd SO50 . . . .57 B1
Summerleigh Wlk PO14 .154 B3
Summers Ave BH11 . . . . . .189 A3
Summers La BH23 . . . . . . .192 B1
Summers St SO14 . . . . .103 B3
Summersfield Cl SO32 . . . .20 C2
Summertrees Ct BH25 . . . .195 B2
Summit Way SO18 . . . . .79 C1
Sumner Rd GU31 . . . . .65 B3
Sun Ct PO5 . . . . .215 C2
Sun St PO1 . . . . .182 A3
Sunbeam Way PO12 . . . . . .181 A2
Sunbury Cl BH11 . . . . .189 A3
Sunbury Ct
8 Bournemouth BH2 . . . .204 C2
Fareham PO15 . . . . .130 C2
Suncourt Villas PO12 . . . . .180 C4
Sunderland Dr BH23 . . . . . .208 A4
Sunderton La PO8 . . . . .88 B3
Sundew Cl
Christchurch BH23 . . . . . . .193 B1
New Milton BH25 . . . . . . .195 B2
Sundew Rd BH18 . . . . .186 C1
Sundridge Cl PO6 . . . . .157 C4
Sunningdale
Christchurch BH23 . . . . . . .206 C3
Hythe SO45 . . . . .125 C2
6 Poole BH15 . . . . .202 C2
Sunningdale Cl
6 Bishopstoke SO50 . . . . .56 C1
Gosport PO13 . . . . .155 B1
Sunningdale Cres BH10 . . .189 B2
Sunningdale Cvn Pk
SO21 . . . . .31 C1
Sunningdale Gdns
Broadstone BH18 . . . . .187 A3
Southampton SO18 . . . . . . .104 A4
Sunningdale Rd
Portchester PO16 . . . . .156 B4
Portsmouth PO3 . . . . .183 A4
Sunny Hill Cl BH22 . . . . . . .203 B3
Sunny Hill Rd BH12 . . . . . .203 B3
Sunny Way SO40 . . . . .100 C4
Sunny Wlk PO1 . . . . .182 A3
Sunnybank Rd BH21 . . . . .164 A3
Sunnybank Way BH21 . . . .164 A3
Sunnydown Rd SO22 . . . . .10 A2
Sunnyfield Rd BH25 . . . . . .210 A4
Sunnyfield Rise SO31 . . . . .105 A1
Sunnyhills PO6 . . . . .158 B4
Sunnyheath PO9 . . . . .135 C2
Sunnyhill Rd BH6 . . . . .206 B3
Sunnylands Ave BH6 . . . . .206 C2
Sunnymead Dr PO7 . . . . . .111 B1
Sunnymoor Rd BH11 . . . . .189 A1
Sunnyside Rd BH21 . . . . . .203 B3
Sunnyside Wlk PO9 . . . . . .135 B4
Sunridge Cl BH12 . . . . .204 A4
Sunrise Ct BH22 . . . . .165 B3
Sunset Ave SO40 . . . . .100 C4
Sunset Lo BH13 . . . . .204 A1
Sunset Rd SO40 . . . . .100 C4
Sunshine Ave PO11 . . . . . .185 A1
Suntrap Gdns PO14 . . . . . .185 A1
Sunvale Cl SO19 . . . . .104 A2
Sunwood Rd PO9 . . . . .135 B3
Surbiton Rd SO50 . . . . .56 A3
Surrey Cl
Christchurch BH23 . . . . . . .191 C1
Totton SO40 . . . . .100 B3
Surrey Ct SO15 . . . . .102 B3
Surrey Gdns BH24 . . . . . . .204 B2
Surrey Ho SO53 . . . . .55 B2

Surrey House Inf Sch
SO19 . . . . .104 B2
Surrey Rd
Bournemouth BH2,BH4 . . .204 A2
Chandler's Ford SO53 . . . . .55 B2
Poole BH12 . . . . .204 A2
Southampton SO19 . . . . . . .103 B1
Surrey Rd S BH4 . . . . .204 B2
Surrey St PO1 . . . . .215 B3
Sussex Cl BH9 . . . . .190 A2
Sussex Ct PO5 . . . . .215 B1
Sussex Gdns GU31 . . . . . . .40 C1
Sussex Pl
Portsmouth PO1 . . . . .215 B4
Portsmouth PO5 . . . . .215 B1
Sussex Rd
Chandler's Ford SO53 . . . . .55 B2
Petersfield GU31 . . . . .41 A1
Portsmouth PO5 . . . . .215 B1
Southampton SO14 . . . . . . .103 A2
Sussex St SO23 . . . . .10 C4
Sussex Terr PO5 . . . . .215 B1
Sutherland Ave BH18 . . . . .187 B3
Sutherland Cl **6** SO51 . . . . .28 A1
Sutherland Ct SO53 . . . . . .55 B3
Sutherland Rd
Portsmouth PO4 . . . . .182 C2
Southampton SO16 . . . . . . .77 C3
Sutherlands Way SO53 . . . .55 A4
Sutton Cl Poole BH17 . . . . .188 A1
Portsmouth PO3 . . . . .158 A2
Sutton Rd
Bournemouth BH9 . . . . . . .190 A1
Poole BH17 . . . . .188 A1
Sutton Gdns SO23 . . . . . . .11 A4
Sutton Pl SO42 . . . . .146 A1
Sutton Rd
Bournemouth BH9 . . . . . . .190 A1
Totton SO40 . . . . .76 C1
Waterlooville PO8 . . . . .111 B2
Swale Dr SO53 . . . . .55 A4
Swallow Cl
Broadstone BH17 . . . . .201 C4
Havant PO9 . . . . .136 A1
Totton SO40 . . . . .100 A3
Swallow Cl Clanfield PO8 . .88 A3
Lee-on-the-Solent PO13 . .179 C2
Swallow Dr SO41 . . . . .211 C2
Swallow Sq SO50 . . . . .55 B1
Swallow Way BH21 . . . . . .164 A4
Swallow Wood PO16 . . . . .131 A2
Swan Cl Emsworth PO10 . .161 A4
Swanwick SO31 . . . . .128 B3
Swan Ct Burslecon SO31 . .128 B4
Gosport PO13 . . . . .155 A2
Swan Ctr The SO50 . . . . . . .56 A1
Swan Gn **8** BH23 . . . . . . .207 A3
Swan La SO23 . . . . .10 C4
Swan Mead BH24 . . . . .141 B3
Swan Quay
Portchester PO16 . . . . .155 B4
Southampton SO18 . . . . . . .103 B4
Swan St GU32 . . . . .40 C2
Swanage Cl SO19 . . . . .104 C2
Swanage Rd PO13 . . . . . . .179 C1
Swancote PO16 . . . . .156 A4
Swanley Cl SO50 . . . . .56 A3
Swanmore Ave SO19 . . . . .104 B2
Swanmore Bsns Pk SO32 .83 C3
Swanmore CE Prim Sch
SO32 . . . . .84 A3
Swanmore Cl
Bournemouth BH7 . . . . . . .206 A4
Winchester SO22 . . . . .1 B2
Swanmore Rd
Bournemouth BH7 . . . . . . .206 A4
Droxford SO32 . . . . .84 C4
Havant PO9 . . . . .135 A3
Swanmore SO32 . . . . .84 A3
Swanmore Sec Sch SO32 . .84 A2
Swans Wlk PO11 . . . . .185 A2
Swansbury Dr BH8 . . . . . . .191 A1
Swanton Cl PO14 . . . . .154 B2
Swanton Gdns SO31 . . . . . .55 A4
Swanwick Bsns Ctr
SO31 . . . . .128 B4
Swanwick La SO31 . . . . . . .128 C4
Swanwick Nature Reserve*
SO31 . . . . .128 B4
Swanwick Shore Rd
SO31 . . . . .128 B4
Swanwick Sta SO31 . . . . . .129 A3
Swarraton Rd PO9 . . . . . . .136 A3
Sway Cl **50** Havant PO9 . . .136 A3
Sway SO41 . . . . .196 B4
Sway Gdns BH8 . . . . .190 B1
Sway Park Ind Est SO41 . .172 A1
Sway Rd
Brockenhurst SO42 . . . . . .172 C4
Hordle SO41 . . . . .197 A3
Lymington SO41 . . . . .197 A4
New Milton BH25 . . . . . . .195 B3
Sway Sta SO41 . . . . .172 A1
Swaythling Prim Sch
SO17 . . . . .79 A2
Swaythling Rd
Havant PO9 . . . . .135 B3
West End SO18,SO30 . . . . .80 A1
Swaythling Sta SO18 . . . . . .79 B2
Swedish Hos SO41 . . . . . . .198 C4
Sweep The BH24 . . . . .140 C4
Sweetbriar Gdns PO7 . . . . .134 C3
Sweethills Cres PO15 . . . . .129 B4
Sweyns Lease SO42 . . . . . .175 B3
Swift Cl Broadstone BH17 . .201 C4
Eastleigh SO50 . . . . .55 B1
Horndean PO8 . . . . .112 A4
Lee-on-the-Solent PO13 . .179 C2
Winchester SO22 . . . . .10 B3

Swift Gdns S019 ....103 B1
Swift Hollow S019 ......103 B1
Swift Rd
  Southampton S019 ....103 B1
  Thorney Island PO10 ....161 A2
Swinburn Gdns PO8 ....111 C2
Swincombe Rise S018 ....80 A1
Swiss Rd PO7 ....134 C4
Switch House Rd S045 ..151 C1
Swivelton La PO17 ....132 A2
Sword Cl Clanfield PO8 ...88 A3
  Gosport PO12 ....180 C1
Sword Sands Rd PO3 ...183 B4
Swordfish Dr BH23 .....208 A4
Sycamore Ave S033 ......30 B1
Sycamore Cl
  Broadstone BH17 ....186 C1
  Bursledon S031 ....127 C4
  Christchurch BH23 ......206 B4
  Clanfield PO8 ....88 B3
  Gosport PO13 ....155 C1
  Milford on Sea S041 ....211 B3
  North Baddesley S052 ...53 C3
  Romsey S051 ....53 B3
  Waterlooville PO8 ......129 B1
Sycamore Ct
  Fordingbridge SP6 ....69 C1
  Ringwood BH24 ....117 B1
Sycamore Dr
  Holbury S045 ....150 A3
  Kings Worthy S023 ....2 A4
  South Hayling PO11 ....184 C2
Sycamore Pl BH21 ......164 B3
Sycamore Rd
  Bishop's Waltham S032 ...83 C4
  Hordle S041 ....195 C2
  Hythe S045 ....125 C2
  Southampton S016 ....78 A1
Sycamore Wlk S030 ....105 C4
Sycamores The 9 S045 .126 A2
Sydenham Ct PO1 ....215 D3
Sydenham Terr
  Portsmouth PO1 ....215 D3
  Westbourne PO10 ....137 A3
Sydling Cl BH17 ....188 A1
Sydmanton Cl S051 ......53 A3
Sydmonton Ct PO9 .....136 A3
Sydney Ave S031 ....127 C2
Sydney Ho PO1 ....215 B4
Sydney Rd
  Bishopstoke S050 ....56 B2
  Broadstone BH18 ....187 A2
  Christchurch BH23 .....191 C1
  Gosport PO12 ....181 A2
  Southampton S015 ....79 B4
Syers Cl GU33 ....20 C2
Syers Rd GU33 ....20 C2
Sylmor Gdns BH9 ....190 A1
Sylvan Ave S019 ....104 B3
Sylvan Cl Hordle S041 ..196 A1
  St Leonards BH24 ......139 B2
Sylvan Dr S052 ....53 C2
Sylvan Fst Sch BH12 ...203 A3
Sylvan La S031 ....128 A1
Sylvan Rd BH12 ....203 A3
Sylvan View PO7 ....134 C3
Sylvans The S045 ......125 B2
Sylvia Cres S040 ....76 C1
Symes Rd
  Hamworthy BH15 ....201 C2
  Romsey S051 ....53 A4
Symonds Cl S033 ....55 B2
Symonds St S023 ....11 A4
Sywell Cres PO3 ....158 B2

T

Tadburn Cl
  Chandler's Ford S053 ...55 B3
  Romsey S051 ....53 A4
Tadburn Gn S051 ....52 C3
Tadburn Rd S051 ....53 A3
Tadden Cotts BH21 ....162 B4
Tadden Wlk BH18 ......186 C1
Tadfield Cres S051 .....53 A4
Tadfield Rd S051 ....53 A4
Tadhurst Ho 4 PO1 ....215 C3
Tait Cl BH17 ....202 C4
Tait Pl PO13 ....155 B1
Talbot Ave BH3 ....204 A4
Talbot Cl Havant PO9 ..135 B2
  Southampton S016 ....78 C2
Talbot Comb Sch BH12 ..204 A4
Talbot Ct
  Bournemouth BH9 .....189 C1
  11 Southampton S014 ...103 A2
Talbot Dr
  Christchurch BH23 ....193 C1
  Poole BH12 ....204 A4
Talbot Heath Sch BH4 .204 B4
Talbot Hill Rd BH9 ....204 B4
Talbot House Prep Sch
  BH9 ....204 C4
Talbot Manor BH3 ....204 B4
Talbot Mdws BH12 ....204 A4
Talbot Mews S014 ....189 A1
Talbot Rd
  Bournemouth BH9 ....204 C4
  Havant PO9 ....135 B2
  Hythe S045 ....125 C1
  Locks Heath PO14 ....129 C1
  Portsmouth PO4 ......182 C2
Talbot Rdbt BH3 ......204 B4
Talbot Rise BH10 .....189 B1
Talisman Bsns Ctr S031 .129 A3
Tall Trees S045 ....203 A3

Talland Rd PO14 ....129 A1
Tamar Cl Ferndown BH22 .166 A3
  Portchester PO16 ......132 A1
Tamar Down PO7 ....135 A4
Tamar Gdns S018 ....80 A1
Tamar Gr S045 ....125 C2
Tamarisk Cl
  Portsmouth PO4 ....183 B2
  Southampton PO14 .....179 B3
  Waterlooville PO7 .....135 A3
Tamarisk Gdns S018 ...103 C4
Tamarisk Rd S030 .....105 A4
Tamella Rd S030 ....105 C3
Tammys Turn PO14 ....154 A4
Tamorisk Dr S040 .....100 B3
Tamworth Ct 8 PO12 ..181 A2
Tamworth Rd
  Bournemouth BH7 ......205 C3
  Portsmouth PO13 ......183 A1
Tan Howse Cl BH7 .....206 A4
Tanfield La PO17 ....108 A2
Tanfield Pk PO17 ......108 A2
Tangier La S032 ....83 A4
Tangier Rd PO3 ....183 A4
Tanglewood
  Fareham PO16 ....131 A2
  Marchwood S040 ....102 A1
Tanglewood Cl PO7 ....134 B2
Tanglewood Ct 11 BH25 .195 A2
Tanglewood La PO17 ...201 C4
Tangley Wlk PO9 ......136 A3
Tangmere Cl BH23 .....208 A3
Tangmere Dr S016 ....78 A2
Tangmere Pl BH17 .....202 C4
Tangyes Cl PO14 ......154 B2
Tanhouse Cl S030 ......105 B3
Tanhouse La
  Botley S030 ....105 B2
  Hedge End S030 ....105 B3
Tankerdale La GU33 .....41 B4
Tankerton Cl 3 PO6 ...157 C4
Tankerville Rd S019 ...103 B2
Tankerville Specl Sch
  S050 ....56 A2
Tanner St 28 S023 ......11 A4
Tanner's Brook Way
  S015 ....101 C3
Tanner's La PO17 ....111 A3
Tanner's Ridge PO7 ...134 C2
Tanneries Ind Est The
  PO9 ....135 C1
Tanners Brook Jun Sch
  S015 ....101 C4
Tanners La Boldre S041 .199 A2
  Gosport PO14 ....154 C3
  Sandleheath SP6 ....68 C2
  West Wellow S051 ....51 B4
Tanners Rd S052 ....54 A2
Tanners The PO14 .....129 B1
Tansy Cl PO7 ....135 A3
Tansy Mdw S053 ....54 C2
Tanyards The S053 ......30 A1
Taplin Dr S030 ....105 B4
Taplings Cl S022 ....1 B2
Taplings Rd S022 ....1 B2
Tapper Ct BH21 ....163 C2
Taranto Rd S016 ....78 B2
Tarbery Cres PO8 .....112 B4
Tardif Ho S016 ....78 A1
Target Rd PO2 ....157 B1
Tarius Cl PO13 ....155 B2
Tarleton Rd PO6 ....133 A1
Tarn Dr BH17 ....201 C4
Tarn Rise PO8 ....189 C1
Tarrant Cl BH17 ......187 C1
Tarrant Gdns PO17 ....135 B2
Tarrant Rd BH9 ....190 A2
Tasman Cl
  Christchurch BH23 ....206 C4
  Southampton S014 ....103 A1
Tasman Cl S014 ....103 A1
Taswell Rd PO5 ....182 B1
Tatchbury La S040 .....76 A1
Tatchbury Mount Hospl
  S040 ....76 A1
Tate Ct S015 ....101 B4
Tate Mews S015 ....101 B4
Tate Rd S015 ....101 B4
Tates Rd Hythe S045 ...126 A1
  Hythe S045 ....126 A1
Tatnam Rd BH15 ....202 B2
Tattenham Rd S042 ...172 C4
Tattershall Cres PO16 .156 A4
Tatum Cres BH15 .....202 B2
Tatwin Cl S019 ....104 B3
Tatwin Cres S019 .....104 B3
Taunton Coll S015 .....78 C1
Taunton Dr S018 ......104 A4
Taunton Row S053 .....55 B2
Tavell's La GU40 ......101 C1
Tavells Cl S040 ....100 A1
Taverner Cl BH15 .....202 B1
Taverners Cl S019 .....104 B2
Tavistock Cl S051 ......28 A1
Tavistock Gdns PO9 ...136 A1
Tavy Cl S053 ....55 A3
Tawny Owl Cl PO14 ...154 A2
Taylor Cl S019 ....103 B1
Taylor Dr BH8 ....190 B2
Taylor Rd PO12 ....181 B1
Taylor Way BH11 .....115 A3
Taylor's Bldgs BH15 ..202 B1
Taylors Cnr S023 ......2 A3
Teachers Terr 6 GU33 ..20 C2
Teachers Way S045 ...150 A2

Teak Cl BH13 ....214 D4
Teal Cl Horndean PO8 ..112 A4
  Portchester PO16 .....155 C4
  South Hayling PO11 ...185 A2
  Totton S040 ....100 B4
Teal Wlk PO13 ....155 A2
Teapot Row PO4 ......183 A1
Teasel Way PO22 .....138 C1
Teazle Cl GU31 ....41 B1
Tebourba Cotts S041 ..172 A1
Tebourba Dr PO12 ....181 A2
Tebourba Ho 6 PO14 .154 C4
Tebourba Way
  Curdridge S030 ....106 B4
  Southampton S016 ....101 C4
Technology Rd BH17 ..202 A4
Ted Kelly Ct 25 PO1 ..182 A3
Tedder Cl BH11 ....189 A2
Tedder Gdns BH11 ....189 A2
Tedder Rd
  Bournemouth BH11 ....189 A2
  Gosport PO13 ....155 B2
  Southampton S018 ....104 A4
Tedder Way S040 .....100 B4
Teddington Rd PO4 ....183 A2
Tees Cl S053 ....55 A4
Tees Farm Rd S021 ....56 C4
Tees Gn 2 S021 ....56 C4
Teg Down GU31 ....41 A2
Teg Down Meads S022 ..1 B1
Teglease Gn PO9 ......135 B4
Teignmouth Rd
  Gosport PO12 ....180 C4
  Portsmouth PO3 ......183 A4
Telegraph Rd S030 ....80 C1
Telegraph Way S021 ...12 A4
Telephone Rd PO4 ....182 C2
Telford Gdns S030 .....81 C1
Telford Rd
  Fareham BH21 ....165 A4
  Portsmouth PO2 ......157 C2
Telford Way PO15 ....129 B3
Teme Cres S016 ....101 C4
Teme Rd S016 ....101 C4
Tempest Ave PO7 .....135 A4
Templar Ct 22 S014 ...103 A4
Templars Mede S053 ...55 A2
Templars Way S053 ....55 A2
Temple Gdns S019 ....103 C1
Temple La GU32 ....63 C4
Temple Mews BH1 ....205 B3
Temple Rd Liss GU33 ...21 A3
  Southampton S019 ....103 C1
Temple St PO1 ....215 B4
Templecombe Rd S040 ..56 C1
Templemere PO14 ....154 A4
Templer Cl BH11 ......188 C1
Templeton Cl PO2 ....157 C2
Tenby Cl S018 ....104 A4
Tenby Dr S053 ....55 A2
Tench Way S051 ....52 C4
Tennyson Cl
  Bishop's Waltham S032 .83 C4
  Holbury S045 ....150 A3
Tennyson Cres PO7 ...111 B1
Tennyson Ct
  22 Southampton S017 ..79 A1
  37 Southampton S017 ..79 A1
Tennyson Gdns PO16 ..131 A1
Tennyson Rd
  Bournemouth BH9 .....189 C1
  Eastleigh S050 ....55 C1
  1 Poole BH14 ....203 A2
  Portsmouth PO2 ......182 C4
  Southampton S017 .....79 A1
  Totton S040 ....79 B1
  Wimborne Minst BH21 ..163 B3
Tensing Cl PO16 ......131 A2
Tensing Rd BH23 .....207 C4
Tenterton Ave S019 ...104 A1
Terence Ave BH17 ....187 B1
Terence Rd PO21 .....186 B3
Terminus Terr S014 ...103 A2
Tern Cl S045 ....126 A1
Tern Ct BH6 ....206 B3
Tern Wlk PO13 ....155 A2
Terne La S016 ....77 B3
Terrace Mews PO2 ....204 C2
Terrace The
  Damerham SP6 ....68 B3
  Rockbourne SP6 ....68 C4
Terrier Cl S030 ....81 B2
Terrington Ave BH23 ..193 C1
Terriote Cl S053 ....55 B4
Test Cl GU31 ....40 C1
Test Ho S051 ....52 B4
Test La S016 ....77 A1
Test Mills S051 ....52 B4
Test Rd S014 ....103 B3
Test Valley Bsns Ctr
  S016 ....77 B1
Test Valley Bsns Pk
  S052 ....54 A3
Testbourne Ave S040 .100 B4
Testbourne Cl S040 ...100 B4
Testcombe Rd PO12 ..181 A2
Testlands Ave S016 ....77 B3
Testwood Ave S040 ....76 C1
Testwood Cres S040 ...76 B1
Testwood La S040 ....101 A4
Testwood Pl S040 ....101 A4
Testwood Rd
  Havant PO9 ....135 B3
  Southampton S015 ...102 A3
Testwood Sch S040 ....76 C1
Tethering Dro SP6 .....47 B2
Tetney Cl S019 ....104 C2
Tetsome Cotts PO17 ..130 C4

Tewkesbury Ave
  Fareham PO15 ....130 B2
  Gosport PO12 ....181 A4
Tewkesbury Cl PO6 ...157 B4
Texas Dr S022 ....10 A2
Thackeray Mall 26
  PO16 ....131 A1
Thackeray Rd S017 ...103 A4
Thackeray Sq 4 PO16 .131 B1
Thacking Gn 3 S021 ...56 C4
Thames Alley 18 BH15 .202 A1
Thames Cl
  Fareham BH22 ....166 A3
  West End S018 ....80 A2
Thames Ct 1 PO8 .....111 C2
Thames Dr PO15 ......130 B2
Thames Mews 17 BH15 .202 A1
Thames Rd S018 ....80 A2
Thamesmead Cl PO12 .180 C4
Thatchers La
  Boldre S041 ....198 C4
  Sopley BH23 ....68 C2
Theatre Mews 2 PO5 .182 B1
Theobold Rd BH24 ....191 A4
Theseus Rd PO13 .....179 B2
Thessaly Cl BH17 .....205 C2
Thetchers Cl BH25 ....195 A3
Thetford Gdns S053 ....55 A4
Thetford Rd
  Gosport PO13 ....180 C4
  Poole BH12 ....203 C3
Thicket The
  Gosport PO13 ....155 C1
  Portchester PO16 .....131 C1
  Portsmouth PO5 ......215 C5
  Romsey S051 ....53 B3
  Waterlooville PO7 ....134 B2
Third Ave Cosham PO6 .157 C4
  Havant PO9 ....136 A1
  Southampton S015 ...101 C3
Thirlmere S050 ....55 C1
Thirlmere Cl PO14 ....154 B2
Thirlmere Ho 68 PO6 ..157 A4
Thirlmere Rd S016 ....77 C1
Thirlstane Firs S053 ...55 A2
Thistle Rd
  Chandler's Ford S053 ..54 C3
  Hedge End S030 ......105 A4
Thistlebarrow Rd BH7 .205 C3
Thistledown PO8 ......112 A3
Thistledowne Gdns
  PO10 ....161 A4
Thomas Cl S040 ......100 B3
Thomas Lewis Way S016,
  S017 ....79 B1
Thomas Lockyer Cl
  BH31 ....115 A3
Thomas Rd S052 ......54 A2
Thompson's La S037 ...63 B4
Thoresby Cl BH25 ....194 C2
Thorn Cl Eastleigh S050 .56 A3
  Petersfield GU31 ......41 B1
Thorn Rd BH17 ....187 B2
Thornbrake Rd PO12 .181 B2
Thornbury 10 BH4 ....204 B2
Thornbury Ave
  Blackfield S045 ....177 C4
  Southampton S015 ...102 C4
Thornbury Cl PO14 ...154 B4
Thornbury Ho 20 PO6 .132 C1
Thornbury Hts S031 ...30 C1
Thornbury Rd BH6 ....207 A2
Thornbury Wood S030 .30 C1
Thorncliff Rd PO3 .....158 A2
Thorncliffe Cl PO2 ....157 C2
Thorncombe Cl
  Bournemouth BH9 ....190 A2
  Poole BH17 ....187 C1
Thorncroft Rd PO11 ..182 C2
Thorndike Sch S053 ...55 C4
Thorndike Cl S016 .....78 A1
Thorndike Rd S016 ....77 C1
Thorne Cl BH31 ....114 C3
Thorne Way BH21 ....139 A3
Thornfield Cl BH23 ...206 C4
Thornfield Dr BH23 ...193 C1
Thorngate Cl S041 ...196 C2
Thorngate Way 22 PO1 .182 A2
Thornham La S031 ....161 B3
Thornham Rd BH25 ...195 B2
Thornhill Ave S019 ...104 B3
Thornhill Cl S045 ....150 C1
Thornhill Park Rd S018 .104 C3
Thornhill Prim Sch
  S019 ....104 B3
Thornhill Rd
  Blackfield S045 ....150 C1
  Southampton S016 .....78 B2

Thorni Ave PO15 ......130 B2
Thornleigh Rd S019 ...103 C1
Thornley Rd BH10 ....189 B2
Thorns La S041 ....199 C3
Thornton Ave S031 ....128 B1
Thornton Cl
  Corfe Mullen BH21 ....186 B3
  Waterlooville PO7 ....134 A1
Thornton Rd PO12 ....181 A4
Thornworthy 4 S045 ..125 C1
Thorogood Ct 2 BH15 .202 C2
Thorold Ct S018 ....79 C1
Thorold Rd
  Chandler's Ford S053 ...30 C1
  Southampton S018 .....79 C1
Three Acre Dr BH25 ..209 C4
Three Acres PO7 .....111 A2
Three Cross Rd BH21,
  BH22 ....138 C3
Three Horse Shoes La
  S024 ....16 C1
Three Legged Cross First Sch
  BH21 ....114 C1
Three Lions Cl 12 BH21 .163 A3
Three Oaks S019 .....104 C2
Three Tun Cl 21 PO1 ..182 A3
Threefield La S014 ....103 A2
Thresher Cl PO7 ......112 B1
Throop Cl BH8 ....191 A1
Throop Rd
  Bournemouth BH8 ....190 C2
  Bournemouth BH8 ....191 A1
Throopside Ave BH9 ..190 B2
Thrush Rd BH12 ......188 B1
Thrush Wlk PO8 ......111 C2
Thruxton Ct S019 ....103 C2
Thruxton Rd PO9 .....135 B3
Thurbern Rd PO2 .....157 C1
Thurmell Cl S030 .....105 B2
Thurmell Wlk S030 ...105 B2
Thurmond Cres S022 ..10 B2
Thurmond Rd S022 ....10 B3
Thursby Rd BH23 .....193 C1
Thurston Cl S033 ......55 B4
Thwaite Rd BH12 .....204 A3
Thyme Ave PO15 .....129 B4
Tichborne Rd
  Eastleigh S050 ....80 A4
  Southampton S018 ...104 B4
Tichborne Way PO13 .155 B1
Tichbourne Ho S030 ..105 B4
Tickleford Dr S019 ...104 A1
Tickner Cl S030 ......105 A4
Ticonderoga Gdns
  S019 ....103 C1
Tidcombe Gn PO9 ....135 B4
Tidemill Cl BH23 .....207 A4
Tides Reach S018 ....103 B4
Tides Way S040 ......101 C1
Tideway Gdns PO4 ...183 B2
Tidworth Rd PO9 .....135 C2
Tiffany Cl S041 ....195 C2
Tiffield Cl PO3 ....158 B2
Tiger Rd PO1 ....181 C4
Tilbrook Rd S015 .....102 A4
Tilburg Rd BH23 .....207 B4
Tilden Rd S021 ....31 B3
Tilebarn La S042 .....173 A3
Tilford Rd PO8 ....111 C3
Tillingbourn PO14 ...129 B2
Tillington Gdns PO8 ...88 B2
Tilmore Gdns GU32 ...40 C3
Tilmore Rd GU32 .....40 C3
Timber La BH17 ......134 B2
Timberlane PO7 ......134 B2
Timberley Ho 2 PO11 .215 C3
Timberley La SP5 .....48 A3
Timberly Cl S045 .....150 B2
Timbermill Ct S041 ...93 C4
Timbers The PO15 ...130 B1
Timor Cl PO15 ....129 B4
Timothy Cl BH10 .....189 B3
Timpson Rd PO2 .....215 D4
Timsbury Cres PO9 ..135 C1
Timsbury Ct S053 ....103 C2
Timsbury Dr S016 ....77 C1
Timson Cl S040 ......100 B3
Tincleton Gdns BH9 ..190 A2
Tindale Rd S016 ....77 C1
Tinker Alley S018 .....80 A4
Tinkers Cross SP6 ....69 C2
Tinneys Cl SP5 ....47 B2
Tintagel Cl S023 ......78 B3
Tintagel Way PO6 ....132 C4
Tintern Cl PO7 ....134 A1
Tintern Ct 15 S015 ...102 C3
Tintern Rd PO12 .....181 A2
Tipner Gn PO2 ....157 B2
Tipner La PO2 ....157 B2
Tipner Rd PO2 ....157 B1
Tiptoe Gn 20 PO9 ....136 A3
Tiptoe Prim Sch S041 .195 B4
Tiptoe Rd BH25 ......171 A1
Tiptop Ho PO5 ....215 B2
Tiptree Cl S050 ....56 A3
Tisted Ct 28 PO9 .....56 A3
Titchbone Gr PO9 ....135 B3
Titchfield Abbey PO15 .130 A1
Titchfield Hill PO14 ..154 A4
Titchfield Industries
  PO14 ....154 A4
Titchfield La PO15, PO17 .130 B2
Titchfield Park Rd PO15 .129 B2
Titchfield Prim Sch
  PO14 ....129 C1

Titchfield Rd P014 ....154 A3
Tithe Barn S041 ....197 C3
Tithe Mead S051 ....27 C1
The The P07 ....110 C2
Tithelands La S024 ....15 C2
Tithewood Cl S053 ....30 A1
Titus Gdns P07 ....135 A4
Tiverton Cl
24 Bournemouth BH4 ......204 B2
1 Fareham PO16 ....131 B1
Tivoli Cl S053 ....55 C4
Toby St P01 ....215 B4
Todber Cl BH11 ....188 C2
Tokar St P04 ....183 A1
Tokio Rd P03 ....158 A1
Tolefrey Gdns S053 ....54 C3
Tollard Cl P014 ....203 C4
Tollbar Way S030 ....81 A1
Tollerford Rd BH17 ....187 B1
Tollgate S053 ....55 B1
Tollgate Ests S051 ....27 A2
Tollgate Rd S031 ....128 B4
Tollgate The 20 S023 ......2 A1
Tolpuddle Gdns BH9 ....190 A2
Tolstoi Rd BH14 ....203 A3
Tomkyns Cl S053 ....54 C3
Tonbridge St P05 ....182 B1
Tonge Rd BH11 ....189 A3
Tonnant Cl P014 ....179 B3
Toogoods Way S051 ....77 B3
Toomer Rd S045 ....150 C1
Toothill Rd S051 ....53 B1
Top La BH24 ....141 A4
Topaz Gr P07 ....135 A4
Topiary Gdns S031 ....129 A2
Tor Cl Portchester PO16 ....131 C1
Waterlooville P07 ....134 C2
Tor Way GU31 ....41 A2
Torbay Rd BH14 ....203 B2
Torberry Dr GU31 ....41 A1
Torch Cl S050 ....57 A1
Torcross Cl S019 ....103 C1
Torfrida Ct P04 ....183 B2
Tormead S045 ....125 C2
Tornay Gr S052 ....53 C2
Toronto Pl P014 ....181 A3
Toronto Rd P02 ....182 C4
Torquay Ave
Gosport P012 ....181 A4
Southampton S015 ....102 B4
Torre Cl S019 ....104 C2
Torre Cl S050 ....56 A3
Torridge Gdns S018 ....80 A2
Torrington Cl S019 ....104 A2
Torrington Rd P02 ....157 C2
Torworth Cl P014 ....154 B4
Torwood Gdns S050 ....56 C1
Tosson Cl S016 ....101 C4
Totland Cl S016 ....101 C4
Totland Ct 8 S041 ....211 B2
Totland Rd Cosham PO6 ....157 C4
Gosport P013 ....155 B1
Totmel Rd BH17 ....188 A1
Totnes Cl S050 ....55 C3
Tottehale Cl S052 ....53 C2
Tottenham Rd P01 ....215 C4
Totton & Eling Heritage Ctr*
S040 ....101 A3
Totton By Pass S040 ....101 A4
Totton Coll S040 ....100 B4
Totton Recn Ctr S040 ......100 C4
Totton Sta S040 ....101 A4
Totton Western By-Pass
S040 ....101 A4
Totton Wlk 18 P09 ....135 B3
Tournerbury La P011 ....185 A2
Tourney Rd BH11 ....188 C3
Tourney Pl S023 ....2 B4
Towans The BH13 ....214 B2
Tower Cl P012 ....180 B2
Tower Ct
Bournemouth BH2 ....204 C1
Locks Heath S031 ....128 B1
10 Winchester S023 ....10 C4
Tower Gdns 4 S016 ....78 C2
Tower Ho S019 ....103 C1
Tower Ind Est The S050 .....56 B1
Toms La BH24 ....56 B1
Wimborne Minst BH21 .....159 A4
Tower Park Rdbt BH15 .....202 C4
Tower Pl S030 ....80 B1
Tower Rd
Bournemouth BH1 ....205 C3
Poole BH13 ....204 A1
Portsmouth P04 ....182 C2
Winchester S022 ....10 C4
Tower Rd W BH13 ....204 A1
Tower St Emsworth PO10 ...161 A4
Portsmouth P01 ....215 A2
Winchester S023 ....10 C4
Tower The 10 P012 ....181 A3
Towers Farm BH21 ....186 B4
Towers Gdn P09 ....159 C3
Towers Way BH21 ....186 B4
Town Hall Rd P09 ....135 C1
Town La GU32 ....41 A3
Town Quay
Portsmouth P01 ....181 C2
Southampton S014 ....103 A2
Towngate Bridge BH15 ....202 B2
Towngate Sh Ctr 1
BH15 ....202 B1
Townhill Inf Sch S018 ......80 A1
Townhill Jun Sch S018 .....80 A1

Townhill Park House (The
Gregg Sch) S018 ....80 A2
Townhill Way S018 ....80 A1
Townsend Cl BH11 ....188 C2
Townsend La SP6 ....42 C2
Townsend Prim & Com Sch
BH8 ....191 A1
Townsville Rd BH9 ....190 A1
Towpath Mead P04 ....183 B2
Toynbee Cl S050 ....56 A2
Toynbee Rd S050 ....56 A2
Toynbee Sch The S053 .....55 C3
Tozer Cl BH11 ....188 C1
Tracey Ct BH23 ....209 A4
Trafalgar Cl S053 ....55 A3
Trafalgar Ct
Christchurch BH23 ....207 C3
Fareham P014 ....154 C4
26 Portsmouth P05 ....182 B1
Trafalgar Pl
Lymington S041 ....197 C2
Portsmouth P01 ....215 D4
Trafalgar Rd
Bournemouth BH9 ....204 C4
Southampton S015 ....102 B3
Trafalgar Sq P012 ....181 A3
Trafalgar St S023 ....10 C4
Trafalgar Way 14 S045 ....126 A1
Trafford Way S030 ....57 B1
Trampers La P017 ....109 A2
Tranby Rd S019 ....103 C2
Tranmere Cl S041 ....197 C1
Tranmere Rd P04 ....183 A2
Treadwheel Rd P08 ....113 A3
Treagore Rd S040 ....76 B1
Trearnan Cl S016 ....101 C4
Treble Cl S022 ....10 A2
Tredegar Rd P04 ....183 A2
Tree Hamlets BH16 ....201 B3
Tree Side Way P07 ....111 C1
Treebys Cl BH23 ....192 B1
Treeside BH23 ....193 B1
Treeside Ave S040 ....101 A4
Treetops 3 BH13 ....214 C4
Trefoil Cl 10 P07 ....135 A4
Trefoil Way S031 ....208 B4
Tregonwell Rd P042 ....184 C1
Treloar Rd P011 ....185 C1
Treloen Ct 3 BH8 ....205 A3
Treloyhan Cl S053 ....55 B2
Tremona Cl S016 ....78 A1
Tremona Rd S016 ....78 A1
Tremley Cl S045 ....150 B2
Trent Cl S018 ....79 C1
Trent Ho 22 S014 ....103 B3
Trent Rd S018 ....79 C1
Trent Way
Fernddown BH22 ....165 C3
Lee-on-the-Solent PO13 ...179 C1
West End S030 ....80 B1
Trent Wlk P016 ....156 A4
Trentham Ave BH7 ....206 A4
Trentham Cl BH7 ....206 A4
Tresillian Cl BH23 ....194 A1
Tresillian Gdns S018 ....80 A1
Tresillian Way BH23 ....194 A1
Trevis Rd P04 ....183 B2
Trevone 18 BH25 ....195 A2
Trevone Cl S040 ....100 C3
Trevor Rd P04 ....182 C2
Trevose Cl
Chandler's Ford S053 ......55 B2
Gosport P013 ....155 B3
Trevose Cres S053 ....55 B3
Trevose Way P014 ....129 A1
Triangle Gdns S016 ....77 B2
Triangle La P014 ....153 C3
Triangle The
Bournemouth BH2 ....204 C2
Upton BH16 ....201 A4
Whiteparish SP5 ....24 A2
Tribe Rd P012 ....181 A3
Tricketts La BH22 ....165 C3
Tricorn The P01 ....215 B4
Trigon Rd BH15 ....202 B4
Trimaran Rd S031 ....128 C1
Trimm's Dro SP6 ....70 C4
Trimmer's Ct P01 ....181 C2
Trinidad Ho 1 S014 ....102 C2
Trinidad Cres P012 ....203 B4
Trinidad Est BH12 ....203 B4
Trinidad Ho S014 ....102 C2
Trinidad Ho BH12 ....203 B4
Trinity 2 BH1 ....205 A2
Trinity Cl P012 ....181 C2
Trinity Ct
Chandler's Ford S053 ......55 B3
2 Southampton S015 ......102 B3
Totton S040 ....76 C1
Trinity Gn P06 ....131 A1
Trinity Gr P012 ....181 C2
Trinity Ind Est
Southampton S015 ....101 C4
Wimborne Minst BH21 ....163 C2
Trinity Rd
Bournemouth BH1 ....205 A2
Southampton S014 ....103 A3
Trinity St P016 ....90 B1
Tripps End Cvn Site
S030 ....105 A4
Tristan Cl S045 ....178 C4
Tristram Cl S053 ....54 C2
Triton Ctr The S051 ....53 B3
Triumph Cl P015 ....130 B1
Triumph Rd P014 ....154 C3
Troak Cl BH23 ....207 C4

Trojan Way P07 ....134 C2
Troon Cres P06 ....134 B1
Troon Rd BH18 ....171 A4
Trooper Bottom GU32 .....19 A2
Trosnant Inf Sch P09 .....135 C2
Trosnant Jun Sch P09 ....135 C1
Trosnant Rd P09 ....135 C1
Trotters La BH21 ....164 A3
Trotts La
Marchwood S040 ....101 B1
Totton S040 ....101 B2
Trowbridge Cl S016 ....77 C3
Trowbridge Ct 16 S023 ....11 A4
Truman Rd BH10 ....189 A2
Truro Ct P013 ....180 B3
Truro Rd P06 ....132 C1
Truro Rise S050 ....56 C2
Truscott Ave BH9 ....205 A4
Trussell Cl S022 ....1 B2
Trussell Cres S022 ....1 B2
Trystworthy ID BH7 ....204 C2
Tuckers La BH15 ....201 C1
Tucks Cl BH23 ....193 A4
Tuckton Cl BH6 ....206 B2
Tuckton Rd BH6 ....206 C2
Tudor Ave P013 ....180 B4
Tudor Cl Alderholt SP6 .....93 A3
Gosport P013 ....180 B4
Southing Poll1 ....184 C1
Totton S040 ....100 B4
Tudor Cres P06 ....157 C3
Tudor Ct
Bournemouth BH1 ....205 A3
8 Cosham P06 ....157 C4
16 Fareham P014 ....154 C4
Poole BH15 ....202 C3
8 Portsmouth P05 ....182 B1
Tudor Gdns S030 ....105 A3
Tudor Ho (Mus)* S014 ....102 C2
Tudor Rd BH18 ....187 A2
Tudor Way S023 ....2 A4
Tudor Wood Cl S016 ....78 C2
Tuffin Cl S016 ....77 B3
Tukes Ave P013 ....155 B2
Tulip Gdns Havant PO9 ....135 B1
Locks Heath S031 ....128 C2
Tulip Rd S016 ....79 B2
Tumulus Cl S019 ....104 C2
Tunstall Rd S019 ....104 C2
Tunworth Ct P09 ....136 A3
Tupman Ho 18 P01 ....182 B4
Tuppenny La P010 ....161 B4
Turbary Ct
Bournemouth BH12 ....189 A1
Ferndown BH22 ....165 C3
Upton BH16 ....201 B4
Turbary Hts S041 ....201 B2
Turbary Park Ave BH11 ...189 A1
Turbary Rd BH12 ....189 A1
Turbary Ret Pk BH11 .....188 C2
Turbury Cl BH12 ....203 B4
Turbury Rd BH12 ....203 B4
Turf Croft Cl BH23 ....194 A1
Turk's La BH10 ....189 A3
Turlin Moor Fst Sch
BH16 ....201 B2
Turlin Moor Mid Sch
BH16 ....201 B2
Turlin Rd BH16 ....201 B2
Turnberry Cl BH23 ....206 C3
Turner Ave P013 ....180 C4
Turner Rd P01 ....182 B4
Turners Farm Cres
S041 ....196 A1
Turners Oak Ct S015 ......78 B1
Turnpike Down S023 ....11 B4
Turnpike Way S030 ....105 A4
Turnstone Gdns S016 ......78 A3
Turnworth Cl BH18 ....187 B2
Turtle Ct P014 ....154 A2
Tury King Ct P07 ....112 C2
Tuscan Wlk S053 ....55 C3
Tuscany Way P07 ....135 A4
Tussocks The S040 ....101 C1
Tutland Rd S052 ....53 C1
Tutt's La S051 ....50 C2
Tweed Cl S053 ....55 A4
Tweed La S041 ....197 B4
Tweedale Rd BH9 ....190 B2
Twemlow Ave BH14 ....202 C2
Twinstead Ho 4 S011 .....128 C2
Twiggs La S040 ....124 B3
Twiggs Lane End S040 ....124 B3
Twin Oaks S019 ....103 C2
Twin Oaks Cl BH18 ....187 A2
Twittens Way P09 ....135 C1
Twyford Ave
Portsmouth P02 ....157 B1
Southampton S015 ....78 B1
Twyford Cl BH8 ....190 B1
Twyford Ct 17 S023 ....2 A1
Twyford Dr P013 ....179 C1
Twyford Ho S015 ....102 C4
Twyford Rd S050 ....56 A3
Twyford Sch S021 ....32 A3
Twyford St Mary CE Prim Sch
S021 ....31 C3
Twyford Way P014 ....187 A1
Twynham Ave BH23 ....207 A4
Twynham Cl SP5 ....46 C3
Twynham Rd BH6 ....206 C2
Twynham Sch BH23 ....207 A3
Twynhams Hill S032 ......108 A4
Tyler Ct P015 ....130 C3
Tylers Cl S041 ....197 B3
Tyleshades The S051 ....53 A3
Tyne Cl S053 ....54 C3

Tynedale Cl
Bournemouth BH9 ....190 A2
Gosport P012 ....180 C4
Tyneham Ave BH12 ....203 B4
Tyrells La BH24 ....142 C2
Tyrrel Lawn P09 ....135 B4
Tyrrel Rd S053 ....55 B4
Tyrrell Gdns BH8 ....191 A1
Tyrrells Ct BH23 ....169 A1
Tyseley Rd P01 ....215 B2
Tytherley Gn
Bournemouth BH8 ....190 B1
24 Havant P09 ....136 A3
Tytherley Rd S018 ....104 B4

U

Ubsdell Cl BH25 ....195 A2
Uddens Dr BH21 ....164 B4
Uddens Trad Est BH21 ....164 C2
Ullswater S050 ....56 A1
Ullswater Ave S018 ....80 A1
Ullswater Rd BH16 P06 ...133 A1
Ullswater Rd
Southampton S016 ....77 C1
Wimborne Minst BH21 ....163 B1
Undercliff Dr BH1, BH5 ....205 B1
Undercliff Gdns BH5 ....205 C2
Undercliff Rd BH5 ....205 C2
Underdown Ave P07 ......134 B1
Undershore S041 ....197 C3
Undershore Rd S041 ......198 A2
Underwood Cl
Poole BH17 ....187 A1
Southampton S016 ....78 C2
Underwood Rd
Bishopstoke S050 ....56 C2
Southampton S016 ....78 C2
Unicorn Rd
Lee-on-the-Solent PO13 ...179 B2
Portsmouth P01 ....215 A4

V

Union La S032 ....61 A1
Union Pl P01 ....215 C4
Union Rd Havant PO9 .....135 C1
Southampton S014 ....103 B3
Unity Ct P012 ....181 A2
Univ of Portsmouth
Portsmouth P01 ....182 A3
Portsmouth P01 ....215 B2
Univ of Portsmouth
(Langstone Campus)
P04 ....183 B3
Univ of Portsmouth (Milton
Campus) P04 ....183 A2
Universal Marina S031 ....128 B3
University Cres S017 ....79 A2
University Parkway S016 ...79 A1
University Rd S017 ....79 A2
University Rdbt BH10 .....204 B4
Unwin Cl S019 ....103 B1
Upham CE Prim Sch
S032 ....58 C3
Upham St S032 ....58 B3
Uphill Rd S022 ....1 B3
Upland La GU33 ....20 A4
Uplands Ave P05 ....210 A4
Uplands Cl BH22 ....166 A4
Uplands Ct P012 ....181 A1
Uplands Prim Sch P016 ...131 A2
Uplands Rd
Bournemouth BH8 ....190 B1
Cosham P06 ....158 B4
Denmead P07 ....110 B3
Rowland's Castle PO9 .....113 B1
West Moors BH22 ....139 A1
Winchester S022 ....1 C2
Uplands Sch BH14 ....203 B2
Uplands Way S017 ....79 A1
Uplyme Cl BH17 ....188 A1
Upmill Cl S018 ....80 A3
Uppark (NT)* GU31 ....90 C4
Upper Arundel St P01 ....215 B3
Upper Banister St 1
S015 ....102 C3
Upper Barn Copse S050 ...57 A2
Upper Bere Wood P07 ....134 C4
Upper Brook Dr S031 .....128 C1
Upper Brook St S023 ......11 A4
Upper Brownhill Rd
S016 ....78 A4
Upper Bugle St S014 .....102 C2
Upper Church Rd S032 ...107 C4
Upper Common Rd
S041 ....196 C2
Upper Crabbick La P07 ...110 B3
Upper Crescent Rd S052 ..53 C3
Upper Deacon Rd S019 ...104 B3
Upper Golf Links Rd
BH18 ....187 A3
Upper Gordon Rd S023 ...194 A1
Upper Heyshott GU31 .....41 A1
Upper High St S023 ....11 A4
Upper Hinton Rd BH1 ....204 C2
Upper House Ct P017 ....108 A2
Upper Market St S050 .....56 A2
Upper Mead Cl 8 S050 ....57 B1
Upper Moors Rd S021 .....56 C4
Upper Mount St GU31 .....41 A2
Upper Mullins La S045 ...125 C2
Upper New Rd S030 ....80 B1
Upper Northam Cl
S030 ....105 A3

Upper Northam Dr
S030 ....104 C3
Upper Northam Rd
S030 ....105 A3
Upper Norwich Rd 13
BH2 ....204 C2
Upper Old St P014 ....154 A2
Upper Piece P07 ....111 A2
Upper Rd S022 ....203 B3
Upper Shaftesbury Ave
S017 ....79 A1
Upper Shirley Ave S015 ...78 B1
Upper Spinney S031 ......152 B4
Upper St Helens Rd
S030 ....105 A3
Upper St Michael's Gr
P014 ....154 C3
Upper Terrace Rd BH2 ....204 C2
Upper Toothill Rd S016 ....77 C4
Upper Wardown S051 ......42 A3
Upper Weston La S019 ...104 A1
Upper Wharf P016 ....155 B3
Uppleby Rd BH12 ....203 B3
Upton Cl Havant PO9 .....135 B4
Upton BH16 ....201 A4
Upton Cres S016 ....157 B4
Upton Cross Mobile Home Pk
BH16 ....201 B4
Upton Ct BH16 ....201 B4
Upton Ctry Pk* BH17 .....201 C3
Upton Grey Cl S022 ....1 B2
Upton Heath Est BH16 ....201 B4
Upton Ho 3 S016 ....78 A1
Upton Inf Sch BH16 ....201 A4
Upton Jun Sch BH16 ......201 A4
Upton La S016 ....77 B3
Upton Rd
Broadstone BH17 ....202 A4
Poole BH17 ....186 C2
Upton Way BH18 ....201 C2
Upwey Ave BH15 ....201 C2
Utrecht Ct BH23 ....207 B4

Vadne Gdns P012 ....181 A3
Vaggs La Hordle S041 .....195 C3
New Milton S041 ....195 B4
Vale Cl BH14 ....203 C2
Vale Dr S018 ....79 C1
Vale Gr P012 ....181 A4
Vale Lo BH1 ....205 B3
Vale Mans 4 BH1 ....205 B2
Vale Rd
Bournemouth BH1 ....205 B2
Poole BH14 ....203 C2
Redlynch SP5 ....47 B3
Winchester S023 ....11 B3
Vale The Horndean P08 .....88 B1
Hythe S045 ....125 C2
Locks Heath S031 ....129 A1
Petersfield GU32 ....41 A3
Portsmouth P05 ....182 B1
Vale View Pk S041 ....195 C4
Valencia Cl P023 ....191 B2
Valentine Ave S019 ....104 B2
Valentine Cl P015 ....130 B1
Valentine Ct
Southampton S019 ....104 B2
Waterlooville P07 ....135 A4
Valentines Inf Sch S019 ..104 B2
Valerian Ave P015 ....129 C2
Valerian Cl S050 ....81 A3
Valerian Rd S030 ....105 B3
Valetta Pk P010 ....160 C4
Valetta Rd P06 ....161 B1
Valette Rd BH9 ....190 A2
Valiant Gdns P02 ....157 B2
Valiant Rd P010 ....161 B1
Valiant Way BH23 ....208 A4
Valkey Cl Blackfield S045 .150 C1
Christchurch BH23 ....191 C2
Colden Common S021 .....56 C4
Redlynch SP5 ....47 B3
Waterlooville P07 ....134 B2
Valley Cl The 4 S022 ......10 B3
Valley La BH23 ....169 C2
Valley Park Dr P08 ....88 B2
Valley Rd
Bournemouth BH8 ....190 C2
Chandler's Ford S053 ......55 B4
Littleton S022 ....1 A3
Totton S040 ....100 C3
Valley Rise S031 ....128 C2
Valley The S022 ....10 B3
Valley View Poole BH12 ...203 A4
Southampton S019 ....104 A2
Valleydene S045 ....125 C1
Vallis Cl BH15 ....202 B1
Valsheba Dr P014 ....179 A3
Vanburgh Way S031 ....30 A1
Vanguard Rd
Bournemouth BH8 ....190 C1
Gosport P012 ....181 B4
Vanstone Rd P013 ....180 B4
Vardy Cl S019 ....104 B2
Varna Rd S015 ....102 B3
Varsity Rd P010 ....161 B1
Vaudrey Cl S015 ....78 B1
Vaughan Cl S019 ....104 C3
Vaughan Rd S045 ....125 B2
Vauxhall Way GU32 ....40 C2
Veal's La S040 ....125 A4
Vear's La S021 ....57 A4
Vecta Cl BH23 ....208 B3

Vectis Ct [1] SO16 78 C2
Vectis Rd
Barton on Sea BH25 209 B4
Gosport PO12 180 C2
Vectis Way PO6 157 C4
Velder Ave PO4 183 A3
Vellan Ct SO16 77 B1
Velmore Rd SO53 55 A2
Velsheda Ct [2] SO45 126 A3
Velvet Lawn Rd BH25 194 C2
Venator Pl BH21 163 B3
Venerable Rd PO14 155 A3
Vengeance Rd PO13 179 C2
Venice Cl PO7 135 A4
Venning Ave BH11 188 C3
Ventnor Ct SO16 79 B3
Ventnor Rd
Gosport PO13 155 A2
Portsmouth PO4 182 C2
Ventnor Way PO16 131 C1
Ventry Cl BH13 203 C2
Ventura Ctr The BH16 201 B3
Ventura Pl BH16 201 B3
Venture Ct PO3 158 A3
Venture Ind Pk PO3 158 A3
Venture Rd SO16 54 B1
Verbena Cres PO8 112 A2
Verbena Way SO30 105 B3
Verdon Ave SO31 127 C2
Verger Cl PO14 129 B2
Verity Cres BH17 188 A1
Vermont Cl SO16 78 C2
Vermont Sch SO16 78 C2
Vernalls Cl BH10 189 B3
Vernalls Ct BH25 195 B3
Vernalls Gdns BH10 189 B3
Verne Rd BH31 115 A3
Verney Cl BH11 189 A2
Verney Rd BH11 189 A2
Vernham Rd SO22 1 C1
Verno La BH23 193 B1
Vernon Ave PO4 183 A3
Vernon Cl
Bishop's Waltham SO32 59 B1
Gosport PO12 181 A3
Vernon Ct [3] PO2 157 C1
Vernon Hill SO32 59 B1
Vernon Mews [2] PO4 183 A3
Vernon Rd Gosport PO12 181 A3
Portsmouth PO3 158 A1
Vernon Wlk [5] SO15 102 C3
Verona Ave BH6 206 B3
Verona Rd SO53 55 C3
Verulam Pl [31] BH1 204 C2
Verulam Rd Poole BH14 202 C2
Southampton SO14 103 A4
Verwood CE First Sch
BH31 114 C3
Verwood Cres BH6 207 A2
Verwood Ind Est BH31 115 A3
Verwood Rd Havant PO9 136 A3
Ibsley BH24 116 A1
St Leonards BH24 140 B4
Three Legged Cross BH21 114 C1
Verwood BH21 114 A4
Woodlands BH21 114 A4
Veryan PO15 130 C1
Vesca Ho SO31 129 A3
Vespasian Ct SO18 103 B4
Vespasian Rd SO18 103 B4
Vespasian Way SO53 55 C4
Vesta Way SO53 55 C4
Vetch Cl BH23 208 B4
Vian Cl PO13 155 B2
Vian Ct BH25 194 C2
Vian Pl SO23 2 B4
Vian Rd PO7 134 C3
Vicarage Cotts BH8 190 C2
Vicarage Dr SO30 105 A3
Vicarage Farm SO50 57 B3
Vicarage Gdns SO41 196 A1
Vicarage La Cadnam SO40 75 A1
Curdridge SO32 106 B4
Hambledon PO7 86 B2
Hordle SO41 196 A1
Stubbington PO14 154 B2
Swanmore SO32 84 B3
Vicarage Pk SP5 47 B3
Vicarage Rd
Bournemouth BH9 189 C1
Marchwood SO40 101 C1
Poole BH15 202 B3
Redlynch SP5 48 A3
Verwood BH31 114 C3
Vicarage Way BH23 192 B1
Vice La SO43 74 A2
Viceroy Rd SO19 104 A2
Vickers Cl BH8 191 A1
Vickery Way BH23 207 B4
Victena Rd SO50 57 B1
Victor Ct SO19 104 B3
Victor Rd
Portsmouth PO1 182 C4
Thorney Island PO10 161 B1
Victor St SO15 78 A1
Victoria Ave
Bournemouth BH9 189 C1
South Hayling PO11 184 C2
Waterlooville PO7 134 A2
Victoria Bldgs SO32 83 A4
Victoria Cl
Corfe Mullen BH21 186 B3
Locks Heath SO31 129 A1
Victoria Cottage Hospl
PO10 160 C4
Victoria Cres BH12 203 B3
Victoria Ct Durley SO32 82 B4
[3] Netley SO31 127 A3
Victoria Ct continued
South Hayling PO11 184 C2
Victoria Gdns
Ferndown BH22 165 B3
Fordingbridge SP6 69 B1
Ringwood BH24 141 A3
Victoria Glade SO31 127 B3
Victoria Gr PO5 215 C1
Victoria Ho [11] PO16 131 A1
Victoria Hospl BH21 163 A3
Victoria Park Rd BH9 189 C1
Victoria Pl
Bournemouth BH1 205 B3
[6] Gosport PO12 181 A2
[2] Lymington SO41 197 C1
Romsey SO51 52 C4
Wimborne Minst BH21 163 A3
Victoria Rd
Bishop's Waltham SO32 83 A4
Bournemouth BH1 205 B3
Christchurch BH23 207 C3
Eastleigh SO50 56 A3
Emsworth PO10 136 C1
Ferndown BH22 165 B3
Fordingbridge SP6 69 B1
Milford on Sea SO41 211 B2
Netley SO31 127 A3
North Hayling PO11 159 C1
Poole BH12 203 B3
Portsmouth PO1 182 A3
Southampton SO19 103 B1
Waterlooville PO7 134 C4
Wimborne Minst BH21 163 A3
Winchester SO23 1 C1
Victoria Rd N PO5 215 C2
Victoria Rd S PO5 182 B1
Victoria Sq PO13 179 C1
Victoria St Gosport PO12 181 B3
Portsmouth PO1 182 B4
Southampton SO14 103 B3
Victoria Terr
[16] Cosham PO6 157 C4
Hermitage PO10 137 A1
Southbourne PO10 161 B4
Westbourne PO10 137 A2
Victoria Wlk SO30 80 C1
Victory Ave PO8 112 A3
Victory Cl
Chandler's Ford SO53 55 A3
Three Legged Cross BH21 139 A3
Victory Cotts SO31 128 B4
Victory Cres SO15 102 A3
Victory Ct PO13 155 B1
Victory Gn PO2 157 B1
Victory Ho PO6 157 A4
Victory Rd
[17] Portsmouth PO1 182 A3
Southampton SO15 102 A3
Stubbington PO14 179 B3
Victory Ret Pk PO2 182 B4
Victory Sq SO15 102 A3
Victory Trad Est PO3 158 A1
Victory Way SO16 77 C4
Viewside Cl BH21 186 B3
Viking Cl Blackfield SO45 177 C4
Bournemouth BH6 207 A2
Southampton SO16 77 C2
Stubbington PO14 154 A2
Viking Way
Bournemouth BH6 207 A2
Christchurch BH23 208 A3
Horndean PO8 88 B2
Vikings The SO51 53 A4
Villa Gdns PO7 134 C4
Village Cl PO14 179 B3
Village Ctr SO40 101 C1
Village Gate PO14 153 C4
Village Rd PO12 180 C1
Village St GU32 41 A3
Ville de Paris Rd PO14 155 A3
Villette Cl BH23 192 A1
Villiers Rd Hythe SO45 149 C4
Portsmouth PO5 182 B1
Southampton SO15 102 B4
Vimoutiers Ct SP6 69 C1
Vimy Ho [3] PO14 154 C4
Vince Cl BH11 189 A3
Vincent Ave SO16 78 B1
Vincent Cl [2] BH25 195 A1
Vincent Gr PO16 156 B4
Vincent Rd
[1] New Milton BH25 195 A1
Southampton SO15 102 B4
Vincent St SO15 102 B4
Vincent's Gr SO15 102 A4
Vincent's Wlk SO14 103 A2
Vine Bank SO18 104 A4
Vine Cl Bournemouth BH7 206 A4
Locks Heath SO31 128 B2
Vine Coppice PO7 134 C2
Vine Ct [22] PO6 157 C4
Vine Farm Cl BH12 204 B4
Vine Farm Rd BH12 204 A4
Vine Hill BH21 162 C3
Vine Ho SO31 129 A3
Vine Rd SO16 78 A2
Vinegar Hill SO41 211 B3
Vineries Cl BH21 163 C3
Vineries The BH21 163 C3
Vinery Gdns SO16 78 B1
Vinery Rd SO16 78 B1
Vinery The BH25 195 A1
Vineside PO13 155 C1
Viney Ave SO51 53 A4
Viney Rd SO41 197 C1
Vineyard Cl SO19 103 B2
Vineyards The SO52 54 A2
Vinnells La GU32 37 B3
Vinneys Cl BH23 192 B1
Vinson Rd GU33 21 A2
Violet Ave PO14 179 A3
Violet Cl SO53 55 A3
Violet Farm Cl BH21 186 B4
Violet La BH25 195 A2
Violet Rd SO16 79 A2
Virginia Cl BH12 203 B4
Virginia Park Rd PO12 180 C3
Viscount Ct BH11 188 B3
Viscount Dr BH23 208 A3
Viscount Wlk BH11 188 B3
Vista Marina BH13 214 B3
Vita Rd PO2 157 C2
Vitre Gdns SO41 197 C1
Vivash Rd PO1 215 D3
Vixen Cl PO14 179 A3
Vixen Wlk BH25 195 A3
Vokes Cl SO19 104 A3
Vulcan Cl SO15 101 C3
Vulcan Rd
Southampton SO15 101 C3
Thorney Island PO10 161 B1
Vulcan Way BH23 208 A4
Vyse La [20] SO14 102 C2

W

Wade Court Rd PO9 160 A4
Wade La PO9 160 A4
Wadham Rd PO2 157 B1
Wadhurst Gdns SO19 127 A4
Wadhurst Rd SO30 105 B3
Wagtail Dr BH25 194 C1
Wagtail Rd PO8 112 A3
Wagtail Way PO16 155 C4
Wainscot Rd PO4 183 A1
Wainsford Cl SO41 197 A1
Wainsford Rd
Hordle SO41 196 C1
Lymington SO41 196 C1
Wainwright Cl PO6 158 B3
Wainwright Gdns SO30 81 B2
Wait End Rd PO7 134 C3
Waite End Prim Sch
PO7 134 C3
Wake Lawn PO4 183 B2
Wakefield Ave
Bournemouth BH10 189 C3
Fareham PO16 130 C2
Wakefield Ct [6] SO18 80 A1
Wakefield Pl PO12 181 A1
Wakefield Rd SO18 80 A1
Wakeford Ct [17] SO51 52 C4
Wakeford Pl SO31 129 A1
Wakefords Way PO9 136 A3
Wakely Gdns BH11 189 A3
Wakely Rd BH11 189 A3
Walberant Bldgs [9]
PO3 157 C2
Walberton Ave PO6 158 A4
Walberton Ct [1] PO6 158 A4
Walcheren Pl BH15 201 B2
Walcott Ave BH23 191 C1
Waldegrave Cl SO19 103 B1
Walden Gdns PO8 112 A4
Walden Rd PO2 157 B1
Walditch Gdns BH17 187 C1
Waldon Gdns SO18 80 A1
Waldren Cl BH15 202 C1
Wales St SO23 11 A4
Walford Bldgs PO3 183 A4
Walford Cl BH21 163 B3
Walford Gdns BH21 163 A3
Walford Mill Craft Ctr*
BH21 163 A3
Walford Rd PO6 133 B1
Walhampton Hill SO41 198 A3
Walker Gdns SO30 81 B1
Walker Pl PO13 155 B1
Walker Rd PO2 157 B1
Walker's La S SO45 177 C4
Walkers Cl SO50 57 B1
Walkers La N SO45 150 C1
Walkford La BH25 194 B2
Walkford Rd BH23 194 B1
Walkford Way BH23 194 A1
Walkingfield La BH15 202 B1
Walkwood Ave BH7 206 A4
Wallace La SO42 175 B3
Wallace Rd
Broadstone BH18 187 A2
Portsmouth PO2 182 C4
Southampton SO19 103 C1
Wallington Ct PO14 154 C3
Wallington Dr SO53 55 A4
Wallington Hill [3] PO16 131 B1
Wallington Rd PO2 157 C1
Wallington Shore Rd
Fareham PO16 131 B1
[14] Portchester PO16 131 B1
Wallington Way PO16 131 B1
Wallis Bglws PO12 180 C2
Wallis Gdns PO7 111 C1
Wallis Rd
Bournemouth BH10 189 A1
Waterlooville PO7 111 C1
Walliscott Rd BH11 189 A1
Wallisdean Ave PO14 154 C4
Wallisdean Jun & Inf Schs
PO14 154 C4
Wallisdean Rd PO3 183 A4
Wallisdown Rd BH10,
BH11 204 B4
Wallisdown Rdbt BH12 189 A1
Wallrock Wlk PO10 136 C2
Walmer Cl SO50 56 A4
Walmer Rd PO1 182 C3
Walnut Ave SO18 79 C3
Walnut Cl
Chandler's Ford SO53 30 B1
New Milton BH25 194 C2
Southampton SO16 77 C1
Walnut Dr PO14 179 A3
Walnut Gr SO16 77 C1
Walnut Tree Cl PO11 184 C2
Walnut Tree Dr PO10 137 C2
Walpole La SO31 128 C4
Walpole Rd
Bournemouth BH1 205 C3
Gosport PO12 181 B2
Winchester SO22 10 B3
Walpole Terr [8] PO12 181 A2
Walsall Rd PO3 183 A3
Walsford Rd BH4 204 B3
Walsingham Cl PO6 133 B1
Walsingham Dene BH7 205 C4
Walsingham Gdns SO18 79 C2
Waltham Bsns Pk SO32 84 A2
Waltham Cl Droxford SO32 61 A1
Portchester PO16 132 B1
Waltham Cres SO16 78 B2
Waltham Rd BH7 206 A3
Waltham St PO5 215 A2
Walton Cl Gosport PO12 181 A2
Waterlooville PO7 134 C3
Walton Ct Fareham PO15 130 B2
[10] Portsmouth PO1 182 A2
Walton Pl SO22 10 B3
Walton Rd
Bournemouth BH10 189 B1
Cosham PO6 158 B3
Gosport PO12 181 A2
Poole BH15 203 A3
Southampton SO19 104 B2
Waltons Ave SO45 150 B2
Wandesford Pl PO12 156 A1
Wandmore Cl SO45 126 A2
Wangfield La SO32 82 B1
Wansbeck Cl SO53 55 A3
Wanstead Cl BH24 117 A1
War Meml Hospl
Gosport PO12 181 A2
Milford on Sea SO41 211 C2
Warbler Cl
Hamworthy BH16 201 A4
Horndean PO8 112 A4
Southampton SO16 78 A3
Warblington Ave PO9 136 A1
Warblington Cl SO53 55 A2
Warblington Ct [2] PO1 182 A2
Warblington Halt Sta
PO9 136 A1
Warblington Rd PO10 160 C4
Warblington Sch PO9 136 A1
Warblington St PO1 182 A2
Warborne La SO41 198 A4
Warbrook Ct [18] PO9 136 A3
Warburton Cl SO19 104 C2
Warburton Rd
Poole BH17 202 C4
Southampton SO19 104 C2
Warburton Way PO8 88 B2
Ward Block PO12 181 B3
Ward Cres PO10 137 A2
Ward Ct PO11 184 C1
Ward Ho [38] PO1 182 A3
Ward Rd PO4 183 A1
Warden Cl SO30 80 B1
Wardens Cl PO11 184 C3
Warders Ct [9] PO12 181 A3
Wardle Rd SO50 56 B4
Wardroom Rd PO2 157 A1
Wareham Ct BH7 206 A3
Wareham Rd BH21 186 B2
Warfield Ave PO7 134 C4
Warfield Cres PO7 134 C4
Warland Way BH21 186 C4
Warlock Cl SO19 104 B2
Warmwell Cl
[9] Bournemouth BH9 190 A2
Poole BH17 187 C1
Warnborough Ct [6]
PO9 136 A3
Warner Ct [11] SO23 2 A1
Warnes La BH24 142 C1
Warnford Cl PO12 180 C2
Warnford Cres PO9 135 B3
Warnford Ct SO15 102 C4
Warnford Rd
Bournemouth BH6, BH7 206 B4
Meonstoke SO32 61 B4
Warren Ave
Chandler's Ford SO53 55 C3
Christchurch BH23 207 C3
Portsmouth PO4 183 A3
Southampton SO16 78 A1
Warren Cl
Chandler's Ford SO53 55 C3
South Hayling PO11 184 B2
Southampton SO16 78 A1
St Leonards BH24 140 B3
Warren Cres SO16 78 A1
Warren Dr BH24 140 B3
Warren Edge Cl BH6 206 C2
Warren Edge Ct BH6 206 C2
Warren Edge Rd BH6 206 C2
Warren Gdns SO51 28 A1
Warren La Beaulieu SO42 200 C4
Froxfield Green GU32 19 A3
Owslebury SO21 33 C4
St Leonards BH24 140 B3
Warren Park Prim Sch
PO9 135 B4
Warren Pk SO41 211 A3
Warren Pl SO40 76 B1
Warren Rd
Bournemouth BH4 204 A1
Liss GU33 21 A4
Poole BH14 203 B2
Winchester SO23 11 B4
Warren The SO45 150 A3
Warren Wlk BH22 165 A4
Warrior Bsns Ctr The
PO6 158 C4
Warrior Cl SO53 55 A2
Warrior Pk SO53 55 A2
Warrys Cl SO45 150 A4
Warsash Cl PO9 135 C3
Warsash Ct SO31 128 B1
Warsash Gr PO13 155 A1
Warsash Maritime Ctr (Soton
Inst) SO31 152 B4
Warsash Rd PO14,SO31 129 A1
Warspite Cl PO2 157 B2
Warton Cl SO42 175 B3
Warwick Ave BH25 195 A2
Warwick Cl
Chandler's Ford SO53 55 A2
Lee-on-the-Solent PO13 180 A2
[18] Winchester SO23 2 A1
Warwick Cres PO5 215 B2
Warwick Ct
[14] Bournemouth BH5 205 C2
[4] Emsworth PO10 160 C4
[14] Winchester SO23 2 A1
Warwick Ho [21] SO14 103 B3
Warwick Pl
[3] Bournemouth BH7 206 A3
West Wellow SO51 50 C2
Warwick Rd
Bournemouth BH7 206 A3
Poole BH14 203 B2
Southampton SO15 78 B1
Totton SO40 100 C4
Warwick Way PO17 108 A2
Wasdale Cl PO8 88 B1
Washbrook Rd PO6 133 B1
Washington Ave BH8 205 B3
Washington Ct [4] PO4 183 A3
Washington Rd
Emsworth PO10 136 C1
Portsmouth PO2 182 B4
Wastwater Ho [25] PO6 133 A1
Watcombe Rd BH6 206 B3
Water Cl SO23 11 A4
Water La
Bournemouth BH6 206 B4
Hythe SO45 125 C1
Totton SO40 100 C4
Winchester SO23 11 A4
Water Lane Farm BH10 189 C3
Water's Edge SO30 105 A3
Waterbeech Dr SO30 105 B4
Waterberry Dr PO7 111 B1
Waterditch Rd
Bransgore BH23 193 A2
Burton BH23 193 A2
Waterford Cl
Lymington SO41 197 C2
Poole BH14 203 A1
Waterford Ct SO41 197 B1
Waterford Gdns BH23 209 A4
Waterford La SO41 197 C1
Waterford Lo BH23 208 A3
Waterford Pl BH23 209 A4
Waterford Rd
Christchurch BH23 209 A4
New Milton BH25 195 B2
Waterfront Mus* BH15 202 A1
Watergate PO12 181 C2
Waterhouse La SO15 102 A4
Waterhouse Way SO15 102 A4
Waterlock Gdns PO4 183 B2
Waterloo Cl PO8 111 B2
Waterloo Ho BH17 187 A1
Waterloo Ind Est SO30 81 A1
Waterloo Rd
Bournemouth BH9 204 C4
Broadstone BH17 202 B4
Corfe Mullen BH21 186 A3
Gosport PO12 181 B1
Havant PO9 135 C1
Lymington SO41 197 C2
Southampton SO15 102 B3
Waterloo Sch The PO7 134 C4
Waterloo St PO5 215 B2
Waterloo Terr SO15 102 C3
Waterloo Way BH24 141 A3
Watermans La SO45 125 C1
Watermead
Christchurch GU21 207 A3
Winchester SO23 10 C3
Watermead Rd PO6 158 C4
Watermill Rd BH23 207 A4
Waters Edge
Lee-on-the-Solent PO13 179 C1
Poole BH13 214 B3
Waters Edge Gdns
PO10 160 C4
Waters Gn SO42 146 A1
Waters Green Ct SO42 146 A1
Waters The PO17 130 C3
Watersedge PO17 108 A2
Watersedge Rd PO6 157 A4
Watershed Ct [2] PO6 133 A1
Watership Dr BH24 141 B3
Waterside
Christchurch BH23 207 C2
[4] Hythe SO45 126 A3

Waterside Cl P014 ... 117 A1
Waterside Gdns P016 ... 131 B1
Waterside La P016 ... 156 C3
Waterside Rd S051 ... 28 A1
Waterside Sch P02 ... 157 A2
Waterside Sch (Unit)
P04 ... 183 B2
Waterside Sq S045 ... 125 C3
Watersmeet
Fareham P016 ... 155 A4
⑯ Winchester S023 ... 11 A4
Waterston Cl BH17 ... 187 B1
Waterworks Rd
Cosham P06 ... 158 B4
Otterbourne S021 ... 31 B2
Petersfield GU32 ... 41 A3
Watery La
Christchurch BH23 ... 208 A4
Upton BH16 ... 201 A4
Watkin Rd
⑩ Bournemouth BH5 ... 205 C2
Hedge End S030 ... 81 B1
Watley Cl S016 ... 77 B3
Watley La S021 ... 32 A3
Watson Wlk S040 ... 100 B4
Watton Cl BH8 ... 191 A1
Watton La S032 ... 61 C1
Watton Rd S045 ... 150 B2
Watts Cl S016 ... 77 C2
Watts Rd
Hedge End S030 ... 105 B4
Portsmouth P01 ... 182 B4
Wavecrest Cl S040 ... 102 A2
Wavell Ave BH17 ... 187 A1
Wavell Rd
Bournemouth BH11 ... 189 A2
Gosport P013 ... 155 B2
Southampton S018 ... 104 A4
Wavell Way S022 ... 10 B3
Wavendon Ave BH25 ... 209 C4
Waveney Cl P013 ... 179 C1
Waveney Gn S016 ... 77 C1
Waveney Way S031 ... 127 B3
Waverley Cl
Fordingbridge SP6 ... 69 C2
Romsey S051 ... 28 A1
Waverley Cres BH15 ... 202 B3
Waverley Cl S031 ... 127 B3
Waverley Gr P04 ... 182 C1
Waverley Ho ⑫ BH25 ... 195 A1
Waverley Path P012 ... 180 C2
Waverley Rd
Cosham P06 ... 158 B4
Fordingbridge SP6 ... 69 C2
New Milton BH25 ... 195 A1
Portsmouth P04 ... 182 C1
Southampton S015 ... 102 B3
Wayfarer Cl
Locks Heath S031 ... 128 C1
Portsmouth P04 ... 183 B3
Wayfarers P013 ... 180 B4
Wayground Rd BH21 ... 162 C1
Waylands Pl S030 ... 105 A2
Wayman Rd BH21 ... 186 C3
Wayne Rd BH12 ... 203 A1
Waynflete Cl ⑪ S032 ... 83 B4
Waynflete Pl S022 ... 10 B3
Wayside S031 ... 128 B4
Wayside Cl S041 ... 211 B3
Wayside Rd
Bournemouth BH6 ... 206 C2
St Leonards BH24 ... 166 C4
Wayte St P06 ... 157 C4
Waytown Cl BH17 ... 187 B1
Weald Cl S031 ... 129 A2
Weardale Rd S053 ... 55 B2
Weavers Cl BH22 ... 138 C1
Weavers Gn P09 ... 136 B2
Weavers Pl S053 ... 55 A4
Weavills Rd S050 ... 57 A1
Webb Cl P011 ... 185 A1
Webb La P011 ... 185 A1
Webb Rd P016 ... 156 B3
Webb's Way BH11 ... 188 C1
Webbers Way P012 ... 181 B1
Webbs Cl BH24 ... 139 B3
Webbs Gn S032 ... 85 B2
Webbs Way BH24 ... 139 C3
Webster Gdns S018 ... 80 A2
Wedburn Rd
Bournemouth BH9 ... 190 A2
Winchester S022 ... 1 A1
Wedgewood Cl
Holbury S045 ... 150 B2
Stubbington P014 ... 179 A3
Wedgewood Way P08 ... 111 C1
Wedgwood Dr BH14 ... 203 A1
Wedgwood Gdns BH23 ... 169 B1
Wedmore Cl S022 ... 10 A2
Weeke Manor Cl S022 ... 1 B1
Weeke Prim Sch S022 ... 1 B1
Weevil La P012 ... 181 B3
Weirs The ⑪ S023 ... 11 A3
Welbeck Ave S017 ... 79 A1
Welburn Cl S018 ... 80 A1
Welch Rd Gosport P012 ... 181 A4
Portsmouth P04 ... 182 C1
Welch Way S016 ... 77 C3
Welchwood Cl P08 ... 111 C3
Weldon Ave BH11 ... 188 C3
Well Cl BH25 ... 194 C1
Well Copse Cl P08 ... 88 B1
Well Hill P07 ... 110 B4
Well House Cl SP6 ... 45 A2
Well House La S022 ... 1 C3

Well La
Hamble-le-Rice S031 ... 128 A1
Poole BH15 ... 202 B2
Swanmore S032 ... 84 A4
Well Mdw P09 ... 135 C3
Welland Gdns S018 ... 80 A1
Welland La S016 ... 101 C4
Welland Rd BH21 ... 163 B2
Wellands Rd S043 ... 122 A3
Wellbrooke Gdns S053 ... 55 A4
Weller Ho ⑯ P01 ... 182 B4
Wellers Cl S040 ... 100 A4
Welles Rd S053 ... 55 B3
Wellesley Ave BH23 ... 208 B4
Wellesley Cl P07 ... 134 C4
Wellington Ave
Christchurch BH23 ... 208 B4
Southampton S018 ... 104 A4
Wellington Cl
Horndean P08 ... 112 B3
Hythe S045 ... 125 B1
Wellington Ct
⑦ Bournemouth, Deane Pk
BH8 ... 205 A3
Bournemouth, Westbourne
BH2 ... 205 A3
⑧ Havant P09 ... 135 C1
New Milton BH25 ... 195 A2
Southampton S015 ... 102 B3
West End S030 ... 80 B1
Wellington Gr P016 ... 156 B4
Wellington Pk S030 ... 81 A1
Wellington Pl S040 ... 98 C4
Wellington Rd
Bournemouth BH1, BH8 ... 205 A3
Poole BH14 ... 203 B2
Southampton S018 ... 79 C1
Wellington St P05 ... 215 B2
Wellington S018 ... 104 A4
Wellman Ct ⑩ S016 ... 78 C2
Wellow Cl Havant P09 ... 135 B2
Southampton S018 ... 104 B4
Wellow Ct ⑧ S018 ... 103 C4
Wellow Dro S051 ... 50 C4
Wellow Gdns P014 ... 129 B1
Wellow Sch S051 ... 50 C2
Wellow Vineyard* S051 ... 51 B4
Wellow Wood Rd S051 ... 50 B4
Wellowbrook Cl S053 ... 55 A3
Wells Cl P015 ... 129 B4
Wells Pl S050 ... 56 A1
Wells Rd S030 ... 81 A1
Wellsmoor P014 ... 129 B1
Wellswood Gdns P09 ... 113 B2
Wellsworth La P09 ... 113 B2
Wembley Gr P06 ... 158 A3
Wembley Way S050 ... 57 B1
Wendover Cl BH25 ... 194 C1
Wendover Rd P09 ... 135 C1
Wendy Cres BH22 ... 138 C1
Wenlock Ct ⑥ BH23 ... 207 C4
Wensley Gdns P010 ... 136 C2
Wentwood Gdns BH25 ... 195 B1
Wentworth BH14 ... 214 B4
Wentworth Ave BH5 ... 206 A2
Wentworth Cl BH5 ... 206 A2
Wentworth Coll BH5 ... 206 A2
Wentworth Dr
Broadstone BH18 ... 187 A3
Christchurch BH23 ... 206 C3
Horndean P08 ... 112 A4
Wentworth Gdns
Holbury S045 ... 150 B2
Southampton S014 ... 103 A1
Wentworth Gr S045 ... 150 B2
Wentworth Grange S022 ... 10 C3
Wescott Way BH11 ... 188 C2
Wesermarsch Rd P08 ... 112 A2
Wesley Cl
⑧ Bournemouth BH8 ... 205 B3
Southampton S019 ... 104 B2
Wesley Ct P01 ... 215 D3
Wesley Gr P013 ... 158 B2
Wesley Grange ⑬ BH4 ... 204 B2
Wesley Ho ⑮ S053 ... 11 A4
Wesley Rd
Kings Worthy S023 ... 2 B4
Poole BH12 ... 203 B3
Wimborne Minst BH21 ... 163 C3
Wessex Ave BH25 ... 195 A1
Wessex Cl
Blackfield S045 ... 177 C4
Christchurch BH23 ... 208 B4
Wessex Ct
Southampton, Sholing
S019 ... 104 A2
⑬ Southampton, Westwood Pk
S019 ... 104 A3
Wessex Dr S022 ... 1 C1
Wessex Est BH24 ... 203 A1
Wessex Gate Ind Est
P08 ... 112 B3
Wessex Gate Ret Pk
BH17 ... 202 A3
Wessex Gdns
Portchester P016 ... 156 A4
Romsey S051 ... 53 A4
Wessex La S018 ... 79 B2
Wessex Maternity Ctr
(private) S018 ... 80 A1
Wessex Nuffield Hospl
S053 ... 31 A1
Wessex Rd Horndean P08 ... 88 B2
Poole BH14 ... 203 A2
Ringwood BH24 ... 140 C4
Wessex Trad Ctr BH12 ... 203 A4
Wessex Way
Bournemouth BH8 ... 205 B3

Wessex Way continued
Colden Common S021 ... 57 A4
West Ave BH21 ... 138 C4
West Bargate ② S014 ... 102 C2
West Battery Rd P02 ... 157 A1
West Bay Rd S015 ... 102 B3
West Block S015 ... 102 B3
West Borough BH21 ... 163 A4
West Butts St ⑪ BH15 ... 202 A1
West Cl Lymington S041 ... 197 B1
Verwood BH31 ... 114 B3
West Cliff Cotts BH2 ... 204 C1
West Cliff Gdns BH2 ... 204 C1
West Cliff Mews BH2 ... 204 C1
West Cliff Rd BH2, BH4 ... 204 B1
West Close Ct BH6 ... 207 A2
West Close Ho BH6 ... 207 A2
West Comm S045 ... 177 C3
West Ct Portsmouth P01 ... 182 C4
Portsmouth, Southsea
P05 ... 183 A2
Southampton S019 ... 103 C1
West Downs Cl P016 ... 131 A2
West Dr S050 ... 56 B2
West End Cl S022 ... 10 C4
West End Cotts ⑧
P016 ... 131 A1
West End Rd
Hedge End S031 ... 104 C2
West End S030 ... 104 A4
West End Terr S022 ... 10 C4
West Haye Rd P011 ... 185 B1
West Hayes
Lymington S041 ... 197 C2
Winchester S022 ... 10 C4
West Hill Ct S015 ... 102 C3
West Hill Dr Hythe S045 ... 125 C3
Winchester S022 ... 10 C4
West Hill Park Sch
P014 ... 153 C4
West Hill Pk S022 ... 10 C4
West Hill Rd ⑩ BH2 ... 204 C1
West Hill Rd BH2 ... 204 C1
West Hoe La S032 ... 83 C4
West Horton Cl S050 ... 56 C1
West Horton La S050 ... 56 C1
West Hove Ct BH11 ... 189 A2
West Howe Ind Est
BH11 ... 188 C2
West La Hordle S041 ... 196 C1
North Baddesley S052 ... 53 C3
North Hayling P011 ... 184 C3
West Links S053 ... 55 B1
West Lodge P013 ... 179 B2
West Mans ⑩ BH4 ... 204 B2
West Marlands Rd
S014 ... 102 C3
West Meon CE Prim Sch
GU32 ... 37 B3
West Mills Rd SP6 ... 69 C1
West Moors Mid Sch
BH22 ... 138 C1
West Moors Rd
Ferndown BH22 ... 165 B4
Three Legged Cross BH21 ... 138 C4
West Moors BH22 ... 138 B3
West Moors St Mary's CE Fst
Sch BH22 ... 138 C1
West Overcliff Dr BH4 ... 204 B1
West Park Dr SP6 ... 68 B3
West Park La SP6 ... 68 B3
West Park Rd S015 ... 102 C3
West Point P013 ... 179 C1
West Quay (Sh Ctr)
S015 ... 102 C2
West Quay Rd
Poole BH15 ... 202 A1
Southampton S015 ... 102 C2
West Rd
Bournemouth BH5 ... 206 A2
Bransgore BH23 ... 193 A4
Emsworth P010 ... 160 C4
Fawley S045 ... 150 B4
Hedge End S030 ... 104 C3
Hythe S045 ... 125 B1
Milford on Sea S041 ... 211 A3
Southampton, Woolston
S019 ... 103 C1
Southwick P017 ... 133 A3
West Row BH21 ... 163 A2
West Row Mews BH21 ... 163 A2
West St Emsworth P010 ... 160 C4
Fareham P016 ... 131 A1
Fordingbridge SP6 ... 69 C1
Hambledon P07 ... 86 B1
Havant P09 ... 135 C1
Hythe S045 ... 125 C3
Poole BH15 ... 202 A1
Portchester P016 ... 156 B4
Portsmouth P01 ... 181 C2
Ringwood BH24 ... 140 C4
Soberton S032 ... 85 B3
Southampton S014 ... 102 C2
Southwick P017 ... 132 C3
Titchfield P014 ... 153 C4
Wimborne Minst BH21 ... 163 A3
West Station Terr BH4 ... 204 B2
West Street Ct ② BH21 ... 163 A3
West Tytherley CE Prim Sch
SP5 ... 7 A4
West View Cotts P010 ... 137 C1
West View Rd
Christchurch BH23 ... 207 C2
Poole BH15 ... 202 B2
West Walk (North) Forest
Wlk* P017 ... 108 C4
West Walk (South) Forest
Wlk* P017 ... 108 C4

West Way
Bournemouth BH9 ... 190 A1
Broadstone BH18 ... 187 A2
Locks Heath P015 ... 129 C2
Lymington S041 ... 197 B1
West Way Cl BH9 ... 190 A1
Westbeams Rd S041 ... 172 A1
Westborn Rd P016 ... 131 A1
Westbourne Ave
Emsworth P010 ... 137 A1
Holbury S045 ... 150 B2
Westbourne Cl
Bournemouth BH4 ... 204 B2
Emsworth P010 ... 137 A1
Westbourne Cres S017 ... 79 A1
Westbourne Ct ⑨ P09 ... 135 C1
Westbourne Cty Prim Sch
P010 ... 137 A2
Westbourne Mans ⑨
S017 ... 79 A1
Westbourne Park Rd
BH4 ... 204 A1
Westbourne Rd
Emsworth P010 ... 137 A2
Portsmouth P02 ... 182 C4
Westbourne P010 ... 137 A2
Westbrook Gdns S051 ... 27 C1
Westbrook Cl
Bournemouth BH10 ... 189 B1
Locks Heath S031 ... 129 A3
Westbrook Ctr The ⑫
P07 ... 112 A1
Westbrook Gr P07 ... 134 B2
Westbrook Rd P016 ... 156 B3
Westbrook Way S018 ... 79 B2
Westbrooke Cl P08 ... 112 A3
Westbury Cl
Barton on Sea BH25 ... 210 A4
Bransgore BH23 ... 193 A4
Christchurch BH23 ... 193 B1
⑪ Cosham P06 ... 133 A1
Westbury Ct
Hedge End S030 ... 105 B3
⑩ Poole BH14 ... 203 A2
Westbury Mall ⑳ P016 ... 131 A1
Westbury Manor Mus*
P016 ... 131 A1
Westbury Rd
Fareham P016 ... 131 A1
Ringwood BH24 ... 141 A4
Southampton S015 ... 101 C4
Westbury Sq ⑳ P016 ... 131 A1
Westby Rd BH5 ... 205 C2
Westcliff P013 ... 179 C2
Westcliff Mews S019 ... 103 B2
Westcliff Rd S045 ... 125 C3
Westcot Rd S045 ... 150 B2
Westcroft Par ⑩ BH25 ... 195 A1
Westcott Pk BH18 ... 187 B2
Westcroft Rd P012 ... 180 C3
Westdown Rd BH11 ... 189 A2
Westerham Cl P06 ... 157 C4
Westerham Rd BH4 ... 204 A2
Westering S051 ... 53 B4
Westerleigh BH4 ... 204 B1
Westerley Cl S031 ... 128 C1
Western Ave
Barton on Sea BH25 ... 209 B4
Bournemouth BH10 ... 189 B2
Emsworth P010 ... 160 B4
Poole BH13 ... 203 C1
Southampton S015 ... 102 A3
Western Cl P08 ... 111 C3
Western Com Hospl
S016 ... 77 C1
Western Ct ⑭ P016 ... 131 A1
Western District Cut
S015 ... 102 B4
Western Downland CE Prim
Sch
Damerham SP6 ... 68 B2
Rockbourne SP6 ... 44 C1
Western Espl S014 ... 102 C2
Western Par
Emsworth P010 ... 160 C4
Portsmouth P05 ... 182 A1
Western Rd
Chandler's Ford S053 ... 30 C1
Cosham P06 ... 157 B4
Fareham P016 ... 131 A1
Fawley S045 ... 150 C1
Havant P09 ... 135 C1
Lymington S041 ... 197 B2
Poole, Canford Cliffs BH13 ... 214 C4
West End S030 ... 80 B1
Winchester S022 ... 10 C4
Western Terr P02 ... 157 B1
Western Way
Fareham P016 ... 131 A1
Gosport P012 ... 180 C2
Portsmouth P01 ... 181 C4
Westerngate BH11 ... 204 A2
Westfield ⑦ BH21 ... 163 A3
Westfield Ave
Fareham P014 ... 154 C4
South Hayling P011 ... 184 C2
Westfield Cl
Fair Oak S050 ... 81 B4
Hamble-le-Rice S031 ... 127 C1
Verwood BH31 ... 163 A3
Westfield Cnr S018 ... 79 C3
Westfield Comm S031 ... 127 C1
Westfield Cres S053 ... 55 B2

Westfield Dr S032 ... 84 B1
Westfield Dro S024 ... 34 C4
Westfield Gdns BH23 ... 193 A1
Westfield Ho S018 ... 79 C2
Westfield Ind Est
Gosport P012 ... 181 A2
Horndean P08 ... 112 B4
Westfield Jun Sch P06 ... 156 C4
Westfield Oaks P011 ... 184 C2
Westfield Rd
Bournemouth BH6 ... 206 C2
Chandler's Ford S053 ... 55 B2
Gosport P012 ... 181 A2
Littleton S022 ... 1 A3
Lymington S041 ... 198 A1
Portsmouth P04 ... 183 A2
Southampton S015 ... 102 A4
Totton S040 ... 100 C4
Westgate P014 ... 179 B3
Westgate Mews S030 ... 80 C1
Westgate Mus* S023 ... 10 C4
Westgate Pk BH4 ... 204 A2
Westgate Sec Sch S022 ... 1 C1
Westgate S031 ... 128 A2
Westgate St S014 ... 102 C2
Westgrove SP6 ... 69 C1
Westhill Gdns P010 ... 160 C4
Westham Cl BH17 ... 187 C2
Westheath Rd BH18 ... 187 A2
Westland Dr P07 ... 134 C2
Westland Gdns P012 ... 181 A2
Westlands Ct BH23 ... 193 A4
Westlands Dr BH13 ... 214 C4
Westlands Gr P016 ... 156 B4
Westley Cl S022 ... 1 B1
Westley Gr P014 ... 154 C4
Westmarch Cl ⑪ S017 ... 79 B1
Westmead Cl P011 ... 184 C2
Westminster Ct BH25 ... 209 C4
Westminster Gate ... 10 A3
Westminster Gdns
P014 ... 129 B2
Westminster Pl P01 ... 182 B4
Westminster Rd
Milford on Sea S041 ... 211 A2
Poole BH13 ... 204 A1
Westminster Rd E BH13 ... 204 A1
Westmoreland Ct S041 ... 195 C2
Westmorland Way S053 ... 55 C3
Weston Ave P04 ... 183 A2
Weston Cl S019 ... 103 C1
Weston Cres S018 ... 104 B4
Weston Dr BH1 ... 205 A2
Weston Grove Rd S019 ... 103 B1
Weston Ho ⑦ GU32 ... 40 C2
Weston Homes ⑦ S019 ... 126 C4
Weston La Buriton GU32 ... 65 B4
Nursling S016 ... 77 A2
Southampton S019 ... 103 C1
Weston Par S019 ... 126 C4
Weston Park Boys Sch
S019 ... 104 A1
Weston Park Inf Sch
S019 ... 104 A1
Weston Park Jun Sch
S019 ... 104 A1
Weston Rd Eastleigh S050 ... 56 A2
Petersfield GU31 ... 41 A2
West End S030 ... 80 B1
S019 ... 126 C4
Westons La ⑧ BH15 ... 202 B1
Westover La BH24 ... 140 B3
Westover Prim Sch
P03 ... 183 A4
Westover Rd
Bournemouth BH1 ... 204 C2
Milford on Sea S041 ... 211 B2
Portsmouth P03 ... 183 A4
Southampton S016 ... 101 B4
Westquay Ho ⑧ P016 ... 131 B1
Westray Hall BH4 ... 204 B1
Westridge Cl S017 ... 79 A1
Westridge Rd S017 ... 103 A4
Westrow Gdns S015 ... 102 C4
Westrow Rd S015 ... 102 C4
Westside View S024 ... 34 C4
Westview Rd S022 ... 1 A1
Westward Rd S030 ... 105 B3
Westways Cosham P06 ... 158 C4
Stubbington P014 ... 179 B3
Westways Cl S016 ... 77 B3
Westwood Ave BH22 ... 165 B3
Westwood Cl P010 ... 137 A1
Westwood Ct
⑫ Southampton S017 ... 103 A4
Totton S040 ... 76 C1
West End S030 ... 80 B1
Westwood Gdns S053 ... 55 C4
Westwood Mans ⑳ S017 ... 79 A1
Westwood Rd
Lyndhurst S043 ... 121 C3
Netley S031 ... 127 A4
Portsmouth P02 ... 157 C2
Southampton S017 ... 103 A4
Westwood View S024 ... 34 C4
Westwoods & Glendene Pk
BH25 ... 194 B3
Wetherby Cl BH18 ... 187 A1
Wetherby Ct S040 ... 100 B4
Wetherdown GU31 ... 41 A2
Weybridge Cl S031 ... 128 C3
Weyhill Cl Havant P09 ... 135 B3
Portchester P016 ... 156 B4
Weyman's Ave BH10 ... 189 B3
Weymans Dr BH10 ... 189 B3
Weymouth Ave P012 ... 180 C4

Weymouth Rd
Poole BH14 . . . . .203 B3
15 Portsmouth PO2 . . . . .157 B1
Whaddon Chase PO14 . .179 A3
Whaddon Dr PO9 . . . . . .135 B3
Whaddon La
Colden Common SO21 . . . .58 A4
Owslebury SO21 . . . . .33 A2
Whale Island Way PO2 . .157 B1
Whalesmead Cl SO50 . . . .56 C1
Whalesmead Rd SO50 . . .56 C1
Whaley Rd PO2 . . . . . . .157 A1
Wharf Cl BH12 . . . . .203 C3
Wharf Hill SO23 . . . . .11 A3
Wharf Mill 2 SO23 . . . . .11 A3
Wharf Rd
Portsmouth PO2 . . . . . . .182 B4
Southampton SO19 . . . . .103 B2
Wharfdale Rd
Bournemouth BH4 . . . . . .204 B2
Poole BH12 . . . . .203 C3
Wharncliffe Ct BH23 . . . .208 C4
Wharncliffe Gdns BH23 . .209 A4
Wharncliffe Ho SO19 . . .103 B2
Wharncliffe Rd
Bournemouth BH5 . . . . . .205 B2
Christchurch BH23 . . . . . .209 A4
Southampton SO19 . . . . .103 B2
Whartons Cl SO40 . . . . .100 B2
Whartons La SO40 . . . . .100 B2
Whatleigh Cl BH15 . . . . .202 B1
Wheat Cl SO53 . . . . .54 C3
Wheatcroft Dr SO18 . . . . .80 A1
Wheatcroft Rd PO13 . . . .179 C1
Wheatear Dr GU31 . . . . . .41 B1
Wheatears Dr SO51 . . . . .50 C2
Wheatland Cl SO22 . . . . . .10 B3
Wheatlands PO14 . . . . . .129 B2
Wheatlands Ave PO11 . . .185 C1
Wheatley Gn 7 PO9 . . . .135 B3
Wheaton Grange BH4 . . .204 B2
Wheaton Rd BH7 . . . . . .206 A3
Wheatplot Park Homes 2
BH10 . . . . .189 C2
Wheatsheaf Ct SO30 . . . .105 A3
Wheatsheaf Dr PO8 . . . .111 B2
Wheatstone Rd PO4 . . . .182 C2
Wheeler Cl PO12 . . . . . .181 A3
Wheeler La BH11 . . . . . .188 B3
Wheelers Wlk SO45 . . . .177 C4
Wheelwright Mews SP5 . .46 C4
Whernside Cl SO16 . . . . .101 C4
Wherwell Ct 13 PO9 . . . .136 A3
Whichers Cl PO9 . . . . . .136 A4
Whichers Gate Rd PO9 . .136 A4
Whimbrel Cl PO4 . . . . . .183 B3
Whimbrel Ct BH23 . . . . .208 A3
Whinchat Cl
Fareham PO15 . . . . .130 B2
Southampton SO16 . . . . . .78 A3
Whincroft Cl BH22 . . . . .165 C4
Whincroft Dr BH22 . . . . .165 C3
Whinfield Rd SO45 . . . . .149 C4
Whinwhistle Rd SO51 . . . .51 A4
Whippingham Cl PO6 . . .157 B4
Whistler Cl SO19 . . . . . .104 B2
Whistler Rd SO19 . . . . . .104 B2
Whitaker Cres SO41 . . . .197 B2
Whitby Ave BH18 . . . . . .187 A1
Whitby Cl BH23 . . . . . . .191 B2
Whitby Cres BH18 . . . . .187 A1
Whitby Ct 4 SO41 . . . . .211 A2
Whitby Rd SO41 . . . . . . .211 A2
Whitchurch Ave BH18 . . .187 B2
Whitchurch Ct SO19 . . . .103 C4
Whitcombe Cl SO40 . . . .100 C4
Whitcombe Gdns PO41 . .198 C2
White Barn Cres SO41 . . .196 A2
White Beam Rise PO8 . . . .88 B3
White Cl BH15 . . . . .202 A2
White Cloud Pk 7 PO4 . .182 C2
White Cloud Pl 8 PO4 . .182 C2
White Dirt La PO8 . . . . . . .88 B2
White Farm Cl BH10 . . . .204 B4
White Gates SO32 . . . . . .82 A3
White Harmony Acres Ind Est
SO30 . . . . .80 C3
White Hart La
Cadnam SO40 . . . . .98 C4
Portchester PO16 . . . . . .156 B4
White Hart Rd
Fair Oak SO50 . . . . .57 B1
4 Gosport PO12 . . . . . .181 A2
Portsmouth PO1 . . . . . . .182 A2
White Heather Ct 1
SO45 . . . . .126 A3
White Ho The SO41 . . . .211 B2
White Horse Dr BH15 . . .202 B3
White Horse La PO7 . . . .111 A3
White Horses BH25 . . . . .209 C4
White House Gdns GU32 . .40 C3
White Knights BH25 . . . .209 C4
White La SO21 . . . . .32 A4
White Ladies SO11 . . . . .204 B2
White Ladies Cl PO9 . . . .136 A1
White Lion Ctyd BH24 . . .140 C4
White Lion Wlk PO12 . . .181 B3
White Lodge BH15 . . . . .202 C2
White Lodge Gdns
PO16 . . . . .130 C2
White Oak Wlk 13 PO7 . .136 A3
White Rd SO50 . . . . .56 B2
White Row SP5 . . . . .46 B4
White Swan Rd PO1 . . . .215 A3
White Way SO32 . . . . .61 A4
White Wings Ho PO7 . . . .110 C2
White's Rd SO19 . . . . . .104 A3

Whiteacres Cl 11 PO12 . .181 A3
Whitebeam Cl
Colden Common SO21 . . . .57 A4
2 Fareham PO14 . . . . . .154 C4
Waterlooville PO8 . . . . . .112 B3
Whitebeam Rd SO30 . . . .105 B3
Whitebeam Way
North Baddesley SO52 . . . .54 A3
Verwood BH31 . . . . .115 A3
Whitechimney Row
PO10 . . . . .137 A2
Whitecliff Cres BH14 . . . .203 A1
Whitecliff Rd BH14 . . . . .202 C1
Whitecliffe Ave PO3 . . . .183 A4
Whitecliffe Ct PO12 . . . .180 B2
Whitecroft SO45 . . . . . . .126 A1
Whitecross Cl BH17 . . . .187 C2
Whitecross Gdns 14
PO2 . . . . .157 C2
Whitefield La 1 BH25 . . .195 A2
Whitefield Rd
Holbury SO45 . . . . .150 B2
New Milton BH25 . . . . . .195 A1
Poole BH14 . . . . .203 A1
Whitehall BH23 . . . . .207 A3
Whitehart Fields 2
BH24 . . . . .141 B4
Whitehaught Ct SO50 . . . .56 B2
Whitehaven
Horndean PO8 . . . . .112 B3
Portchester PO16 . . . . . .156 A4
Whitehaven Home Pk
SO45 . . . . .177 C4
Whitehayes Cl BH23 . . . .192 B1
Whitehayes Rd BH23 . . . .192 B1
Whitehill Cl SO18 . . . . . .104 B4
Whitehorn Dr SP5 . . . . . .73 B4
Whitehouse Gdns SO15 . .102 A3
Whitehouse Rd BH21 . . . .163 B1
Whitelands
Bransgore BH23 . . . . . . .169 B2
Droxford SO32 . . . . .85 A4
Whitelaw Rd SO15 . . . . .102 A4
Whiteleaf La PO7 . . . . . . .86 B4
Whiteley Rd BH10 . . . . . .189 C3
Whiteley La
Locks Heath PO15 . . . . . .129 C3
Swanwick PO15,SO31 . . .106 B1
Whiteley Prim Sch
PO15 . . . . .129 B4
Whiteley Way PO15 . . . . .129 B3
Whitemoor La SO40,SO51 . .75 C2
Whitemoor Rd SO40 . . . .145 B1
Whitenap Cl SO51 . . . . . .53 A3
Whitenap La SO51 . . . . . .53 A3
Whiteparish All Saints CE
Prim Sch SP5 . . . . .24 A2
Whites Cl 10 PO2 . . . . . .157 B1
Whites Hill SO21 . . . . .33 A2
Whites La SO45 . . . . . . .126 C3
Whiteshoot SP5 . . . . .47 C2
Whiteshoot Hill SP5 . . . . .47 C2
Whiteshute La SO23 . . . . .10 C3
Whitestone Cl SO16 . . . .101 C4
Whitethorn Rd PO11 . . . .184 C3
Whitewater Rise SO45 . . .125 C1
Whiteways BH21 . . . . . . .163 C3
Whitfield Park BH24 . . . .140 A3
Whitingham Ct 8 BH5 . .206 A3
Whitley Cl PO10 . . . . . . .137 A4
Whitley Row PO4 . . . . . .183 B3
Whitley Way BH25 . . . . .195 A3
Whitmore La BH21 . . . . .114 A4
Whitsbury Cl BH8 . . . . . .190 B1
Whitsbury Cross SP6 . . . .69 B4
Whitsbury Rd
Fordingbridge SP6 . . . . . .69 C2
Havant PO9 . . . . .136 A3
Whitstable Rd PO6 . . . . .157 C4
Whittington Cl SO45 . . . .125 C2
Whittington Ct PO10 . . . .160 C4
Whittle Ave PO15 . . . . . .129 B3
Whittle Rd BH21 . . . . . . .164 C4
Whittles Way BH15 . . . . .202 A1
Whitwell SO31 . . . . .127 B4
Whitweil Rd PO4 . . . . . . .182 C1
Whitworth Cl PO12 . . . . .181 A2
Whitworth Cres SO18 . . .103 B4
Whitworth Rd
Gosport PO13 . . . . .181 A3
Portsmouth PO2 . . . . . . .182 C4
Southampton SO18 . . . . .103 B4
Whyke Ct 3 PO9 . . . . . .135 C1
Whyte Cl SO45 . . . . .150 A2
Whyteways SO50 . . . . . . .56 A2
Wick 1 Ind Est BH25 . . . .194 C1
Wick 2 Ind Est BH25 . . . .194 C1
Wick Dr BH25 . . . . .194 C1
Wick Farm BH6 . . . . . . .207 A3
Wick La
Bournemouth BH6 . . . . . .207 A3
Christchurch BH23 . . . . . .207 A3
Downton SP5 . . . . .46 A4
Wicket Rd BH10 . . . . . . .189 C3
Wicket The SO45 . . . . . .125 C1
Wickfield Ave BH23 . . . . .207 A3
Wickfield Cl BH23 . . . . . .207 A3
Wickford Ho BH23 . . . . .207 A4
Wickham CE Prim Sch
PO17 . . . . .108 A2
Wickham Croft PO17 . . . .108 A2
Wickham Ct
Ferndown BH22 . . . . . . .165 C3
Gosport PO12 . . . . .180 B2
Wickham Dr BH21 . . . . . .186 B2

Wickham Ho
17 Southampton SO17 . . . .79 A1
18 Southampton SO17 . . . .79 A1
Wickham Rd
Bournemouth BH7 . . . . . .206 A3
Droxford SO32 . . . . .85 A3
Fareham PO16,PO17 . . . .131 A3
Wickham St PO1 . . . . . . .182 A3
Wickham Vineyard*
SO32 . . . . .107 A4
Wicklea Rd BH6 . . . . . . .207 A2
Wicklow Dr SO53 . . . . . . .55 A3
Wickmeads Rd BH6 . . . . .207 A2
Wickor Cl PO10 . . . . . . .137 A1
Wickor Way PO10 . . . . . .137 A1
Wicor Mill La PO16 . . . . .156 A4
Wicor Path PO16 . . . . . .156 B3
Widbrook Prim Sch PO16 .156 A4
Widbury Rd SO41 . . . . . .197 B1
Widden Cl SO41 . . . . . . .172 A1
Widdicombe Ave BH14 . . .203 C1
Wide La SO18 . . . . .79 C3
Wide Lane Cl SO42 . . . . .145 C1
Widecombe Dr SO45 . . . .125 C2
Widgeon Cl
Gosport PO13 . . . . .181 A4
Southampton SO16 . . . . . .78 A3
Widgeon Ct PO16 . . . . . .155 C4
Widget Cl BH11 . . . . .189 A3
Widlers La SO32 . . . . .58 C3
Widley Court Dr PO6 . . . .158 A4
Widley Ct
4 Cosham PO6 . . . . . . .158 A4
Fareham PO14 . . . . .155 A3
Widley Gdns PO7 . . . . . .134 B2
Widley Rd Cosham PO6 . .158 A4
Portsmouth PO2 . . . . . . .157 B1
Widley Wlk PO6,PO7 . . . .133 C2
Widworthy Dr BH18 . . . .186 C3
Widworthy Ct PO9 . . . . . .135 B2
Wigan Cres PO9 . . . . . . .135 A1
Wight View
Lee-on-the-Solent PO13 . .179 B2
South Hayling PO11 . . . . .185 B2
Wight Wlk PO22 . . . . . . .165 C1
Wightway Mews SO31 . . .128 B1
Wigmore Ho PO1 . . . . . .215 C4
Wilberforce Cl 2 SO22 . . .10 B3
Wilberforce Rd
Gosport PO12 . . . . .181 B1
Portsmouth PO5 . . . . . . .215 B1
Wilby La PO3 . . . . .158 B2
Wild Arum Way SO53 . . . .54 C3
Wild Cherry Way SO53 . . .55 A3
Wild Grounds Nature Reserve
PO13 . . . . .180 B3
Wild Ridings PO14 . . . . .154 B4
Wild Rose Cres SO31 . . .128 C1
Wildburn Cl SO40 . . . . . . .76 B1
Wilde Cl SO40 . . . . .100 B4
Wildern Cl SO31 . . . . . . .128 C2
Wildern Ct SO30 . . . . . . .105 A4
Wildern La SO30 . . . . . . .105 A4
Wildern Sec Sch SO30 . . .105 B4
Wilderness Hts SO18 . . . .80 B1
Wilderton Rd BH13 . . . . .203 C2
Wilderton Rd W BH13 . . .204 A2
Wildfell Cl BH23 . . . . . . .192 A1
Wildground Inf Sch
SO45 . . . . .125 C1
Wildground Jun Sch
SO45 . . . . .125 C1
Wildmoor Wlk PO9 . . . . .136 A3
Wildown Gdns BH6 . . . . .207 A2
Wildown Rd BH6 . . . . . . .207 A2
Wilfred Rd BH5 . . . . .205 C2
Wilkins Cl PO8 . . . . .88 A3
Wilkins Way BH15 . . . . . .202 A1
Wilkinson Dr BH8 . . . . . .191 A1
Wilkinson Ho PO4 . . . . . .183 A1
Wilks Cl SO16 . . . . .77 B3
Willersley Cl PO6 . . . . . .133 B1
Willett Rd BH21 . . . . . . .163 A1
William Booth Ho 17
PO4 . . . . .182 A3
William Cl
Christchurch BH23 . . . . . .194 A1
Stubbington PO14 . . . . . .179 B3
William Ct 17 BH23 . . . . .209 A4
William George Ct 9
PO13 . . . . .179 C1
William Gilpin CE Prim Sch
SO41 . . . . .173 C1
William Macleod Way
SO16 . . . . .78 A1
William Price Gdns
PO16 . . . . .131 A1
William Rd
Bournemouth BH7 . . . . . .205 C4
Lymington SO41 . . . . . . .197 C3
11 Winchester SO14 . . . .103 B3
William's Ind Pk BH25 . . .194 C1
Williams Cl
Gosport PO13 . . . . .180 B4
Holbury SO45 . . . . .150 B2
Williams Rd PO3 . . . . . . .158 A2
Willis Ave SO52 . . . . .54 A2
Willis Rd Gosport PO12 . .181 B2
Portsmouth PO1 . . . . . . .215 B3
Southampton SO16 . . . . . .79 B3
Williton Gr BH12 . . . . . . .203 A4
Willis Wages SO23 . . . . . .11 B3
Willment Marine & Bsns Pk
SO19 . . . . .103 B3
Willow Ave SP6 . . . . .69 C1
Willow Cl
Bournemouth BH4 . . . . . .204 A3

Willow Cl continued
Havant PO9 . . . . .136 A1
Hedge End SO30 . . . . . .105 B3
St Leonards BH24 . . . . . .139 B2
Upton BH16 . . . . .201 B3
West End SO30 . . . . .80 C2
Willow Ct
Bournemouth BH7 . . . . . .206 B3
Fareham PO14 . . . . .130 B1
Southampton SO16 . . . . . .78 A2
Willow Dr
Christchurch BH23 . . . . . .207 A3
Marchwood SO40 . . . . . .124 A2
Ringwood BH24 . . . . . . .141 A3
Wimborne Minst BH21 . . .164 B3
Willow Gdns
North Baddesley SO52 . . . .53 C3
Westbourne BH10 . . . . . .137 A2
Willow Gn SO21 . . . . .57 A4
Willow Gr 11 SO50 . . . . .57 B1
Willow Herb Cl SO31 . . .128 C1
Willow La BH23 . . . . .169 B2
Willow Mead
Bournemouth BH8 . . . . . .190 B2
Hedge End SO30 . . . . . .105 A4
Willow Pk BH14 . . . . . . .203 A2
Willow Pl
Christchurch BH23 . . . . . .207 B3
Gosport PO13 . . . . .181 A3
Willow Rd
Bishop's Waltham SO32 . . .83 C4
Liss GU33 . . . . .21 A2
Willow Tree Ave PO8 . . . .112 A2
Willow Tree Gdns PO14 . .154 C4
Willow Tree Ho SO41 . . . .197 B1
Willow Tree Rise BH11 . . .189 A2
Willow Tree Wlk SO19 . . .104 A2
Willow View BH16 . . . . . .201 B2
Willow Way
Christchurch BH23 . . . . . .207 A3
Ferndown BH22 . . . . . . .165 B4
Willow Wlk BH25 . . . . . . .210 A4
Willow Wood Rd PO11 . . .185 A2
Willowdale Cl GU32 . . . . .40 A2
Willowdene Cl
Havant PO9 . . . . .135 A2
New Milton BH25 . . . . . .195 B2
Willows The
Fareham SO30 . . . . .210 A4
Chandler's Ford SO53 . . . .55 B2
Denmead PO7 . . . . .110 C2
Wills Cl BH21 . . . . .186 B2
Wills Rd BH12 . . . . .203 C2
Wills Way SO51 . . . . .53 A3
Willwood Cl BH17 . . . . . .187 C2
Wilmcote Gdns 5 PO1 . .215 C3
Wilmcote Ho PO1 . . . . . .215 C3
Wilmer Rd SO50 . . . . .56 A1
Wilmington Ct SO18 . . . . .79 C2
Wilmot Cl SO50 . . . . .56 C3
Wilmott Cl PO12 . . . . . . .180 C3
Wilmott La PO12 . . . . . . .180 C3
Wilmur Cres BH15 . . . . . .202 C3
Wilson Ct Fair Oak SO50 . .81 B4
Fordingbridge SP6 . . . . . .69 C1
Wilson Gr PO5 . . . . .215 B1
Wilson Rd
Bournemouth BH1 . . . . . .205 C3
Poole BH14 . . . . .203 B2
Portsmouth PO1 . . . . . . .157 B1
Wilson St SO14 . . . . .103 B3
Wilton Ave SO15 . . . . . . .102 C3
Wilton Cl
Christchurch BH23 . . . . . .191 B1
Gosport PO12 . . . . .180 C2
Wilton Cres SO15 . . . . . . .78 B1
Wilton Ct SO15 . . . . .102 B4
Wilton Dr PO8 . . . . .112 A3
Wilton Rd
Bournemouth BH7 . . . . . .205 C3
Southampton SO15 . . . . . .78 B1
Wilton Terr PO5 . . . . . . .182 B1
Wiltshire Gdns BH23 . . . .192 C4
Wiltshire Rd
Bransgore BH23 . . . . . . .192 C4
Chandler's Ford SO53 . . . .55 B2
Wiltshire St PO5 . . . . . . .215 A2
Wilverley Ave
Bournemouth BH8 . . . . . .190 C1
Havant PO9 . . . . .136 A2
Wilverley Cl SO41 . . . . . .197 A1
Wilverley Pl SO45 . . . . . .150 C1
Wilverley Rd
Brockenhurst SO42 . . . . .145 C1
Brockenhurst, Wootton
BH25 . . . . .170 C2
Christchurch BH23 . . . . . .208 A4
Wimbledon Park Rd
PO5 . . . . .182 B1
Wimborne Fst Sch
BH21 . . . . .163 A3
Wimborne Ho PO1 . . . . . .77 C1
Wimborne Inf & Jun Schs
PO4 . . . . .183 A2
Wimborne Minster Model
Town & Gdns* BH21 . . .163 A2
Wimborne Rd
Bournemouth BH10,BH11,
BH2,BH3,BH9 . . . . .204 C3
Bournemouth, Kinson
BH10,BH11,BH2,BH3,
BH9 . . . . .189 B3
Broadstone BH21 . . . . . .162 C1

Wimborne Rd continued
Poole BH15 . . . . .202 B3
Portsmouth PO4 . . . . . . .183 A2
Wimborne Minst BH21 . . .163 A3
Wimborne Minster, Colehill
BH21 . . . . .163 A2
Wimborne Rd E BH22 . . .165 B3
Wimborne Rd W
Ferndown BH21 . . . . . . .164 B3
Wimborne Minst BH21 . . .164 B3
Wimpole Ct PO1 . . . . . . .215 C4
Wimpole St PO1 . . . . . . .215 C4
Wimpson Gdns SO16 . . . .77 C1
Wimpson La SO16 . . . . . .101 C4
Wincanton Way PO7 . . . .112 A1
Winchcombe Rd PO6 . . . .133 A1
Winchelsea Sch BH14 . . .188 B1
Winchester Cath* SO23 . .11 A4
Winchester City 7 SO31 . .127 A3
Winchester Coll
Winchester SO22 . . . . . . .10 C3
Winchester SO23 . . . . . . .11 A3
Winchester Ct
Gosport PO13 . . . . .180 B3
5 Romsey SO51 . . . . . . .28 A1
Southampton SO15 . . . . . .78 B1
Winchester City Mill*
SO23 . . . . .11 A4
Winchester Ho SO15 . . . .53 A4
Winchester Ho 10 SO51 . .53 A4
Winchester Ho 8 SO51 . . .136 A3
Winchester Ho 9 BH15 . .202 B1
Winchester Rd
Bishop's Waltham SO32 . . .83 A4
Chandler's Ford SO53 . . . .55 C4
Durley SO32 . . . . .81 C2
Langrish GU32 . . . . .39 C2
Langrish GU32 . . . . .39 C2
New Milton BH25 . . . . . .195 B2
Owslebury SO21, SO32 . . .58 B2
Petersfield GU32 . . . . . . .40 B2
Portsmouth PO2 . . . . . . .182 C4
Romsey SO51 . . . . .52 C4
Romsey, Woodley SO51 . . .28 B1
Southampton SO16 . . . . . .78 B1
Upham SO32 . . . . .58 B2
Waltham Chase SO32 . . . .83 C1
Winchester Sch of Art
SO23 . . . . .11 A4
Winchester St
Botley SO30 . . . . .106 A4
4 Southampton SO15 . . .102 C3
Winchester Sta SO22 . . . .10 C4
Winchester Way SO40 . . .100 B4
Winchfield Cl SO19 . . . . .104 A1
Winchfield Cres PO9 . . . .135 B2
Winchfield Ho PO12 . . . .181 C2
Wincombe Cl BH22 . . . . .165 B2
Wincombe Dr BH22 . . . . .165 B2
Windbury Rd SO16 . . . . . .77 C1
Windermere Ave
Southampton SO16 . . . . . .77 C1
Stubbington PO14 . . . . . .154 B2
Windermere Gdns SO40 . .100 C4
Windermere Ho PO6 . . . .157 A4
Windermere Rd
Bournemouth BH5 . . . . . .205 A4
Portsmouth PO2 . . . . . . .157 C2
West End SO30 . . . . .80 A1
Windfield Dr SO51 . . . . . .53 A4
Windgreen Est BH21 . . . .186 C4
Windham Mews BH1 . . . .205 B3
Windham Rd BH1 . . . . . .205 B3
Windhill Field PO7 . . . . . .111 A2
Windmill Cl Clanfield PO8 . .88 B3
4 Milford on Sea SO41 . .211 B3
St Leonards BH24 . . . . . .140 B2
Windmill Copse SO45 . . .125 C1
Windmill Gr PO16 . . . . . .156 B3
Windmill La
Bursledon SO31 . . . . . . .105 A1
St Leonards BH24 . . . . . .140 B2
Windover Cl SO19 . . . . . .104 B3
Windrush Gdns PO7 . . . .134 B4
Windrush Rd SO16 . . . . .101 C4
Windrush Way SO45 . . . .126 A2
Windsor Cl SO40 . . . . . . .195 C2
St Leonards BH24 . . . . . .139 C2
Windsor Ct
5 Christchurch BH23 . . . .209 A4
Cosham PO6 . . . . .157 C4
Poole BH14 . . . . .203 A2
14 Southampton SO17 . .103 A4
15 Southampton, Bitterne
SO18 . . . . .103 C4
Southampton, Millbrook
SO15 . . . . .102 A3
8 Southampton, Westwood Pk
SO17 . . . . .103 A4
Windsor Gate SO50 . . . . .56 A3
Windsor Ho
7 Portsmouth PO1 . . . . .215 C3
22 Winchester SO23 . . . .11 A4
Windsor Rd
Bournemouth BH5 . . . . . .205 C2
Christchurch BH23 . . . . . .206 C4
Gosport PO12 . . . . .181 A2
Petersfield GU32 . . . . . . .40 C2
Poole BH14 . . . . .203 A2
Portchester PO16 . . . . . .156 B3
Windsor Way SP6 . . . . . .93 A3
Windward Ct 11 PO12 . . .181 B2
Wine Cross PO17 . . . . . .109 A1

Winecross PO17 109 A1
Winfield Way PO10 136 C2
Winfrid Ho SO40 100 B4
Winfrith Cres BH12 203 C4
Winfrith Way SO16 77 B3
Wingate Dr SO19 104 A3
Wingate Rd
Gosport PO12 155 C1
Totton SO40 100 B4
Wingfield Ave
Christchurch BH23 193 B1
Poole BH15 202 B3
Wingfield Ct BH1 205 B2
Wingfield St PO1 182 B4
Wingrove Rd SO40 100 B2
Winifred Cl SO50 57 B2
Winifred Rd Poole BH15 202 C3
Waterlooville PO7 134 C4
Winkfield Row PO8 112 A3
Winkle St SO14 103 A1
Winkton Cl Burton BH23 192 B2
Havant PO9 135 B2
Winkton Ho BH23 192 B2
Winn Ct SO17 102 C4
Winn Mans 25 SO17 79 A1
Winn Rd SO17 79 A1
Winnall Cl SO23 2 B1
Winnall Manor Rd SO23 11 B4
Winnall Prim Sch SO23 11 B4
Winnall Trad Est SO23 11 B4
Winnall Valley Rd SO23 11 B4
Winnards Cl BH22 165 C1
Winnards Pk SO31 128 B2
Winnham Dr PO16 132 A1
Winnington PO15 130 B2
Winnington Cl PO15 130 B2
Winscombe Ave PO8 112 A1
Winsford Ave SO50 57 A1
Winsford Cl
Bishopstoke SO50 57 A1
Christchurch BH23 193 B1
Winsford Gdns SO50 57 A1
Winslade Rd Havant PO9 135 B3
Winchester SO22 1 B2
Winsley Ave BH6 206 B2
Winslow Ct PO6 158 B4
Winsor Cl PO11 185 B1
Winsor Ct SO50 56 B2
Winsor La SO40 99 C4
Winsor Rd Cadnam SO40 75 B1
Totton SO40 101 A3
Waterlooville PO7 111 B1
Winspit Cl BH15 201 C2
Winstanley Rd
Nursling SO16 77 B3
Portsmouth PO2 157 B1
Winston Ave BH12 204 A3
Winston Churchill Ave
PO5 215 B2
Winston Cl Eastleigh SO50 56 A2
South Hayling PO11 184 C2
Southampton SO16 77 C1
Winston Ct
1 Christchurch BH23 207 A4
20 New Milton BH25 195 A1
Winston Gdns BH12 204 A3
Winston Par 22 BH25 195 A1
Winston Pk BH12 204 A3
Winston Rd BH9 190 A2
Winston Way BH24 141 A4
Winstone Bldgs SO16 78 C2
Winstone Cres SO52 54 A2
Winter Rd PO4 183 A2
Winterbarrow Cotts
SO32 36 C2
Winterbourne Cl BH15 202 B2
Winterbourne Rd
Cosham PO6 132 C1
Poole BH15 202 B3
Romsey SO51 28 A1
Winterhayes Cl BH17 187 C2
Winterhill Rd PO6 157 B4
Winters Cl SO45 150 B2
Winters Hill
Bishop's Waltham SO32 82 C4
Durley SO32 82 C4
Winters Rd SO32 84 A1
Winterslow Dr PO9 135 C3
Winton (Boys) Sch
BH10 189 B1
Winton Cl
Lymington SO41 197 C2
Winchester SO22 1 C1
Winton Ct
11 Petersfield GU32 40 C2
West End SO30 80 B1
Winton Prim Sch BH9 189 C1
Winton Rd
Petersfield GU32 40 C2
Portsmouth PO2 157 C1
Winton St 14 SO14 103 A3
Winton Way
Bournemouth BH10 189 B1
New Milton BH25 195 A3
Wisbech Way SO41 195 C2
Wisborough Rd PO5 182 C1
Wises Ct PO12 181 C2
Wish Pl PO5 215 D1
Wishart Gdns BH9 190 A3
Wistaria Ho 7 BH10 189 C2
Wisteria Dr BH31 115 B2
Wisteria Gdns PO9 136 A2
Witchampton Cl PO9 136 A3
Witchampton Rd BH18 186 C1
Witham Cl SO53 55 A3
Withedwood Ave SO15 102 B4
Witherbed La
Locks Heath PO15 129 B2
Locks Heath PO15 129 C3
Withermoor Rd BH9 204 C4
Withers La SO42 175 B4
Withewood Mans 2
SO15 102 B4
Withies Rd PO13 180 B4
Withingham Rd BH13 203 C2
Withington Cl 8 PO6 133 A1
Withy Cl SO51 52 C4
Witley BH14 214 B4
Witley Rd PO8 111 C3
Witney Rd BH17 187 B1
Witt Rd SO50 57 B1
Wittensford La SO43 98 B4
Wittering Rd
South Hayling PO11 185 C1
Southampton SO16 78 A2
Witts Hill SO18 79 C1
Woburn Cl SO50 56 A3
Woburn Ct PO13 179 C1
Woburn Rd SO16 78 B3
Wode Cl PO8 88 B2
Wodehouse Rd SO19 103 C2
Woking Rd BH14 203 B2
Wolfe Cl
Christchurch BH23 207 B4
Winchester SO22 10 B3
Wollaston Rd BH6 206 C2
Wollaton Cres BH22 165 B2
Wollaton Rd BH22 165 B2
Wollstonecraft Rd 25
BH5 205 C2
Wolseley Rd Poole BH12 203 B3
Southampton SO15 102 B4
Wolsey Way SO41 211 B3
Wolterton Rd BH12 204 A3
Wolverley Ct
16 Bournemouth BH4 204 B2
Southampton SO16 78 B2
Wolverton Rd
Bournemouth BH7 205 C3
Havant PO9 135 C3
Southampton SO14 103 A3
Wolvesey Castle (Old
Bishop's Palace)*
SO23 11 A3
Wolvesey Pl SO53 55 A2
Wolvesey Terr 3 SO23 11 A3
Wonderholm Par BH11 189 A1
Wonston Ct PO9 136 B3
Wonston Rd SO16 78 A2
Wood Cl SO19 104 B2
Wood End Rd BH24 141 C3
Wood End Way SO53 55 A3
Wood Glade Cl SO40 101 C1
Wood House La SO41 174 A1
Wood La
Bournemouth BH11 188 C3
Bramdean SO24 15 C3
Milford on Sea SO41 211 B2
Southwick PO17 133 A3
Wood Lark Gdns GU31 41 B2
Wood Lawn Cl BH25 209 C4
Wood Lodge SO40 76 A1
Wood Rd SO40 100 A1
Wood Row BH9 190 C2
Wood View BH21 164 A4
Wood's Cnr BH24 143 B3
Woodacre Gdns BH22 165 C2
Woodberry La PO9,PO10 136 C4
Woodbind Wlk SO31 128 C1
Woodbourne Cl
Fareham PO15 130 B1
Liss GU33 21 A2
Woodbury
Bournemouth BH1 205 A1
Brockenhurst SO42 145 B1
Woodbury Ave
Bournemouth BH8 190 C1
Havant PO9 159 C4
Petersfield GU32 40 C3
Woodbury Cl BH23 191 C2
Woodbury Gr PO8 111 C3
Woodcock La SO41 196 A2
Woodcocks Cres BH7 206 A4
Woodcot Cres PO9 136 A3
Woodcot Prim Sch
PO13 155 A2
Woodcote Cotts SO24 15 B2
Woodcote Dr BH16 201 A3
Woodcote La PO14 155 A2
Woodcote Rd SO17 79 B2
Woodcroft Gdns PO8 111 C3
Woodcroft La PO8 111 C3
Woodend Rd BH9 204 C4
Wooderson Cl SO50 57 A2
Woodfern SP6 70 B1
Woodfield Ave PO6 134 C1
Woodfield Cotts GU32 19 A2
Woodfield Dr SO22 10 A3
Woodfield Gdns BH23 193 B1
Woodfield Ho 22 PO2 157 C2
Woodfield Park Rd
PO10 161 A4
Woodfield Rd BH11 189 A3
Woodford Cl BH24 141 B4
Woodford Ho PO15 130 B1
Woodford Rd BH1 205 B2
Woodgaston La PO11 160 B1
Woodgreen Ave PO9 135 B2
Woodgreen Dr BH11 188 B2
Woodgreen Rd SO22 1 B2
Woodgreen Wlk SO40 76 A1
Woodhall Way PO15 130 C2
Woodhay SO43 121 C3
Woodhay Wlk 22 PO9 136 A3
Woodhayes Ave BH23 193 C1
Woodhill Sch
Botley SO30 105 C4
Chandler's Ford SO53 55 B4
Woodhouse La
Finchdean PO8 113 A3
Hedge End SO30 105 C4
Rowland's Castle PO8,
PO9 113 B2
Woodhouse Rd PO8 112 C4
Woodington Cl 55 PO9 136 A3
Woodington Rd SO51 51 B3
Woodlake Cl BH17 187 B1
Woodland Ave BH5 206 A2
Woodland Cl
Southampton SO18 104 B4
Verwood BH31 114 C4
West Wellow SO51 51 A1
Woodland Ct BH7 205 C3
Woodland Dro SO21 32 A2
Woodland Mans BH14 203 A3
Woodland Mews SO30 80 B1
Woodland Pl 18 SO15 102 C4
Woodland St PO1 215 D4
Woodland Vale SO19 104 A2
Woodland View
Bursledon SO31 127 C4
Horndean PO8 111 C3
Woodland Way
Christchurch BH23 208 B4
Milford on Sea SO41 211 B2
Woodland Wlk
Bournemouth BH5 206 A2
Ferndown BH22 165 C4
* Mottisfont SO51 5 B2
Woodlands PO16 131 B1
Woodlands Ave
Emsworth PO10 136 C2
Hamworthy BH15 201 C2
Woodlands Cl
Bransgore BH23 193 A4
Chandler's Ford SO53 30 B1
Gosport PO13 180 B3
Hythe SO45 125 C1
Locks Heath SO31 128 C3
Woodlands Com Sch
SO18 104 B4
Woodlands Cres BH15 201 C2
Woodlands Ct
5 Hythe SO45 125 C1
18 Winchester SO23 2 A1
Woodlands Dr SO31 127 B3
Woodlands Dro SO40 99 C2
Woodlands Gdns 8
SO51 28 A1
Woodlands Gr PO7 134 B3
Woodlands La Liss GU33 21 A2
South Hayling PO11 184 C3
Woodlands Prim Sch
PO8 111 B2
Woodlands Rd
Ashurst SO40 99 C2
Barton on Sea BH25 209 C4
Brockenhurst SO42 172 C4
Netley Marsh SO40 99 C2
Woodlands The
Chandler's Ford SO53 30 A1
Kings Worthy SO23 2 B3
Woodlands Way
Bursledon SO31 127 C4
Havant PO9 135 C2
New Milton BH25 195 A3
North Baddesley SO52 53 C2
Southampton SO15 102 C4
St Leonards BH24 139 C2
Woodlane Cl SO24 15 B3
Woodlea Cl SO22 1 C1
Woodlea Gdns SO30 80 C1
Woodlea Ho SO53 55 B2
Woodlea Way SO51 29 C1
Woodleaze Cl BH18 187 A3
Woodleigh Cl PO9 136 B2
Woodley Cl SO51 28 B1
Woodley Close Flats
SO51 28 B1
Woodley Gdns SO41 197 B3
Woodley La SO51 28 A1
Woodley Rd
Gosport PO12 181 B2
Southampton SO19 103 B2
Woodley Way SO51 28 B1
Woodling Cres SP6 70 B1
Woodlinken Cl BH31 115 A2
Woodlinken Dr BH31 115 A3
Woodlinken Way BH31 115 B2
Woodmancote La PO10 137 C2
Woodmancote Rd PO4 183 A2
Woodmill La SO18 79 C1
Woodmoor Cl SO40 102 A1
Woodpath PO5 215 B1
Woodpath Ho PO5 215 B1
Woodpecker Cl
Havant PO9 136 A1
Verwood BH31 114 C3
Woodpecker Copse
SO31 129 A2
Woodpecker Dr
Broadstone BH17 201 C4
Marchwood SO40 101 C1
Woodpecker Way
Eastleigh SO50 55 B1
Portsmouth PO3 158 A2
Woodpeckers Dr SO22 1 B1
Woodrisings BH13 214 A2
Woodrisings The BH2 204 B2
Woodroffe Wlk PO10 136 C2
Woodrow PO7 110 C2
Woodruff Cl BH23 208 B4
Woodrush Cres SO31 128 C1
Woods Ho 5 GU32 40 C2
Woods View Rd BH9 204 B4
Woodsedge PO7 135 A3
Woodside
Brockenhurst SO42 173 A4
Chilworth SO16 54 C1
Gosport PO13 155 A3
Portsmouth PO5 215 B1
Woodside Ave
Eastleigh SO50 56 A3
Lymington SO41 197 C1
Woodside Cl
Ferndown BH22 165 C3
13 Lymington SO41 197 C1
Marchwood SO40 101 C1
Woodside Cres SO16 54 C1
Woodside Ct 23 SO17 103 A4
Woodside Gdns SO40 100 B2
Woodside La SO41 197 C1
Woodside Rd
Bournemouth BH5 206 A2
Eastleigh SO50 55 C2
Ferndown BH22 165 C3
North Baddesley SO52 53 C2
Poole BH14 203 B2
Southampton SO17 103 A4
West Moors BH22 138 B2
Woodside Way SO30 105 A3
Woodstock Ave PO8 112 A3
Woodstock Cl
Fareham PO15 130 C1
Hedge End SO30 105 B3
Poole BH14 203 A1
Woodstock Ct BH22 165 C2
Woodstock Dr SO17 79 A1
Woodstock La BH24 141 A3
Woodstock Rd
Burton BH23 192 B1
Gosport PO12 181 B2
Havant PO9 135 B1
Poole BH14 203 A1
Woodthorpe Gdns SO31 128 C3
Woodvale PO15 130 B1
Woodvale Gdns BH25 195 B2
Woodview Cl SO16 79 A3
Woodville Dr PO1 182 A2
Woodville Rd
Fawley SO45 151 A2
Havant PO9 135 A1
Woodward Cl PO12 180 C2
Woofferton Rd PO6 133 A1
Wool Rd BH12 203 A4
Woolfield La GU32,GU34 18 A2
Woolford Cl 1 SO22 10 B3
Woolley Ho 17 SO14 103 A3
Woolmer Ct 30 PO9 136 A3
Woolmer La BH24 117 A1
Woolmer St PO10 136 C2
Woolner Ave
Cosham PO6 158 A4
Petersfield GU32 40 C2
Woolsbridge Ind Est
BH21 139 A3
Woolsbridge Rd BH24 139 C3
Woolslope Cl BH22 138 C1
Woolslope Gdns BH22 138 C1
Woolslope Rd BH22 138 C1
Woolston Ct PO12 180 B2
Woolston Inf Sch SO19 103 C1
Woolston Rd Havant PO9 135 B3
Netley SO31 127 B4
Woolston Sch (Annexe)
SO19 103 C2
Woolston Sec Sch SO19 103 C1
Woolston Sta SO19 103 B2
Woolven Cl BH14 203 A3
Woolwich Cl SO31 104 C1
Wootton SO31 127 B4
Wootton Farm Rd BH25 170 C1
Wootton Gdns BH1 205 A2
Wootton Mount BH1 205 A2
Wootton Rd
Lee-on-the-Solent PO13 180 A2
New Milton BH25 195 B4
Wootton Rough BH25 195 A4
Wootton St PO6 157 C4
Worbarrow Gdns BH12 203 B4
Worcester Cl 5 PO1 215 C2
Worcester Ct PO13 180 B3
Worcester Pl
7 Lymington SO41 197 C1
Southampton SO19 104 A1
Wordsworth Ave
Bournemouth BH8 190 C1
Portchester PO6 132 C1
Wordsworth Cl
Bishop's Waltham SO32 83 C4
Winchester SO22 10 B4
Wordsworth Inf Sch
SO15 78 A1
Wordsworth Pl PO15 106 B1
Wordsworth Rd SO15 78 B1
Worgret Rd BH15 202 B4
Workhouse La GU32 38 B1
Worldham Rd PO9 136 A3
Worrell Dr BH12 203 B4
Worsley Rd PO5 215 B1
Worsley St PO4 183 A1
Worth The PO5 182 B1
Worthing Ave PO12 180 C4
Worthing Rd PO5 182 B1
Worthington Cres BH14 203 A2
Worthy Ct 46 PO9 136 A3
Worthy Ho SO16 78 A1
Worthy La SO23 1 C1
Worthy Rd
New Milton BH25 195 A1
Winchester SO23 2 A1
Wortley Rd BH23 209 A4
Wr Twr Rd BH18 187 B2
Wraxall Cl BH17 187 B1
Wraysbury Park Dr
PO10 136 C2
Wren Cl
Christchurch BH23 208 A3
New Milton BH25 194 C1
Ringwood BH24 141 B3
Winchester SO22 10 B3
Wren Cres BH12 204 A3
Wren Ctr The PO10 137 A2
Wren Gdns SP6 93 A3
Wren Rd SO50 55 C1
Wrenway PO16 155 C4
Wrexham Gr PO8 88 A1
Wright Way SO45 151 C1
Wright's Hill SO19 104 A1
Wrights Wlk SO31 104 C1
Wriothesley Ct PO14 153 C4
Wroxham Rd BH12 203 C3
Wryneck Cl SO16 78 A3
Wuthering Hts SO22 10 C3
Wyatts Cl BH21 186 B3
Wyatts La BH21 186 B3
Wyborn Cl PO11 185 A1
Wych La PO13 155 A2
Wychwood Cl BH2 204 C2
Wychwood Dr
Blackfield SO45 177 C4
Bournemouth BH2 204 C2
Wychwood Gr SO53 55 C4
Wychwood Grange 1
BH2 204 C2
Wycliffe Rd
Bournemouth BH9 204 C4
Southampton SO18 80 A1
Wycote Rd PO13 155 A2
Wyeford Cl 4 PO9 136 A3
Wyelands Ave BH21 164 B3
Wykeham Ave PO2 157 C1
Wykeham Cl
6 Netley SO31 127 A3
Poole BH17 202 C4
Southampton SO16 78 C2
Wykeham Field PO17 108 A2
Wykeham House Sch
PO16 131 B1
Wykeham Ind Est The
SO23 2 B2
Wykeham Lo BH13 214 C3
Wykeham Pk SO21 12 A4
Wykeham Pl
Lymington SO41 197 C2
Winchester SO22 10 B3
Wykeham Rd
Netley SO31 127 A3
Portsmouth PO2 157 C1
Wyld Green La GU33 21 A3
Wylds La GU32 65 B4
Wyllie Rd PO2 157 C2
Wylye Cl SO18 80 A2
Wymering La PO6 133 C1
Wymering Manor (Youth
Hostel) PO6 157 B4
Wymering Manor Cl 9
PO6 157 B4
Wymering Rd PO2 182 C4
Wyn Sutcliffe Ct 9 PO4 183 A2
Wyncombe Rd BH5 206 A3
Wyndcliffe Rd PO4 182 C2
Wyndham Cl
Christchurch BH23 194 A1
Waterlooville PO8 112 A2
Wyndham Ct SO15 102 C3
Wyndham Mews PO1 182 A2
Wyndham Pl 14 SO15 102 C3
Wyndham Rd
Christchurch BH23 194 A1
Poole BH14 203 A2
Wynford Ind Pk SO51 27 C2
Wynford Rd
Bournemouth BH9 190 A2
Poole BH14 203 B2
Wynne Cl BH18 186 C2
Wynter Cl BH7 205 C4
Wynter Rd SO18 104 A4
Wynton Way PO15 130 B2
Wynyards Gap SO52 53 C2
Wyre Cl SO53 55 A3
Wyvern Cl
Chandler's Ford SO53 55 B3
Poole BH12 203 B4
Wyvern Tech Coll SO50 57 B1

Y

Yachtsman Cl SO31 128 B4
Yaldhurst Ct 23 PO9 136 A3
Yaldhurst La SO41 197 A2
Yapton St PO1 215 B3
Yarborough Rd PO5 215 B1
Yardlea Cl PO9 113 A1
Yardley Cl PO3 158 B2
Yardley Rd SO30 105 B3
Yarmouth Cl BH12 204 A3
Yarmouth Gdns 14 SO15 78 A1
Yarmouth Rd BH12 203 C3
Yarrell Mead SO41 197 A2
Yarrells Cl BH16 201 B3
Yarrells Dr BH16 201 A4
Yarrells La BH16 201 B3
Yarrells Sch BH16 201 A4
Yarrow Cl BH23 208 A4

Yarrow Rd BH12 ....203 A4
Yarrow Way SO31 ......128 C1
Yateley Cl PO9 ....135 B3
Yaverland SO31 ....127 B3
Yeatminster Rd BH17 ..187 C1
Yeatton Ho SO41 ....196 A1
Yelverton Ave SO45 ....150 A4
Yelverton Rd 28 BH1 ..204 C2
Yeo Ct PO4 ....183 B2
Yeoman Pk SO16 ....77 B1
Yeomans Ind Pk BH8 ..190 C1
Yeomans Rd BH8 ......190 C2
Yeomans Way
  Bournemouth BH8 .....190 C1
  Totton SO40 ....100 C4
Yeovil Chase SO18 .....104 A4
Yeovilton Cl SO41 .....196 C1
Yerville Gdns SO41 .....195 C2
Yew La BH25 ....195 B2

Yew Rd SO18 ....104 A4
Yew Tree Ave PO8 ......112 A1
Yew Tree Cl
  Fair Oak SO50 ....57 B2
  Hedge End SO30 ......105 A3
  Wimborne Minst BH21 ..163 B3
Yew Tree Ct
  Fordingbridge SP6 ......93 C4
  Locks Heath PO15 ....129 A4
  50 New Milton BH25 ...195 A1
Yew Tree Dr PO15 ......129 A4
Yew Tree Gdns
  Denmead PO7 ....110 C2
  3 Ringwood BH24 .....141 A3
Yew Tree Pl GU33 ....21 A2
Yew Tree Rd PO11 .....185 A4
Yewberry Way SO53 .....54 C3
Yews The PO8 ....112 B4
Yewside PO13 ....155 B1

Yewtree Cl SO45 ....150 A4
Yewtree La SO16 ....77 B2
Yoells Cres PO8 ....111 C3
Yoells La PO8 ....111 C3
Yokesford Hill SO51 ....27 C2
Yokesford Hill Est SO51 .27 C3
Yonge Cl SO50 ....56 A2
York Ave BH25 ....195 A2
York Bldgs SO14 ....103 A2
York Cl Broadstone BH18 .187 A1
  Chandler's Ford SO53 ...54 C2
  Christchurch BH23 .....206 C4
  Fair Oak SO50 ....81 B4
  Petersfield GU32 ....40 B2
  Southampton SO14 ....103 B3
  Totton SO40 ....101 A4
York Cres PO13 ....180 A2
York Dro Nomansland SP5 .73 B4
  Southampton SO18 ....104 A4

York Gdns PO16 ....156 C3
York Ho 30 Gosport PO12 .181 B2
  7 Southampton SO14 ...103 B3
  32 Winchester SO23 .....2 A1
York Pl Bournemouth BH7 .206 A3
  17 New Milton BH25 ...195 A2
  Portsmouth PO1 ....182 A3
York Rd
  Bournemouth BH1 .....205 A2
  Broadstone BH18 ......187 A1
  Eastleigh SO50 ....80 A4
  Netley SO31 ....127 A3
  Southampton SO15 ....102 B4
York Terr PO2 ....157 C3
Yorkdale SO31 ....128 B2
Yorke St PO5 ....215 A2
Yorke Way SO31 ....127 C2
Yorkwood GU33 ....20 C2

Youngbridge Ct 16
  PO16 ....155 A4
Youngs Rd BH11 ....189 A3
Yves Mews PO5 ....182 B1

Zamek Cl BH11 ....189 A3
Zetland Ct BH4 ....204 A1
Zetland Rd Cosham PO6 ..158 B4
  Gosport PO12 ....181 A3
Zeus La PO7 ....134 C2
Zinnia Cl BH10 ....189 C1

NG NH NJ NK

NM NN NO NP

NR NS NT NU

NX NY NZ

SC SD SE TA

SH SJ SK TF TG

SM SN SO SP TL TM

SR SS ST SU TQ TR

SW SX SY SZ TV

Any feature in this atlas can be given a unique reference to help you find the same feature on other Ordnance Survey maps of the area, or to help someone else locate you if they do not have a Street Atlas.

The grid squares in this atlas match the Ordnance Survey National Grid and are at 1 kilometre intervals. The small figures at the bottom and sides of every other grid line are the National Grid kilometre values (**00** to **99** km) and are repeated across the country every 100 km (see left).

To give a unique National Grid reference you need to locate where in the country you are. The country is divided into 100 km squares with each square given a unique two-letter reference. Use the administrative map to determine in which 100 km square a particular page of this atlas falls.

The bold letters and numbers between each grid line (**A** to **C**, **1** to **4**) are for use within a specific Street Atlas only, and when used with the page number, are a convenient way of referencing these grid squares.

Example The railway bridge over *DARLEY GREEN RD* in grid square A1

Step 1: Identify the two-letter reference, in this example the page is in **SP**

Step 2: Identify the 1 km square in which the railway bridge falls. Use the figures in the southwest corner of this square: Eastings **17**, Northings **74**. This gives a unique reference: **SP 17 74**, accurate to 1 km.

Step 3: To give a more precise reference accurate to 100 m you need to estimate how many tenths along and how many tenths up this 1 km square the feature is. This makes the bridge about **8** tenths along and about **1** tenth up from the southwest corner.

This gives a unique reference: **SP 178 741**, accurate to 100 m.

Eastings (read from left to right along the bottom) come before Northings (read from bottom to top). If you have trouble remembering say to yourself "Along the hall, THEN up the stairs"!

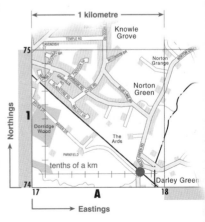

Addresses

Name and Address	Telephone	Page	Grid reference